The West in the World

A Mid-Length Narrative History

Volume II: From 1600

D1307736

DENNIS SHERMAN

John Jay College of Criminal Justice
City University of New York

JOYCE SALISBURY

University of Wisconsin–Green Bay

Boston   Burr Ridge, IL   Dubuque, IA   Madison, WI   New York   San Francisco   St. Louis
Bangkok   Bogotá   Caracas   Lisbon   London   Madrid
Mexico City   Milan   New Delhi   Seoul   Singapore   Sydney   Taipei   Toronto

McGraw-Hill Higher Education

*A Division of The **McGraw-Hill** Companies*

THE WEST IN THE WORLD, VOLUME II: FROM 1600

Published by McGraw-Hill, an imprint of The McGraw-Hill Companies, Inc., 1221 Avenue of the Americas, New York, NY 10020. Copyright © 2001 by The McGraw-Hill Companies, Inc. All rights reserved. No part of this publication may be reproduced or distributed in any form or by any means, or stored in a database or retrieval system, without the prior written consent of The McGraw-Hill Companies, Inc., including, but not limited to, in any network or other electronic storage or transmission, or broadcast for distance learning.

Some ancillaries, including electronic and print components, may not be available to customers outside the United States.

This book is printed on acid-free paper.

2 3 4 5 6 7 8 9 0 VNH/VNH 0 9 8 7 6 5 4 3 2 1

ISBN 0–07–289541–1

Vice president and editor-in-chief: *Thalia Dorwick*
Editorial director: *Jane E. Vaicunas*
Senior sponsoring editor: *Lyn Uhl*
Developmental editor: *Burrston House/Anne Sachs*
Marketing manager: *Janise A. Fry*
Senior project manager: *Jayne Klein*
Lead media producer: *David Edwards*
Production supervisor: *Sandy Ludovissy*
Senior designer: *Jennifer McQueen Hollingsworth*
Senior photo research coordinator: *Lori Hancock*
Photo research: *Barbara Salz*
Supplement coordinator: *Stacy A. Patch*
Compositor: *GTS Graphics, Inc.*
Typeface: *10.5/12 Goudy*
Printer: *Von Hoffmann Press, Inc.*

The credits section for this book begins on page C-1 and is considered an extension of the copyright page.

Library of Congress has cataloged the combined version as follows:

Sherman, Dennis.
     The West in the world / Dennis Sherman, Joyce E. Salisbury — 1st ed.
          p.   cm.
     Includes bibliographical references and index.
     ISBN 0–07–059983–1
     1. Civilization, Western—History.   2. Civilization, Modern—European influences.
3. World history.   I. Salisbury, Joyce E.   II. Title.

CB245 .S465   2001
909′.09821—dc21   00–039421
                                                            CIP

www.mhhe.com

We live in the present with
what remains of the past,
scarcely knowing all that we
take for granted

About the Authors

DENNIS SHERMAN

Dennis Sherman is Professor of History at John Jay College of Criminal Justice, the City University of New York. He received his B.A. (1962) and J.D. (1965) from the University of California at Berkeley, and his Ph.D. (1970) from the University of Michigan. He was visiting Professor at the University of Paris (1978–1979; 1985). He has received the Ford Foundation Prize Fellowship, the Council for Research on Economic History fellowship, and fellowships from the National Endowment for the Humanities. His publications include *A Short History of Western Civilization*, Eighth Edition (co-author); *Western Civilization: Sources, Images, and Interpretations*, Fifth Edition; *World Civilizations: Sources, Images, and Interpretations*, Second Edition (co-author); a series of introductions in the Garland Library of War and Peace; several articles and reviews on nineteenth-century French economic and social history in American and European journals; and short stories in literary reviews.

JOYCE SALISBURY

Joyce Salisbury is Frankenthal Professor of History at the University of Wisconsin–Green Bay where she has taught undergraduates for almost twenty years. She received a PhD in medieval history from Rutgers University in New Jersey. She is a respected historian who has published many articles and has written or edited eight books, including the critically acclaimed *Perpetua's Passion: Death and Memory of a Young Roman Woman*; and *The Beast Within: Animals in the Middle Ages*. Salisbury is also an award-winning teacher, who was named *"Professor of the Year for Wisconsin in 1991"* by CASE (Council for Advancement and Support of Education), a prestigious national organization.

Brief Contents

Contents

CHAPTER 15

Competing for Power and Wealth: The Old Regime, 1715–1789   499

CHAPTER 16

Overturning the Political and Social Order: The French Revolution and Napoleon, 1789–1815   535

CHAPTER 17
Factories, Cities, and Families in the Industrial Age: The Industrial Revolution, 1780–1850   569

CHAPTER 18
Coping with Change: Ideology, Politics, and Revolution, 1815–1850   601

CHAPTER 19

Nationalism and Statebuilding: Unifying Nations, 1850–1870   637

CHAPTER 20

Mass Politics and Imperial Domination: Democracy and the New Imperialism, 1870–1914   659

List of Maps

Preface

WHAT'S DIFFERENT AND WHY

Western civilization influences—and is influenced by—peoples all over the world today; it remains a fascinating (and at times controversial) subject. While many have studied the strong contributions of the West to the world, too often the reverse influences have not been stressed. In fact, one of the hallmarks of Western civilization has been its power to be transformed through contact with people outside its center. This quality has contributed to the West's capacity to keep changing as it embraces new ideas, new people, and new challenges. We chose the title of this book—*The West in the World*—to emphasize this characteristic, and we have written the story of the West in a way that reveals its complex interactions with the surrounding world.

When we first prepared to write this book, we set five goals for ourselves:

- To demonstrate the complex relationship between Western and world history
- To weave a strong social-history "thread" into the political/cultural framework
- To write a book that would hold readers' attention and that would convey the drama and interest inherent in the story of the past
- To integrate some unique features that would enhance the narrative and support learning on the part of readers
- To make the book an attractive, manageable length

With each chapter and each round of revision, we reminded ourselves of these five goals and asked our reviewers to hold us accountable for achieving them.

To address the first goal, we dealt with the thorny issue of the relationship between Western and world history. In doing so, we chose to present the concept of Western civilization as an ever-changing pattern of culture that first emerged in the ancient Middle East and that then moved west through the Mediterranean lands, north to Europe, and, in the sixteenth century, across the Atlantic. Throughout the narrative we have tried to emphasize the importance of the interactions—economic, social, and cultural as well as political—that have created our modern civilization that in the twenty-first century is in many ways a world civilization.

Civilizations grow and are shaped through the decisions and actions of people, and we have kept this idea in mind as we wove the story of the West. To meet our second goal, we integrated social history, including women's history, throughout this text, acknowledging that people of all ages and walks of life have affected the course of history. Social historians have sometimes written about "the masses" while losing touch with the individual men and women whose lives have shaped the past. We frequently "stop the music" for a moment to let the words and experiences of individuals illustrate broad developments, and in addition we have presented biographical portraits of people who experienced some of the developments discussed in each chapter.

To meet our third goal, we sought to capture both the art and science of history. We strove for an engaging narrative of Western civilization (the "art") that would also analyze the events, individuals, ideas, and developments (the "science"). We designed the book to draw students in as they follow the unfolding of Western culture from its earliest roots to the present.

As scholars who care as much about teaching as we do about history, and to fulfill our fourth goal, we have designed a number of unique pedagogical features to complement and support the narrative. For example, we treat art works and maps in an unusual way. Each illustration is discussed in the text itself rather than presented as a separate, optional feature or mere ornamentation. This approach not only brings the past alive for today's highly visual audience, it also helps teach students how to interpret art works and other illustrations. Maps are also treated as more than a visual aid. Each map comes with an analytical guide that encourages readers to consider connections between geography, politics, and other developments. A picture by itself is not worth a thousand words, but in this text the illustrations and maps serve as a central feature for learning.

THINKING ABOUT GEOGRAPHY

MAP 2.3 *The Persian Wars, 490–480 B.C.*
This map shows the routes of invasions and the major battles of the wars between Persia and the Greek poleis. ■ **Notice** the two routes through which the Persians tried to invade Greece. **Consider** the particular advantages and disadvantages posed by the land and sea routes. ■ **Notice also** the narrow land and sea areas where the Persians engaged the Greeks. **Consider** how the narrow spaces served as a disadvantage to the more numerous Persian forces.

To achieve our final goal of making this book an attractive size, we selected a length that is unusual for a Western civilization textbook. Long texts, while of great value, can be intimidating to students in their level of detail and can make the assigning of supplementary readings difficult, if not impossible—we've all had this experience. Brief texts, while leaving plenty of time for additional readings, are typically lacking in necessary coverage and detail, thus making it a remarkable challenge for the authors to achieve the kind of braided, nuanced narrative that history deserves. Medium in length, *The West in the World* is long enough to present a strong, rich narrative while allowing instructors the flexibility to use other sources and books as supplements.

ORGANIZATION AND COVERAGE

The West in the World is organized in a way that reflects the typical Western civilization course. The twenty-five chapters follow the history of Western civilization chronologically, and the subheadings allow professors to select portions of chapters to suit their syllabi. The text is divided in two volumes, with overlapping chapters that cover the seventeenth and eighteenth centuries to provide flexibility for two-semester courses. While this organization makes it easy for instructors to use this text, it also allows us to cover traditional topics in fresh ways.

Narrative

Students and instructors often complain that history texts are dry. We agree. The strong narrative approach of this book reflects our belief that the various dimensions of an historical era—political, intellectual, social, and cultural—are best presented as part of an integrated whole rather than separate chapters or occasionally referenced in a discussion. The story of the West is a compelling one, and we have worked hard to tell it in a lively way that includes analysis (the "why" of history) as well as events and ideas (the "what"). For example, in Chapter 7, the discussion of Charlemagne's wars and his relation with the papacy are framed in a larger theoretical discussion of the benefits of linking politics with religion. Similarly, in Chapter 11, a chronology of warfare is informed by an analysis of technological and social change.

Integration of Political and Social History

History is about people, and we keep that point "front and center" in our narrative, which integrates political and social history. Women, families, peasants, and workers are not treated as an afterthought, but as essential players in the evolving story. Our "Biography" feature as well as illustrative anecdotes throughout, regularly reminds readers that the human past emerged through the interaction of all members of society and that human agency is an essential component of the past. For example, Chapter 17 begins by comparing the differing experiences of industrialization for a middle-class couple with that of a railroad worker. That comparison is then used to reflect broader developments and leads to an analysis of the causes of the Industrial Revolution. The same theme is echoed in the chapter's *Biography* section, *The Cadburys*.

Art and Culture

In addition to written evidence, paintings, sculpture, ceramics, photographs, and buildings all provide valuable historical information. In this book, the examples of material culture and art do far more than just beautify the presentation. Each visual source is discussed and interpreted within the narrative. For example, we analyze a painting of a nineteenth-century middle-class family to show gender roles, attitudes toward children, the place of servants, and relationships to the outside world. Similarly, we use a beautiful Rubens painting of the miracles of Saint Ignatius Loyola to comment on the theology and sensibilities of sixteenth-century Catholicism. All this is discussed within the narrative of the text. Visuals serve as sources of history and encourage students to arrive at richer insights than they would have gained solely through reading the text.

Science and Medicine

An enthusiasm for science and technology has been a hallmark of Western civilization. Like many developments in the story of the West, this enthusiasm has ebbed and flowed over time. To meet the growing interest among today's students and scholars, we emphasize these topics throughout the narrative. For example, a discussion of medieval technology reveals the significant inventions that brought mechanical power to a central point in society, and students will also see how other cultures—like early Muslim societies—performed surgery, dispensed drugs, and established hospitals. Even in the modern period, we discuss the experience of going to a doctor in addition to reporting on new developments in medicine, such as antiseptics, anesthetics, and antibiotics. Consistent with our use of art as history, illustrations such as Caroline Naudet's "Journey of a Dying Man to the Other World" are used to reveal both typical medical practices and common attitudes toward physicians.

Wall painting of a woman playing a cithara

The Romans believed that their greatness derived first from the family, in which aristocratic fathers and mothers were educated and devoted to instilling traditional values in their children. This illustration shows one such cultured mother playing a cithara for her child.

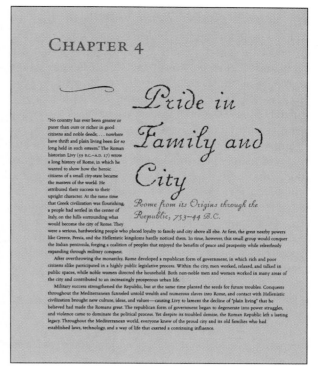

CHAPTER 4

Pride in Family and City

Rome from its Origins through the Republic, 753–44 B.C.

"No country has ever been greater or purer than ours or richer in good citizens and noble deeds, . . . nowhere have thrift and plain living been for so long held in such esteem." The Roman historian Livy (59 B.C.–A.D. 17) wrote a long history of Rome, in which he wanted to show how the heroic citizens of a small city-state became the masters of the world. He attributed their success to their upright character. At the same time that Greek civilization was flourishing, a people had settled in the center of Italy, on the hills surrounding what would become the city of Rome. They were a serious, hardworking people who placed loyalty to family and city above all else. At first, the great nearby powers like Greece, Persia, and the Hellenistic kingdoms hardly noticed them. In time, however, this small group would conquer the Italian peninsula, forging a coalition of peoples that enjoyed the benefits of peace and prosperity while relentlessly expanding through military conquest.

After overthrowing the monarchy, Rome developed a republican form of government, in which rich and poor citizens alike participated in a highly public legislative process. Within the city, men worked, relaxed, and talked in public spaces, while noble women directed the household. Both non-noble men and women worked in many areas of the city and contributed to an increasingly prosperous urban life.

Military success strengthened the Republic, but at the same time planted the seeds for future troubles. Conquests throughout the Mediterranean funneled untold wealth and numerous slaves into Rome, and contact with Hellenistic civilization brought new culture, ideas, and values—causing Livy to lament the decline of "plain living" that he believed had made the Romans great. The republican form of government began to degenerate into power struggles, and violence came to dominate the political process. Yet despite its troubled demise, the Roman Republic left a lasting legacy. Throughout the Mediterranean world, everyone knew of the proud city and its old families who had established laws, technology, and a way of life that exerted a continuing influence.

PEDAGOGICAL FEATURES

We believe that telling a good story is only part of the task facing those who teach the history of the West. Instructors also have to engage students in the enterprise of learning, and the more actively engaged they are, the more they learn. Therefore, we have designed and included a number of pedagogical features to help students participate actively in the learning process. These can be used by students alone or become part of classroom activity.

· Chapter Previews and Summaries

Each chapter opens with a short preview and telling anecdote that, together, set the stage for understanding the material. Chapters then end with a summary of key themes. Rather than dry outlines, these features instead preserve the engaging narrative style while satisfying the pedagogical dictum: "tell them what they'll learn; teach them; then tell them what they have learned." The chapter previews and reviews help students stay focused on the main themes in the narrative.

peace seemed to come at the price of the traditional Republic, and at the expense of the old power structure. Some conspirators were simply self-serving, hoping to increase their own power. Sixty senators with various motives entered into a conspiracy to murder their leader. Even Brutus, a friend and protégé of Caesar, joined in the plot. He would be like the Brutus of early Rome who had avenged Lucretia and freed Rome from the Etruscan kings. This Brutus would save Rome from a new king—Caesar.

Caesar was planning a military campaign for March 18, 44 B.C., so the assassins had to move quickly. On March 15, the date the Romans called the "ides," or middle of the month, they surrounded the unwary dictator as he approached the Senate meeting place. Suddenly they drew knives from the folds of their togas and plunged them into his body. He died at the foot of the statue of Pompey, his old enemy. Most of the killers seem to have genuinely believed they had done what was best for Rome. They saw themselves as "liberators," who had freed Rome from a dictator and who would restore the Republic. In 43 B.C. they issued the coin shown in Figure 4.13. The coin depicts the assassins' daggers and reads "Ides of March." On the other side of the coin is a portrait of Brutus.

Caesar's murder

This attempt to celebrate a great victory on the coin was mere propaganda. The conspirators had no real plan beyond the murder. They apparently had made no provision for control of the army, nor for ensuring peace in the city. In the end, their claim to "save the Republic" rang hollow. After Caesar's death, one of his friends supposedly lamented, "If Caesar for all his genius, could not find a way out, who is going to find one now?"

FIGURE 4.13
Coin commemorating the murder of Caesar, 43 B.C.

Summary

The Republic of Rome, with its emphasis on family and city, rose to great power from 509 B.C. to the death of Caesar in 44 B.C. By that year, Rome controlled much of the Mediterranean world, and a system of wealthy slave owners and a large standing army had replaced the farmer-soldier who had laid the foundation for the Republic's success. Whereas the early Romans had emphasized the ties between citizens, now violent power struggles tore at the social fabric. A people who preserved stories of serious Roman heroes began to treasure Greek models of beauty and individualism.

Julius Caesar became a central figure in Rome's transformation from republic to empire. Since Caesar's death, historians have argued about his qualities. Was he a great man who detected the inability of the republican form of government—designed to govern a city-state—to adapt to the changed circumstances of empire and social unrest? Or was he a power-hungry politician who craved control and blocked his fellow citizens from having any political involvement in the Republic? The truth no doubt falls somewhere between these extremes. One thing is certain: Despite the assassins' confident claims, Caesar's murder did not solve anything. More violence would ensue until a leader arose who could establish a new form of government that would endure even longer than the Republic.

• Timelines and Reminder Dates

Many instructors and reviewers have told us that students lack a sense of chronology. We believe that this problem stems in part from the way history texts are written—as the narrative progresses in a linear way, students lose track of simultaneous developments, and indeed of the dates themselves. We have added several features to strengthen readers' sense of chronology. For example, we include dates in the chapter titles and many of the chapter subheadings. We have also sprinkled important dates throughout the narrative and whenever key individuals are named.

As a significant feature to address the understanding of chronology, we have included timelines at the beginning and end of each chapter. The beginning lines that we have called "The Big Picture" show blocks that indicate the large events, periods, or dynasties that will be covered within the chapter.

The ending lines, called "A Closer Look," detail events and people that were covered within the text. Both these lines depict simultaneous developments in a memorable, visual way and provide a sense of broad chronological context. Finally, we have made sure that the timelines draw from the material in the previous and forthcoming chapters. Again, this technique emphasizes connectedness and continuity in the story of Western civilization.

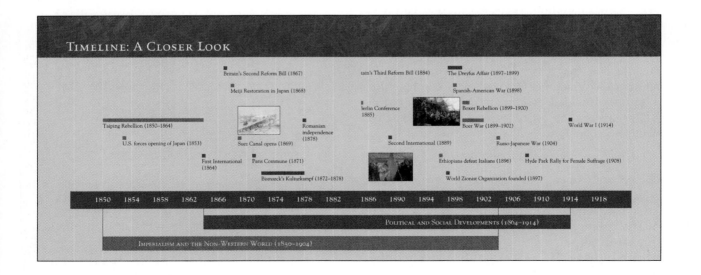

· Map Exercises

Because a sense of geography is essential to the study of history, we have included a wealth of full-color maps, and we treat them uniquely. As instructors know very well, too often students just glance at maps without understanding them or engaging them critically. To address this, we have included a feature called "Thinking About Geography," which provides analytical exercises that invite students to delve into the meaning of each map. We hope this approach will not only help students remember particular maps, but will also get them into the habit of actively seeking to understand how geographic features shape human events.

· Biographies

Each chapter features a biographical essay of a man or woman who embodies major themes from the chapter. The individuals selected are not necessarily the most celebrated nor the most typical, but instead are powerful illustrative examples. Each biography serves as a reminder of the major themes—another kind of review—and provides a concrete way to discuss some of the more abstract concepts covered, and each biogra-

THINKING ABOUT GEOGRAPHY

MAP 16.4   *Europe, 1810*

This map shows Europe at the height of Napoleon's empire. ● Notice the extent of area Napoleon controlled—directly and indirectly. Where would you expect Napoleon's rule to exert the greatest impact? What geographical problems did Napoleon face trying to control his empire? ● Locate those areas that remained hostile to Napoleon. How might geography help explain why those areas retained their independence?

phy includes questions that guide students to think critically about the individual's life and connect it with the chapter's themes. We designed the biographies to bring the past to life, as well as to encourage students to think about how large developments affect individuals. For example, the biography of Isabelle D'Este, found in Chapter 10, illustrates the Renaissance by her patronage of the arts, her political struggles, and her strong family ties. Similarly, the biography of Jean-Jacques Rousseau in Chapter 14 analyzes his life as well as how it reflects the broad themes of the enlightenment.

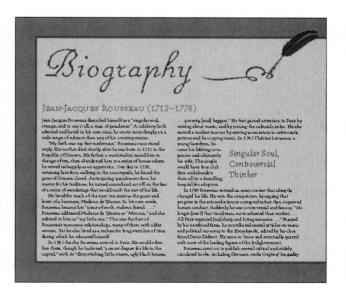

• Clear Headings and Marginal Notes

Each chapter has clear thematic titles and precise headings that guide students through the narrative. Throughout, brief marginal notes help students focus on the key concepts, terms, and events and provide a tool for reviewing the chapter.

• Review, Analyze, and Anticipate

At the end of each chapter are questions that not only ask students to think about the material discussed within the chapter, but also encourage them to place the material within the context of what has come before and what is coming next. The summary paragraphs included within these sections offer continuous reviews and previews of material, once again helping students to retain the larger picture while learning new details.

• Glossary and Pronunciation Guide

Important terms are briefly defined in the Glossary at the end of the book (that is conveniently marked by a color border to make it easy to locate). All the words, except the most simple, come with a pronunciation guide. This feature allows students to review terms readily, while giving them the confidence in pronunciation to help make the terms part of their vocabulary.

ning jenny, which revolutionized thread production. By 1812 one spinner could produce as much cotton thread as 200 spinners had in 1760. Other inventions, such as Richard Arkwright's (1732–1792) water frame and Edmund Cartwright's (1743–1823) power loom, allowed weavers to turn cotton into cloth in tremendous quantities. Two American developments added to the acceleration in textile production: Eli Whitney's (1765–1825) cotton gin (1793), which efficiently removed seeds from raw cotton; and the expanding slave plantation system in the South. Indeed, British manufacturers' growing demand for cotton became an important force perpetuating slavery in the cotton-growing areas of the United States.

Weaving and spinning

By 1850, British cotton manufacturers had boosted cloth production from less than 40 million yards per year during the 1780s to over 2,000 million yards per year. Cotton had become hugely popular and, alone, accounted for some 40 percent of British exports.

IRON: NEW PROCESSES TRANSFORM PRODUCTION

Machines for the new cotton industry were just one source of a growing demand for iron. Armies needed guns and cannon; civilians needed nails and pans. Until the eighteenth century, British iron makers were limited by the island nation's dwindling forests, for they knew how to smelt iron ore only with charcoal, which came from wood. Even during the days of plentiful charcoal, ironworkers had only their own and their animals' muscle power with which to work the iron into usable forms. Figure 17.2, a painting by the British artist Joseph Wright of Derby (1734–1797), shows a typical eighteenth-century iron forge. As this picture suggests, most production came out of small family firms or homes of artisans. The men—posing proudly—use only hand-powered tools to transform the iron, while women and children stand by, averting their eyes or turning away from the white-hot metal.

Abraham Darby's (1678?–1717) discovery in 1708 of an efficient way to smelt iron with coal in a blast *Smelting with coal* furnace started the iron industry down a new path. By the end of the century, other novel processes enabled iron makers to double production again and again in the years that followed. Foundry workers began using the steam engine to operate smelting furnaces, drive forge hammers to shape the iron, and roll the iron into sheets.

By 1850, ironworks, with their tall, smoke-belching furnaces, had joined cotton factories as a pillar of the industrial revolution.

THE STEAM ENGINE AND THE FACTORY SYSTEM

Both the cotton and the iron industries created ever higher demand for power. At the beginning of the eighteenth century, people had to rely on muscle, wind, and water to supply the energy to do their work. Early mills used water power, which meant that their owners had to build them near waterfalls. A drought in the summer or a cold snap in the winter could threaten to dry up or freeze this essential power source.

The steam engine, first used in the early eighteenth century to pump water out of deepening coal mines, provided a solution and would become the industrial revolution's most important technological advance. Portable and easily controlled, the earliest models were nevertheless not yet efficient enough for widespread application. Over the course of the eighteenth century, inventors such as Thomas Newcomen (1663–1729) and James Watt (1736–1819) improved the power and efficiency of these engines. Watt, a skilled craftsman backed by the daring entrepreneur Matthew Boulton (1728–1809), worked for years on the engine, making several design changes and eventually converting the

FIGURE 17.2
Joseph Wright of Derby, *The Iron Forge*, 1772.

575

Summary — Through the sixteenth century, the monarchs of the unified states of Europe—England, France, Spain, and the Holy Roman Empire—struggled to snatch power, wealth, and land from each other. The wars that resulted accomplished little except to bankrupt some of the kings, leave the European countryside in ruins, and inflict misery on the people. Meanwhile, religious revolutionaries stepped up their criticism of the thousand-year history of Christian tradition. These Protestants effected a reformation that spurred a century-long religious war and that split Christendom as people followed their own paths to God. The religious quest had political ramifications as well—kings involved themselves in the Catholics' and Protestants' conflict in part to try to exert religious hegemony over their own lands and to gain land from their neighbors.

When the century of religious wars in Europe ended, it left a legacy of economic devastation, social and political change, and an intellectual revolution that transformed Western culture. More boys and girls in village schools began to read and write, men and women hoped to find love in marriage, and people began to take more pride in work over leisure. Nevertheless, the Protestant revolution failed to stop the competition for Christian souls. In the centuries to come, Europeans would take the battle between Protestants and Catholics across the seas, as they discovered lands that were new to them.

REVIEW, ANALYZE, AND ANTICIPATE

REVIEW THE PREVIOUS CHAPTER

Chapter 10—"A New Spirit in the West"—described the characteristics that we have come to identify with the Renaissance. In addition, Chapter 10 also discussed the complex political structure of Italy that engaged popes as well as princes in power politics.

1. Which Renaissance characteristics also describe the ideas of Protestant reformers? Consider how the Renaissance influenced the Protestant Reformation.
2. Review the policies of Renaissance popes as they strove to become political powers in Italy. How did those policies contribute to the Reformation?

ANALYZE THIS CHAPTER

Chapter 11—"Alone Before God"—follows the expansion of warfare until it engulfed all of Europe in the sixteenth century. It also looks at the new religious ideas that split the Catholic Church and brought about a change in social life in the West.

1. Review the various religious beliefs of the different Protestant sects, and consider the relationship of these ideas to the different social and economic groups who were attracted to them.
2. How did the differing appeal help lead to the century of religious warfare? What were the results of this warfare?
3. Review the reform movements of the Catholic Church. How did the church respond to the critique of the Protestants?
4. How did the Reformation help contribute to changing social and cultural patterns that marked seventeenth-century Europe?

ANTICIPATE THE NEXT CHAPTER

Chapter 12—"Faith, Fortune, and Fame"—looks at the European expansion into much of the rest of the world that took place at the same time Europe was wracked with the religious wars discussed in Chapter 11.

1. Based on the strengths and weaknesses of the various states discussed in Chapter 11, which countries do you think might take the lead in the explorations, and which might be left behind? Why?
2. Which Christian churches do you think might be most vigorous in missionary activities? Review Chapter 11's discussion of the characteristics of each sect's relative theology as you decide.

390

SUPPLEMENTS

For the Instructor

Instructor's Manual, by Carol Bresnahan Menning, The University of Toledo

Test Bank, by David Hudson, California State University at Fresno

The Instructor's Manual portion of this combined Instructor's Manual/Test Bank includes chapter summaries, main themes, points for discussion, map exercises, essay questions, terms for identification, and a pronunciation guide. In addition, the Instructor's Manual draws on some of the unique features of the text, including a guide to visual analysis, discussion questions derived from the book's integrated coverage of visual material and boxed biographies, World Wide Web-related exercises accompanied by a listing of relevant websites for each chapter, and video suggestions.

The Test Bank includes short answer and essay questions, identification questions, multiple choice, fill-in-the-blank questions, mapping exercises, true/false questions and chronology exercises. Like the Instructor's Manual, it offers a range of questions that highlight the distinctive features of the text.

Computerized Test Bank Available for both Macintosh and IBM-compatible computers, this on-disk version of the test bank allows instructors to customize each test to suit any course syllabus.

Overhead Transparencies This comprehensive packet of approximately 140 transparencies is designed to support the text's unique integrated art program. Fine art, photos, and maps—many pulled directly from the text— allow instructors to easily illustrate classroom lectures.

Slide Set Available through your McGraw-Hill sales representative, instructors can choose from a list of hundreds of fine art slides to create a customized slide set to complement the text and enhance classroom lectures.

Presentation Manager The McGraw-Hill presentation manager organizes a diverse range of instructor's tools on one CD. Instructors can illustrate classroom lectures and discussions with text-specific PowerPoint presentations including outlines, maps, and photos for each chapter. The Instructor's Manual and Test Bank are also included on this CD, as well as links to web-based research assignments.

Instructor's Online Learning Center

www.mhhe.com/sherman

At the homepage to the text-specific website, instructors will find a series of online tools to meet a range of classroom needs. The Instructor's Manual and most PowerPoint shows can be downloaded by instructors, but are password-protected to prevent tampering. Instructors can also create web-based homework assignments or classroom activities by linking to the Student Online Learning Center, and can create an interactive course syllabus using McGraw-Hill's **PageOut** (*www.mhhe.com/pageout*).

PageOut

www.mhhe.com/pageout

On the PageOut website, instructors can create their own course websites. PageOut requires no prior knowledge of HTML, no long hours of coding, and no design skills on the instructor's part. Simply plug the course information into a template and click on one of 16 designs. The process takes no time at all and leaves instructors with a professionally designed website. Powerful features include an interactive course syllabus that lets instructors post content and links, an online gradebook, lecture notes, bookmarks, and even a discussion board where instructors and students can discuss course-related topics.

Videos Created and narrated by Joyce Salisbury, this three-video collection illuminates the author's lectures on the Middle Ages with the sculpture and fine art of the times. Available to adopters through your local McGraw-Hill sales representative, this unique series contains a video on each of the following topics: medieval women, medieval Judaism, and medieval life.

A wide range of videos on classic and contemporary topics in history is available through the Films for the Humanities and Sciences collection. Instructors can illustrate classroom discussion and enhance lectures by selecting from a series of videos that are correlated to complement **The West in the World.** Contact your local McGraw-Hill sales representative for further information.

For the Student

Student Study Guide, by Bruce Venarde, University of Pittsburgh, Megan McLean, University of Pittsburgh, and Melissa McGary, University of Pittsburgh

Available in two volumes, this guide helps students to process and master important concepts covered in the text. For each chapter of the text, the study guide offers valuable pedagogical tools such as chapter summaries and reviews, chapter outlines that include the main theme of each chapter, objective questions, short answer and essay questions, and mapping exercises. Visual learning exercises, chronology exercises based on the text's timeline, and questions that make use of the text's many biography sections highlight some of most distinctive features found in **The West in the World.** A unique guide to history on the Internet can be found at the front of the study guide.

Map Workbooks Students need all the work they can get on geography, and this supplement offers the opportunity for extra mapping practice. The workbooks are available in two volumes, and each builds upon the many unique map exercises found throughout the text.

Making the Grade Student CD-ROM, by Peter Seelig, The University of Wisconsin, Green Bay, and Benjamin Reilly, University of Pittsburgh

Packaged free with each new copy of the book, this interactive study tool allows students to test their mastery of text material with chapter-by-chapter quizzes. Multiple choice questions, fill-in-the-blank questions, and true/false questions test students on key facts and concepts. All quizzes are graded instantly, and each includes directive feedback to explain the correct response. In addition to quizzing, the CD offers a Learning Styles Assessment to help students understand how they learn, and based on that assessment, how they can use their study time most effectively. The CD also offers two different guides to the web. The Internet Primer

explains the essentials of online research, including how to get online and how to find information once you are there. For more experienced web researchers, the CD also contains the McGraw-Hill Guide to Electronic Research, which guides students through using web-based information databases and explains how to evaluate the quality of information gathered online.

Student Online Learning Center
www.mhhe.com/sherman

At the homepage to the text-specific website, students can link to an interactive study guide, including online essay questions, timelines, mapping exercises, and a variety of objective questions to guide students through the text material. Links to related websites make the student Online Learning Center a great place to begin web-based research.

Qualifications As a full service publisher of quality education products, McGraw-Hill does much more than just sell textbooks to your students. We create and publish an extensive array of print, video, and digital supplements to support instruction on your campus. Orders of new (versus used) textbooks help us to defray the cost of developing such supplements, which is substantial. Please consult your local McGraw-Hill sales representative to learn about the availability of the supplements that accompany *The West in the World.*

ACKNOWLEDGMENTS

We have nurtured this book through many drafts, and every page has benefited from the advice of numerous reviewers, some of whom we have gone back to several times. For their thoughtful comments and generous contribution of time and expertise, we would like to thank the following reviewers:

Edward Anson
University of Arkansas

William S. Arnett
West Virginia University

Richard Berthold
University of New Mexico

Robert Blackey
California State University—San Bernardino

Hugh Boyer
Michigan Technical University

Carol Bresnahan-Menning
University of Toledo

April Brooks
South Dakota State University

Nathan Brooks
New Mexico State University

Blaine T. Browne
Broward Community College

Donald Butts
Gordon College

Frederick Corney
University of Florida

Jeffrey Cox
University of Iowa

Florin Curta
University of Florida

Norman Delaney
Del Mar College

Robert Dise
University of Northern Iowa

Chris Drake
Houston Community College–Northwest

Lawrence G. Duggan
University of Delaware

Laird Easton
California State University–Chico

Gregory Elder
Riverside Community College

Nancy Erickson
Erskine College

Chiarella Esposito
University of Mississippi

Gary Ferngren
Oregon State University

Nancy Fitch
California State University–Fullerton

Elizabeth Lane Furdell
University of North Florida

Frank Garosi
California State University–Sacramento

Don Gawronski
Mesa Community College

Paul Goodwin
University of Connecticut

Anita Guerrini
University of California –Santa Barbara

Louis Haas
Duquesne University

Alice Henderson
University of South Carolina–Spartanburg

Jennifer Hevelone-Harper
Gordon College

Steven Hill
Wake Technical Community College

Laura J. Hilton
Ohio State University

Karen Holland
Providence College

David Hudson
California State University–Fresno

Gary Johnson
University of Southern Maine

Jonathan G. Katz
Oregon State University

Andrew Keitt
University of Alabama–Birmingham

Charles Killinger
Valencia Community College

Lisa Lane
Mira Costa College

John Livingston
University of Denver

David Longfellow
Baylor University

Donna Maier
University of Northern Iowa

James I. Martin, Sr.
Campbell University

Carol Miller
Tallahassee Community College

Eileen Moore
University of Alabama–Birmingham

Frederick I. Murphy
Western Kentucky University

Max J. Okenfuss
Washington University

Michael Osborne
University of California–Santa Barbara

John P. Pesda
Camden County College

Russell Quinlan
Northern Arizona University

Patricia Ranft
Central Michigan University

Roger Reese
Texas A&M University

Harry Rosenberg
Colorado State University

Constance M. Rousseau
Providence College

Jay Rubenstein
University of New Mexico

Claire Sanders
Texas Christian College

Alan Schaffer
Clemson University

Daryl Schuster
University of Central Florida

Marc Schwarz
University of New Hampshire

David Shearer
University of Delaware

Arlene Sindelar
University of Central Arkansas

James Sisson
Central Texas College

Ronald D. Smith
Arizona State University

Saulius Suziedelis
Millersville University of Pennsylvania

Hunt Tooley
Austin College

Kevin Uhalde
Northern Illinois University

David Ulbrich
Kansas State University

Bruce Venarde
University of Pittsburgh

Charlotte Wells
University of Northern Iowa

Michael Wilson
University of Texas–Dallas

Robert Wise
University of Northern Iowa

Bill Wrightson
American River College

We would also like to offer a special thank-you to the reviewer focus group participants. We appreciate your generous contribution of time and attention to this book, from its inception to the final design touches.

In addition, we would like to thank Lauren Johnson, who served as the developmental editor, for her detailed line-by-line editing, and Peter Seelig, Karen Lewis, and William Whiting for their research assistance.

Last, but certainly not least, we would like to thank the many professors who choose to use this text in their classrooms. It is they who will fulfill our hope for this text—that it will bring the past to life for many undergraduates and will perhaps awaken in them a love for history and an awareness that understanding the past is the key to our future.

Charles Lebrun, *Chancellor Seguier*

Chancellor Pierre Seguier (1588–1672) was an ambitious courtier to the French king Louis XIV, and a member of France's new nobility that earned position by service to the crown, the noblesse de robe. In this painting, Seguier's office is symbolized by the formal robes he wears, rather than by arms. Several well-dressed pages surround him, one holding an umbrella over his head as if he were a minor monarch. His face conveys a sense of pleased assurance with the position he has gained. Charles Lebrun (1619–1690), like several other leading artists of the day, served as painter to Louis XIV and for eighteen years created decorations for the king's Versailles palace.

CHAPTER 13

The Struggle for Survival and Sovereignty

Europe's Social and Political Order, 1600–1715

"This poor country is a horrible sight," wrote the abbess of a French town in January 1649. "[I]t is stripped of everything. The soldiers take possession of the farms . . . there are no more horses . . . the peasants are reduced to sleeping in the woods . . . and if they only had enough bread to half satisfy their hunger, they would indeed count themselves happy." France had just emerged a victor from the Thirty Years' War (discussed in Chapter 11) only to find itself embroiled in a series of internal revolts. These revolts, like many others erupting throughout Europe, signaled new strains on European society from the bottom to the top of the traditional order.

For the vast majority—peasants who worked the fields—pressures came from powers outside their control. The landowning aristocracy required service and obedience; governmental officials demanded ever more taxes and military service; and the impersonal forces that most people attributed to luck, fate, or God brought bad weather, failed harvests, and plagues. Sometimes peasants fled their aristocratic masters or turned violently against isolated governmental officials. However, against the fates and well-armed soldiers, they were powerless.

For those at the top of society, the pressures came from central governments and monarchs. Kings, struggling with the increasingly heavy burdens of war and governance, chipped away at aristocratic independence year after year. They argued that "the royal power is absolute. . . . The prince [king] need render account of his acts to no one." Elites insisted that "our privileges and liberties are our right and due inheritance, no less than our very lands and goods." This contention between monarch and aristocrat sometimes broke out in violence, other times led to compromises, and often severely strained the elite order.

These two struggles—the first faced by the vast majority on the bottom, the second by the dominant elites on top—colored the West's social and political life during the seventeenth and early eighteenth centuries. This chapter follows these intertwined conflicts in four areas—France, eastern Europe, England, and the Netherlands—where the story took different turns.

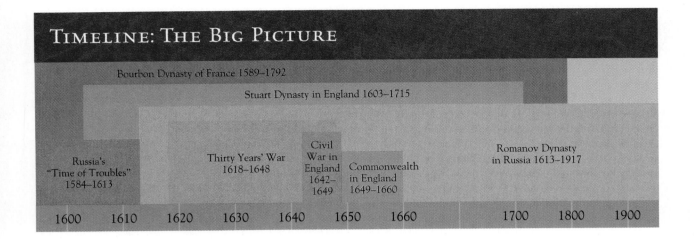

Bourbon Dynasty of France 1589–1792

Stuart Dynasty in England 1603–1715

Civil War in England 1642–1649

Russia's "Time of Troubles" 1584–1613

Thirty Years' War 1618–1648

Commonwealth in England 1649–1660

Romanov Dynasty in Russia 1613–1917

1600   1610   1620   1630   1640   1650   1660   1700   1800   1900

Stresses in Traditional Society

"It is necessary that some command and others obey," explained a French judge and legal scholar in 1610. "Sovereign lords address their commands to the great; the great to the middling, the middling to the small, and the small to the people." This description captures the traditional social order that reigned in the West during the seventeenth century. Indeed, people took this order for granted. The structure was based on a hierarchy of ranks, and each rank, from nobility to peasantry, had its set status and occupations. Within each rank were subranks. For example, a hierarchy of titles and offices determined position among the nobility. Artisans divided themselves into masters, journeymen, and apprentices. Within the peasantry, landholders stood above laborers, and all looked down on serfs. Each rank distinguished itself through conventions, dress, duties, and etiquette. Finally, within all these ranks position went hand in hand with family, itself ranked with men at the top, followed by women, and then children at the bottom.

Together the ranks made up the "body politic," with kings and nobles serving as the head and arms, and artisans and peasants as hands and feet. All worked together to perpetuate life as an organic whole. Everywhere the church and religious sentiments sanctified this organic social hierarchy. Indeed, the social structure paralleled what westerners saw as the larger, hierarchical order of the universe—the Great Chain of Being. In the Great Chain, everything—from God to the angels, humans, animals, and plants—existed in an ordered, permanent arrangement. During the seventeenth century, new forces tested the smooth running of this traditional society.

MOUNTING DEMANDS ON RURAL LIFE

Facing new demands from many quarters, rural life declined. At the beginning of the century, life for most Europeans typically centered on small, self-sufficient villages that contained a few to a hundred families. A church or manor served as the center of communal activities. Strangers attracted intense scrutiny, and most authorities were local people whom everyone knew. When bad harvests, plagues, or war struck, the villagers received little help from the outside.

The majority of people lived in crowded one-room houses made of timber, thatch, and mud, with one or two narrow windows. At one end of the house stood a stone hearth used for light, cooking, and heat. Wood and peat, which fired the stove, were often in short supply, and the villagers struggled to stay warm during the winters. Grain, in the form of black bread and porridge, made up most meals, though in some areas meat, vegetables, fruits, and dairy products supplemented diets. A few treasured pots, pans, and utensils served all.

In Figure 13.1, Louis le Nain (1593–1648), a French artist known for his realistic paintings of peasant life, shows a farmyard scene in rural France. Here women and children of varying ages stand on a cart or tend a few animals. One woman sits with her baby on the ground; another has slung a large pot over her back, perhaps in preparation for gathering water. In the background stands a modest house. The faces of these people express a grimness; clearly they have known hard times and would endure difficulties again and again. Many seventeenth-century Europeans were poorer even than those in this painting. According to one observer in 1696, "They suffer from exposure: winter and summer, three-fourths of them are dressed in nothing but half-rotting tattered linen, and wear throughout the year wooden shoes and no other covering for the foot."

As in past centuries, the family functioned as both a social and an *The family* economic unit. Women and men married for practical as well as sentimental reasons. The land, wealth, skills, and position one held counted for much in a potential marriage partner. Husband, wife, and children lived together, and most marriages, whether happy or not, lasted until death. At various times, relatives, domestics, and laborers might live for a while in the household. Finally, although everyone worked together in the fields, men generally did the heaviest work, while women gardened, raised poultry, and supervised dairy producing.

FIGURE 13.1
Louis le Nain, *The Cart*, 1641.

Fathers, older children, and other relatives might also participate with mothers in raising and socializing young children. Nevertheless, children were not considered at the center of family life, and girls were less valued than boys. Indeed, parents often sent children away to other households to work as apprentices, domestics, or laborers if they could earn more there. Infant mortality ran high; of the five or more children to whom a woman was likely to give birth, only two or three lived beyond five years. Parents valued and cared for their children, but in a time of grinding poverty, it is not surprising that parents also viewed children as either assets or liabilities in the struggle for survival; great emotional entanglements with them were risky.

The stresses on these common people are strikingly revealed by the population decreases that occurred during the first half of the *Population changes* seventeenth century. The devastation from the seemingly endless wars took many lives, especially in German lands. The old enemies—poverty, disease, and famine—also roared through these decades. Severe winters left their mark, and wet summers destroyed crops. Suffering, malnutrition, illness, and too often death, followed. "The staple dish here consists of mice, which the inhabitants hunt, so

desperate are they from hunger," reported provincial officials in northern France in 1651. "They devour roots which the animals cannot eat . . . not a day passes but at least 200 people die of famine in the two provinces."

Bad times also meant postponed marriages, fewer births, and an increase in the number of deaths among infants and children. Europeans already married late compared to the rest of the world. On average, men waited until their late twenties to wed; women until their mid-twenties. Sometimes so many people died, wandered away in search of food, or fled to the cities that whole villages were abandoned. Conditions improved a bit during the second half of the century, though only enough for the European population to maintain itself and perhaps grow slightly. Life expectancy, which varied by social class and region, was probably less than thirty years (in part, due to high infant mortality).

New demands from central governments cut into traditional patterns of rural life. With every new outbreak of war, governmental officials intruded more and more into villages in search of army conscripts. People resisted, and for good reason. Military service took men out of the fields, increasing the burden on

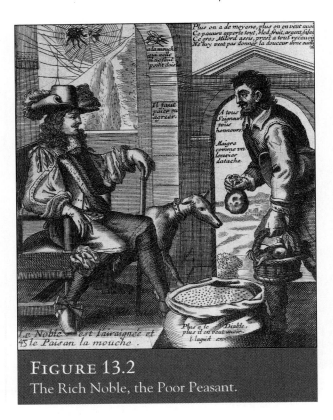

FIGURE 13.2
The Rich Noble, the Poor Peasant.

the women, children, and elderly who had to shoulder the men's share of the labor. Soldiers embroiled in nearby battles plundered what they could from the villages they passed.

Officials also came with new tax assessments, even though peasants already owed much to those above them. Traditional taxes to the government, tithes to the church, and rents to large landowners used up more than half of the already scant wealth peasants produced. Figure 13.2, a mid-seventeenth-century print, caustically depicts some of the peasants' grievances. On the left, the well-dressed noble sits authoritatively on his padded chair to receive the peasant ("thin as the noble's terrier"), who is bringing money in his right hand, fruits and vegetables in his left hand, and a sack of wheat at his feet. Above the noble is a spider and a fly caught in its web. As the caption on the lower left states, "The noble is the spider and the peasant the fly." The noble says, "You must pay or serve." The peasant can only reply, "To all masters, all honors."

Peasants avoided collectors and hid what assets they could. In countless incidents, peasants and city-dwellers across Europe rose against increasing taxes and attacked the hated collectors. In the 1630s, for example, French peasants rose against tax increases and forced temporary concessions from local officials, only to have those victories reversed by the state. Farther south, in 1647, women demanding more bread led riots that swept through the city of Palermo in Spanish-occupied Italy. Rebels in the city chanted, "down with taxes!" As in France, government forces eventually reversed early victories and crushed the revolt.

Tax revolts

Other intrusions further eroded the traditional isolation that characterized rural life. Officials and merchants ventured more and more often to the countryside to buy grain for cities, creating food shortages in rural villages. Moreover, as members of the local nobility departed for capital cities and the king's court, new officials appeared and began administering affairs and rendering judgments in courts. For good or ill, villagers found themselves increasingly drawn into the web of national affairs.

PRESSURES ON THE UPPER ORDERS

Monarchs faced pressures of their own, especially the demands of war. In the competition for territory and status, kings won by fielding ever larger armies and mustering the resources needed to support them. During the seventeenth century, armies doubled and redoubled in size, as did the central governments that supported them (see Chapter 11). The costs of making war and supporting government increased accordingly. Governments devoted half or more of their income to the military, and monarchs desperate for money levied more and more taxes just to stay even. The ability to collect taxes could make or break a ruler. More than anything else, a king's unrelenting demands for more taxes sparked widespread resistance to his rule.

Competing centers of power added to the kings' problems. Independent town officials, church leaders, and provincial officials tried to hold on to their authority over local matters. Religious dissidents, for their part, guarded what independence they could. Finally, those who resented the royal tax collectors resisted the crown's reach. But the greatest threat to monarchical power came from aristocrats, who tried to retain as much of their social and economic dominance as possible. These nobles often challenged

Competing centers of power

royal policies and decried royal "tyranny" as a violation of divine law. They guarded their traditional rights and local authority, and many of them refused to give up their tax exemptions. Should the crown falter, they stood ready to take back any powers they might have lost.

Monarchs argued with, fought, and schemed against these forms of opposition. They justified their power as a divine right, because they represented God on Earth, and surrounded themselves with compliant advisors and admirers. Their favored supporters, such as France's court preacher and royal tutor, Bishop Jacques Bossuet (1627–1704), backed them. As Bossuet declared, "The whole state is included in him [the monarch], the will of all the people is enclosed within his own."

Yet the kings used more than words and "yes-men" in this power struggle. Bypassing representative institutions, they sent their royal law courts into the provinces as a way to extend their authority. Sometimes they appointed new local leaders to gain allies. Other times, they attracted aristocrats from the provinces to the royal court, thereby creating a power vacuum that they then filled with their own men. When great nobles resisted being turned into obedient officials, rulers often turned to the lesser nobility or members of the wealthy middle class—men such as Chancellor Seguier, whom we met in the photo on p. 426. Such royal servants received titles or land and were elevated to high office as compensation for their loyalty.

Women also became entwined in these struggles between monarchs and aristocrats. With the royal courts growing in size, many women became important friends and unofficial advisors to kings and influential aristocrats. They used their intelligence, wit, services, and advice to gain privileged positions in royal courts. Once there, they won titles, offices, lands, money, and advantageous marriages for themselves and their families. Mothers encouraged their daughters not to let good marriage opportunities pass by. "It is true that [the proposed groom] is some fifteen years older than you," wrote one aristocratic mother in 1622. "[B]ut . . . you are going to marry a man . . . who has spent his life honorably at court and at the wars and has been granted considerable payments by the king." Royal mistresses also achieved important positions in the king's household. Françoise d'Aubigné (Marquise de Maintenon), mistress (and, secretly, wife) of France's king Louis XIV, influenced

court appointments and founded a royal school for the daughters of impoverished nobles in 1686. Some mistresses even persuaded kings to acknowledge their children as "royal bastards" and grant them titles and privileges.

This system of elevated royal authority has been called "royal absolutism," because the kings of the day commanded more loyalty, control, *Royal absolutism* and resources than their predecessors had, and because they justified their right to rule as an absolute. However no monarch gained true absolute power. Most people understood that even the strongest ruler, divinely ordained, was vaguely subject to tradition and law. As one seventeenth-century French jurist explained, the king's power "seems to place him above the law, . . . [but] his rank obliges him to subordinate his personal interests to the general good of the state." Further, with so many local centers of power, scores of nobles who persisted in their independent ways, and too much information to control, no king in this era could hope to dominate everything. Some monarchs even found themselves on losing ends of internal battles for power.

Royal Absolutism in France

In western Europe, the efforts of French kings to maximize their power exemplified the development of royal absolutism. Building upon the work of predecessors who had enhanced the power of the monarchy, Louis XIV (r. 1643–1715) took personal control of the French monarchy in 1661. By then, France had supplanted Spain as the most powerful nation in Europe. Under Louis' long rule, royal absolutism reached its peak and inspired other monarchs to emulate his style.

HENRY IV SECURES THE MONARCHY

French absolutism had its immediate roots in the reign of Henry IV (r.1589–1610). When Henry IV ascended the French throne in 1589, his country had endured several decades of wars between Protestants and Catholics combined with conflicts between different political factions. Law and order had broken down, and powerful nobles had reasserted their authority. The finances of the central government lay in disarray, and French prestige abroad had sunk to a low ebb.

The talented, witty Henry, in his prime at thirty-six, set out to change all this. He defused the religious turmoil by issuing the Edict of Nantes (see Chapter 11), which granted to Huguenots (French Protestants) religious toleration and control of some 200 fortified cities and towns as a guarantee against future oppression. He appealed to the traditional nobility by developing an image as a cultured warrior-king who could be trusted to enforce the law. He catered to rich lawyers, merchants, and landowners by selling new governmental offices, which often came with ennoblement as well as prestige. This growing elite became known as the nobility of the robe, because their robes of office, rather than the arms borne by the traditional nobility of the sword, represented their power (see p. 426). Many of these nobles gladly paid annual fees for the right to pass their offices on to heirs. For the peasantry, Henry suggested that prosperity should bring "a chicken in the pot of every peasant for Sunday dinner." Not surprisingly, Henry's authority and popularity soared.

With the help of his able, methodical administrator, the duke of Sully (1560–1641), Henry also launched a comprehensive program of economic reconstruction. Agriculture and commerce benefitted from the increased security of life and property brought by better law enforcement; from improved transportation facilitated by the repair of roads, bridges, and harbors; and from the freeing of trade thanks to lower internal tariff barriers. The monarchy even subsidized and protected new industries that produced luxuries such as glass, porcelain, lace, silk, tapestries, fine leather, and textiles. Sully's efficient collection of taxes and administration of expenditures produced a rare budget surplus.

Henry also dreamed of making France secure from ambitious foreign states and of ensuring his country a supreme position in all of Europe. However, the powerful Spanish and Austrian Habsburgs on France's borders stood in his way. In 1610, he prepared to join his armies for a campaign against his rivals. Yet before he could set out, he was assassinated by a fanatic, and his plans died with him.

RICHELIEU ELEVATES ROYAL AUTHORITY

For several years after Henry's death, his Italian wife, Marie de Médicis (1573–1642), ruled as regent for their son, the young Louis XIII (r.1610–1643). Marie kept opponents at arm's length, but made little new headway in strengthening the position of the monarchy. Then in 1624, one of her favorite advisors, Cardinal Richelieu (1585–1642), became chief minister and began exercising power from behind the throne. Having come from a minor noble family and possessing a keen intellect, the arrogant and calculating Richelieu handled the young king deftly and controlled others through a skillful blend of patronage and punishment. His twofold policy was to make royal power supreme in France, and to maneuver France into a position of dominance in Europe. To Louis XIII, Richelieu promised "to ruin the Huguenot party, to abase the pride of the nobles, to bring back all your subjects to their duty, and to elevate your name among foreign nations to the point where it belongs."

With the royal army at his disposal, Richelieu boldly destroyed the castles of nobles who opposed the king, disbanded their private armies, and executed a number of the most recalcitrant among them. When Huguenot nobles in the southwest rebelled, Richelieu sent in the army and stripped the Huguenots of the special military and political privileges that Henry IV had granted them. Only their religious liberties remained intact. To dilute local centers of political power, the dynamic minister divided France into some thirty administrative districts, placing each under the control of a powerful *intendant*, who was an agent of the crown. He chose these intendants from the ranks of the middle class and recently ennobled people and shifted them around frequently lest they become too sympathetic with their localities. Finally, Richelieu plunged France into the Thirty Years' War in Germany (see Chapter 11). His purpose was to weaken the Habsburgs, chief rivals of the French monarchs for European supremacy.

By the time of his death in 1642, Richelieu had firmly secured royal power in France and elevated France's position in Europe. Nevertheless, the imperious cardinal, having more than doubled taxes to promote his policies, had gained few friends. Far more French subjects rejoiced in his death than mourned his passing.

MAZARIN OVERCOMES THE OPPOSITION

Richelieu was succeeded by his protégé, Cardinal Jules Mazarin (1602–1661). Louis XIII's death in 1643, a few months after that of his great minister, left the throne to Louis XIV, a child of five. Mazarin, who began his career as a gambler and diplomat, played the same role in the early reign of Louis XIV and his regent, Anne of Austria (1601–1666), that Richelieu had played during the reign of Louis XIII.

Early on, Mazarin, Anne, and the child-king faced a series of wide-ranging, uncoordinated revolts that **The Fronde** forced them to flee Paris. Known collectively as the Fronde (the name of a child's slingshot game, which implied that the participants were childish), these revolts stemmed primarily from French subjects' objections to high taxes and increasing royal power. Between 1648 and 1653, ambitious nobles, footloose soldiers returning from war, urban artisans, and even some peasants fought the monarchy and its supporters in what amounted to a civil war at times. Bad harvests only added to the chaos and suffering: "People massacre each other daily with every sort of cruelty," wrote an observer in 1652. "The soldiers steal from one another when they have denuded everyone else . . . all the armies are equally undisciplined and vie with one another in lawlessness." Nobles conspired and shifted alliances for their own gains, resulting in growing disillusionment with their cause. Gaining support from city-dwellers and peasants longing for peace, and shrewdly buying off one noble after another, Mazarin quashed the revolts by 1653. The crown gradually reasserted itself as the basis for order in France.

The Fronde was paralleled by other revolts during the 1640s in Spain, the Italian states, and much more seriously, in England. In each case, the catalysts included new taxes, the demand for more men and supplies for the military, and monarchies' efforts to acquire more power. In the Spanish provinces of Catalonia and Portugal, as well as in the Italian states of Naples and Sicily, rebels murdered tax officials, peasants took up arms, and local nobles joined the fray. Localities demanded and sometimes got concessions, but many of these victories proved short lived when the crown reasserted its authority. As we will see, matters grew much worse in England. Taken together, these midcentury rebellions served as a warning to monarchs not to push unpopular policies too far—and to the aristocracy not to underestimate the power of the crown.

THE SUN KING RISES

Upon Mazarin's death in 1661, the twenty-three-year-old Louis XIV finally stepped forward to rule in his own right. "Up to this moment I have been pleased to entrust the government of my affairs to the late Cardinal," he announced. "It is now time that I govern them myself." With his regal bearing and stolid build, young Louis fit the part well. His lack of intellectual brilliance was offset by a sharp memory, a sense of responsibility, and a capacity for tedious work. "One reigns only by dint of hard work," he warned his own son. Haunted by childhood memories of fleeing in terror across the tiled rooftops of Paris during the Fronde revolts, he remained determined to prevent further challenges from rebellious aristocrats. By his mother, Mazarin, and a succession of tutors, Louis had been convinced that he was God's appointed deputy for France. Supporting him was the most famous exponent of royal absolutism, Bishop Bossuet, who argued that the monarchy "is sacred, it is paternal, it is absolute, and it is subject to reason . . . the royal throne is not that of a man but the throne of God Himself." In words commonly attributed to Louis, "*L'état, c'est moi*" ("I am the state").

However, Louis could not possibly perform all the functions of government personally. The great bulk of the details were handled by a series of councils and bureaus and administered locally by the intendants. Distrusting the traditional nobility, Louis instead usually appointed members of modest noble backgrounds to the important offices of his government. Well supervised by the industrious king, the administrative machinery hummed along.

To raise his stature, Louis XIV initiated massive public-works projects that glorified him, his government, and his reign. His greatest architectural project was a new palace. Hating the **Versailles** tumult of Paris, with its streets teeming with commoners, he selected Versailles, eleven miles southwest of the city, as the new seat of government. There, as many as 35,000 workmen toiled for over forty years to turn marshes and sand into Europe's most splendid palace and grounds.

Figure 13.3 shows Versailles in 1668. Over the next forty-three years, successive teams of workers added rear gardens and more than doubled the size of the buildings. This painting, which shows the roads, paths, and gardens of Versailles geometrically laid out, gives a sense of the scale of the project. In the foreground to the right, the royal coach, with its train of followers, arrives at the front gates. The exterior of Versailles was designed in long, horizontal, classic lines. The interior boasted a lavish baroque style with richly colored marbles, mosaics, inlaid

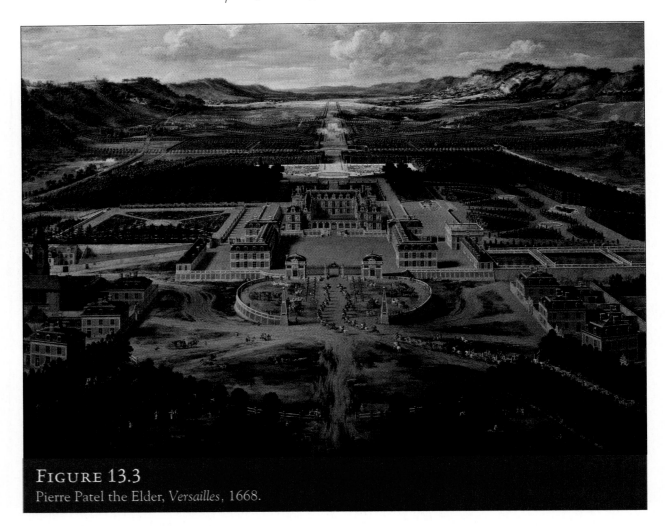

FIGURE 13.3
Pierre Patel the Elder, *Versailles*, 1668.

woods, gilt, silver, silk, velvet, and brocade. Ceiling-to-floor windows and mirrors, and crystal chandeliers holding thousands of candles illuminated the salons and halls. In terms of sheer capacity, the palace could house 5,000 people and serve thousands more visitors each day. It faced hundreds of acres of groves, walks, canals, pools, terraces, fountains, statues, flower beds, and clipped shrubs—all laid out in formal geometric patterns symbolizing the triumph of engineering over nature. So dazzling was this hallmark of royal absolutism that other European monarchs soon attempted to copy it.

Louis used Versailles, images of himself, and symbols to enhance his authority among the nobility and everyone else. "The peoples over whom we reign, being unable to apprehend the basic reality of things, usually derive their opinions from what they can see

with their eyes," he explained. Figure 13.4, a painting by an anonymous seventeenth-century artist, shows Louis—in the center astride a white horse—as he rides into the gardens at Versailles. His favored courtiers throng around him, hoping to be seen by him and others more than to see him. Servants mingle in the crowd as well. Above is the king's chosen symbol, the sun, with its light radiating out. As Louis put it, "The symbol that I have adopted and that you see all around you represents the duties of a Prince . . . endlessly promoting life, joy and growth." It is "the most dazzling and most beautiful image of the monarch."

The "Sun King" finally moved to Versailles in 1682. Once established there, he lured the men and women of the nobility away from their local centers of power where they might make trouble and turned them into domesticated court "butterflies." He subjected them to a complex system of etiquette and favoritism that made every aspect of Louis' daily life the center of their concern. Court became a theatre where those already in favor, as well as aspiring favorites, had to scheme for gifts, patronage, and position. Winners might secure lucrative rewards, losers might spend themselves broke trying to stay in the race.

Versailles critics

Despite the grandeur of Versailles, this glittering monument to royal absolutism had its critics. In her novel *The Princess of Clèves* (1678), the Countess de Lafayette complained that at Versailles "everybody was busily trying to better their position by pleasing, by helping, or by hindering somebody else." The court reportedly seethed with gossip, scandal, and intrigue. Critics such as Pierre Jurieu, a French Calvinist pastor who fled to Holland, lamented that the king "is the idol to which are sacrificed princes, great men and small, families, provinces, cities, finances and generally everything." Resentful nobles once proudly drawing high status from their lands and lineage came to depend on the approval of and service to the king as the primary route to power. Many hard-toiling, heavily taxed French commoners also grumbled about living in the reflected glory of a pretentious monarch.

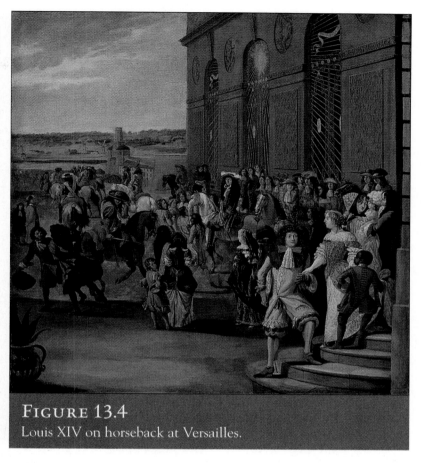

FIGURE 13.4
Louis XIV on horseback at Versailles.

"Classical" literature

To enhance the glory of his court, Louis XIV subsidized and attracted to Versailles leading French artists and literary figures. The elegance, the sense of order, and the formalism of royalty all found expression in much of the literature of this "classical" period in French culture. Pierre Corneille (1606–1684), for example, wrote elegant plays modeled on the ancient Greek tragedies. Human beings' conflicts with their own nature and with the workings of fate and the universe furnished the plots. Even more exquisite were the perfectly rhymed and metered couplets of Jean Racine's (1639–1699) dramas. Finally, in his profound comedies, Jean-Baptiste Molière (1622–1673) satirized pompous scholars, social climbers, false priests, and quack physicians. Louis and his court had little to fear from this literature. On the contrary, they appreciated its formal order and laughed along with other audiences at its satire, which was aimed at humankind in general rather than at specific ruling regimes.

At court and elsewhere, many members of the elite also read historical romances. Perhaps the most popular of these was *Grand Cyrus* by Madeleine de Scudéry (1608–1701), a writer who rose from an impoverished background. The fact that this book was published under the name of the author's brother, Georges, hints at the difficulties women faced in expressing their cultural talents. Other forms of literature included letters and memoirs. The courtier Madame de Sévigné (1626–1696), for example, wrote almost 2000 letters to her daughter that reported what the king said and

FIGURE 13.5
Claude Lorraine, *The Marriage of Isaac and Rebekah (The Mill)*, 1640.

did as well as news of marriages, deaths, gossip, fads, and conspiracies that marked life at the court of Louis XIV. The duke of Saint-Simon (1675–1755), who like many nobles felt slighted and grew to resent the king, chronicled life at Versailles in his forty volume *Memoirs*.

While the literature of the seventeenth century amused monarchs, the visual arts of the period positively glorified them. Kings and aristocrats **Visual arts** still favored the baroque style of painting and architecture (see Chapter 11). As they saw it, the baroque's swirling forms and massive, ornamental elegance perfectly reflected their wealth and power. Yet during the second half of the seventeenth century, classicism, with its emphasis on control and restraint,

began to gain favor. The appealing paintings of French artists Claude Lorraine (1600–1682) and Nicolas Poussin (1594–1665) helped classicism win official approval in France. Both men spent much time in Italy, studying the Renaissance masters and the Italian landscape. Figure 13.5 embodies their style. In this painting, Lorraine has framed the foreground figures with trees under a radiant sky. The Italian landscape is geometrically balanced, the figures are in classic dress, and the scene exudes calm and discipline. Here is an idyllic vision, a scene designed to elevate the minds of viewers. Compared to the baroque, the classical style shows a logic that echoed the sense of order pervading the Versailles court of the Sun King.

Versailles, the arts, and all other aspects of government cost money. Louis assigned the talented Jean-Baptiste Colbert (1619–1683) to manage his finances.

Colbert An engine of efficiency, Colbert toiled endlessly, supervising the details of the French economy while also promoting culture by founding the Royal Academy of Sciences in 1666 and subsidizing the arts. In keeping with his bourgeois origins, he chose service to the king as his means of advancement. His family shared in his success, becoming ministers, gaining high offices in the church, marrying well, and securing top positions in the military.

Promoting mercantilistic economic policies (see Chapter 12), Colbert protected industries with high tariffs while subsidizing exports and new industries. To encourage France's growing empire and the commerce it generated, he built a large navy. Finally, Colbert worked to ensure a worldwide reputation for the uniformly high quality of French products. He subjected manufacturing to the most minute regulation and supervision: So many threads of such and such quality and color must go into every inch of this textile and that lace. Although Colbert's restrictive mercantilistic controls in the long run stifled initiative and economic change, French products earned wide acclaim for their quality. By his death in 1683, Colbert had balanced the budget and promoted relative prosperity despite Louis XIV's lavish expenditures.

During the following decades, however, Louis embarked on policies that undermined much of what Colbert had accomplished. The king's demands for religious conformity and his military ambitions ranked among the most destructive of these policies. Huguenots (French Protestants) paid the highest price for his religious intolerance. In 1685 Louis revoked the Edict of Nantes, which in 1598 had granted tolerance to the Protestant minority. Then he outlawed Protestantism and ordered Protestant churches demolished. The duke of Saint-Simon lamented that the "ultimate results [of the reversal] were the depopulation of a fourth part of the kingdom and the ruin of our commerce . . . the country was given over to the authorized ravages of dragoons [armed troops], which caused the death of, literally, thousands of innocent people of all ages and both sexes." Although Huguenots were forbidden to emigrate, perhaps as many as 200,000 did, taking their wealth and skills with them to Protestant-friendly areas in Europe and America, "enriching them and causing their cities to flourish at the expense of France," according to Saint-Simon. Up to a million Huguenots who remained in France went underground.

Nor was Louis content to rule in peace as the leader of Europe's most powerful nation. During the last four decades of his *Wars of aggression* seventy-two-year reign, he fought four wars of aggression. The same old reasons prompted him to lead France into battle: more territory, more glory, and more wealth. He set his sights on the Spanish and Austrian Habsburg lands on France's eastern borders and on the Dutch, France's most powerful commercial rivals on the Continent. He put his war minister, the marquis of Louvois (1639–1691), in charge of organizing France's huge military establishment on the model of a complex business, replete with supply depots and hospitals. While Louvois introduced strict discipline, uniforms, and promotions based on merit, Sébastien de Vauban (1633–1707) designed sturdy fortifications and brilliant siege operations. It was a common saying that whereas a city defended by Vauban was safe, one besieged by Vauban was doomed.

Louis initiated his foreign adventures in the War of Devolution (1667–1668), waged against Spain for French claims in the Spanish Netherlands and Franche-Comté (Burgundy). When victory seemed within reach, the United Provinces, England, and Sweden joined Spain to prevent France from upsetting the balance of power. The Treaty of Aix-la-Chapelle (1668) brought Louis only minor gains (see Map 13.1). In 1672 Louis turned against the Dutch, who he blamed for organizing the alliance against him and who were France's chief trade competitors. The Dutch stopped the invading French only by opening the dikes and flooding the land. Dutch diplomacy brought Spain, Sweden, Brandenburg, and the Holy Roman Empire into an alliance against the French. Louis fought them to a standstill, and gained some valuable territories in the Peace of Nijmegen (1679). In the following years, Louis made enemies of the Austrians by refusing to help in their war against the Turks, and he alienated Europe's Protestants by turning against the Huguenots. Fearful that he intended to upset the balance of power and dominate the Continent, much of Europe formed the Grand Alliance against him. The eight-year War of the League of Augsburg (1689–1697) gained France little territory at the cost of much bloodshed and misery. Louis' final struggle, the War of the Spanish Succession, was

THINKING ABOUT GEOGRAPHY

MAP 13.1 *France under Louis XIV, 1661–1715*

This map shows France's provinces and the territorial gains it made during the reign of Louis XIV.
⬧ **Notice** that most of Louis' gains came from Spanish lands and German states on France's eastern border. **What** might this imply about vulnerable areas of Europe and changing power relationships?
⬧ **Consider** how little France's gains were despite almost endless, costly wars. **What** were the likely consequences for France's finances and the popularity of its monarch?

fought over French claims to the Spanish throne and the partition of Spanish holdings in the Netherlands and Italy. The war lasted eleven years (1702–1713), and the Grand Alliance defeated French and Spanish forces in a series of battles. Beaten, impoverished, and facing revolts fueled by despair and opposition to tax-

ation, Louis XIV was forced to accept the Peace of Utrecht (1713), which ended Louis' ambitions to create a partnership of Bourbon monarchs in France and Spain—with France the senior partner. Map 13.1 depicts France in 1661, when Louis XIV took control of the monarchy, and the territories he eventually acquired. In the end, he possessed little more than what he had started with some fifty years earlier, and had even fewer holdings in North America.

Louis XIV died only two years after the Peace of Utrecht. He had long outlived his popularity. One widely circulated letter from an aristocratic critic, Archbishop Fénélon, complained that "for thirty years, your principal ministers have . . . overthrown all the ancient maxims of the state in order to increase your authority beyond all bounds. . . . For the sake of getting and keeping vain conquests abroad, you have destroyed half the real strength of your own state." As the coffin carrying Louis XIV's body was drawn through the streets of Paris, some of his abused subjects cursed his name.

The Sun King had built the French state into the envy of Europe, and his glittering court at Versailles outshone all others. His success relied on knowing how to use the old system, modified by preceding state-builders such as Richelieu, to his advantage. He tamed rather than fought the nobility, who at the same time remained the crown's most important ally and potent competitor. Clearly, strong central governments enjoyed advantages, and none were stronger than France's under Louis XIV. For many monarchs, France under Louis XIV became the model of absolutism. However his expenditures and wars created unprecedented misery for most commoners saddled with relentlessly rising taxes, more military service, and famines. Recognizing that the continued power of the state required some support of the people, Louis' successors would try to avoid his mistakes and ameliorate the worst threats to the lives of French people.

Assessing Louis XIV

The Struggle for Sovereignty in Eastern Europe

In eastern Europe, people struggled just as fiercely to survive and to define sovereignty as they did in the west. However, the two regions differed sharply, and those differences affected the outcomes of battles over these issues. States east of the Elbe River (see Map 13.2) were less commercially developed than those in western Europe. Instead of farms worked by legally free and mobile peasants, estate agriculture (large landed estates owned by lords and worked by their serfs) dominated those economies. By the six-

teenth century, the nobles who owned these estates had reversed the medieval trends toward greater freedom for the peasantry and the growth of towns. Most people who worked the fields sank into serfdom, bound to the land and owing ever increasing services to their lords. The middle classes in the towns also declined, failing to gain in numbers and wealth like their counterparts in western Europe. Finally, most central governments at the beginning of the seventeenth century proved weaker than those in western European states, as powerful nobles retained much independence. Despite all this, several monarchs decided to change things in their own favor.

CENTRALIZING THE STATE IN BRANDENBURG-PRUSSIA

In Brandenburg-Prussia, the "Great Elector" Frederick William (r. 1640–1688) inherited a scattered patchwork of poorly managed lands weakened by years of war and population decline. He faced a number of other problems as well. His army was tiny—too weak to keep foreign forces out of his lands or to discipline internal opponents. His nobles, or *Junkers*, had an independent streak and had found ways to avoid most taxes. Finally, his cities remained uncooperative, asserting their long-established political and economic independence.

Frederick William set out to correct the situation. He believed that the key was to strengthen his standing army. Only then could he gain control of his lands and make Brandenburg-Prussia a desired ally in international affairs. During the 1640s he more than tripled the size of his army. This new strength and effective diplomacy won him several new territories at the end of the Thirty Years' War (see Map 13.2). With energy and skill, he next centralized and administered the governments of his fragmented holdings—while continuing to boost the size of his army. He prevailed over the Estates—the representative assemblies of the realm—and acquired the crucial authority to collect taxes. He then used his newly powerful army to enforce tax payments and organize state resources. In a pivotal compromise with landed aristocrats, he allowed them complete control over their serfs in return for support and service in his bureaucracy and army. Through mercantilistic policies, he protected industries, improved communications, and promoted

THINKING ABOUT GEOGRAPHY

MAP 13.2 *Central and Eastern Europe, 1648*

This map shows the border between the western and eastern agrarian zones, running from the mouth of the Elbe River south to Trieste on the Adriatic Sea. ◈ **Notice** which states are to the east of this line. **What** might this imply about social differences between eastern and western European states? **What** problems might these differences pose for eastern European states such as Austria and Brandenburg-Prussia, which controlled provinces to the west of this line?

agriculture. Though he could not afford a lavish court like that of Louis XIV, Frederick William's policies ratcheted up his power. "Hold fast to the eminence of your superior position . . . [and] rely on your own strength," he advised his son. At the Great Elector's death in 1688, Brandenburg-Prussia was well on the road to becoming a major player in European politics. He also left a legacy of military values and reliance on armed might that would influence much of Prussia's subsequent history.

In 1701, his son, Frederick I (r. 1688–1713), increased the dynasty's status by acquiring the title of king of Prussia in return for helping the Holy Roman Emperor in a war against France. He used state revenues to turn his Berlin court into a great social and cultural center. By his death in 1713, Brandenburg-Prussia had become a respected force in eastern Europe.

AUSTRIA'S HABSBURGS EXPAND THEIR CONTROL

Austria's Leopold I (r. 1657–1705), facing extreme local, language, and ethnic differences within his diverse lands, could not hope to acquire the same power as that enjoyed by Louis XIV in France or even Frederick William in Prussia. Localities retained considerable autonomy, especially in matters of taxation. The practical Leopold focused on securing his own Habsburg lands rather than cementing the minimal control he had over the Holy Roman Empire, and allied himself closely with the Catholic Church. He gained the allegiance of the nobles by making them his chief advisors and granting them rights to exploit lands and the peasants on them. Some peasants revolted, but as elsewhere in Europe, they did not pose a serious challenge to authorities.

With the help of Poland's king, Jan Sobieski (r. 1674–1696), Leopold also fought the Ottoman Turks, who controlled most of Hungary and laid siege to Austria's capital, Vienna, in 1683. Leopold's and Sobieski's forces saved the city and then brought most of Hungary under Austrian control (see Map 13.3 on page 444). The Austrian king next tried to install his own nobility in Hungarian lands and ally himself with powerful Hungarian nobles at the expense of the peasantry. He succeeded only partially, and the still independent Hungarian nobles remained a thorn in the side of the Austrian monarchy. Facing west, Leopold helped build a coalition that stood against Louis XIV. By the Austrian king's death in 1705, the Habsburg state had become one of the most powerful in Europe.

RUSSIA AND ITS TSARS GAIN PROMINENCE

Even farther east, the Russian monarchy slowly rose to prominence. Already in the sixteenth century, Ivan IV ("the Terrible") (r. 1533–1584) had added both to the authority of the Russian *tsars* (*caesars,* or emperors) and to the span of territories over which they ruled. He destroyed the remaining power of the Mongols in southeastern Russia and annexed most of their territory. Next he began Russia's conquest of Siberia. Half a century later, Russians planted their flag on the shores of the Pacific. Within his expanding state, Ivan ruled as a ruthless autocrat, creating his own service gentry to bypass powerful nobles and using torture and terror to silence all he saw as his opponents.

A difficult period known as the "Time of Troubles" (1584–1613) followed Ivan IV's death. Ivan's feeble-minded son Fydor ruled ineffectively and left no successor upon his death in 1598. Great nobles vied for power among themselves and against weak tsars. To end the political chaos, a group of leading nobles in 1613 chose the seventeen-year-old Michael Romanov (r. 1613–1645) to rule as tsar. He began a dynasty that would rule Russia for over 300 years.

The Romanovs

Despite the political stability Michael and his immediate successors brought, discontent among those below the tsar and the nobility mounted during the century as the authorities increasingly restricted the freedom of the masses. The notorious Law Code of 1649, for example, merged peasants and slaves into a class of serfs, and gave the landowning nobility the power to treat them as property. In a spate of uprisings between the late 1640s and early 1670s, the lower classes rebelled against landowners and officials by killing them and looting or burning their estates. The discontent reached a climax in the late 1660s and early 1670s with the revolts of Cossacks ("free warriors") in south Russia led by Stenka Razin. A shrewd, seasoned warrior, Razin claimed to "fight only the boyars and the wealthy lords. As for the poor and the plain folk, I shall treat them as brothers." His rebel army marched north, and many towns opened their gates to welcome Razin's forces, now swelling with the addition of discontented peasants and the urban poor. Russian soldiers finally caught, tortured, and executed Razin, and the uprisings tapered off.

By the final decades of the seventeenth century, the Romanov tsars had shored up the government's central administration and extended their authority throughout the country. Moreover, through increased trade and travel, Russia's commercial and cultural contacts with the West expanded, bringing new European goods and ideas into the country. The stage was set for a dynamic tsar to propel Russia more fully into European affairs.

This new, energetic emperor came in the person of Peter I ("the Great") (r. 1689–1725). Standing nearly seven feet tall, Peter seemed born to rule. At the age of seventeen, he seized the reins of government from his elder sister. He soon concluded that the best way to bolster his own political and military power was to copy Western practices. To this end, he traveled to western Europe and learned as much as he could about Western politics, customs, and technology.

Peter the Great

Back home, he took decisive steps to solidify his authority. In 1698 he crushed a revolt of his body-guards and silenced critics with a ruthlessness that cowed all potential troublemakers. "Every day was deemed fit and lawful for torturing," wrote an observer. He also made five years of education away from home and state service requirements for the nobility, and allowed movement within the ranks only through merit. Peter applied the bureaucratic system of western European monarchs to both central and local government to secure his rule. He also brought Western technicians to Russia in large numbers and protected new industries with mercantilistic policies. Western social customs were introduced to the upper and middle classes of Russian society, such as bringing Russian women out of seclusion to appear in Western dresses at official dinners and social gatherings. In addition, Peter banned the long beards and flowing Oriental robes that Russian men traditionally wore. When the patriarch of the Russian Orthodox Church opposed the tsar's authority and some of his westernizing policies, Peter took control of the church and confiscated much of its wealth. Henceforth, the Orthodox Church served as a powerful instrument of the Russian government.

All these reforms left the peasantry in even worse straits than before. Peasants made up 97 percent of Russia's population during Peter's reign, and they became tied down in a system of serfdom bordering on slavery. The taxes they were forced to pay ballooned by a whopping 500 percent, and their feudal obligations and military service only increased. Nowhere was peasant life harsher than in Russia, and Peter's efforts to westernize the nobility only widened the gap between the educated elites and the enserfed peasantry.

To keep Russia in step with the West and support his ambitions for territorial expansion, Peter devoted particular attention to his military establishment. He built a navy and patterned his expanded and modernized conscript army on the model of Prussia. Recruits were drafted for life and even branded with a cross on their left hand to deter desertion. Officials arbitrarily assigned serfs to work in mines and manufacturing establishments to supply the military with equipment and arms.

Russia's military establishment

Peter meant to use his new military might. Figure 13.6 depicts the clean-shaven tsar Peter the Great in heroic military pose. Clad in armor and carrying a sword, Peter asserts his authority over all potential rivals, who offer him their swords. Beneath the feet of his horse lays a defeated dragon. Above, an angel crowns Peter with divine authority. The tsar waged numerous military campaigns over his long reign, and he designed many of his great reforms to strengthen and modernize his armed forces. In the background of the painting, his troops surge to victory in a mighty battle.

Lacking warm-water access to the west, Peter tried to seize lands bordering the Black Sea that the Ottoman Turks held. Though they had weakened during the seventeenth century, the Ottoman Turks remained a formidable obstacle, and Peter's armies could not dislodge them. Frustrated, Peter turned northwest toward Sweden, which controlled lands bordering the Baltic Sea. Under King Gustavus Adolphus (r. 1611–1632), this Nordic country had become the dominant military power in northeastern Europe in the early seventeenth century (see Chapter 11). At the opening of the eighteenth century, Sweden held large areas east and south of the Baltic in addition to the homeland, and ranked second only to Russia in size. However, it lacked the population and resources to hold its far-flung territories for very long. Though Peter initially lost battle after battle to his brilliant Swedish adversary, Charles XII (r. 1697–1718), his persistence finally paid off. In the Battle of Poltava (1709), the Russians destroyed the Swedish army and managed to wound Charles.

Through the Treaty of Nystad in 1721, Russia received the Swedish Baltic provinces and some Polish territories (see Map 13.3). On the shores of the Baltic Sea, Peter triumphantly built a modern capital, St. Petersburg, that faced west. Reigning from this new court, he emulated the cultured, royal ways of the West to enhance his personal authority. At his death in 1725, Russia had taken its place as a major player on the European stage.

THE VICTORY OF THE NOBILITY IN POLAND

Not all the eastern European states drifted toward monarchical absolutism. In Poland, the competition between the monarchy and the nobility took a different turn—with severe consequences for the nation. In the sixteenth and seventeenth centuries, Poland seemed poised to become a major power. Taking advantage of Russia's "Time of Troubles" (1584–1613), the Poles had captured Moscow for a few years until the Russians finally drove them out in 1613. In reality, however, the Polish nation, which included Lithuania in a dual kingdom, was far from strong. Sprawling over a large area between Russia and the German states, it had no natural, protective boundaries either to the east or to the west. Ethnic and religious divisions undermined the Polish rulers' hopes for unity, and the economy had stumbled. In the late Middle Ages, a sizable overland commerce between the Black and Baltic Seas had flowed across Poland. However, with the

FIGURE 13.6
Louis Karavack. *Peter the Great.*

shifting of commercial routes and centers to the west in the sixteenth century, Poland's commerce withered. Worse, the Polish nobility, protective of its own power and fearful of an alliance between merchants and the king, deliberately penalized merchants by passing legislation to restrict trade. The great mass of the Polish people remained serfs, bound to the estates of the powerful nobility.

In the face of such forces, only a strong central government could have ensured stability for Poland. Yet this was precisely where Poland proved weakest. For many years, Poland's nobles had been gaining the upper hand and closely guarded their power to elect the king. When King Sigismund II died in 1572, end-

ing the long-ruling Jagellon dynasty, the nobles saw to it that no strong king ascended the throne. They monopolized the legislative body (the "Diet") and, to safeguard their rights, required a unanimous vote to pass any measure. This system guaranteed political anarchy.

Over the course of the seventeenth century, revolts by Ukrainian Cossack warriors and wars with Russia, Sweden, and Brandenburg-Prussia resulted in the loss of Polish territories. Rivalries among the Polish nobles only worsened the chaos. Moreover, Tatar slave raiders carried off many people. Incursions and internal wars destroyed towns, and the once thriving

Legend:
- Brandenburg-Prussia
- Prussian acquisitions in 1688
- Russian territory in 1693
- Seized by Peter the Great from Sweden, 1694–1725
- Austrian Habsburg territory in 1657
- Austrian Habsburg territory in 1718
- Ottoman Empire in 1699
- —— Boundary of the Holy Roman Empire

THINKING ABOUT GEOGRAPHY

MAP 13.3   *Central and Eastern Europe, 1640–1725*

This map shows the changing political landscape in central and eastern Europe during the seventeenth and early eighteenth centuries. ❧ **Notice** how Russia's expansion to the west increased its contact with European commerce and affairs. **How** might this alter the balance of power in Europe? ❧ **Notice** the gains made by the Austrian Habsburgs against the Ottomans. **What** might the declining fortunes of the Ottoman Empire have implied for the future of this part of the Western world? ❧ **Locate** Poland-Lithuania. **What** problems face this country, hemmed in by three growing powers?

Jewish populations were pushed from their homes and often slaughtered. Tens of thousands of Jews were murdered in the pogroms (organized persecutions) that swept through Poland between 1648 and 1658. Protestants also suffered at the hands of the Catholic majority. Not surprisingly, Poland's population declined sharply in these years. By the beginning of the eighteenth century, it lay vulnerable to surrounding powers that boasted stronger central governments.

The Triumph of Constitutionalism

As the tendency toward absolutism intensified in central Europe, another major struggle began to unfold in a tiny island nation far to the west. Kings desiring absolute power in England faced a situation significantly different from that in France. In France, the nobility had little history of common action between classes, and lost their solitary struggle against absolutism. In England, however, there had been a tradition of joint parliamentary action by nobles and commoners who owned land, and this helped contribute to a different outcome in the struggle for sovereignty. Instead of government residing in the person of an absolute monarch, it rested in written law—constitutions, not kings, would come to rule.

THE NOBILITY LOSES RESPECT

For over 1,000 years, the English had taken for granted the idea of separate social classes. Peasants and members of the middle classes showed the high nobility an unmistakable deference, turning out to greet them when they emerged, and gazing downward and holding their hats respectfully in their hands. Even upwardly mobile landowners with some wealth (the "gentry") knew that they ranked well below the "peers" (the old nobility). In England, there were only about 400 noble families and they jealously guarded their exclusive position. Commentators wrote that "nobility is a precious gift" and accepted this privilege as the natural order of things: "Men naturally favor nobility."

By the beginning of the seventeenth century, several disturbing incidents pointed to ominous cracks in the wall of privilege. One member of the gentry actually jostled and swore at an earl as the two passed in a narrow passageway, and some tenant farmers neglected to turn out, hats in hand, to welcome passing noblemen. Later, a Protestant sect, the Quakers, enacted a religious policy that forbade members to take off their hats to men in authority. Something had changed and nobles no longer seemed so essential, or so noble.

What explained this apparent loss of respect for the English upper crust? We can find a partial answer in the shifting role of money. In the early modern world, the old wealth of the nobility had declined relative to the "new money" of merchants and other enterprising individuals. Furthermore, the medieval base of noble power, the military, had also declined. No longer were nobles in charge of defending the realm; mercenary armies made up of commoners now took care of these matters. England had a relatively large sector of independent craftsmen compared to other countries, and noblemen depended more on "free labor"—that is, on wage laborers who could enter into contracts for their labor. These differences led commoners increasingly to feel they could control their own lives rather than defer to their "betters." In addition, education had become the key to upward mobility. More and more, knowledge and service, rather than birth, seemed the measure of a man.

New wealth

The members of the nobility did not relinquish their traditional place easily. Indeed, critics complained that noblemen were becoming more arrogant than ever in exerting their privileges. Sometimes, nobles even exceeded the bounds of propriety. In 1635 the earl of Arundel lost his temper when the mayor of a city did not turn out to greet him in the traditional way. The earl sought out the mayor, grabbed his staff of office, and proceeded to beat him with it, shouting, "I will teach you to . . . attend Peers of the Realm!"

As early as the sixteenth century, laws throughout Europe had begun to supplement tradition in keeping the social classes separate, and England was no different. Governments issued sumptuary laws to regulate what kinds of clothing were appropriate for members of each social class. For example, an individual could not wear velvet unless he had an independent income of over 100 pounds a year, and laborers could not wear cloth costing more than two shillings a yard. These laws were supposed to preserve social distinction, but the newly

Sumptuary laws

FIGURE 13.7

Anthony Van Dyck, *James Stuart, Duke of Richmond and Lennox*, ca. 1630.

new mandates even allowed them to set lethal trap-guns to kill poachers. Not surprisingly, these laws only exacerbated the common people's anger, as the poor continued to poach simply to survive in times of hunger. Still, many members of the nobility tried to hang on to their privilege while others pressed to undo them.

The portrait of James Stuart, a member of the royal family, shown in Figure 13.7 captures the arrogance and complacency of the typical English nobleman of 1630, who was oblivious to the gathering social storm that would soon disrupt his idyllic world. James stands proudly dressed in the opulent clothing of the nobility that the sumptuary laws carefully tried to preserve. His stockings are made of the finest silk, and the lace at his throat is expensive and handcrafted. Adorning his jacket sleeve is a sun image embroidered in silver thread—an early forerunner of Louis XIV's trademark symbol. The painting portrays James with his huge hunting dog, again proclaiming his privileged position through his hunting rights. The dog gazes up adoringly at his master with the kind of deference that James had come to expect. Sadly for members of the nobility, they would receive fewer and fewer admiring glances from their fellow humans.

PROTESTANTISM REVITALIZED

A good deal of social criticism also came from Protestants, many of whom believed that the implementation of Reformation ideas in England had not gone far enough. Because many Protestants were involved in the increasingly lucrative commerce, their wealth helped make their concerns more visible. For many, the compromise of Elizabeth I (discussed in Chapter 11) that allowed worshipers of many beliefs to share one Church of England was unacceptable. These critics believed that the Church of England (the Anglican Church) should be "purified"—that is, trimmed of any practice that lacked biblical precedent or smacked of Catholicism. They especially objected to priestly garments and the elaborate rituals of the Anglican Church. Some wanted to eliminate bishops altogether, preferring rule by church elders instead. (This was the practice common in Scotland, where Protestant churches became called "Presbyterian"—"ruled by elders").

In their zeal, many Protestants became increasingly anti-Catholic, and their political actions would be shaped by this prejudice. Other Protestants even

rich recognized that the path to gaining social respect lay in part in *looking* noble. Thus, men and women insisted on purchasing luxurious clothing to rival that of the highest classes. In 1714 a Sicilian traveler observed: "Nothing makes noble persons despise the gilded costume so much as to see it on the bodies of the lowest men in the world." Now, it seemed, there was no visual marker of a person's noble status.

The nobles had more success in guarding their property rights than their fashion privileges. In 1671, Parliament passed game laws giving the nobility the exclusive prerogative to hunt on their own lands. The wanted to purify daily life, objecting to theater, cock-fights, and other seemingly frivolous activities. While individuals disagreed among themselves on exactly how they wanted the Church of England purified, they all concurred that change was essential. Many members of this loose group of critics, called Puritans, became influential members of Parliament.

Puritans in England reconsidered the political relationship between monarchs and their subjects, wondering about competing loyalties between law and conscience, for example. These questions formed the backdrop of a struggle for sovereignty that would dominate the seventeenth century. As early as 1561, the Scottish reformer John Knox warned Queen Mary of Scotland that monarchs were responsible to their subjects: "If their princes exceed their bounds, Madam, no doubt they may be resisted, even by power." This was tantamount to a call to revolution. Knox later pushed his point even further, asking, "But who may punish the king . . . if it be not the whole body of the people to whom the king swears and obliges himself?" As Puritans gathered to discuss the purification of the church, they could not help but consider the possibility of political action.

JAMES I INVOKES THE DIVINE RIGHT OF KINGS

Because Queen Elizabeth I had died childless, the throne went to her cousin, the king of Scotland, who became King James I of England (r. 1603–1625). As soon as James heard of Elizabeth's death, he rushed to England brimming with great plans. He made promises to many who greeted him on his way south to London, rapidly knighted thousands of gentry, and even ordered an accused thief hanged without a trial—assuming incorrectly that as king he had the right to do so. Many of his subjects turned out to see their affable new monarch, but, unfortunately for him, he would not prove as popular, nor as politically shrewd as "Good Queen Bess."

The honeymoon of the new monarch and his people faded rather quickly, for unlike his predecessor he *Religious problems* was unable to mollify the varying religious beliefs of his people. He was a Calvinist, yet he favored Anglicanism, and his most enduring heritage was the translation of the Bible he commissioned, the King James Bible, which remains widely admired as both religion and beautiful literature. However, the king managed to offend his subjects who hoped for his support for religious change. At the beginning of his reign, Calvinists approached the king hoping to eliminate the Anglican episcopal system and bring it in line with the Presbyterian Scottish practice with which the king was familiar. They were sadly disappointed, for James threatened to "harry them out of the land" if they did not conform to Anglicanism.

James also offended his Catholic subjects, banning Jesuits and seminary priests. In 1605, a conspiracy of Catholics planned to blow up Parliament while it was in session. The plot failed and the conspirators were executed. Yet, the "gunpowder plot" as it came to be known increased the anti-Catholic feelings in the country, which were exacerbated when James planned a political marriage between his son and a Catholic Spanish princess. Although the marriage negotiations fell through, the attempt alienated Calvinists and Anglicans alike.

Thus by 1610, there was much animosity between the king and many of his subjects. James thought the English ungrateful and they found him *Divine right* arbitrary and arrogant. Unlike Elizabeth before him, James was disinclined to compromise his theoretical notions of divine right monarchy. Even before he ascended the throne, James had written two treatises in which he asserted the divine right of kings, and in 1610 he presented this position to a skeptical Parliament. As he put it, "Kings have power of . . . life and death; [they are] judges over all their subjects and in all causes, and yet accountable to none but God." This position was consistent with his hasty execution of the accused thief, but it offended many Puritans in the House of Commons, as well as many Lords who viewed the king as subject to the law of the land.

During James' rule, the English colonies in North America grew. In part, the attention to the New World stemmed from James' financial difficulties: The first permanent English *Colonies* colony, named Jamestown after the monarch, was founded in Virginia in 1607. James hoped to generate new income from the Virginia colonies, which in 1619 had imported slaves from Africa to grow tobacco, an increasingly popular crop. Colonial settlement was also forwarded by James' high-handed attitude toward religious dissidents. When the king threatened to harry nonconformists out of the land, some took him literally, and emigrated to North America to establish colonies. They avoided Jamestown, which was sympathetic to the Church of England, and instead landed farther north, founding their first colony in Plymouth, Massachusetts, in 1620. The New World was not to be the solution to either James' religious or fiscal problems. He died leaving a shortage of money and an oversupply of ill will among both Parliament and Protestants.

CHARLES I ALIENATES PARLIAMENT

James' son, Charles I (r. 1625–1649), inherited both his father's rule and his policies. This sober monarch, continuing to invoke the divine right of kings, considered himself answerable only to God, not Parliament. His relationship with his subjects deteriorated rapidly. He approached Parliament in the same way his father had—calling it when he needed money and disbanding it when the members demanded concessions.

Showing a remarkable insensitivity to his Protestant subjects, Charles married a sister of the Catholic king Louis XIII of France. Soon after his wedding, *Concessions to Catholics* Charles granted concessions to English Catholics, even allowing the queen and her entourage to practice Catholic rituals in the court itself. English Protestants were horrified at what they saw as outrageous behavior by the family of the titular head of the Church of England. Charles responded to critics by persecuting Puritans, whom he viewed as disloyal. More Puritans fled to North America, settling so many colonies in the northeast that the region came to be called New England. Meanwhile, the situation in old England grew more desperate.

As we saw in Chapter 11, warfare had become extremely expensive, and Charles' costly and fruitless *Parliament gains power* wars with Spain and France had so strained his finances that he even tried to pawn the crown jewels. The king called Parliament several times in the 1620s, only to disband them repeatedly. Things came to a head in 1640, when the Scots, who also objected to the king's high-handed religious policies, invaded the north of England. To raise the army and funds he needed to fight the Scots, Charles called Parliament again. This time, Parliament forced him to agree that he could not disband them without their consent.

The first crack in Charles' armor of divine right had appeared. The "Long Parliament," as it came to be called, continued to meet from 1640 to 1653. Over time, it acquired a measure of power and established protections for the religious freedom of Anglicans and Puritans alike.

However, the temporary compromise between the king and Parliament came to an end when troubles in Ireland caused both to agree to send troops. However, their alliance ended there. The question of who would command the army remained. Parliament did not trust the king to suppress his Catholic sympathies, and the king did not trust Parliament to share control of any army it raised. In the end, Parliament appointed officers to raise an army, and Charles withdrew from London to raise an army of his own. The Irish no longer seemed the immediate enemy for either side.

"GOD MADE MEN AND THE DEVIL MADE KINGS": CIVIL WAR, 1642–1649

As Map 13.4 shows, the alignments in the English civil war show some divisions in English life. The rural areas were more likely to support the king, and the Puritan strongholds in the cities followed the forces of Parliament. In response to Charles' call for support, noblemen, cavalry officers, and Irish Catholics rallied to his banner. His royalist supporters were called Cavaliers, or horsemen, as a reference to medieval knights who fought for their kings. Back in London, Parliament recruited an army 13,000 strong, drawn from the commoners, merchants, a few noblemen, Scots, and Puritans. All these generalizations, however, are drawn in broad strokes, and frequently the choice to support one side or another derived from private decisions based sometimes on religion and sometimes on long-standing personal grudges against neighbors.

The strength of the parliamentary forces, called Roundheads for their short haircuts, stemmed mainly from their skilled infantry, the support of major sections of the navy, and their religious conviction. Parliament's forces also benefited from the leadership of Oliver Cromwell, a Puritan who not only forwarded the cause of revolutionary change in Parliament, but who took charge of the army and forged it into a formidable force called the New Model Army. The royalists had more experience in battles, and more

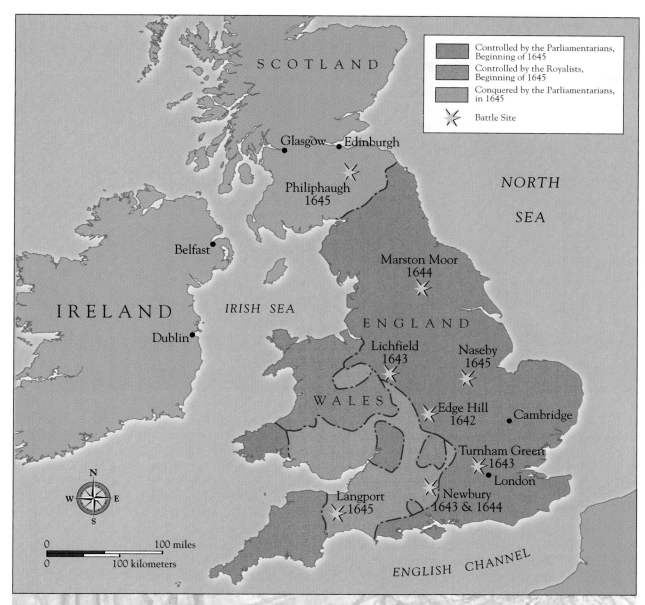

Legend:
- Controlled by the Parliamentarians, Beginning of 1645
- Controlled by the Royalists, Beginning of 1645
- Conquered by the Parliamentarians, in 1645
- ✶ Battle Site

SCOTLAND

Glasgow • Edinburgh

Philiphaugh 1645

NORTH SEA

Belfast

Marston Moor 1644

IRELAND

IRISH SEA

ENGLAND

Dublin

Lichfield 1643

Naseby 1645

WALES

Edge Hill 1642

Cambridge

Turnham Green 1643

London

Langport 1645

Newbury 1643 & 1644

ENGLISH CHANNEL

0   100 miles
0   100 kilometers

THINKING ABOUT GEOGRAPHY

MAP 13.4   The English Civil War, 1642–1649

This map shows England during the civil war years, the locations of the parliament and royalist supporters, and the major battles. ❧ **Notice** the scale of the map and **consider** how this might have affected the progress of the war. ❧ **Notice** the regions that initially supported the king and **consider** why the royalists drew from rural rather than the urban centers. ❧ **Notice** the locations of Ireland, Scotland, and Wales, which would be incorporated into what would become Great Britain.

FIGURE 13.8
Weesop, *Execution of Charles I*, 1649.

skilled generals. The lines were drawn—the royalist forces led by the king fought a civil war against the forces led by Cromwell.

By 1646 Parliament forces had won a series of victories, and Charles surrendered to the Scots, who later turned him over to Parliament in exchange for their back military pay. However, the temporary end to the hostilities then permitted divisions within the Roundheads to widen. Members of Parliament could not agree on the religious organization that should govern the Church of England, and quarreled about the degree of hierarchy that should exist. While the king was moved from prison to prison as royalists conspired to free him, leaders of Parliament confronted new challenges: a series of social upheavals as more and more people were drawn into the turbulent events of the 1640s.

Charles captured

Women from all social groups participated in unprecedented numbers in the English civil war. In their husbands' absence, a number of noble women defended their fortified castles against parliamentary forces, inspiring many accounts of "great heroics" considered surprising in the "weaker sex." Working women disguised as men also passed themselves off as Roundhead soldiers. In 1643, Charles issued a proclamation intending to prevent women from joining the army: "Let no woman presume to counterfeit her sex by wearing man's apparel under pain of the severest punishment which law shall inflict." However, the king was in no position to enforce this edict, and women continued to serve as soldiers. It is impossible to know exactly how many women fought for their cause, but the fact that Charles tried to legislate their exclusion suggests that at least he and his advisors thought the numbers significant.

Women in war

Women were well suited as spies, because people expected them to be noncombatants. One such woman, Jane Whorwood, dedicated herself fiercely to the king's cause. The tall redhead repeatedly tried to free Charles during his imprisonment after 1646. She smuggled money to him and once brought in acid to weaken the metal bars so that he could break free. One of Charles' aides described Whorwood as "the most loyal person to King Charles I in his miseries."

Other previously uninvolved members of society also jumped into the fray. After 1646, radicals, both men and women, raised new demands for social justice. Their complaints stemmed mostly from the severe economic problems that had hamstrung England in the 1640s. A series of bad harvests caused food shortages and rising prices, and disabled soldiers returning home discovered they could no longer earn a living. Crime increased as people stole to feed their families, and the social order deteriorated. **Levellers** One contemporary observed: "Necessity dissolves all laws and government, and hunger will break through stone walls." From these difficult circumstances, groups of radical Protestants arose. Known as Levellers, they insisted that social justice become part of Parliament's agenda. A pamphlet sympathetic to their cause claimed that "God made men and the Devil made kings."

Levellers were as varied a group as the Puritans, encompassing people with a broad array of agendas. In general, however, they harked back to a tradition of English religious radicals like John Ball (see Chapter 9), and espoused as their goal to "level" social differences. To that end, they advocated some reforms of Parliament. For example, they believed Parliament should be chosen by the vote of all male heads of households, which would represent a dramatic broadening of the vote. Furthermore, they wanted members of Parliament to be paid, so that even those with no independent income could serve. While these ideas may seem natural to us, they posed a major threat to those who believed that only property brought privilege.

THE KING LAID LOW

In the midst of these controversies, the civil war broke out again in 1648 as Charles encouraged his supporters to rise up to free him. Cromwell's forces promptly crushed the uprisings, and some army leaders concluded that they would never come to peaceful terms with the king. With Cromwell's support, they demanded that he be tried for treason. The majority of Parliament members refused to take this extreme step, but in December 1648 invading soldiers purged Parliament of the cautious. The remaining members, scornfully called the Rump Parliament by opponents and historians, brought the king to trial.

The Rump Parliament tried Charles as a king, rather than deposing him first and then trying him as a private citizen. In other words, they wanted to find the *king* guilty, not just the man. This bold act represented a direct clash between two theories of government—one claiming that the king stood above Parliament, the other declaring that he must answer to it. This unprecedented, highly public trial became the first in history to receive full press coverage. Newspapers had initially emerged in England in 1641, on the eve of the civil war; by 1649, six licensed newspapers recorded the testimony in the trial and provided differing opinions on the proceedings.

Charles was accused of claiming to rule by divine right: He who had been "trusted with a limited power to govern . . . according to the law of the land . . . had conceived a wicked design to . . . uphold in himself an unlimited and tyrannical power to rule according to his will. . . ." Though he genuinely believed in divine right, Charles refused to answer this or any other charge. Instead he claimed that Parliament had no right to bring charges against him at all. He gained much popular support over the few days of the trial as he consistently reiterated his position, rising above a stutter that had plagued him all his life in order to express his views firmly and with dignity. He challenged Parliament to justify "by what power I am called hither . . . by what authority [you bring charges]." Both sides clearly understood the magnitude of the trial's central question: Who had sovereignty? Charles claimed that God had sovereignty and had delegated it to the king; the Puritans in Parliament claimed that they had sovereignty. There was no room for compromise, and neither side gave way. Charles was found guilty and sentenced to die.

On January 30, 1649, the condemned king was led to a scaffold erected in front of Whitehall Palace. His public execution inspired a rash of etchings and paintings. Figure 13.8 **Charles executed** depicts the crowds who gathered to watch, including women, whose interest in the execution seemed remarkable to contemporary commentators. Many in the crowd were sympathetic to their king. Jane Whorwood, for example, who had worked tirelessly to free Charles, ran forward to greet the king as he walked to the scaffold. Figure 13.8 shows some of these sympathizers; note the old man in the foreground leaning on his cane and crying, and the woman fainting on the left.

Charles bravely addressed the few people near him on the scaffold, and repeated his views on sovereignty: "I must tell you that the liberty and freedom [of the people] consists in having a government. . . . It is not for having a share in government. Sir, that is nothing pertaining to them. A subject and a sovereign are clear different things." Charles then laid his head on the block, and the executioner severed it cleanly with one blow. The man on the side of the platform in Figure 13.8 holds the king's head up to show the crowd. The monarchy had ended, and a new form of government arose to take its place: a republic in which sovereignty rested with representatives of those who owned property. England called its new republic the Commonwealth.

FIGURE 13.9
The Royal Oak of Britain, 1649.

A PURITAN REPUBLIC IS BORN: THE COMMONWEALTH, 1649–1660

As the Rump Parliament began to rule the republic, chaos erupted throughout the realm. The new commonwealth faced warfare outside its borders and dissension within. Fortunately, Parliament had an able champion in Oliver Cromwell (1599–1658). While Parliament ruled, Cromwell with his army controlled the policies.

Rebellions broke out in Catholic Ireland and Protestant Scotland, and Cromwell led his army to those lands, putting down the revolts so brutally that the Irish still remember his invasion with anger. However, Cromwell was effective and brought Scotland and Ireland tightly under English rule. Yet Parliament had more to worry about than just these expensive wars.

Within England, Levellers continued to agitate for social reform, and many of their leaders were imprisoned. Then, in 1649, a gathering of women entered the House of Commons bringing a petition asking for "those rights and freedoms of the nation that you promised us." One member of Parliament taunted the women,

Domestic distress

saying their public stance was "strange," to which a petitioner responded, "It was strange that you cut off the king's head." These were odd times indeed, and many wondered whether Parliament's victory in the civil war had created more disorder than it had resolved.

The 1649 cartoon in Figure 13.9 expresses the fears of royalists and moderates alike during this difficult era, and serves to illustrate the tumultuous times of the Commonwealth. In this complex image, ax-wielding men (representing the Roundheads) chop down "the Royal Oak of Britain," England's longtime symbol of authority and tradition. The oak teeters, threatening to fall and take with it the Bible, the Magna Carta, and the traditional rule of law. Soldiers assist the woodsmen in destroying the tree and the order it represents. The pigs in the center symbolize the common people, being "fattened for the slaughter." Oliver Cromwell stands at the left, supervising the destruction. Below his feet is hell, though he is oblivious to how close he is to damnation. While this cartoon clearly vilifies Cromwell and all he embodied, it also reveals the disorder that had torn at England since the civil war began. Could the parliamentary forces under Oliver Cromwell resolve these fears and tensions?

Parliament seemed incapable of uniting the various constituents that demanded action after Charles'

Lord Protector death. In 1653, when the House of Commons considered a proposal to dismantle Cromwell's large army, the general lost patience. He disbanded Parliament altogether, named himself "Lord Protector" of the Commonwealth of England, Scotland, and Ireland, and established a military dictatorship—the ideal of the republic remained only as an ideal. Cromwell faced the same problems that had confronted Parliament and the king—foreign wars and religious struggles. A pious Puritan, Cromwell set out to make England the model of a Protestant land, banning horse races, cockfights, and even theater. He ultimately proved as intolerant of Anglicans as they had been of Puritans, and alienated most of the population with his intrusive policies. The brief experiment with a rule purely by Parliament had failed, and a military dictatorship could not be popular in a land with such a tradition of participatory government.

WHO HAS THE POWER TO RULE?

Charles' trial and execution, and the disorder that followed, did not resolve the issue of who had the ul-

Thomas Hobbes timate power in England. In 1651, the English philosopher Thomas Hobbes (1588–1679) wrote a political treatise, *The Leviathan*, that offered an answer to this question in the form of a new theory of government. Perhaps shaken by the chaos of the civil war, Hobbes harbored a pessimistic view of human nature. He claimed that everyone was driven by a quest for power, and that given the chance, people would try to exercise their power at the expense of their neighbors—even if it meant taking their property and their lives. In this "state of nature" where there was no controlling authority, Hobbes described human life as "solitary, poor, nasty, brutish and short." However, he held out a ray of hope. Humans, he explained, recognized their inability to live peacefully, so they created a "social contract" by which they erected a ruler above them. By this contract, subjects willingly surrendered their sovereignty to a ruler who in turn agreed to rule over them absolutely.

With this explanation, Hobbes reconciled the Protestant views of sovereignty—in which the people held the right to rule—with absolute monarchy,

FIGURE 13.10

Frontispiece of *The Leviathan* by Thomas Hobbes, 1651.

where the ruler (the king or "Lord Protector") possessed sole sovereignty. In the famous frontispiece of *The Leviathan*, shown in Figure 13.10, Hobbes visually portrayed the benefits of his system. The ruler is shown at the top wielding the sword and scepter of absolute power. Even more significant, he comprises all the people of the land—he is the "body politic." The king derives his power from his subjects, without whom he would not exist. However, with this delegated power, he presides over an orderly and peaceful countryside and village. Church, state, the army, and Parliament are all neatly ordered along the sides of the page. This tidy, comforting vision stands in stark contrast to the chaos shown in Figure 13.9, and reveals

Biography

SAMUEL PEPYS (1633–1703)

Samuel Pepys was born in London on February 23, 1633, the fifth of eleven children. Only he and two of his siblings survived childhood. Samuel's father was a relatively modest tailor and his mother, the sister of a butcher. Nevertheless, the family had relatives who included landed gentry, lawyers, and a physician. The Pepyses were Puritans, and although Samuel uncharitably recalled his mother as "quarrelsome and feeble-minded" and his father as "always needing some kind of aid," the family did provide him with the educational opportunities he needed to succeed.

As a young boy, Pepys was sent to live with an uncle and attend the same grammar school where the young Oliver Cromwell had been educated. Samuel must have seemed a promising student, for when he was about thirteen he returned to London to attend St. Paul's School, a stronghold of Puritanism and classical learning. He won scholarships to attend Cambridge University and received his bachelor's degree in 1654. After graduating, he found a job as secretary to a distant relative who had taken an important position in Cromwell's new Commonwealth.

A year later, Pepys married Elizabeth, the fifteen-year-old daughter of a French Protestant refugee. She brought no dowry to the marriage, though Samuel was probably drawn to her beauty—throughout his diary, he repeatedly made notes about attractive women. His domestic life proved stormy, but he wrote often about being pleased with his marriage during the more harmonious times in his household. Pepys complained that Elizabeth was untidy and that she mismanaged the household. For his part, Samuel was no model husband; he always kept his wife short of money and was relentlessly unfaithful to her. He recorded the details of his infidelities and of Elizabeth's pained reactions to them. Elizabeth died young and childless in 1669, and Samuel never remarried.

Through the late seventeenth century, Pepys was an active participant and a careful chronicler of the major events of the era. While still at Cambridge, he witnessed the execution of Charles I and supported the Commonwealth as a clerk. However, he must have harbored royalist sympathies, for his political career blossomed in 1660 with the Restoration. Pepys had accompanied the fleet that escorted the new monarch back to England, and his contacts on that journey ensured him a position suited to his many talents.

Pepys began his diary in 1660 and for nine years detailed the events of his times both great and small. In this extraordinary text, we have an eyewitness account of the devastating plague that scourged London in 1665, followed by the great fire the year after. Pepys juxtaposed historical events with the most intimate details of his daily life, from the food he ate to the arguments he had with his wife. He stopped keeping his diary in 1669 because his eyesight was failing him.

Pepys took an active role in political life by working in the naval office. In 1685 he was even elected to the House of Commons. He continued to receive the benefits of royal patronage under the reigns of Charles II and James II, but the Glorious Revolution of 1688 caused his fortunes to change. He lost the parliamentary election in 1689, and in the following year he was even arrested on suspicion that he supported the deposed James II. Pepys had always been more interested in observing political events rather than engaging passionately in them, and when he was released from prison he removed himself from political life. He spent the rest of his years reading, playing music, and exchanging letters with friends, including such eminent scholars as Isaac Newton. His last years were devoted to building a substantial library

Enterprising Clerk, Member of Parliament, and Diarist

that he bequeathed at his death to his alma mater, where it still remains intact and unaltered. He died peacefully in 1703.

Pepys wrote his diary in a shorthand that was used by clerks in the seventeenth century; Newton used the same shorthand for taking his notes. The four-volume, handwritten, leatherbound diary written in a forgotten code lay ignored on the library shelves until the nineteenth century. Then, an undergraduate of the college took on the gigantic task of transcribing the diary (omitting the erotic passages) and it became an instant success. Modern editions of the complete diary continue to engage readers with its direct picture of seventeenth-century England. It has ensured that Samuel Pepys will not be forgotten.

❧ **Notice** that Pepys' diary shows how the political events of the day—the Glorious Revolution and the growing importance of Parliament—affected his life. ❧ **Consider** the effects of educational opportunities on the lives of seventeenth-century people.

Hobbes' hope that absolute monarchy would guarantee peace in the land.

Hobbes omitted a key point in his thesis: Absolute rule is only as effective as the ruler. Although Cromwell preserved order (albeit while offending many), he failed to develop an institution that could maintain the Puritan republic. When he died in 1658, he named his son Richard his successor. However, the young man could not lead with the same energy and fervor that his father had shown. Under pressure from members of Parliament, Richard resigned, and the right to govern once again returned to the people's representatives.

THE MONARCHY RESTORED, 1660–1688

Sobered by the chaos that had followed Charles' execution, Parliament decided to reinstate the monarchy. It invited Charles II (r. 1660–1685), son of the executed king, to resume the throne. Ships sailed from England to Holland to escort the king home from his place of exile. Among those in attendance when the king returned was Samuel Pepys (see Biography), an English diarist who became noted for the detailed accounts he kept of events from 1660 to 1669. According to Pepys, the people of England greeted their new king with much fanfare and excitement. Charles II came home to a restored monarchy that had all the luxury that his father had enjoyed— and all the problems that had plagued this troubled institution.

Samuel Pepys devoted several pages of his diary to Charles' coronation in 1661. "So glorious was the show with gold and silver," he wrote, "that we were not able to look at it, our eyes at last being so much overcome with it." Like most of his countrymen, Pepys drank ale with wild abandon during the celebration—the years of Puritan temperance seemed to melt away in a haze of drunkenness.

Yet, not everyone got caught up in the celebration. Former Cromwell supporters saw the Restoration in a very different light. John *John Bunyan* Bunyan (1628–1688), for example, who had fought with Cromwell, was imprisoned in 1660 for preaching against the Restoration. His original sentence of three months was extended to twelve years because he refused to stop preaching. After his release in 1672, he continued to preach and wrote his masterpiece, *Pilgrim's Progress* in 1678.

Probably the most widely read book by an English author, *Pilgrim's Progress* tells of a hero named Christian and his search for salvation through an allegorical world. This tale of hope and confidence in the human power to prevail through times of tribulation was balanced by Bunyan's lesser-known work, *The Life and Death of Mr. Badman* (1680). In this allegory, Bunyan criticized the loose life of Restoration England by describing the journey of a man who goes straight to hell. Bunyan's works strongly suggested that the Restoration had definitely not solved the political struggles of England.

Charles II grappled with the same fiscal problems that had plagued James I and Charles I, but he had to face a Parliament that had proven its strength during the civil wars. The *Fiscal problems* king was bound by law to call Parliament at least every three years, and the members of Parliament had severely curtailed royal power over taxation. Like his predecessors, Charles needed money, and to buttress his revenues without the restrictions Parliament imposed, the new king tried to exert more control over the colonies in North America. He increased the customs duties permitted by the Navigation Acts (imposed in 1651), and fought a war with the Dutch in 1665. This conflict ended in a treaty that gave the English New York in exchange for Dutch control of Surinam in South America.

Charles' international dealings were hampered by disasters at home. In 1665, England experienced a plague of frightening intensity— *Plague and fire* 70,000 people died in London alone. The following year, a devastating fire broke out in London, engulfing the city and destroying 13,000 dwellings and eighty-seven churches, including the venerable St. Paul's Cathedral. Pepys described the horror of the fire in detail: "We saw the fire grow; . . . and in corners and upon steeples and between churches and homes, as far as we could see up the hill of the city, in a most horrid, malicious, bloody flame. . . ." After the fire had died out, Charles ordered the city rebuilt, and hired the skilled architect Sir Christopher Wren to redesign the main buildings. Wren's masterpiece, the new St. Paul's Cathedral still marks the London skyline.

In addition to these disasters, the issue of religion once again came to the fore. Charles had Catholic sympathies, and to circumvent Parliament he had several times turned to the Catholic king Louis XIV of

France for help and money. The Protestant Parliament, wary of Charles' granting concessions to Catholics, passed the "Test Act" in 1673. The law required an oath of Protestant loyalties that would prevent Catholics from holding public offices, but legislation could not affect the king's conscience, nor alleviate Parliament's fears of Catholicism. In 1685, Charles died after converting to Roman Catholicism on his deathbed.

Charles' successor, his brother James II (r. 1685–1688), would not be able to avoid direct confrontation with the Protestant Parliament. A Catholic, James demanded in vain that Parliament repeal the Test Act, and proceeded to place Catholics in high office in violation of Parliament's law. Many English feared that James would adopt Louis XIV's policies against Protestants and even try to institute absolute rule. They may well have been right, but the members of Parliament were not going to wait and see. In 1688, when James' Catholic wife produced a Catholic heir to the throne of England, leading members of Parliament took action.

THE GLORIOUS REVOLUTION

To preempt James, Parliamentary leaders turned to the king's eldest daughter, Mary, a Protestant and the wife of William of Orange of the Netherlands. William staunchly opposed the policies of the Catholic Louis XIV, so both his politics and his religion suited the English Protestants. William gathered a fleet and an army of 14,000 men and landed in England in November 1688. He marched slowly *William and Mary* and peacefully toward London, while most of the English population rallied to his side. Recalling Charles I's fate, James decided to flee to France "for the security of my person." Louis XIV received his Catholic counterpart with kindness.

The Irish Catholics did not welcome the new Protestant king. Indeed, they thought of James II as a Catholic hero, and Irish leaders conspired with James to help him retake his throne while the French king helped fund this enterprise. Early in his reign William led an army into Ireland and ruthlessly suppressed what he saw as Catholic treason. Abandoning both Ireland and his claim to the throne, James lived out his life in lavish exile in France, leaving the Irish to bear the brunt of William's wrath. The new king reduced Ireland

to colonial status, and offered new opportunity for English landlords to take possession of Irish Catholic lands. Irish anger toward the English festered and would grow, but William's victory was cheered in England.

William and Parliament turned to the immediate task of establishing the legitimacy of his kingship. Parliament decided that James' flight from England *England's Bill of Rights* constituted an abdication of the throne. The sovereignty that, according to Hobbes, the people had surrendered to their king had been returned to parliament, who now had the right to install a new monarch. Parliament determined to clarify its relationship with the king. In 1689 it passed a Bill of Rights firmly stating that kings were subject to the laws of the land, thus creating a constitutional monarchy—the triumph of constitutionalism. Within the Bill of Rights, William agreed to "deliver this kingdom from popery [Catholicism] and arbitrary power" and to preserve freedom of speech, election, and the rule of law. The bill secured the position of Protestantism in England by ruling that "no person embracing Catholicism or married to a Catholic is eligible to succeed to the throne." Through this bloodless "Glorious Revolution," Parliament had finally demonstrated that the power to rule rested with the people through their representatives, rather than absolutely with the king. After this, Parliament began to meet annually, which was a practical way to secure its authority.

ROYALISM RECONSIDERED: JOHN LOCKE

Just as the civil war spawned Hobbes' highly pessimistic view of the need for absolute monarchy, the circumstances of the Glorious Revolution inspired a more positive political theory of popular sovereignty. In *The Second Treatise of Government* (1690), the English philosopher John Locke (1623–1704) articulated a new relationship between the king and his subjects. Like Hobbes, Locke believed that power originally rested with the people and that citizens themselves established a monarchy to keep order. However, whereas Hobbes had said that the people turned over their sovereignty completely to the monarch, Locke claimed that they retained it but created a contract of mutual obligations with their ruler. Locke argued that if the king broke the contract, the people had the right to depose him and install a new monarch, just as Parliament had done during the Glorious Revolution.

Locke's political theories were not intended to support full democracies—in his time, the "people" meant only those who owned property. He did not intend for individuals such as the landless Levellers to threaten property owners. Nor did he view women as sharing in the popular sovereignty of the privileged social orders. Locke's highly influential rhetoric, in which he claimed natural rights of "life, liberty, and property" actually applied to relatively few people in 1690. However, in time his theory would broaden to form the basis for democracy as well as constitutional monarchy.

Parliament soon had the opportunity to exert its king-making authority once again. William and Mary died without an heir, so the crown went to James II's Protestant daughter, Anne. Queen Anne (r. 1701–1714) also died without an heir, whereby the Protestant Stuart dynasty evaporated. Parliament then passed the crown to George I (r. 1714–1727), a great-grandson of James I, who ruled the German principality of Hanover, introducing the Hanoverian dynasty to England. This peaceful transition demonstrated once and for all that the struggle for sovereignty in England was over—Parliament ruled.

THE NETHERLANDS: THE SOVEREIGNTY OF LOCAL AUTHORITY

The English nobles asserted their rights over the king by exercising their authority through a parliament that ruled over a highly centralized government. This struggle created a strong constitutional monarchy that preserved popular sovereignty while creating a state that would prove highly stable. Another way for people to preserve their sovereignty was to resist a strong central government in order to strengthen local institutions. In the seventeenth century, the Netherlands developed this political structure that also gave power to the people instead of to absolute rulers. They instituted another form of constitutionalism that structured the government around consent of the propertied.

When the Low Countries split in 1609, the southern Catholic regions remained subject to the absolutist monarch, Philip II of Spain (see Chapter 11). Map 13.5 shows the division of the Low Countries in 1609.

THINKING ABOUT GEOGRAPHY

MAP 13.5   *The United Provinces and the Spanish Netherlands, 1609*

This map shows the location of the Netherlands in Europe and its division into two separate states. ◘ **Notice** the scale of this map. **Consider** how small the United Provinces were. **What** about their location contributed to their wealth and importance in the seventeenth century? ◘ **Notice** the proximity of the Catholic Spanish Netherlands to France. **Consider** how this region might have served as a buffer for the Protestant United Provinces.

The Spanish Netherlands of the south (now Belgium) formed a buffer between the United Provinces of the north and the divine right monarchy of France. In the United Provinces, which became largely Calvinist after the wars with Catholic Spain, a Protestant state developed that successfully resisted any attempts at royal absolutism. The United Provinces—also known as the

The United Provinces

Dutch Republic—became a republic in which sovereignty remained with the people and power stayed at the local level. Figure 13.11 shows how little central authority there was, and how this authority was effectively controlled by the provincial assemblies. The 1648 Treaty of Westphalia that ended the Thirty Years' War (see Chapter 11) formally recognized the Republic of the United Provinces.

What were the special circumstances that led the Netherlands *Dutch prosperity* to develop and maintain this strong sense of local sovereignty when other areas of Europe were moving to centralized governments? In large part, such political independence was facilitated by prosperity. The seventeenth century has been called the "golden age" of the United Provinces, for this small region was a tremendous European and colonial power. Amsterdam became the commercial and financial center of Europe as ships brought huge quantities of herring from the North Sea, as well as sugar, tobacco, glass, and many other items from around the world, through the bustling port. Figure 13.12, a contemporary painting of busy merchants and shoppers in the central square of seventeenth-century Amsterdam, reveals the prosperity of this wealthy city.

The Dutch also grew rich from their activities as major slave traders in the New World. The population of Amsterdam grew from about 30,000 people in 1570 to 200,000 by 1660, and the growth was testimony to the wealth and opportunities people saw there. Its financial importance was secured in 1609 by the foundation of the Exchange Bank of Amsterdam, the greatest public bank in northern Europe. Europeans were astonished by the prosperity and enterprise of the Dutch, and one English traveler (John Keymer) analyzed their culture to try to urge the Eng-

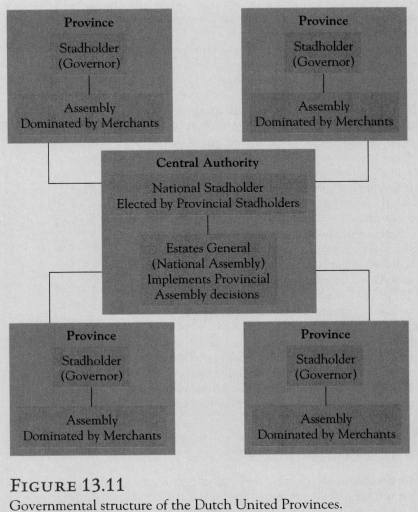

FIGURE 13.11

Governmental structure of the Dutch United Provinces.

lish to emulate it and thus also prosper. Keymer noted their industry, hard work, and the "liberty of free traffic for strangers to buy and sell. . . ." He recognized that there was an intimate link between prosperity and freedom.

The Dutch had other elements that contributed to their resistance of absolutism. The Dutch aristocracy was not as wealthy as that of England or France, for example. Their wealth lay more in commerce than in land, so the aristocracy had more in common with the merchants of their land than they did with the landed gentry in England or with the nobility at the court of Versailles. Furthermore, in the United

Provinces the Protestant faith cultivated an ideology of moderation—rather than the aristocratic excess that marked the nobility of other states. That is not to say that the seventeenth-century United Provinces espoused notions of egalitarian democracy—the nobility were as interested in trying to increase their power as those of other countries. They were just not able to exert much centralized control over the prosperous, Protestant residents that were the wonder of Europe.

Overall, the Dutch exhibited an unusual degree of religious toleration for their time. They even allowed Catholics and Jews to practice their

Religious toleration

religions, a policy that encouraged religious refugees to flock to the Netherlands from all over Europe. These refugees greatly enriched the cultural and economic life of the republic. Not only did the United Provinces attract intellectuals, such as René Descartes from France and John Locke from England, but the open-minded assemblies stimulated the spread of ideas through the press. The United Provinces became a leading center for book publishing and transmitted ideas, even revolutionary ones, all over Europe. In 1649, for example, an anonymous pamphlet published in the Netherlands attacked Cromwell's government for not supporting the ideas of the Levellers. The pamphlet called for an "equality of goods and lands" and condemned the government that "hangs a poor man if he do steal, when they have wrongfully taken from him all his maintenance."

The refugees streaming into the Netherlands included some destitute travelers and in some ways burdened the small country. The Dutch, however, generously assisted the needy, who never sank to the same depths of hardship that faced the poor in many other European cities. In his brief stay in the Netherlands, Samuel Pepys recorded in his diary the provisions the Dutch made for the poor. He observed a guesthouse, "where it was very pleasant to see what neat preparation there is for the poor." He further noted that there were special entertainment taxes to provide for the needy.

FIGURE 13.12
Jacob van der Ulft, *Dam Square in Amsterdam*, 1659.

The wealthy middle classes treated themselves well also. For example, they commissioned paintings that depicted their unique way of life. The Dutch artist Jan Vermeer (see Chapter 12) was one of several whose talents flourished in the free Dutch environment. Even more celebrated was the Dutch artist Rembrandt van Rijn (1606–1669), whose brilliant use of light and forceful expressiveness made him among the greatest of western European painters.

In the painting *Syndics of the Cloth Guild* (Figure 13.13) Rembrandt portrays the serious, successful merchants who had been chosen to manage the wealthy guild. The artist captures the proud intensity with which they work over a book on the table. In the uniformity in their clothing, they stand in striking contrast to the man in Figure 13.7 on page 446, who boasts luxurious designs and fabrics that set him apart from people precisely like these successful syndics. Rembrandt offered this painting to the cloth guild in thanks for their charity—the painter, who had fallen on hard times, needed coal to heat his house for the

Timeline: A Closer Look

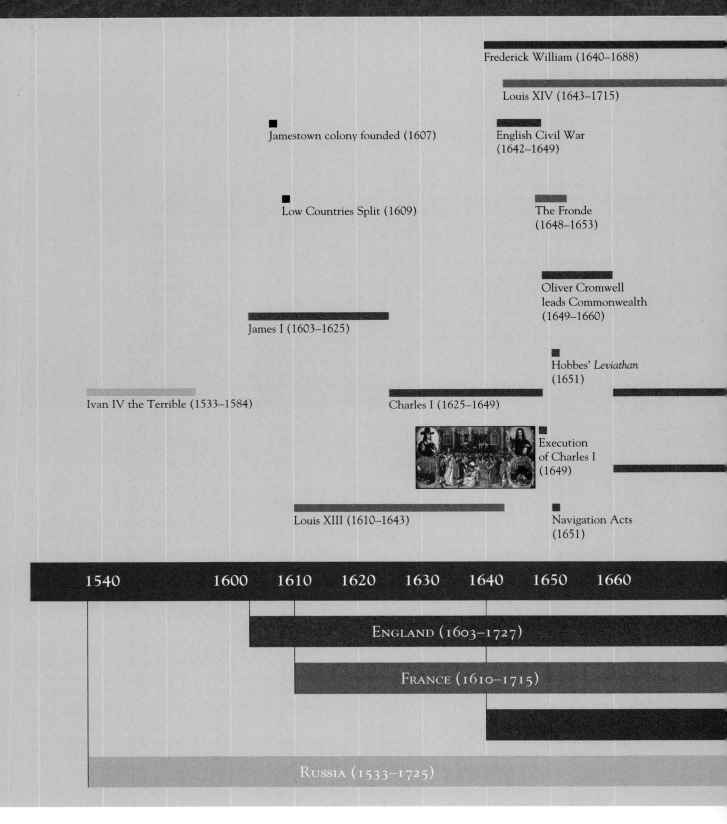

Frederick William (1640–1688)

Louis XIV (1643–1715)

Jamestown colony founded (1607)

English Civil War
(1642–1649)

Low Countries Split (1609)

The Fronde
(1648–1653)

Oliver Cromwell
leads Commonwealth
(1649–1660)

James I (1603–1625)

Hobbes' *Leviathan*
(1651)

Ivan IV the Terrible (1533–1584)

Charles I (1625–1649)

Execution
of Charles I
(1649)

Louis XIII (1610–1643)

Navigation Acts
(1651)

| 1540 | 1600 | 1610 | 1620 | 1630 | 1640 | 1650 | 1660 |

ENGLAND (1603–1727)

FRANCE (1610–1715)

RUSSIA (1533–1725)

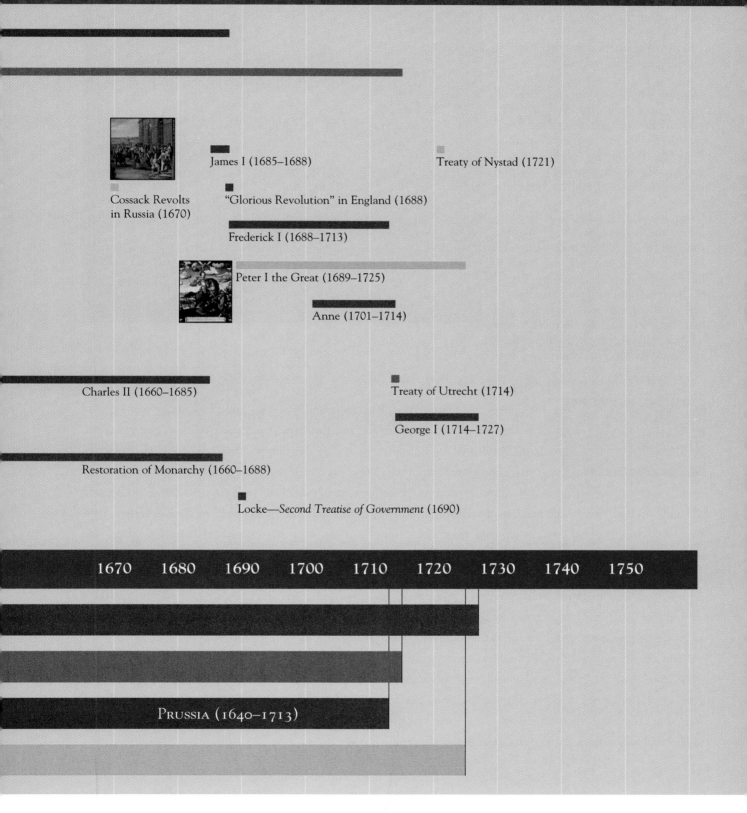

James I (1685–1688)

Treaty of Nystad (1721)

Cossack Revolts
in Russia (1670)

"Glorious Revolution" in England (1688)

Frederick I (1688–1713)

Peter I the Great (1689–1725)

Anne (1701–1714)

Charles II (1660–1685)

Treaty of Utrecht (1714)

George I (1714–1727)

Restoration of Monarchy (1660–1688)

Locke—*Second Treatise of Government* (1690)

| 1670 | 1680 | 1690 | 1700 | 1710 | 1720 | 1730 | 1740 | 1750 |

PRUSSIA (1640–1713)

winter, and the cloth guild had provided it.

The preeminence of the Dutch in the seventeenth century began to wane by the beginning of the next century. The economies of England and France had gathered strength both in Europe and abroad, and encroached on the commercial empire forged by the Dutch. Yet the two geographically small countries of England and the Netherlands had contributed much to the political development of the West. Both established the sovereignty of the people through constitutionalism—England through Parliament, and the Netherlands through local autonomy. For all their tremendous impact for the future, at the opening of the eighteenth century both nations seemed hardly whispers in a Europe dominated by strong monarchs proclaiming a divine right to rule.

FIGURE 13.13
Rembrandt van Rijn, *Syndics of the Cloth Guild.*

Summary

For upper-crust members of Western societies, the seventeenth century was a period of both comfort and struggle. The comfort came from these elites' continued dominance. From the beginning to the end of the century, they held most of the riches, status, and power. Those below them sometimes revolted, but the real threats came from competing colleagues and the monarch above. The efforts by monarchs to increase their power, to become "absolute" in both theory and practice, sparked intense struggles within states. In some places, such as France, Prussia, and Russia, strong monarchs offering order and stability won. In other places, such as Poland, England, and the Netherlands, powerful nobles—sometimes allied with commoners—overcame kings.

For the vast majority who toiled the fields, the period offered struggle without much comfort. In western Europe, demands from expanding central governments for taxes and conscripts only aggravated the hardships wrought by unusually bad harvests and disease. In eastern Europe, landowning nobles added to these problems by burdening peasants under an increasingly heavy yoke of serfdom.

Thus the structure of this hierarchical society may have loosened enough for some people in western Europe to improve their lot. However, that structure only tightened in eastern Europe. For all of Europe, war, revolt, and even revolution shook societies without breaking the traditional hierarchies. Nevertheless, some traditions had started to crumble. Important changes in science and thought were already afoot that would soon transform the intellectual foundations of Western society.

REVIEW, ANALYZE, AND ANTICIPATE

REVIEW THE PREVIOUS CHAPTER

In Chapter 11—"Alone Before God"—the Reformation, which shattered the unity of Western Christendom, and the entwined religious and dynastic wars that followed were examined. Chapter 12—"Faith, Fortune, and Fame"—told how several European powers expanded overseas during this same period and grew rich from the commerce developed in their colonies.

1. *Analyze how the religious divisions and wars of the 16th and 17th centuries lay the groundwork for both the growth of absolutism in France and central Europe as well as the struggle against it in England and the Netherlands.*

2. *In what ways might the competition for overseas empires and the commerce that resulted have affected the power of central governments and their responsibilities? How might the Netherlands' political structure have contributed to its commercial expansion?*

ANALYZE THIS CHAPTER

Chapter 13—"The Struggle for Survival and Sovereignty"—describes how kings and nobles battled for power, the resolutions of those struggles, and their impact on the millions of people outside the elites.

1. *Analyze the ways monarchs tried to increase their power.*

2. *What groups opposed the increase in monarchical power, and what political theories were developed to support their positions?*

3. *How do you explain why in some areas monarchs won the battle for sovereignty, while in others they lost?*

4. *Describe the struggles peasants throughout Europe faced during the seventeenth century. How did their conditions differ in western and eastern Europe?*

ANTICIPATE THE NEXT CHAPTER

In Chapter 14—"A New World of Reason and Reform"—the changing intellectual foundations of the West will be examined.

1. *What kinds of intellectual changes do you think might undermine the traditional social and political order during the seventeenth and eighteenth centuries? Why?*

2. *What groups and institutions are most likely to be threatened by or resist intellectual changes? Why?*

BEYOND THE CLASSROOM

STRESSES IN TRADITIONAL SOCIETY

Braudel, Fernand. *Civilization and Capitalism: The Structures of Everyday Life*. New York: Harper & Row, 1981. An excellent survey by an important historian that details the transformations in economic and social history.

Bush, Michael. *Noble Privilege*. New York: Holmes & Meier, 1983. Analyzes the role of the nobility in the seventeenth century.

Chartier, Roger, ed. *A History of Private Life, Vol. III: Passions of the Renaissance*. Cambridge, MA: Harvard University Press, 1989. Part of a fine series that describes the creation of the sphere of private life.

Gottlieb, Beatrice. *The Family in the Western World from the Black Death to the Industrial Age*. Oxford: Oxford University Press, 1994. A thorough survey of the transformations in family life.

ROYAL ABSOLUTISM IN FRANCE

Bercé, Yves-Marie. *The Birth of Absolutism*. London: Macmillan, 1996. A solid examination of French absolutism from the reign of Louis XIV to 1789.

Campbell, Peter R. *Louis XIV, 1661–1715*. London: Longman, 1993. A brief examination of the subject with supporting documents and a good bibliography.

Muchembled, Robert. *Popular Culture and Elite Culture in France, 1400–1750*. Baton Rouge, LA: Louisiana State University Press, 1985. Examines popular culture and the means by which higher authorities attempted to destroy it.

THE STRUGGLE FOR SOVEREIGNTY IN EASTERN EUROPE

Bérenger, Jean. *A History of the Habsburg Empire, 1273–1700*. London: Longman, 1990. A useful survey, particularly for this period.

Hughes, Lindsey. *Russia in the Age of Peter the Great*. New Haven, CT: Yale University Press, 1998. The most recent study of this important figure.

Kirby, David G. *Northern Europe in the Early Modern Period: The Baltic World, 1492–1772*. London: Longman, 1990. A good survey of the region during this period.

Vierhaus, Rudolf. *Germany in the Age of Absolutism*. New York: Cambridge University Press, 1988. An informative discussion of the German states during the seventeenth century.

THE TRIUMPH OF CONSTITUTIONALISM

Coward, Barry. *The Stuart Age: A History of England, 1603–1714*. White Plains, NY: Longman Publishing Group, 1995. Provides a readable and balanced narrative of the whole course of the history of England.

van Deursen, Arie Theodorus. *Plain Lives in a Golden Age: Popular Culture, Religion, and Society in Seventeenth-Century Holland*. Trans. M. Ultree. New York: Cambridge University Press, 1991. A fascinating analysis of how laborers, peasants, and sailors made their living.

Durston, Christopher, ed. *Culture of English Puritanism, 1560–1700*. New York: Saint Martin's Press, 1996. A look into the lives and times of the English Puritans.

Fraser, Antonia. *The Weaker Vessel*. New York: Alfred A. Knopf, 1984. A detailed, illustrated, and comprehensive study of women in seventeenth-century England.

Gaunt, Peter. *Oliver Cromwell*. Cambridge, MA: Blackwell Publishers, 1995. A good study on the life and career of the Lord Protector.

Geyl, Pieter. *History of the Low Countries: Episodes and Problems*. New York: St. Martin's Press, 1964. A collection of essays by a preeminent scholar that illuminates this important period in the Low Countries.

Hill, Christopher. *A Nation of Change and Novelty: Radical Politics, Religion, and Literature in Seventeenth-Century England*. London: Routledge, 1990. The standard history of the revolution by an eminent historian.

Miller, John. *Restoration and the England of Charles II*, 2nd ed. White Plains, NY: Longman Publishing Group, 1997. Clarifies the complex issues of the major political and religious themes surrounding the Restoration.

Sharpe, Kevin. *Culture and Politics in Early Stuart England*. Stanford, CA: Stanford University Press, 1994. A revisionist look at the culture and politics in England at this time.

Unfamiliar words? See our Glossary at the back for pronunciation and definitions.

See our Web Page at www.mhhe.com/sherman for more information and review exercises.

Frontispiece to Marco Vincenzo Coronelli's Atlas, 1691

In this frontispiece from an atlas, a globe and ship occupy center stage and
represent the West's exploration of the world. Just above, the banner of a
trumpeting angel reads, "Yet farther"—words that contrast sharply with the
traditional medieval expression "No farther." Drawings of the numerous
instruments that characterized the new age of exploration and science occupy
the periphery of the image.

A New World of Reason and Reform

The Scientific Revolution and the Enlightenment, 1600–1800

In 1655, French scientist Blaise Pascal (1623–1662) retired from his studies and began recording his thoughts in writing. "Man is but a reed, the most feeble thing in nature; but he is a thinking reed," he wrote. "All our dignity consists, then, in thought . . . by thought I comprehend the world." Pascal's words hint at the changes emerging in scholars' thinking about ideas, the world, and the place of humans in it.

We can detect more clues about these changes in the artwork on page 466. The 1691 world atlas itself, published by the accomplished Venetian mapmaker and mathematician Marco Coronelli (1650–1718), echoes the overseas expansion of Europe, already two centuries old. It also reveals the underlying culture of the Renaissance, which stressed learning and exploration through reading and art. Coronelli chose this illustration to open his new atlas. With the images of a ship, the earth, scientific instruments, and the provocative phrasing "Yet farther," he declared the end of limits to the search for knowledge. The entire illustration suggests a people proudly using science to fuel their growing power— over other peoples as well as nature itself.

Buoyed by the accumulation of scientific discoveries, this optimism about the power of thought and the search for knowledge grew and spread throughout the West during the eighteenth century. Widening circles of intellectuals and the reading public learned about the new ways of thinking being applied to all fields, from politics and religion to economics and criminology. Despite resistance from church and state, this dawning of what became known as the Age of Reason would gather strength, filter down through the ranks of society, and form the intellectual foundation for life in the modern West. During this same period, the Islamic, Chinese, Japanese, and other civilizations of the world declined to question their traditional ways. Only westerners challenged the standard assumptions of their civilization. The power and attitudes that the West gained from this intellectual exploration helped redefine Western civilization and distinguish it from the non-Western world.

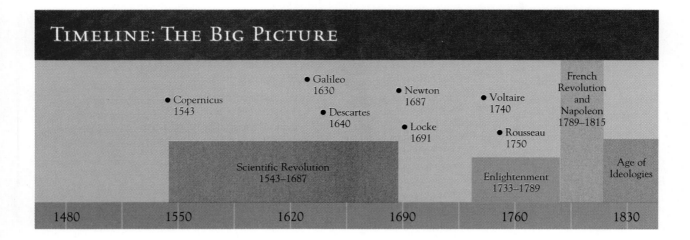

	● Copernicus 1543	● Galileo 1630 ● Descartes 1640	● Newton 1687 ● Locke 1691	● Voltaire 1740 ● Rousseau 1750	French Revolution and Napoleon 1789–1815		Age of Ideologies
		Scientific Revolution 1543–1687		Enlightenment 1733–1789			
1480	1550	1620	1690	1760		1830	

Questioning Truth and Authority

On June 22, 1633, the well-known Italian scientist Galileo Galilei (1564–1642) knelt in a Roman convent before the cardinals who served as judges of the Inquisition. The cardinals informed Galileo that he was "vehemently suspected of heresy." They also showed him the customary instruments of torture, though they did not use them. Next, they ordered him to deny "the false opinion that the sun is the center of the universe and immovable, and that the earth is not the center of the same"—views that Galileo had supported in a book he published the previous year. Threatened with being tried and burned as a heretic, Galileo had to denounce his views as heresy. The court and papacy sentenced Galileo to house arrest in Florence for the rest of his life and forbade him to publish on the topic again. Nevertheless, Galileo would not change his mind. The sequence of events leading to Galileo's trial and conviction is a story of its own, but the conflict lay at the core of a major development of the age: the scientific revolution.

THE OLD VIEW

Until the sixteenth century, most European scholars shared the standard medieval understanding of the physical nature of the earth and the universe. This understanding was based on a long legacy stretching back to the views of the fourth-century B.C. Greek philosopher Aristotle. His ideas had been modified in the second century A.D. by Ptolemy of Alexandria and then passed on through Byzantine and Arab scholars to medieval European thinkers. After the thirteenth century, Europeans translated Aristotle's works into Latin and merged his thinking with Christian ideas about the universe.

According to this Christian medieval understanding, illustrated in the woodcut in Figure 14.1, the earth rested at the center of an unchanging universe. Around it in ascending order rose the perfect spheres of air, fire, the sun, the planets, and the stars (the "firmament"), with God (the "prime mover") just beyond. The signs of the zodiac are recorded on one band in the illustration, revealing the importance of astrology. Westerners accounted for the succession of day and night by explaining that this finite universe rotated in precise circles around the earth once every twenty-four hours. The heavenly abode of angels consisted of pure matter, while the earthly home of humans was made of changeable, corrupt matter. This universe was clear, finite, and satisfyingly focused on the earthly center of God's concern.

The Earth-centered universe

Common sense supported this worldview. A glance at the sky confirmed that the sun and stars indeed circled around the earth each day. Under foot, the earth felt motionless. To careful observers, the motion of planets, whose position often changed, was more perplexing. To explain this mystery, Ptolemy and others had modified their theories, concluding that planets moved in small, individual orbits as they traveled predictably around the earth. People had lived by the wisdom of the ancients and authoritative interpretations of the Bible for centuries. Accordingly, investigation of the physical universe generally consisted of making deductions from these long-accepted guides.

FIGURE 14.1

The medieval view of the universe, 1559.

According to Hermetic doctrine, based on writings mistakenly attributed to Hermes Trismegistus (supposedly an ancient Egyptian priest), all matter contained the divine spirit, which humans ought to seek to understand. *Hermetic doctrine* Among many scholars, this doctrine stimulated intense interest in botany, chemistry, metallurgy, and other studies that promised to help people unlock the secrets of nature. The Hermetic approach also held that mathematical harmonies helped explain the divine spirit and represented a crucial pathway to understanding God's physical world. This approach encouraged scholars to use mathematics and to measure, map, and quantify nature. Moreover, Hermetic doctrine also held that the sun was the most important agency for transmission of the divine spirit, and thus rightly occupied the center of the universe. Finally, these beliefs fostered the idea of the natural magician who could unleash the powers of nature through alchemy (the study of how to purify and transform metals, such as turning common minerals into gold), astrology (the study of how stars affect people), and magic. Scholars often saw no distinction between

UNDERMINING THE OLD VIEW

During the fifteenth and sixteenth centuries, new problems began undermining this traditional view. Authorities of all kinds—including Aristotle—came into question during the Renaissance. Some of this questioning stemmed from the Renaissance search for classical writings, which led scholars to discover and read the works of Greek authorities who contradicted Aristotle. Neoplatonism, based on the ideas of Plato, stressed the belief that one should search beyond appearances for true knowledge; truth about both nature and God could be found in abstract reasoning and be best expressed by mathematics. Neoplatonic Hermetic doctrine provided especially powerful alternatives to Aristotelian thought.

FIGURE 14.2

Heinrich Khunrath, The Laboratory and the Chapel, 1609.

seeking to understand the harmony, oneness, and spiritual aspects of the natural world, and what we would call scientific observation and experimentation. While Hermetic doctrine often proved unuseful, all these ideas encouraged investigators to question traditionally accepted knowledge.

Figure 14.2, an illustration from a book on alchemy by the German Heinrich Khunrath, shows these close connections between spiritual beliefs and the "science" or "Hermetic art" of alchemy. At the left, the author prays in a small chapel. Lettering on the drapery of the chapel states, "When we attend strictly to our work, God himself will help us." At the center, musical instruments and a pair of scales rest on a table, representing the links among music, harmony, and number so characteristic in alchemy. The inscription on the table reads, "Sacred music disperses sadness in evil spirits." On the floor lie containers and other apparatus used to mix materials, and at the upper right are flasks and other storage containers.

In addition to new ideas and beliefs, geographic exploration during the Renaissance also upset traditional assumptions. The discovery of the New World, *Exploration* for example, disproved Ptolemaic geography. Furthermore, overseas voyages stimulated demand for new instruments and precise measurements for navigation. This demand in turn encouraged research, especially in astronomy and mathematics.

Finally, the recently invented printing press enabled even out-of-favor scholars to publish their findings, which spread new ideas and *The printing press* discoveries even further. Renaissance rulers supported all these efforts in hopes of gaining prestige as well as practical tools for war, construction, and mining. Church authorities did the same at times, especially backing astronomical research in the hopes of improving the calendar to date Easter more accurately.

Like the Renaissance, the Reformation also unleashed forces that provoked the questioning of long-held views. Most researchers had religious motives for their work, though those motives were not necessarily grounded in tradition. In particular, they yearned for insights into the perfection of God's universe. As we read in Chapter 11, the Reformation shattered confidence in religious authorities. By upsetting hallowed certainties, sixteenth- and seventeenth-century scholars hoped to establish new, even sounder certainties and thereby regain a sense of mastery over nature.

Developing a Modern Scientific View

Even with these rumblings of change, no sudden breakthrough cleared away the centuries-old understanding of nature. Most scientific work still proceeded slowly, as did scholarly and public acceptance of its findings. Investigators had to demonstrate the effectiveness of their new methods again and again to convince even their colleagues. Indeed, few scholars suggested a wholesale rejection of traditional authorities; most simply chipped away at old notions. By the end of the seventeenth century, however, an entirely new scientific view of reality, initiated by just a handful of scholars, had replaced the traditional view. To understand this startling shift, we need to trace developments in astronomy, physics, and scientific methodology.

ASTRONOMY AND PHYSICS: FROM COPERNICUS TO NEWTON

During the sixteenth and seventeenth centuries, astronomy and physics attracted the most systematic attention from scholars. Researchers in these fields became particularly dissatisfied with the inability of Aristotelian theory to explain, simply and efficiently, careful observations and mathematical calculations of the stars. The Ptolemaic system for predicting planetary movements seemed overly complex and cumbersome to these scholars. Their findings would dramatically alter westerners' perceptions of nature and of the earth's place in the universe. As the English poet John Donne complained in 1611, "New philosophy calls all in doubt."

Nicolaus Copernicus (1473–1543), a Polish clergyman with an interest in astronomy, astrology, mathematics, and church law, took the first steps in this intel- *Nicolaus Copernicus* lectual adventure. Like so many other northern European scholars, he crossed the Alps to study in an Italian university. There he became influenced by the rediscovery of Greek scholarship, Neoplatonism, and the Hermetic doctrine. Copernicus sought a simpler mathematical formulation to explain how the universe operated. His search convinced him that the earth was *not* at the center of the universe. Instead, he believed that the sun "sits upon a royal throne" in that location, "ruling his children, the planets which circle around him." Moreover, Copernicus concluded that the earth was not stationary: "What appears to be a motion of the sun is in truth a motion of the earth." According to Copernicus, the earth moved in perfect, "divine" circles around the sun, as did other bodies in the universe. Day passed into night because the earth turned on its axis. Figure 14.3 shows this view of the universe. At the center is the sun, circled by the earth ("this globe of mortality") and other planets, all bounded by an infinity of stars ("fixed" and "immovable") and the heavens ("the palace of happiness . . . the habitat for the elect"). This change from an Earth-centered (geocentric) to a sun-centered (heliocentric) universe would become known as the Copernican revolution.

Copernicus worked on his heliocentric model of the universe for almost twenty-five years. However, fearing ridicule and disapproval from the clergy, he waited until 1543—what became the year of his death—to publish it. Few people outside a limited circle of scholars knew of his views, and even fewer accepted them. Nevertheless, Catholic and Protestant authorities who were wedded to the Earth-centered system soon recognized the threat to the Christian conception of the universe that these ideas represented. They denounced the Copernican system as illogical, unbiblical, and unsettling to the Christian faith. One Protestant associate of Martin Luther complained that "certain men . . . have concluded that the earth moves. . . . It is want of honesty and decency to assert such notions publicly. . . . It is part of a good mind to accept the truth as revealed by God and to acquiesce in it."

Still, Copernicus' thinking had some supporters. An Italian monk, Giordano Bruno (1548–1600), tested Catholic authorities by openly teaching and extending Copernican thought, arguing that "the universe is entirely infinite because it has neither edge, limit, nor surfaces." Bruno also professed a se-

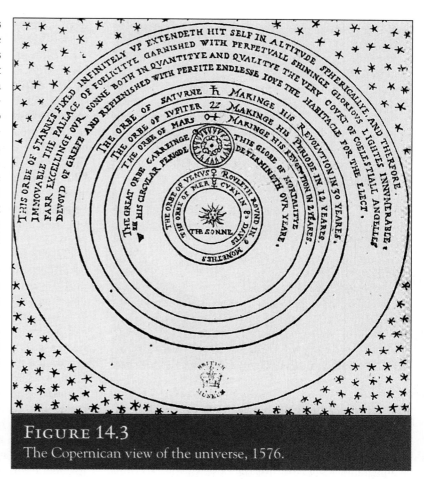

FIGURE 14.3
The Copernican view of the universe, 1576.

ries of unusual religious notions. Outraged, the Catholic Inquisition burned Bruno at the stake. Nevertheless, Copernicus' views began to influence other scholars who were investigating the physical nature of the universe.

The Danish aristocrat Tycho Brahe (1546–1601) did not share Copernicus' belief in a heliocentric universe, nor did he grasp the sophisticated mathematics of the day. Still, he became the next most important astronomer of the *Tycho Brahe* sixteenth century. He persuaded the king of Denmark to build for him the most advanced astronomy laboratory in Europe. There he recorded thousands of unusually accurate, detailed observations about the planets and stars over a period of twenty years—all without a telescope. His discoveries of a new star in 1572 and a comet in 1577 undermined the Aristotelian belief in a sky of fixed, unalterable stars

FIGURE 14.4
Galileo Galilei, The Moon, 1610.

Kepler thus showed "that the celestial machine . . . is the likeness of [a] clock," further undermining the Aristotelian view and extending the Copernican revolution.

In 1597, Kepler responded to a letter from Galileo Galilei, the Italian astronomer, physicist, and mathematician discussed at the beginning of this chapter. Although Galileo expressed a reluctance to publicize his beliefs in Copernican ideas, Kepler encouraged him to take the risk. "Be of good cheer, Galileo, and appear in public. If I am not mistaken there are only a few among the distinguished mathematicians of Europe who would dissociate themselves from us. So great is the power of truth."

Galileo Galilei

Galileo already believed that the world could be described in purely mathematical terms. "Philosophy," he wrote, "is written in this grand book, the universe, which stands continually open to our gaze. . . . It is written in the language of mathematics, and its characters are triangles, circles, and other geometric figures without which it is humanly impossible to understand a single word of it. . . ." Galileo also felt that harmonies could be discovered through experimentation and mathematics. By conducting controlled experiments such as rolling balls down inclines, he demonstrated how motion could be described mathematically. He rejected the old view that objects in their natural state were at rest and that all motion needed a purpose. Instead, he formulated the principle of inertia, showing that bodies, once set into motion, will tend to stay in motion. He thus overturned Aristotelian ideas and established rules for experimental physics.

Galileo, hearing about the recent invention of the telescope, then studied the skies through a telescope that he built in 1609 out of a long tube and magnifying lenses. Figure 14.4 shows what he saw. He sketched this illustration of the moon for his book *Starry Messenger*. Instead of being a perfect, smooth heavenly body, the moon's surface was rugged (like the earth's), with craters and mountains indicated by lines and shading. The telescope also revealed that Jupiter had moons, and that the sun had spots. These observations confirmed the view that other heavenly bodies besides the earth were imperfect, and further convinced him of the validity of Copernicus' hypothesis. For years Galileo had feared the disapproval of the Catholic Church. Now, however, he was ready to

moving in crystalline spheres. Although Brahe mistakenly concluded that some planets revolved around the sun, which itself moved around the earth, other astronomers with better understandings of mathematics would use his observations to draw very different conclusions.

Tycho Brahe's assistant, Johannes Kepler (1571–1630), built on Brahe's observations to support the Copernican heliocentric theory. A German Lutheran from an aristocratic family, Kepler—like other Hermetic scholars—believed in an underlying mathematical harmony of mystical significance to the physical universe. He sought one harmony that would fit with Brahe's observations. Between 1609 and 1619, he announced his most important findings: the three laws of planetary motion. After determining the first law—which stated that the planets moved in ellipses around the sun—he excitedly wrote, "It was as if I had awaken from a sleep." The second law declared that the planets' velocity varied according to their distance from the sun. The third law concluded that the physical relationship between the moving planets could be expressed mathematically.

Johannes Kepler

publicly argue that "in discussions of physical problems we ought to begin not from the authority of scriptural passages, but from sense-experiences and necessary demonstrations." Galileo published his findings in 1610.

Six years later the church attacked his proposition that "the earth is not the center of the world nor immovable, but moves as a whole, and also with a daily motion." This statement, the church said, was "foolish and absurd philosophically, and formally heretical." To back up its claim, the church cited the authority of both the Bible and itself. For the next several years, Galileo kept his thoughts to himself. In 1632, believing that the church might be more open, he decided once again to present his views. To avoid challenging the church, he submitted his book to the official church censors and agreed to some changes they demanded. Finally he published his *Dialogue on the Two Chief Systems of the World*—in Italian rather than the less accessible Latin. This text advocated Copernicanism, portrayed opponents of the Copernican system (such as the Jesuits) as simpletons, and brought Galileo directly into public conflict with conservative forces in the Catholic Church. Because Galileo could show that his book had already been approved by church officials, prosecutors had to use questionable evidence against him. As we saw at the beginning of the chapter, the Roman Inquisition ultimately forced him to renounce his views.

News of Galileo's sensational trial spread throughout Europe, as did fear of publishing other radical views. Soon, however, his book was translated and published elsewhere in Europe, and his views began to win acceptance by other scientists. Even though Galileo admitted that the new science was beyond the grasp of "the shallow minds of the common people," he effectively communicated its ideas to his peers. By the time of his death in 1642, Europe's intellectual elite had begun to embrace the Copernican outlook.

In England, Isaac Newton (1642–1727) picked up the trail blazed by Copernicus, Brahe, Kepler, and Galileo. Late in life, Newton described *Isaac Newton* his career modestly: "I do not know what I may appear to the world; but to myself I seem to have been only like a boy playing on the sea-shore, and diverting myself in now and then finding a smoother pebble or a prettier shell than ordinary, while the great ocean of truth lay all undiscovered before me." Newton may have held himself in humble

regard, but his accomplishments were astonishing.

In 1661 Newton entered Cambridge University, where he studied the ideas of Copernicus and Galileo as well as the advantages of scientific investigation. He distinguished himself enough in mathematics to be chosen to stay on as a professor after his graduation. Like most other figures of the scientific revolution, Newton was also profoundly religious and hoped to harmonize his Christian beliefs with the principles of science. He also believed in alchemy and elements of Hermeticism.

Starting in his early twenties, Newton made some of the most important discoveries in the history of science. He developed calculus and investigated the nature of *Newton's Principia* light, and also formulated and mathematically described three laws of motion: inertia, acceleration, and action/reaction. Yet he is best known for discovering the law of universal attraction, or gravitation. After working on the concept for years, he finally published it in 1687 in his great work *Principia (The Mathematical Principles of Natural Knowledge)*. In the book, he stated the law with simplicity and precision: "Every particle of matter in the universe attracts every other particle with a force varying inversely as the square of the distance between them and directly proportional to the product of their masses." In his view, this law applied equally to all objects, from the most massive planet to a small apple falling from a tree.

Newton had managed to synthesize the new findings in astronomy and physics into a systematic explanation of physical laws that applied to the earth as well as the heavens. This Newtonian universe was infinite and had no center. Uniform and mathematically describable, it was held together by explainable forces and was atomic in nature. Essentially, everything in the universe consisted of only one thing: matter in motion.

THE REVOLUTION SPREADS: MEDICINE, ANATOMY, AND CHEMISTRY

While astronomy and physics led the way in dramatic scientific findings, researchers in other fields made important discoveries as well. Many of these advances also had roots in the sixteenth century. For example, several scholars developed new ideas in the related fields of medicine, anatomy, and chemistry.

ANDREAE VESALII.

FIGURE 14.5
Andreas Vesalius, 1543.

In medicine, a flamboyant Swiss alchemist-physician known as Paracelsus (1493–1541) strongly influenced the healing arts. A believer in *Paracelsus* Hermetic doctrine, Paracelsus openly opposed medical orthodoxy and taught that healers should not look for truth in libraries ("the more learned, the more perverted," he warned) but in the Book of Nature. "I have not been ashamed to learn from tramps, butchers, and barbers," he boasted. As a teacher and wandering practitioner, he treated patients, experimented with chemicals, recorded his observations, and developed new theories. Paracelsus concluded that all matter was composed of salt, sulfur, and mercury—not the traditional earth, water,

fire, and air. Rejecting the standard view that an imbalance in the humors of the body caused disease, he instead looked to specific chemical imbalances to explain what caused each illness. He also encouraged research and experimentation to find natural remedies for bodily disorders, such as administering mercury or arsenic at astrologically correct moments. Though rejected by most established physicians, Paracelsus' ideas became particularly popular among common practitioners and would later influence the study of chemistry.

Other researchers founded the modern science of anatomy. In the sixteenth century, Andreas Vesalius (1514–1564), a Fleming living in Italy, wrote the first comprehensive *Andreas Vesalius* textbook on the structure of the human body based on careful observation. Figure 14.5 shows the twenty-eight-year-old Vesalius displaying one of his studies on human anatomy from his 1543 treatise, *On the Fabric of the Human Body*. This figure is one of more than 200 woodcut illustrations showing the composition of the body, stage by stage. Vesalius himself dissected cadavers, as suggested by the scalpel resting on the table. A notable aspect of this illustration is that Vesalius boldly looks the viewer in the eye, perhaps to challenge directly the old, authoritative assumptions about human anatomy. Nevertheless, his dissections of human bodies brought him into conflict with traditional physicians and scholars. Disgusted, he finally gave up his scientific studies and became the personal physician to Emperor Charles V.

Despite relentless criticism, other scholars continued anatomical research. A line from a poem written for the opening of the Amsterdam Anatomical Theatre in the early *William Harvey* seventeenth century reflects the sense that this research needed special justification: "Evil doers who while living have done damage are of benefit after their death." In other words, the body parts of criminals "afford a lesson to you, the Living." The most important of these researchers was William Harvey (1578–1657), an Englishman who, like Vesalius, studied at the University of Padua in Italy. Harvey dissected hundreds of animals, including dogs, pigs, lobsters, shrimp, and snakes. He discovered that the human heart worked like a pump, with valves that allowed blood to circulate through the body: "The movement of the blood occurs constantly in a circular manner and is the result of the beating of the heart." Yet, despite this mechanistic view, he also considered the heart the physical and spiritual center of life—in his words, "the sovereign of everything."

By the seventeenth century, anatomists and others benefitted from several newly invented scientific instruments, such as the microscope. Anton van Leeuwenhoek (1632–1723), a Dutchman, became

Anton van Leeuwenhoek

the chief pioneer in the use of this instrument. In observations during the 1670s, he described seeing "little animals or animalcules" in water from a lake. "It was wonderful to see: and I judge that some of these little creatures were above a thousand times smaller than the smallest ones I have ever yet seen, upon the rind of cheese, in wheaten flour, mould and the like." Leeuwenhoek discovered what would later be identified as bacteria in his own saliva: "little eels or worms, lying all huddled up together and wriggling . . . This was for me, among all the marvels that I have discovered in nature, the most marvellous of all."

Around this same time, Robert Boyle (1627–1691), an Irish nobleman particularly interested in medical

Robert Boyle

chemistry, helped lay the foundations for modern chemistry. Drawing inspiration from Paracelsus, Boyle attacked many assumptions inherited from the ancients and began a systematic search for the basic elements of matter. Relying on the experimental method and using new instruments, he argued that all matter was composed of indestructible atoms that behaved in predictable ways. Boyle also discovered a law—which still bears his name—that governs the pressure of gases. His exacting procedures set a standard for the scientific practice of chemistry.

THE METHODOLOGY OF SCIENCE EMERGES

The scientists who challenged traditional views in their fields also used new methods of discovery—of uncovering how things worked and of determining "truth." Indeed, this innovative methodology lay at the heart of the scientific revolution. Earlier techniques for ascertaining the truth—by referring to long-trusted authorities and making deductions from their propositions—became unacceptable to the new scientists. They instead emphasized systematic skepticism, experimentation, and reasoning based solely on observed facts and mathematical laws. The two most important philosophers of this methodology were Francis Bacon and René Descartes.

Francis Bacon (1561–1626), an English politician who was once lord chancellor of England under James I, took a passionate interest in the new science. He rejected reliance

Francis Bacon

on ancient authorities and advocated the collection of data without preconceived notions. From such data, he explained, scientific conclusions could be reached through inductive reasoning—drawing general conclusions from particular concrete observations. "Deriv[ing] axioms from . . . particulars, rising by gradual and unbroken ascent, so that it arrives at the most general axioms of all. This is the true way," he proclaimed. In addition, Bacon argued that scientific knowledge would be useful knowledge: "I am laboring to lay the foundation not of any sect or doctrine, but of human utility and power." He believed that science would benefit commerce and industry and improve the human condition by giving people unprecedented power over their environment.

Figure 14.6, the title page from Bacon's 1620 book *New Instrument*, graphically depicts these views. The illustration shows a ship of discovery sailing out from the western end of the Mediterranean Sea into the unknown. Below is the quotation, "Many shall venture forth and science shall be increased." Here is an optimistic assertion that knowledge is limitless and that science constitutes a voyage of discovery—a view that would be echoed again and again, as we saw in the picture at the beginning of this chapter. Bacon thus became a noted propagandist for the new science as well as a proponent of the empirical method.

Despite his brilliance, Bacon did not have a thorough understanding of mathematics and the role it could play in the new science. His contemporary, René Descartes (1596–1650), would

René Descartes

be the one to excel in this arena. Born in France, René Descartes received training in scholastic philosophy and mathematics at one of France's best Jesuit schools, and took a degree in law. He entered military service and served during the Thirty Years' War. During his travels, he met a Dutch mathematician and became interested in the new science. An ecstatic experience in 1619 convinced him to commit to a life of the mind. He spent his most productive years as a mathematician, physicist, and metaphysical philosopher in Holland. In 1637, he published his philosophy and scientific methodology in the *Discourse on Method*—in French, not Latin. The book presented an eloquent defense of skepticism and of abstract deductive reasoning—deriving point. From there he followed a rigorous process of deductive reasoning to draw a variety of conclusions, including the existence of God and the physical world. He argued that there were two kinds of reality: mind, or subjective thinking and experiencing; and body, or objective physical matter. According to this philosophy, known as Cartesian dualism, the objective physical universe could be understood in terms of extension (matter occupying space) and motion (matter in motion). "Give me extension and motion," vowed Descartes, "and I will create the universe." He considered the body nothing more than "an earthen machine." In his opinion, only the mind was exempt from mechanical laws.

Descartes emphasized the power of the detached, reasoning individual mind to discover truths about nature. Unlike Bacon, he put his faith in mathematical reasoning, not empirical investigation. By challenging all established authority, by accepting as truth only what could be known by reason, and by assuming a purely mechanical physical universe, Descartes established a philosophy and methodology that became the core of the new science.

Supporting and Spreading Science

Only a small group of people actually participated in the scientific revolution. Of these, a handful of women managed to overcome barriers to take part as patrons for scientists or as scientists themselves. Men ignored or discounted their work, and scientific societies usually excluded them. The few women engaged in science had to rely on their own resources or work in collaboration with their husbands.

Few scientific scholars—whether male or female—got far without calling on a network of peers and soliciting the support of wealthy patrons. To spread their ideas, these scientists needed to publish their works, interact with like-minded colleagues, and gain the backing of prestigious elites. Fortunately for them, these elites were eager to comply.

COURTS AND SALONS

Governments and wealthy aristocrats served as benefactors and employers of scientists. Kepler, for example, received help from the imperial court, serving in

FIGURE 14.6
Title page of Francis Bacon's *New Instrument*, 1620.

conclusions that logically flowed from a premise. "Inquiries should be directed, not to what others have thought, nor to what we ourselves conjecture, but to what we can clearly and perspicuously behold and with certainty deduce; for knowledge is not won in any other way."

Descartes questioned all forms of authority, no matter how venerable—be it Aristotle or even the Bible. He tried to remove systematically all assumptions about knowledge, and advocated doubting the senses, which he claimed could be deceptive. Taken to its logical conclusion, his argument left him with one God-given experiential fact—that he was thinking. "I think, therefore I am" became his starting

Bohemia as Rudolf II's official mathematician. Galileo became court mathematician to Cosimo de' Medici in Tuscany. Vesalius served as physician to Holy Roman Emperor Charles V, and Harvey as royal physician in England.

Queen Christina of Sweden, like several other monarchs, invited scholars and artists to her court. Figure 14.7 shows her in 1649 with the French philosopher and mathematician René Descartes (on the right pointing to papers). Books, papers, and instruments attest to the importance of the new science at this meeting. In this Protestant country, the religious figure on the far right seems to indicate that there is little conflict between science and religion. The artist portrays Christina, a deeply religious person (who would later become a Catholic), as an interested and gracious benefactor helping to bring to light scientific findings.

Rulers had their own motives—namely practicality and prestige—for assisting scholars and scientists. Royals especially hoped that scholarship and scientific inquiry would yield discoveries that would enhance the strength and prosperity of the state. For example, they sought experts in building projects, armaments, mapmaking, navigation, and mining. They also tried to burnish their own reputations as powerful, educated people by patronizing scholarship, science, and the arts. In this way, support of science became a supposed hallmark of good government. Enticed by this assistance, learned people gathered at royal courts, which gradually filled rooms with new tools, machines, exotic plants and animals, and books.

Beyond the court, people formed private salons and local academies where those interested in science could meet. In the 1540s, the first academy for scientific study was established in Naples. Women ran several important salons where scientists discussed their findings along with literature, art, and politics. Some scientists even found benefactors at these meetings.

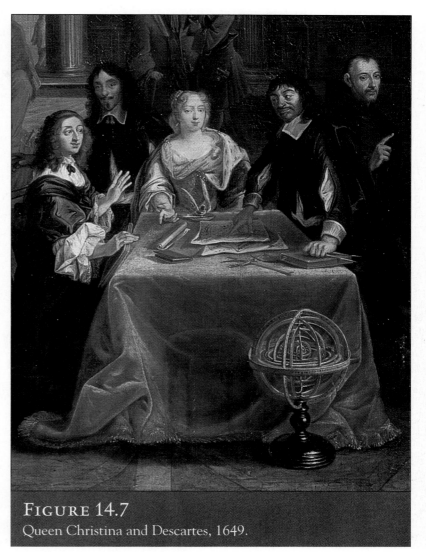

FIGURE 14.7
Queen Christina and Descartes, 1649.

THE RISE OF ROYAL SOCIETIES

During the second half of the seventeenth century, central governments stepped up their support of scientific experimentation, publications, and academies. In 1662, for example, Charles II chartered the Royal Society in England; four years later, Louis XIV's finance minister, Jean Baptiste Colbert, founded the Académie des Sciences in France. Figure 14.8 illustrates royal interest in these academies. Here Louis XIV, boasting a plumed hat, visits the Académie. At Louis' left, Colbert points to a plan for improved military fortifications. Throughout the room are instruments and specimens for studies in cartography, geography, astronomy, physics, chemistry, and natural history—all supported by the Académie. Through the window on the right we can see a new Royal Observatory being built. These organizations and others patterned after them furnished laboratories, granted subsidies, brought scientists together to exchange ideas, published their findings, and honored scientific achievements. This governmental support of science added to the growing prestige of science and the scientific community.

RELIGION AND THE NEW SCIENCE

Religious organizations played a mixed role in the spread of the new science. Traditionally, the Catholic Church supported scholarship and learning in general, including natural science. Moreover, religious orders staffed most universities, and many key figures of the scientific revolution held university positions. Numerous leading scholars also felt a profound sense of spirituality. Copernicus, for example, who dedicated his work to the pope, was a cleric, as were many other natural scientists. While we may be tempted to assume that the skepticism inherent in the scientific method would lead to atheism, the great scientists attacked neither faith nor established religion. Nor were they dispassionate investigators holding themselves apart from the spiritual nature of their age. They often believed in magic, ghosts, and witchcraft, and typically considered alchemy, astrology, and numerology (predicting events from numbers) valuable components of natural science. Galileo, though he

FIGURE 14.8
Sebastien Le Clerc, *Louis XIV at the Academy of Sciences*, 1671.

later decried his trial as the triumph of "ignorance, impiety, fraud and deceit," remained a believing Catholic. Even Robert Boyle, who like others came to think of the universe as a machine, attributed its origin to God: "God, indeed, gave motion to matter . . . and established those rules of motion, and that order amongst things . . . which we call the laws of nature." Newton agreed: "This most beautiful system of the sun, planets, and comets, could only proceed from the counsel and dominion of an intelligent and powerful Being. . . . He endures forever, and is everywhere present. . . ."

Nevertheless, the new science did challenge certain tenets of faith and the traditional Christian conception of God's place in the ordering of the world. Neither Protestant nor Catholic leaders welcomed Copernican ideas and the implications of the new science. The Catholic Church, itself ordered in a hierarchy that paralleled the old view of the universe, stayed particularly committed to established authorities. Moreover the church's condemnation of Galileo in 1633 discouraged scientific investigations throughout much of Catholic Europe. Descartes was not alone in deciding not to publish ideas incorporating Copernican assumptions. As he explained in 1634, "It is not my temperament to set sail against the wind . . . I want to be able to live in peace . . . out of sight." Although the French government would actively promote science, after the mid-seventeenth century most scientific work and publishing took place in Protestant areas—particularly in England and the Netherlands.

THE NEW WORLDVIEW

By the end of the seventeenth century, the accumulation of convincing scientific findings and the support for those findings among the educated elites had broken the Aristotelian-medieval worldview and replaced it with the Copernican-Newtonian paradigm. According to the new view, the earth, along with the planets, moved around the sun in an infinite universe of other similar bodies. The natural order consisted of matter in motion, acting according to mathematically expressible laws. Scientific truths came from observing, measuring, experimenting, and making reasoned conclusions through the use of sophisticated mathematics. Religious truths still had their place, and the orderliness of nature reflected God's design. However, science now claimed precedence in explaining the material world.

In the sixteenth and early seventeenth centuries, great thinkers such as Copernicus and Galileo had been ridiculed and persecuted for their ideas. By the late seventeenth and early eighteenth centuries, Isaac Newton's fate revealed the acceptance of the new paradigm among educated elites. Famous and popular, Newton became a member of Parliament, served for many years as director of the Royal Mint, and was knighted by Queen Anne.

The Copernican-Newtonian paradigm

Laying the Foundations for the Enlightenment

In the course of the eighteenth century, the ideas of the scientific revolution spread widely and were applied in stunning new ways. With this broadening, the eighteenth century witnessed the birth of a major cultural movement known as the Enlightenment. At the heart of this movement lay the firm conviction—especially among intellectuals—that human reason should determine understanding of the world and the rules of social life. "[H]ave the courage to use your own intelligence," and leave your "self-caused immaturity," exhorted the German philosopher Immanuel Kant (1724–1804). "All that is required for this enlightenment is freedom, and particularly . . . the freedom for man to make public use of his reason in all matters."

The Enlightenment hit its full stride in the middle decades of the eighteenth century, when it particularly influenced literate elites of Europe and North America. Yet, its roots stretched back to the end of the seventeenth century. At that time, the thinking that would characterize the Enlightenment emerged in the writings of people who popularized science, applied a skeptical attitude toward religious standards of truth, and criticized accepted traditions and authorities.

SCIENCE POPULARIZED

Unevenly educated and facing challenging findings, members of scientific societies often struggled to understand one another's work. For the nonscientific public, the problem of communicating new, complex ideas was even worse. Late in the seventeenth century, several talented writers, nonscientists themselves but believing that science had established a new standard of truth, began explaining in clear language the meaning of science to the literate public. For example, the French writer Bernard de Fontenelle (1657–1757) enjoyed a long, brilliant career as a popularizer of science. In *Conversations on the Plurality of Worlds* (1686), he presented the Copernican view of the universe in a series of conversations between an aristocratic woman and her lover under starry skies. Other writers targeted more specific audiences. In 1737, for example, *Newtonianism for Women* was published in Naples and soon translated into English. Writings such as these helped make science fashionable in elite circles.

FIGURE 14.9
Science, education, and enlightenment, 1759.

portance of natural history. Atop the bookcase and on the floor are seminal instruments of science—an air pump, a microscope, a telescope, and a globe. A human skeleton hangs in the closet.

Soon scientific ideas were being taught to children of the middle and upper classes. For example, the year 1761 saw the publication of *The Newtonian System of Philosophy, Adapted to the Capacities of Young Gentlemen and Ladies*, a book engagingly advertised as the "Philosophy of Tops and Balls." In it, a fictional boy named Tom Telescope gave lectures on science topics to children while also teaching the virtues of good manners and citizenship. The book proved immensely popular, going through many editions in Britain and in other countries.

Many of these books emphasized Newton—and for understandable reasons. Enlightenment thinkers saw this brilliant Englishman as the great syn-

Glorifying Newton: Reason and nature

thesizer of the scientific revolution, an astute observer who rightly described the universe as ordered, mechanical, material, and set into motion by God. From Newton, they concluded that reason and nature were compatible: Nature functioned logically and discernibly; therefore, what was natural was also reasonable. Many writers of the day agreed with the spirit of a poem written for Newton by the English author Alexander Pope upon the scientist's death in 1727:

> *Nature and Nature's Laws lay hid in Night.*
> *God said, "Let Newton be," and all was Light.*

In simple terms, Newton had become a European cultural hero, as Figure 14.10 suggests. At the left-center of this allegorical painting, a great urn "wherein is supposed to be deposited the Remains of the deceased Hero" is displayed. Above the urn shines a beam of light, broken into the colors of the spectrum by a prism—a bow to Newton's famous prism experiments.

By the mid-eighteenth century, this popularization of science merged with another foundation of Enlightenment thinking: the belief that every educated man and woman should be familiar with the nature and methods of science. Figure 14.9, an illustration from a British book on the arts and sciences, depicts this connection between science and education. Here a teacher instructs three young men in the principles of astronomy by demonstrating the planetary movements on a new machine—the orrery. The stuffed animals hanging from the ceiling underscore the im-

Teaching science

At the right are pages filled with mathematical calculations; below them, a globe and measuring instruments. Various figures in classical dress admire these objects and perhaps discuss Newton's ideas. The entire painting glorifies not only Newton, but all of science.

Enlightenment thinkers also admired the ideas of Newton's compatriot John Locke (1632–1704), who *The psychology of John Locke* applied scientific thinking to human psychology. This English philosopher did not hold the mind exempt from the mechanical laws of the material universe. In his *Essay Concerning Human Understanding* (1690), Locke pictured the human brain at birth as a blank sheet of paper that sensory perception and reason filled as a person aged. "Our observation, employed either about external sensible objects or about the internal operations of our minds perceived and reflected on by ourselves, is that which supplies our understanding with all the materials of thinking." Locke's empirical psychology rejected the notion that human beings were born with innate ideas or that revelation was a reliable source of truth. What we become, he argued, depends solely on our experiences—on the information received through the senses. Schools and social institutions should therefore play a major role in molding the individual from childhood to adulthood. These ideas, like those of Newton and the scientific revolution, also set the stage for the skeptical questioning of received wisdom.

FIGURE 14.10
Giovanni Battista Pittori, Allegorical Monument to Isaac Newton, 1727–1730.

SKEPTICISM AND RELIGION

Locke's ideas, along with those of Newton and the scientific revolution, set the stage for the questioning of established wisdom that came to define the Enlightenment. Among several writers, skepticism—or doubts about religious dogmas—mounted. Pierre Bayle (1647–1706), a French Huguenot forced to flee to the Dutch Republic because of Louis XIV's religious persecutions, became the leading proponent of skepticism in the late seventeenth century.

Pierre Bayle In his *News from the Republic of Letters* (1684), Bayle bitterly attacked the intolerance of the French monarchy and the Catholic Church. In most of Europe, where religious principles shared by ruler and ruled underlay all political systems, nonconformity was a major challenge. Therefore, the book earned him condemnation in Paris and Rome. Eventually, however, Bayle would have the last word. In 1697 he published the *Historical and Critical Dictionary*, which contained a list of religious views and beliefs that Bayle maintained did not stand up to criticism. Bayle cited human reason and common sense as his standard of criticism: "Any particular dogma, whatever it may be, whether it is advanced on the authority of the Scriptures, or whatever else may be its origins, is to be regarded as false if it clashes with the clear and definite conclusions of the natural understanding." Bayle also argued that "morals and religion, far from being inseparable, are completely independent of each other." For Bayle, a person's moral behavior had little to do with any particular religious doctrine or creed. With these stands, Bayle pushed much harder than Galileo in challenging the Catholic Church and other religious beliefs. He became recognized as an international authority on religious toleration and skeptical criticism of the Bible.

New information and arguments added weight to Bayle's criticism of biblical authority. For example, geo-

David Hume logical discoveries suggested that life on Earth had actually begun earlier than biblical accounts claimed. Investigators also began casting doubt on reports of miracles and prophecies. David Hume (1711–1776), a first-rate Scottish philosopher and historian, carried the skeptical argument even further. In *An Essay Concerning Human Understanding* (1748), he insisted that nothing—not even the existence of God or our own existence—could be known for sure. Reality consisted only of human perceptions. To Hume, established religions were based on nothing but "hope and fear." Reason demanded that people live with skeptical uncertainty rather than dogmatic faith.

BROADENING CRITICISM OF AUTHORITY AND TRADITION

Several writers—among them Baron de Montesquieu (1689–1755), a wealthy judge in a provin-

cial French court, and the French author Voltaire (1694–1778)—used comparisons of place and time to criticize authority and tradition during the early decades of the eighteenth century. Journeying abroad and writing about their experiences gave such people a new perspective on their home societies. Montesquieu and Voltaire, for their part, chastised Eu-

Travel writings of Montesquieu and Voltaire

ropean customs in general and French institutions in particular for being contrary to reason and good ethics.

Both presented the traveler as an objective observer. In his best-selling book *Persian Letters* (1721), Montesquieu bitingly satirized the customs, morals, and practices of Europeans, especially the French, from the point of view of two Persian travelers. Through this comparative perspective, Montesquieu painted the French as lacking in both good morals and effective government. Voltaire, in his widely read *Letters Concerning the English Nation* (1733), similarly criticized French politics and Catholic intolerance by describing his travels in England. In the island nation, "one thinks freely and nobly without being held back by any servile fear." Like many people, Voltaire idealized England because it allowed greater individual freedom, religious differences, and political reform than most other countries, especially France. England was also enviably prosperous, and was the home of Newton and Locke, so admired in France. Many French intellectuals wanted for their own country what the English already seemed to have.

Other writers took a new historical perspective to criticize tradition and trumpet rapid change. For them, the tools of science and reason enabled people to surpass

History and progress

their historical predecessors, even the admired Greeks and Romans of antiquity. History became a story of relentless human progress, and people living in the eighteenth century stood on the brink of unprecedented historical achievements. The eighteenth century was the beginning of a new, "modern" epoch. Some people, such as the American scientist and philosopher Benjamin Franklin (1706–1790), embraced the idea of progress with an almost religious fervor: "The rapid Progress of *true* Science now occasions my regretting sometimes that I was born so soon. It is impossible to imagine the Height to which may be carried . . . the Power of Man over Matter, . . . all diseases may by sure means be prevented, . . . and our lives lengthened at pleasure."

The Enlightenment in Full Stride

Building on the foundations of science, skepticism, and criticism, Western intellectuals systematically investigated the ethical, political, social, and economic implications of science after the 1730s. For them, nature—with its laws, order, simplicity, and rationality—served as a guide for human thought and society. "The source of man's unhappiness is his ignorance of Nature," claimed France's influential Baron d'Holbach (1723–1789). These optimistic intellectuals pushed for reform and change, using critical and empirical reasoning to back up their arguments. Specifically, they urged people to shrug off the shackles of tradition and custom and to participate in the accelerating progress of civilization. The spark of reason, they explained, would soon dispel ignorance and enlighten all human understanding. Indeed, it was this image that lent the Enlightenment its name.

THE PHILOSOPHES

Although Enlightenment ideas bubbled up throughout Europe and North America, France was the true heart of the movement. There Enlightenment thinkers came to be called *philosophes*, the French term for "philosophers." In a sense, the questions these thinkers grappled with were philosophical: How do we discover truth? How should we live our lives? Yet the philosophes were not traditional philosophers. Coming from both noble and middle-class origins, they were intellectuals—though often not formally trained by or associated with a university. They tended to extend, apply, or propagandize others' ideas rather than initiate new concepts themselves. They also wrote more plays, satires, histories, novels, encyclopedia entries, and short pamphlets than formal philosophical treatises. Finally, they considered themselves part of a common intellectual culture, an international "republic of letters" held together by literature, correspondence, and private gatherings. In the eyes of leading philosophes such as Jean Le Rond d'Alembert (1717–1783), this republic of letters should "establish the laws of philosophy and taste for the rest of the nation."

The witty, versatile François Arouet, who took the pen name Voltaire (1694–1778), best represented the philosophes. The son of a Parisian lawyer, Voltaire received a fine classical education from the Jesuits and soon denounced their religious doctrine. He became the idol of French intellectuals while only in his twenties, and the enemy of many others. He soon ran afoul of state authorities, who imprisoned him in the Bastille for writing verses that criticized the crown. Released, he became embroiled in a dangerous conflict with a prominent nobleman and again landed in the Bastille. By promising to leave the country, he gained his freedom. In England he encountered the ideas of Newton and Locke and came to admire English parliamentary government and the nation's religious tolerance. As we saw, he popularized Newton's and Locke's ideas and extolled the virtues of English society in his writings.

Voltaire

Slipping back into France, Voltaire hid for a time under the protection of Emile du Châtelet (1706–1749), a wealthy woman who became his lover and match. Châtelet had already shown brilliance as a child. By the age of twelve, she could speak four languages and had already translated Greek and Latin texts. Her mother worried that she would not find a mate because she "flaunts her mind, and frightens away the suitors her other excesses have not driven off." In 1733, she insisted on joining a group of male intellectuals who met regularly at a Parisian coffeehouse, donning men's clothes after the management refused to admit her because of her gender. In an unusual arrangement, Voltaire lived openly with Châtelet and her husband. In the great hall of their country chateau, she hung rods, pipes, and balls from the ceiling for her experiments in physics. She made her reputation by publishing a three-volume work on the German mathematician and philosopher Leibnitz and translating Newton's *Principles of Mathematics*. A philosophe, accomplished scientist, and leading proponent of Newtonian thought in her own right, Châtelet helped Voltaire gain a better understanding of the sciences and their significance. When she died in childbirth in 1749, the despondent Voltaire accepted an invitation from King Frederick II of Prussia to join his court.

Emile du Châtelet

Figure 14.11 shows the two men together in Prussia. Voltaire, seated, talks with Frederick, who has just arrived on horseback and who seems to bend deferentially to the learned writer. This engraving reveals the image of the great Enlightenment thinker at work with books, papers, and pen and with the international stature sufficient to gain the ear of "enlightened" monarchs such as Frederick. However, they soon argued, and Voltaire returned to France.

Having made both a fortune in financial speculations and a rich network of friends and acquaintances, Voltaire was not without resources. He wrote poetry, drama, history, essays, letters, and scientific treatises— ninety volumes in all. The novel *Candide* (1759) became his best-known work. In this dark satire, Voltaire created the epitome of the "ivory-tower" intellectual, ridiculed the pretensions of the nobility and clergy, and skewered the naiveté of optimists who believed that "this is the best of all possible worlds and all things turn out for the best." He aimed his cynical wit especially at the Catholic church and Christian institutions. His *Philosophical Dictionary* became the most famous, wide-ranging attack on supernatural religion and churches. Voltaire mounted several campaigns for religious toleration, coming to the defense of individuals attacked by prejudice. In his *Treatise on Tolerance* (1763), he attacked the mentality that led to the torture and murder of a Protestant merchant, Jean Calas, on the false charges of murdering his son for threatening to convert to Catholicism. "Christians ought to tolerate one another. I will go even further and say that we ought to look upon all men as our brothers. What! call a Turk, a Jew, a Siamese, my brother? Yes, of course, for are we not all children of the same father, and the creatures of the same God?" Celebrated as a national hero and lionized internationally, Voltaire's popularity reveals the widespread acceptance of Enlightenment thought throughout the West by the late eighteenth century.

THE ENCYCLOPEDIA

No work better summarizes the philosophy of the Enlightenment than the *Encyclopedia*, a collaborative effort by many philosophes under the editorship of De-

FIGURE 14.11
Voltaire and Frederick II of Prussia.

nis Diderot (1713–1774) and Jean le Rond d'Alembert. In the preface, the editors stated their aim: "to overturn the barriers that reason never erected" and "contribute to the certitude and progress of human knowledge." The *Encyclopedia* embodied the notion that reason alone could be used to discover, understand, or clarify almost anything. This massive work explored the complete spectrum of knowledge, offering articles on subjects ranging from music to machinery interpreted through the "lens" of the philosophes' criticism and empiricism. The authors wrote with supreme self-importance: "I can assure you," said d'Alembert in a 1752 letter, "that while writing this work I had posterity before my eyes at every line."

The first volume of the *Encyclopedia* was published in 1751. Figure 14.12 shows one of its many illustrations. In this image of a chemical laboratory, two chemists and their assistants work. Each piece of equipment is numbered in the illustration and labeled in the text. At the bottom of the picture is a "table of affinities," a system used to organize and symbolize each chemical substance. The illustration conveys a sense of both the practicality of chemistry and its ordered progress. Although the study of chemistry and the hundreds of other topics covered in the *Encyclopedia* at first glance may appear innocent enough, they were saturated with the philosophy of the Enlightenment. Church authorities and their governmental allies therefore saw the *Encyclopedia* as a direct threat to the status quo. They censored it, halted its publication, and harassed its editors. Thanks in great part to the persistence of Diderot, who fought the authorities and managed a difficult group of contributing authors, the project was finally completed in 1772.

FIGURE 14.12
Chemistry, the *Encyclopedia*, 1751.

BATTLING THE CHURCH

Diderot's struggle to publish the *Encyclopedia* was part of a wider conflict between the philosophes and the church. Both sides spent much time and effort attacking each other. In countries such as France and Italy, where clerics were strongly entrenched in government, officials censored the writings of the philosophes and threatened to imprison or exile them. Governmental censorship was usually more nominal than real. However Diderot and others trying to publish "offensive" books constantly worried about these threats: "How many times did we awake uncertain if . . . we would be torn from our families, our friends, our fellow citizens. . . ." French authors often sent their works to Holland or Switzerland for publication, and private companies then made a business of smuggling the books back into France across Swiss or Dutch borders.

Sometimes the philosophes' "crime" was promoting toleration of religious minorities, whether Christian or otherwise. Montesquieu and Voltaire in France were among several who attacked discrimination against Jews, for example. These views were par-

ticularly controversial because religious tolerance—formal and informal—was not the rule. Most governments maintained a state religion, rooted in law and viewed as the custodian of received views, that discriminated against nonmembers. For example Denmark barred Catholic priests from entering the country, and the Catholic Inquisition remained active in Spain.

Some philosophes such as Baron d'Holbach and David Hume, verged on atheism in their attacks on organized religion. "The Christian religion not only was at first attended by miracles, but even now cannot be believed by any reasonable person without one," Hume claimed. However, few Enlightenment thinkers pushed matters that far. Most believed in some form of deism—that an impersonal, infinite Divine Being created the universe but did not interfere with the world of human affairs. The prominent author and political philosopher Thomas Paine (1737–1809) stated, "I believe in one God, and no more; and I hope for happiness beyond this life. . . . I do not believe in the creed professed by the Jewish church, by the Roman church, by the Greek church, by the Turkish church, by the Protestant church, nor by any church that I know of. My own mind is my own church." These ideas, like

Deism

Biography

JEAN-JACQUES ROUSSEAU (1712–1778)

Jean-Jacques Rousseau described himself as a "singular soul, strange, and to say it all, a man of paradoxes." A celebrity both admired and hated in his own time, he wrote more deeply on a wide range of subjects than any of his contemporaries.

"My birth was my first misfortune," Rousseau once stated wryly. His mother died shortly after he was born in 1712 in the Republic of Geneva. His father, a watchmaker, raised him to the age of ten, then abandoned him to a series of homes where he served unhappily as an apprentice. One day in 1728, returning late from walking in the countryside, he found the gates of Geneva closed. Anticipating punishment from his master for his tardiness, he turned around and set off on the first of a series of wanderings that would mark the rest of his life.

He lived for much of the next ten years as the guest and lover of a baroness, Madame de Warens. In his own words, Rousseau became her "piece of work, student, friend. . . ." Rousseau addressed Madame de Warens as "Momma," and she referred to him as "my little one." This was the first of Rousseau's numerous relationships, many of them with older women. Yet he also lived as a recluse for long stretches of time during which he educated himself.

In 1742 the shy Rousseau arrived in Paris. He would often live there, though he harbored "a secret disgust for life in the capital," with its "dirty stinking little streets, ugly black houses, . . . poverty, [and] beggars." He first gained attention in Paris by writing about music, and by joining the cultural circles. He also earned a modest income by serving as secretary to aristocratic patrons and by copying music. In 1745 Thérèse Levasseur, a young laundress, became his lifelong companion and ultimately his wife. The couple would have four children and abandon them all to a foundling hospital for adoption.

Singular Soul, Controversial Thinker

In 1749 Rousseau entered an essay contest that abruptly changed his life. He won the competition by arguing that progress in the arts and sciences corrupted rather than improved human conduct. Suddenly he was controversial and famous. "No longer [was I] that timid man, more ashamed than modest. . . . All Paris repeated [my] sharp and biting sarcasms. . . ." Buoyed by his newfound fame, he contributed several articles on music and political economy to the *Encyclopedia*, edited by his close friend Denis Diderot. He came to know and eventually quarrel with most of the leading figures of the Enlightenment.

Rousseau went on to publish several critical and widely circulated books, including *Discourse on the Origin of Inequality*

---

other ideas of the Enlightenment, gained momentum over the course of the eighteenth century. In the long run, the church probably lost more supporters among the upper and middle classes than it gained by so ardently attacking the philosophes and their ideas.

 REFORMING SOCIETY

The philosophes thought long and hard about reforming society. They wrote and argued about the relationship between the individual and society, and reevaluated the functioning of traditional social institutions.

Political thought: Montesquieu and Rousseau

Applying their critical reasoning to fields from government to education, they generated influential ideas for reform.

The most important political thinkers of the Enlightenment—Montesquieu and the Swiss-born writer Jean-Jacques Rousseau (1712–1778)—built on John Locke's work. Locke had pleaded eloquently for the

(1755), *Julie* or *The New Heloise* (1761), *Émile* (1762), and *The Social Contract* (1762). These writings inspired not only learned responses, but ardent mail from ordinary readers. One reader of

FIGURE 14.13

Allan Ramsay, *Jean-Jacques Rousseau*, 1766.

The New Heloise, a novel focusing on the conflict between social demands and personal feelings, wrote, "Ever since I read your blessed book I have burned with love of virtue. . . . Feeling has taken over once again." Yet the books also inspired scorn. Peasants once stoned Rousseau's house, for example, after a pastor attacked him from the pulpit. Authorities issued more serious threats. In 1762 Parisian officials ordered *The Social Contract* burned and Rousseau arrested. He fled to Geneva, only to discover that officials there were also seeking his arrest. Again he escaped, moving from place to place and finding shelter with friends whom he quickly lost after bitter arguments. Figure 14.13 shows him in the distinctive fur hat and collar he often wore during this period, when he was a guest of the English philosopher David Hume.

In the last fifteen years of his life, Rousseau felt persecuted and depressed. "I appear," he wrote, "as the enemy of the Nation." He published stunning, often exaggerated self-revelations in his *Confessions*, disclosing his affairs, lies, and quarrels.

A difficult man and a tortured soul, Rousseau was also a superb writer whose *New Heloise* became the most widely read novel of his age. He counts among the most important educational theorists in history and became an accomplished composer and musical theorist. Author of one of the most striking autobiographical works ever written, he also proved an extremely influential philosopher and political theorist. "I am different," he wrote, "alone on earth. . . . Whether nature did well or ill to break the mould in which she formed me, this is something one can only judge after reading me." Sixteen years after Rousseau's death in 1778, France's revolutionary government moved his body to a place of honor near Voltaire's burial site in Paris.

❑ Consider how Rousseau's work and life reflect the ideas and efforts of other Enlightenment thinkers.

"natural rights"— life, liberty, and property—of human beings. In his *Second Treatise on Civil Government* (1690), Locke had argued that to safeguard these rights, individuals agree to surrender a certain amount of their sovereignty to government. However, the powers of the government, whether it be monarchical or popular, were strictly limited. No government was allowed to violate the individual's right to life, liberty, and property. If it did, the people who set it up could and should overthrow it—something the English had done in their Glorious Revolution, according to Locke.

An admirer of Locke and the English system of government, Baron de Montesquieu analyzed political systems from a relativistic perspective. In his widely acclaimed political masterpiece *The Spirit of the Laws* (1748), Montesquieu argued that political institutions should conform to the climate, customs, beliefs, and economy of a particular country. For instance, limited monarchy is most appropriate for countries of moderate size, like France; and republics for small states, like Venice or ancient Athens. Each form of government had its virtues and vices.

Not only did Montesquieu approve of Locke's doctrine of limited sovereignty, but he specified how it could best be secured—by a separation of powers and a system of checks and balances. The alternative, he warned, was tyranny and an end to liberty: "There would be an end to everything, were the same man or the same body, whether of the nobles or of the people, to exercise those three powers, that of enacting laws, that of executing the public resolutions, and of trying the causes of individuals." This theory, equally applicable to monarchies and to democracies, became Montesquieu's greatest practical contribution to political thought. In North America, framers of the U.S. Constitution would incorporate his ideas into their structuring of the United States government, creating separate executive, judicial, and legislative branches of government.

Rousseau offered a more radical political theory than Montesquieu's (See Biography). In his *Discourse on the Origin of Inequality* (1755), Rousseau argued that people in the "primitive" state of "noble savagery" were free, equal, and relatively happy. Only when some of them began marking off plots of ground, claiming them as their own and thereby founding civil society, did the troubles begin. Private property created inequality and the need for laws and governments to protect people from crime and wars. In *The Social Contract* (1762), Rousseau began by challenging his contemporaries: "Man is born free; and everywhere he is in chains." He then offered a solution to this conflict between individual freedom and social restrictions. In an ideal state, he argued, people entered into a compact with one another, agreeing to surrender their individual liberty, which was driven by self-interest, to the whole society. In return, the individual gained freedom by virtue of being part of the society's "general will," which was driven by the common good. "This means nothing less than that [the individual] will be forced to be free," explained Rousseau. Although Rousseau never made it clear just how the general will operated in practice, he believed that the people themselves—rather than a monarch or a parliamentary body—should make laws. His controversial ideas would powerfully influence the development of democratic theory over the next two centuries. For some, *The Social Contract* would support participatory democracy, while for others Rousseau's emphasis on conforming to the general will would justify authoritarian political systems.

Although critical and combative, neither Rousseau, Montesquieu, nor the other philosophes were political or social revolutionaries. They did not champion the lower classes, whom they dismissed as ignorant, prone to violence, and, in Voltaire's words, "inaccessible to the progress of reason and over whom fanaticism maintains its atrocious hold." Diderot, of humble parents, admitted that he wrote "only for those with whom I should enjoy conversing . . . the philosophers; so far as I am concerned, there is no one else in the world." Most philosophes hoped for painless change from above rather than a revolutionary transfer of power to the still-unenlightened "masses." Many shared Voltaire's belief that enlightened absolutism—rule by a well-educated, enlightened monarch—offered the best chance for the enactment of Enlightenment reforms such as religious toleration, rule subject to impartial laws, and freedom of speech (see Chapter 15).

If the functioning of the universe and politics could be described by understandable, rational laws,

Economic ideas: The Physiocrats and Adam Smith

why should the same not hold true for economic activity? Several Enlightenment thinkers turned their thoughts to this question and attacked mercantilism, the system of regulated national economics that still operated throughout much of Europe. A group of French thinkers known as Physiocrats, led by François Quesnay, personal physician to Louis XV, began to teach that economics had its own set of natural laws. The Physiocrats believed that the most basic of these laws was that of supply and demand, and that these laws operated best under only minimal governmental regulation of private economic activity. This doctrine, which became known as *laissez-faire* (noninterference), favored free trade and enterprise. In France, the Physiocrats saw land and agriculture as the main source of national wealth. Other economists would build on their ideas and apply them to different settings.

In 1776, Adam Smith (1723–1790), a Scottish professor of philosophy who associated with the Physiocrats while traveling in France, published *Wealth of Nations*. The book became the bible of laissez-faire economics. By nature, Smith argued, individuals who were allowed to pursue rationally their own economic self-interest would benefit society as well as themselves. Focusing on Britain's economy, Smith emphasized commerce, manufacturing, and labor rather than agriculture as the primary sources of national wealth. Anticipating the industrial age that would first emerge in Britain, he concluded that "the greatest improvement in the productive powers of labor . . . have been the effects of the division of labor." For Smith as well as the Physiocrats, laissez-faire economics held the key to national wealth—whether a nation was built on agriculture or industry.

What Smith and the Physiocrats did for economics, the Italian Cesare Beccaria (1738–1794) did for criminology and penology. Beccaria wrote *On Crimes and Punishments* (1764), an international best-seller, to protest "the cruelty of punishments and the irregularities of criminal procedures, . . . to demolish the accumulated errors of centuries." He argued that criminal laws and punishments, like all other aspects of life, should incorporate reason and natural law. Good laws, he explained, promoted "the greatest happiness divided among the greatest number." Criminal law should strive to deter crime and rehabilitate criminals rather than merely punish wrongdoers. In Beccaria's view, torture and capital punishment made no sense; indeed, only new penal institutions that mirrored natural law could transform convicted criminals.

Criminology, penology, and slavery

Other Enlightenment thinkers used similar arguments to denounce slavery. Abbé Guillaume Raynal (1713–1796), an outspoken and widely read critic of slavery, argued that this institution and many other practices of European and American colonists were irrational and inhumane. In the name of natural rights, he called for a slave rebellion. An article in the authoritative *Encyclopedia* asserted similar views, declaring that all enslaved individuals "have the right to be declared free. . . ." These arguments, like the ideas of Beccaria and, in politics, of Montesquieu and Rousseau, would resound again and again through eighteenth-century Western society.

Becoming "enlightened" required education. Diderot claimed that the *Encyclopedia* was written so "that our children, by becoming more educated, may at the same time become more virtuous and happier . . ." Many Enlightenment thinkers based their ideas on the psychological ideas of John Locke, which emphasized the power of education to mold the child into the adult. These thinkers often attacked organized religion in particular for controlling education.

Education

Rousseau became the outstanding critic of traditional education. In *Émile*, he argued that teachers should appeal to children's natural interests and goodness rather than impose discipline and punishment. "Hold childhood in reverence," he counseled. "Give nature time to work." He also pushed for less "artificial" schools, maintaining that nature and experience were better guides to independent thinking and practical knowledge—at least for males. "I hate books," he pointed out. "They only teach us to talk about things we know nothing about." By emphasizing practical education, learning by doing, and motivating rather than requiring the child to learn, Rousseau's *Émile* became one of the most influential works on modern education. His ideas on the education of females, however, were not so modern. Like most men of his time ("enlightened" or not), he believed that girls should be educated to fulfill their traditional domestic roles as wives and mothers.

In theory at least, the Enlightenment emphasis on individualism opened the door to the idea of equality between men and women. Several intellectuals explored this controversial issue. Early in the period, some challenging books on the "woman question" were published by female authors. In one of the best-known of these, *A Serious Proposal to the Ladies* (1694), the English writer Mary Astell (1666–1731) argued that women should be educated according to the ideas of the new science—reason and debate—rather than tradition. In other writings, she questioned the inequality of men's and women's roles: "If all Men are born Free, how is it that all Women are born Slaves?" Later in the eighteenth century, the British author Mary Wollstonecraft (1759–1797) published *Vindication of the Rights of Women* (1792), in which she analyzed the condition of women and argued forcefully for equal rights for all human beings. Like Astell, Wollstonecraft stressed the need to educate women: "If she be not prepared by education to become the companion of man, she will stop the progress of knowledge and virtue; for truth must be common to all, or it will be inefficacious with respect to its influence on general practice."

The "woman question"

Few male writers went that far. Although some men supported better education for women, most held the traditional view that women were weaker than men and best suited for domestic rather than public affairs. According to Immanuel Kant, who spoke so optimistically and eloquently about education and enlightenment, "laborious learning or

FIGURE 14.14

Anicet Charles Lemonnier, *An Evening at Madame Geoffrin's in 1755*, 1812.

painful pondering, even if a woman should greatly succeed in it, destroy the merits that are proper to her sex." The editors of the *Encyclopedia* also ignored contributions from women, instead praising those who remained at home. Some of Rousseau's writings were particularly influential among women, primarily because they glorified child rearing, maternalism, and emotional life. Rousseau never suggested that women were independent beings equal to men. For him, "Woman is made to please and to be subjugated to man."

THE CULTURE AND SPREAD OF THE ENLIGHTENMENT

The Enlightenment glittered especially in Paris, and salon meetings became the chief social setting for this intellectual culture. These meetings were hosted by wealthy Parisian patrons, usually women of the aristocracy or upper middle class. In an environment lush with art, music, and wealth, the philosophes, powerful nobles, diplomats, statesmen, artists, and well-educated conversationalists gathered regularly to read, listen to, and debate the ideas of the Enlightenment. They also discussed—and sometimes influenced—economic policies, wars, and the king's choice of ministers. The German critic Friedrich Grimm (1723–1807), who published a private newsletter on Parisian life, described the salons of Julie de Lespinasse, who lived openly with the philosophe d'Alembert: "Her circle met daily from five o'clock until nine in the evening. There we were sure to find choice men of all orders in the State, the Church, the Court—military men, foreigners, and the most distinguished men of letters. Politics, religion, philosophy, anecdotes, news, nothing was

Salon meetings

FIGURE 14.15

Léonard Defrance, *At the Sign of Minerva*, 1781.

excluded from the conversation." These salon meetings became self-conscious forums for arbitrating and molding public opinion through the open use of reason.

As leaders, patrons, and intellectual contributors to these gatherings, women played a particularly important role in the Enlightenment. Independent, witty, powerful women governed the potentially unruly meetings and discussions by enforcing rules of polite conversation. One of the most famous of these patrons was Madame Marie-Thérèse Geoffrin (1699–1777), a rich middle-class widow who served as a model and mentor for other women leaders of salons. Figure 14.14, a painting by Anicet Charles Lemonnier, shows a salon meeting at her home in 1755. Madame Geoffrin, wearing a blue dress and looking at the viewer, sits at the left next to Bernard de Fontenelle, ninety-eight-year-old popularizer of science. Above is a bust of Voltaire, the Enlighten-

ment hero living in exile at the time. Women with the right intellectual and social qualifications attended this and other salons, but the star invitees were usually men.

Smaller meetings in other French and foreign cities, from Berlin to Philadelphia, paralleled the Parisian salon meetings. Moreover, all these meetings went hand in hand with an extensive international correspondence carried out by participants. For some, letter writing, like good conversation in the salons, was an art. People also read and discussed Enlightenment ideas in local academies, Freemason lodges, societies, libraries, and coffeehouses. In addition, most municipalities had clubs where the social and intellectual elites could mingle.

Even bookstores, where people could purchase books or pay small fees to read recent works, became hotbeds of Enlightenment ideas. Figure 14.15

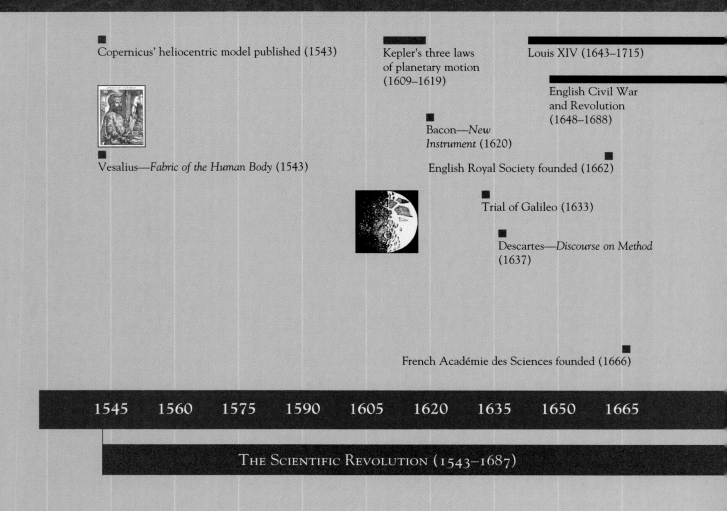

Copernicus' heliocentric model published (1543)

Vesalius—*Fabric of the Human Body* (1543)

Kepler's three laws
of planetary motion
(1609–1619)

Bacon—*New
Instrument* (1620)

English Royal Society founded (1662)

Trial of Galileo (1633)

Descartes—*Discourse on Method*
(1637)

Louis XIV (1643–1715)

English Civil War
and Revolution
(1648–1688)

French Académie des Sciences founded (1666)

| 1545 | 1560 | 1575 | 1590 | 1605 | 1620 | 1635 | 1650 | 1665 |

THE SCIENTIFIC REVOLUTION (1543–1687)

shows an eighteenth-century bookstore. In the doorway stand two women, reading books. Just outside are packages of books being delivered from or to Spain, Portugal, Rome, and Naples. In the street, apparently drawn to the bookstore, are people of all classes, from a peasant with his scythe at the left to a cleric in his white robes at the center. The name of the bookstore,

Bookstores

"The Shield of Minerva," refers to the Roman goddess of wisdom. In a growing number of bookstores such as this, all sorts of works became increasingly available, from religious tracts and chivalric tales to new novels and Enlightenment literature.

These gatherings and interchanges spread the ideas of the Enlightenment throughout society and enhanced the social respectability of intellectuals.

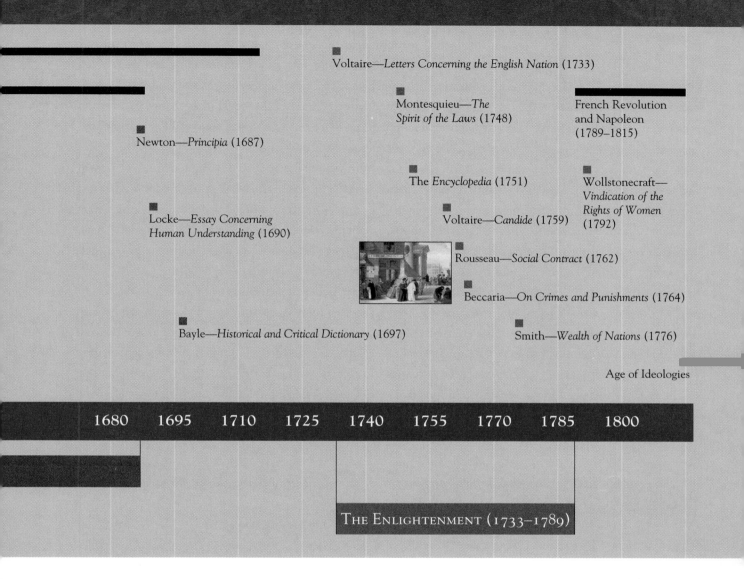

Voltaire—*Letters Concerning the English Nation* (1733)

Montesquieu—*The Spirit of the Laws* (1748)

French Revolution and Napoleon (1789–1815)

Newton—*Principia* (1687)

The *Encyclopedia* (1751)

Wollstonecraft— *Vindication of the Rights of Women* (1792)

Locke—*Essay Concerning Human Understanding* (1690)

Voltaire—*Candide* (1759)

Rousseau—*Social Contract* (1762)

Beccaria—*On Crimes and Punishments* (1764)

Bayle—*Historical and Critical Dictionary* (1697)

Smith—*Wealth of Nations* (1776)

Age of Ideologies

| 1680 | 1695 | 1710 | 1725 | 1740 | 1755 | 1770 | 1785 | 1800 |

THE ENLIGHTENMENT (1733–1789)

They also helped create a common intellectual culture that crossed class lines and political borders and that contributed to an informed body of public opinion. People who participated in these interchanges came to sense that they could freely express ideas as well as debate political and social issues. By the last quarter of the eighteenth century, Enlightenment ideas could be heard even in the camps of the philosophes' traditional opponents—the clergy, governmental officials, and monarchs. As we will see, these ideas pushed some monarchs to enact "enlightened" reforms and encouraged many other people to demand revolutionary change.

The great intellectual revolution of the seventeenth and eighteenth centuries was fueled by advances in science. Brimming with new scientific ideas and discoveries, Western civilization relinquished its medieval assumptions and embarked on an innovative journey unique among the cultures of the world. This change in direction became one of the main forces behind the power and dynamism that came to characterize the West. Through science, westerners hoped to gain greater control over the material world and nature.

Enlightenment thinkers carried these daring aspirations further, self-consciously leading a mission of reform and freedom from the shackles of tradition. By striking the match of reason, they believed, people could at last dispel the darkness of the past and liberate themselves as never before. Thus enlightened, humanity as a whole could move from childhood to adulthood. As the philosophe Baron d'Holbach proclaimed, "The *enlightened man*, is man in his maturity, in his perfection; who is capable of pursuing his own happiness; because he has learned to examine, to think for himself, and not to take that for truth upon the authority of others."

Many participants in Enlightenment circles have since been criticized as self-concerned dilettantes reluctant to take on the risks of real reform. Most historians, however, see the philosophes as thoughtful, sincere, and sometimes brilliant thinkers. The philosophes clearly left a mark on Western culture. Their ideas, like those of the seventeenth-century scientists, threatened the traditional order, especially the church. As their primary legacy, they widened the gap between religiously influenced doctrines and accepted scholarly thought. Equally significant, they set the intellectual stage for a series of revolutions that would soon sweep America and Europe. Above all, their way of thinking—stressing reason, individualism, and progress—would form the intellectual foundation of modern Western society and further distinguish this civilization from its non-Western counterparts.

REVIEW, ANALYZE, AND ANTICIPATE

REVIEW THE PREVIOUS CHAPTER

Chapter 12—"Faith, Fortune, and Fame"—told how several European powers expanded overseas during the fifteenth, sixteenth, and seventeenth centuries and grew rich from the commerce. Chapter 13—"The Struggle for Survival and Sovereignty"—focused on how kings and nobles battled for power, the resolutions of those struggles, and their impact on the millions of people outside the elite.

1. Analyze how the expansion of Europe might have stimulated scientific research.

2. In what ways did the effort of monarchs to increase their power and create stability relate to the promotion of science and the desire for greater intellectual certainty?

ANALYZE THIS CHAPTER

Chapter 14—"A New World of Reason and Reform"—examines the changing intellectual foundations of the West.

1. List and analyze the differences between the new scientific views of the world and traditional medieval views. How did standards for ascertaining the "truth" differ between these two perspectives?

2. Analyze the beliefs and motives of three central figures in the scientific revolution. What barriers did they have to overcome to present their views?

3. Do you think the Enlightenment merely popularized the scientific revolution, or did it accomplish something more?

4. *In what ways did the Enlightenment threaten traditional views and authorities?*

Anticipate the Next Chapter

In Chapter 15—"Competing for Power and Wealth" —the struggles of Western powers over land, position, and commerce, as well as the economic and social changes affecting life in several Western societies during the eighteenth century, will be examined.

1. *What kinds of reforms—actual changes in governments and institutions—would most likely flow from Enlightenment ideas?*

2. *What social groups might try to adopt the ideas of the Enlightenment as a basis for demanding political and social reforms? Why might some monarchs consider enacting Enlightenment ideas?*

Beyond the Classroom

Questioning Truth and Authority

Debus, Allen. *Man and Nature in the Renaissance.* Cambridge: Cambridge University Press, 1978. A solid, thoughtful analysis of the intellectual roots of scientific thought.

Kuhn, Thomas S. *The Structure of Scientific Revolutions,* 2nd ed. Chicago: University of Chicago Press, 1970. A landmark analysis of the nature, causes, and consequences of transformations in scientific concepts.

Mandrou, Robert. *From Humanism to Science.* Atlantic Highlands, NJ: Humanities Press, 1979. Describes how the role of intellectuals changed between 1480 and 1700.

Developing a Modern Scientific View

Cohen, H.F. *The Scientific Revolution.* Chicago: University of Chicago Press, 1994. An analysis of when and where modern science began.

Hall, Rupert A. *The Revolution in Science, 1500–1750.* London: Longman, 1983. A useful introduction to the developments in science during this period.

Schiebinger, Londa. *The Mind Has No Sex? Women in the Origins of Modern Science.* Cambridge, MA: Harvard University Press, 1990. Examines the participation of women in science and stresses how science reflected male biases.

Webster, Charles. *The Great Instauration: Science, Medicine, and Reform.* New York: Holmes & Meier Publishers, 1976. An excellent study that connects the development of scientific attitudes to England's Puritan revolution.

Westfall, Richard. *The Construction of Modern Science: Mechanisms and Mechanics.* New York: Cambridge University Press, 1977. A good survey of scientific developments during the seventeenth century that emphasizes the importance of mathematics and mechanics.

Westfall, Richard. *The Life of Isaac Newton.* Cambridge: Cambridge University Press, 1993. A full-scale biography of Isaac Newton.

Supporting and Spreading Science

Jacob, Margaret C. *The Cultural Meaning of the Scientific Revolution.* New York: Alfred A. Knopf, 1988. Examines the evolution of science within its political, social, and cultural context.

Moran, Bruce T., ed. *Patronage and Institutions: Science, Technology and Medicine at the European Court, 1500–1750.* Rochester, NY: Boydell Press, 1991. Examines the role of royal courts in supporting and shaping science during this period.

Laying the Foundations for the Enlightenment

Hampson, Norman. *The Enlightenment.* London: Penguin Books, 1982. A thorough survey that relates the Enlightenment to contemporary events.

Imhof, Ulrich. *The Enlightenment.* Oxford: Blackwell, 1994. A recent examination and evaluation of the Enlightenment.

Sklar, Judith. *Montesquieu.* Oxford: Oxford University Press, 1987. A concise, well-written study of Montesquieu and his ideas.

The Enlightenment in Full Stride

Besterman, Theodore. *Voltaire,* 3rd ed. Chicago: University of Chicago Press, 1976. A useful biography of this major Enlightenment figure.

Chartier, Roger. *The Cultural Uses of Print in Early Modern France.* Princeton, NJ: Princeton University Press, 1987. Examines changing reading habits and the connections between culture and society in eighteenth-century France.

Darton, Robert. *The Business of Enlightenment: A Publishing History of the Encyclopedia, 1775–1800.* Cambridge, Mass.: Belknap Press, 1979. A well-written social history and analysis of the publication of the Encyclopedia.

Gay, Peter. *The Enlightenment: An Interpretation,* 2 volumes. New York: Alfred A. Knopf, 1966–1969. A classic study, exhaustive, but with a strong point of view.

Goodman, Dena. *The Republic of Letters: A Cultural History of the French Enlightenment.* Ithaca, NY: Cornell University Press, 1994. A study of the cultural and intellectual life of eighteenth-century France that concentrates on the role played by the salons.

Lougee, Carolyn. *Le Paradis des Femmes. Women, Salons, and Social Stratification in Seventeenth-Century France.* Princeton, N.J.: Princeton University Press, 1976. Analyzes the foundations and importance of the French salons, emphasizing the role played by women in them.

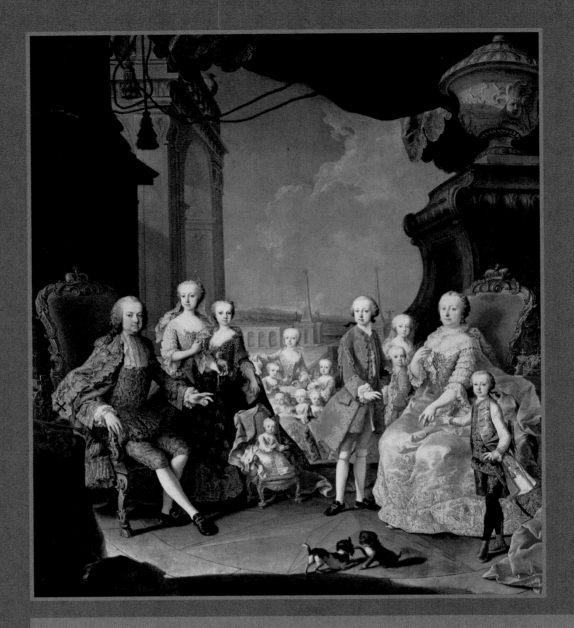

Martin Meytens, Maria Theresa and Her Family, 1750

In 1750 Habsburg court artist Martin Meytens (1695–1770) painted Austria's powerful monarch, Maria Theresa (1717–1780), with her husband (seated on the left) and thirteen of her sixteen children. Her son, Joseph, heir to the throne, stands in a favored place at the center of the star floor. As this painting suggests, even though she led Austria through two major wars, Maria Theresa often chose to present herself as a good mother to both her family and her nation.

CHAPTER 15

Competing for Power and Wealth

The Old Regime, 1715–1789

"A reasonable man is always happy if he has what is necessary for him according to his condition [social rank], that is to say, if he has the protection of the laws, and can live as his father lived before him," wrote a French observer in 1747. The political lesson behind these words was clear: "Essential . . . to the good of a nation is being governed in one constant and uniform manner." Most people living in the eighteenth century would have nodded their heads in agreement. Indeed, they actively upheld the social order—ranked, governed, and sanctioned as it was by tradition and Christian teachings.

Despite this affirmation of stability, change was afoot in these years, even among monarchs such as Austria's Maria Theresa (r. 1740–1780) (p. 498). During the seventeenth century, kings and queens had struggled with nobles in their own countries for control and with other monarchs to increase their nations' sway. In their continuing competition for power and wealth, eighteenth-century kings and queens tried to strengthen their states while gaining status—often through war—in the international arena. Below them, ambitious aristocrats flexed their muscles, sometimes challenging their monarchs, sometimes forging alliances with them, and often reveling in the new wealth and culture that now lay within their reach. They, along with the growing number of commoners, began to see much promise in the new ways to produce food and organize manufacturing, all fueled by accelerating commerce—especially with overseas colonies. Moreover, many elites—including some monarchs themselves—also recognized the strength of Enlightenment ideas and began to think of ways to institute "enlightened" reforms. At the base of Western society, the mass of peasants and workers toiled, as they always had. However, their numbers were increasing, and their ways of life were slowly adjusting to the pressures of change. This society and its politics would later be known as the Old Regime, but many living at the time detected the quickening pulse of a new era.

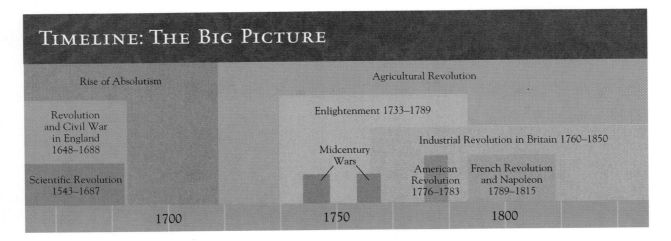

Rise of Absolutism

Agricultural Revolution

Revolution
and Civil War
in England
1648–1688

Enlightenment 1733–1789

Industrial Revolution in Britain 1760–1850

Midcentury
Wars

Scientific Revolution
1543–1687

American
Revolution
1776–1783

French Revolution
and Napoleon
1789–1815

1700   1750   1800

Statebuilding and War

In August 1715, the old and sad Louis XIV fell ill. His legs swelled and turned black as gangrene set in. Remarkably, he had outlived both his son and grandson. On his deathbed, Louis warned his five-year-old great-grandson, who would succeed him as Louis XV (r. 1715–1774), not to "imitate my love of building nor my liking of war." Neither Louis XV nor many other rulers of the time managed to follow this advice for long. War and building might cost lives and drain royal treasuries, but they made a spectacular show of power in a competitive world. The rulers of Europe clung to their statebuilding ways, straining to secure their central governments and ensure their own position at the top.

During the seventeenth century, this competitiveness had plunged Europe into a series of bloody conflicts—the very battles Louis XIV regretted on his deathbed (see Chapter 13). In western Europe, the violence stopped with the Peace of Utrecht in 1713–1714. Seven years later, the Treaty of Nystad (1721) ended the conflicts in eastern Europe (see Map 15.1). For a while, the two treaties held. Monarchs throughout Europe tried to adhere to the principle of a balance of power to prevent any one state or alliance from dominating the others. Nevertheless, anyone hoping for an extended period free of war would be sorely disappointed. Up-and-coming states such as Prussia and Britain bristled with ambition and vied with their established competitors for power, prestige, and wealth. Their struggles spread beyond the borders of Europe to overseas colonies on continents from North America to Asia, in this sense turning European wars into global conflicts. As we will see, this competition subjected millions of people to a fresh round of hardship and irrevocably altered the fate and fortunes of nations throughout the West.

RISING AMBITIONS IN EASTERN EUROPE

Within Europe, the fiercest competition took place in eastern Europe. There Russia and Brandenburg-Prussia were on the rise. Under Peter the Great, Russia had already defeated Sweden, grabbing much of the northeastern Baltic coast in the process. Russia next hoped to take advantage of the sprawling but weak Polish state farther west (see Chapter 13), and to benefit from the decline of the Ottoman Empire, which controlled the Black Sea to Russia's south. Brandenburg-Prussia also saw opportunities in Poland, which divided and bordered its lands. This militaristic state also coveted some of the holdings of the bloated Austro-Hungarian Empire to the south, which in turn intended to hold its own in the power struggle. Someone would have to pay the price for all these ambitions.

Peter the Great had done much to turn Russia toward the west and make it a great power. By the time of his death in 1725, he had modernized Russia's government and military, established Russia as the dominant power in northeastern Europe, and pressured the Russian nobility into the state bureaucracy and army officer corps. In the process, he made many enemies, from the peasants who paid dearly for Peter's accomplishments to all those who had a stake in the very social, cultural, and religious traditions that Peter attacked. His successors would have to face these enemies and shoulder the task of sustaining Russia's expansion to the south and west.

Six mediocre rulers followed Peter—including an infant, a boy of twelve, and a mentally unstable tsar. Despite this shaky leadership, Russia held its ground.

From 1725 to 1762, its population increased, and the landowning elite grew wealthier than ever. The nobility took back some of the authority it had lost to Peter, diminishing the service it owed to the state; in 1762 nobles freed themselves of

New leadership in expanding Russia

all such obligations. Nevertheless, they still staffed the bureaucracy and military officer corps. Moreover, nobles cracked down even more on their serfs, reducing their status to that of mere property. The 1767 Decree on Serfs made the situation crystal clear: "Serfs and peasants . . . owe their landlords proper

THINKING ABOUT GEOGRAPHY

MAP 15.1 *Europe, 1721*

This map shows Europe after the Treaties of Utrecht (1714) and Nystad (1721). ▧ **Notice** that although France and Spain are ruled by Bourbon monarchs, the two nations remain separate. **How** might their union have altered the balance of power in Europe? ▧ **Locate** the large states in eastern Europe. **Which** of these states, despite their size, are declining powers? ▧ **Notice** the lands controlled by Austria. **Why** might this power's holdings be vulnerable?

submission and absolute obedience in all matters."

The decades of weak leadership ended when a dynamic new leader ascended the Russian throne. Catherine the Great (r. 1762–1796) grew up an obscure princess from one of the little German states. For

Catherine the Great

political reasons, her family married her to young Peter III (r. 1762), the tyrannical and intellectually limited grandson of Peter the Great and heir to the Russian crown. He soon rejected her in all ways, and once he became tsar he quickly lost most of his supporters as well. Catherine had no intention of languishing in obscurity. "I did not care about Peter," she later wrote, "but I did care about the crown." Less than a year after he took the throne, Catherine conspired with a group of aristocratic army officers, who assassinated him and declared Catherine tsarina of Russia.

The new empress used her striking intelligence, charm, and political talent to assert her own power and expand Russian territory and might. In contrast to Maria Theresa (see p. 498), she chose to have herself portrayed as a warrior. Figure 15.1 depicts Catherine on a stallion with sword in hand. Her pose and outfit mimic the style and dress of western European rulers, reflecting her respect for western European culture.

Well educated, she thought of herself as attuned to Enlightenment ideas. She often corresponded with French philosophes such as Denis Diderot, who spent some time at St. Petersburg as her guest. In 1766 she congratulated Voltaire for triumphing "against the enemies of mankind: superstition, fanaticism, ignorance, quibbling, evil judges, and the power that rest in their hands." Voltaire returned the favor with constant praise for Catherine. She relaxed the traditionally tight constraints on the press in Russia and confiscated church lands—policies that seemed in line with Enlightenment thinking. Her educational reforms, by which she established new local schools, teachers' colleges, and schools for girls, also suggested a forward-thinking monarch. Most stunningly, Catherine convened a legislative commission, half of whose members were commoners (some even peasants), to reform Russia's legal code. She wrote the *Instruction* (1767) to that commission herself, relying on the works of key Enlightenment figures such as Montesquieu and Beccaria. Her *Instruction* called for equality before the law, the abolition of torture, and other liberal reforms.

These programs promised more than they delivered. The commission members squabbled among themselves, and in the end the effort yielded only minor reforms before it was finally abandoned. Catherine's early talk of easing the burdens on the peasantry also came to little; in return for the support of noble landowners, she allowed them to subjugate the peasants even further. When one critic argued, "What good does it do the country that every year a few thousand more bushels of grain are grown, if those who produce it are valued on a par with the ox whose job it is to break the heavy furrow?", Catherine imprisoned him.

In 1768, Catherine provoked a war against the Ottoman Empire. The event seems to have signaled her turn away from enlightened reform and toward power politics. A massive insurrection by Russian serfs in 1773 under the leadership of a Don Cossack, Yemelyan Pugachev (1726–1775), further soured her on reform. Pugachev claimed to be Catherine's murdered husband, a "redeemer tsar," and promised his followers land and freedom. Thousands of serfs in southwestern Russia turned against their masters—slaughtering hundreds of landlords and officials—and demanded an

FIGURE 15.1
Catherine the Great, 1762.

end to their plight. Catherine's army managed to put down the rebellion, but only with great difficulty. When some disgruntled followers betrayed Pugachev, the army captured him and tortured him to death.

Catherine proved more successful in her ambitious foreign policy. She defeated the Turks in 1774, extending Russia to the Black Sea and the Balkan Peninsula. Map 15.2 shows Russia's expansion to the

	Boundary of Poland to 1772
	Boundary of the Three Powers at 1795
	Russian Gains 1721–1795
	Poland 1793–1795

THINKING ABOUT GEOGRAPHY

MAP 15.2   *The Expansion of Russia and the Partition of Poland, 1721–1795*

This map shows eastern Europe during the eighteenth century. **Notice** the division of Poland. **In what ways** did the partition of Poland benefit Russia, Prussia, and Austria? **How might** Poland's decline change the balance of power? **Notice** the expansion of Russia and Prussia. **Where** might these rising powers look for further expansion?

south and west during the eighteenth century. For the Ottoman Empire, this defeat marked the beginning of an unstoppable decline.

Catherine then turned on Poland. At the beginning of the eighteenth century, Poland was the third largest country in Europe. Yet, as we saw in Chapter 13, it lacked natural boundaries and a strong central government. Weak and without allies, it became a power vacuum that proved all too tempting to its ambitious neighbors. In 1772, Russia, Prussia, and Austria—having plotted Poland's demise among themselves—annexed slices of Polish territory. This aggression at long last stirred the Polish government to action. The Diet passed sweeping reforms, improved the lot of commoners, and gave the central government power to act effectively. These changes came too late. Poland still could not match the combined armies of its enemies, and in 1795 the three aggressors divided the remainder of the hapless nation among themselves. Map 15.2 shows the eventual dismemberment of Poland, which left Russia, Prussia, and Austria the dominant powers in eastern Europe. When Catherine died in 1796 after thirty-five years of rule, Russia had grown to an ominous size and had taken its place as a major power in world affairs.

The Partition of Poland

In east-central Europe, the small but rising Brandenburg-Prussia set its sights on the Austrian Empire, a large

Forging a military state in Prussia

power struggling to maintain control over its far-flung lands. From 1713 to 1740, the vigorous Frederick William I ruled Prussia. The king was obsessed with unquestioned absolutism, centralized bureaucratic administration, and above all, the military. His martial uniforms and preoccupation with Prussian soldiery earned him the label the "Sergeant King."

Frederick William's mental image of the perfect military dominated his policies and Prussian society. While he employed his army for road and canal building as well as traditional military service, some 70 percent of the state's budget went to the armed forces, whose size he more than doubled dur-

ing his reign. Rather than relying on mercenaries, the king required all men to register for military service in local units commanded by German noble officers. The localities in turn had to recruit and support these regiments, and soldiers were billeted among the civilian population.

As Figure 15.2 suggests, drills and parades were common sights. The tight formation shown in the illustration resembles the fighting formations the Prussians strove to achieve in actual battle. Here is an image of near-perfect discipline and order, mastered through endless drill and professional command. The wooden horse at the left was used to punish undisciplined soldiers. The presence of the townspeople in the background on the right suggests that exercises such as these typically took place within towns rather than separate military centers. No other state in Europe could boast such a high proportion of men, from peasant to noble, in the military. Nor could any other state point to such a regimented society. In Prussia, the higher ranks of the military and state bureaucracy were reserved for the nobility; the middle classes were clearly prevented from rising to noble status; and the peasantry was a subordinate, overburdened people,

FIGURE 15.2
Prussian troops at drill.

often still serfs living in almost slavelike relationships to their landowning masters.

Despite the martial tenor of life in Prussia, the king left a surprisingly progressive legacy. Frederick William I avoided wars, promoted a strong economy, welcomed Protestant and Jewish refugees, and filled the treasury. In 1740 he passed all that he had built, intact, on to his talented son Frederick II (r. 1740–1786), later known as Frederick the Great. The new king soon used this army—the fourth largest in Europe—and the money his father had accumulated to make a bold bid for Austrian lands.

In the same year that Frederick II ascended the throne in Prussia, Maria Theresa (r. 1740–1780) became empress of the Austrian Habsburg dominions.

Austria tries to hold on Austria was not a tightly controlled, militaristic state like Prussia. Rather, it had already lost most of the indirect control it once held over the central German states as head of the Holy Roman Empire. Austria's own lands contained a complex array of language groups and consisted of some semiautonomous territories. Austria could barely control Hungary, and its nobility fully dominated its serfs, who paid most taxes directly to their lords rather than to the crown. As a result, Maria Theresa could afford only a relatively small army.

The empress' father had feared that these weaknesses might prove Austria's undoing when he died. Moreover, there was only weak precedent for a female ruler of Habsburg lands. Therefore he spent the final twenty years of his life securing agreement among all the European powers (embodied in a document called the Pragmatic Sanction) that his daughter would succeed him without question. In spite of his diligence, once he died in 1740, competitors arose to challenge her authority. As for the principle of balance of power among states implying a desire for peace, Frederick II of Prussia dismissed the idea bluntly: "The fundamental rule of governments is the principle of extending their territories."

As soon as Maria Theresa took the crown, Frederick challenged her authority, a common occurrence

The midcentury land wars when a succession was questionable in any way. Acting on his maxim that "the safety and greater good for the state demands that treaties should be broken under certain circumstances," the Prussian king marched his troops into Silesia (see Map 15.3),

the richest of the Habsburg provinces. He also shrewdly forged alliances with other German states against Austria. His aggressive scheming plunged most of the major European states into a series of wars for the mastery of central Europe.

The War of the Austrian Succession dragged on for eight years (1740–1748). Maria Theresa rallied Hungarian arms to her defense and repelled Prussia's allies—the Bavarians, Saxons, French, and Spanish. The conflict eventually turned into a military stalemate, which led to a 1748 peace treaty that ended the hostilities. Maria Theresa had managed to preserve the Habsburg state as a major power, but she had been unable to dislodge Frederick from Silesia.

Neither she nor her advisors intended to tolerate this robbery of their fair province by the upstart *The Diplomatic Revolution* Prussians—even if it meant starting negotiations for an alliance with their traditional rival, France. Frederick grew fearful of being isolated by his enemies and left vulnerable to invasions. In 1756, when he signed an alliance with Great Britain—Prussia's opponent only a few years earlier—Maria Theresa solidified a new alliance with France. This astounding shift of alliances—the so-called Diplomatic Revolution—suddenly transformed former enemies into friends. Meanwhile, Maria Theresa shored up Austria's internal resources by honing her government's control over taxation, diminishing burdens on the peasantry, and reorganizing the bureaucracy. All this strengthened her position as a ruler who could command strong forces and who enjoyed backing from a powerful ally.

Not one to wait for his enemies to strike first, Frederick reopened hostilities by overrunning Saxony in 1756, initiating the Seven Years' War (1756–1763). However, Frederick soon found himself at bay as France and Austria—now joined by Russia and Sweden, both of which hoped to gain lands at Prussia's expense—closed in on him from all directions. His only backing came from Britain, which saw an opportunity to weaken its longtime opponent, France. After holding off his enemies for six years, the exhausted Prussian king finally seemed near defeat. "I believe all is lost," he confessed in private. Then in 1762 his luck revived. The Russian tsarina Elizabeth, one of his most reviled enemies, died. Her successor, the weak Peter III, happened to admire Frederick and suddenly pulled Russia out of the war. The remaining allies soon lost stomach for the fight. The peace in 1763 left

THINKING ABOUT GEOGRAPHY

MAP 15.3 *Prussia and the Austrian Empire, 1721–1772*

This map shows two growing eighteenth-century powers, Prussia and Austria. ❧ **Compare** the holdings of these two states. **Which** do you think might be considered the stronger? **What** problems face both in creating a strong, unified state? ❧ **Notice** France to the west and Russia to the east—both large and unified states. **Where** are Austria and Prussia most likely to compete with each other or expand?

matters much as they had been before the war began, but as we will see (p. 514), the fighting in Europe spread to India, the Caribbean, and North America.

Having narrowly escaped destruction, Frederick spent the remaining twenty-three years of his life reconstructing his war-ravaged territories. He encouraged agriculture, subsidized and protected industry, and invited immigrants into his well-governed territories. At no time, though, did he neglect his army or lose his sense of practicality. Indeed, in 1772 he

joined Austria and Russia in the first partition of Poland. Map 15.3 shows Prussia's expansion under Frederick, first at the expense of the Austrian Empire when he took Silesia, then at the expense of Poland as he used the territory to unify the main portions of his country. The map also shows Prussia's chief competitor, Austria, with its more far-flung territories. By the time of his death in 1786, Frederick had raised Prussia to the status of a great power and shared the leadership of central Europe with Austria.

WARFARE IN THE EIGHTEENTH CENTURY

The nature of wars fought by these eighteenth-century nations had evolved and changed from earlier times. Now armies consisted primarily of professional forces whose size and elaborate organization mirrored the centralized, bureaucratic governments they served. Officers were paid as full-time servants of the state in both peace and war. However, the troops they commanded were not all so "professional." Conscripts, volunteers, mercenaries, and even criminals made up their rank and file. In this sense, armies served as a depository for men without means and for those seen as threats to the social order. Officers tried to tame these motley groups by stressing harsh discipline and incessant drilling (see Figure 15.2).

Weapons and tactics were also changing. Reliable muskets; bayonets that no longer hindered fire; mobile cannons; and skilled coordination of troops, artillery, and cavalry all made warfare potentially more destructive than ever. Still, generals typically avoided all-out battles, preferring to expend their resources judiciously. "I do not favor pitched battles, especially at the beginning of a war," said Marshall Saxe, a leading French officer and writer on war tactics, in 1732. "I am convinced that a skillful general could make war all his life without being forced into one." Even Frederick the Great—not one to shy away from warfare—expressed this preference in his *Instructions for His Generals* (1747): "The greatest secret of war and the masterpiece of a skillful general is to starve his enemy." Instead of embarking on grand, decisive battles, then, eighteenth-century generals focused on building fortifications, initiating and maintaining sieges, securing supply lines, gaining superior positions, and piling up small advantages. Moreover, most military campaigns lasted only four or five months a year. Meanwhile, life outside the military—commerce, farming, culture, travel, and politics—went on as usual.

Yet, as Frederick the Great recognized, "war is [ultimately] decided only by battles and is not finished except by them." Outright fighting, when it finally occurred, took a heavy toll in human lives. Typically, soldiers arranged themselves in dense rows at least three men deep and fired their muskets, row by row, on command. Each side hurled artillery fire into the opposing troops and sent the cavalry charging in. Casualties mounted, but at the end of the day generals usually pulled their forces back from the battle with enough survivors to fight again.

Maritime battles cost fewer lives than land wars but could be crucial in the overall outcome of war. The largest ships of war in the eighteenth century carried up to 100 cannon. Figure 15.3, a cutaway view

FIGURE 15.3
An eighteenth-century French warship. *Iconographic Encyclopaedia*, 1851.

of a French warship, shows cannon poking out of the top three decks. Sailors are depicted at drill and at rest. At the upper right are officers' quarters, while the bottom decks house supplies, including livestock. Often firing at each other at point-blank range, many warships were destroyed or suffered grievous damage in these brutal clashes, and thousands of sailors perished.

A single battle, whether on land or sea, rarely led to a definitive outcome. More likely, the relentless draining away of money and men prompted diplomats to come to the bargaining table and end the war. This hemorrhaging of money and men was not missed by critics of the military, especially Enlightenment thinkers, who denigrated the old warrior culture as irrational and wasteful. Their criticisms, however, could neither prevent nor end wars in a society in which most people still regarded war as a normal—perhaps necessary—part of life.

WESTERN EUROPE AND THE GREAT COLONIAL RIVALRY

Like eastern Europe, western Europe experienced its own brand of statebuilding and rivalry for power. In this region as well as overseas, France and Britain uneasily shared dominance. Their seventeenth-century rivals, Spain and Holland, were declining. On the Continent, Spain—lacking the finances, manpower, and royal leadership that made it such a power in the late sixteenth and early seventeenth centuries—could no longer threaten France. Holland—damaged by three Anglo-Dutch wars and economic warfare with Britain during the seventeenth century—had gradually lost much of its trade and international position. Overseas, however, Spain as well as Portugal had managed to hold onto most of their lands. In the Americas, they remained great colonial powers, controlling most of the territory stretching from Mexico to the South American continent. There, they dominated the Amerindians, disrupting their cultures and turning them into laborers on large plantations and in mines, which still produced massive loads of gold and silver for shipment to Europe. Holland also had retained its Pacific colonies, which supported a valuable coffee and spice trade. However, the Dutch had lost some of their empire in Asia and much of their sea power to the British. With Spain and Holland thus occupied, France and Britain became the primary colonial rivals (see Map 15.4).

Louis XIV had made France a model of absolutism. However, the French monarchy never again achieved the clout it had enjoyed under his guidance. To be sure, France remained a first-rank power with *The French monarchy in decline* a large army, a centralized bureaucracy, and a growing economy. Yet, even during the last decades of his reign, Louis XIV's stature diminished. Thoughtful people criticized him for dragging France into what they saw as meaningless foreign conflicts. Louis' expensive wars and unreformed taxation policies also depleted the treasury. As Voltaire reported in 1751, "In the minds of the majority of his subjects, he lost during the last three years of his life all the prestige of the great and memorable things he had accomplished. . . ."

After Louis' death in 1715, French nobles in governmental councils and France's *parlements*—the thirteen judicial courts that had to sign royal decrees before those documents could become law—angled for a restoration of the powers they had lost to the king. The *parlements* claimed to speak for the nation, though in fact they voiced only the interests of the elites. The nobles bargained with the crown, sometimes to the point of open defiance. They faced a stubborn opponent. The young Louis XV, who had ascended the throne at the age of five, would rule for almost sixty years. Like Louis XIV, he asserted that "sovereign power resides in my person only . . . my courts [*parlements*] derive their existence and their authority from me alone . . . to me alone belongs legislative power without subordination and undivided."

Despite his longevity and support from some able ministers, Louis XV governed far less effectively than his predecessor had. Ignoring administrative matters, he allowed his royal bureaucracy to weaken. As resistance from the *parlements* ate away at the king's authority, France's fiscal pressures from old debts and continued military expenditures grew. The rising tensions centered on the issue of taxes. Specifically, the crown wanted to tap France's wealth by raising taxes, but the nobility sidestepped this move by using the *parlements* to protect their tax exemptions. Moreover, private tax farmers still controlled the collection of taxes, keeping one-third for themselves. Clearly, the monarchy was missing out on large sources of revenue. In 1716, the crown had tried to change this system. The effort led to the creation of a private bank, promoted by a brilliant Scottish financier, John Law, with the power to produce its own notes as legal tender and to monopolize overseas commerce. Within

Map showing British, Danish, Dutch, French, Portuguese, Russian, and Spanish colonial holdings and trade routes. Locations and goods labeled include: CANADA, BRITISH NORTH AMERICA (Furs, Timber, Tobacco), CARIBBEAN ISLANDS (Sugar, Slaves), PERU (Gold, Silver), ANGOLA (Slaves), GREAT BRITAIN, FRANCE, PORTUGAL, SPAIN, DENMARK-NORWAY, SWEDEN, OTTOMAN EMPIRE, RUSSIAN EMPIRE, QING EMPIRE (Tea, Porcelain, Silk, Lacquer ware), JAPAN, JAVA, Bombay (British), Calcutta (British), Pondicherry (French), Cape of Good Hope. Trade goods: Manufactured goods, Gold, Silver, Slaves, Sugar, Coffee, Silk, Coffee, Gems, Cinnamon, Pearls, Silk, Cotton, Gems, Pepper, Spices, Ebony, Slaves.

THINKING ABOUT GEOGRAPHY

MAP 15.4   Overseas Colonies and Trade, 1740

This map shows Europe's colonies and overseas trade patterns during the mid-eighteenth century.
⬧ **Locate** British and French holdings. **Where** are conflicts most likely to break out between these two powers? ⬧ **Identify** the triangular trade structure across the Atlantic. **Why** was slavery so central to this structure? ⬧ **Notice** what goods dominated trade. **Which** goods were Europeans most interested in selling and buying? **Why?**

just a few years, however, overspeculation in his Mississippi Company had brought the bank to ruin the "Mississippi Bubble," leaving France saddled once again with its inefficient old system.

Nothing drained money from the treasury more than wars. By avoiding major wars until 1740, the crown achieved relative financial stability. Thereafter the story changed, as France was drawn into a series of costly conflicts with continental and colonial rivals. Struggling to fund these endeavors, and lacking the appropriate financial institutions and taxable resources, France staggered under a relentlessly expanding debt.

In the 1770s, the king and his chancellor finally dissolved the *parlements* and tried to enact an ambitious program of reform. The move came too late. The inept Louis XV had never projected the image of a dynamic, reforming, enlightened monarch. On the contrary, he had a reputation for living lavishly within his opulent court. Underground pamphlets accused him of allowing his mistress and his sexual taste for girls to distract him from attending properly to courtly matters and the demanding business of managing the state. By the end of his reign, he had earned the dislike and even hatred of his subjects. Louis XV's death in 1774 was met with conspicuous silence, and his tardy reform program evaporated.

Hoping to gain popularity, Louis' successor, Louis XVI (r. 1774–1792), quickly restored the *parlements* and their powers. Once more, these aristocratic bodies thwarted new plans for financial reform—even those offered by talented ministers. In France, unlike in most other European powers, the crown and the nobility failed to find a satisfactory way of working together. Again and again, reform efforts faltered, annoying those hoping for change. As frustrations intensified, the crown became more and more isolated from traditional sources of support within the country.

France needed all the strength it could muster to compete for colonies and stature with Great Britain, where a much different situation had evolved. In 1714, a year before Louis XIV's death, Queen Anne had died. The crown passed to George I (r. 1714–1727), the first of the German Hanoverian line. The British monarchy had already sustained damage from the civil war and revolution of the seventeenth century (see Chapter 13). Though the king remained the chief executive of the state, ordained by God and tradition, Parliament now had the upper hand. Divided into the House of Lords (for nobles only) and House of Commons (elected representatives of commoners), Parliament controlled critical functions such as taxation, lawmaking, and the process for bringing grievances to the monarchy. Clearly, king and Parliament had to find a way to work together rather than in opposition.

The answer came in the form of a new institution: the cabinet system. Under this structure, the king chose members of Parliament, usually from the House of Commons, to serve as his ministers. If he hoped to enact policies, he had to select ministers who could command plenty of votes. These men tended to be the leaders of the major groups, or parties, in the House of Commons. By the eighteenth century, two groups dominated the House. Whigs, favoring commercial interests and a strong Parliament, remained staunchly opposed to any return of the Catholic Stuarts to the crown. Whigs also championed popular rights more than the conservative Tories did. Tories usually favored large landowners and a strong monarchy, and had stood less firmly against the Stuarts than the Whigs had.

Differences between the two groups came to a head in 1714. That year, the Tories considered supporting James, a Catholic Stuart raised in France, against George I. An unsuccessful rebellion in favor of James discredited the Tories in the eyes of the monarchy. In 1746 the English army put down another rebellion in Scotland that had attempted to support a Catholic Stuart. This latest fiasco further alienated the Tory leadership from the British crown.

For these reasons, George I and his son George II (r. 1727–1760) selected their ministers from the Whigs rather than the Tories. The two kings' lack of talent and public support made them all the more dependent on Whig leadership for governance. That leadership came in the person of Robert Walpole (1676–1745). Already recognized as a superb speaker and leading Whig in the House of Commons, Walpole became First Lord of the Treasury and the most important minister in George I's Privy Council in 1721. Much of Walpole's prominence derived from his successful handling of a financial crisis after an overseas trading company collapsed in 1720 (the South Sea Bubble). After that coup, he brought in other Whigs who could control votes in Parliament. He flattered and "managed" the monarch to remain in favor. Through patronage—control over money, contracts, offices, and honors—and the manipulation of elections, he ensured the dominance of the Whigs and his own leadership for twenty years.

Many complained about this pattern of political corruption, which both Whigs and Tories used. One critic—the British artist, William Hogarth (1697–1764)—produced many prints lambasting British political and social life. In Figure 15.4, one of a series of works on British elections, Hogarth shows a corrupt political campaign in progress. At the center, a voter emerges drunk from a riotous tavern. He has been bribed and is being instructed how to vote, which at the time was done publicly. At the left, the Tory candidate is purchasing cheap jewelry for a woman on the balcony. He makes his purchase from a Jewish merchant, despite his own anti-Jewish record in Parliament.

Walpole's successors continued his strategy of patronage to ensure parliamentary support, and the Whigs held office for another twenty years. By the middle of the eighteenth century a pattern had emerged. A group of ministers—themselves led by a prime minister, chosen from Parliament, who could command enough votes in the House of Commons to pass legislation—served the monarch and remained responsible to Parliament. Unlike in France, where

Making the British system work

most political debate took place outside the government, in Britain debate occurred within Parliament between the party in power and the "loyal opposition." People thus perceived the nation as being governed by the rule of law rather than the whim of a monarch. This system often moved slowly, but it worked.

While Britain's government may have been more representative than France's, it was far from democratic. Only some 200,000—most of them the wealthiest males—could vote. Rich landowners and powerful local elites staffed the government. Not surprisingly, Parliament listened most carefully to representatives of the 400 families whose massive estates included one-fourth of Britain's arable land. British officials did not

FIGURE 15.4
William Hogarth, *Canvassing for Votes—The Election*, 1754.

seek to exempt themselves from taxation, as did most of their counterparts in France, but instead ruled along with the crown by controlling Parliament.

Prosperity formed the foundation of Britain's strong position in these years. The middle class in particular agreed with the popular British author and observer Daniel Defoe, that "the greatness of the British nation is not owing to war and conquests . . . it is all owing to trade, to the increase of our commerce at home, and the extending it abroad." Goods poured into Britain from India and North America. The nation transformed itself into an agricultural exporter and a flourishing manufacturing center. By the middle of the eighteenth century, Great Britain had become Europe's leading economic power. It pursued its interest in European affairs through diplomacy, alliances, and the subsidizing of its allies' arms. Its naval dominance alone made it a formidable opponent. After 1740, Britain used both its economic strength and its military might in the great midcentury wars with France that stretched across three continents. To un-

derstand this story, we must shift our attention to the West's overseas colonies and the nature of trade among them.

More than anything else, France and Britain fought over colonies. For both countries, foreign trade quadrupled in the eighteenth century, and a large part of that increase derived from transactions *Colonies, trade, and war* with colonies. The two nations also made their greatest profits from trade across the Atlantic. However, their overseas presence differed crucially. The French had only 56,000 colonists living in North America in 1740—a fraction of the British colonial population. Yet French colonists carried out an extensive, highly profitable fur trade. Further, because of their small numbers and trade arrangements, they experienced limited conflict with Amerindians.

British colonists, clustered along the eastern seaboard, had a different experience. First, they grew rapidly—from 250,000 in 1700 to 1.7 million in 1760. As they occupied and exploited more and more land, they pushed the Amerindians out. Their expansion, combined with resistance from local tribes, led to savage battles. The fighting in turn convinced the colonists that removing or even exterminating the Amerindians was justified. As they became more firmly established, the British colonists bought manufactured goods from Britain in return for tobacco, rice, cotton, and indigo dye, much of which Britain re-exported to the European continent.

These North American colonists participated in the even more lucrative triangle of trade that connected *The triangle of trade* Europe, Africa, and the Americas, and that centered on the Caribbean (see Map 15.4). The British and French, along with the Dutch and Spanish, held islands there that supported a sugar, rum, coffee, and dyestuffs trade produced by slave labor. In particular, the demand for sugar and coffee seemed endless. European craving for these items grew so much that, for many, they became necessities rather than occasional luxuries.

At the heart of this thriving colonial commerce was the slave trade (see Chapter 11). Slavery was long common throughout Africa and in other societies.

For centuries, Islamic merchants had purchased slaves through well-established African networks and transported them by caravan across *The slave trade* the Sahara Desert to the Mediterranean basin or by ship from east African ports across the Indian Ocean to Asia.

By the eighteenth century, the dramatic demand for slaves in the Americas shifted Africa's slave trade westward to the Atlantic coast. Ships from Europe carried manufactured goods (most notably, guns) and gin to western Africa and traded them for slaves—two-thirds of them males, because they best provided heavy labor. Usually captured by African middlemen, slaves languished in pens in towns or forts on the African coast. European trading ships then carried them across the Atlantic in a perilous two-month sea voyage known as the Middle Passage.

Figure 15.5, an 1846 watercolor, suggests what conditions were like below decks on a slave ship. Typically, slaves were packed like cargo into the holds of ships "where the light of day does not penetrate." As many as 700 slaves—naked, branded, and shackled—might be crammed in one ship. A French writer describing these voyages told of a "continuous state of alarm on the part of the white men, who fear a revolt, and . . . a cruel state of uncertainty on the part of the Negroes, who do not know the fate awaiting them."

Traders took most of their slaves to the West Indies and Brazil; less than 10 percent went to North American destinations. After unloading their human cargo, the ships filled up with sugar, rum, and other goods—sometimes stopping farther north in the American colonies to take on additional products such as cotton, tobacco, timber, and furs. From there, the ships returned to Europe. Merchants then re-exported many of these products to other European nations.

FIGURE 15.5
A transatlantic slave ship.

Disease, abuse, and suicide took the lives of many slaves. In addition, African women often suffered the horror of rape by their captors. Those who survived the "middle passage" were then sold for profit and put to work on a plantation or in the mines or households of colonists. Figure 15.6 depicts slaves harvesting sugar cane on a West Indies plantation. Men, women, and children share the difficult work. In the foreground, a manager on horseback gives orders to a slave, who looks up deferentially to his master. On the right, sugar cane is being loaded into a cart, to be carried to the mill in the distant background. Slaves suffered from poor diets, inadequate housing, broken families, and stiff corporal punishment. The uprooting, the trauma of transportation, and the harsh conditions in the colonies stripped much away from these people. Still, salves often resisted their masters by working slowly, sabotaging equipment, running away, and revolting. Despite their lack of freedom, slaves built hybrid cultural traditions from African, American, and European sources.

Within the slave societies of Brazil, the West Indies, and North America, the notion of race was becoming tied to slavery, adding to earlier notions of racial prejudice. The unprecedented dependence on slavery and the associated development of racism would stain these societies in ways that would persist to this day.

The consequences of the slave trade also rippled through sub-Saharan Africa. Traditional trade routes north to the Mediterranean and east to the Indian Ocean disintegrated as more lucrative commerce shifted west to the Atlantic coast of Africa. To supply more human cargo to the Europeans, West African kingdoms raided inland tribes. Bloody internal wars erupted—more deadly than ever thanks to the guns supplied by Europeans to the Africans.

Because many slaves perished in the Americas and the plantations that depended on them kept expanding, the demand for fresh supplies of slaves increased relentlessly. This rising need in turn perpetuated the triangular commerce among Europe, Africa, and the Americas. European

traders took 50,000 to 100,000 slaves across the Atlantic each year during most of the eighteenth century. By the time slave trafficking abated in the mid-nineteenth century, more than 11 million Africans had been ripped from their homes, transported across the Atlantic, and sold into slavery. Another 4 million died resisting seizure or while in transport.

Planters and merchants on both sides of the Atlantic profited from this trade, and European cities serving as slave-trade ports flourished, particularly in England. The coastal town of Liverpool, for example, grew from a small town to a major city in the eighteenth century. In 1750 its slave merchants and fleet of almost 200 ships carried almost half of Europe's slave trade. Thousands of men from Liverpool worked on both merchant and naval ships, and more than a dozen banks and several insurance companies served slave-trade merchants. The wealth spread outward from Liverpool, helping to finance Britain's burgeoning industry as well as its rising position on the world stage. "Our West-Indies and African Trades are the most nationally beneficial of any we carry on. . . . The Trade to Africa is the branch which renders our American Colonies and Plantations so advantageous to Great Britain," argued one British defender of the slave system in 1746. "The daily bread of the most considerable part of our British Manufacturers are

FIGURE 15.6
A West Indies sugar plantation, 1823.

owing primarily to the labor of Negroes." While the statement may be an exaggeration, slavery generated much commerce and wealth in this eighteenth-century Atlantic economy, whether by direct or indirect means.

As Europeans' commercial activities, profits, and presence increased in the Americas, so did competition and friction, especially between the French and British. In North Amer-

Fighting on three continents

ica, British colonists along the eastern seaboard pushed inland, beyond the Appalachian Mountains into the Ohio Valley. The French strengthened their holdings by building forts along the Great Lakes and the large rivers of the St. Lawrence and Mississippi valleys. When the War of the Austrian Succession broke out in Europe in 1740, Britain and France soon locked horns on the Continent as well as overseas. Most of the fighting took place in the Americas, however. Wins and losses on each side balanced out, and by the time the conflict ended in 1748, each side had settled for what it had held in the beginning.

The peace would not last long. In 1755, war—sometimes known as the French and Indian War—erupted again, this time initiated by a British offensive against a French stronghold near Pittsburgh in North America. At the same time, the two powers were also competing in India, each trying to take advantage of the declining power of the Moguls (India's Muslim rulers). To gain support and position, France and Britain each allied themselves with opposing Indian princes and political factions. The competition developed into an undeclared war that, after 1756, coalesced with the hostilities breaking out across Europe, the Caribbean, and North America.

In this widespread war, which involved Asians and Amerindians as well as Europeans, France invested most of its energy and resources in the European arena, while Britain focused on the battle overseas. Initially, the French, assisted by the Amerindian allies they had gained, held their own in North America. Then the British, with their superior navy and more extensive population, began capturing French strongholds one by one. The fall of Quebec in 1759 opened all of Canada to British forces. British naval power overwhelmed the French and their Spanish allies in the Caribbean as well. In India, the British also prevailed, crushing the French and subduing several resisting Indian states.

Maps 15.5 and 15.6 show the changing fortunes of France and Britain in North America between 1755 and 1763. The Treaty of Paris, which ended the fighting in 1763, gave Britain control of Canada and of France's holdings east of the Mississippi. Britain also received France's West Indian possessions, except for Guadeloupe and Martinique, and most of France's holdings in India. British control over most of India dates from this period. France and several other nations still retained important overseas colonies, but Britain now reigned as the top colonial and commercial power. This "great war for empire" paved the way for the British to establish their worldwide empire in the nineteenth century.

The Twilight of Monarchies? The Question of Enlightened Absolutism

In both Britain and France, the eighteenth-century monarchies were in decline, but for different reasons. In Britain, the monarchs ruled in partnership with Parliament. However, the kings were undistinguished, and Parliament continued to gain the upper hand. In France, the successors to Louis XIV lacked the interest, talent, and support to make the monarchy dynamic or popular. The twin threats to the crown in these nations—the growing complexity of effective governance, and demands from elites to share power—arose elsewhere as well.

However, in several other nations monarchs managed to maintain their authority—often by justifying their rule in innovative ways and instituting new policies. In the second half of the eighteenth century, some of these monarchs styled themselves as "enlightened," or attuned to Enlightenment beliefs and willing to initiate reforms for the good of the state and its people. Some historians have distinguished these rulers from their predecessors, calling them "enlightened absolutists" or simply "enlightened." Yet, how valid is this characterization? Several historians claim that these monarchs primarily followed the long tradition of trying to buttress the central government's power and efficiency. Other historians argue that they genuinely initiated reforms in line with Enlightenment thinking.

THINKING ABOUT GEOGRAPHY

MAPS 15.5 AND 15.6   *North America, 1755 and 1763*

These maps show North America before and after the Seven Years' War. ❊ **Notice** France's large holdings in 1755. **What** advantages helped the British defeat France in this part of the world? **What** new problems faced Britain as a result of this victory? ❊ **Notice** what other competitors to the British remained in North America after 1763. **Assess** their relative strength.

The most sensational of the self-described enlightened monarchs was Frederick the Great (Frederick II) of Prussia. Even as a boy, Frederick had loved music,

Frederick the Great   poetry, and philosophy. After ascending to the throne, he still found time to perform in concerts as an accomplished flutist in his Palace of San Souci. There he also hobnobbed with towering cultural figures such as Voltaire, savored books in his library, and carried on a lively correspondence with leading French intellectuals. He knew and spoke the phrases of the Enlightenment. Like several other monarchs, he also wanted to display his awareness of culture and intellectual life to

help justify his position as monarch. He described "the good monarch" as one who behaved "as if he were each moment liable to render an account of his administration to his fellow citizens." He claimed to act only in the common interest of the people, declaring himself to be "the first servant of the state" rather than a divinely appointed ruler.

At the end of the Seven Years' War (1756–1763), the second of his two wars of aggression, Frederick made some attempts at "enlightened" reforms. For example, he initiated codification of the laws, abolished torture, and ended most capital punishment. Believing that "all religions, if one examines them, are founded on superstitious systems, more or less absurd," he proclaimed religious toleration. Nevertheless, he considered Jews "useless to the state," and taxed them heavily. He advocated public education, but spent very little on it compared with what he spent on his army. In his economic policy, Frederick did share the Physiocrats' appreciation of the importance of agriculture and tried to introduce new methods of cultivation (see p. 488). Yet he did nothing to free the serfs or lessen their burdens. Both his wars and his involvement in the partition of Poland revealed no hint of "enlightened" principles different from the monarchs who preceded him.

No one tried more sincerely to be "enlightened" than Joseph II of Austria (r. 1780–1790). "Since I have ascended the throne," he said in 1781, "I have made *philosophy* the legislator of my empire." Viewing his rule as a moral and holy calling, Joseph issued thousands of decrees. Unfortunately, he lacked the practical sense of Frederick the Great. He did change laws that had previously limited freedom of the press and religion (including Judaism). He also restricted the death penalty, promoted education, and enacted and tried to enforce equality before the law.

Nevertheless, Joseph still ruled as an autocrat, antagonizing most of the powerful groups in his lands. Even peasants, unable to understand exactly what all the decrees meant, failed to support him. His well-meaning but ill-conceived efforts—to centralize the administration of the widely dispersed Habsburg territories, to replace the numerous languages of his subjects with German, to subordinate the strongly entrenched Roman Catholic Church, and to free the serfs in a society still based on feudalism—all backfired. Opposition and even open revolt swelled in his lands. In 1787 Joseph lamented, "[I] hope that when I am no more, posterity will examine, and judge more equitably . . . all that I have done for my people." His vision would not come to pass. Within a few years of his death in 1790, most of his reforms were abolished and the Habsburg lands reacquired their old, conservative ways.

Other monarchs, such as those of Sweden, Sardinia, Spain, and Portugal, attempted or enacted reforms that could be seen as enlightened. In Russia, Catherine the Great certainly prided herself on being "enlightened" (see pp. 502–504). She once described the true aim of monarchy as "not to deprive People of their natural Liberty; but to correct their Actions, in order to attain

Joseph II

the supreme good." Ultimately, however, Catherine failed to put most of her reforms into practice. Instead, she resorted to the tried-and-true tactic of appeasing elites at a price paid by the peasantry.

Certainly these monarchs found it easier to manifest their "enlightenment" in style rather than substance. Moreover, they rarely lost sight of traditional goals: to increase their own military and economic power. Few attempted to enact fundamental social, political, or economic reforms dictated by Enlightenment thought. Even those who tried, such as Joseph II in Austria, generally failed to overcome opposition to those reforms from tradition-minded people.

Style, substance, or survival?

Nevertheless, thoughtful observers of the eighteenth century—looking for tendencies and possibilities for reform rather than revolutionary change—believed that several rulers displayed the enlightened spirit of the times. Despite great obstacles to reform within the traditional order, some of these rulers made progress toward fulfilling the philosophes' agenda of promoting more religious tolerance, humane social institutions, and rational administration. In the eyes of contemporaries, they earned the label "enlightened."

Finally, from another perspective, "enlightened absolutism" also may have reflected a growing sense that, in the long run, monarchs could no longer *claim* to embody the state. The need for governmental efficiency had grown too much to be entrusted to a poorly qualified individual who happened to be a king or queen. If the institution of monarchy were to survive, kings and queens had to justify their position in these new, ostensibly "enlightened" ways.

Changes in Country and City Life

Eighteenth-century European monarchs and officials faced not only the risky politics and wars of their times, but also the changes unfolding in their very societies. Especially in western Europe, new economic and social forces began to upset old traditions (see Chapter 13). For some, these changes created a sense that life was improving and would continue to do so. For others, the changes only deepened their misery. The greatest shifts emerged in the countryside, where the vast majority of the population (some 80 percent) lived and depended on agriculture for their livelihood and very survival.

Historically, toiling in the fields within Europe's traditional subsistence economies produced little more than enough food to survive. During the late seventeenth and eighteenth centuries, new methods of agricultural production that had originated in Holland spread to England and then to other areas of western Europe. These innovative methods allowed fewer people to work the fields and still produce far more food than they needed. The new techniques and the changes flowing from them became so important that they are known as the agricultural revolution.

THE AGRICULTURAL REVOLUTION

Most early-eighteenth-century farmers used methods that differed only marginally from those employed in previous centuries. They grew the same crops year after year, left one-third to one-half of the land fallow (unplanted) to allow the soil to replenish itself with nutrients for the next planting, and saved only enough fodder to feed small numbers of domestic animals during the winters. Individual families worked small strips of land, while large, uncultivated fields, brushlands, and forests (the "commons") were reserved for general use by the community. Traditional community practices usually determined decisions about crops, animals, and land use. Overall, only a small minority of people made their living outside of agriculture, and an even smaller percentage had the good fortune to afford luxuries.

This traditional, agricultural economy had the potential to support a limited measure of population growth. In the eighteenth century, population increases stepped up the demand for food, and hence for hands to clear fields, drain swamps, terrace hillsides, carry water, and till the soil. Most of these efforts were simply an intensification of old methods for increasing agricultural yields, and the growing population consumed most of the extra food they produced. Something had to change if large numbers of Europeans hoped to increase their standard of living and provide enough food for people living in the cities as well as the countryside.

At the heart of the agricultural revolution lay two developments: first, the introduction of new crops and the use of new farming techniques that dramatically boosted agricultural yields; and second, the transformation of rural lands farmed for subsistence into large, controlled properties that produced crops for commerce. The primary agricultural advances *New crops and techniques* came first in Holland and Britain, where farmers began experimenting with new crops such as clover, turnips, and legumes, as well as the potato from America. These crops replenished the soil rather than depleting it, and therefore could be grown on lands that farmers periodically had to leave fallow. Farmers now used the new crops to feed livestock during the hard winters. More cattle meant more protein-rich dairy products; more horses and oxen eased the workload for humans and provided transportation; and more sheep produced more wool. All this livestock, improving with new crossbreeding practices, yielded more meat, leather, and soap as well as manure with which to fertilize fields. Other new foods, such as nutrient-rich potatoes, also made the land more productive than ever before. Some landowners became renowned for their farming innovations. In England, for example, Charles "Turnip" Townshend (1674–1738) experimented with crop rotation and growing turnips. His compatriot, Jethro Tull (1674–1741), advocated the use of a seed drill and manure, which made planting more efficient and productive.

Not all farmers adopted the new agricultural methods. For many, traditional ways were comfortably familiar. Even those who realized how much profit they might make by selling their surpluses in the cities and other distant markets needed money to fund the new farming methods. They also required control over larger tracts of land to introduce the new crops, apply the innovative methods, and specialize in certain products—whether sheep for wool, grain for flour, or cattle for meat and dairy.

By all means, fair and foul, these market-oriented landowners dispossessed individuals of their small plots and communities of their commons *Enclosures* to enclose land with fences, hedges, and walls as their own. After 1750, Britain's Parliament furthered this trend by authorizing a wave of these enclosures. Over the decades, wealthy landowners created large, controlled tracts that yielded products for the market. They reserved only a small part of their land for their own needs or bought their food elsewhere. Through this process, thousands of small, independent landowners, sharecroppers, and tenant farmers lost their land—and the status and security that had come with it. Rural communities disintegrated, eroding the support and human interactions that had so characterized life in the country.

MANUFACTURING SPREADS IN THE COUNTRYSIDE: COTTAGE INDUSTRY

The spreading agricultural revolution became one force pushing, forcing, or freeing people to work more in nonagricultural jobs. When families lost their self-sufficient farms, they had to find new sources of income to supplement the meager day-labor wages their landowning employers paid them. Manufacturing seemed to offer a solution. Growing commerce, particularly overseas trade, had heightened demand for manufactured goods—and thus workers to produce them. Traditionally, well-paid urban artisans had done this sort of work. Now, with demand high and rural workers available by the thousands, merchants turned to the countryside to increase production and take advantage of the cheap labor. Moreover, by shifting more production itself to the countryside, merchants avoided urban guild regulations that historically had controlled wages and the quantity and quality of goods.

All these changes stimulated the growth of "cottage industry," also known as the "putting-out system." This system, which had already existed in the sixteenth and seventeenth centuries but to a much smaller degree, worked in a specific way. An entrepre-

neur provided raw materials (usually for production of textiles such as wool or linen) and sometimes equipment (such as a handloom or spinning wheel) to peasants. The entrepreneur might be anyone—from a city merchant to a rural landowner—who managed to amass enough money to make an initial investment in raw materials and perhaps equipment. Peasants, who sought employment during times of the year when there was less need for agricultural labor, worked in their homes (hence the term "cottage industry") to turn these raw materials into finished products. Mainly, they spun wool into yarn and wove the yarn into cloth. Sometimes enterprising peasants contracted out raw material to other spinners to keep weavers busy, since weavers depended on spinners to provide a steady supply of yarn. Women and children often worked while men were off performing day-labor for large landowners. The entrepreneur periodically returned, paid for the peasants' labor by the piece, and distributed the finished products to distant markets.

As Figure 15.7 shows, whole families participated in cottage-industry work. Women and children usually washed, combed, and spun the raw material into thread, while men often wove the yarn on looms. In this print, members of a rural household in Ireland beat and comb flax into linen, which will later be spun and woven. The light streaming in from the open window, the smiling laborers, and the little girl playing with a dog all distract our attention from the realities of the work: the dark, cramped quarters of single-room cottages and the tedious nature of this labor.

Cottage industry spread rapidly during the eighteenth century, particularly in Great Britain and parts of France and Germany. In addition to textiles, all sorts of goods—from buttons and housewares to knives, nails, and clocks—were produced through this system. The quality of these products varied, and relations between merchants and laborers often broke down over accusations of theft and disputes over wages. Still, more and more people came to depend on the system. For many of these workers, cottage-industry labor changed from a part-time to a full-time occupation.

The primary appeal of the work was its availability. Cottage industry allowed many people to remain in rural areas in a time of shrinking demand for farm workers. It also helped large families keep up, and enabled young people to get an earlier start on marriage. On the other hand, the pay rarely rose above starvation wages, and the labor was drudgery.

Wherever it spread, cottage industry extended the money economy and the web of the commercial mar-

FIGURE 15.7
Cottage industry.

ketplace. Along with the agricultural revolution, the growth of cottage industry helped set the stage for an even greater economic transformation that would eventually sweep from Britain throughout the West and into the non-Western world: the industrial revolution.

§ MORE PEOPLE, LONGER LIVES

As these new economic and social forces began to alter traditional ways of life, Europe's population jumped from approximately 110 million in 1700 to 190 million in 1800. Figure 15.8 *Population growth* reveals the population growth throughout most of Europe during the eighteenth century. Relatively large populations help explain the strength of three major powers—England (along with Ireland), France, and Russia (note that much of Russia's increased population came from territorial expansion). Earlier marriages, more and better food, and fewer plagues raised the birthrate and lowered the death rate. Agricultural and commercial prosperity, along with improvements in the transportation of food, reduced the number and severity of famines in many areas. In particular, the widespread cultivation of the potato during the second half of the eighteenth century made this cheap, nutritious food available to millions. A spate of good weather helped to improve harvests. In some areas, new urban sanitation practices—cleaning wells, draining swampy areas, and burying refuse—probably improved health as well.

Surprisingly, medical practices rarely contributed to better health. Certainly the medical field saw some advances. Inoculation against smallpox, for example, spread to Europe from the Middle East during the eighteenth century, *Eighteenth-century medicine* though it was not used widely until the end of the century. Surgeons also made some improvements in the treatment of battlefield injuries. For instance, they learned to treat soldiers for shock before operating, and to clean wounds around the trauma.

Despite these signs of progress, eighteenth-century medicine was still dangerous. Figure 15.9 provides a glimpse into a German hospital. In just one room, a bewildering array of medical procedures takes place. At the center, a surgeon saws off the leg of a patient. At the right lies a woman with a grotesquely swollen leg; just behind her, a woman prepares to give

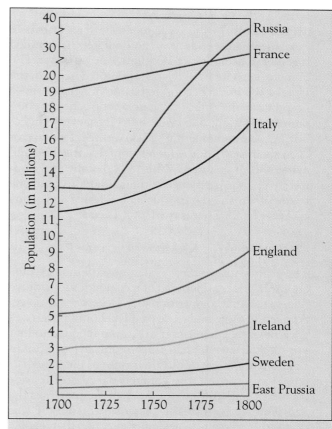

FIGURE 15.8
Population growth in Europe, 1700–1800.

FIGURE 15.9
A German hospital, 1746.

birth. At the far left, a priest administers last rites to a dying patient. In the background, women distribute food, men haul a body away, and sufferers lie crowded together in beds. French hospitals were no better. The French encyclopedist Denis Diderot described the Hôtel-Dieu in Paris, considered one of France's finest hospitals at the time: "Imagine a long series of communicating wards filled with sufferers of every kind of disease who are sometimes packed three, four, five or even six into a bed, the living alongside the dead and dying, the air polluted by this mass of unhealthy bodies, passing the pestilence of their afflictions from one to the other, and the spectacle of suffering and agony on every hand. That is the Hôtel-Dieu."

Deepening Misery for the Poor

The eighteenth-century population explosion exacted an ironic price. Stiffening competition for food drove prices up, while competition for jobs kept wages down. As a result, more and more people fell into poverty. A governmental commission in Austria reported to Empress Maria Theresa that "the peasants live in a condition of real slavery. . . . In their ruinous huts, the parents sleep on straw, the children naked on the wide shelves of earthenware stoves . . . all the charges of the Kingdom are born by the peasants, who are the sole taxpayers." Despite a widespread sense that people were better off than ever and that things would improve, in truth more people meant more misery.

In a desperate attempt to survive, poor people fled to the cities, hoping to find work in trade and manufacturing or as day-laborers and domestics. Only some of them managed to find jobs; the rest were left to fend for themselves. A large percentage of urban dwellers missed out on the new wealth and opportunities of the cities. They eked out a living at little more than a subsistence level, and their lot worsened as more and more of them crowded in from the countryside.

Indeed, the surplus of workers; inflation; and disasters such as war, disease, and failed harvests hit the poor in cities and countryside alike. In France, economist Jacques Turgot (1727–1781) described the disastrous harvest of 1769: "The people could exist only by exhausting their resources, by selling at a miserable price their articles of furniture and even their clothes. Many of the inhabitants have been obliged to disperse themselves through other provinces to seek work or to beg, leaving their wives and children to the charity of the parishes. . . ." One Spanish official

described how "wives and children are without work, and all, piled together in cities or large towns, live at the expense of charity . . . " Even for those who found steady employment, wages simply did not keep pace with escalating prices.

In bad times, food riots and tax revolts broke out in cities and rural areas across Europe. A rise in the price of grain often sparked attacks on merchants, granaries, and convoys of grain slated for armies. People turned on officials as well, blaming them for not keeping grain prices affordable or for allowing food to be shipped out to higher bidders elsewhere. Crime increased and more people slept along the sides of rural roads and city streets. Crowds of mothers pushed into foundling hospitals, desperate to leave children they could not care for. Some foundling hospitals established lotteries to determine which children they could afford to take in. Others found ways to make it easier for women to give up their children. Figure 15.10 depicts a woman abandoning her baby at an Italian foundling home. Desperate mothers could give up a baby at any time of day without embarrassing questions by placing the child on a revolving table. The nun or nurse on duty would then rotate the table and take in the child. Here the worried mother looks back to see if anyone is looking. Scenes such as this took place in many countries during the eighteenth century.

This deepening of poverty put a huge strain on traditional systems for aiding the poor, such as through the church or private charity. Some people were reduced to begging, and to teaching their children this dubious art. Some authorities sympathized; others turned a blind eye. As one French official put it, "Beggary is the apprenticeship of crime; it begins by creating a love of idleness . . . in this state the beggar does not long resist the temptation to steal." A few countries devised legislation, such as the English Poor Laws, that required the impoverished to work on public projects or in workhouses. Officials used these sorts of laws more to control and discipline the poor than to help them. Often the same institution served as a workshop for the unfortunate, a hospital, and a prison. True, the poor had always suffered. Now, however, the population boom pushed their numbers to overwhelming new heights.

Prosperity and the Bourgeoisie

Like the agricultural revolution, urban growth made life worse for some and better for others. Those who gained most during this era were the middle and aristocratic classes, particularly those who seized opportunities in commerce and industry and in the expanding governmental bureaucracies. The urban middle class—in French, the *bourgeoisie*—expanded and found itself in a particularly odd situation. Wealthier than most, the bourgeoisie lived off their investments in trade, manufacturing, or land rather than working with their hands like their fellow commoners. They also found ways to avoid the restrictions of the guild system of production. While those laboring "below" them envied and resented their success, the bourgeoisie tried to distance themselves from "less respectable" commoners.

Middle-class people also had difficult relationships with those above them—the aristocracy. Successful members of the bourgeoisie resented the privileges enjoyed by the aristocracy, but—even more strongly—they wanted those privileges for themselves. They longed to join the aristocracy, and they were willing to spend money to do it. Money got them titles and offices, large estates, and judicious marriages—the trappings of success that they hoped would earn them acceptance into the ranks of the aristocracy. The aristocrats, for their part, viewed this method of "social climbing"—and the people who attempted it—with disdain. As they saw it, true nobility derived from birth, not wealth.

Nevertheless, the bourgeoisie persisted and thrived. These merchants, manufacturers, and professionals made money, expanded their businesses, invested in government bonds, and took chances on shaky financial schemes. They valued hard work and the accumulation of money. Moreover, they had the means to purchase a vast variety of luxuries, from coffee and chocolate to wallpaper, cotton clothing, and watch chains—goods produced outside the home, often even outside the country. For them, the market—rather than the household—supplied staples as well as conveniences and luxuries.

Over time, the richest among the bourgeoisie might manage to gain entrance into the aristocracy. Yet even if they could not get into the courts, estates, and homes of the aristocracy, the bourgeoisie developed a public culture of their own. They educated their children at universities, and attended public theaters, music halls, and galleries. They filled tearooms, coffeehouses, literary societies, and clubs, and devoured newspapers, journals, and books written especially for them. Over time, they acquired their own sense of identity, as well as an impatience when further opportunities to rise in society were denied them.

FIGURE 15.10
Abandoning children.

The Culture of the Elite: Combining the Old and the New

The culture of the bourgeoisie and the aristocracy reflected the continuance of old trends along with the new developments that characterized the eighteenth century. For example, the courts of Europe still sponsored painters, composers, and musicians. In their private halls, aristocrats savored these artists' paintings, concerts, and operas. The prevailing spirit remained classical, inspired by the Greek and Roman appreciation for formal symmetry, proportion, and reason. On the other hand, artistic styles were changing. Several artists and authors put a new emphasis on emotion and nature in their works, an artistic trend sometimes referred to as the "cult of sensibility." Audiences for these new cultural forms expanded, and the stream of literature being published for the growing numbers of literate westerners swelled.

THE ADVENT OF THE MODERN NOVEL

Much of the reading public consisted of members of the middle class, and not surprisingly the modern novel reflected middle-class tastes. A compelling story, complex and varied characters, and realistic social situations formed the core of this new literary form. Novels also conveyed current ideas, manners, news, and information in witty and dramatic ways. In several popular novels, the English writer Daniel Defoe (1660–1731) wrote about individuals who planned ahead and used their entrepreneurial skills to meet challenges. The adventures of a character in a Defoe novel might take place at home in England, or on exotic islands, as in *Robinson Crusoe* (1719). Similarly, Defoe's book *Moll Flanders* (1722) tells of a woman of lower-class origins who manages to navigate through all sorts of difficult situations, from prisons to a position in high society, in England and America.

Samuel Richardson (1689–1761) and Henry Fielding (1707–1754), also British, used the novel to analyze human personality, emotions, and psychology. In *Pamela, or Virtue Rewarded* (1740), Richardson recounts the story of a servant girl who tries to retain her "virtue" in the face of her wealthy employer's sexual advances. The book's characters and circumstances powerfully reflected contemporary realities, and the novel inspired a wave of similar works. Henry Fielding, for one, expanded on Richardson's effort, weaving a rich tapestry of English society in his novel *Tom Jones* (1749).

FIGURE 15.11
Antoine Watteau, *A Pilgrimage to Cythera*, 1717.

Many novels appealed particularly to women readers. British writer Fanny Burney (1752–1840) gained fame with the publication of her novel *Evelina or A Young Lady's Entrance into the World* (1778). The book portrays a provincial girl who makes a life for herself in London. Although the story ends with a marriage, it also reveals the social restrictions and dangers facing eighteenth-century women who tried to live an independent life. Burney would go on to publish several other popular novels.

During the second half of the century, novels and works of poetry by authors such as Jean-Jacques Rousseau in France and Johann Wolfgang von Goethe (1749–1832) in the German states emphasized emotion, relationships, and social problems. These authors presented the emotions as natural virtues, rejecting the artificiality of formal manners. Their style, which would become known as romanticism, grew in popularity during the last quarter of the century.

PRIDE AND SENTIMENT IN ART AND ARCHITECTURE

Unlike literature, the fine arts still typically reflected the tastes of the dominant aristocracy. Artists vied with one another for commissions to paint the portraits of royals and aristocrats, depicting their proud subjects adorned with plumes, buckles, silks, brocades, and laces. The scenes might include children and dogs and, in the background, lavish estate grounds. The distinctive clothing, haughty poses, and elaborate settings marked subjects as members of the landowning elite.

Many paintings showed intimate scenes of aristocratic private life— meetings, picnics, flirtations, and conversations among the upper classes. In Antoine Watteau's (1684–1721) popular paintings, for example, the context might be classical mythology, but the figures were eighteenth-century aristocrats. In *A Pilgrimage to Cythera* (a mythical island of love), shown in Figure 15.11, aristocrats wander leisurely through an idyllic garden of nature. Cupids at the left and Venus at the right bless the scene. The line between life, mythology, and the social roles played by the subjects blurs in this lush scene. The painting also has an underlying seriousness, as the lovers, reluctantly preparing to depart to the everyday world, enjoy a moment of life that will pass too quickly.

Whereas the aristocracy tended to populate Watteau's works, other artists painted well-received, sentimental scenes of ordinary people experiencing dramatic moments. Figure 15.12, a painting by the French artist Jean-Baptiste Greuze (1725–1805), shows one of these works. Here the father at the left curses his departing son, who is determined to find his own way through life by joining the army. The young man's mother and other members of the family try in vain to reconcile the two men and to prevent the breakup of the family on such a painful note. In an accompanying painting, the grief-stricken son returns to find his father on his death bed. William Hogarth's engravings (see Figures 15.4 and 15.14) also explored everyday experiences in the lives of ordinary people, but usually from a satirical or moralistic perspective.

Eighteenth-century architecture could not portray sentiments in the same detail as paintings, but buildings in the baroque style still expressed well the gaudy

FIGURE 15.12
Jean-Baptiste Greuze, *The Father's Curse*.

Biography

WOLFGANG AMADEUS MOZART (1756–1791)

Musicians quickly recognized the young Wolfgang Amadeus Mozart as a unique genius. His father Leopold, a well-known Austrian composer and violinist, called him the "miracle which God let be born in Salzburg." Born in 1756, Wolfgang wrote his first compositions when he was just five years old. He embarked on the first of many tours throughout Europe as a six-year-old child-prodigy, playing the clavier with his elder sister Nannerl, also a child-prodigy, and his father. (see Figure 15.13). They played at several royal courts for monarchs such as Louis XV of France, Maria Theresa of Austria, and George III of Britain. They also performed at the homes of leading nobles as well as in public theaters. Wolfgang's father, always eager to promote his young son, wrote that "our great and mighty Wolfgang seems to know everything at the age of seven that a man acquires at the age of forty."

By the time he had reached fourteen, Mozart had composed several concertos, sonatas, and an opera. Announcements for his performances stressed his virtuosity. For example, for a concert in Italy, the fourteen year old would play "A Symphony of his own composition; a harpsichord concerto which will be handed to him, and which he will play on first sight; a sonata handed him in like manner, which he will provide with variations, and afterwards repeat in another key. . . ." The boy could play the organ and violin almost as well. After hearing Mozart in 1771, one well-known composer said, "This boy will cause us all to be forgotten." The prestigious Haydn, who strongly influenced Wolfgang's music, would later tell Wolfgang's father that "your son is the greatest composer known to me. . . ."

Child-Prodigy, Musical Genius

In 1781 Mozart settled in Vienna as a teacher and composer. Short, slim, with engaging blue eyes and a full head of fine hair, the young man enjoyed an active social life, including billiards and dancing. Yet music preoccupied him. He wrote, "You know that I am, so to speak, swallowed up in music, that I am busy with it all day—speculating, studying,

---

splendor of the eighteenth-century monarchs and their courts. At the same time, architects began de-emphasizing size and instead relied on multiple curves and lacy, shell-like ornamentation to convey a sense of pleasing luxury. This style is usually referred to as rococo. Some new government buildings and urban residences followed a more neoclassical style, which stressed clarity of line and form modeled on Greek and Roman ideals.

Gardens complemented the buildings they accompanied, extending them and reflecting the mix of old and new tastes. As we saw in Louis XIV's Versailles palace (see Chapter 13), the French garden in particular emphasized rational, geometric forms marked off by hedges. Here nature was shown completely tamed by human power and reason. By contrast, the eighteenth-century English garden looked freer and more natural.

In fact, these gardens were not natural at all. Landscape architects designed them to imitate a vision of nature or to turn the grounds of an estate into an idealized version of nature. This managing of nature in English gardens was a compromise between old and new ideas about human beings' place in the natural world.

REACHING NEW HEIGHTS IN MUSIC

Of all the eighteenth-century arts, music left the most profound legacy. Much of it reflected the tastes of its royal, aristocratic, and ecclesiastical patrons. Composers and musicians, therefore, usually stuck to established forms and music was typically heard as a pleasing background to conversations, balls, and other social occasions in the bastions of the aristocracy. Increasingly, however, music was played in pubconsidering." Keenly aware of his own talents, he at times arrogantly criticized other musicians' limitations. He felt certain that he could outshine any rival.

In 1782, despite the doubts of his father and sister, Mozart married Constanze Weber, a singer. Mozart wrote that "as soon as we were married, my wife and I both began to weep" for joy. Their marriage seems to have been happy. They would have six children, of whom only two survived. Neither parent managed the family finances well. Even though Mozart became brilliantly successful as a composer, a virtuoso pianist, and a teacher; received numerous commissions and fees; and attained appointment as royal chamber composer to Emperor Joseph II of Austria, he continually borrowed money to support his growing family.

Wolfgang could never quite satisfy his demanding and increasingly distant father. Hearing that Leopold had fallen seriously ill in 1787, Mozart wrote a letter of consolation that included his own views on death: "As death . . . is the true goal of our existence, I have formed during the last few years such close relations with this best and truest friend of mankind that his image is no longer terrifying to me but rather very soothing and consoling." Leopold died a month later. In July 1791, a stranger appeared at Wolfgang's door with a commission to write a Requiem in secrecy. Mozart was still working on the project in December when he died in relative poverty. He was just thirty-five. Although he probably had succumbed to an infection and fever, unsubstantiated rumors circulated for years that a competitor had poisoned him.

FIGURE 15.13
The Mozarts.

⬧ **Consider** how Mozart's career reflected eighteenth-century society—still dominated by the aristocracy but with a growing middle class interested in the culture of the day.

lic concert halls to a larger audience. Opera houses opened everywhere, and composers could now hope to make money from paying audiences as well as from court and aristocratic patronage. Several cities became well-known musical centers, but Vienna topped them all. This Austrian city became the musical heart of Europe, drawing hundreds of musicians who competed for favor there.

The first half of the eighteenth century saw the high point of baroque music, a style that had originated in the seventeenth century and that was still favored in royal courts and aristocratic homes. The greatest practitioners of the baroque style were Johann Sebastian Bach (1685–1750) and George Frideric Handel (1685–1759). Bach was a member of a German family long distinguished by its musical talent. Noted in his

Baroque music

own lifetime chiefly as an organist rather than a composer, he created a vast array of great music for organ, harpsichord, clavichord (forerunner of the piano), orchestra, and chorus. Sadly, much of Bach's work has been lost. Most of Bach's compositions were religiously inspired. Handel was born in central Germany in the same year and same region as Bach. He studied Italian opera in Germany and Italy and wrote forty-six operas himself. He also became court musician in Hanover. Later, he made his home in England, as did the elector, who became King George I of England. Handel wrote an enormous quantity of music—both instrumental and vocal—all of it marked by dignity, formal elegance, and harmony.

During the last decades of the century, the restrained baroque style gave way to the more melodic "classical" style, with its striking depth, structure, and emotion. Franz Joseph Haydn (1732–1809) and Wolfgang Amadeus Mozart (1756–1791) led the way. Their most stunning work was the symphony; by the end of their careers, they had created symphonies of rich *The classical style* harmonic complexity and emotional depth within the restrained classical form. During his long career in Vienna, Haydn wrote more than a hundred symphonies in addition to scores of compositions for other forms, particularly chamber music. Toward the end of his career, he became so popular that he left noble patrons and signed a lucrative contract with his music publisher.

Haydn became a friend and a source of inspiration for the young Mozart (see Biography). Figure 15.13 shows the seven-year-old Wolfgang playing the piano. Accompanying him are his father on the violin and his sister, who is singing. Here the performers are exquisitely dressed for their aristocratic audience. Ultimately, Mozart composed more than 600 works and excelled in all forms, but he became most appreciated for his symphonies, piano concertos, and operas. His music was stunningly clear, melodic, elegant, and graceful. In his hands, the classical style reached its peak.

THE GRAND TOUR

The music, art, and literature of the elites was part of a broader, cosmopolitan culture that spilled across national boundaries. This culture manifested itself in elaborate styles of dress, polished manners, and highly structured conversation. French was its international language. The growing popularity of travel and travel literature added to the sense of a common European cultural identity, at least among elites. Indeed, the wealthy often considered the "grand tour" a necessary part of education. Travelers on the tour stopped in main cities to indulge in coffeehouses, storefront window displays, public gardens, theaters, opera houses, and galleries. They might also visit art dealers or public auctions to purchase quality paintings. Family connections offered them accommodations and introduced them to local society, Enlightenment salons, or potential candidates for marriage. The tour usually continued to historical ruins, which featured revered models of Greek and Roman antiquity that further strengthened the viewers' sense of a common cultural identity.

Culture for the Lower Classes

The lower classes were not without cultural outlets that fit their lives and provided a sense of common identity. For peasants, artisans, and the urban poor, culture typically came in the form of shared recreation, songs, tales, and the passing down of wisdom at gatherings and celebrations. Many of these activities also coincided with religious gatherings and celebrations.

FESTIVALS AND POPULAR LITERATURE

Villagers both worked together and celebrated together—at fairs, harvests, plowings, weddings, and religious holidays. Numerous festivals and public ceremonies had seasonal themes that were of particular importance and interest to people so dependent on agriculture. Other celebratory events related to the Christian calendar and centered on holidays, such as Christmas and Easter. Traditional weddings involved a community procession and festivities as well as a religious ceremony, and featured music, dancing, feasts, games, and play. In the cities, artisans participated in their own organizations that combined recreational activities with mutual aid and religious celebrations.

Certain forms of literature also became popular among ordinary people. Literacy was growing, thanks to the printing press, the demands of business, and an increase in the number of primary schools. By the end of the eighteenth century, some 40 to 60 percent of the population in England and France could read (more of them men than women). With the rise in literacy, popular literature also expanded. Stirring religious tracts, almanacs, and tales of chivalric valor—typically, small, cheap booklets—circulated widely. More often, however, the "literature" of ordinary people was passed on orally. At night, people might gather to share folktales and songs that told of traditional wisdom, the hardships of everyday life, the hopes of common people, the dangers of life in the forests or of strangers who could be monsters or princes, and the ways to get along in life.

In the past, elites had fully participated in this popular culture, but during the eighteenth century they increasingly abandoned it to the lower classes. The "respectable" classes now often considered the leisure activities of ordinary people too disorderly and crude. Nevertheless, the middle and upper classes read some of the same popular literature enjoyed by the lower classes. Moreover, everyone—aristocrats and peasants alike—might be found at village festivals, fairs, and sporting events or enjoying jugglers, acrobats, magic lantern shows, and touring troops of actors. Men of all classes watched and wagered on cockfights and dogfights. Other sports, such as soccer and cricket, gained popularity and drew large, animated crowds.

GIN AND BEER

All the social classes also engaged in drinking—whether wine or brandy in the privacy of a wealthy home, or gin and beer in popular taverns. Especially in England, the ravages of drinking gin seemed to grow to alarming proportions. Figure 15.14, another moralistic work by William Hogarth, graphically depicts the evils of gin drinking in England. At the center a pox-ridden, impoverished, and drunk woman lets her baby fall over a wooden rail. Near her, a man slowly starves to death. In the background, workers haul bodies away, a man hangs himself in an upstairs tenement, children drink glasses of gin, and buildings collapse for want of repair. The scene is one of physical, social, and moral decay from excessive alcohol consumption. Though this image is an exaggeration, the actual problems caused by drinking were so extensive that in 1751 the British government passed a heavy tax on cheap gin to curtail its consumption.

RELIGIOUS REVIVALS

Popular culture also merged with deeply felt spiritual beliefs and religious activities. Despite the many secular trends of the period, Christianity still stood at the center of Western culture and life. Churches rather than the state ran the schools and hospitals. The poor, aged, and crippled relied on churches for social services. Church bells announced the time of day everywhere and religious holidays marked the year.

Within this Western religious culture, popular piety persisted. Indeed, especially among Protestants, a sense grew among ordinary churchgoers that official *Pietism* churches were becoming bureaucratized, complacent and unresponsive to peoples' spiritual needs. In response, religious revivals spread from community to community and across national borders. In the German and Scandinavian states, pietism—which minimized dogma and formal ritual in favor of inner piety, holy living, and the private emotional experience of worshiping—gained strength. Revival movements in Britain and its North American colonies attracted thousands to huge gatherings.

The greatest of these revival movements was Methodism, founded in England by John Wesley (1703–1791). While studying for the Anglican ministry at Oxford, Wesley and a band of fellow students became disillusioned with the spiritual emptiness that had fallen upon the Anglican Church as well as its subservience to the government and the aristocracy. The group's lives became such examples of piety and moderate regularity that their fellow students branded them "Methodists" in derision. Methodism stressed humble faith, abstinence, and hard work.

FIGURE 15.14
William Hogarth, *Gin Lane*, 1750.

Barred from preaching in the Anglican churches, Wesley rode horseback from one end of England to the other until well into his eighties, preaching the "glad tidings" of salvation in thousands of sermons in streets, fields, and anywhere else he could find even a small audience. He claimed "to lower religion to the level of the lowest people's capacities."

Among Catholics, similar movements—such as Jansenism in France and Italy, and Quietism in Spain—spread among elites and others. East European Jews had their own revivalist movement with the founding of the Hasidic sect in the 1740s. Hasidim (meaning "most pious") spread throughout Poland, rejecting formalism, stressing simplicity, and engaging in loud, joyful singing prayers. These religious movements revealed the power with which spiritual matters still influenced people in the West. Nevertheless, like the broader cultural forms of the time, religious revivals left the overall social order intact.

Foreshadowing Upheaval: The American Revolution

For most of the eighteenth century, neither wars, colonial rivalries, nor changes in country and city life upset the fundamental social and political stability of Western societies. In the last quarter of the eighteenth century, however, new forces erupted that would ultimately transform the West. The first of these disturbances occurred in Britain's thirteen North American colonies. This upheaval shifted the tide of events in North America and foreshadowed a far deeper and broader revolution that would strike at the heart of Europe itself.

INSULTS, INTERESTS, AND PRINCIPLES: THE SEEDS OF REVOLT

By the mid-eighteenth century, over 2 million people lived in the colonies. The seaboard cities in particular flourished, benefiting from a thriving commerce with Europe, Africa, and the West Indies. The colonists thought of themselves as British. Furthermore, the thirteen colonies in theory were part of Great Britain, governed in the same way and therefore subject to British trade regulations. In practice, however, the colonists often acted as they pleased, even if that meant quietly ignoring those regulations. They developed their own patterns of local government, manipulated British governors, and worked around British mercantilist policies.

Tensions between the island nation and these prospering colonies arose just after the Seven Years' War ended in 1763. Feeling *New commercial regulations and taxes* that they had helped defend the American colonists against the hostile French and Indians, the British expected the colonists to help pay off the huge debt incurred in the fighting. To tighten their control over the colonial empire for which Britain had just fought so long and hard, British officials enacted new commercial regulations and taxes. Perhaps the most irritating of these was the Stamp Act of 1765, which taxed printed documents such as newspapers, pamphlets, and wills.

The colonists reacted to the new policies with complaints, boycotts, protest meetings, outrage, and sometimes riots. Because colonists were not represented in Britain's Parliament, headlines in newspapers and pamphlets screamed, "No taxation without representation!" In their Stamp Act Congress of 1765, colonists announced that they were "entitled to all the inherent rights and liberties of his [the king's] natural born subjects within the kingdom of Great Britain." Local circumstances and the distance from Britain meant that "the only representatives of these colonies are persons chosen therein by themselves, and that no taxes ever have been, or can be constitutionally imposed on them, but by their respective legislatures." The British compromised, repealing most of the taxes, but many colonists were still not satisfied.

Figure 15.15 is a portrait of one of these dissatisfied colonists, Paul Revere (1735–1818), before he became a hero of the American Revolution. This neoclassical painting by John Singleton Copley (1738–1815), one of America's outstanding artists, shows the thirty-three-year-old Revere as a well-known, confident silversmith. Here he proudly holds one of his silver teapots; his engraving tools lie nearby on the table. This ambitious, up-and-coming merchant-craftsman created products that competed directly with similar items from England, and he rebelled against British efforts to tax and control American commerce.

Both sides translated their disagreements into ideological terms. American newspapers, propagandists, and political groups, echoing Enlightenment ideas, argued that violation of their fundamental rights justified a fight for independence. Most people in Britain stood against rebellion and for parliamentary sovereignty as a matter of principle. They argued that they were making only reasonable and minimal demands on the colonies.

In the end, each side felt backed into a corner. The notion of full independence gained appeal among the colonists. American political leaders who were critical of British policies organized the First Continental Congress in 1774, hoping to persuade Parliament to abandon its efforts to directly control colonial affairs. In response, King George III increased British armed forces in America, convinced that "blows must decide whether they are to be subject to the Country or Independent."

A War for Independence

The first "blows" were exchanged in 1775 between British troops and American militiamen in New England. The Second Continental Congress appointed George Washington (1732–1799) its military commander, setting the course for armed rebellion and independence. On July 4, 1776, that Congress issued the Declaration of Independence, written primarily by Thomas Jefferson (1743–1826) and based on the ideas of John Locke and other Enlightenment thinkers. Citing "self-evident" truths; "inalienable" natural rights such as "Life, Liberty, and the pursuit of Happiness"; and "a long train of abuses" to reduce the people under "absolute Despotism," the Declaration passionately justified rebellion.

Odds favored the stronger British forces, and at first they had the upper hand. Indeed, many British leaders viewed the rebel troops with disdain, one official calling the rebels a "rude rabble without a plan." Nevertheless, despite much internal division, an American victory at Saratoga in 1777 persuaded the French to help the Americans with money, ships, and troops against France's longtime enemy. The Dutch and Spanish eventually declared war on Britain, increasing the stakes for the British. Now British possessions in the West Indies, the Mediterranean, and perhaps even India hung in the balance. In 1781 the victory of the French fleet off Virginia forced a large British army to surrender at Yorktown. This indignity convinced the British that the effort to keep the American colonies was not worth the costs. After two years of negotiations, the combatants drew up the Treaty of Paris in

1783. Britain agreed to recognize American independence, and ceded to the United States the lands between the Mississippi River to the west, Canada to the north, and Spanish Florida to the south.

Creating the New Nation

By 1787 a new American constitution established a central government balanced by a separation of powers and strong states' rights. A Bill of Rights was soon enacted, protecting individual liberties and separating church and state. These principles, though lofty, did not apply to everyone. While the Declaration of Independence had proclaimed that "all men are created equal" as a "self-evident" truth, one-fifth of the people remained slaves, and only property owners and men could vote. Nevertheless, the new nation had instituted—to an unprecedented degree—popular control, personal freedom, and formal toleration.

Figure 15.15
John Singleton Copley, *Paul Revere*, 1768–1770.

TIMELINE: A CLOSER LOOK

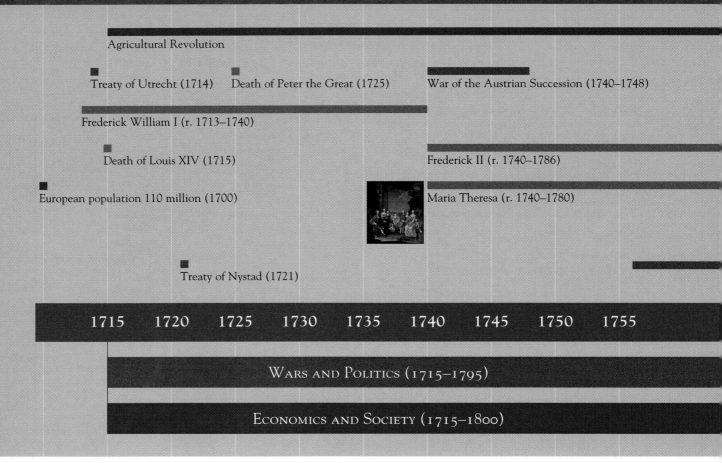

Agricultural Revolution

Treaty of Utrecht (1714) Death of Peter the Great (1725) War of the Austrian Succession (1740–1748)

Frederick William I (r. 1713–1740)

Death of Louis XIV (1715) Frederick II (r. 1740–1786)

European population 110 million (1700) Maria Theresa (r. 1740–1780)

Treaty of Nystad (1721)

| 1715 | 1720 | 1725 | 1730 | 1735 | 1740 | 1745 | 1750 | 1755 |

WARS AND POLITICS (1715–1795)

ECONOMICS AND SOCIETY (1715–1800)

Some historians deem the American rebellion a war for independence, while others call it a revolution. At the time, people throughout the West—not just in America and Great Britain—viewed the events as dramatic and significant. A growing body of European readers avidly followed the action in newspaper accounts. Many of these readers saw the American Revolution as a victory for Enlightenment ideas. The French in particular celebrated the Revolution as a triumph in their own competition with their British rivals. They did not realize at the time that the debts incurred by France and the ideas promoted by the American Revolution would soon come back to haunt the French monarchy.

War for independence or revolution?

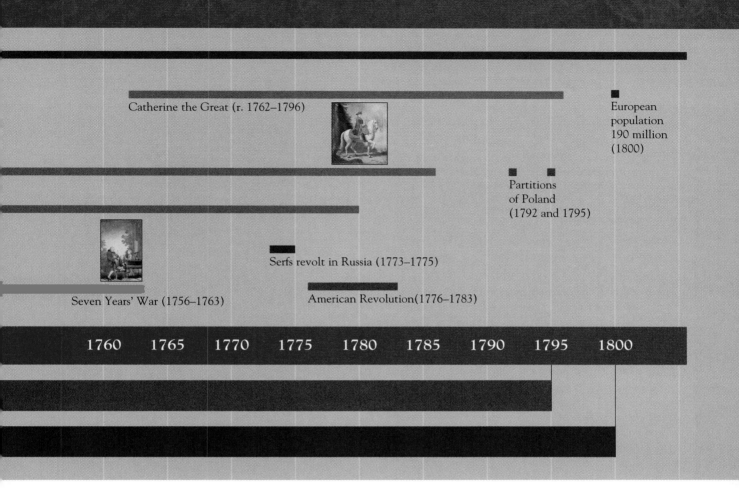

Catherine the Great (r. 1762–1796)

European population 190 million (1800)

Partitions of Poland (1792 and 1795)

Serfs revolt in Russia (1773–1775)

Seven Years' War (1756–1763)

American Revolution(1776–1783)

| 1760 | 1765 | 1770 | 1775 | 1780 | 1785 | 1790 | 1795 | 1800 |

Summary

On the surface, life between 1715 and 1789 seemed to change only incrementally for most westerners. The vast majority still lived in the countryside and worked the fields. Moreover, society and politics in the so-called Old Regime remained dominated by the aristocracy and, in most places, the monarchy. As in the seventeenth century, cultural forms still reflected elite tastes and the traditional values of commoners below them.

Below the surface, however, the West changed in crucial ways during this period. The political balance of power shifted as Russia and Prussia rose in the east while Britain gained prominence in the west. Success in the international arena often reflected how well central governments conducted their internal affairs. Some monarchs managed to dominate or work with the nobility, enact reforms, and even take on the trappings of "enlightened" rulers, while others—such as the French kings—failed in these ways. More important, mushrooming commerce, the agricultural revolution, and the spreading of cottage industry altered the ways by which millions of people earned a living, and generated enormous new wealth. Finally, across the Atlantic in Britain's North American colonies, the American Revolution posed a challenge to the status quo that the French would soon take up in a much more fundamental way. These developments, combined with the spread of Enlightenment ideas, mark the eighteenth century as a period in which westerners—knowingly or not—laid foundations for the great transformations to come.

REVIEW, ANALYZE, AND ANTICIPATE

REVIEW THE PREVIOUS CHAPTER

Chapter 13—"The Struggle for Survival and Sovereignty"—told the story of kings and nobles battling for power, the results of those struggles, and their impact on millions of people throughout the West. Chapter 14—"A New World of Reason and Reform"—shifted focus to the changing intellectual foundations of the West.

1. *In what ways was the eighteenth century a continuation of the struggle between monarchs and elites that had marked the seventeenth century?*

2. *Analyze how Enlightenment ideas—themselves stemming from the scientific revolution—affected Western society and especially politics during the eighteenth century.*

ANALYZE THIS CHAPTER

Chapter 15—"Competing for Power and Wealth"— examines the battles of Western powers over land, position, and commerce, as well as the economic and social changes affecting eighteenth-century life in the West.

1. *Which nations do you think were the biggest winners, and which the biggest losers in this period? How do you explain their varying fortunes?*

2. *How did eighteenth-century rulers try to shore up and justify their own powers and those of their central governments?*

3. *Analyze the benefits and costs of the growing commerce, the agricultural revolution, and cottage industry.*

4. *Why might this period be considered one of both growing prosperity and deepening social misery?*

5. *Delineate the differences between elite and popular culture during this period. How do you explain those differences?*

ANTICIPATE THE NEXT CHAPTER

Chapter 16—"Overturning the Political and Social Order"—will examine the great upheaval in France that shook and transformed the West.

1. *Why might the French monarchy have been particularly vulnerable to a revolution?*

2. *In what ways might the American Revolution—as a revolution and in its principles—have foreshadowed the political upheaval that would break out in France?*

BEYOND THE CLASSROOM

STATEBUILDING AND WAR

Anderson, M.S. *Europe in the Eighteenth Century, 1713–1783*, 3rd ed. London: Longman, 1987. A thorough survey of the period.

Clark, J.C.D. *English Society, 1688–1832*. Cambridge: Cambridge University Press, 1985. A major reinterpretation of political thought and behavior that emphasizes the role of religion in English political life.

Davis, Ralph. *The Rise of the Atlantic Economies*. Ithaca, NY: Cornell University Press, 1973. A survey of the early modern economic history of the countries on the Western fringe of Europe and their colonies in North and South America.

de Madariaga, Isabel. *Catherine the Great: A Short History*. New Haven, CT: Yale University Press, 1990. A solid, useful study.

Manning, Patrick. *Slavery and African Life: Occidental, Oriental and African Slave Trades*. Cambridge: Cambridge University Press, 1990. A wide-ranging study that demonstrates how the external slave trade affected African societies.

Ritter, Gerhard. *Frederick the Great*. Berkeley, CA: University of California Press, 1968. More of an extended essay than a standard biography, but useful.

Weigley, R.F. *The Age of Battles: The Quest for Decisive Warfare from Breitenfeld to Waterloo*. Bloomington: Indiana University Press. 1991. A study of the period between 1631 and 1815 when economic, social, and technological circumstances enabled governments to concentrate large forces in the field.

THE TWILIGHT OF MONARCHIES? THE QUESTION OF ENLIGHTENED ABSOLUTISM

Gagliardo, John G. *Enlightened Despotism*. Arlington Heights, IL: AHM Publishing Co., 1967. A respected examination of the topic in its European context.

Scott, H.M., ed. *Enlightened Despotism*. Ann Arbor, MI: University of Michigan Press, 1990. Essays by leading historians analyzing Europe's rulers and nobility.

CHANGES IN COUNTRY AND CITY LIFE

Blum, Jerome. *The End of the Old Order in Rural Europe*. Princeton, NJ: Princeton University Press, 1978. A comprehensive study of life in rural Europe from the early eighteenth to the mid-nineteenth century; especially good on the abolition of serfdom.

Chambers, J.D. and G.E. Mingay. *The Agricultural Revolution*. London: Batsord, 1966. Covers various aspects of the agricultural revolution such as enclosures and technological improvements, and relates agriculture to the socioeconomic life of the period.

Clarkson, Leslie A. *Proto-Industrialization: The First Phase of Industrialization?* London: Macmillan, 1985. Stresses the importance of cottage industry for the beginning of industrialization.

THE CULTURE OF THE ELITE: COMBINING THE OLD AND THE NEW

Black, Jeremy. *Eighteenth-Century Europe*. London: Macmillan, 1990. A thorough survey of the period.

Watt, Ian. *The Rise of the Novel*. Berkeley, CA: University of California Press, 1957. A study of the intellectual and social conditions that produced the novel in eighteenth-century England.

CULTURE FOR THE LOWER CLASSES

Burke, Peter. *Popular Culture in Early Modern Europe*. New York: Harper & Row, 1978. Surveys popular culture from the Renaissance to the French Revolution.

Muchembled, Robert. *Popular Culture and Elite Culture in France, 1400–1750*. Baton Rouge, LA: Louisiana State University Press, 1985. Examines popular culture and the means higher authorities used to destroy it.

FORESHADOWING UPHEAVAL: THE AMERICAN REVOLUTION

Countryman, Edward. *The American Revolution*. New York: Hill and Wang, 1985. A social history of the American Revolution.

Middlekauff, Robert. *The Glorious Cause: The American Revolution, 1763–1789*. New York: Oxford University Press, 1981. A narrative account of the Anglo-American conflict.

Storming the Bastille

On July 14, 1789, a crowd of Parisians stormed the Bastille, a castle-prison that stood as a symbol of all that was oppressive under the Old Regime. For most people, this event marked the beginning of the French Revolution.

CHAPTER 16

Overturning the Political and Social Order

The French Revolution and Napoleon, 1789–1815

France was beginning to stir. On October 17, 1787, Arthur Young, a British farmer and diarist traveling through France, described "a great ferment amongst all ranks of men, who are eager for some change, without knowing what to look to, or to hope for." People whom Young talked with in Paris concluded that "they are on the eve of some great revolution in the government."

Two years later, the French Revolution brought the French monarchy to its knees. During the following ten years, revolutionaries eliminated the monarchy, overturned the social system of France's Old Regime, and transformed France's institutions. Moreover, the Revolution, with its compelling banner of "Liberty, Equality, Fraternity," proved so potent that its impact spread far beyond the borders of France. It soon spawned wars that engulfed most of Europe for more than two decades. Riding the twin forces of revolutionary turmoil and war, one individual—Napoleon Bonaparte—would rise to a legendary pinnacle of power. He would rule over a new French Empire and a nearly conquered continent. In the process, Napoleon spread the ideals of the French Revolution well beyond France. This tide of change, turmoil, and war mounted by the French Revolution and Napoleon would eventually subside, but for France—and for much of Western civilization—the course of history had shifted permanently.

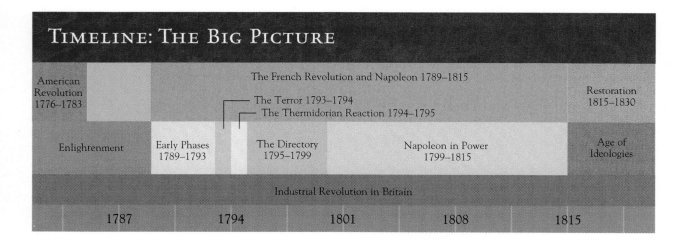

TIMELINE: THE BIG PICTURE

American Revolution 1776–1783		The French Revolution and Napoleon 1789–1815		Restoration 1815–1830

The Terror 1793–1794
The Thermidorian Reaction 1794–1795

| Enlightenment | Early Phases 1789–1793 | The Directory 1795–1799 | Napoleon in Power 1799–1815 | Age of Ideologies |

Industrial Revolution in Britain

| 1787 | 1794 | 1801 | 1808 | 1815 |

"A Great Ferment": Trouble Brewing in France

Arthur Young recognized discontent percolating among the French population, but there was good reason for people everywhere to assume that any crises would pass without a fundamental change in the monarchy or social order. The French monarchy had remained intact for centuries. Both Louis XVI and his predecessor, Louis XV, ruled over the leading nation on the Continent—a country more populous, wealthy, and educated than ever. Although neither king could claim much popularity, Louis XVI could at least bask in the glory of supporting the American revolutionaries in their victory over the British, France's chief competitor.

Then what caused the "great ferment" in France described by our British traveler? Below the surface bubbled growing complaints within France's social orders. Members of the aristocracy and middle classes, many influenced by the ideas of the Enlightenment, wanted more rights and power from the monarchy. Peasants suffered hardships that could, as in the past, create disorder and uprisings. However, the immediate, visible problem came from a conflict over France's finances.

THE FINANCIAL CRISIS WEAKENS THE MONARCHY

When Louis XVI ascended the throne in 1774, he inherited a large—and constantly growing—national debt. Much of that debt had been incurred financing wars and maintaining the military (see Chapter 15).

Yet this debt should not have broken a nation as rich as France. Great Britain and the Netherlands had higher per-capita debts than France, but these countries also boasted taxation systems and banks to support their *The taxation system* debts. France lacked an adequate banking system, and most of the national debt was short term and privately held. Moreover, France's taxation system offered little help. The French nobility, clergy, and much of the bourgeoisie controlled the bulk of France's wealth and had long been exempt from most taxes. Nearly all direct taxes fell on the struggling peasantry. There was no consistent set of rules or method for collecting taxes throughout the country, and private tax collectors diverted much revenue from the treasury into their own pockets. Unless something was done, royal bankruptcy loomed ahead.

To stave off financial ruin, Louis XVI appointed the Physiocrat Jacques Turgot (1727–1781), a friend of Voltaire, as his minister of finance in 1774. Turgot proposed to abolish guilds, eliminate *Reform efforts* restriction on the commerce in grain, institute a small new tax on landowners, and cut down on expenses at court. However, people who benefited from the old system soon engineered his dismissal, and his modest reform measures were rescinded. A succession of ministers tried all kinds of temporary solutions, but to no avail. Costs incurred to support the Americans in their war of independence against England made matters worse. Now interest payments on the debt ate up half of all government expenditures. Bankers began refusing to lend the government money.

Desperate, Louis called an Assembly of Notables in 1787 and pleaded with these selected nobles, clergy, and officials to consent to new taxes and financial reforms. Still they refused, as did the judges (all members of the nobility) in the *parlement*, or law court, of Paris when Louis turned to them. Instead, leading nobles and officials demanded a meeting of an old representative institution, the Estates General. They fully expected to control these proceedings and thereby assert their own interests. With bankruptcy imminent and nowhere else to turn for help, the king gave in. No one knew it at the time, but Louis' decision set the stage for turning France's financial crisis into a political and social movement of epic proportions.

THE UNDERLYING CAUSES OF THE REVOLUTION

Louis' financial woes were just the most visible part of France's problems. When these tensions combined with the conflicts tugging at the fabric of French society, a dangerous blend resulted. One of the most troubling conflicts stemmed from the relationship between the monarchy and the nobility. For centuries, the French nobility, less than 2 percent of the population, had been the foundation on which the monarchy established its rule. However, the nobility was also the monarchy's chief rival for power, and it had grown increasingly assertive during the eighteenth century (see Chapter 15). Through institutions such as the *parlements* that they controlled, nobles resisted ministerial efforts to tax them. More and more, nobles claimed to be protecting their rights as well as France itself from "ministerial despotism." So when the monarchy turned to this group for financial help, the nobles refused for two reasons. First, they wanted to protect their own financial interests. Second, they used the crisis to assert their independence. Indeed, they argued that they represented the nation. They established a price for their cooperation: a greater share of power. Understandably, France's kings refused to pay that price. Thus, when the Assembly of Notables turned a deaf ear to Louis' pleas in 1787 and instead demanded a meeting of the Estates General, the king faced a financial crisis that was linked to a virtual revolt of his own nobility.

Revolt of the nobility

Louis might have thought he could find allies within the middle class in his standoff with the nobility. After all, French and other European kings had occasionally turned to wealthy members of this class for support in the past. Nevertheless, as events would prove

Middle class demands

in the tumultuous months of 1789, the middle class had changed—it now nursed its own set of grievances. This growing social sector—having almost tripled during the century to some 9 percent of the population—had benefited greatly from France's general prosperity and population boom after 1715. Many talented, wealthy, and ambitious members of the middle class managed to gain the high offices, titles, and privileges enjoyed by the nobility. Others rubbed shoulders and shared ideas with the nobility in salons and did their best to copy the nobles' style of life. Moreover, most had found ways to avoid paying heavy taxes.

However, numerous members of the bourgeoisie—particularly younger administrators, lawyers, journalists, and intellectuals—had encountered frustrating barriers to the offices and prestige enjoyed by the nobility. They also had grown impatient with the monarchy's failure to enact reforms that would benefit them specifically. By 1789, many applauded broad attacks on the privileged orders and the status quo. An example of such an attack was Abbé Emmanuel-Joseph Sieyès' widely circulated pamphlet *What Is the Third Estate?* According to Sieyès, "If the privileged order should be abolished, the nation would be nothing less, but something more." The sorts of reforms that these middle-class critics had in mind were no more palatable to the monarchy than those of the nobility.

People from both the middle class and the nobility had begun expressing ideas and using highly charged political terms that profoundly threatened the monarchy. In the decades before 1789, salon meetings and new publications had spread key ideas of the Enlightenment to an increasingly literate public, particularly the aristocratic and middle-class elite in Paris and other French cities (see Chapter 14). These ideas emphasized the validity of reason and natural rights and questioned long-established institutions. They also undermined notions of the divine rights of kings and traditional ways of life—all while intensifying expectations of rapid reforms. In addition, terms such as "nation," "citizen," and "general will" had increasingly cropped up in the political discourse and reflected a growing sense that politics should include more than the concerns of the monarch and a tiny elite. So, when nobles asserted their own interests against the king, they often used language and ideas that attacked monarchical

Enlightenment ideas and language

absolutists as unjustified tyrants and that accused the king's minister of "despotism." Middle-class men and women shared these sentiments and later extended them to demands for legal equality.

Thus, given all the resentments brewing among the nobility and the middle class, Louis and his often unpopular ministers risked much once they exposed themselves to discussions of reform within the Estates General. Three other developments—all beyond the powers of the king, nobility, and middle class—added an underlying sense of disappointment, desperation, and disorder among the French people in these decades.

First, a gap opened between rosy expectations and frightening realities. Before 1770, France had enjoyed a long period of prosperity. *Disappointed expectations* This growing wealth engendered a sense of rising expectations—that economically things would keep getting better and better. After 1770, a series of economic depressions struck, turning these high expectations into bitter disappointment and frustration. Worse, in 1788 the countryside suffered unusually bad harvests. In May and July of that year, hailstorms wiped out crops throughout France. Drought and then the most severe winter in decades followed. The price of bread soared, and with it came hunger, desperation, and even starvation. Droves of peasants crowded into the cities in search of jobs and help, but the agricultural depression had already spread there and had thrown thousands of artisans and laborers out of work. In the spring of 1789, peasants and urban poor looking for food turned to violence in France's cities and villages. Women led groups demanding grain and lower prices for flour. Desperate people attacked bakeries and stores of grain wherever they could find them. Arthur Young wrote, "the want of bread is terrible: accounts arrive every moment from the provinces of riots and disturbances, and calling in the military, to preserve the peace of the markets." The populace angrily blamed governmental figures and "parasitical agents" of the Old Regime for their plight.

By 1789, many pamphlets and cartoons portraying the connection between suffering and France's privileged orders circulated throughout France. Figure 16.1 is an apt example of these publications. This illustration shows the thin "common man," who represents the vast majority of the people, carrying three heavy figures from the privileged classes on his back. In front, wielding a whip and claiming feudal rights, is an aristocrat or perhaps the king himself. Just above him is a clergyman in robes, brandishing papers representing the threat of an inquisition and clerical privileges. In back rides a judge with a list of the jealously guarded rights of the noble-controlled *parlements*. The illustration depicts the common man as a naked beast kept under control by reins, chains, and a blindfold. He crawls pitifully across barren fields, bleeding from the hands, knees, and loins, while his tormentors spur him on.

The second unsettling development came with the increasing demands for political participation and governmental reform throughout *Demands for political participation* the West in the years before 1789. These movements, arising in various countries, were led by ambitious elites. In Poland, agitation for independence from Russian influence surfaced between 1772 and 1792. Across the Atlantic, what started as a tax revolt in Britain's North American colonies turned into the American Revolution and war for independence that directly involved French aristocrats and common sol-

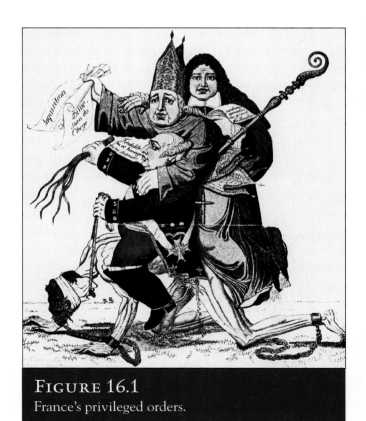

FIGURE 16.1
France's privileged orders.

diers alike, and led to government without a king (see Chapter 15). In the Dutch Republic, demands for reform in the 1780s erupted into open revolt in 1787. In the Austrian Netherlands (Belgium and Luxembourg), elites rose against the reforms initiated by Emperor Joseph II in 1787. Well-informed French elites, keeping abreast of these disturbances, began to surmise that they, too, might successfully challenge the political status quo.

The economic hardship and political uprisings across Europe were damaging enough. A third problem—the French people's disrespect for their own king—only made matters worse.

Unpopular kings For much of the eighteenth century, France had been ruled by the unremarkable, unpopular, and long-lived King Louis XV. Unlike some of his European counterparts, neither he nor his successor, Louis XVI, managed to forge an effective alliance with the nobility or consistently assert their authority over it. Nor did they succeed in enacting reforms or even give the impression of being "enlightened" monarchs. Louis XVI had little particular taste or talent for rule, and his unpopular Austrian wife, Queen Marie Antoinette, increasingly drew fire for her supposed extravagance and indifference to those below her. According to a widely circulated story, she dismissed reports that the poor could not buy bread with the phrase, "Let them eat cake!" Though the story was untrue, it reflected the growing anger against the king and queen.

Desperate to stave off the immediate threat of bankruptcy, the relatively weak Louis XVI looked for support. Instead of able allies, he found a jealous nobility, a disgruntled middle class, a bitter and frustrated peasantry, and an urban poor made desperate by hunger.

THE "TENNIS COURT OATH"

In this ominous atmosphere, Louis XVI summoned the Estates General in 1788. This representative body, which had not met since 1614, was divided into France's three traditional orders,

The Estates General or estates: the first estate, the clergy, owned over 10 percent of France's best land; the second estate, the nobility, owned more than 20 percent of the land; and the third estate, the so-called commoners, included the bourgeoisie, the peasantry, and the urban populace. During the early months of

1789, elections of representatives to the Estates General were held. All men who had reached the age of twenty-five and paid taxes could vote. In thousands of meetings to draw up lists of grievances to present to the king, people found their political voices and connected their dissatisfactions with inflating expectations of reform. Hundreds of pamphlets appeared and public debate spread widely. Each of the three estates elected their own representatives. Because the third estate made up more than nine-tenths of the total population, Louis XVI agreed to grant it as many seats as the other two estates combined. However, by tradition, the three estates sat separately, and each group had one vote.

In April 1789, delegates began streaming into Versailles armed only with *cahiers*, or the lists of grievances from all classes of people, that had been called for by the king. Of the 600 representatives of the third estate, not one came from the peasantry. Except for a handful of liberal clergy and nobles elected to the third estate, these delegates—mostly ambitious lawyers, petty officials, administrators, and other professionals—were all members of the bourgeoisie. They fully expected to solve the financial crisis quickly and then move on to addressing the long lists of complaints that they had been accumulating for years. Most bourgeois representatives, like many liberal nobles, wanted to create a constitutional government with a national assembly that would meet regularly to pass taxes and laws.

After religious services and a solemn procession in Paris, the delegates met in Versailles on May 5. Immediately they debated the voting system. The two privileged estates demanded that, according to custom, the three estates meet separately and vote by order—that is, each estate cast one vote. This procedure would place power squarely in the hands of the nobility, which controlled most of the first estate as well as its own order. The third estate demanded that all the orders meet jointly and that delegates vote by head. This method would favor the third estate, for not only did this order boast as many members as the other two combined, but a number of liberal clergy and nobles in the first and second estates sympathized with the reforms called for by the third estate. All sides realized that the outcome of this voting issue would be decisive.

The delegates haggled for six weeks. Louis waffled from one side to the other. Finally the third estate, backed by some clergy from the first estate, took action and declared itself the National Assembly of

The National Assembly

France on June 17 and invited the other two estates to join it in enacting legislation. Three days later, when the third estate deputies arrived at their meeting hall, they found it locked. Adjourning to a nearby building that served as an indoor tennis court, they took the "Tennis Court Oath," vowing not to disband until France had a constitution.

Figure 16.2 dramatizes and glorifies this act of defiance. The painting is usually attributed to Jacques-Louis David (1748–1825), a talented contemporary painter and active supporter of the Revolution. In the center of the picture, the presiding officer Jean-Sylvain Bailly (1736–1793) (soon to become mayor of Paris), raises his arm in a pledge and reads the oath aloud. Below him, a robed member of the clergy represents the first estate, and a finely dressed noble represents the second estate. In the middle, a figure in a black suit represents the third estate. All three figures join, symbolizing the transformation of the meeting into the newly formed National Assembly. Around these figures, representatives also take the oath. From above, light streams through billowing curtains as if blessing the heroic activities below, and members of the populace approvingly watch the scene.

FIGURE 16.2
Jacques-Louis David, *The Tennis Court Oath.*

On June 23 the king met with the three estates in a royal session. He offered many reforms but also commanded the estates to meet separately and vote by order. Then the king, his ministers, and members of the first two estates regally filed out. The third estate representatives, however, defiantly remained seated. When the royal master of ceremonies returned to remind them of the king's orders, Count Mirabeau (1749–1791), a liberal nobleman elected by the third estate, jumped to his feet. "Go and tell those who sent you," he shouted, "that we are here by the will of the people and will not leave this place except at the point of the bayonet!" When the startled courtier dutifully repeated these words to his master, Louis XVI, with characteristic weakness, replied, "They mean to stay. Well, damn it, let them stay." A few days later, the king reversed himself and ordered the three estates to meet jointly and vote by head. The third estate had won the first round.

STORMING THE BASTILLE

The monarchy might have been able to reassert control had not the new National Assembly received unexpected support from two sources: the Parisian populace and the French peasantry. Both groups had been suffering from the unusually poor economic conditions initiated by bad harvests. Revolutionary events raised expectations in hard times, making these people in the city and countryside particularly volatile. The first important disturbances broke out in Paris, whose population of 600,000 made it one of the largest cities in Europe. In early July, rumors that the king was calling the professional troops of the frontier garrison to Versailles raced through the streets of Paris. Alarmed, residents concluded that the king meant to use force against them. Then Louis dismissed his popular finance minister, Jacques Necker (1732–1804). This move seemed to confirm the fears of the third estate, who saw Necker as an ally.

At this critical juncture, the common people of Paris acted on their own. On July 14 riotous crowds of men and women searching for arms marched on the Bastille, a gloomy old fortress-prison in a working-class quarter. Few people were actually in the weakly guarded Bastille, but it symbolized the old order. Many died in the confused battle. With the help of mutinous troops, however, the crowd eventually took the Bastille, hacked its governor to death, and paraded around Paris with his head on a pike. "This glorious day must amaze our enemies, and finally usher in for us the triumph of justice and liberty," proclaimed a Paris newspaper.

The scene on page 534, one of many paintings and drawings made to celebrate this event, reveals the importance of this famous battle. The Bastille is portrayed as a massive castle that, against all odds, has come under attack by commoners and troops who have rallied to the side of the people. Only a few cannon seem necessary, for the people supposedly have heroic revolutionary spirit and numbers enough to surge forward and somehow storm across the bridge toward the Bastille entrance. The picture poignantly captures the symbolism of the act—the Bastille, representing the old feudal regime of the past, falls because of corruption within and the heroic power of an outraged people fighting under the revolutionary banner of Liberty, Equality, and Fraternity. In fact, this show of force by the artisans, shop owners, and laborers of Paris stayed the king's hand and sparked uprisings in other cities across France. Under pressure, royal authority began to crumble.

Uprisings in the countryside echoed events in Paris. That July and August, peasants throughout France revolted against their lords. Burning tax rolls, the peasantry attacked manors, reoccupied enclosed lands, and rejected the traditional rights of noble landowners—dues on land, flour mills, wine presses, and law courts, and the tithes (taxes) landlords charged their tenants. These revolts intensified with the spreading of unfounded rumors that bands of brigands, perhaps assembled by nobles, were on the loose in the countryside. Panicked by this "Great Fear," many nobles—including one of the king's brothers—fled France and became known as the *émigrés* (exiles).

Peasant revolts

The "Great Fear"

THE END OF THE OLD ORDER

Now the nobility as well as the monarchy was in retreat. The National Assembly—dominated by the middle-class deputies from the third estate but now including many deputies from the clergy and nobility—tried to pacify the aroused peasantry. On August 4, during a night session of the National Assembly, one nobleman after another stood up and renounced his traditional rights and privileges in an effort to make the best of a bad situation. A leader of the Assembly hailed the "end of feudalism." Quickly the National Assembly decreed the end of serfdom, traditional dues owed to landlords, special taxation rights, and privileged access to official posts. The peasantry seemed pacified for the time being.

Success spurred the National Assembly to take further steps. The most important of these actions occurred on August 26, when the Assembly proclaimed the Declaration of Rights of Man and Citizen. Enlightenment ideas and phrases similar to those in the American Declaration of Independence filled this document. "Men are born and remain free and equal in rights," it stated. The natural rights included "liberty, property, security, and resistance to oppression." Sovereignty—supreme authority—rested with the nation as a whole, not the monarchy. Enacted laws should express the "general will"—a term and idea made popular by Jean-Jacques Rousseau (see Chapter 14). The document proclaimed freedom of opinion "even in religion," freedom of the press, and freedom from arbitrary arrest. In 1791, this spirit would lead to the liberation of France's Jews from old legal disabilities.

Declaration of Rights of Man and Citizen

Some of these rights, such as freedom of the press, applied to women as well as men, but only men gained the full measure of new social and political rights. In the months and years that followed, many women objected to this limitation. Organizing groups and writing petitions and pamphlets, these women demanded to be included. In 1791, Olympe de Gouges (1748–1793), a writer and strong supporter of the Revolution, wrote one of the best-known and more challenging pamphlets, the *Declaration of the Rights of Women*. She argued that women should have the same political and social rights as men: "The only limits on the exercise of the natural rights of woman are perpetual male tyranny; these limits are to be reformed by the laws of nature and reason." Some members of the government, such as the marquis de Condorcet (1743–1794) voiced similar demands. However, their arguments fell on deaf ears.

Despite this rising tide of defiance, Louis refused to sign the August decrees. Instead, he once more assembled troops around Versailles and Paris. In answer to this new threat of force, on October 5 and 6 a huge crowd of Parisian women, already infuriated by high bread prices and food shortages, marched eleven miles through the rain to Versailles. The contemporary print shown in Figure 16.3 depicts the marchers, armed with picks, axes, swords, and cannon. With the exception of the well-dressed, reluctant figure at the left, their faces express a striking determination and authority. (Notice the woman riding in the cart with the cannon and the woman at the front to the far right).

March to Versailles

At Versailles, the marchers surrounded the palace. With the help of members of the recently formed National Guard—units of armed civilians under Lafayette—they forced the king and his family to accompany them back to Paris, bringing him closer to the people and away from the protected isolation of Versailles and the king's aristocratic advisors. As the carriage bearing the royal family rolled toward the capital, where the royal family would be virtually imprisoned in the Tuileries Palace, the surrounding crowd of women and men shouted jubilantly, "We have the baker [the king], the baker's wife, and the little cook boy! Now we shall have bread!" While this image of women taking political action into their own hands made them heroines of the Revolution in some eyes, others would nervously look back on the women's behavior as something inappropriate and even frightening. Most men were not ready to accept such a change in women's traditional roles.

A few days later, the National Assembly moved its sessions to Paris. The third estate, building on the anger and hunger of the peasantry and the urban poor, had triumphed. The old order had disintegrated.

The Constitutional Monarchy: Establishing a New Order

Flushed with success, the National Assembly now turned to the task of transforming French institutions. Guiding principles were represented by the revolutionary banner "Liberty, Equality, and Fraternity." At that time, the idea of liberty meant freedom from arbitrary authority and freedom of speech, press, conscience, assembly, and profession. Equality meant equal treatment under the law and equality of economic opportunity—at least for men. Fraternity meant comradeship as citizens of the nation. During the next two years, the Assembly passed a series of sweeping reforms that altered almost all aspects of life in France.

Liberty, Equality, Fraternity

The central government, now based on national sovereignty, was transformed into what amounted to a constitutional monarchy. The National Assembly served as its legislature, and the king (still an important symbol of authority for many) remained its chief executive officer. Because only tax-paying males could vote and win election to office, the bourgeoisie firmly held the reins of power. For the time being, the governance of France was decentralized. To undermine old loyalties and the power of the provincial nobility, the National Assembly created eighty-three newly named departments, each almost equal in size and administered by locally elected assemblies and officials (Maps 16.1 and 16.2). Similarly, the National Assem-

Constitutional monarchy

FIGURE 16.3
Parisian women march to Versailles.

bly took France's judicial system out of the hands of the nobility and clergy. It created new civil and criminal courts, with elected judges. France's complex, unequal system of taxation was also swept away, replaced by uniform taxes on land and the profits of trade and industry.

The new government linked reform of the Catholic Church with the financial problems it faced. Repudiating France's debt was out of the question since part of it was owed to members of the bourgeoisie. To pay for its expenditures, the National Assembly issued what amounted to paper money called *assignats*. To back up the *assignats*, pay off the debt, and at the same time bring the church under governmental control, government officials confiscated and sold church property.

This seizure of property constituted a major step toward the nationalization of the church. Next the As-

sembly dissolved all convents and monasteries and prohibited the taking of religious vows. People would elect the clergy, including non-Roman Catholics, and the state would pay their salaries. These measures were incorporated in the Civil Constitution of the Clergy, to which all members of the clergy were required to take an oath of allegiance in order to perform their functions and draw their salaries. This last step proved too much for many religious officials, for it threatened the very independence of the clergy. Pope Pius VI called the oath of allegiance "the poisoned fountainhead and source of all errors." Approximately half the clergy of France, including nearly all the bishops, refused to take the oath. This defection of the "nonjuring clergy" created a long-lasting division among France's Catholic population. Many, especially rural women, fought against this disturbance of their

Civil Constitution of the Clergy

THINKING ABOUT GEOGRAPHY

MAPS 16.1 AND 16.2   *Reorganizing France in 1789*

These maps show France's historic provinces, each with its own political identity, and the nation's revolutionary departments after 1789. ◙ **Notice** the different sizes of the old provinces and the almost equal size of the new departments. ◙ **Notice** that the historic names of the provinces have been eliminated, and most of the new departments are named for geographical features (mountains, such as the Alps; rivers, such as the Seine). **Consider** why France's Assembly reorganized the nation in this way.

religious life, vowing to defend their faith "with the last drop" of blood. The Revolution would lose the support of many French citizens who felt loyal to the old church and their local priests.

THE KING DISCREDITED

Louis XVI must have bitterly resented these changes, for they diluted his power and put Paris under the control of his former subjects. Nonetheless, he managed to make things even worse for himself. On June 20, 1791, the royal family, in disguise, escaped from Paris and headed by coach to France's eastern frontier, where Louis hoped to find supporters and perhaps reverse the tide of events. Unfortunately for him and his family, a postmaster recognized them just before they could reach safety. Officials arrested the royal family in Varennes and returned them to Paris. To save face, the government concocted a thin story about the royal family being kidnapped, but in many eyes the king and queen had now become traitors.

Flight of the royal family

In October 1791, the National Assembly gave way to the Legislative Assembly, with all new representatives elected under the new rules. In only two years, and with relatively little bloodshed, France had been made over. A written constitution ruled supreme over the diminished monarchy. The church lost its independence from the state. The nobility forfeited its special rights and privileges. Men gained individual rights and liberties and legal equality. Though excluded by the reformers, women would nevertheless continue to voice demands for political and social rights and play important roles as the Revolution evolved. France now boasted a more democratic electoral system than England or the United States. Events had already gone well beyond anything our British traveler, Arthur Young, might have imagined two years earlier.

REACTIONS OUTSIDE FRANCE

Outside France, writers and reformers in Europe and the United States hailed the French Revolution or the principles underlying it. In elegant salons, elites spiritedly discussed these dramatic events, and in newspapers and pamphlets, writers dissected and debated their meaning. Supporters established societies in Britain and in states along France's eastern borders. Some activists, such as the American writer Tom Paine, traveled to Paris to participate directly. In Britain, Charles Fox, a leader of the Whigs, called the Revolution "much the greatest event that ever happened, and much the best." Others argued against the French Revolution. The most famous attack was launched by Edmund Burke in his *Reflections on the Revolution in France* (1790). This British statesman argued that France moved too quickly in the name of abstract notions of natural rights and justice. As a result, revolutionaries replaced a despotic monarchy with anarchy. In his view, societies should evolve slowly, drawing reforms from the long historical experience of a national culture. Good government came from good habits. Reforms worked well when based on a nation's best traditions.

Most governments opposed the Revolution when they realized the threat it posed to their own security. If a revolution could rise in France, end aristocratic privileges, and undermine the monarchy, the same might happen elsewhere. Officials welcomed and listened to the aristocratic émigrés who fled France. They suppressed pro-revolutionary groups within their borders. Within a few years, most states joined coalitions to fight against the revolutionary armies.

To the Radical Republic and Back

The new government, launched with such optimism in October 1791, lasted less than a year. Up to that point, the bourgeoisie and the peasants had been the primary beneficiaries of the Revolution. The bourgeoisie had gained political control over the country and social mobility. The peasantry had won freedom from feudal obligations. To the many peasant landowners who owned their land before the Revolution were now added others who had seized the lands of émigré nobles or had purchased confiscated church lands (though many of these lands went to middle-class buyers).

However, other groups remained quite dissatisfied. The royal family and much of the aristocracy and high clergy yearned for the restoration of their traditional positions. On the other hand, many Parisians urged a more radical approach to the Revolution.

These shopkeepers, artisans, bakers, innkeepers, and workers had won little beyond theoretical rights and legal equality. Those who owned no property still could not vote, yet they had supplied much of the physical force and anger that had saved the third estate and made the reforms possible. Increasingly these men and women formed organizations, held meetings, and intently discussed the numerous pamphlets, petitions, and newspapers printed daily in Paris. Some of these clubs became egalitarian meeting places for women and men; others such as the Society of Revolutionary Republican Women insisted that women should participate more fully in the Revolution. Many of the most politically active came to be known as the *sans-culottes* because they wore long pants instead of the fashionable knee breeches of the elites. A pamphlet described a *sans-culotte* as "a man who has no mansions, no lackeys to wait on him, and who lives quite simply. . . . He is useful, because he knows how to plough a field, handle a forge, a saw, or a file, how to cover a roof or how to make shoes and to shed his blood to the last drop to save the Republic." Typically the *sans-culottes* carried pikes and addressed people as "Citizen" or "Citizenesse." Eventually they and their supporters gained control over the municipal government of Paris—the Commune.

Sans-culottes

Leadership for this urban populace fell into the hands of radical members of the bourgeoisie, who allied themselves with the *sans-culottes* and favored overthrow of the monarchy and extension of the Revolution. Well organized and ably led, these radicals came together in numerous clubs that formed to debate and plan political matters. The Jacobin Club, which had hundreds of affiliated clubs outside of Paris, became the most important of these political organizations. Its membership included more than 200 deputies, and over time, militant radicals gained strength within the organization.

The Jacobin Club

◊ WAR AND THE BREAKDOWN OF ORDER

Events—particularly the rumors of war that had begun circulating throughout France—soon played into the hands of the Parisian radicals. The monarchs of Austria and Prussia, fearing the spread of revolutionary ideas to their own lands and urged on by French émigrés, began to make threatening moves and to issue meddlesome warnings to the French revolutionaries. In France, many groups welcomed the prospect of war, though for different reasons. The royal family and its supporters believed a French victory would enhance the prestige and power of the throne; even a French defeat could help by restoring the Old Regime and royal power. Radicals, who wanted to turn France into a republic, believed that war would expose the inefficiency and disloyalty of the king and topple the monarchy.

The war that broke out in April 1792, became the first of a series of conflicts that would span twenty-three years and ultimately embroil most of the Western world. At first, inflation, food shortages, and breakdowns of order hampered France's war effort. The French armies suffered from lack of experienced leadership, since nearly all the high-ranking officers were members of the nobility and had either fled or been deposed. The Austrian and Prussian armies badly defeated the French and advanced toward Paris. Panic broke out in the city. "Everywhere you hear the cry that the king is betraying us, the generals are betraying us, that nobody is to be trusted . . . that Paris will be taken," exclaimed an observer. When the Prussian commander, the duke of Brunswick, announced that he would deliver the royal family "from their captivity," French radicals rightly accused Louis XVI and Marie Antoinette of being in treasonable communication with the enemy. On August 10, local leaders in Paris organized a huge Parisian crowd of men and women who attacked the king's palace. The royal family fled for their lives to the Legislative Assembly. The invading crowd wrecked the interior of the palace and slaughtered hundreds of the king's guards. The Legislative Assembly suspended and imprisoned the hapless Louis XVI. Under pressure from the people of Paris, it called elections—this time with almost all men enjoying the right to vote—for a National Convention to draw up a new, more radical constitution.

Meanwhile, one of the Jacobin leaders, Georges-Jacques Danton (1759–1794), used his great skills as an orator and organizer to gather recruits for the army and rush them to the front. As the recruits prepared to leave Paris to meet the invading Prussians, rumors—spurred by the propaganda of radical journalists like Jean-Paul Marat (1743–1793)—spread that reactionary clergy and nobles planned to murder their wives and children. Frightened and enraged people began murdering members of the nonjuring clergy (who would not swear allegiance to the new order) and nobles being held in the prisons of Paris. During

Panic and massacres

the first 3 weeks of September 1792, more than a thousand fell victim to these massacres.

In the elections for the National Convention, held amid this hysteria, republicans—favoring elimination of the monarchy altogether and the creation of a French republic—won a sweeping victory. Most of the conservative elements fearfully stayed away from the polls. This Convention would rule France for the next three years, taking the Revolution down a new, more radical road.

National Convention

Radical Republicans Struggle for Power

The struggle for political dominance among the different Jacobin factions intensified after the election. The Girondins, so called because many of their leaders came from the vicinity of Bordeaux in the department of the Gironde, had once been the most powerful and radical faction of the Legislative Assembly. Because they had sat on the speaker's left, they had come to be known as "the Left." In the new National Convention the Girondins found themselves on the Right as the more conservative faction. Now the Left consisted mostly of members of the Jacobin political club from Paris. These Jacobins came to be called "the Mountain," because they occupied the highest seats in the convention hall.

Girondins and Jacobins

On September 22, 1792, the National Convention declared France a republic. The government then disposed of the king, who had squandered most of his support since his flight to Varennes in 1791. The Convention tried Louis, and found him guilty of treasonable communication with the enemy. An extended debate ensued over whether to execute the king, with most of the Girondins opposed and the Mountain in favor. On January 21, 1793, the Convention voted by a narrow margin to execute Louis.

The Republic

Figure 16.4 depicts the scene of Louis' execution. An eyewitness described how the executioners "dragged him under the axe of the guillotine, which with one stroke severed his head from his body." The revolutionary government adopted the newly invented guillotine as its instrument of choice because it considered the device more efficient and therefore humane than other methods of execution, such as hanging and the axe. Here an executioner holds up the

Execution of the king

head of the king for the troops and crowd to view. An observer reported that a few seconds later, "cries of 'Vive la Républic' [long live the Republic] were heard . . . and in less than ten minutes this cry, a thousand times repeated, became the universal shout of the multitude, and every hat was in the air." The troops, with their backs to the crowd, are there to witness what is presented as a patriotic event. While other executions would not have the same significance or draw the same crowds, this scene would be repeated thousands of times over the next two years. Beheadings not only served as affirmations of revolutionary justice, they also provided entertainment—people often rented chairs and purchased food, drinks, and souvenirs, including miniature guillotines. Those who could not attend might purchase widely sold prints such as the one pictured.

Ten months later the queen, Marie Antoinette, followed Louis XVI to the guillotine. These executions sent a shudder of horror through the royal courts of Europe, as did the new French army recruits' surprising success against the Austrian and Prussian coalition. The hastily assembled revolutionary armies, swelling with numbers and enthusiasm, had checked the advancing Austrian and Prussian armies at Valmy in September 1792. France now went on the offensive. Alarmed, Britain, the Dutch Netherlands, Spain, Portugal, Sardinia, and Naples joined Austria and Prussia in a great coalition against France. This new external threat was compounded by internal threats to the revolutionary government. The peasants of the Vendée region in western France, stirred up by the nonjuring clergy and others, rebelled against the republican government. "We want our king, our priests and the Old Regime," cried the rebels. The uprising spread until some sixty of the eighty-three departments suffered revolts. Lyons, France's second largest city, rose against the government in May. Toulon, the chief French naval base on the Mediterranean, invited in the British fleet to help in the fight against France's radical government. All-too-real enemies outside and within France's borders surged forward to fight against the Revolution.

Internal and external enemies

The Terror

Faced with a seemingly inevitable demise of their cause and threatened by radical demands from the *sans-culottes*, the leaders of the Mountain decided to take drastic action. For support they turned to the

Paris Commune, as the city government was called, which radicals and the *sans-culottes* controlled. The *sans-culottes* wanted to carry the Revolution even further toward more direct democracy and governmental controls over the price of bread. While the Mountain's leaders did not fully agree with the *sans-culottes*, they were willing to work with them to gain supremacy.

The National Convention, now dominated by the Mountain and surrounded by a threatening Parisian crowd of women and men urged on by *sans-culotte* leaders, voted the expulsion and arrest of their chief competitors, the Girondin leaders, on June 2, 1793. To pacify the *sans-culottes*, the National Convention also agreed to enact the Law of the Maximum to control the price of bread, flour, and other essentials. Finally, the Convention drafted a democratic constitution based on universal male suffrage that promised rights to education and even subsistence (a job or poor relief). However, the Conven-

Committee of Public Safety

tion soon suspended the constitution and formed the twelve-member Committee of Public Safety to guide the country. The committee had two main tasks: to secure the Republic against its enemies—both internal and external—and to carry out a radical republican program. With the vast authority granted by the Convention, it enjoyed dictatorial powers. The committee came under the ideological leadership of the gifted and feared Maximilien Robespierre (1758–1794). A lawyer from the provinces when elected to the Estates General in 1789, he quickly rose to head the Jacobin Club in Paris. This stern, determined idealist was influenced by Rousseau and bent upon the creation of a virtuous republic. In pursuit of this dream, Robespierre and his fellow committee members struggled to both appease and control the unpredictable, threatening *sans-culottes*.

To protect the Republic from its internal enemies and to satisfy demands from the *sans-culottes* for immediate action, the Committee of Public Safety insti-

FIGURE 16.4
Execution of Louis XVI.

Biography

MANON ROLAND (1754–1793)

Manon Roland, describing herself as a "friend of humanity" and "lover of liberty," welcomed the French Revolution "with rapture." Born in 1754 into the family of a Parisian engraver, she learned to read by the age of four. By her early twenties, she was fluent in two foreign languages, had mastered the Greek and Roman classics, and embraced the ideas of Rousseau. She also rejected her Catholic faith and formed a lasting hatred for the pretensions of the aristocracy—and of the royal family in particular. She married a lawyer twenty years her senior who gained a position as inspector of manufacturers in Lyons. At the outbreak of the Revolution in 1789, she was at the center of a group of idealistic intellectuals and admirers who met regularly in Lyons. She argued for a republic rather than a constitutional monarchy and demanded that the royal family be put on trial.

The turmoil of revolutionary events created opportunities for the couple. In 1791, the city government of Lyons sent Manon's husband to Paris as a negotiator. Manon accompanied him, thrilled to be at the political center of France. They attended meetings of the Jacobin Club, and Manon quickly gathered around her a social circle of men, including Robespierre, whom she would later describe as "ardent, jealous, avid for popularity." The Rolands also associated with Girondins.

Manon's husband often attended gatherings of this circle, and Manon let him do all the public speaking for both of them. Upholding the traditional, formal role of a proper wife, mother, and homemaker, she mostly listened. "I knew the role that suited my sex, and I never abandoned it," she noted. Similarly, she did not argue for the rights of women or even invite other women to these gatherings, but she often resented men's attitudes toward women: it takes "a great deal of patience or vanity to hear with cool head, from men's own mouths, the value they attach to their superiority over us." Yet she was more politically and intellectually ambitious than her husband. Often, she was the force behind her husband's words and the author of writings that came out under his name. Figure 16.5 shows this strong woman looking directly at the viewer, pen in hand.

In 1792, with the rise to power of the Girondins, Manon's husband was offered the high post of minister of the interior. She talked him into accepting it and, from behind the scenes, shared his new position of power and prominence. It was she who did most of the necessary writing—the instructions, circulars, and public announcements—and who accepted visitors eager to get an audience with the busy minister.

---

tuted a Reign of Terror. "We must annihilate the enemies of the Republic at home and abroad, or else we shall perish," Robespierre warned. He justified the Terror by arguing that in this time of revolution, "the first maxim of our politics ought to be to lead the people by means of reason and the enemies of the people by terror." Accordingly, agents of the committee searched out and summarily tried anyone suspected of being counterrevolutionaries. Even those who had once supported the Revolution—such as the Girondins, whose views had fallen out of favor—were arrested and executed.

Reign of Terror

Jean-Sylvain Bailly, shown leading the 1789 Tennis Court Oath in Figure 16.2; Manon Roland (see Biography); and Olympe de Gouges, the woman who argued so strongly for revolutionary principles in the beginning, fell to the guillotine. Though many people became victims of arbitrary justice, officials used the Terror most often where real threats arose—regions in revolt and vulnerable areas near France's borders. During this violent phase of the Revolution, probably between 200,000 and 400,000 victims of the Terror went to prison. Some 25,000 to 50,000 died in jail or at the hands of executioners.

Events, however, moved too rapidly for Manon Roland as her life and the Revolution took more radical turns. She fell in love with Buzot, a young Girondin in her circle. She told her husband of her feelings, and although the two honored the form of their marriage out of a sense of propriety and discipline, they were miserable together. Manon made new political enemies, particularly Danton and the more radical Jacobins. The radical press called her a whore and her salon a hotbed of intrigue. Then the Girondins began to lose power, and Manon's husband's career stumbled as well. He resigned from office two days after the execution of the king in early 1793. The Revolution had gone too far even for Manon Roland, who wrote that she was "ashamed of it. It has been dishonored by scoundrels." Over the next few months both Rolands drew criticism from the press and their political enemies. Threatening groups of *sans-culottes* lurked in front of their apartment.

Too late, the Rolands tried to flee Paris. On May 31, 1793, Manon's husband, like many other Girondins, was arrested. He soon escaped, but then Manon suffered the same fate. After languishing in jail for months and writing her memoirs (modeled on Rousseau's *Memoirs*), she was tried on November 8, 1793, and found guilty of crimes against the Republic. That same day, she was escorted to the very guillotine where her longtime enemies Louis XVI and Marie Antoinette had perished. On the platform, she raised her eyes to David's statue representing liberty and lamented, "O Liberty, what crimes are committed in thy name." Upon hearing of her death, her husband committed suicide. Just weeks later, her love, Buzot, facing arrest himself, also committed suicide.

Revolutionary events that had drawn Manon to Paris and initially fulfilled her hopes quickly spun out of control. At the forefront of change in 1789, she found herself left behind and labeled an enemy of the Revolution just four years later. For Manon Roland and so many like her who rose with the Revolution, the wry statement of a moderate observer held true: "The Revolution . . . devours its children."

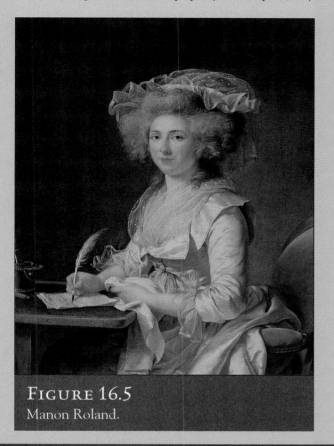

FIGURE 16.5
Manon Roland.

▧ **Consider** what Manon Roland's life reveals about the attitudes underlying the Revolution and the rapidly changing events that disrupted people's lives.

To secure the Republic against external enemies, the government ordered a *levée en masse*, or general call-up of all men, women, and children to serve the nation. As able-bodied young men were rapidly trained and rushed to the front, the army swelled to 850,000 men—a number that far exceeded the forces of France's opponents. Everyone else was supposed to contribute to the war effort by collecting or manufacturing supplies for the troops and by bolstering spirit. Women stitched clothing and served as nurses, children made bandages, and old men delivered stirring, patriotic speeches. This united activity for defense of the country produced an intense national patriotism. One soldier wrote home from the front to explain his feelings: "When *la patrie* calls us to her defense, we ought to fly there. . . . Our life, our wealth, and our talents do not belong to us. It is to the nation, *la patrie*, that all that belongs." With the officer corps now open to talent and the massive mobilization of men, materials, and spirit, the citizen armies turned back coalition forces by the end of 1793. By the summer of the following year, they carried the war beyond France's borders.

| Levée en masse |

THE REPUBLIC OF VIRTUE

While fighting this war, Robespierre and the Committee of Public Safety carried out their radical republican program. They attempted to reform institutions and infuse all aspects of French life with revolutionary politics. They intended to create a Republic of Virtue based on Rousseauian ideas of reason and natural law.

First, they targeted those institutions that, in their view, represented the worst of the Old Regime. Many officials saw the *Attacking the Catholic Church* Catholic Church in this negative light, and sold church buildings, turned them into warehouses, or rededicated them as "temples of reason." Angry radicals disfigured religious statues, even sending some wooden figures of saints to the guillotine and melting down church treasures. The most enthusiastic radicals searched out nonjuring clergy for prosecution and pressured even the clergy that had sworn to uphold the Revolution to leave their vocations. Some radical leaders hoped that the new festivals established to celebrate the Revolution would provide a sufficient substitute for Christian rituals. Other revolutionaries tried to create new beliefs, such as the Cult of Reason, to replace Christianity. Robespierre tried in vain to institute his own deistic Cult of the Supreme Being.

The National Convention also enacted legislation that took the rules governing family life and education away from the church *Family life and education* and placed them in state hands. Marriage became a civil rather than a religiously ordained act. New rules for divorce allowed thousands of couples to end marriages they would have been bound to under church rules. Births were registered at city halls rather than local churches. Women could sue for equal inheritance for the first time. Education became a responsibility of the state. New legislation mandated free primary schooling for all girls and boys and state-run secondary schooling, though in fact the government had neither the funds nor enough trained teachers to support such a system.

Women—especially those living in the cities—welcomed the new marriage, divorce, inheritance, and education laws, for they increased women's rights. However, the Jacobins had no desire to free women from their traditional role in the private sphere. Rather, they rejected women's participation in politics and outlawed female associations such as the Society of Revolutionary Republican Women. Jacobins declared that women's primary duties lay in nurturing children. They concluded that women had no proper role as active citizens and that women's political groups only disrupted the republican order. As one member of the government explained, "It is horrible, it is contrary to all laws of nature for a woman to want to make herself a man."

The new government went far beyond simply rooting out opponents of the Revolution and attacking institutions tied to the Old Regime. It also tried to create *Revolutionary symbols* support for the Republic by infusing the objects and activities of everyday life with revolutionary symbols. The figure of Liberty replaced royal symbols on everything from coins and statues to plates and posters. Patriotic groups planted liberty trees throughout France. Women adopted the flowing robes and hairstyles of ancient Greece that reflected rejection of the traditional social order. People sported revolutionary ribbons on their hats. Songs such as the Marseillaise, rallying the "children of the nation . . . against . . . the bloody standard of tyranny!" rang out among crowds and troops. Plays and paintings that supported the Revolution were encouraged. Officials promoted festivals that featured revolutionary symbols, mass loyalty oaths, and patriotic celebrations. Titles of all kinds were discarded and replaced with the terms "citizen" and "citizeness."

Pamphlets and posters spread throughout France proclaiming what the Republic stood for. The 1792 poster shown in Figure 16.6, printed just after France became a republic, is a typical example. The poster announces principles at the core of the Republic: "Unity, indivisibility of the Republic. Liberty, equality, fraternity, or death." A triangle of authorities—"God, People, Law"—shines its blessings on these principles. Also blessed are the liberty trees that symbolize the Revolution, the one at the left topped by a "liberty cap"; the one at the right, by a helmet from France's citizen army.

In the name of reason and revolutionary principles, the government revamped the calendar, making the months equal in length and naming them after the seasons. Weeks were made ten days long, with one day of rest. (This change eliminated Sunday, a day of traditional Christian importance.) September 22, 1792—the date of the declaration of the Republic—became the first day of Year I. The new metric system of weights and measures based on

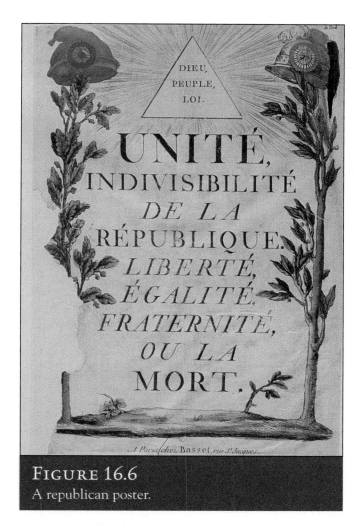

FIGURE 16.6
A republican poster.

field enabled France to set up "sister" republics in Holland, Switzerland, and Italy. To these areas, the French brought their own Enlightenment-inspired revolutionary principles and legislation. However, the gains carried a tremendous price tag. Hundreds of thousands died in the fighting, and the constant warfare disrupted trade and created shortages of essential goods.

The Revolution also powerfully influenced opinion outside France. Initially many groups in nearby countries supported the Revolution and its principles. However, part of that support rested on seeing France, a powerful rival, weakened. As people began to understand the seriousness of the attacks on monarchy and aristocracy and the threat to their own political independence, support waned. Still, many intellectuals and liberal political groups continued to uphold the ideals of the Revolution, at least until 1793 when the Revolution took a more radical turn.

Outside opinion

The Revolution helped promote other developments farther away. In Poland, patriots tried to use inspiration from France to assert independence from Russia. Despite some initial successes, however, their efforts failed. In Ireland, the revolutionary doctrines of liberty, equality, and natural rights touched many, encouraging them to rise against their British lords and make Ireland a republic. Irish patriots even anticipated a French invasion to help their own rebellion, though the invasion never took place.

Uprisings

In the Caribbean, slaves in France's lucrative colony of St. Domingue (Haiti) took heart from revolutionary principles and revolted. As Figure 16.7, a French print, reveals, the 1791 slave uprising struck fear in the hearts of white settlers. Salves, outnumbering white settlers, attack a plantation. Women and men fall under the knives, swords, and cannon of the revolting slaves, while plantation buildings go up in flames. Reports from French settlers, such as the wealthy Madame de Rouvray, described how the slaves "slaughtered and torched much of the countryside hereabouts," and warned, "how can we stay in a country where slaves have raised their hands against their masters?"

After much maneuvering and the abolishing of slavery by the National Convention in February 1794, the rebel leader Toussaint L'Ouverture and his black generals gained control of St. Domingue. The determined

units of ten was introduced and eventually would spread beyond France's borders to countries throughout the world.

THE REVOLUTION SPREADS OUTSIDE OF FRANCE

Since 1792, France had fended off various coalitions of European powers. After initial defeats, France's citizen armies had gone on the offensive. During the struggles that ensued, the France incorporated lands on its northern and eastern borders, claiming that these additions conformed to France's "natural boundaries" of the Rhine and the Alps. By 1799, more victories on the battle-

Sister republics

FIGURE 16.7
Slave rebellion in St. Domingue (Haiti), 1791.

Figure 16.8 reveals another form of resistance and the symbols of conflict during the radical phase of the Revolution. The painting, by the politically active artist Jacques-Louis David, depicts the death of Jean-Paul Marat, a journalist and leading radical deputy, in July 1793. Marat was working in his bathtub when Charlotte Corday, a supporter of the Girondins, assassinated him. Corday felt that it was her duty to kill Marat because of his persistent demands for more executions. This painting shows the mortally wounded Marat with pen and paper still in his hands and Corday's knife on the floor. David and others eulogized Marat as a martyr for the Revolution. On the side of his writing stand are the words, "Not having been able to corrupt me, they assassinated me." Corday, widely denounced but convinced that she had "avenged many innocent victims," was soon guillotined.

Meanwhile, discontent with Robespierre and his policies increased. With the defeat of the invading coalition armies and the suppression of internal rebel-

group would go on to oppose successfully English, Spanish, and French armies, turning the island into the independent republic of Haiti in 1804.

RESISTANCE TO THE REPUBLIC RISES

Despite the Reign of Terror and efforts to establish a Republic of Virtue, violent resistance to the Republic persisted and in some cases grew. Its leadership consisted primarily of local aristocrats and notables, officials who had fallen out of favor with the Jacobins, Girondin sympathizers, and members of the nonjuring clergy who had gone underground. They gathered additional support from remaining royalists, conservative peasants who had already gained most of what they wanted, opponents of military conscription, and the many citizens who remained loyal to Catholicism and their nonjuring priests. Of the many armed revolts that broke out across France, the most important occurred in the Vendée, a region in western France. In what amounted to a regional civil war that raged for most of 1793 and dragged on for years thereafter, both sides committed atrocities and thousands lost their lives before republican soldiers gained the upper hand.

FIGURE 16.8
Jacques-Louis David, *The Death of Marat*, 1793.

lion, most people no longer saw any need for the Terror—yet the Terror only intensified. When the influential Danton counseled moderation, Robespierre sent him and his most prominent followers to the guillotine. No one, not even *Thermidorian reaction* the members of the National Convention, felt safe. Finally, on July 27, 1794 (9 Thermidor on the Revolutionary calendar, and thus referred to as the "Thermidorian reaction"), the Convention overthrew Robespierre. In an ironic ending, the Jacobin leader died by the guillotine: the same device to which he had sent so many others to their deaths.

REACTION: THE "WHITE" TERROR AND THE DIRECTORY

With the leader of the Terror now dead, the propertied bourgeoisie quickly gained control of the government. Eliminating the "Red" Terror of the Committee of Public Safety, they replaced it with the "White" Terror of reaction. They executed the former terrorists and imprisoned many supporters of Robespierre, including the painter, Jacques-Louis David. Armed bands of bourgeois hirelings roved around beating and killing Jacobins. Restrictive measures of Robespierre's regime were repealed, and many individuals, weary of the Republic's code of discipline and restraint, reveled in an outburst of licentious living. Middle- and upper-class women wore more revealing clothing; mistresses appeared more publicly, even in the political arena. On the other hand, women of the poor in the small towns and countryside often turned back to the Catholic Church. They hoped that a return to God would end the turmoil of the revolutionary years.

A new constitution in 1795 reflected conservative reaction. The right to vote for members of the legislative bodies was limited to the wealthier property owners. Executive functions were placed in the hands of five directors—the Directory.

Men of reasonable competence staffed the Directory (1795–1799), but they failed to restore tranquility. War dragged on, governmental finances unraveled further, and brigands terrorized the countryside and the cities. The five directors tried to balance threats from the royalists on the Right and the Jacobins on the Left. They turned against the *sans-culottes* by removing price controls and had to be saved by governmental forces when the *sans-culottes* stormed the Convention in May 1795. Five months later, the government barely put down a royalist uprising, thanks to a quick-acting artillery officer named Napoleon Bonaparte. The directors finally resorted to purges to control the legislature and increasingly relied on the army for support. All in all, the situation was ripe for the arrival of a strongman who could bring both order at home and peace abroad.

Napoleon Bonaparte

Within France, the Revolution provided unprecedented opportunities for ambitious soldiers of talent. Most prerevolutionary army officers had come from the nobility, and had fled the country or lost their commands as the Revolution gathered momentum. This leadership drain, as well as the need to expand the army, created a huge demand for skilled officers. Napoleon Bonaparte, a talented artillery officer, stepped in to take full advantage of these opportunities.

NAPOLEON'S RISE TO POWER

Born into a poor but well-known family on Corsica in 1769, just a few months after the Mediterranean island was transferred from the Republic of Genoa to France, Napoleon was hardworking, assertive, independent, and even arrogant as a youth. These qualities would stay with him for the rest of his life. The young Napoleon attended French military school (where he proved particularly strong in mathematics) and received his commission as second lieutenant when he was just sixteen. When the Revolution broke out in 1789, Napoleon was already familiar with Enlightenment ideas and resented the aristocratic pretensions of those around him. He quickly sided with the revolutionaries. In 1793, he attracted attention during the recapture of Toulon. Two years later, when he happened to be in Paris, the National Convention called on him to quell a threatening Parisian crowd. Using artillery—his legendary "whiff of grape-shot"—Napoleon quickly dispersed the crowd and became the hero of the Convention. He fell in love with and married the politically well-connected Josephine de Beauharnais (1763–1814), a thirty-two-year-old widow eager to provide security for her children.

Napoleon then used his growing prominence to secure command of the French army still fighting in northern Italy. Calling his forces "soldiers of liberty" and announcing to the people of Italy that "the French army comes to break your chains," he skillfully galvanized the lethargic French forces into de-

Italian campaign feating the Austrians and Sardinians. Along with loads of Italian art, Napoleon sent home glowing reports of his exploits. In 1797, he personally negotiated a favorable Treaty of Campo Formio with Austria, which recognized French expansion and the creation of the Cisalpine Republic in northern Italy (Map 16.3). Over the next two years, French armies moved south, helping to set up more French-controlled republics throughout the Italian peninsula. Napoleon's successes in Italy established his reputation as a brilliant military leader and able statesman.

Turning toward the British, Napoleon and the Directory concluded that an expedition to Egypt would

Expedition to Egypt deal a telling blow to British commerce with its colonies in Asia. Egypt could also serve as the foundation for a new French colony. Moreover, a conquest there might enhance Napoleon's image as a daring, heroic conqueror. Yet, despite some spectacular battlefield successes, the expedition failed; Admiral Nelson (1758–1805), who became one of Britain's most admired naval commanders, destroyed the French fleet at the Battle of the Nile on August 1, 1798. Even so, Napoleon avoided personal disaster by slipping back to France with a few chosen followers, cleverly controlling the reports from Egypt, and emphasizing the expedition's scientific explorations and exotic discoveries.

Meanwhile, matters took a bad turn for France's government, the Directory. The expedition to Egypt prompted Great Britain, Austria, and Russia to join

Coup d'état in a new coalition. These allies inflicted defeats on French armies and threatened to invade France itself. Eyeing this foreign threat, as well as bankruptcy, insubordinate army commanders, and disruptions in the countryside, rival factions within France vied for power. One conservative faction, led by a member of the Directory, Abbé Sieyès, concluded that a coup d'état would gain them needed control over the government. This situation provided Napoleon with another opportunity to advance his career. Sieyès and others conspired with him to overthrow the Directory on November 9, 1799 (18 Brumaire). The conspirators expected that the thirty-year-old military hero would make a popular figurehead representing authority, while they would

actually govern the country. As events would prove, they were very mistaken.

NAPOLEON CONSOLIDATES CONTROL

Napoleon quickly outmaneuvered his partners. He had a new "short and obscure" constitution drawn up and accepted by members of the old legis-

First consul lature. In a national plebiscite where people could vote to accept or reject the new constitution, the French overwhelmingly approved it (though the government falsified the results to give it a more lopsided victory). As one observer explained, people "believed quite sincerely that Bonaparte . . . would save us from the perils of anarchy." Napoleon named himself "first consul" and assumed the powers necessary to rule—all with the ready support of the Senate. The remaining two consuls, as well as voters and the handpicked legislative bodies they thought they were electing, had only minimal powers. Next, Napoleon placed each of France's eighty-three departments under the control of a powerful agent of the central government—the *prefect*. Thus at both the local and national level, Napoleon ended meaningful democracy in France.

With the touch of a skilled authoritarian politician, Napoleon proceeded to gather support. He welcomed former Old Regime officials as well as moderate Jacobins into his service. By approving the end of serfdom and feudal privileges as well as all transfers of property that had occurred during the Revolution, he won favor with the peasantry. He gained the backing of the middle class by affirming the property rights and formal equality before the law that adult males had secured during the Revolution. He welcomed back to France all but the most reactionary émigrés, most of whom had come from France's old aristocracy. The educated elite admired Napoleon for patronizing science and inviting leading scientists to join him in his government. To deter opposition, he created a secret police force, suppressed independent political organizations, and censored newspapers and artistic works. Finally, for those who displayed the highest loyalty and the most spectacular achievements (particularly in the military), he created the prestigious Legion of Honor.

Keenly aware of the political and social importance of religion—once calling religion "excellent stuff for keeping the common people quiet"— Napoleon made peace with the pope and ended the

THINKING ABOUT GEOGRAPHY

MAP 16.3 *France and Its Sister Republics*

This map shows the expansion of France and the creation of its sister republics between 1792 and 1798.
▣ **Notice** the dates of annexation and creation of sister republics. **Consider** who was most threatened by these developments. ▣ **Notice** the arrow indicating Napoleon's invasion of Egypt in 1798. **Why** might Napoleon have moved against British interests in Egypt rather than Great Britain itself?

ten-year struggle between the French revolutionary governments and the Roman Catholic church. Their Concordat (formal agreement) of 1801 declared the

The Concordat Catholic religion the religion of the majority of the French people, but ensured freedom for Protestants. Later Napoleon would grant new rights to Jews as well. Under his rule, the clergy was paid by the state and required to take an oath of allegiance to the state. Confiscated Catholic Church property was not returned.

Reforming France

Napoleon followed up this pattern of blending compromise and authoritarian control with a remaking of France's legal, financial, and educational systems. The Civil Code of 1804 (the Napoleonic Code), for

Napoleonic Code example, generally affirmed the Enlightenment-inspired legal reforms that the early French revolutionaries had sought. Progressives throughout Europe and even overseas would embrace this law code. For men, the code guaranteed legal equality, careers open to talent, and paternal authority over women, children, and property. In particular, it catered to middle-class employers by forbidding strikes and trade unions. At the same time, the code rejected many of the rights and liberties gained in 1789 as well as the more radical measures enacted after 1792. For women, the code represented a clear defeat. Rather than granting them legal or political equality, it gave power over property and the family to men and left married women legally and economically dependent on their husbands. The code also severely restricted the right to divorce, particularly for women. These measures reflected Napoleon's belief that women belonged in the home and that their concerns should center on domestic life.

To stabilize France financially, Napoleon established the Bank of France to handle governmental funds and issue money. To promote economic health,

Finance and education he involved the state in a huge program of public works, supported certain industries, and established price controls. To restructure educational institutions, he created a long-lasting system of secondary schools tied to the University of France and infused it with patriotic trappings. Napoleon also actively supported scientific research and rewarded surgeons, chemists, mathematicians, and other scientists with governmental posts and honors.

Creating the Empire

Napoleon's rise to power hinged on his ability to remove external military threats as well as internal disruptions. This he managed by crossing the Alps in 1800 with a French army to crush the Austrian forces in Northern Italy and knock Austria out of the coalition of powers opposing France. Next, he made peace with Russia and persuaded Great Britain to sign the Peace of Amiens in 1802.

In the first five years of his rule, Napoleon scored spectacular successes. Law and order reigned at home, and he secured peace abroad. Public morale was high. Napoleon's vision of a centralized, paternalistic state that would make France the model of a modern nation through reason, authority, and science seemed almost real.

However, two problems lurked beneath this promising exterior. First, Napoleon had an insatiable craving for public recognition and legitimacy. He satisfied this need at least partially with a *Emperor Napoleon* bold move in 1804. That year, with the approval of the Senate and the French people in a lopsided plebiscite, Napoleon formally established France as an empire—and then crowned himself emperor.

As Jacques-Louis David's painting in Figure 16.9 reveals, Napoleon controlled all aspects of the coronation. Although he invited Pope Pius VII (seated behind him) to preside over the ceremony, it is Napoleon—ever the self-made man—who takes matters into his own hands. As splendidly dressed spectators look on, Napoleon raises a crown, preparing to place it on the kneeling Josephine's head to make her his empress. He has already boldly crowned himself emperor with a laurel wreath that alludes back to Roman emperors and Charlemagne, crowned emperor by the pope in the year 800. Aware of the importance of details, Napoleon had shrewdly instructed his ardent supporter David to paint the reluctant pope raising his hand in blessing.

The new emperor then elevated members of his family to princely status and granted new titles and honors to his wealthy supporters who had proved themselves, usually as officers on the battlefield. Later, he divorced empress Josephine, whose relationship with Napoleon became more formal than intimate, and who failed to produce a male heir. He married Princess Marie-Louise of Austria, giving him a stronger image as legitimate royalty.

FIGURE 16.9
Jacques-Louis David, *Napoleon's Coronation.*

1805, the ambitious Napoleon had to battle a new coalition of European powers. That year, he marched to the English Channel with a huge army and seemed poised to invade England. Before him stretched twenty-four miles of water and British sea power. To overcome those barriers, Napoleon amassed a combined French and Spanish fleet and plotted his next move. Alert for any opportunity, he suddenly turned his army eastward, surrounded an exposed Austrian army, and on October 20, forced it to surrender. The next day, however, England's Admiral Nelson sighted the combined French and Spanish fleets off Cape Trafalgar on the southwest point of Spain and annihilated them. Although Nelson perished early in the battle, his navy's victory saved Great Britain from the menace of an invasion and limited Napoleon's conquests to the European continent.

Battle of Trafalgar

On land, Napoleon fared much better—in fact, he seemed invincible. His success stemmed in part from his independent units that could move quickly and then join in a mass attack. Equally important, he possessed an unusually talented officer corps, and enjoyed the loyalty of a large number of nationalistic citizen-soldiers. The strategy of sending a mass of spirited soldiers in a column of attack aimed at dividing opposing forces served Napoleon well. Fighting alongside his troops, he cleverly used these military strengths to crush the combined forces of Austria and Russia at Austerlitz in December 1805. Prussia made the mistake of declaring war on France after it was too late to join the Austrians and Russians. As the French troops moved east through villages and cities, people reported how "the dreadful cry was heard in the streets, 'the French are coming!' " Napoleon virtually obliterated the Prussian forces. When the Russian troops began massing again, Napoleon moved eastward and decisively defeated them in the great Battle of Friedland (1807). Although the resulting Treaties of Tilsit (July 1807) were technically between equals, they actually left Russia only a junior partner to France. France commanded the greater resources, and Napoleon expected to have his way on the European continent.

Military strengths

In addition to his hunger for formal recognition, Napoleon had a second problem. He had risen to prominence and power through his military conquests. "I am an upstart soldier," he admitted. "My domination will not survive the day when I cease to be strong, and therefore feared." These martial ties would push Napoleon to seek still greater conquests on the battlefield. "Conquest has made me what I am; only conquest can maintain me." Yet even when battle after battle brought him victory, war also came at great cost and risk.

Need for conquests

WAR AND CONQUEST

The interests of Great Britain and Napoleon clashed too often for their peace to last long. By the end of 1803, the two countries were again at war, and by

Despite all these triumphs, Napoleon still could not find a way to get his troops across the Channel to attack England directly. He finally hit on an alternate plan—the "Continental System"—that he hoped would destroy his rival's commercial economy by pre-

The Continental System

venting the importation of British goods into continental Europe. To implement the plan, he ordered a continent-wide blockade against British ships, confiscated all British goods, and set French privateers upon British merchant ships. Britain responded with new regulations that amounted to its own blockade on shipping to continental ports. Now the naval war between France and Britain affected even neutral states, including the United States.

By 1810, Napoleon had redrawn the map of Europe (Map 16.4) and the political balance of power. He had dismembered Prussia and abolished the Holy

THINKING ABOUT GEOGRAPHY

MAP 16.4 *Europe, 1810*

This map shows Europe at the height of Napoleon's empire. ◼ **Notice** the extent of area Napoleon controlled—directly and indirectly. **Where** would you expect Napoleon's rule to exert the greatest impact? **What** geographical problems did Napoleon face trying to control his empire? ◼ **Locate** those areas that remained hostile to Napoleon. **How** might geography help explain why those areas retained their independence?

Roman Empire. Now most German states were unified into the Confederation of the Rhine. Holland and the Italian peninsula had come under French

The new European order control. Spain was a dependent state, and Austria, Russia, and a diminished Prussia had become reluctant allies of France. Only Great Britain and still-defiant parts of Spain and Portugal remained active opponents.

In those areas annexed to France, Napoleon ruled directly and imposed all of France's laws and institutions. In dependent states, he installed French-controlled governments to rule with the help of local elites. He usually made members of his family monarchs in these areas—his brother Louis king of Holland, his brother Jérôme king of Westphalia, and his brother Joseph king of Spain. To varying degrees, France's "enlightened" institutions and policies were introduced. These usually included constitutional government, equality before the law, careers open to talent, the Napoleonic Civil Code, civil rights to Jews and other religious minorities, and the creation of similar public works improvements—schools, roads, bridges—that Napoleon supported in France. Wherever Napoleon conquered, except Russia, he abolished serfdom. At the same time, the reforms included tax increases and conscription quotas to help finance and provide soldiers for Napoleon's armies.

THE IMPACT OVERSEAS

Naturally, Napoleon's policies exerted their greatest impact in Europe, but other areas—particularly in the Western Hemisphere and the British Empire—also felt the effects of his rule and expansion. In the Caribbean, Napoleon failed to put down the black population's struggle for independence and freedom in Saint Domingue (Haiti) (see pp. 551–552). He also cut his losses in North America and sold Louisiana to the United States.

The Napoleonic Wars had dramatic consequences in the colonies of Spain and Portugal in the Americas. Discontent with colonial rule had been mounting dur-

Revolt in Latin America ing the eighteenth century. In particular, the colonists resented the economic and political restrictions imposed by the "mother" country. As the native-born "Creoles" began to outnumber the Spanish- and Portuguese-born settlers, the ties of loyalty to home countries weakened. The successful revolt of the English

colonies to the north and the birth of the United States also impressed colonial liberals and intellectuals. Spanish colonists' attachment to Spain faltered further when Napoleon overthrew the Spanish king and placed his own brother, Joseph Bonaparte, on the throne. By 1810 many colonists were in open revolt.

Over the next ten years, Spain struggled to regain its colonies. In 1814 Argentina drove off a Spanish army and won its independence. Elsewhere, Simón Bolívar (1783–1830), known as "The Liberator," led the fight for independence against Spanish forces. Figure 16.10 shows him in heroic pose, probably to symbolize his military campaigns in Venezuela, Colombia, Ecuador, and Peru. The painting is modeled on a well-known work by David that portrays Napoleon leading his troops across the Alps. Bolívar points upward while a wind blows at his back—a traditional posture of victory.

As Map 16.5 shows, by 1822 almost all of Spain's colonies, as well as Portugal's huge colony of Brazil, had gained their independence. Nevertheless, Bolí-

FIGURE 16.10
Simón Bolívar.

THINKING ABOUT GEOGRAPHY

MAP 16.5 Latin America After Independence

This map shows that within a twelve-year period Spain and Portugal lost most of their possessions in the Americas. ◗ **Notice** that in several areas there are differences between the date of independence from the colonial power and the date of separation from other states. **What** might these differences mean? ◗ **Locate** those territories still held by European nations. **What** might differ these territories from those that gained their independence?

var's and other's hopes for unity within Spain's old colonies soon faded as various South American regions began dividing into separate states. Most of these new states would adopt the Napoleonic Code as their basis of civil law, and oppressive white minorities would rule them for many years.

Napoleon's dominance over the European continent inspired England to step up its overseas expansion *England's overseas expansion* and tighten control over its own colonies and areas of influence. Sea power enabled it to capture and take over French and Dutch colonies in Africa, Asia, and America. In addition, England began trading more briskly with South America. However, one of England's strategies—its counterblockade of Napoleonic Europe—had a major, unintended drawback. By enforcing the blockade, England ended up embroiled in the War of 1812 with the United States. That war, in turn, spread further north when the United States invaded Britain's loyal colonies in Canada.

Finally, in the decades that followed, states from Asia to the Americas that reformed their own governments and laws *Adopting the Napoleonic Code* would look to the Napoleonic Code and adopt parts of it. In this way, some of the ideals of the Enlightenment and the French Revolution would be translated through the Napoleonic Code to many areas around the globe.

DECLINE AND FALL

Napoleon had an even more ambitious vision—to rule Europe as the head of a single imperial administration. Before he could make his vision real, new problems cropped up to plague him. Even at the height of his power, Napoleon and his empire suffered from dangerous weaknesses. Between 1808 and 1812, three crucial vulnerabilities—flawed policies, resistance to his rule, and overextension of his military reach—would intensify and erode Napoleon's power.

The Continental System that Napoleon devised to cripple England economically was not working well enough. With control of the sea, Great Britain applied an effective counterblockade *Flawed policies* against the Napoleon-dominated Continent. Port cities and industries relying on external commerce suffered. Smuggling further weakened the system. In some areas, such as Holland and Russia, the restrictions of the system became a constant source of irritation and resentment against the French. In the long run, the Continental System stiffened opposition to Napoleon on the Continent and failed to weaken England. Again and again, that island nation would finance Napoleon's enemies.

People across Europe had other reasons besides the Continental System to resist Napoleon's rule. In the wake of France's conquering armies, a new national spirit developed among many subject peoples. In Spain, for ex- *Growing resistance* ample, Napoleon had no sooner placed his brother Joseph on the Spanish throne when his unwilling subjects rose up against him. The painting in Figure 16.11 by the influential Spanish artist Francisco de Goya depicts the popular resistance in Spain to the Napoleonic occupation and the reprisals that resulted. Here, in a night scene on May 3, 1808, a firing squad of anonymous French soldiers brutally executes citizens in retaliation for riots against French troops in Madrid. The magnitude of the French atrocity is emphasized by the central figure, who resembles a crucified Christ about to be shot. Monks and commoners, selected at random for execution, surround the man at the center, and the bodies of those already executed lie scattered on the bloody earth around him. Goya, who painted this scene six years after the actual event, intended the work as a statement against the evils of war.

The Madrid rebellion and reprisals by Napoleon's soldiers inspired other Spanish uprisings and organized resistance against French troops in the years to come. Larger French armies, even when led by Napoleon himself, managed only limited success against the hit-and-run guerrilla tactics used by the Spanish. England took advantage of the situation by sending supplies and troops to Spain under the duke of Wellington (1769–1852), the British commander who would plague Napoleon's forces to the end. Spain became a running abscess that drained Napoleon's military strength.

In Prussia, similar national sentiments encouraged the government—partly in secret—to modernize its army and civil institutions in preparation for liberation from France. In Austria, the government again declared war on Napoleon in a premature effort to free itself from subservience to the French emperor. In Holland, opposition to Napoleon's policies ran so strong that in 1810 he had to annex the country to France to bring it under control. All this resistance drained French forces and raised the specter of open revolt at the least opportunity.

FIGURE 16.11
Francicso de Goya, *The Third of May, 1808.*

Napoleon himself created that opportunity by overextending his imperial reach. Successes on the battlefield added to his growing dreams of creating an empire ruled from Paris that would encompass all of Europe. Russia, already chafing against the commer- *Overextension* cial restrictions of the Continental System and harboring its own ambitions for expansion in eastern Europe, stood as the main barrier to Napoleon's dreams. In 1812, these conflicting ambitions soured the alliance between Russia and France. Against the advice of his closest associates, Napoleon decided to invade Russia. Amassing an immense army of over 600,000, he plunged into the vastness of Russia. Half of his troops, however, were unenthusiastic conscripts from dependent states. The Russian *Invasion of Russia* army retreated into the interior of their huge country, following a scorched-earth policy and luring Napoleon ever farther from his base of supplies. "We believed that once in Russia, we need do nothing but forage—which, however, proved to be an illusion. . . . All the villages were already stripped before we could enter," wrote Jakob Walter, a German conscript in Napoleon's army. One of Napoleon's aides explained the deepening problem: "We were in the heart of inhabited Russia and yet we were like a vessel without a compass in the midst of a vast ocean, knowing nothing of what was happening around us." At Borodino the Russians turned and made a stand. In one of the bloodiest battles of the nineteenth century—taking a toll of more than 80,000 casualties—the two armies fought until the Russians withdrew.

The French army may have won the battle, but it failed to destroy Russia's forces. In September, Napoleon's Grand Army, weakened by battlefield losses and even more so by hunger, fatigue, and disease, finally entered Moscow. Tsar Alexander I, however, refused to capitulate. The future looked even worse for the French when a fire destroyed much of Moscow, leaving the invaders without enough shelter or supplies to ride out the notorious Russian winter. "Here in the white country we'll all have to die of hunger," wrote Hohann Wärncke, a German soldier in Napoleon's army. Napoleon began his retreat, but too late. The winter caught his forces overburdened with loot. Tens of thousands of them froze, starved, or succumbed to disease. Russian Cossacks, riding out of the blizzards, cut down or captured thousands more. Many of Napoleon's men surrendered to Russian forces. Of the original 600,000 who marched into Russia, fewer than 100,000 struggled home.

Napoleon himself was able to dash back to France. Behind him, one nation after another, aided by British money, joined the Russians in a war of liberation. Back home, **Defeat at Leipzig** Napoleon raised new conscripts for his army and once again rushed them eastward. At Leipzig in central Germany, in October 1813, allied armies at last decisively defeated Napoleon. The next year, the allies entered Paris and exiled Napoleon to the island of Elba, off the coast of Italy.

Napoleon still had some fight left in him. While the allies squabbled over the peace settlement and discontent weakened France's new government under Louis XVIII, Napoleon escaped back **Waterloo** to France. "Soldiers! In exile I heard your voice," he announced. "Now I have landed [in France]." He quickly raised yet another army from the remains of his old, still loyal supporters. However he was finally defeated in June 1815 by British and Prussian forces at Waterloo in Belgium. This time his captors imprisoned him on the bleak island of St. Helena in the South Atlantic, where six years later Napoleon died of stomach cancer.

Summary

In 1815, a king from the old house of Bourbon once again ruled France. Many aristocrats and royalists hoped to turn back the clock to the days before 1789, when they enjoyed unchallenged power and prestige. However, too much had changed. The Revolution had destroyed a French monarchy based on the divine right of kings. French aristocrats might still boast impressive titles, but the revolutionaries and Napoleon had secured legal equality for French men, if not women. Members of the middle class, though no longer enjoying the control they had exercised during the revolutionary years, would not relinquish the opportunities for position and prestige that they had gained. The peasantry, which had played such an important role during the early months of the Revolution, would never again be burdened by the traditional dues and services they once owed to lords. Finally, the Catholic Church had forever lost the lands and position it had once possessed before the Revolution.

Napoleon's connection to the Revolution was contradictory. He subverted key elements of the Revolution by removing the substance from representative institutions and eliminating freedom of speech and press. On the other hand, he preserved other elements of the Revolution by affirming the end of feudalism, protecting the rights of property, and insuring equality before the law for men; through his conquests, he spread the ideas and institutions of the Revolution beyond France's borders. When he maximized the political and military power of the state by rationalizing the government, he acted like an eighteenth-century enlightened despot.

Finally, the French Revolution and Napoleon created two potent, long-lasting images. First, people had learned

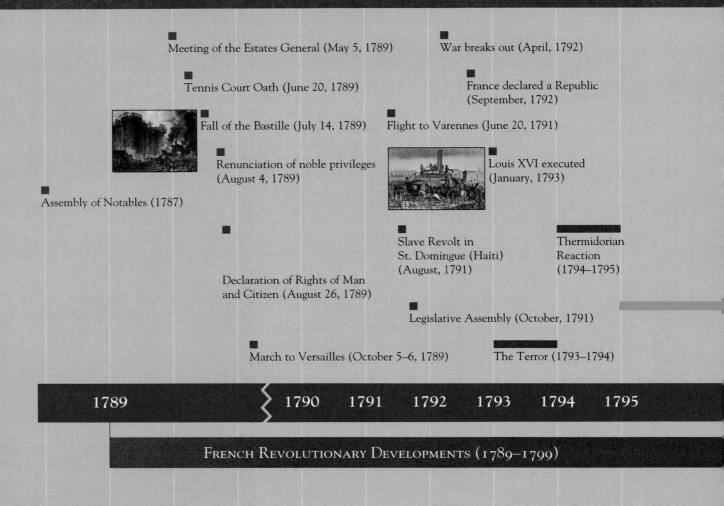

Meeting of the Estates General (May 5, 1789)

War breaks out (April, 1792)

Tennis Court Oath (June 20, 1789)

France declared a Republic (September, 1792)

Fall of the Bastille (July 14, 1789)

Flight to Varennes (June 20, 1791)

Renunciation of noble privileges (August 4, 1789)

Louis XVI executed (January, 1793)

Assembly of Notables (1787)

Slave Revolt in St. Domingue (Haiti) (August, 1791)

Thermidorian Reaction (1794–1795)

Declaration of Rights of Man and Citizen (August 26, 1789)

Legislative Assembly (October, 1791)

March to Versailles (October 5–6, 1789)

The Terror (1793–1794)

| 1789 | 1790 | 1791 | 1792 | 1793 | 1794 | 1795 |

FRENCH REVOLUTIONARY DEVELOPMENTS (1789–1799)

that a popular revolution could topple the government and social order of even the most powerful country. This image would inspire revolutionaries and unnerve those representing the status quo for decades to come. Second, westerners also saw in Napoleon a nationalistic, charismatic leader who could suddenly seize power and exert his will with ease. This compelling image would inspire other individuals who envisioned themselves as potential Napoleons. Perhaps even more important, it would seduce people who yearned for easy, decisive solutions to complex problems.

After 1815, the old forces of order tried desperately to reassert their control. Although they scored some temporary successes, the ideas and institutions of the Revolution, spread by the armies of the French Republic and Napoleon, had taken root permanently in France and beyond its borders. The French Revolution had become a watershed event, and those who ignored it did so at peril.

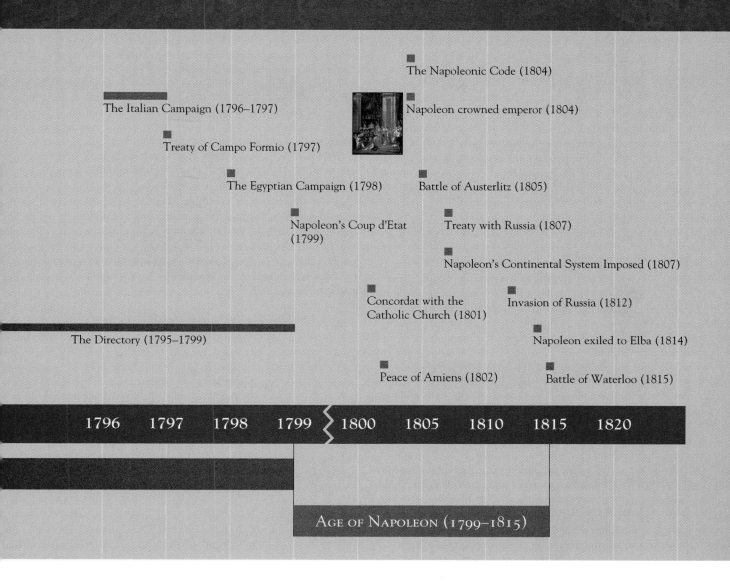

The Napoleonic Code (1804)

The Italian Campaign (1796–1797)

Napoleon crowned emperor (1804)

Treaty of Campo Formio (1797)

The Egyptian Campaign (1798)

Battle of Austerlitz (1805)

Napoleon's Coup d'Etat (1799)

Treaty with Russia (1807)

Napoleon's Continental System Imposed (1807)

Concordat with the Catholic Church (1801)

Invasion of Russia (1812)

The Directory (1795–1799)

Napoleon exiled to Elba (1814)

Peace of Amiens (1802)

Battle of Waterloo (1815)

| 1796 | 1797 | 1798 | 1799 | 1800 | 1805 | 1810 | 1815 | 1820 |

AGE OF NAPOLEON (1799–1815)

REVIEW, ANALYZE, AND ANTICIPATE

REVIEW THE PREVIOUS CHAPTERS

Chapter 14—"A New World of Reason and Reform"—revealed how Enlightenment ideas challenged traditional values and institutions in the West. Chapter 15—"Competing for Power and Wealth"—followed the battles of Western powers over land, position, and commerce as well as the economic and social changes affecting eighteenth-century life in the West.

1. *In what ways were Enlightenment ideas reflected in the values and reforms of the French Revolution?*

2. *Do you think the French Revolution conformed to or contradicted the main political trends of the eighteenth century?*

3. *In what ways did Napoleon embody the eighteenth-century trend toward "Enlightened Absolutism"?*

ANALYZE THIS CHAPTER

Chapter 16—"Overturning the Political and Social Order"—examines the great upheaval in France that shocked and transformed the West.

1. *Analyze the roles of France's aristocracy, bourgeoisie, and poor in causing the French Revolution.*

2. *Why do you think the Revolution turned more radical, resulting in the establishment of a republic and leading to the Reign of Terror?*

3. *How do you explain Napoleon's rise? Was his rise a logical consequence of revolutionary events?*

4. *Analyze Napoleon's accomplishments. Do you think they were worth the costs?*

ANTICIPATE THE NEXT CHAPTER

In Chapter 17—"Factories, Cities, and Families in the Industrial Age"—the industrial revolution and its accompanying social changes will be examined.

1. *With the industrial revolution beginning in Britain at about the same period as the French Revolution on the Continent, in what ways should this period be considered a watershed ushering in the modern era?*

BEYOND THE CLASSROOM

"A GREAT FERMENT": TROUBLE BREWING IN FRANCE

Chartier, Roger. *The Cultural Origins of the French Revolution.* Trans. Lydia G. Cochrane. Durham, NC: Duke University Press, 1991. Examines the developments that contributed to the cultural destabilization of the Old Regime.

Furet, Francois. *Interpreting the French Revolution.* Cambridge: Cambridge University Press, 1981. An important book that refutes the traditional theory of the French Revolution as a bourgeois revolution.

Landes, Joan. *Women and the Public Sphere in the Age of the French Revolution.* Ithaca, NY: Cornell University Press, 1988. Explores the historical evolution of the male-oriented public sphere and the consignment of women to the private realm of domesticity.

Lefebvre, George. *The Coming of the French Revolution.* Trans. R.R. Palmer. Princeton, NJ: Princeton University Press, 1947. A landmark analysis of the social structure of prerevolutionary France and the opening phase of the Revolution.

Lucas, Colin, ed. *Rewriting the French Revolution.* Oxford: Clarendon Press, 1991. Essays on social development, politics, religion, and ideas during the French Revolution by eight scholars.

Sutherland, Donald M.G. *France, 1789–1815: Revolution and Counter-Revolution.* New York: Oxford University Press, 1986. A departure from the traditional theory of the French Revolution as an attempt by the bourgeoisie to overthrow the aristocracy and install a capitalist order.

THE CONSTITUTIONAL MONARCHY: ESTABLISHING A NEW ORDER

Hunt, Lynn. *Politics, Culture and Class in the French Revolution.* Berkeley, CA: University of California Press, 1984. Focuses on the political culture of language, dress, and festivals created by the revolutionaries.

Jones, P. *The Peasantry in the French Revolution.* New York: Cambridge University Press, 1988. Examines the role of the peasantry in the revolutionary events from 1789–1799.

Rudé, George. *The Crowd in the French Revolution.* Oxford: Clarendon Press, 1959. A study of the composition of the crowds that participated in revolutionary events such as the storming of the Bastille.

TO THE RADICAL REPUBLIC AND BACK

Bertaud, Jean-Paul. *The Army of the French Revolution.* Princeton, NJ: Princeton University Press, 1988. Analyzes the role of the army in overthrowing the Old Regime and how the army changed during the revolutionary years.

Hufton, Olwen. *Women and the Limits of Citizenship in the French Revolution.* Toronto: University of Toronto Press, 1992. Analyzes attitudes toward women during the French Revolution that led to female exclusion from the rights of citizenship.

Kennedy, Emmet. *A Cultural History of the French Revolution.* New Haven, CT: Yale University Press, 1989. Examines the role of the arts, clubs, and intellectual institutions during the Revolution.

Lyons, Martyn. *France Under the Directory.* New York: Cambridge University Press, 1975. A brief yet wide-ranging survey of the Directory period.

Palmer, Robert R. *Twelve Who Ruled: The Committee of Public Safety During the Terror.* Princeton, NJ: Princeton University Press, 1970. A well-written account of the Terror and its leaders.

NAPOLEON BONAPARTE

Connelly, Owen. *Blundering to Glory: Napoleon's Military Campaigns.* Wilmington, DE: Scholarly Resources, 1987. An assessment of Napoleon's military strategy and achievements.

Kafker, Frank A., and James M. Laux, eds. *Napoleon and His Times: Selected Interpretations.* Malabar, FL: Krieger Publishing Co., 1989. A fine collection of articles on many aspects of Napoleon's regime.

Lyons, Martyn. *Napoleon Bonaparte and the Legacy of the French Revolution.* New York: St. Martin's Press, 1994. A solid reevaluation of Napoleon and his legacy.

Industrial Manchester, 1851

By 1851, Manchester in northern England had grown into an industrial city of some 400,000 inhabitants. The city "chiefly consists of dense masses of houses, inhabited by the population engaged in the great manufactories of the cotton trade," explained James Kay, a contemporary observer, "but the opulent merchants chiefly reside in the country." This painting captures the common vision of industrial cities standing in stark contrast to the surrounding countryside.

CHAPTER 17

Factories, Cities, and Families in the Industrial Age

The Industrial Revolution, 1780–1850

In 1828 a German visitor described Britain as a land where the "new creations springing into life every year bordered on the fabulous." These creations were the machines and factories of the industrial revolution that were replacing agriculture and handicrafts as the basis of the traditional economy. They turned industrial cities like Manchester into what the French writer Alexis de Tocqueville called "the greatest stream of human industry" that "flows out to fertilize the whole world."

However, this wave of industrial developments, which made Britain wealthy and envied, brought disturbing consequences in its wake: great swings of economic prosperity and depression and a new working class harnessed to the rhythm of machines. A British journal in 1826 spoke of a growing "accumulation of misery endured by thousands" in industrial areas. A few years later, the French consul in Edinburgh argued, "Who would want the prosperity of Liverpool and Manchester in France ... beside these base miseries offered by manufacturing establishments?"

These "miseries" haunted not only the new factories and mines. Workers hoping for jobs crowded into unprepared cities. There, life for them as well as for middle-class employers, professionals, and shopkeepers was rapidly changing. In bad times, unemployment and business failures made urban life particularly harsh. In prosperous times, filth and disease still marked these cities. Here even the family, which for so long labored together as a cooperating unit of economic life, was shifting under the weight of new ideas and pressures. Western societies were entering the industrial age.

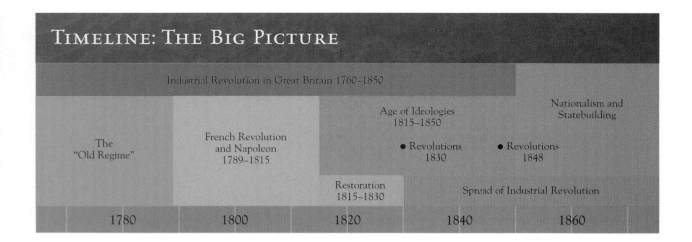

TIMELINE: THE BIG PICTURE

Industrial Revolution in Great Britain 1760–1850

Nationalism and
Statebuilding

Age of Ideologies
1815–1850

The
"Old Regime"

French Revolution
and Napoleon
1789–1815

● Revolutions
1830

● Revolutions
1848

Restoration
1815–1830

Spread of Industrial Revolution

1780   1800   1820   1840   1860

The Industrial Revolution Begins

In this new era, Britain led the way. There a middle-class couple such as Richard and Elizabeth Cadbury (see the Biography on pages 592–593) might expect to work hard and see the cloth and dry goods store they opened in 1794 support them and their several children. Thirty-five years later their sons Benjamin and John had become wealthy retailers and manufacturers.

Others did not consider the industrial age such a boon. One railroad worker told of a day when 2000 of his coworkers lost their jobs: "They were all starving, the heap of them, or next door to it." This worker had recently injured his leg at work and was laid up for one month, living "all that time on charity; on what the chaps would come and give me. When I could get about again, the work was all stopped, and I couldn't get none to do. . . . I went to a lodginghouse in the Borough, and I sold all my things—shovel and grafting-tool and all, to have a meal of food. When all my things was gone, I didn't know where to go. . . . Now I'm dead beat, though I'm only twenty-eight next August."

Stories about successful merchants like the Cadburys and less fortunate laborers like this railroad worker give us a glimpse at the two faces of Britain's industrial revolution. Year by year, the work and home lives of these people and others changed only gradually. However, between the 1780s and 1850s—little more than a single lifetime—astonishing developments transformed economic and social life in Britain.

The scene pictured on page 568 captures some of what that transformation meant to people. In the foreground of this 1851 painting is a romanticized vision of nature and the countryside, featuring trees, bushes, rock formations, hills, and a road winding around a lake. On the left, a couple, perhaps enjoying a picnic, relax with their dog—all apparently at one with nature. In the distance looms Manchester, which between 1780 and 1851 grew from a small country town to a large, industrialized city. Manchester's numerous factory chimneys belch clouds of smoke into the air. The sense of contrast is striking: In the city, people grind out the new wealth of this civilization, all while enduring crowds and filth away from the imagined delights of nature and the rural life they once knew.

In the mid-eighteenth century, most British people had lived in the countryside. Women and men who laboriously spun fibers into thread and yarn and then wove it into cloth with the aid of only simple tools and handlooms barely noticed the few new machines that could quickly spin American cotton into thread and weave it into cloth by the thousands of yards. At the edges of forests where wood was available for smelting iron, most iron masters still forged metal using slow methods inherited from their ancestors. To transport their goods to markets, these people, like their predecessors from centuries back, relied on coaches drawn by horses over rutted dirt roads, and on wooden ships pushed by currents and winds across the seas. Steam engines, already present for several decades, were inefficient and rare outside of coal mines.

By 1850 things had changed dramatically. About half of Britain's population, which had more than doubled during the period, now lived in cities. Cotton factories churned out hundreds of millions of yards of cloth that were sold throughout the world every year and were driving those who still made cloth the old way out of business. New mines, machines, and production techniques made vast quantities of iron cheap to produce, easy to work, and available everywhere. Railroads carried people and merchandise to their destinations quickly, inexpensively, and reliably. Recent generations of efficient coal-burning steam engines powered these factories, foundries, and railroads. Waves of inventions and innovations built on earlier breakthroughs cheapened production while improving quality. Entrepreneurs and business organizations applied these machines and production methods to other industries in Britain and elsewhere in the West. Although marked by periodic crises and downturns, a self-sustaining process of economic growth and tech-

nological change had been achieved and would continue through the decades after 1850.

Figure 17.1, an 1830 British print, reveals the impact on people's imaginations of the new industrial age. In this fanciful view, all sorts of vehicles powered by smoke-belching steam engines race down one of London's main streets—White Chapel Road. The old mixes oddly with the new: The street remains unpaved, some of the vehicles are little different than the horse-drawn carts and coaches of the period, and despite the jam of traffic there is still room for dogs to roam down the road at a leisurely pace. Yet the image is one of life in the process of being transformed by the new technology.

FIGURE 17.1
Technology transforming life.

What created this phenomenon—which French observers in the 1820s termed an "industrial revolution"—and why did it happen first in the West and particularly in Britain?

A BOOMING COMMERCIAL ECONOMY IN THE WEST

Why the industrial revolution emerged first in the West rather than in other civilizations such as China or India is difficult to say. Before 1500, Europeans enjoyed no fundamental advantages in how they produced goods over their Asian counterparts; in some areas, such as iron and steel production, they even lagged behind. Many qualities, such as intellectual traditions and politics, differed Eastern civilizations from the West and may help explain the early appearance of the industrial revolution in the West. However, the rise of commerce during the sixteenth, seventeenth, and eighteenth centuries distinguished the West economically. Civilizations elsewhere usually participated in this growing commerce only reluctantly. China, for example, may have produced luxury goods dearly desired by westerners, but, except for gold and silver, the Chinese wanted little in trade from the West. Moreover, the occupation of merchant had a low social status in China, further discouraging any potential bloom of commerce in that part of the world. In the West, however, the growth of commerce encouraged people to produce more agricultural and manufactured goods and sell them for a profit in the marketplace. Merchants and entrepreneurs became devoted to "buying low" and "selling high," thereby amassing more and more wealth. The growth of commerce helped create the potential markets, producers, entrepreneurs, and capitalists that would fuel the industrial revolution in the West.

The Western and non-Western worlds

BRITAIN'S UNIQUE SET OF ADVANTAGES

Commerce also helps explain why Britain industrialized first. During the sixteenth and seventeenth centuries, commercial activity in England intensified along with English sea power and overseas holdings. In the eighteenth century, Britain became Europe's leading commercial and colonial power (see Chapter 15).

Commercial vigor

Britain's economy efficiently turned out goods for export, and the island nation enjoyed considerable access to expanding markets—both internal, from its rapidly growing and relatively wealthy population, and external, from its colonies and established commercial connections.

Commercial vigor, however, is not enough to answer the question of why Britain led the industrial revolution. Other areas of Europe enjoyed advantages that would be important for industrialization. For example, during the first half of the eighteenth century, Holland's agriculture and financial institutions were second to none. France was the wealthiest nation in the West. Britain, however, boasted a unique combination of advantages that, when added to its commercial leadership, laid a solid foundation for the birth of the industrial revolution.

Water transportation—far cheaper and quicker than overland shipping—would play a crucial role in moving the coal, iron, cloth, and machines pumped out by Britain's new factories and mines. Already crisscrossed with countless navigable rivers (see Map 17.1), Britain enhanced its natural internal transportation system even more by building an extensive network of canals after 1760.

Transportation

Certain raw materials—above all coal, iron, and cotton—also had an essential part in the island's industrialization. Britain's American colonies harvested large quantities of cotton. The British countryside not only contained plentiful deposits of coal, but they were often conveniently located near iron deposits where foundry workers used the two materials in the newer processes of smelting to make iron products.

Raw materials

An expanding population and a particularly large and mobile force of both skilled and unskilled workers gave Britain another advantage. Already less tied to villages than others in many parts of the Continent, this class of rural laborers grew as waves of enclosures in the eighteenth century made many small farmers landless (see Chapter 15). These men and women could fill the rising demand for cheap industrial labor in the cities.

Labor

Britain had the capital to invest in industry for several reasons. First, its growing agricultural and commercial prosperity made it one of the wealthiest countries—per capita—in Europe. Second, it gained an unusual ability to amass and mobilize that wealth into capital for potential investment

Capital

thanks to the development of a national banking system. Third, unlike most of its continental competitors, Britain was long free of internal tariff barriers, had a uniform and stable monetary system, and—since the Glorious Revolution of 1688 (see Chapter 13)—had a government that sympathized with business interests. All this encouraged wealthy individuals and families to risk money on commerce and industry. Therefore, inventors, innovators, and those who saw an opportunity could more easily find the means to start an industrial enterprise in Britain than elsewhere in Europe.

Finally, and according to some analysts, most importantly, entrepreneurship—at the heart of industrialization—was more socially acceptable in England than elsewhere. Members of England's aristocratic families—especially younger sons left without inherited lands—often sought careers in commerce and manufacturing. Social barriers between them and the business-minded middle class were lower than elsewhere. More than in most European nations, British merchants and entrepreneurs occupied a strong, respected place in society. On the other hand, in France, for example, most elites looked on commerce and industry as a means—often regrettable—to gain money to purchase office, estates, and aristocratic status; as soon as possible, French aristocrats usually left commerce or distanced themselves from their businesses.

Entrepreneurship

In short, Britain had the most potential both to nurture and to take advantage of Europe's first industrial stirrings. Yet, what was it that finally transformed this potential into reality? Oddly, the crucial development came with advances in agriculture.

A REVOLUTION IN AGRICULTURE

The agricultural revolution, with its new crops, methods of rotating crops, breeding of animals, and enclosures of open fields, spread in Britain during the late seventeenth and eighteenth centuries (see Chapter 15). Production increased, as did profits for the

THINKING ABOUT GEOGRAPHY

MAP 17.1 *Eighteenth-Century England*

This map shows England's system of navigable waterways and areas of coal and iron production in the eighteenth century.
● **Consider** the advantages of England's natural resources for industrialization. **How** did the English add to those advantages during the second half of the eighteenth century?

large landowners who shipped their crops to markets near and far. Declining food prices enabled more British families to purchase manufactured goods such as shoes, knives, and cloth. As the agricultural revolution picked up speed, fewer and fewer people produced more and more food. The new, large-scale farmers grew crops and livestock to feed the growing number of people working in factories, digging in the mines, and building their lives in the cities. Moreover, these well-to-do, enterprising landowners could use their profits to invest in the many business and commercial opportunities becoming available.

By 1850 the majority of Britain's population no longer raised food or lived in the countryside. Most lived and worked in cities and factory towns. Whether people were better off in these urban centers is a question we will turn to later. For now, the stage was set for Britain's industrial revolution.

New Markets, Machines, and Power

As wealth increased and people moved away from subsistence farming toward the burgeoning urban centers, the demand for manufactured goods reached unheard-of levels. Inventors and entrepreneurs rushed to fill this demand, dreaming up new machines and designing novel manufacturing methods. The machines, gaining complexity almost every year, seemed like mechanical wonders. The methods of production transformed the workplace. Coal and steam provided all the power necessary to make these machines and production methods work. Manufactured goods poured forth, available to all with the money to purchase them.

The Rising Demand for Goods

The old methods of production—slow, unreliable, and costly—could not satisfy the rising clamor for manufactured goods. In fact, the population growth in Britain and Europe alone created an ever expanding pool of potential customers for low-cost clothing, nails, pottery, knives, and so forth. Eager overseas buyers, particularly in the colonies, offered raw materials in return for Britain's manufactured goods. At home, Britain's own successful farmers and merchants added to the demand.

Between the middle decades of the eighteenth century and 1850, inventors and entrepreneurs introduced new machines and methods that began to sat-

isfy these hungry markets. Most inventors were practical men who embodied the widespread British interest in devices, gadgets, and machines of all kinds, and had more talent as curious tinkerers than as scientific thinkers. Industrial entrepreneurs were also practical. Sometimes inventors themselves, they more often used the new devices and processes invented by others. Entrepreneurs purchased machines and employed workers, ran factories and mines, and found the necessary capital and markets.

Inventors and entrepreneurs

Some entrepreneurs were landowning aristocrats, others rose from rags to riches. Many were Protestant dissenters, such as Calvinists and Quakers, who had been discriminated against by the dominant Anglican Church. Denied careers in government, they jumped at the opportunities presented by commerce and industry. Most, however, came from the middle classes. They took advantage of journals that promoted new techniques and ideas, divided and redivided the processes of production, and trained a work force unaccustomed to working with machines in factory conditions. Buying raw materials from both local and distant suppliers, they promoted their products to the public. Through their resourcefulness and sometimes outright greed, they pursued profits. Navigating a risky competitive environment, they often reinvested their profits in their shops and factories, buying new machines and boosting production. The story of how they took advantage of new markets in the early decades of the industrial revolution is a narrative of new developments in cotton, iron, and steam.

Cotton Leads the Way

Changes in cotton production came first and with dramatic results. Before 1750, most thread and yarn was spun by women and woven into cloth by men who worked in rural cottages or small urban shops. Using only simple spinning wheels and handlooms, these laborers produced thread, yarn, and cloth of uneven quality. How much they produced was limited by many things—the supply of fiber, farmwork that took them away from their spinning and weaving, the wages paid by the entrepreneurs who organized much of this work, and, above all, the tools and methods they used.

In 1733, John Kay (1704–1764) invented a device called the flying shuttle, which doubled the speed at which cloth could be woven on a loom. The shuttle in turn intensified the demand for thread. In the 1760s, James Hargreaves (d. 1778) invented the spinning jenny, which revolutionized thread production. By 1812 one spinner could produce as much cotton

Weaving and spinning thread as 200 spinners had in 1760. Other inventions, such as Richard Arkwright's (1732–1792) water frame and Edmund Cartwright's (1743–1823) power loom, allowed weavers to turn cotton into cloth in tremendous quantities. Two American developments added to the acceleration in textile production: Eli Whitney's (1765–1825) cotton gin (1793), which efficiently removed seeds from raw cotton; and the expanding slave plantation system in the South. Indeed, British manufacturers' growing demand for cotton became an important force perpetuating slavery in the cotton-growing areas of the United States.

By 1850, British cotton manufacturers had boosted cloth production from less than 40 million yards per year during the 1780s to over 2,000 million yards per year. Cotton had become hugely popular and, alone, accounted for some 40 percent of British exports.

§ IRON: NEW PROCESSES TRANSFORM PRODUCTION

Machines for the new cotton industry were just one source of a growing demand for iron. Armies needed guns and cannon; civilians needed nails and pans. Until the eighteenth century, British iron makers were limited by the island nation's dwindling forests, for they knew how to smelt iron ore only with charcoal, which came from wood. Even during the days of plentiful charcoal, ironworkers had only their own and their animals' muscle power with which to work the iron into usable forms. Figure 17.2, a painting by the British artist Joseph Wright of Derby (1734–1797), shows a typical eighteenth-century iron forge. As this picture suggests, most production came out of small family firms or homes of artisans. The men—posing proudly—use only hand-powered tools to transform the iron, while women and children stand by, averting their eyes or turning away from the white-hot metal.

Abraham Darby's (1678?–1717) discovery in 1708 of an efficient way to smelt iron with coal in a blast

Smelting with coal furnace started the iron industry down a new path. By the end of the century, other novel processes enabled iron makers to double production again and again in the years that followed. Foundry workers began using the steam engine to operate smelting furnaces, drive forge hammers to shape the iron, and roll the iron into sheets.

By 1850, ironworks, with their tall, smoke-belching furnaces, had joined cotton factories as a pillar of the industrial revolution.

§ THE STEAM ENGINE AND THE FACTORY SYSTEM

Both the cotton and the iron industries created ever higher demand for power. At the beginning of the eighteenth century, people had to rely on muscle, wind, and water to supply the energy to do their work. Early mills used water power, which meant that their owners had to build them near waterfalls. A drought in the summer or a cold snap in the winter could threaten to dry up or freeze this essential power source.

The steam engine, first used in the early eighteenth century to pump water out of deepening coal mines, provided a solution and would become the industrial revolution's most important technological advance. Portable and easily controlled, the earliest models were nevertheless not yet efficient enough for widespread application. Over the course of the eighteenth century, inventors such as Thomas Newcomen (1663–1729) and James Watt (1736–1819) improved the power and efficiency of these engines. Watt, a skilled craftsman backed by the daring entrepreneur Matthew Boulton (1728–1809), worked for years on the engine, making several design changes and eventually converting the

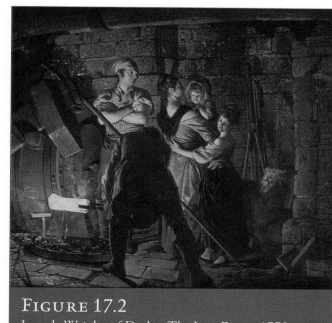

FIGURE 17.2

Joseph Wright of Derby, *The Iron Forge*, 1772.

reciprocal motion of the piston into a rotary motion. Now steam engines could be used not only to pump coal mines but also to drive the other new machines of the day, such as powering bellows for iron forges, mills for grains, and looms for textiles. Figure 17.1 indicates that the steam engine came to symbolize the new industrial age.

Reliable power from steam engines also made it possible for entrepreneurs to locate factories away from water power sites and build even larger cotton, iron, and other factories. In huge buildings, entrepreneurs hoped to guard their industrial secrets and mold a new labor force. Hundreds of workers, who produced goods in a repetitive series of steps and specialized tasks, tended rows of machines. The factory system had emerged. "The principle of the factory system . . . is to substitute mechanical science for hand skill, and the partition of a process into its essential constituents, for the division or graduation of labor," explained Andrew Ure, a professor of applied science, in 1835. As we will see, factories generated unprecedented wealth for their owners and investors, but brought new hardships for the people who toiled in them.

Figure 17.3 reveals the nature of the factory system. This realistic 1859 painting of a factory interior in France shows the mixture of raw materials (zinc ore), machines, and division of labor that epitomized factories in the industrial age. In the upper left and center, workers bring ore from the mines and dump it into machines for initial washing and processing. After the ore is split and sorted, workers shovel it into large ovens to be melted down. Men, women, and children work together in this hot, noisy building; the men have the more authoritative and skilled jobs (a foreman sits in the rear to the left), while the women and children are assigned to sorting and splitting chunks of ore.

FIGURE 17.3
Francois Bonhomme, *Workshop with Mechanical Sieves*, 1859.

COAL: FUELING THE REVOLUTION

As the industrial revolution hit its stride, the demand for coal also intensified. Steam engines devoured coal as fuel. Iron makers required more and more coal to run their furnaces. Britain's doubling population needed coal to heat their homes.

People poured huge amounts of money and labor into digging mines, extracting the coal, and developing the roads, canals, and rails necessary to transport the mineral to waiting customers. Coal not only fueled the industrial revolution; mining and manufacturing became so entwined that it was hard for people to think of one without the other.

 RAILROADS: CARRYING INDUSTRIALIZATION ACROSS THE LAND

The advent of the railroad age brought everything together. In the eighteenth century, horses had pulled carts along rails radiating out from mines, hauled barges along the growing network of canals, and pulled carriages along roads. Only wind in the sails of ships could move heavy cargoes and passengers across the seas.

During the 1820s, as steam engines began to power ships, the British inventor George Stephenson (1781–1848) developed the practical modern railroad. In 1830 his new train, "the Rocket," initiated the Liverpool-to-Manchester railway line. The Rocket's speed (sixteen miles per hour) and reliability excited the imaginations of everyone. People eagerly invested in railway companies, rode the new lines out of curiosity, and traveled by rail to vacation spots.

The railway carried heavy freight with unprecedented ease and speed. By 1850 trains were chugging over 2,000 miles of track in Britain, reaching astonishing speeds of up to fifty miles an hour. Steaming across bridges and through tunnels to the railway stations dotting the land, the new locomotives embodied the power and the promise that seemed to characterize the industrial age.

Figure 17.4, a lithograph by the British industrial artist John Cooke Bourne, portrays the drama of the railroad age. The piece shows a locomotive on the Great Western Railway, with its shining copper haystack boiler, bursting out of a newly built tunnel into daylight near Bristol in 1846. The image captures the combination of power, practicality, science, and art that characterized the early years of the railroads. Painted at the height of a speculative boom in railway stocks, it reflects the visions of optimistic ob-

servers such as the British politician Edward Stanley, who argued that "of all the promoters of civilization, the Railway System of communication will be amongst the foremost in its effects, for it cannot fail to produce many and mighty changes in manufactures, in commerce, in trade, and in science."

The railroad seemed to pull together all the trends that emerged during the industrial revolution. It ignited demand for an array of related products—coal-thirsty steam engines to power the trains, iron to build the rails *Effects of the railroad* and cars, cloth and leather to make furnishings, and bricks and glass to erect the new stations. Like the cotton factories, iron foundries, and coal mines, the railroad industry created new jobs while destroying old ones. In addition, it left is own permanent mark on the land and neighborhoods it affected. As Charles

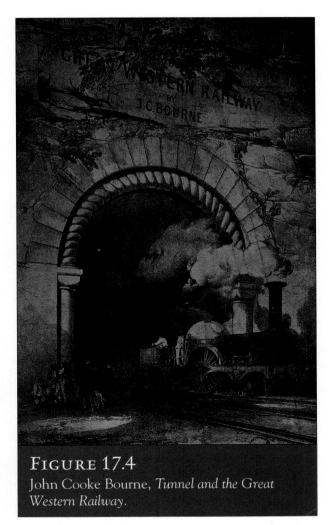

FIGURE 17.4
John Cooke Bourne, *Tunnel and the Great Western Railway.*

Dickens (1812–1870) described in *Dombey and Son* (1846), a new rail line meant that "houses were knocked down; streets broken through and stopped; deep pits and trenches dug in the ground; enormous heaps of earth and clay thrown up . . . everywhere carcasses of ragged tenements, and fragments of unfinished walls and arches, and piles of scaffolding, and wilderness of bricks, . . . mounds of ashes blocked up rights of way." All this "wholly changed the law and custom of the neighborhood," before the railroad "trailed smoothly away, upon its mighty course of civilization and improvement."

Finally, like the other new industries, the railroads could be a risky investment opportunity. Some owners and investors grew fabulously wealthy; others suffered devastating financial losses. Just as the cotton and iron industries continued to face competition from older methods such as the putting-out system (cottage industry), handicrafts, small family firms, and agriculture, the railroads had to fight to steal business from the roads and canal systems that were expanding across Britain at the same time. Those who had thrown their lot in with the railroads need not have worried too long about the wisdom of their investment, however. Like the cotton and iron factories, the railways were the wave of the future, and they rolled inexorably across the British landscape.

BRITAIN'S TRIUMPH: THE CRYSTAL PALACE EXHIBITION

In 1851, that shining future was put on display for all the world to admire. That year, London hosted the first international industrial fair at the glass-and-iron

FIGURE 17.5
The Crystal Palace Exhibition.

Crystal Palace. At this dazzling exhibit, millions of visitors came to gaze reverently at the British miracle.

Figure 17.5 shows the interior of the Crystal Palace—its arching glass roof like a cathedral, its steel framing a testament to modern engineering. Matthew Wyatt, one of the directors of the exhibition, proudly described the construction of the palace as an industrial triumph: "But for the perfect system of discipline, which frequent practice in directing the labour of masses of workmen has now made general throughout England, it would have been impossible to have fashioned, in so short a time, so novel and so vast a structure . . . the gates of which may . . . be thrown open to the world at large, for many years to come." To Wyatt and many others in 1851, the Crystal Palace was at once an architectural masterpiece and a jewel of mass production that could not help but appeal to popular taste. In addition to admiring the building itself, visitors could view displays from various nations. No exhibit was more impressive, however, than the British-manufactured products and machines. Figure 17.6 shows one of these British triumphs, a lathe for forming railway wheels.

The awe-inspiring palace confirmed economic realities. Britain produced more than half the world's cotton cloth and iron, and, despite periodic downturns, the nation enjoyed sustained economic growth. Britain had become the world's first industrialized nation.

Industrialization Spreads to the Continent

It was not until after 1830 that industrialization spread with much force outside Britain (see Figure 17.7). Before then, people from France, the German states, and elsewhere were interested in Britain's economic wonders. Some traveled to Britain to copy machines, while others enticed British technicians and capital to their own countries. A few modern industrial shops and machines sprang up on the Continent, but overall, agriculture and tradition still dominated economic life there.

After 1830, industrialization spread to certain regions, especially Belgium, northeastern France, the northern German states, and northwestern Italy (see Figure 17.7). These areas had plenty of urban laborers, deposits of iron and coal, and developed transportation facilities. Envious of British wealth, pressured by British competition, and recognizing the military potential of cheap iron and rail transportation, continental governments took a more active role in supporting industrialization than British rulers had. They enacted tariffs to protect their manufactures from British goods and subsidized new industries. Railroads, partially financed by governments and foreign capital, led rather than followed the advent of other industries, widening markets and creating demand for coal and iron. These countries could not yet hope to catch up to Britain. At midcentury, a German official complained that Germany would never "be able to reach the level of production of coal and iron currently attained in England." But soon Germany and other nations would manage to industrialize more selectively and quickly, thanks to the groundwork that Britain had laid.

Governmental aid

As Map 17.2 indicates, by 1850 large industrial centers had arisen in Belgium, France, and those areas of northern Germany bounded by the 1834 *Zollverein* (a customs union that eliminated tariffs between independent German states). Other regions, particularly around Milan in northern Italy and in the northeastern United States, had also begun to industrialize.

Most of southern, central, and eastern Europe, however, remained virtually untouched by industrial development. Lacking well-placed resources, efficient transportation, mobile work forces, commercialized agriculture, and capital for investment,

Remaining traditional economies

FIGURE 17.6
British machinery displayed at the Crystal Palace Exhibition.

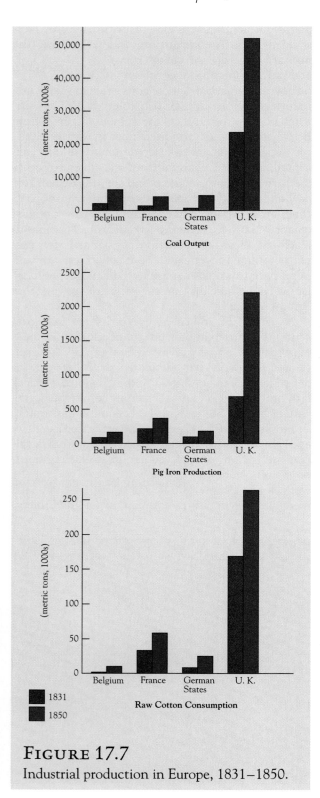

FIGURE 17.7
Industrial production in Europe, 1831–1850.

these regions retained their traditional and rural character. The vast majority of people in these areas remained in the countryside tied to subsistence farms or, especially in the east, large agricultural estates. Small villages rather than booming cities were the rule. Wealthy urban elites might purchase manufactured goods from industrial regions to the west, but their own countries could not produce them in the same way. Governments and perhaps a few ambitious and wealthy individuals sometimes imported the latest machines and built a few railroad lines, but these signs of industrialization primarily had symbolic or military value. Relying on old methods of production, merchants in these lands had trouble selling their manufactured goods in international markets. Nations, such as Spain and Russia, that once exported cloth saw their sales dry up in the face of British textiles.

There were a few exceptions in these traditional economies. For example, Austria's Bohemian lands developed a spinning industry, and a few factories sprang up around St. Petersburg and Moscow in Russia. Even so, British technicians and industrialists were often needed to support these limited efforts. On the whole, all these countries would have to wait before experiencing both the benefits and the burdens of the industrial revolution.

Balancing Benefits and Burdens of Industrialization

How did industrialization affect everyday life for Europeans? To answer this complex question, we might first explore the impact of the new machines, factories, and railroads on people's work conditions, home lives, and social relationships. It is also important to ask who received the lion's share of the new wealth.

Foreign observers marveled at Britain's wealth; indeed, to this day many of us associate machines, factories, and railroads with prosperity. Statistics seem to confirm this impression: Britain's national product rose more than threefold between 1780 and 1850. The population in Europe also surged during the same period and absorbed some of the new wealth. Probably thanks to better food supplies (especially cultivation of the potato), earlier marriages, and declining mortality rates, Europe's population ballooned from fewer than 175 million in 1780 to 266

New wealth

Population growth

million in 1850. During this same period, Britain's population more than doubled.

These startling numbers suggest a sense of economic well-being on the part of Europeans, but they also frightened some contemporaries. In his influential *Essay on the Principle of Population* (1798), British economist Thomas Malthus (1766–1834) warned that population growth would inevitably outstrip food supplies. A few years later another well-known economist, David Ricardo (1772–1823), argued that overpopulation would restrict wages to no more than subsistence levels.

Nevertheless, industrialization generated new wealth so rapidly that personal income rose faster than population growth in these years. Between 1800 and 1850, per-capita income skyrocketed by a whopping 75 percent in Britain. As other countries—such as Belgium, Germany, and France—industrialized, they too enjoyed similar gains. But who exactly was receiving these new riches?

THE MIDDLE CLASS

The middle classes (bourgeoisie), still a minority of the population even in Britain, prospered. The newest, most dynamic group within the middle classes were the industrial entrepreneurs—the factory and mine owners. They gained the most, some

THINKING ABOUT GEOGRAPHY

MAP 17.2 *The Industrial Revolution in Europe, 1850*

This map reveals the spread of industrialization in Europe by 1850. ◼ **Locate** industrial areas. **What** connections are there between these areas, resources—such as coalfields—and access to transportation by water or rail? **Compare** the extent of British industrialization to that in continental nations. ◼ **Notice** the location of railways. **What** does this suggest about the kinds of areas that early railways were intended to serve?

amassing enormous fortunes. Many bankers, smaller factory owners, professionals, merchants, and shop-keepers enjoyed more modest gains, as did those who earned interest and profits from investing their savings in industrial and commercial ventures. All investments, however, did not pay off. Some loans were not repaid. People took financial risks, and some lost their bets. Firms failed all the time, and periodic economic downturns spawned a string of losses and bankruptcies.

Still, over the long haul, the middle class as a whole benefited the most from industrialization. As their wealth and numbers grew, so did their prestige, political power, and cultural influence. The middle class, marked by their modest, sober clothing, gradually displaced the once glittering aristocracy who were still tied by tradition to the land. This process unfolded slowly, and some aristocrats and landowners managed to adjust quite well to the change.

THE WORKING CLASSES

The picture is far less clear for the working classes—those who labored in the factories, tended the machines, and toiled in the mines. For people who shifted from the agricultural life or jobs as artisans to work as factory laborers, industrialization may have hurt more than it helped, especially in its earlier decades. These people worked six days a week, twelve to sixteen hours a day, earning only subsistence level wages. William Harter, a British silk manufacturer, justified the long hours to a parliamentary commission: Reducing the hours of labor "would instantly much reduce the value of my mill and machines . . . every machine is valuable in proportion to the quantity of work which it will turn off in a given time." In textile factories, whole families typically labored together. Women's earnings were between one-third and two-thirds of men's, and children's wages were a mere fraction of that. As a result, factory owners employed women and children whenever possible to save money, and even contracted with orphanages to provide cheap child laborers.

Figure 17.8, an 1853 woodcut, shows the interior of a cotton factory. Here the supervisor of an English

Factory labor cotton factory whips a boy as a woman in tattered clothing looks on. Whipping was one way in which supervisors disciplined child workers to the rhythms of the machinery. In the

scene's background, women and men tend the spinning machines while three other men talk, apparently unconcerned by the violence. Middle-class reformers such as Frances Trollope (1780–1863) used pictures like these to decry the harsh treatment of children in the cotton mills. One governmental investigation of child labor described how children "were rendered pale, weak and unhealthy" from "labouring for hours like little slaves." Employers, anxious to keep their machines running and wages low, replied that "it was absolutely necessary that the children should be employed within the mills from six o'clock in the morning till seven in the evening, summer and winter."

After the 1820s, factory workers' wages started to climb. By the 1840s or 1850s, they were earning more

FIGURE 17.8
Factory labor, 1853.

than their agricultural counterparts. This change did not make them rich, however, for most of them had to spend some two-thirds of their income on food alone.

Money was only one variable in the quality-of-life equation. Industrial workers faced job insecurity, phys-

Insecurity

ical dangers, and painful changes unique to their way of life. The worst insecurity centered on employment itself. Even in good times, some firms failed. During economic downturns and crises, such as the "Great Hunger" of the 1840s, wages plummeted below subsistence levels, and many workers lost their jobs. For these industrial laborers there was no unemployment insurance to turn to, and no foraging, cottage industry, or gardening that people living in the countryside could resort to in hard times.

The work itself carried a high risk of severe physical injury. Factory owners made no provisions for safety. In cotton factories, children regularly climbed under and

Risks of injury

on top of the equipment to free jammed machines, collect cotton, and tie broken threads; many young workers suffered terrible injuries to their hands and even lost fingers. Long hours and exposure to chemicals, dust, smoke, and industrial residue all led to ill health. Indeed, industrial populations had a far shorter life expectancy and higher incidence of disease and deformity than rural populations. In the 1840s, the military turned down 90 percent of volunteers from some urban areas for health reasons—double the rate of rejection for rural volunteers.

Besides job insecurity, injury, and ill health, the new industrial age brought other lifestyle changes that are harder to evaluate. Industrial workers experienced a new rhythm of labor that no longer bore any

Lifestyle changes

resemblance to the natural rhythms of daylight and seasonal changes. Now, workers toiled unrelentingly to keep pace with the machines and schedules of the factory owner. Employers and their stewards maintained workplace discipline with fines, curses, and whippings. Children who could not keep up were beaten at times (see Figure 17.8); some were even chained to their machines. There were no slack days, like the traditional Monday of preindustrial times. Wages took the form of cash, which workers had to save and apportion carefully over the week for food and housing despite the temptations of alcohol and other leisure activities. At the end of the long workday, laborers trudged home to poor housing clustered around noisy mills or mine entrances, or to cheap, overcrowded rooms and cellars of industrial cities.

The question remains: Did the overall quality of life improve for the working classes in the early decades of the industrial revolution? One way to judge is to ask what would have happened to these people without industrialization. Communal villages and agricultural labor had their advantages. In a widely popular poem, "The Deserted Village," (1770) Oliver Goldsmith lamented the loss of rural life:

> *Ill fares the land, to hastening ills a prey*
> *Where wealth accumulated . . .*
> *But a bold peasantry, their country's pride*
> *When once destroyed, can never be supplied.*

People growing up on farms and in small villages at least had traditions they could rely on. But this traditional life also had its own harsh side. Poverty was no stranger to the countryside, nor was child labor, cold, uncertainty, and squalor in windowless hovels. One contemporary, Frederick Eden, argued that the difficulties experienced by small farmers and villagers were only "temporary," and a small price to pay for "the greater good which may be expected from the improvement." However we evaluate all this, life in the city did give the working class something no one could have foreseen: a new sense of class consciousness, an awareness of their own unique burdens and hardships that emboldened them into action and alarmed the onlooking middle classes.

DEVELOPING WORKING-CLASS CONSCIOUSNESS

As industrial workers lived in the same areas, labored in the same oppressive buildings, grappled with similar problems, socialized and commiserated together, and joined the same trade or civic organizations, they began to see themselves as a separate class. This sense of solidarity came partly from a tradition among artisans and craftsmen of mem-

Workers' organizations

bership in guilds. Although guilds were being made illegal after 1791 and opposed by middle-class people committed to gaining control over the workplace, other workers' organizations such as fraternal societies, trade organizations, and mutual aid societies persisted. These groups would lay the foundation for the emergence of trade unions, made legal (though severely restricted) in England in 1824 and elsewhere after 1850.

Figure 17.9, a nineteenth-century trade union membership certificate, reveals the pride and values in union labor during this industrial age. Like most unions of the period, the Associated Shipwright's Society—a British shipbuilders' union—was made up of skilled workers. Toward the top of this membership certificate is a blue shield; above it are two hands clasped in brotherhood, below it are the words, "WE ARE AS ONE." In the center is a construction site where ships are being built. Just above are pictures of ships, particularly the steamships that carried people and commerce throughout the world. On the bottom of the certificate are pictures of some of the typical benefits of union membership, including accident insurance, retirement income, and death payments. By midcentury, labor leaders had formed the beginnings of

national unions, such as the Grand National Consolidated Trades Union in Britain in 1834, the National Trades Union in the United States in 1834, and the General Workers' Brotherhood in Germany in 1848.

Sometimes workers turned to violence against what they saw as threats from industrialization by destroying the new machines. After 1811, English hand weavers, losing their work to the new power looms, went on rampages smashing the machines to pieces or campaigning to get rid of them. Glove makers, too, destroyed the new stocking frames that threatened their jobs. These forms of protest came to be known as Luddism in honor of a legendary (and perhaps fictitious) leader, Ned Ludd. The British Parliament quickly named industrial sabotage a capital offense and heavily suppressed the violence. Nevertheless, sporadic episodes of violence continued to erupt for several years, not only in Britain but elsewhere as the industrial revolution spread. In the 1830s, silk workers in Lyons, France, rose up against attempts to lower their pay. In 1836 Spanish workers burned a textile factory in Barcelona. During the 1840s, several governments had to call out troops against strikers.

Luddism

Most of these efforts brought few concrete results in the period before 1850. In addition to the power wielded by wealthier classes and governments, many internally divisive forces chipped away at the fledgling working-class solidarity. Labor leaders, for example, who usually came from the more skilled trades—the cabinetmakers, printers, tailors, masons, and blacksmiths—tended to look down on unskilled industrial workers. Most women were not invited to join worker organizations, though they forged some of their own trade associations. Other loyalties based on religion, region, trade, or even neighborhood undermined worker unity. Sometimes the only connection holding laborers together was a sense of shared problems, the belief that workers had a right to a "just wage," and the impression that their employers were exploiters rather than economic partners.

Despite the forces dividing them, workers' sense of themselves as a separate, unique class strengthened over time. Increasingly, members of the middle class began to see them as dangerous and even savage. As we will see in following chapters, with the sharpening of working-class consciousness, the power of the traditional artisan groups and the peasantry would decline—quickly in the decades after 1850, especially in highly industrialized places such as Britain, Belgium, and parts of Germany. The process would unfold more gradually in moderately industrialized

FIGURE 17.9
Trade Union membership certificate.

places such as France, and slowly in most of southern and eastern Europe.

For good or ill, industrialization was transforming everyday life across Europe. The economic and human balance shifted from the countryside to the city. Now the dramatic social transformations took place in the growing urban centers where, as one young worker described London in the 1820s, "a wilderness of human beings" lived.

Life in the Growing Cities

The unprecedented growth of cities from 1780 to 1850 stemmed from a combination of forces. Population was increasing in both urban and rural areas. Enclosures of land by market-oriented landowners that dispossessed individuals of their small farms and communities of their commons further uprooted rural families. These pressures pushed people from the land. At the same time, the cities, with their promise of jobs and the lure of beer halls and theaters, attracted people in droves. Industrial towns sprang up where none had existed before. Towns ballooned into cities, and already large cities grew even more imposing. Some of the most spectacular urban growth happened in industrial cities such as Manchester, which expanded from 25,000 in 1772 to 367,000 in 1850; and Birmingham, Leeds, and St. Etienne in France, which more than tripled in size. Other already substantial cities, such as London and Paris, became increasingly crowded and sprouted new suburbs.

Urban growth

Most cities flourished through industrial activity, such as mining and manufacturing. Other areas scarcely touched by industrialization, such as Naples, St. Petersburg, and Vienna, also grew dramatically through the expansion of governmental bureaucracies and traditional commerce.

THE PROMISE AND PITFALLS OF WORK IN THE CITIES

Industry, however, had the strongest pull. It inevitably attracted new commerce and gave rise to a broad range of consumer and service needs. Women flocked to the textile factories, but even more women living in the cities worked as domestics. Many young women came for what jobs they could find, perhaps hoping to send home part of their pay and still save enough to start a new life. The building trades drew growing numbers of men, who sometimes left their wives and children in the countryside to survive on a patch of land and dwindling cottage industry employment. Many men periodically returned to the countryside, particularly in winter when construction slowed, or during planting and harvest times.

LIVING WITH URBAN GROWTH

Industrialization and urbanization also altered the landscape that people traveled through to reach the cities. Forests shrank as people cut down more and more trees for construction of cities, mines, factories, and railroads. The same mines and railroads cut scars into the land, while the cities and factories ate up rural landscapes. Rivers once fit for fish or drinking now were polluted with industrial and human wastes.

Approaching the cities, travelers saw smoke in the air from the dirty coal fires used to heat buildings and from the engines of industry. Once in the city, and particularly in the poor working-class areas, the air smelled foul, for there were no modern sewers, sorely inadequate toilet facilities, and not enough clean water. Garbage and animal waste collected in the streets until heavy rains washed them away. In Manchester, only two-thirds of the houses had toilets, and many of those flushed into inadequate cesspools. Human and animal waste mixed in rivers that people used for drinking water. Charles Dickens' description of the fictionalized Coketown in his novel *Hard Times* (1854) would have struck a familiar chord for nineteenth-century travelers to Britain's industrial cities: "It was a town of machinery and tall chimneys, out of which interminable serpents of smoke trailed themselves for ever and ever. . . . It had a black canal in it, and a river that ran purple with ill-smelling dye, and vast piles of buildings full of windows where there was a rattling and a trembling all day long, and where the piston of the steam-engine worked monotonously up and down."

Environmental changes

Overwhelmed by these surroundings, newcomers to the cities tended to settle in areas where they knew someone else. Whole neighborhoods grew up populated by people who had come from the same rural region. This tendency led to a sense of segregation and separate identities within the cities, as people familiar with one another clustered together.

Few neighborhoods were planned. Indeed, the expansion of most cities became increasingly uncontrolled. The rampant growth created far more problems for the working class than for anyone else. The middle classes, for example, most likely lived in lower-floor apartments in the more desirable sections of town, and *Different neighborhoods* had the benefit of some running water. They also could afford to employ servants. It was in the working-class sections and poverty-stricken areas that the social ills and squalor of the age reached their worst levels. As the manufacturer and socialist, Frederich Engels (1820–1895) described, "The houses are packed from cellar to attic and they are as dirty inside as outside." In the Irish quarter of London, as many as thirty-eight people crowded into small buildings down narrow alleys where the walls were crumbling and "piles of refuse and ashes lie all over the place and the slops thrown out into the street collect in pools which emit a foul stench." In the bad quarters lived "the poorest of the poor. Here the worst-paid workers rub shoulders with thieves, rogues and prostitutes."

Figure 17.10, a mid-nineteenth-century woodcut by the French artist Gustave Doré (1832–1883), portrays the squalor and crowding of a London slum. In the center, a young child carries a baby, perhaps because her mother is working. Around her in the alley, dejected men, women, and children stand listlessly. Dark tenements tower over them, and laundry sags from clotheslines. Though criticized for overdramatizing the plight of the poor, Doré effectively conveys the anguish of unemployment, poverty, and crowding marring this rich city. As this and other works by novelists such as Charles Dickens, Elizabeth Gaskell, Frances Trollope, and Honoré de Balzac showed, the burgeoning cities were fostering a whole set of social concerns.

WORRYING ABOUT URBAN SOCIETY: RISING CRIME

One of those social concerns centered on patterns of criminal behavior. People in the upper classes complained about crime and the social disorder it implied. Had cities become hotbeds of crime, as some middle-class observers claimed, or were these critics simply overly worried about their own safety and well-being?

Crime certainly plagued people in the West long before the industrial revolution. In rural areas, along highways, and in the preindustrial cities of Europe, crimes ranging from pickpocketing to murder occurred all too frequently. Professional thieves reportedly ran rampant in Germany, England, and France in past centuries.

FIGURE 17.10
Gustave Doré, *A London Slum.*

In the early stages of industrialization, theft and robbery in particular did rise in the cities. Crowds provided prime opportunities for pickpockets. In urban taverns and dance halls, men sometimes fell into violent brawling, sometimes over women. In these establishments, alcohol flowed freely and almost certainly played a role in outbreaks of fighting. The widening gaps between rich and poor and the desperation of living in hard times also made tempers short. Finally, the anonymity of life in the city and the tempting array of luxury items to steal made crime harder to resist.

Whether justified by the realities of more crime or not, the specter of urban crime and fear of disorder prompted new efforts to improve law enforcement. In 1828 Parliament, under the leadership of Robert Peel, passed a law establishing the first modern police force in London. Peel's new police, called "Bobbies"

Crime and law enforcement

in his honor, emphasized regular patrols by uniformed officers as a way to deter crime and present a visual image of security. Both the middle and the working classes accepted the Bobbies, in part because the police were not allowed to be engaged for political purposes such as domestic espionage, and in part because people saw them as the first line of defense against all disorder. By the early 1830s, there were some 3,000 uniformed officers in the force.

The frightening consequences of rapid urbanization were becoming all too apparent. Year by year, the cities grew more densely packed and seemingly more dangerous. In bad times, they teemed with desperate people hoping to find jobs; in good times, they drew even more people eager to take advantage of the available work and other opportunities. Contemporaries associated the cities with overcrowding, filth, crime, moral degeneracy, and an unruly working class. "They [the working class] live precisely like brutes . . . they eat, drink, breed, work and die," complained a middle-class British observer in 1850. "The richer and more intelligent classes are obliged to guard them with police." Perhaps most disturbing, however, was the disease and death that haunted urban centers.

Public Health and Medicine in the Industrial Age

People had good reason to fear for their health and safety in the growing cities, especially in the poorer sections of town. On average, city-dwellers fell ill more often and died at a far earlier age than their rural counterparts. Within the cities, the poor lived half as long as the rich.

Industrialization itself was dangerous. The new machines maimed factory workers, and cave-ins, floods, and explosions killed miners. Various diseases stemmed directly from mining and manufacturing. Coal miners became ill and died from black-lung disease. Cotton workers developed brown-lung disease. In textile factories, women suffered particularly high mortality rates. Metalworkers, especially grinders, developed lung diseases from inhaling shavings. Poisonings from mercury, lead, and phosphorus used in industrial processes also increased.

THINKING ABOUT GEOGRAPHY
MAP 17.3   *The Spread of a Cholera Epidemic*

This map shows the spread of a cholera epidemic, which originally broke out in eastern India in 1817. ◨ **Notice** how, over time, the epidemic spread north and west. **Consider** what this reveals about the growing connections between the Western and non-Western worlds.

TO THE INHABITANTS OF THE PARISH OF
CLERKENWELL.

His Majesty's Privy Council having approved of precautions proposed by the Board of Health in London, on the alarming approach OF THE

INDIAN CHOLERA

It is deemed proper to call the attention of the Inhabitants to some of the Symptoms and Remedies mentioned by them as printed, and now in circulation.

Symptoms of the Disorder;

Giddiness, sickness, nervous agitation, slow pulse, cramp beginning at the fingers and toes and rapidly approaching the trunk, change of colour to a leaden blue, purple, black or brown; the skin dreadfully cold, and often damp, the tongue moist and loaded but flabby and chilly, the voice much affected, and respiration quick and irregular.

REMEDIES:

All means tending to restore circulation and to maintain the warmth of the body should be had recourse to without the least delay.

The patient should be immediately put to bed, wrapped up in hot blankets, and warmth should be sustained by other external applications, such as repeated frictions with flannels and camphorated spirits, poultices of mustard and linseed (equal parts) to the stomach, particularly where pain and vomiting exist, and similar poultices to the feet and legs to restore their warmth. The returning heat of the body may be promoted by bags containing hot salt or bran applied to different parts, and for the same purpose of restoring and sustaining the circulation white wine wey with spice, hot brandy and water, or salvolatile in a dose of a tea spoon full in hot water, frequently repeated; or from 5 to 20 drops of some of the essential oils, as peppermint, cloves or cajeput, in a wine glass of water may be administered with the same view. Where the stomach will bear it, warm broth with spice may be employed. In every severe case or where medical aid is difficult to be obtained, from 20 to 40 drops of laudanum may be given in any of the warm drinks previously recommended.

These simple means are proposed as resources in the incipient stages of the Disease, until Medical aid can be had.

THOS. KEY,
GEO. TINDALL, } *Churchwardens.*

Sir GILBERT BLANE, Bart. in a pamphlet written by him on the subject of this Disease, recommends persons to guard against its approach by moderate and temperate living, and to have in readiness the prescribed remedies; and in case of attack to resort thereto immediately but the great precautative he states, is found to consist in a *due regard to Cleanliness and Ventilation.*

N.B. It is particularly requested that this Paper may be preserved, and that the Inmates generally, in the House where it is left may be made acquainted with its contents.

NOV. 1st, 1831.

T. GOODE, PRINTER, CROSS STREET, WILDERNESS ROW.

FIGURE 17.11
A cholera warning, 1831.

THE DANGER OF DISEASE

The greatest danger came from infectious diseases. They were the great causes of sickness and death before the nineteenth century, and the rapid growth of crowded cities that lacked sanitation facilities made matters worse. People living in working-class quarters and urban slums were most vulnerable. Tuberculosis and diphtheria thrived in the most heavily populated areas and killed millions during the nineteenth century.

Worse, plagues periodically swept through cities. Cholera epidemics struck Europe several times, causing great panic as people in city after city awaited the arrival of the illness (see Map 17.3). Figure 17.11, a poster circulated throughout London in 1831, warned of the approaching disease and described its symptoms. Suggested remedies included taking several measures to restore warmth to the body, giving laudanum (opium dissolved in alcohol), and seeking medical aid. In 1831 alone, cholera killed some 100,000 in France and 50,000 in England.

People disagreed about the causes of diseases. Some observers blamed illnesses on physical weakness and immorality of individuals. In these critics' view, disease was rooted in *Causes of disease* inferior genetic background, overindulgence, degenerate lifestyle, poor hygiene, and irresponsibility. Only self-help could solve the problem, they argued.

Other commentators and some doctors theorized that disease spread through contagion—that people caught diseases from one another. This theory had more to do with magic, belief in the devil, or a desire to keep the ill out of sight than any notion of modern germ theory. It seemed to explain sexually transmitted diseases like syphilis, but could not answer the question of why some people contracted various diseases while others did not. In these commentators' minds, quarantine offered the best solution to fighting contagious diseases.

Most doctors eventually concluded that disease stemmed less from personal contact than from environmental forces. They believed in "miasma," the centuries-old notion that people caught diseases by breathing fumes given off by human waste, rotting vegetables, decaying flesh, marshes, or stagnant ponds. They also blamed poor diets for weakening resistance to these sources of disease. In a widely respected 1840 study, the French physician Louis Villermé attributed the prevalence of disease in the working-class slums of Lille to the cellars and crowded rooms where "the air is never renewed," where "everywhere are piles of garbage, of ashes, of debris from vegetables picked up from the streets, of rotten straw," where "one is exhausted in these hovels by a stale, nauseating, . . . odor of filth, odor of garbage." This helped him and others explain why people living in barracks, workhouses, and the worst parts of cities more often fell ill and died.

SEEKING MEDICAL CARE

None of these theories about disease aided individuals seeking medical care. Doctors may have been well-meaning, but in 1850, anyone visiting a doctor was more likely to be hurt than helped. Most people consulted physicians reluctantly and had *Doctors* little trust in the power of treatments or medicine. To our twentieth-century sensibilities, medicine in the early 1800s can indeed seem quite alarming. To alleviate a fever, for example, doctors often turned to traditional cures such as initiating bloodletting by opening a vein or applying leeches to the skin, or recommending laxatives to purge the "bad humors" and fluids from the body. Physicians routinely prescribed pills that at best did nothing and more likely contained toxic substances such as mercury. Frequently, the addictive drug laudanum was suggested for the treatment of pain, sleeping problems, difficulties with children, and a variety of other complaints. Such treatments more often led to fluid depletion, poisoning, and addiction than any improvement of the patient's condition.

More benignly, doctors might recommend fresh-air cures or "taking the waters" at health spas. Many of the wealthy traveled to coastal resorts and centers in Caldas da Rainha in Portugal, Bath in England, and Baden Baden in Germany for these health

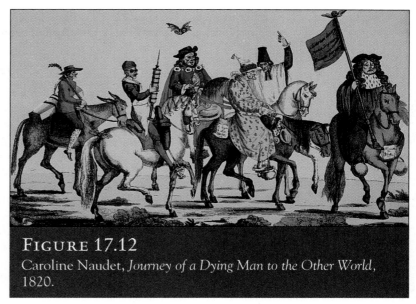

FIGURE 17.12
Caroline Naudet, *Journey of a Dying Man to the Other World,* 1820.

cures. They may have gained some temporary relief from conditions such as arthritis, but they more likely enjoyed the lively social events and casinos that also attracted them to these spas.

Figure 17.12, an 1820 print by the French artist Caroline Naudet (1775–1839), reveals popular attitudes toward physicians. Entitled *Journey of a Dying Man to the Other World,* the print depicts a wealthy doctor in black robes leading a procession that includes a dying man, a clergyman pointing up, a surgeon with a fluttering bat over his head, a sinister-looking apothecary carrying an enema device, and an undertaker. The solemn physician carries a banner that describes the traditional treatment for diseases: "To give a clyster [enema], after that to bleed, finally to purge."

Many sufferers looked for treatments opposed by ordinary doctors to cure their ailments. Homeopathy,

Alternative medicine which emphasized the use of herbal drugs and natural remedies, gained in popularity during the period. Other options—from vegetable laxatives, claimed to be effective for all ills, to faith healers—saw wide use. These alternatives at least gave sufferers a sense of controlling their own health.

As for surgery, people turned to this option only as a last resort. Surgical methods became safer in the

Surgery first half of the nineteenth century, but anesthesia and antiseptics still lay in the future. Those who managed to survive the pain of an opera-

tion faced a likelihood of dying from an infection afterward.

PROMISING DEVELOPMENTS FOR PUBLIC HEALTH

Despite all the dangers, the period had a few bright spots for the future of public health. Improvements in diet probably held the most promise. Many nutritious foods had become more available than ever, especially potatoes, which were an affordable, rich source of vitamin C and minerals; dairy products, which helped newborns survive infancy and childhood; and meat, which contained high-grade proteins. Inexpensive cotton underwear, thanks to the new cotton mills, kept people warmer and cleaner than before. The smallpox vaccine, developed during the eighteenth century and made into a safe form in 1796 by Edward Jenner in England, would virtually erase a disease that had once afflicted almost 80 percent of Europeans and killed millions. The discovery of anesthetics—nitrous oxide and, after 1846, ether and chloroform—began to make surgical trauma bearable.

Other developments showed some potential as well. Following the lead of a small group of influential French physicians, European doctors applied scientific methods to medicine and made great strides in pathology and physiology. Hospitals proliferated and increasingly became places to observe the sick and gather information. New laboratories allowed doctors to conduct more experiments. Professional organizations and educational institutions for doctors and nurses formed, and governments, particularly in France, began taking some responsibility for medical education and licensing.

New developments in medicine

Many doctors no longer relied solely on a patient's description of the problem. Physical examinations became common—feeling the pulse, sounding the chest, taking the blood pressure, looking down the throat. Some doctors used the new stethoscope, which became a crucial tool for diagnosing bronchitis, pneumonia, and pulmonary tuberculosis (commonly referred to as consumption). Among the upper classes, the family physician was even gaining some favor as a respected social contact and confidant.

In England, Edwin Chadwick (1800–1890) initiated a campaign to improve public health. In his 1842 report for a parliamentary commission, *The Sanitary Condition of the Laboring Population of Britain,* he emphasized that the accumulation of human and animal waste near people's dwellings was a crucial cause of disease. He proposed a system of underground tunnels that would allow constantly running water to carry waste out of the city.

Nevertheless, the gains from these promising new developments would not come until the second half of the nineteenth century. In Britain, one of every three people still died of contagious diseases in the decades surrounding 1850. Health therefore remained a great public and private concern. It was not the only concern that crossed the lines between public and private life, however. The day-to-day events in everybody's lives, whether in illness or health, unfolded within a crucial setting: the family. In this period of industrialization and urbanization, the family as an institution and the roles within it would begin to shift in the face of enormous economic and social pressures.

Family Ideals and Realities

The ways that people come together into families and the roles they play in their families usually evolve slowly, if at all. During this period, however, the middle class redefined accepted notions of the family, and working-class families struggled under the new pressures beleaguering them. In subtle but important ways, family ideals and realities were changing.

MIDDLE-CLASS IDEALS: AFFECTION, CHILDREN, AND PRIVACY

With their numbers, wealth, and status in urban societies rising, the middle class not only developed its own ideas about what the proper family should be; it propagated those ideas as the norm for everyone else. The result was an evolution of, rather than a break from, old notions about the family. Compared with families of earlier times, the ideal middle-class family emphasized emotional bonds, attention to children, and privacy.

People were supposed to marry because of affection, love, and emotional compatibility. Social rank and wealth remained important, but these values exerted less influence than they had in the past. Love could bridge social and economic gaps. Indeed, one of the great themes in the flood of new novels that appeared during the nineteenth century centered on this very conflict: the tension between love and money in marriage. In stories that ended happily, love won out—though most characters in these plots never were relegated to a life of poverty as a consequence of their choice.

Marriage

The new middle-class family was smaller and more child-centered than before. Europeans were choosing to limit the size of their families, and by midcentury this preference led to declining rates of population growth. Women gave birth to fewer children—two or three rather than the five or six of an earlier era—and more infants than ever survived the first, riskiest years of life. Unlike workers and peasants, middle-class parents did not have to view their children as economic assets—as hands to work the fields, help with the crafts, or labor in the factories. Wealthier urban parents could afford to raise perhaps just two or three children as fulfilling products of a good home. More than ever, children came to be seen as innocent, impressionable, vulnerable persons who should be separated from the corrupting influences of adult society. Mothers and fathers began investing more time, effort, and other resources in child rearing. Boys, especially, needed training and education designed to ensure their success as adults in the changing urban world. To arm them with these essentials, parents extended the time period of childhood and economic dependence. All this re-

Family size

Children

quired planning and intensified emotional ties between parents and children. Parents increasingly centered their attention and family activities on children.

More than ever, mothers and fathers idealized their home as a private "haven in a heartless world," separate from and above the world of paid work. The home **The home** represented the reward for competing on the job, a protected, glorified place for a satisfying personal life. There husband and wife could enjoy the delights of material possessions and, hopefully, the rewarding intimacy of family life. As indicated by the growing number of popular books by authors such as Jane Austen (1775–1817), Mary Ann Evans (1819–1880) (writing under the pen name George Eliot), and Charlotte Brontë (1816–1855), home was a setting of many appealing, moralizing dramas where the virtues of prudence, love, sacrifice, self-reliance, and persistence could usually overcome all obstacles.

SEPARATE SPHERES: CHANGING ROLES FOR MIDDLE-CLASS WOMEN AND MEN

With the rise of industrialization and urban life, the roles of middle-class husbands and wives grew more and more separate. In the seventeenth and eighteenth centuries, most middle-class families had worked together as one economic unit—sharing the responsibilities of running a shop or business, and living near their place of work in back rooms, upstairs, or next door. During the nineteenth century, the tasks assigned to men and women, and the private world of home and the public place of paid work, became increasingly distinct. As the locus of work shifted from the home to the factory, store, or office, women lost their traditional employments that contributed to the family economy. Paid employees working outside the home now occupied the role previously played by women who had run thriving family businesses. The new economic growth also allowed middle-class families to afford the homes, servants, and leisure previously reserved for the elite. Eventually, the ability of middle-class women to devote more time to their homes and families without having to do paid work, and to hire servants to lighten domestic burdens, became symbols of social success. The home became women's sphere, and within the home, child rearing began requiring far more maternal attention than ever. As the task of raising children and socializing them with the values and training needed for success expanded, so did the responsibilities of motherhood. Becoming "rational mothers," fully able

to meet the new demands of child rearing, turned into a revered duty.

The man was supposed to be the respected economic provider who operated primarily in his sphere: the competitive world of work outside the home. He was expected to behave in an authoritative, competent, and controlled manner. These qualities reflected the legal and economic realities of the time. Under British common law and the Napoleonic Code on the Continent, for example, a man had legal authority over his wife and children. He also had control over his wife's personal property as well as over any money earned by her. Furthermore, only men could vote. Most positions in the middle-class world of work were reserved for men. Those jobs usually required specialized skills in planning and information managing—abilities that came primarily from formal schooling. Young men were more likely than women to receive a formal education in areas of study such as accounting or law. Through apprenticeships and clerkships in commerce, industry, or finance, men also found many opportunities to equip themselves for success in the growing industrial-urban economy.

Women faced a very different set of cultural expectations. A host of marriage manuals, medical tracts, advice books, and religious dictates reminded women that their place was within **The woman's domestic sphere** the domestic sphere. A woman should provide emotional support for her husband and cultivate a virtuous home environment to

FIGURE 17.13
Carolus-Duran, *Merrymakers*, 1838.

Biography

THE CADBURYS

By the late eighteenth century, the Cadburys were a well-established Quaker family of shopkeepers in western England. Young Richard Tapper Cadbury used his father's connections to find positions as an apprentice and journeyman to drapers (selling retail cloth and dry goods) in Gloucester and London. In 1794 his father helped him again, giving him money to start his own cloth and dry goods store on a main street in Birmingham, one of Britain's leading industrial cities.

In 1800, Richard, his wife Elizabeth, and their growing family moved into an apartment above their shop on Bull Street. Middle-class families such as the Cadburys typically lived in the same building as their business until they could afford to buy a separate home.

Elizabeth Cadbury, like most middle-class women of moderate means, worked in the family enterprise but had received no professional training. She picked up skills on the job, helping rather than leading, and taking over for her husband when he was away. As a married woman, Elizabeth had no independent legal identity and could not have owned a business on her own. Formally, their family business belonged to Richard, but like many businesses during the period, it also functioned as an informal partnership between the couple. In addition to working in the business, Elizabeth was also responsible for running the household, which included eight children and young apprentices.

Draper retailers such as the Cadbury family played a major role in the revolution of Britain's textile industries. Like producers, retailers benefited from the new sources of supply and expanding demand for cloth. The Cadbury shop expanded and brought in enough income for Richard and Elizabeth to rent a house and land for a garden on the outskirts of Birmingham in 1812. The younger children, their nurse, and their pets moved there. Elizabeth and her older daughters traveled back and forth managing the two households.

A Rising Middle-Class Family

Richard's and Elizabeth's sons eventually apprenticed in retail businesses in different cities—Benjamin as a draper, John as a tea and coffee dealer. The daughters had no such training. Instead they learned what they could from their mother as they helped in the shop, house, and garden.

John (1801–1889) opened a tea and coffee store next door to his parents' shop (see Figure 17.14). He and his first wife, who died in 1828, lived over the shop. When John accumulated enough money, he also opened a plant to manufacture the cocoa and chocolate for which the family name would become so famous. In 1834 John and his second wife, Candia, moved their home away from the city, with its filth and crowds, to a new planned middle-class suburb just

counteract the amoral, competitive marketplace. She should care for the children, make sure the house was clean and the meals served, supervise domestic servants (a requirement for any middle-class home), and manage other domestic tasks from sewing to administering household accounts.

In the 1838 painting shown in Figure 17.13, Carolus-Duran depicts two middle-class women at home. The center of the women's attention, and the painting, is a playful child sitting on her mother's lap and reaching for a pet bird or figurine. Across the table from the two well-dressed women, a maid or house servant leans toward the child with a folded paper figurine, perhaps in mock play with the bird. On the lower right are more petlike figurines. Indeed, middle-class families often considered pets as much a part of domestic life as the food and drink on the table.

In some ways, a middle-class woman's domestic sphere extended outside the home. She might manage the family's social life, for example, or lead in reoutside of Birmingham. Candia generally stayed at home, busy with her domestic tasks and gardening, while John rode to town every day to take care of business and political affairs.

FIGURE 17.14
E. Wall Cousins, *The Cadbury Shops*, 1824.

Candia could not look after the family business as her mother-in-law Elizabeth had, for the demands of child rearing had grown and the training necessary for John's more complex business had increased. John and Candia's spheres were much more distinct that the elder Cadburys' had been.

In 1861, John's sons, Richard and George, took over their father's failing business. They visited a chocolate factory in Holland that was using a new process to transform cocoa beans into cocoa and chocolate. In 1866, they successfully introduced that process into their own factory. This new technique helped them to break the near monopoly that French chocolate products had previously enjoyed in the British market. In the decades that followed, the brothers built Cadbury into a prosperous cocoa and chocolate manufacturing firm. Richard painted the designs for fancy Cadbury chocolate boxes that idealized children and their innocence, using his own children as models.

In 1879, the brothers moved their firm from industrialized Birmingham to a rural site they called Bournville. There they introduced improved conditions for their workers and a private social security program, reforms well ahead of their time. George, holding firmly to the Quaker views of his parents and grandparents, had long taught in a Birmingham "adult school" for workingmen. Concluding that poor housing lay at the root of many social evils, he began building high-quality working-class housing that featured gardens. By 1900, that community included 313 houses and served as a model for British "garden cities" and "garden suburbs."

In 1901 George and members of his family acquired the *London Daily News* and other newspapers, which they used to express their Liberal Party views. By this time, Cadbury, which had grown unevenly from the seeds planted by Richard and Elizabeth in 1794, had become a vast, worldwide company.

▣ **Consider** why the Cadburys benefitted so greatly from the industrial revolution and how members of the family exhibited typical nineteenth-century middle-class values.

ligious matters. If she had the time and means, she might also participate in philanthropic activities, social movements such as temperance or the abolition of slavery, and certain cultural events—but only as long as these activities added to her image as virtuous, dutiful, maternal, supportive, and sensitive. These activities put women in a position of power as representatives of the family in religious, social, and cultural matters, and often gave them the last word on such matters within the family.

Involvement in politics was out of the question for most women. A few middle-class women joined movements to gain political and legal rights, but their efforts did not lead to real reforms during this period. Nor did paid work fit the domestic image. While a woman might serve without wages as a clerk or secretary in her husband's store or office, paid work outside the home was considered inappropriate and generally not available to married women. Even for unmarried women, only occupations directly connected to the domestic role such as governess, elementary school-teacher, lady's companion, or seller of women's clothing were deemed acceptable. There were exceptions, especially in cultural fields such as painting and writing, but most people raised a skeptical, disapproving eyebrow at women who had such careers.

At home, a wife was expected to be the counterpart to her controlled, strong husband. "In every thing . . . that women attempt, they should show their consciousness of dependence" on men, explained Elizabeth Poole Sandford in her widely read book *Woman in her Social and Domestic Character* (1842). Law hindered most married women from acquiring economic independence and generally placed them, as well as children, under the formal power and protection of men. Women were to be emotional and even frail, and therefore capable of only domestic tasks. The training of young women reinforced these qualities. Instead of a secondary schooling or professional education, women's formal training focused on religion, music, and perhaps languages. Any other skills a young woman might need, she picked up at home.

Educators and scientists generally agreed that women were ill suited for occupations outside the home and that they lacked the emotional control, mental acuity, and assertiveness of men. Doctors usually held the same views, and even believed that menstruation incapacitated women and that women had no interest in sex. Clothing, too, emphasized this vision of women's proper role. Middle-class husbands wore prudent and practical clothing for the world of work—trousers and jackets in modest black or gray. Their wives endured tight corsets and full decorative skirts more suited for display than action.

In short, the middle-class ideal was a small, private family bonded by love and authority. In such a family, the wife and husband willingly fulfilled the expected roles of their separate spheres. Families measured their success in achieving this ideal by the luxury items they bought, collected, and self-consciously displayed; by the accomplishments of their children; by how well their lives matched the uplifting dramas that the novels and paintings of the day depicted; and by their participation in appropriate social, religious, and philanthropic activities.

Middle-class success is well illustrated by the economic and social rise of wealthy commercial and industrial families such as the Cadburys (see Biography). The 1824 drawing by E. Wall Cousins in Figure 17.14 shows the still-modest Cadbury shops on Bull Street in Birmingham. To the right is Richard's original dry-goods (linens) store; to the left, his son John's tea and coffee shop. The plate-glass windows and the dress of people on the street indicate the store's intention to appeal to middle-class and wealthy clients. Above are the family's apartments, which include plants and pets. When the business expanded, the Cadburys moved away from this store to a suburban house, with separate nursery and schoolrooms for the children. The idea of separate rooms for eating, cooking, children, reading, and socializing was new and reflected the growing wealth of the middle class and how the idea of differentiation—separate areas for different tasks and the division of labor—already spreading in the industrial world affected the domestic sphere as well.

Middle-class success

WORKING-CLASS REALITIES

The middle class assumed that its vision of the proper family served as the standard for all. However, this vision did not fit the urban and industrial realities facing the far more numerous working classes.

Industrialization pulled many working-class women away from their homes and into factory jobs. Employers preferred to hire women because they worked for lower salaries and seemed more pliable than men. In the early decades, young children often accompanied their mothers, providing even cheaper labor and falling victim to the harsh, disciplined factory environment. During the 1830s and 1840s, public outcry against child labor (led by middle-class reformers, not the working class) prompted women to leave their younger children at home in care of an older child or neglectful "babyfarmers," women who took in far too many children. Many mothers resorted to drugging their children with laudanum to keep them out of harm's way while the adults were at work.

Women workers

Middle-class critics demanded reforms that would limit women's ability to work away from home, though working-class women objected that they had no better alternatives. As one group of women factory workers from Manchester pointed out, "Hand loom has been almost totally superseded by power loom weaving, and no inconsiderable number of females, who must depend on their own exertions, . . . have been forced . . . into the manufactories, from their total inability to earn a livelihood at home." During recessions, women's plight worsened. Employers laid off the more highly paid men first, leaving women with the overwhelming burden of managing both a paid job and all the domestic tasks at home.

Working-class and peasant families were being pulled apart in other ways as well. Adolescent boys left home to seek work in the mines or cities. Daughters, too, sought jobs as factory laborers or as domestics in middle- or upper-class homes. In the cities, women were all the more vulnerable during economic downturns when low-paying jobs disappeared.

PROSTITUTION

Hard times left both unmarried and married women in particularly desperate straits. To survive, some women turned to prostitution, which grew along with Europe's mushrooming cities. In 1850 there were probably some 30,000 prostitutes in Paris, and 50,000 in London. Unemployment and the dangers of solitude were probably the main forces driving women to prostitution. Many prostitutes had come from outside the cities and had no family to help them. Others were out-of-work domestics, seamstresses in need of income during a slow season, daughters of unemployed workers, or women abandoned after being impregnated by masters or lovers. Low wages also led to prostitution; a woman earned as much money in one night prostituting herself as she could acquire after an entire week of work at the factory.

Many of these women worked as prostitutes for relatively short periods, and only part time. While the work helped them financially, it also exposed them to venereal disease, which ran rampant during this period. Finally, in some people's minds, prostitution linked working-class women to images of urban crime and immorality. To middle-class moralists, prostitutes embodied unrestrained sexuality and therefore were the ultimate outcasts. However, despite its dangers, prostitution would persist as a sign of the difficulties that many working families faced in Europe's growing cities.

STRESS AND SURVIVAL IN THE WORKING CLASSES

The new tensions swirling through working-class family life had severe consequences for some. Peasant, artisan, and working-class families had worked together as economic units for longer than the middle class had, and industrialization and urbanization corroded this unity. The stresses proved so great that some families broke apart, leaving a growing number of women to work and manage households on their own.

However, the picture was not all bleak. As a rule, the family survived, providing a haven for workers and a home for children. Like peasants' and artisans' families, many working-class families clung to the old putting-out system or the newer piece-work system, in which entrepreneurs distributed jobs, such as tailoring or decorating, to workers at their homes. Unions, better wages, and new social policies would ease the burdens on workers in the decades after 1850. In the end, most families adjusted and found ways to meet the many challenges of the industrial age.

Industrialization meant unprecedented, sustained economic growth, and it soon became a measure of whether people considered a society "modern" or "traditional." Carrying in its wake fundamental changes in literally all aspects of life, industrialization altered the ways people worked, what they could buy, how they lived their lives, and where they stood on the social ladder. Its railroads, dams, bridges, factories, and mines transformed the land, the rivers, and the air. Nations that industrialized left others behind in the competition for wealth. That wealth was all too easily translated into power, leaving traditional agrarian societies in the West vulnerable to their industrialized neighbors.

The new riches pumped out by the machines of industry also propelled the West into an even stronger position

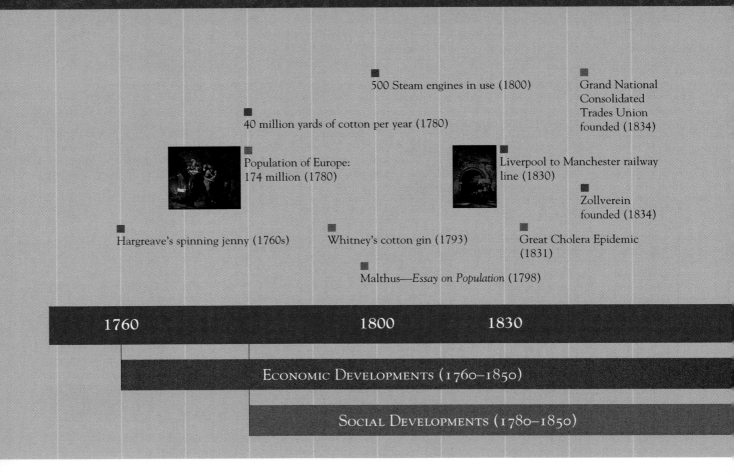

500 Steam engines in use (1800)

Grand National Consolidated Trades Union founded (1834)

40 million yards of cotton per year (1780)

Population of Europe: 174 million (1780)

Liverpool to Manchester railway line (1830)

Zollverein founded (1834)

Hargreave's spinning jenny (1760s)

Whitney's cotton gin (1793)

Great Cholera Epidemic (1831)

Malthus—*Essay on Population* (1798)

| 1760 | 1800 | 1830 |

ECONOMIC DEVELOPMENTS (1760–1850)

SOCIAL DEVELOPMENTS (1780–1850)

to dominate over unindustrialized, non-Western societies throughout the world. Decade after decade, a widening gap of wealth and power opened up between the industrializing regions of the West and nonindustrializing regions of Asia, Africa, and Latin America.

At the same time, the cities grew. There, old ties to traditional communities and beliefs loosened; long-established religions even lost some of their influence. Despite a host of social problems, the cities had a vibrancy and an image of opportunity that continued to attract people. While some people lost when they migrated to the cities, others gained, whether by hard work, luck, or the advantages of birth. Perhaps life in the countryside, with its slower pace and simpler pleasures, simply could not compete with what the city promised.

Through these decades, most families found ways to adapt to new circumstances. Middle-class families responded to their improving positions by developing a compelling new set of ideals about how men and women should behave. Working-class families did their best to hold themselves together in the face of divisive forces; looking to the future, workers began seeing themselves as a new class of people who just might have the power to determine their own fate.

This growing awareness by both classes added to the fundamental changes being wrought by industrialism.

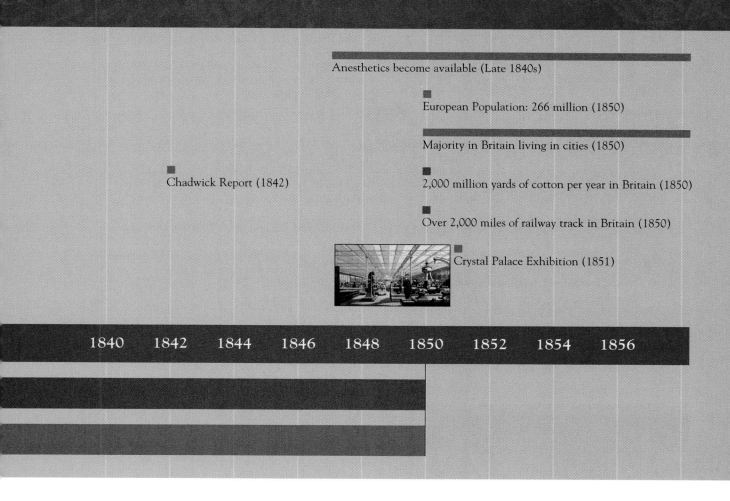

Anesthetics become available (Late 1840s)

European Population: 266 million (1850)

Majority in Britain living in cities (1850)

Chadwick Report (1842)

2,000 million yards of cotton per year in Britain (1850)

Over 2,000 miles of railway track in Britain (1850)

Crystal Palace Exhibition (1851)

| 1840 | 1842 | 1844 | 1846 | 1848 | 1850 | 1852 | 1854 | 1856 |

Conflict—whether in an intellectual realm, at the work site, in the courts, or on the barricades—would often be the result. These conflicts, along with those stemming from the French Revolution, would profoundly shape social and political life in the West in the decades to come.

REVIEW, ANALYZE, AND ANTICIPATE

REVIEW THE PREVIOUS CHAPTER

Chapter 16—"Overturning the Political and Social Order"—examined the revolution that transformed France and whose consequences were felt throughout the West. The chapter also focused on the role Napoleon played during that period and the battles he waged throughout Europe until his final defeat in 1815.

1. *Who do you think were the main beneficiaries of the French Revolution and the industrial revolution? Were they the same groups?*

2. *In what ways might the French Revolution and the industrial revolution be related?*

ANALYZE THIS CHAPTER

Chapter 17—"Factories, Cities, and Families in the Industrial Age"—analyzes the industrial revolution and urbanization.

1. *How do you explain why Britain was the first to industrialize?*

2. Compare the consequences of industrialization for the middle class and the working class.

3. In what ways did moving from the countryside to the city change people's lives during this period?

4. Analyze how the family and ideas about women's and men's roles altered within the middle class. In what ways were circumstances different for working-class families?

ANTICIPATE THE NEXT CHAPTER

In Chapter 18—"Coping with Change"—we will examine the political developments, theories of change, and revolutionary movements of the period between 1815 and 1850.

1. What sorts of problems do you think the industrial revolution will pose for governments? What policies might they adopt to solve those problems?

2. Consider which ideas about the industrial revolution might be favored by people sympathetic to the workers. What about people sympathetic to middle-class employers?

BEYOND THE CLASSROOM

THE INDUSTRIAL REVOLUTION BEGINS

Brown, Richard. *Society and Economy in Modern Britain, 1700–1850.* New York: Routledge, 1991. Argues that Britain's industrial development was gradual and quite regionally varied.

Mathias, Peter. *The First Industrial Nation,* 2nd ed. London: Methuen, 1983. Attempts to account for the origins of industrialization in eighteenth-century Britain and traces its development during the nineteenth century.

O'Brien, Patrick K., and Roland Quinault, eds. *The Industrial Revolution and British Society.* Cambridge: Cambridge University Press, 1993. Essays by noted scholars that stress the origins and consequences of the industrial revolution in Britain.

NEW MARKETS, MACHINES, AND POWER

Deane, Phyllis. *The First Industrial Revolution,* 2nd ed. Cambridge: Cambridge University Press, 1979. A respected account of British industrialization and its consequences.

Goodman, Jordan, and Katrina Honeyman. *Gainful Pursuits: The Making of Industrial Europe, 1600–1914.* London: Edward Arnold, 1988. A wide-ranging examination.

Landes, David S. *The Unbound Prometheus: Technological Change and Industrial Development in Western Europe from 1750 to the Present.* London: Cambridge University Press, 1969. A classic treatment of technological development in a broad social and economic context.

Mokyr, Joel. *The Lever of Riches: Technological Creativity and Economic Progress.* New York: Oxford University Press, 1992. Attempts to explain why technological creativity occurred in some places and not in others.

INDUSTRIALIZATION SPREADS TO THE CONTINENT

Pollard, Sidney. *Peaceful Conquest: The Industrialization of Europe, 1760–1970.* Oxford: Oxford University Press, 1981. Charts the process of industrialization as it spread from Britain to the European continent.

Sylla, Richard, and Gianni Toniolo, eds. *Patterns of European Industrialization.* London: Routledge, 1993. A comparative analysis of industrialization in Europe.

BALANCING THE BENEFITS AND BURDENS OF INDUSTRIALIZATION

Chinn, Carl. *Poverty Amidst Prosperity: The Urban Poor in England, 1834–1914.* Manchester: Manchester University Press, 1995. Focuses on the poverty created by the industrial revolution.

Nardinelli, Clark. *Child Labor and the Industrial Revolution.* Bloomington, IN: Indiana University Press, 1990. A sympathetic portrait of the topic.

Thompson, E.P. *The Making of the English Working Class.* New York: Random House, 1966. A remarkable book of sympathy and insight that has been hugely controversial and influential.

LIFE IN THE GROWING CITIES

Lawton, Richard, and Robert Lee, eds. *Urban Population Development in Western Europe from the Late Eighteenth to the Early Twentieth Century.* Liverpool: Liverpool University Press, 1989. Examines urban growth throughout western Europe.

Traugott, Mark, ed. *The French Worker: Autobiographies from the Early Industrial Era.* Berkeley, CA: University of California Press, 1993. Presents a working-class perspective on the effects of industrialization.

PUBLIC HEALTH AND MEDICINE IN THE INDUSTRIAL AGE

Porter, Roy. *A Medical History of Humanity.* New York: W.W. Norton & Co., 1998. A wide-ranging and interesting survey that covers the period well.

Family Ideals and Realities

Davidoff, Leonore, and Catherine Hall. *Family Fortunes: Men and Women of the English Middle Class, 1750–1850*. Chicago: University of Chicago Press, 1987. An interesting analysis of the interaction between gender and class that reconstructs every dimension of middle-class life.

Maynes, Mary Jo. *Taking the Hard Road*. Chapel Hill, NC: University of North Carolina Press, 1995. Examines German and French workers' lives during the industrial revolution.

Tilly, Louise, and Joan Scott. *Women, Work and Family*. New York: Holt, Rinehart and Winston, 1978. A classic study of the family as an economic unit, especially during the first half of the nineteenth century.

Anton Ziegler, *The Barricade in Michaeler Square on the Night of May 26th*

This painting by the Austrian artist Anton Ziegler depicts the "glory days" of the 1848 revolutions. In the image, men and women of various classes in Vienna guard a revolutionary barricade made of paving stones, timbers, and carts. Behind the barricade, a community of people stand ready to help one another politely in the common effort (notice the man aiding a woman across a wooden footbridge). The atmosphere has an almost festive quality, and nothing in the picture hints at the violence and loss of life that came with this turbulent year.

CHAPTER 18

Coping With Change

Ideology, Politics, and Revolution, 1815–1850

Prince Clemens von Metternich (1773–1859), Austria's conservative and powerful minister of foreign affairs, discussed ideas in candlelit salons as easily as he wielded power in somber cabinet meetings. Like other cosmopolitan aristocrats born into traditional eighteenth-century societies, he spoke French as well as the German of his birthplace. In 1820, five years after the fall of Napoleon, he wrote to his ally, Tsar Alexander I (r. 1801–1825) of Russia. "Kings have to calculate the chances of their very existence in the immediate future," he complained. "Passions are let loose and league together to overthrow everything which society respects as the basis of its existence; religion, public morality, laws, customs, rights, and duties, all are attacked, confounded, overthrown, or called to question."

Metternich, Alexander I, and people everywhere were struggling to adjust to the political and social forces unleashed by the French Revolution and Napoleon's domination of Europe. The industrial revolution, wherever it set its roots, spawned another set of problems along with the wealth it created. Together, these waves of change were undermining traditional political, social, and economic orders.

Some, such as Metternich, fought to maintain the old order; others, displaying the "passions" Metternich complained about, fought for all-encompassing reforms. People on all sides turned to ideologies—sets of ideas, attitudes, and beliefs about how the world is and should be—to try to cope with the new realities of Western life in the nineteenth century. One of those realities was the possibility of revolution again raising its unpredictable head. The outcomes of these struggles of ideologies and politics would profoundly shape much of nineteenth-century history.

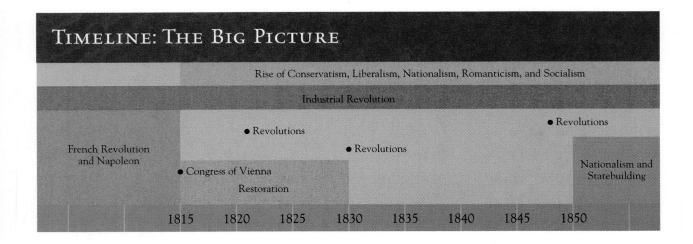

Rise of Conservatism, Liberalism, Nationalism, Romanticism, and Socialism

Industrial Revolution

• Revolutions

• Revolutions

French Revolution and Napoleon

• Revolutions

• Congress of Vienna

Restoration

Nationalism and Statebuilding

1815   1820   1825   1830   1835   1840   1845   1850

The Congress Of Vienna: A Gathering Of Victors

In the autumn of 1814, the leaders of the powers who had finally vanquished Napoleon gathered to redraw territorial boundaries and fashion a lasting peace. The conference also attracted representatives of every state in Europe, hundreds of dispossessed princes, agents of every interest, and adventurers. Nearly everyone who thought he or she was somebody of importance in "high circles" attended. The representatives reveled in the glittering gatherings and entertainments. In addition to the public conferences, many private meetings took place—though just how private remains uncertain, for Austrian spies regularly opened letters and searched wastebaskets. Elsewhere, in newspapers from St. Petersburg, Rome, and Paris to London and even Boston, people closely followed the daily events in the beautiful Austrian capital. Something immensely important and exciting seemed to be unfolding there.

The four major victors over Napoleon—Great Britain, Prussia, Russia, and Austria—set peace terms with France around the time of Napoleon's overthrow in April, and these four dominated the congress. The able Lord Castlereagh (1769–1822) represented Great Britain and the experienced Baron Hardenberg (1750–1822) represented Prussia. Russia's tsar, the unsteady Alexander I, headed his own delegation. The elegant, arrogant Metternich led the Austrian delegation and became the most influential figure of the congress.

Jean-Baptiste Isabey's formal portrait of the principal figures at the Congress of Vienna (Figure 18.1)

The victors

gives a sense of the seriousness of this event and the ideals that the victors represented. From left to right, Austria's polished Metternich stands before a chair, Great Britain's Castlereagh sits with crossed legs, and the elderly Talleyrand (1754–1838) of France rests with his right arm on the table. In a fine but businesslike eighteenth-century salon, these powerful men are gathered around a table to participate in the reading and signing of crucial documents. Their clothing marks them as members of the aristocracy: almost all the men sport gold trim and knee breeches with high stockings, some wear military coats and carry swords reflecting victory in the field over Napoleon. Most display medals symbolizing their achievements and position. Yet these clothes also hint at change: most of the figures in the painting lack the more elegant clothing and wigs of the eighteenth century. Above the men, as if approving of what they are doing, hangs a symbol of the restoration of the old regime: a portrait of a king draped in regal robes.

As guiding principles in the negotiations, the conferees decided on "legitimacy" and "stability." By *legitimacy* they meant that territories should once more be placed under the control of the old ruling houses of the

Legitimacy and stability

traditional order. By *stability* they meant establishing and maintaining a balance of power within Europe, with particular focus on restraining France. The main powers agreed that the settlement should apply to all of Europe.

Yet the conferees proved lenient in their settlement toward France. Thanks to the victors' desire to turn France into an ally rather than a resentful enemy and to Talleyrand's diplomatic skills, France, the original force behind all the turmoil, escaped the proceedings

Kongreß zu Wien. Sitzung der Bevollmächtigten der acht an dem Pariser Frieden beteiligten Mächte.
Nach dem Bilde von Isabey gestochen von Godefroy.

FIGURE 18.1
Jean-Baptiste Isabey, *The Congress of Vienna.*

with only light penalties. Having already restored the French throne to the Bourbons, the powers merely reduced France roughly to its 1789 boundaries. Because of Napoleon's 100-day return (see p. 563), they also required France to pay an indemnity of 700 million francs, return stolen art treasures, and submit to occupation by allied forces until the indemnity was paid.

To confine France within its frontiers and discourage future French aggression, the powers established *Territorial arrangements* strong buffer states along France's borders. As Map 18.1 shows, Prussia received a sizable block of territory along the Rhine, the Austrian Netherlands (Belgium) and the Dutch Netherlands were unified, Piedmont-Sardinia in northern Italy was enlarged, and the old monarchy was restored in Spain.

Trading among themselves, the four main powers took new territories. Great Britain gained several strategic islands and colonies, all of which boosted its sea power and overseas dominance. Prussia added some areas in central Europe. Russia acquired control over a reduced, nominally independent Poland, thereby edging farther into the heart of central Europe. Russia also took Finland from Sweden, which in turn got Norway at the expense of Napoleon's ally, Denmark. Austria gained Lombardy and Venetia in northern Italy as well as the permanent presidency over the weak German Confederation—the thirty-nine German states that remained after Napoleon's destruction of the Holy Roman Empire.

Although they displayed little concern for the wishes of the peoples being placed under the control of one power or the other, the conferees did produce a settlement that contributed to a century of freedom from Europe-wide war. Moreover, thanks to the persistent efforts of the British, the powers agreed in principle to abolish the slave trade. They also achieved—at least temporarily—their conservative goals of promoting legitimacy and stability that meant so much to them.

THINKING ABOUT GEOGRAPHY

MAP 18.1 *Europe, 1815*

This map shows Europe after the Congress of Vienna in 1815. ▧ **Compare** this map with that of Napoleon's empire in Chapter 16 (Map 16.4). **What** are the main changes? ▧ **Locate** the enlarged states—the Netherlands, Prussia, and Piedmont-Sardinia. **Why** did the Congress of Vienna strengthen these states? ▧ **Consider** the effect of the settlement on the major European powers. **Did** the settlement severely punish France?

THE CONCERT OF EUROPE: SECURING THE VIENNA SETTLEMENT

Metternich and his colleagues, pleased with their handiwork, set up the political machinery for perpetuating the Vienna settlement. Conveniently at hand was the Holy Alliance, conceived by Alexander I to establish and safeguard the principles of Christianity. Russia, Austria, and Prussia—the three bastions of conservatism—formed the nucleus of this alliance. Though Metternich and professional diplomats put little faith in it, the Holy Alliance did symbolize a commitment to preserving the Vienna settlement. Perhaps more important, it suggested a possible willingness to intervene in other countries in support of its conservative principles.

The Holy Alliance

The Quadruple Alliance, also known as the Concert of Europe, proved a much more earthly agency for perpetuating the Vienna settlement. Austria, Russia, Prussia, and Great Britain created this military alliance in November 1815 to guarantee the Vienna settlement. The powers agreed to hold periodic meetings to discuss common problems. In 1818 France completed its payment of indemnities and joined the Alliance.

The Concert of Europe

Soon this conservative partnership showed its strength. In 1821 it authorized an Austrian army to put down an insurrection in Naples against King Ferdinand I. The Neapolitan liberal rebels, no match for the Austrian troops, were soon defeated and their leaders executed, imprisoned, or exiled. In 1822 the Alliance, despite Britain's withdrawal, authorized France to intervene against a liberal revolt in Spain. A French army streamed across the Pyrenees and easily crushed the rebellion. That same year, the conservative powers supported Alexander's proposal to send a Russian fleet to help put down the revolt of Spain's Latin American colonies (see Chapter 16).

The great strength of the Alliance, however, remained bound within the European continent. Across the Atlantic Ocean, President Monroe of the United States announced what would come to be called the Monroe Doctrine: The United States would regard any interference on the part of European powers in the affairs of the Western Hemisphere as an "unfriendly act." British support of the doctrine—stemming from Britain's own economic interests in Latin America—killed any further thought of Holy Alliance intervention in the Western Hemisphere, for Great Britain enjoyed unchallenged dominance of the seas.

Ideologies: How the World Should Be

The principles underlying the settlement at Vienna and the international cooperation to enforce it reflected the deep conservatism of Metternich and many others during these years. Their conservatism was more than just a whim or political mood. Under the impact of the French Revolution and the industrial revolution, the centuries-old aristocratic order and agriculturally based society had started to crumble. Intellectuals in particular tried to grasp these changes by exploring ideologies, or sets of beliefs about the world and how it should be. These ideologies exerted immense power. People wrote, marched, fought, and died for them. Indeed, they fueled many of the struggles that would erupt in the years to come, and ultimately would shape our very definition of the modern world.

CONSERVATISM: RESTORING THE TRADITIONAL ORDER

The changes initiated during the French Revolution and supported by Enlightenment ideas threatened and even terrified conservatives. They wanted desperately to preserve the traditional way of life. Conservatism provided the ideas to refute Enlightenment and revolutionary principles and all those who stood behind them. At the heart of conservatism lay a belief in order and hierarchy. The social and political order, conservatives believed, should be based on a hierarchy of authoritative institutions whose legitimacy rested on God and tradition. As conservatives saw it, the revolutionary notion of equality was wrong. The elite was equipped to rule; the rest were not. The most formidable enemy was the bourgeoisie, "this intermediary class" ready to "abandon itself with a blind fury and animosity . . . to all the means which seem proper to assuage its thirst for power," according to Metternich. Conservatives also warned that the idea of individualism promoted by the Enlightenment and favored by the rising middle class would fragment society and lead to anarchy. In the mind of a conservative, all change was suspect. If change did come, it should take the form of slow evolution of social and political institutions.

In 1790, the influential Anglo-Irish writer and statesman Edmund Burke (1729–1797), horrified with the outbreak of the French Revolution, outlined some of the principles of conservatism (see p. *Burke* 544). He argued that the revolutionaries' radical reforms based on abstract reason and notions of equality unraveled hard-won victories against savagery: "[I]t is with infinite caution that any man ought to venture upon pulling down an edifice which has answered . . . for ages the common purposes of society." The monarchy and nobility should be preserved because they, like the church, were established links to an organic past and the best hopes for preserving the order necessary for societies to thrive.

The French writers Joseph de Maistre (1753–1821) and Louis de Bonald (1754–1840) represented a later generation of conservative thinkers who proved more rigid and ultraroyalist than Burke. *de Maistre and de Bonald* They attacked everything about the French Revolution and Enlightenment as contrary to religion, order, and civilization. De Maistre called the French Revolution an "insurrection against God." Both writers argued that authority rightly rests in the monarchy and the church, both of which derive that authority from God. "When monarchy and Christianity are both attacked, society returns to savagery," declared de Bonald. These conservatives felt that deep down, humans were more wicked than good, more irrational than rational. Only the time-tested traditions and institutions could hold the bad impulses of humans in check. All means, including fear and violence, should be used to roll back the changes from the French revolutionary and Napoleonic periods and return to societies dominated by monarchs, aristocrats, and clergy.

Not surprisingly, people from these same three groups found conservatism most appealing. Conservatism also attracted many who believed in a Christian view of society, particularly members of the established churches rather than religious minorities. Some even saw the revolutionary and Napoleonic periods as divine retribution for *Appeal of conservatism* the presumption and evil that had long marred human beings. In the international field, conservatism was epitomized by Metternich's policies, the Holy Alliance, and the Concert of Europe. In domestic policies, this conservatism was characterized by the restoration of power to the traditional monarchs and aristocrats, the renewed influence of Christianity, and the suppression of liberal and nationalistic movements.

However, conservatives faced formidable opponents even during the early years after the fall of Napoleon. The French Revolution had turned the ideas of liberalism into a powerful, persistent force. The clash between conservatism and liberalism had just begun and would endure into the twentieth century.

LIBERALISM: INDIVIDUAL FREEDOM AND POLITICAL REFORM

In contrast to conservatism, liberalism drew on the promises of the French Revolution and the Enlightenment. Conservatives sought to maintain traditional society; liberals fought to change it. Liberals wanted a society that promoted individual freedom, or liberty. However, many laws, customs, and conditions of the traditional order stood in their way. Liberals therefore opposed the dominance of politics and society by monarchs, aristocrats, and clergy, and governments' arbitrary interference with individual liberty. To the extent that these elements of the traditional order remained in place, liberals demanded reform and fought resisting conservatives.

From the Enlightenment and the theories of John Locke, liberals adopted ideas about natural laws, natural rights, toleration, and the application of reason to human affairs (see Chapter 14). From political thinkers such as Montesquieu, they took the idea that governmental powers should be *Sources of liberalism* separated and restricted by checks and balances. From the French and American Revolutions, they drew on the principles of freedom, equality before the law, popular sovereignty, and sanctity of property.

Liberalism reflected the aspirations of the middle class, which was gaining wealth but lacked political and social power in the traditional order. Not surprisingly, then, liberals advocated government limited by written constitutions, the elimination of political and social privileges, and extension of voting rights to men of some property and education (most liberals stopped short of suggesting universal male suffrage or extension of the vote to women.) In addition, liberals desired representative institutions where none existed, and an extension of the right to participate in representative institutions that remained the preserve of the aristocratic and wealthy elite. They demanded that governments guarantee the sanctity of property and individual rights, such as freedom of the press, speech, assembly, and religion.

Certain economic policies also had great importance to liberals and reflected the stake that the middle class had in commerce and industry. The Scottish economist Adam Smith (1723–1790) formulated the ideas that guided economic liberalism (see pp. 488–489). In *The Wealth of Nations* (1776), **Smith** Smith argued that economics, like the physical world, had its own natural laws. The most basic economic law was of supply and demand, he explained. When left to operate alone, economic laws, like an "invisible hand," would keep the economy in balance and, in the long run, create the most wealth. According to Smith, self-interest—even greed—was the engine that motivated people to work hard and produce wealth. Governments should therefore follow a policy of laissez-faire (hands-off), limiting their involvement in the economy to little more than maintaining law and order so that an unfettered marketplace could flourish.

Other liberal economic thinkers extended Smith's ideas. The British economist Thomas Malthus (1766–1834) cast gloom on hopes for progress among workers. He argued that population would always increase more than food supplies, resulting in poverty **Malthus and Ricardo** and death by "the whole train of common disease, and epidemics, wars, plague and famine." Malthus concluded that workers themselves are "the cause of their own poverty," because they lacked the moral discipline to avoid sexual activity. The politically influential Englishman David Ricardo (1772–1823) refined Malthus' arguments into the "iron law of wages," explaining that wages would always sink to subsistence levels or below because higher salaries just caused workers to multiply, thereby glutting the labor market and lowering wages. He emphasized that the economy was controlled by objective laws. The lessons for these "classical" liberals (to distinguish them from modern American liberals, who usually favor government programs to regulate certain economic and social affairs) were clear: No intervention in economic matters by government, no tariffs or unions that artificially raise prices or wages, and no restrictions on individual enterprise.

Over time, liberalism evolved and developed several variations. The English philosopher Jeremy Bentham (1748–1832) and his followers advocated a kind of liberalism that became particularly influential in Britain. Known as utilitarianism, it held that all activities and policies should be judged by the standard of usefulness. "Nature has placed mankind **Bentham** under the governance of two sovereign masters, *pain* and *pleasure*," explained Bentham. What was useful, the utilitarians decreed, was what created more pleasure than pain; the best laws and policies were therefore those that promoted "the greatest good for the greatest number" of people. Bentham's utilitarians fought for more governmental intervention in economic and social affairs than other liberals. For example, they supported reforms to protect women and children workers in factories and to improve urban sanitation. Democracy was implicit in utilitarianism, for the best way for the greatest number to maximize their own happiness was for each person to vote. Nevertheless, most liberals during this period actually opposed democracy. They feared the supposedly unruly "masses" and hoped to keep government in the hands of the propertied and well educated. They would not start to embrace demo- **Mill** cratic reforms until the middle of the nineteenth century. At that time, some of them, such as John Stuart Mill (1806–1873) (see Biography), would also begin arguing for major social programs to protect workers and even the right to vote for women.

As we saw earlier, liberalism appealed especially to the rising middle classes, who were prospering from commerce and industry and wanted political power along with their growing wealth and confidence. Liberals had faith that history was on their side, that liberalism, like progress, was inevitable and that the forces they opposed were of the past. That optimism gave them strength to fight against the conservative forces of tradition and rally to protect their gains.

NATIONALISM: A COMMON IDENTITY AND NATIONAL LIBERATION

Like the liberals, nationalists harbored a spirit of optimism. They too were aroused by the French Revolution, for it promoted the idea that sovereignty rested not in a monarch or church, but in the people, and that they, banded together, constituted the nation. Nationalism promised to unify nations, liberate subject peoples from foreign rule, create a sense of fraternity among members of a national community, and lead that community to a common destiny. At its core was a feeling of cultural identity among distinct

Biography

JOHN STUART MILL (1806–1873) AND HARRIET TAYLOR (1807–1858)

John Stuart Mill and Harriet Taylor were one of the most famous and extraordinary couples of the nineteenth century. Born in 1806, John described his own childhood as "remarkable." His father, the well-known liberal philosopher James Mill (1773–1836), raised John according to the cut-and-dried principles of Jeremy Bentham's utilitarianism. John learned Greek at the age of three, Latin when he was seven, logic at twelve, and economics at thirteen. On their daily walks, James encouraged little John to summarize assigned readings for him. He wanted to turn John's mind into a logical machine for radical thought and utilitarian reform.

In 1822, John and several other young men founded the liberal Utilitarian Society. John, like other liberals, had great faith in the power of knowledge and reason to right human errors: "Knowledge has triumphed. It has worked the downfall of much that is mischievous." For the young Mill, utilitarianism was virtually "a religion." In 1823, John took his first job with the East India Company, the vehicle of British rule in India. He would remain with that company for thirty-five years, reading dispatches from the company's agents in India and drafting replies.

In 1826 he suffered a "crisis." Recoiling from his sterile, intellectualized upbringing, John came to doubt the value of his education and ambition, concluding that neither of these qualities led to happiness. He turned to romanticism—a movement that featured the lush music and especially the writings of Wordsworth, Goethe, and other cultural icons of the day. In time, he came to believe that "poetry is higher than logic, and . . . the union of the two is philosophy."

During these same years, nineteen-year-old Harriet Hardy had married John Taylor, a wealthy partner in a wholesale drug firm. Taylor adored his intellectual wife, who was bolder and more brilliant than he. However, after giving birth to two children, Harriet began to lose interest in John. She increasingly found sex with him an unpleasant imposition and criticized marriage as a sexual contract that was unfair to women.

Extraordinary Victorians

In 1830 Harriet Taylor and John Stuart Mill met. They became "intimate and confidential friends." Mill was a constant visitor to the Taylor household and a frequent companion to Harriet in London. Although their relationship created a scandal in London society, John Taylor, unwilling to see his wife unhappy, acquiesced in it.

In 1843, Mill published *A System of Logic*, the first of several major works that marked him as one of the leading thinkers of the nineteenth century. In 1851 Harriet published anonymously *The Enfranchisement of Women*, which argued for universal suffrage and more equal companionship between men and women. Mill would go on to publish *On Liberty*

---

groups of people who shared a common language and traditions and who belonged in a nation-state of their own.

France became an early source of nationalist sentiments. There a sense of membership in the state became especially important when the Revolution transformed the kingdom into a nation. Popular sovereignty, wider political participation, and abolition of old provincial boundary lines gave the French a feeling of solidarity among themselves and with the national government. Universal conscription into the revolutionary armies added to feelings of fraternity in a righteous cause and helped make those armies strong. Powerful new symbols, such as the tricolor flag, stood for national unity and willingness to sacrifice for the sake of the nation.

The French Revolution

(1859), his most famous political work, in which he argued for freedom of thought and warned against the tyranny of the majority. In 1869 he published *The Subjection of Women*, which made him one of the leading feminists of the century. It is fundamentally wrong, he said, for society to "ordain that to be born a girl instead of a boy, any more than to be born black instead of white, or a commoner instead of a nobleman, shall decide the person's position through all life."

Mill was happy to describe most of his works as jointly produced by himself and Harriet. But Mill may have been too generous in his praise of her role. Just how much she contributed has long been a matter of heated debate. In 1849, two discreet years after John Taylor's death, Mill and Harriet Taylor married. They were proud that their relationship was based on rationality, intellectual companionship, affection, and intimacy, but not sex. They imagined their marriage as a utopian union of equals. It lasted until 1858, when Harriet died.

In the years before his death in 1873, Mill was elected to the House of Commons, where he argued for liberal reforms such as the abolition of capital punishment, feminist reforms such as the extension of suffrage to women and socialist reforms such as poor relief. Figure 18.2 shows a caricature drawing of Mill that was published in the widely read journal *Punch* in 1867. Readers could easily recognize the famous liberal intellectual (depicted with an unusually large head). The illustration shows him leading women, who are demanding the right to vote, by pushing aside resisting men with his arm and his logical arguments. He concluded that "the social problem of the future" would center on "how to unite the greatest individual liberty of action with a common ownership in the raw material of the globe."

Thus Harriet and John embodied many nineteenth-century trends. Liberalism,

romanticism, and socialism all played a role in their lives. In addition, what brought them together was the middle-class ideal—affection, companionship, the shared life at home. In other ways, however, they did not reflect the times at all. Their views on marriage and relations between men and women, for example, the long triangular relationship with John Taylor, and the intensity of their intellectual collaboration all alarmed many of their contemporaries. Only in the decades to come would these unusual views gain more favor.

◙ **Consider** why Mill is labeled a leading proponent of liberalism. ◙ **Compare** the Mill family and the Cadbury family discussed in Chapter 17.

FIGURE 18.2
John Stuart Mill.

Nationalism also moved people who did not yet share a state. In the German-speaking areas, for example, scholars and intellectuals developed a cultural basis for nationalism. Writers such as Johann Gottfried von Herder (1744–1803) fostered a sense of common national identity arising from German folk culture and oral traditions. Georg Wilhelm Friedrich Hegel (1770–1831)

Cultural nationalism

provided philosophical and historical bases for German nationalism and the importance of the national state. Romantics such as Ernst Moritz Arndt (1769–1860) urged Prussians, Austrians, Bavarians, and others with common roots to "be Germans, be one, will to be one by love and loyalty, and no devil will vanquish you." Groups and secret societies like Young Germany—usually composed of students, intellectuals, and members of the middle class—promoted a sense of national identity and unity.

In Italy, Poland, and elsewhere, nationalists formed similar organizations while intellectuals created interest in national languages and folk culture. Scholars resurrected and developed languages from previous eras and elevated myths to national histories. Schoolteachers taught these languages and histories to their students and thereby spread a sense of ethnic unity. Nationalists used this growing interest in language and history to proclaim their nation's special mission—for example, of the Czechs to become leaders of the Slavs, or the Italians to lead Europe again as it had during Roman times.

Nationalism promised a new sense of community as the old order with its traditional allegiances declined. It offered a sense of strength and unity that appealed to many peoples: to those
Sense of community threatened with foreign domination, such as the Spaniards and Italians under the French during the Napoleonic era; to those dissatisfied with the dominance of one ethnic group, such as Czechs, Magyars, or Serbs under the Germans within the Habsburg Empire; and to those feeling suppressed by what they considered foreign domination, such as the Greeks under the Ottomans, the Poles under the Russians, and the Italians under the Austrians.

From such sources, it was a short step to calls for national liberation and political unification. Nationalism soon acquired attributes of a religion and became a
National liberation and unification powerful political force. For example, the Italian nationalist Giuseppe Mazzini (1805–1872), who founded the revolutionary Young Italy movement in 1831, called Italy "the purpose, the soul, the consolation of our thoughts, the country chosen of God and oppressed by men." Some nationalist leaders such as Mazzini began demanding loyalty and solidarity from members of their organizations.

Before 1848, most nationalists supported liberal causes, for liberals also struggled for national rights. Both liberals and nationalists typically believed that sovereignty should rest with the people, united by common loyalties and language. They also had faith that change would bring political, social, and economic progress. Campaigns by liberals to promote agricultural improvement and industrial development often merged into German, Italian, and Hungarian calls for national unity.

Later, nationalists would ally themselves with conservatives, for both believed in the value of historical traditions and in an organic society over the rights of the individual. Nationalism would also become more entwined with notions of national superiority and special national missions that so often appealed to conservatives. All nationalists, however, insisted that each nation of people, unified into a self-governing state, should be the primary focus of political loyalty, and that the political boundaries of the state should be the same as ethnic boundaries of the people. The widespread political and emotional appeal of nationalism made it an increasingly powerful ideology over the course of the century.

ROMANTICISM: FREEDOM, INSTINCT, AND SPONTANEITY

The origins of nationalism in literature and history also made it attractive to believers in romanticism. This ideology became the dominant spirit in literature and art during the first half of the nineteenth century. Its significance stretched beyond culture, however. Romanticism reflected a new recognition that human beings were complex, emotional, and only sometimes rational creatures. In a civilization that was growing ever more scientific, materialistic, industrial, and urban, romanticism became a counterweight for the human experience. It stood against eighteenth-century classicism and the Enlightenment, and the ideals of reason and order that so characterized those eras. Instead, romanticism emphasized individual freedom and spontaneity.

Origins of romanticism can be traced back to Jean-Jacques Rousseau, the acclaimed writer and philosopher we met in Chapter 14. Though a central figure of the Enlightenment, Rousseau had stressed
Rousseau feeling, instinct, emotions, and love of nature. He described walking away from the city into the fields and woods, stretching himself out on the ground, digging his fingers and toes into the dirt, kissing the earth, and weeping for joy. In several of his most widely read writings, he seemed to idealize love, childhood, and "the noble savage."

Other strands of romanticism came from the German "storm and stress" literature of the late eighteenth century. German writers gave much weight to inner feelings fully experienced and expressed by sensitive individuals. Johann Wolfgang von Goethe provided a model of the emotional individual searching for love and self-understanding in his novel *The Sorrows of the Young Werther* (1774). Like Rousseau, Goethe had many interests. He delved into philosophy, science, and public affairs as well as literature. His masterpiece, the philosophical drama *Faust*, featured a medieval scholar who, dissatisfied with the fruits of knowledge, sells his soul to the devil in return for earthly pleasure and wisdom. In Goethe's medieval interests, his emotional spontaneity, and his love of nature and of individual personality, this renowned writer exemplified the heart of romanticism.

"Storm and stress" literature

All of these qualities explored by Rousseau and Goethe came to characterize the work of succeeding romantic writers and artists. Many romantics expressed a new interest in the Middle Ages. They revived the popularity of medieval tales, Gothic architecture, the Knights of the Round Table, and heroic figures, thereby turning the medieval era from the "Dark Ages" into the "Age of Faith."

Reviving the Middle Ages

This fascination with the Middle Ages reflected romanticism's passionate concern with the drama of history. Written by scholars such as Thomas Babington Macaulay (1800–1859) in Great Britain, history was literary and exciting, featuring heroic individuals, great accomplishments, and national struggles. These same themes were explored by the Prussian philosopher Hegel. In Hegel's view, history was a great spiritual drama of heroic individuals that would lead to a new sense of national identity and freedom.

History

Romanticism also stressed the emotion of Christianity and the mystical presence of God in nature. According to romantic theologians, the important part of religion was the feeling of dependence on an infinite God rather than religious dogma or institutions. In his widely read book, *The Genius of Christianity*, the French writer François Auguste-René de Chateaubriand (1768–1848) described in lush words how "every thing in a Gothic church reminds you of the labyrinths of a forest; every thing excites a feeling of religious awe, of mystery, and of the Divinity." In part, religious revivals during the late eighteenth and early nineteenth centuries, with their stress on piety and emotional outpourings, reflected these spiritual qualities of romanticism.

Christianity

The connections among the love of nature, the spiritual presence of God, and the power of emotions were most striking in the romantic literature, art, and music of the period. In the literary realm, the English poets William Wordsworth (1770–1850) and Samuel Taylor Coleridge (1772–1834) became closely associated with the beautiful lake country of northwest England, Wordsworth by birth and Coleridge by adoption. Together the two men traveled to Germany, where they fell under the influence of German romanticists. They collaborated on *Lyrical Ballads* (1798), which included Wordsworth's "Lines Composed a Few Miles Above Tintern Abbey" and Coleridge's "Rime of the Ancient Mariner." Both writers glorified nature and sensed a brooding, mystical presence of the divine. Wordsworth saw in nature a higher wisdom than what scholars might offer:

Literature

> *One impulse from a vernal wood*
> *May teach you more of man,*
> *Of moral evil and of good*
> *Than all the sages can.*

Wordsworth's and Coleridge's ardent appreciation of nature, their introspective concern for the individual, and their preoccupation with the spiritual rather than the material made them leaders among Britain's many romantic poets.

In France, Germaine de Staël (1766–1817) led the romantic movement in literature. Although she admired the passionate Rousseau, she attacked most Enlightenment thinkers for not being free enough. She turned to writing in order to grapple with her own emotional experiences with several lovers, and to argue for living the passionate life. Often writing about female heroes and genius in works such as *Corinne*, de Staël also looked to history for a vision of another, better world. She and other romantics created an image of the ideal romantic heroine, who followed her emotions rather than tradition or reason—a model that some tried to follow in life. Also in France, George Sand (Amandine Dupin Dudevant) (1804–1876) became an extraordinarily creative writer and an unconventional, even threatening woman. Abandoning her tyrannical husband for an independent life in Paris, Sand became an intellectual leader whose private life included several love affairs with well-known people. At her own convenience, she dressed as a man or woman (see Figure 18.5). Like several other women writers, she also took a male pseudonym to add legitimacy to her writings. Several of her novels explored romantic love and featured strong, intensely emotional heroines.

Leading romantic painters also stressed emotional images. Figure 18.3, an oil painting by the German artist Karl Friedrich Schinkel, shows an idealized image **Art** of a medieval town at twilight. In the center stands a magnificent Gothic cathedral, its spires stretching toward the heavens above. The parting clouds and setting sun seem to bless this church and town. Below, humble workers bring abundant supplies from the river. They are dwarfed by the cathedral, the central stairs leading up to the cathedral, the high-arching bridge that echoes the arches of the cathedral, their finely built town on the right, and nature above. The painting contains the key elements of romanticism: glorification of nature, religious mysticism, adoration of an idealized medieval era, and expression of emotion.

The romantic love of magnificent landscapes can be found in Figure 18.4. This 1817 painting emphasizes the theme of the poet both immersed in nature and conjuring up a majestic natural setting like a god. Here the robed poet with his harp stands on a cliff, his arm stretched out to the swirling heavens above. Below him, waters rage and a knight on a white horse (lower left) gallops off into the distance. In the background stands a medieval castle built into the mountains.

In music, a number of romantic composers followed in the footsteps of Ludwig van Beethoven (1770–1827). The music of this famed German composer overflowed the bounds of clas- **Music** sic forms, becoming freer, more individualistic, and emotional than anything that had come before.

FIGURE 18.3
Karl Friedrich Schinkel, *Medieval Town on a River*, 1815.

FIGURE 18.4
John Martin, *The Bard*, 1817.

Beethoven composed his *Pastoral Symphony* as a musical link to nature. "How happy I am," he wrote in 1810, "to be able to stroll in the woods, among the trees, bushes, wild flowers and rocks. No one can love the country as much as I do." The lyrics to one of his choral works explain his feelings about music:

> *When the magic of sound holds sway*
> *and works bring inspiration,*
> *glorious things must appear,*
> *darkness and turmoil become light.*

One critic explained that romantic music should "paint to the eyes of the soul the splendors of nature, the delights of contemplation, the character of nations, the tumult of their passions, and the languor of their sufferings. . . ."

The painting by the Austrian artist Josef Danhauser shown in Figure 18.5 brings together leading figures of romantic art and literature. At the center, the Hungarian virtuoso and composer Franz Liszt

plays the piano for his friends. Standing, from left to right, are the French writer Victor Hugo, the Italian violinist Niccolò Paganini, and the composer Antonio Rossini. Sitting are the French writers Alexandre Dumas, George Sand (characteristically in men's clothing), and Daniel Stern (Marie d'Agoult, who had a long-term liaison with Liszt). Above the group hangs a portrait of Lord Byron and a bust of Beethoven, the deceased "saints" of romantic poetry and music.

Through much of romanticism, strands from all the ideologies combined and recombined in a variety of ways. Nationalism, for example, played a prominent role in some roman-tics' lives. In the 1820s, *Connections to nationalism* England's romantic poet Lord Byron (1788–1824) fought for Greek national independence against the Turks (see Figure 18.8). Some of Frederic Chopin's (1810–1849) dramatic music self-consciously evoked nationalistic sentiments for his native Poland, which was still under Russian rule. The Italian Giuseppe Verdi (1813–1901) and the German Richard Wagner (1813–1883), who developed the opera into a fully integrated artform of music, theater, ballet, and special effects, were among many other composers whose works brought together romantic and openly nationalistic themes.

Liberals, too, found comfort in various aspects of romanticism, which helps explain the movement's wide appeal. By breaking sharply with past forms, romanticism attracted liberal *Connections to liberalism* and revolutionary spirits. Indeed, many romantic writers and artists sided with liberal causes. Germaine de Staël, for example, in her own life as well as in her novels, histories, and political tracts, fostered romanticism and liberalism in France. Few liberal romantics, however, were more popular than the French writer Victor Hugo (1802–1885), who idealized the masses of underprivileged humanity and preached redemption and purification through suffering.

At the same time, certain dimensions of romanticism appealed to conservatives as well—especially the return to the past, *Connections to conservatism* the emphasis on Christianity, and the stand against the rationalism of the Enlightenment. Sir Walter Scott (1771–1832), who in novel and verse glorified the Middle Ages and his native Scotland, was a conservative. So was the

Figure 18.5
Josef Danhauser, *Liszt at the Piano,* 1840.

French writer François Auguste-René de Chateaubriand, who advocated a return to mystic Catholicism and dreamed of noble Indians in tropical America.

Romanticism found expression in many cultural forms—in the new English gardens that imitated nature rather than confining it to geometric forms, in the image of the artist as a nonconforming genius, in the glorification of walks down wooded lanes, in the popularity of the Grimm fairy tales that evoked images of medieval life, and in the sentimentalization of love in life and literature. In its qualities, its popularity, and its persistence, romanticism proved to be more than a casual change of taste or a mood. It reflected the revolutionary social, political, and intellectual developments of the era.

Early Socialism: Ending Competition and Inequities

Romantics questioned the existing system from cultural and emotional perspectives. Socialists questioned it from social and economic perspectives. As socialists saw it, the common people—the workers—were missing out on the astounding power and wealth generated by the industrial revolution. Socialists called for a reordering of society so as to end the competition and class divisions that caused inequalities and suffering. Such calls made the socialists enemies of both the conservative and liberal camps.

During the early decades of the nineteenth century, a few intellectuals—some of whom came to be called Utopian Socialists—contended that society should be based on cooperation rather than competitive individualism and that property should be owned communally. One of the first of these early socialists

Utopian Socialists was the French nobleman Henri de Saint-Simon (1760–1825). During the French Revolution, Saint-Simon abandoned his noble title. Turning to land speculation, he made and lost a fortune. He and his followers believed that society should be reorganized on the basis of a "religion of humanity," that all people should work, and that the inheritance of private property should be abolished. In Saint-Simon's ideal world, women

Saint-Simon would be elevated from their inferior social positions. Superior artists, scientists, engineers, and business people would be rewarded according to the formula: "from each according to his capacity, to each according to his desserts." Saint-Simon's influential followers became convinced that the best scientists and managers could use their expertise to plan and run prosperous societies for the benefit of everyone.

Charles Fourier (1772–1837) was also an early Utopian Socialist who, like Saint Simon, gathered a following. A Frenchman who had been a traveling

Fourier salesman, he advocated doing away with economic competition, which he saw as the very source of evil. In his utopian society, agriculture and industry would be carried on by voluntary cooperatives whose members would pool their resources and live in communal apartment houses (*phalansteries*). Housework and child care would be a shared responsibility of the community. Women, like men, would have the right to work and to control their own money. Fourier also considered traditional marriage too restrictive sexually. Work and pleasure would merge as people did as they pleased while still carrying out the tasks their society required to survive. People would be paid according to the labor, capital, and talent that each contributed.

Figure 18.6 reveals the dream of Fourier and his followers. In the background, an imagined phalanstery—geometrically ordered and laid out in a style reminiscent of the palace at Versailles—rests in an idyllic setting away from large cities. A classical temple on the shoreline offers tranquillity to people arriving in boats. On a hill in the foreground, Fourier—depicted as a saintly father figure with his arm lovingly around a child—instructs his followers. In fact, the communities that Fourier's followers es-

tablished in the United States and Europe rarely lasted for long. Fourier's ideas, however, inspired many people looking for a more joyful, communal alternative to the competitive industrial societies spreading in the West.

Robert Owen (1771–1858) had different ideas. Born in Wales, Owen quickly made an industrial fortune in Manchester and bought large cotton mills in New Lanark, Scotland. Early in the nine-

Owen teenth century, he set out to make New Lanark a model community. He raised wages, shortened work hours, improved working conditions, abolished child labor, provided educational and recreational facilities for employees, and established sickness and old-age insurance. Productivity in his mills soared, and profits rose. Owen spent years drawing up plans for model socialist communities, which he envisioned as being located in rural settings and as mostly self-sufficient. The plans called for community members to raise children together and for women to share in governing. Like Fourier, Owen advocated loosening the bounds of marriage to create greater sexual freedom for women and men. Several such communities were established in America, most notably New Harmony, Indiana. However, all soon succumbed to internal disagreements and economic difficulties. The efforts cost Owen most of his fortune. He retained his fame, especially within the labor movement and among those establishing modest workers' cooperatives. However, he died in 1858 without having created a lasting alternative to the harsh industrial capitalism he deplored.

In the 1830s, several French women began linking socialist demands with calls for the emancipation of women. The most famous of these women was Flora Tristan (1801–1844), a French woman influ-

Tristan enced by Fourier's ideas. French law discriminated against women in many ways, including automatically awarding custody of children to fathers after a marital separation. When Tristan's abusive husband was awarded their children, she fought back. Eventually she turned this dispute into a campaign to end discrimination against women within marriage, in the law, and on the job. She traveled throughout Europe and Latin America, speaking passionately for unions and the creation of centers for the care and education of workers. In her *Worker's Union* (1843), she argued that equality between women and men could free the whole working class and transform civilization.

FIGURE 18.6
Fourier and his phalanstery.

These and other early socialists recognized both the significance of the industrial revolution and its possibilities. They attacked the unbridled pursuit of profits in an unregulated, industrial economy. Only a well-organized society, they explained, could eliminate the misery of industrial capitalism and promote happiness. Most also attacked middle-class restrictions on women, emphasized the importance of sensual pleasure, and questioned traditional Christianity. The wave of socialist thought that these leaders unleashed became profoundly influential by the middle decades of the nineteenth century. As it evolved, it took on a more revolutionary quality, and it bore the distinctive stamp of one of the most authoritative thinkers of the nineteenth century: Karl Marx.

"SCIENTIFIC SOCIALISM": KARL MARX AND THE COMMUNIST MANIFESTO

"A specter is haunting Europe—the specter of Communism," announced Karl Marx (1818–1883) in 1848. "Let the ruling classes tremble at a Communist revolution." Born into a German middle-class family, his father was a Jewish lawyer who had converted to Christianity. A brilliant student, Marx attained his doctorate in philosophy and history, but he was denied an academic position because of his radical views. After embarking on a career in journalism, he was exiled from Germany for his attacks on censorship and his economic views; later France exiled him because of his revolutionary socialist ideas. He spent the last thirty-four years of his life in London researching, writing, and trying to build organizations to put his ideas into action. Marx collaborated with his friend Friedrich Engels (1820–1895), son of a wealthy German manufacturer, in writing the seminal work, *The Communist Manifesto* (1848). This treatise, along with the later *Das Kapital,* contained the fundamentals of what Marx called "scientific socialism."

Marx argued that economic interest, more than anything else, drove human behavior. He also thought that the dominant characteristic of each his-

Economic interest torical epoch was its prevailing system of economic production— how people made a living. In his view, politics, religion, and culture were all shaped mainly by economic and social realities.

Marx also described how human societies in each historical era became divided into the "haves" and the "have-nots." The haves owned the means of eco-

Class struggle nomic production—in nineteenth century Britain, for example, the industrial capitalists who owned the machines and factories. They also controlled the state and the ideas that dominated their societies. The have-nots were the exploited laborers—for example, Britain's industrial working class. Each side consisted of classes of people with opposing interests. As Marx wrote, "[T]he history of all hitherto existing society is the history of class struggle." At a certain point, economic and social change would bring these class struggles to a revolutionary crisis. The French Revolution, he explained, was an example of one of those conflicts coming to a violent head, as the bourgeoisie (the middle-class capitalists) overcame the aristocracy (the feudal landlords.)

Marx focused much of his analysis on his own industrial society of the nineteenth century. In this society, he explained, the bourgeoisie (capitalists) ex-

Industrial capitalism ploited workers by paying them only subsistence wages rather than compensating them for the true value created by their work. "These labourers, who must sell themselves piecemeal, are a commodity, like every other article of commerce," Marx lamented. At the same time, Marx saw capitalists as locked in a competitive struggle with one another. This contest forced them continually to introduce new, costly machines and build larger factories: "Constant revolutionizing of production, uninterrupted disturbance of all social

conditions, ever-lasting uncertainty and agitation distinguish the bourgeois epoch from all earlier ones." Soon, Marx warned, greater and greater quantities of goods would be produced by a system running out of control. Eventually, the relentless competition and the periodic economic crises that plague industrial societies would thin the ranks of the bourgeoisie. At the same time, the working class would grow stronger as its numbers and consciousness would increase. Inevitably, the workers—with "nothing to lose but their chains" and with "a world to win"—would revolt, seize the factories, destroy the capitalist system, abolish private property, and establish a classless socialist society.

Marx only hinted at the general nature of this new socialist society. His writings suggest that the elimination of capitalism would end the division of society into classes of haves (capitalists) and have-nots (workers). The state itself *Socialist society* would eventually wither away, for its only purpose was to protect the interests of the haves against the have-nots. Freed from exploitation and the pressures of capitalist competition, all people would lead more varied, cooperative, creative lives—in this sense, free and truly human.

Marx's socialism gained immense appeal. Because he based much of his analysis on evidence and logic, it attracted intellectuals and students. Because his socialism reflected the social and emotional turmoil being produced *Appeal of socialism* by the industrial revolution, especially the suffering of the working poor, it spoke convincingly to workers and their leaders. During the second half of the nineteenth century, Marx's socialism would become a major force in the West.

Restoration and Repression

Socialism as well as the other ideologies reflected the political and social realities of their era, particularly the efforts of people to understand and cope with changes that either threatened them or offered promise. In the three decades following 1815, however, socialism played only a limited part in the great struggles for policies and power. During these years, it was the forces representing conservatism, liberalism, and nationalism that instead took center stage.

The struggles for influence and power among believers of these ideologies took place in pamphlets and newspapers, in courts and parliaments, in universities and police barracks, and in streets and fields throughout Europe. In the first years after the defeat of Napoleon, conservatism held sway in international and diplomatic affairs. The Vienna agreements and the cooperative arrangements to repress the threat of revolution in Europe epitomized this ideology. Conservatism also prevailed in domestic politics across most of Europe.

THE RETURN OF THE BOURBONS IN FRANCE

When the victorious armies of the coalition powers entered France and deposed Napoleon in the spring of 1814, they brought "in their baggage" the members

Louis XVIII

of the Bourbon royal family who had fled the Revolution. In their wake trooped the émigré nobility. The brother of the guillotined Louis XVI was placed on the throne as Louis XVIII (r. 1814–1824). (The son of Louis XVI, who had died in prison without having ruled, was considered Louis XVII.)

The "restored" king ruled with an odd mixture of conservatism and moderation. He issued a charter that retained Napoleon's administrative and legal system as well as civil and religious liberties. He also placed lawmaking in the hands of a two-chamber legislature. However, only a small, wealthy elite could vote, and the king kept most of the power.

Nevertheless, Louis XVIII used his authority with moderation, thinking that a mild leadership style would help ensure his hold on the crown and tranquillity in France. Most of the returned émigrés, however, had little appreciation for his relaxed rule—they were more conservative and angry than he was and wanted action. Led by the king's younger brother, Comte d'Artois, these ultraroyalists controlled the legislature. Through the rest of Louis XVIII's reign, they agitated for a return of their privileges and indemnification for their lost lands.

After Louis XVIII's death in 1824, d'Artois was crowned King Charles X (r. 1824–1830), and followed more conservative policies that favored the old

Charles X

aristocracy and the Catholic Church. He offered money to indemnify those who had lost land in the Revolution and gave the church greater control over education. Those policies provoked growing opposition to his rule. When elections increased the size of the opposition, he dissolved the

Chamber of Deputies. In the face of still increasing opposition, he abolished freedom of the press and drastically restricted the right to vote.

REACTION AND REPRESSION IN THE GERMAN STATES

The Germanies in 1815 consisted of thirty-seven little states and two large ones—Prussia and Austria. All belonged to the German Confederation, which lacked an army, a treasury, and even a flag. Austria and Prussia dominated politically the German lands. Both states were firmly conservative if not reactionary.

In multilingual Austria, the Habsburg emperor and Metternich, the conservative diplomat we met at the beginning of the chapter, held sway. The Austrian leaders had good reason to fear liberalism and nationalism like the plague, for the

Metternich

empire included many ethnic groups—including Hungarians, Czechs, Serbs, and Italians—with their own languages and customs. In the wake of the French Revolution, they began to stir with national consciousness. Metternich used all means—police, spies, censorship, and travel restrictions—to ensure the status quo. The only possible threats to conservative control came from within some of the small states in the weak German Confederation, and Austria enjoyed permanent presidency over that organization.

When students and professors formed organizations and staged festivals that supported liberal and nationalistic principles, conservative officials became alarmed. "We want a constitution for the people that fits in with the spirit of the times and with people's own level of enlightenment," explained one student. "[A]bove all, we want Germany to be considered *one* land and the people *one* people."

The murder of a conservative dramatist by a member of a student organization, Karl Sand, gave Metternich his opportunity to strike. After Sand's trial and public execution, Metternich called the princes of the leading German

Carlsbad Decrees

states to Carlsbad and had them draw up a set of harsh decrees outlawing the organizations. He also issued an ominous warning: "The duty of especial watchfulness in this matter should be impressed upon the special agents of the government." The Carlsbad Decrees established strict censorship and supervision of classrooms and libraries. Spies and police terrorized liberal students and professors. Although Sand became a political martyr in the eyes of many young nationalists, the crackdown worked: the small liberal and nationalistic movements evaporated.

In Prussia, the conservative, militaristic Hohenzollern kings reigned. Behind them stood the equally conservative landed aristocracy, the *Junkers*. The Junkers served as officers in the Prussian army and filled the key posts in the civil service and administration. They had no sympathy for any reforms that seemed even faintly liberal or nationalistic, and they reversed many of the changes of the Napoleonic era. However, in order to better connect its separated territories, Prussia began making commercial treaties with its smaller German neighbors, providing for the free flow of trade among them. By 1834, nearly all the states of the German Confederation except Austria had joined the Prussian-sponsored *Zollverein* (customs union), which would prove of great importance in the march toward national unity.

> Prussia

RESTORATION IN ITALY

Austria dominated Italy even more completely than Germany. Metternich described Italy as only a "geographical expression." Austria annexed the northern states of Lombardy and Venetia outright. Most other states were ruled by Austrian princes or under Austria's protection and guidance. Piedmont-Sardinia in the northwest was free from Austrian control, but its ruling House of Savoy was no less conservative than Metternich.

In 1815 the deposed aristocracy and clericals trooped back to the Italian states intent on regaining their old positions. They and their Austrian masters soon sent nearly all the Italian intelligentsia to prison or exile. When revolts in Naples, Sicily, and Piedmont flared up in 1820, the forces of order quickly used overwhelming force to put them down.

The Papal States in central Italy were no exception in this period of restoration. Pope Pius VII revived the Inquisition, reconstituted the *Index* of prohibited books, annulled Napoleonic laws of religious toleration, and even did away with French innovations such as street lighting. His successor, Pius VIII, followed equally conservative ideas. In 1829, he condemned almost everything even faintly liberal, including secular education and civil marriage.

CONSERVATISM IN RUSSIA

Russia remained a vast agricultural nation with a feudal social structure and a tiny urban bourgeoisie. The Orthodox Christian Church, dominated by an upper clergy drawn from the aristocracy, served as an arm of the government. After fighting against the French, suffering a ravaging invasion in 1812, and playing a major role in Napoleon's defeat, Russia commanded considerable respect and power in Europe. Russia's tsar was the unstable Alexander I—at first a man open to reform, such granting the Poles a constitution and proclaiming religious toleration, and later more of a reactionary mystic who resumed religious repression. He fell under the influence of Metternich in international affairs and his own aristocratic magnates at home. At his death in 1825, Russia remained a champion of autocracy and conservatism.

His successor, Nicholas I (r. 1825–1855), was an austere autocrat whose military career wedded him to the concepts of discipline and authority. When he assumed the throne in December, 1825, a group of his young liberal military officers—hoping to write a constitution and free the serfs—revolted. Nicholas immediately crushed these "Decembrists" and bitterly turned against any hints of liberalism. He followed a policy of demanding submission of everyone to the autocracy and to the Orthodox Church. Although the Decembrists would later gain a reputation as liberal political martyrs, Russia's government now stood as a bastion of conservatism and would remain so for many decades.

HOLDING THE LINE IN GREAT BRITAIN

Although Great Britain had for years been a home of representative government, conservatives dominated its government in 1815. Property qualifications so severely restricted the suffrage that only about 5 percent of adult males could vote. The distribution of seats in Parliament was so distorted that a relatively small number of families dominated the House of Commons. Furthermore, the emerging industrial cities of the north were scarcely represented at all. The conservative landed aristocracy and the Tory Party, which had seen the country through the Napoleonic Wars, had a firm grip on power.

Things became even more restricted when an economic depression left thousands of returning veterans jobless. Luddite riots (see p. 584) and the specter of revolutionary activity prompted the government to take strong measures against the restless workers. The climax came in 1819 when troops fired on a crowd that had assembled in St. Peter's Fields, outside Manchester, to listen to reform speeches. A number were killed and hundreds injured in this "Peterloo Massacre."

Peterloo Massacre

Figure 18.7, a print by George Cruikshank, shows the troops of the conservative British government breaking up this rally for liberal and radical political reform. On the platform women and men wave banners demanding universal suffrage, religious freedom, and liberty; their banners are topped with liberty caps, a radical symbol from the French Revolution. This depiction of the violence that erupted at St. Peter's Fields near Manchester seeks to evoke sympathy for the reformers. It portrays merciless troops on horseback striking down and trampling nonresisting women, men, and children. An army officer on horseback repeats orders from a higher authority, "Cut them down." A participant confirmed this depiction: "Women, white-vested maids, and tender youths, were indiscriminately sabred or trampled. . . . In ten minutes from the commencement of the havoc the field was an open and almost deserted space." Parliament would not back down. It soon passed the Six Acts of 1819, which further restricted public meetings and facilitated prosecution of radicals.

The government treated the Irish no less harshly. The Irish had long been ruled and exploited as a conquered people. In the 1801 Act of Union, Britain formally absorbed Ireland into the United Kingdom. In this predominantly Catholic land, the Protestant minority controlled most the of land and political power. The Catholic peasantry suffered from such acute poverty that the threat of famine was not uncommon. Irish nationalists organized to agitate for the right to send elected Catholic representatives to Parliament. In 1829, fearing a civil war in Ireland, the conservative British government reluctantly passed the Catholic Emancipation Act, which allowed Roman Catholics to become members of Parliament.

Ireland

A Wave of Revolution and Reform

Despite conservative efforts to maintain order and halt change during the years after 1815, liberal and nationalistic causes simmered just under the surface. The demands for greater political participation and recognition of national identity strengthened and spread. Moreover, Europeans could no longer ignore the changes stemming from early industrialization and urbanization. In some cases, revolts and revolutions broke out. In other cases, people clamored for and gained major reforms.

THE GREEK WAR FOR INDEPENDENCE

A hint of the problems to come occurred during the 1820s, when Greeks mounted a national liberation movement against their Ottoman Turk overlords. After the Turks met Greek insurrections with force and atrocities, romantic and liberal idealists formed an international movement to support Greek independence. Britain's well-known romantic poet Lord Byron was one of several who traveled to Greece to contribute to the cause. He brought money and enlisted in a regiment, but lost his life to malaria at Missolonghi.

Figure 18.8, by the romantic French artist Eugène Delacroix (1798–1863),

FIGURE 18.7
George Cruikshank, *The Peterloo Massacre*, 1819.

FIGURE 18.8
Eugène Delacroix, *Greece Dying on the Ruins of Missolonghi.*

In the end, intervention by Great Britain, France, and Russia finally secured Greek independence. While Europeans thought of Greece sympathetically as Christian and the birthplace of European civilization, these countries' motives had more to do with their own greedy hopes of gains at the expense of the Turks than genuinely supporting the Greek revolutionaries. They achieved their objective, but this dramatic chapter in Greek history still revealed the strength of nationalistic movements and the power of liberal and romantic ideals to fuel these movements.

LIBERAL TRIUMPHS IN WESTERN EUROPE

In 1830 a new series of revolutions tested and sometimes overwhelmed established governments. In France, a struggle arose for liberal reforms against the reactionary King Charles X. Since ascending the throne in 1824, Charles had tried to reverse the moderate policies of his predecessor, Louis XVIII, and return France to the days before the French Revolution. He aligned himself with the most extreme ultraroyalists and the Catholic Church, angering the wealthy bourgeoisie and even the peasantry with his reactionary policies. Support for his regime weakened and he lost control over the Chamber of Deputies, the most representative of France's two-chamber legislature. His efforts to dissolve the Chamber, *The July Revolution in France* censor the press, and narrow the electoral laws only stiffened liberal opposition. In July 1830, things came to a head. Liberals in Paris joined with workers outraged by rising food prices. Workers took to the streets of Paris and set up barriers against the king's unenthusiastic troops. Uprisings—fueled by hunger, suspicions of hoarding, and resentment against taxes—spread throughout France. After three days of haphazard fighting, the insurgents gained the upper hand. Charles X, the last Bourbon king of France, fled to Great Britain.

Figure 18.9, a painting by Gustave Wappers, reveals how the victors in France's revolution of 1830 interpreted the dramatic events of that year. In the center of the painting, the new constitutional monarch, Louis-Philippe, rides victoriously to the Hôtel de Ville (city hall), the seat of power in Paris. Before him a man carries the French revolutionary tricolor flag, replacing the old Bourbon flag of Charles X. Louis-Philippe's horse picks his way through the paving stones, which

captures Greece's struggle for independence. Delacroix was well known for his rich, exotic, historical works. In this painting, entitled *Greece Dying on the Ruins of Missolonghi*, Greece is symbolized as a beautiful, defenseless peasant woman and a classical symbol of liberty. She kneels on the stone remains of Greek culture in a desperate appeal for aid. But it is already too late for the martyred freedom fighter (perhaps evoking the memory of the fallen Byron), whose arm is thrust forward toward the viewer. Behind the woman, a Turkish soldier strikes a victorious pose. The painting, like the Greek cause in Europe, blends the themes of romanticism, liberalism, and nationalism that so characterized the era.

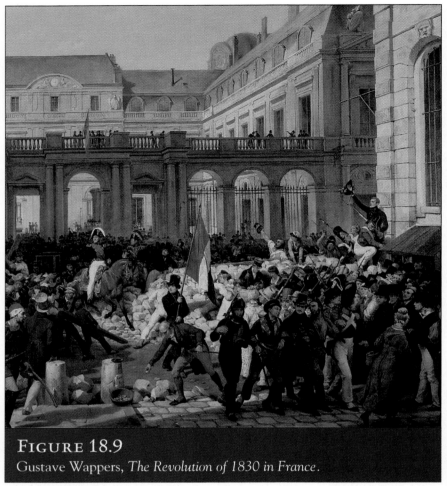

FIGURE 18.9
Gustave Wappers, *The Revolution of 1830 in France.*

doubling the electorate (though still only the property-owning elite could vote).

The year 1830 also brought revolutionary trouble in the Belgian provinces of the kingdom of the Netherlands. The union forced on Belgium (predominantly *Revolution in Belgium* Catholic) and the Netherlands (mainly Calvinist) at Vienna had never been a happy one. Although numerically a minority, the Dutch staffed most of the country's political institutions. As one Belgian nationalist put it in 1830, "By what right do two million Dutchmen command four million Belgians?" Desires for national liberation combined with tensions over high food prices to fuel a revolt in August 1830. When the half-hearted efforts of the Dutch government failed to suppress the revolt, Austria and Russia threatened to intervene. Britain and France resisted the intervention and secured Belgian independence. Belgium soon adopted a liberal constitution.

By that time, liberal reformers had also scored successes in Switzerland, making that country the first to grant *Switzerland and Spain* universal male suffrage. In 1834, a new constitution introduced at least the form of liberal institutions to Spain as well.

TESTING AUTHORITY IN EASTERN AND SOUTHERN EUROPE

As Map 18.2 shows, revolutionaries also tested regimes in eastern and southern Europe. In November 1830, a Polish nationalistic movement led *Poland* by students and army cadets tried to end Russian rule. They managed to establish a provisional government in Warsaw, but conflict within different social groups and among reformers weakened that

the people of Paris had used to construct barricades and hurl at the royal troops. In the foreground, rich and poor walk arm-in-arm with regular and irregular soldiers in victory; a wealthy man stops to drop alms into a basket for the poor or fallen. Women and men of all classes hail the new king and the revolutionary cause.

While many in France had hoped for a republic to replace the Bourbon monarchy, more conservative liberals took control and created a constitutional "Bourgeois monarchy" under Charles X's cousin, Louis-Philippe (r. 1830–1848). Recognizing that a new, more liberal era had dawned in France, Louis-Philippe assumed the role of "citizen king," casting aside the clothes and ornaments of royalty and dressing in the style of his Parisian upper-middle-class supporters. He reduced property qualifications for voting, thereby

Sites of Revolts, 1820-1831

Boundary of
German Confederation

St. Petersburg
1825

SWEDEN

NORTH
SEA

DENMARK

BALTIC SEA

RUSSIA

GREAT
BRITAIN

BRUNSWICK
1830

NETH.

P R U S S I A

Warsaw

POLAND
1830-1831

ATLANTIC

OCEAN

Brussels

BELGIUM
1830

SAXONY
1830

HESSE
1830

GERMAN
CONFEDERATION

AUSTRIA-
HUNGARY

Paris

FRANCE
1830

SWITZ.

PIEDMONT
1821

PARMA
1831

MODENA
1831

PAPAL
STATES
1831

Rome

OTTOMAN EMPIRE

PORTUGAL
1820

Madrid

Naples
1820

KINGDOM
OF NAPLES

SPAIN
1820

MEDITERRANEAN   SEA   SICILY

GREECE
1821-1829

0   500 miles

0   500 kilometers

THINKING ABOUT GEOGRAPHY

MAP 18.2   *European Revolts, 1820–1831*

This map shows the locations of revolts in Europe between 1820 and 1831. ◙ **Notice** the geographic extent of these revolts. **What** problems might this have posed for the efforts of the Concert of Europe to maintain the status quo through international cooperation? ◙ **Consider** which of these revolts had the most lasting consequences.

government. Russian troops soon defeated the revolutionaries. Nicholas sent thousands of Poles to Siberia in chains and began a harsh program of Russification to crush any hint of Polish independence.

In Italy, nationalists began gathering in secret societies called *Carbonari*. (The word means "charcoal burners," suggesting an image of common people meeting around charcoal fires.) The Carbonari had long plotted for political freedom and national unification. In 1831 liberal and nationalist revolutions broke out in central Italy, but Austrian forces promptly suppressed them. The movement again went underground, but was kept alive under the leadership of the romantic nationalist Giuseppe Mazzini (1805–1872).

Italy

LIBERAL DEMANDS IN GREAT BRITAIN

In Britain, conservatives had to contend not only with demands for liberal reforms but also with pressures rising from early industrialization and urbanization. Despite the Peterloo Massacre and the restrictive Six Acts, Britain had already shown signs of political flexibility in response to public opinion in the 1820s. By 1822, it had deserted the conservative Concert of Europe. The government repealed laws preventing laborers from organizing unions and removed civil restrictions against nonconforming Protestants and Catholics. Yet these measures, however encouraging to liberals, did not get at the fundamental issue that had raised reform demands for decades: broadening popular participation in the government.

Now the industrial middle class, gaining in wealth and number, added weight to radicals' demands to extend the right to vote and relocate political strength from the countryside to the underrepresented industrial cities. However, the conser-

Reform Bill of 1832

vative Tories, who controlled Parliament, remained unwilling or unable to effect electoral reform. In 1830, elections brought the more liberal Whigs to power. These Whigs believed that moderate reform rather than reactionary intransigence was the best way to preserve elite institutions from revolutionary change. Worried that the July Revolution in France might spread to Britain, and facing increasing public demonstrations for reform as well as violent acts of protest, the Whigs decided to bend rather than break. They introduced the Reform Bill of 1832, which answered some of the demands. Speaking in favor of the bill, the English historian and politician Thomas Babington Macaulay warned that "now, while the crash of the proudest throne of the Continent [France] is still resounding in our ears . . . now, while the heart of England is still sound," the Reform Bill must be passed.

After considerable effort, the Whigs finally enacted the new law. Figure 18.10, an engraving from the April 15, 1832 issue of *Bell's Weekly Messenger*, depicts the successful struggle to enact the liberal Reform Bill. At the top, under the banner of reform, Whig leaders unite with the king to pass the bill. At the bottom, the British lion (with the help of figures of justice on the right) uses reform to defeat the fleeing Tories and the dragon representing the rotten borough system. In the background, a crowd of citizens raise their arms in triumph.

The Reform Bill did not grant the universal manhood suffrage called for by radicals, but it lowered property qualifications so that most upper-middle-class men (still a small minority) could vote. More important, the bill redistributed electoral districts, taking power away from the "rotten boroughs" (no-longer-important towns and rural areas) and giving it to the underrepresented cities where commercial and industrial elites dominated. The political struggle to pass the bill enabled the House of Commons to gain power over the House of Lords, which had opposed the law. The long era of dominance by the conservative landed aristocracy was ending. More liberal property owners, including the commercial and industrial bourgeoisie, rose to power. From that point on, Britain's leading political groups realigned themselves into the modern Conservative and Liberal parties.

FIGURE 18.10
The Reform Bill of 1832.

Britain's government soon turned to other reforms. Britain had for several decades led in the antislavery movement, abolishing its own slave trade in 1807 and pushing the Congress of Vienna to declare against the trade in 1815. Europeans, however, often violated principled declarations against slavery and shipped hundreds of thousands more African slaves to the Americas—especially to the Caribbean and Brazil. In 1833, Parliament bowed to humanitarian radicals and Protestant reformers and abolished slavery in Britain's colonies. Fifteen years later, France would follow suit by abolishing slavery in its colonies, and in 1888, Brazil joined the list, ending slavery in the Americas.

Antislavery

Britain's Parliament and reformers also tried to cope with growing pressures exerted by the industrial revolution. Several new laws aimed to ease some of the disturbing harshness of industrial employment. Between 1833 and 1847, Parliament forbade the employment of women and children in underground mines, prohibited the employment of children under nine in textile mills, and limited children nine or older and women to ten hours a day in those factories. Other legislation also reflected the British economy's shift from agriculture to industry. In the name of free trade and lower bread prices, liberals mounted a major attack on the Corn Laws, which imposed tariffs on grain imports. An anti-Corn Law movement spread throughout the country, accusing the aristocratic landowners who benefitted from the Corn Laws of being enemies of the middle and working classes. Victory for the movement came in 1846 with the repeal of the Corn Laws. The repeal reduced the price of bread, but it also opened up the possibility that employers—knowing that workers could afford the cheaper bread—would slash wages.

Economic and social reforms

Corn Laws

These liberal principles and reforms, however, only added to the suffering of millions facing the horrible potato famine in Ireland. This mostly rural and impoverished population relied on the potato for food. In 1845, a new, unknown fungus attacked potato plants, ruining the crop. Famine spread as the crops failed year after year. Despite pleas for help, Britain's liberal government concluded that the state should not meddle in the economy. More than a million died in Ireland and another million fled overseas while Britain's liberals—often sympathetic and believing that the

Irish famine

free market would alleviate the distress—held fast to their principles and did almost nothing.

Nor were liberal reforms enough for the hard-pressed urban workers. They were bitterly aware that they had been bypassed by the Reform Bill of 1832: "The Reform Act has effected a transfer of power from one domineering faction to another, and left the people as helpless as before," explained one of their leaders. They also complained that Britain's unprecedented national prosperity had not benefitted workers: "With all these elements of national prosperity, and with every disposition and capacity to take advantage of them, we find ourselves overwhelmed with public and private suffering." In 1838 working-class leaders took action and drew up The People's Charter. The document called for several democratic reforms, including universal male suffrage, election by secret ballot, and the removal of property qualifications for office. "We perform the duties of freemen; we must have the privileges of freemen," announced the charter.

Chartism

The so-called Chartists presented their demands twice to Parliament, which summarily rejected them. Nevertheless, the movement persisted within the working class for years. Women aided the cause by raising money and passing petitions for signatures. They also, unsuccessfully, demanded that the charter include provisions for female suffrage. Finally, in April 1848, the Chartists planned a huge demonstration in London to back up their petition. The frightened government and middle classes prepared to use force to control the gathering, as they had several times against strikes and workers' protests. However, when the reforms were refused once more, only a few mild protests arose, and the Chartist movement sputtered out. Nevertheless, Britain's political parties were becoming aware of the growing influence of the working classes, and began considering ways to win their favor.

In Britain, then, reforms designed to meet demands for broader representation and manage the social consequences of industrialization and urbanization were under way by the 1840s. Under pressure, Britain's government bent enough to satisfy much of the middle class. The discontented working classes were not yet powerful enough to force their views on the resisting government. Liberalism, the strongest ideology challenging Britain's traditional order, remained a force for reform rather than revolution.

On the Continent, however, nations followed a different path. Throughout western Europe, liberal and nationalistic movements gained stunning successes in these same years. In eastern and southern Europe, these two ideologies also rose and served notice, but, with the exception of Greece, the conservative forces of order beat them down. In 1848, however, the complicated interplay among all these movements finally reached a volatile turning point.

The Dam Bursts: 1848

On New Year's Day, 1848, one could look back to 1830 and conclude that the forces that had opened the gates to a wave of revolutions and reforms had since been held under control. In February, 1848, everything would change.

Trouble had already been brewing across Europe. In 1846 and 1847, poor harvests had driven up food prices and even brought famine. These disasters, along with financial crises, undermined markets for manufactured goods, created business failures, and left thousands of workers jobless. Governments tried to maintain order, but the growing resentments of liberals, nationalists, and now socialists, who blamed governments for failing to enact overdue reforms, made things even more difficult.

Antigovernment groups had also begun taking on a disturbing complexity and variety. Some protesters wanted only to widen political participation and institute accepted liberal reforms; others demanded full democracy. Several ethnic groups desired national autonomy; workers wanted jobs and rights. Together, the potential opposition to established governments not only loomed large but also cut across class and ideological lines. Intense, shared opposition to the status quo masked any differences these groups might have had. As the pressure of their frustration mounted, the economic crisis threatened to unlock the floodgates.

The "Glory Days"

The dam broke first in France. Louis-Philippe's constitutional monarchy had allied moderate conservatives and moderate liberals into a regime of wealthy property owners. Presenting itself as the bearer of national patriotism and political caution, the govern-

ment managed to quiet both conservative and radical opponents during the 1830s. However, beneath the surface of this apparently stable regime, discontent grew. The king and his chief minister during the 1840s—the moderately liberal historian Francois Guizot—opposed any further extension of the suffrage. Workers, who had not shared in the relative prosperity of the period, clamored for the right to vote and the right to organize unions, but got neither. The poor harvests and financial crises in 1846 and 1847 heightened frustration with the regime. In Paris, more than 40 percent of the workforce were without a job. One Parisian radical complained, "While half of the population of Paris dies of starvation, the other half eats for two."

France

The parliamentary opposition and bourgeois reformers began holding banquets to rally support for widening the right to vote. When a banquet to be held in Paris on February 22 in honor of George Washington's birthday (the United States served as a symbol of democracy in this period) promised to attract thousands of sympathetic workers, the government tried to prohibit the event. Opposition erupted in the Parisian streets. King Louis-Philippe tried to quiet people down by dismissing his unpopular prime minister, Francois Guizot (1787–1874). Long in office, Guizot's response to those not rich enough to have the right to vote was, "Get rich, then you can vote." The king's effort at appeasement failed. A shot fired during a brawl between a crowd and troops guarding government houses unnerved the troops, who fired a murderous volley into the mob and set off a full-scale insurrection. Barricades against governmental troops flew up all over Paris, and when the king's citizen militia, the National Guard, began taking the rebels' side, Louis-Philippe followed Guizot into exile.

Figure 18.11 depicts the triumph of the revolutionaries and the already simmering political battles to come. In the center, the well-dressed liberal and romantic poet Alphonse de Lamartine (1790–1869) stands with his arm raised in front of the Paris city hall. He persuades the crowd to keep the tricolor flag to represent the new republic rather than the more radical red flag, carried by a woman in plain dress riding a white horse on the left. On the right, troops and ordinary citizens march under the flag in unity. On the left, citizens bring objects of wealth gathered to support the new republic. At the bottom are the paving stones used in the battle and a fallen victim of the struggle.

FIGURE 18.11
Revolutionary triumph in Paris, 1848.

Lamartine and a group of bourgeois liberals proclaimed the Second Republic and hastily set up a provisional government. The new ruling body was republican in sentiment, but tellingly, it had only one prominent radical member: the socialist writer Louis Blanc (1811–1882). The provisional government immediately called for the election by universal male suffrage of an assembly to draw up a new constitution. Yet that government turned down demands for political and economic rights by the new woman's newspaper, *The Voice of Women,* and by women's political clubs. Under the pressure of the Paris populace, the provisional government did admit workers to the National Guard, and therefore access to arms.

In response to popular demand for the "right to work," the government also set up national workshops. The workshops—an idea once proposed by

National workshops Louis Blanc—however, were a parody of Blanc's socialist vision. Blanc lamented that they were deliberately planned so as to ensure failure. In this ill-designed undertaking, laborers were assigned to hastily arranged projects. When more laborers enrolled than could be used, the surplus workers were paid almost as much as the employed ones to remain idle. To make matters worse, tens of thousands of job-hungry laborers rushed to Paris to join the workshops. The resulting demoralization of labor and the cost to the taxpayers frightened peasant and bourgeois property owners alike. Elections held in April 1848 swept conservative republicans and monarchists back into office.

As Map 18.3 reveals, the February explosion in Paris set central Europe aflame with revolt. One core of the revolutions settled in Vienna, the seat of the Habsburg government. After news of the **Austria** Paris events arrived in Vienna, Austrian students, middle-class reformers, and workers charged into the streets, clamoring for an end to Metternich's system. There, as elsewhere in the streets of Europe's cities, women joined men in the effort, building the barricades, taking care of the wounded, supplying the fighters with meals, and sometimes taking part in battles against armed forces. The painting on page 600 captures the flavor of this revolutionary activity. As the uprising gained momentum, Metternich fled for his life. The Habsburg emperor, Ferdinand I, hastily abolished the country's most repressive laws, ended serfdom, and promised constitutional reform.

In Hungary, the Magyars, under the leadership of the eloquent Louis Kossuth (1802–1894), rose and

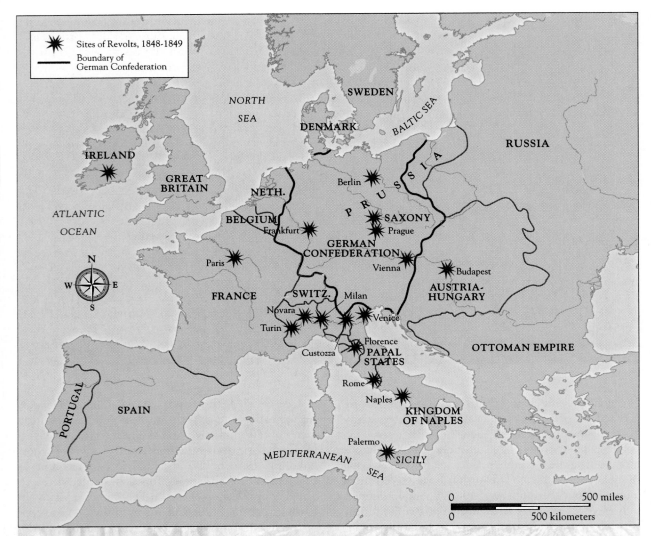

THINKING ABOUT GEOGRAPHY

MAP 18.3 *European Revolts, 1848–1849*

This map shows the location of the 1848 revolutions. ◼ **Consider** the possible reasons for the eruption of so many revolutions over this wide geographic area. ◼ **Compare** this map with Map 18.2. **What** do the two maps reveal about the breath of revolutionary activity between 1820 and 1848 and the challenges faced by the conservative forces of order?

demanded national autonomy from Austria. The Czechs followed suit in Bohemia and called for a Pan-Slavic congress to meet at Prague. In Austria's Italian provinces of Lombardy and Venetia, the rebellious populace drove the Austrian forces into defensive fortresses and declared their in-

Hungary

dependence. By June 1848, it appeared that the Habsburg Empire was splintering along ethnic lines and that its German core would commit to liberal reforms.

When the Hohenzollern ruler of Prussia, Frederick William IV (r. 1840–1861), heard of events in Austria, he granted some reforms and promised a liberal constitution. Nevertheless, the news from Paris and Vienna sent middle-class liberals and artisans demon-

Prussia strating in the streets of Berlin, the capital of Prussia. Frederick William sent in the troops, but their brutality only stiffened support for the revolutionary cause. A few days later he withdrew his troops and promised more reforms and support for German national unity. Hohenzollern Prussia, like Habsburg Austria, appeared on the road to liberal government.

In several other German states, rulers quickly gave in to revolutionary demands. Then a self-appointed group of liberal leaders made a bold move: they called

Frankfurt Assembly for a popularly elected assembly representing all German states to meet at Frankfurt to construct a liberal German nation. "[A]t last the great opportunity had arrived for giving to the German people the liberty which was their birthright and to the German fatherland its unity and greatness," explained a participant. Three crucial questions confronted the Frankfurt Assembly: (1) whether German-speaking portions of the multilingual Habsburg Empire and other states should be included in the projected German nation, (2) what should be done with non-German ethnic groups living within German states, and (3) who should head the new nation. After almost a year of debate, the assembly decided on a smaller Germany and offered the crown to the king of Prussia.

Meanwhile, in Italy several states established new constitutions. The movement for national unification

Italy kept alive by the idealist Giuseppi Mazzini found additional strength. He backed up his ideas with action: "Insurrection—by means of guerrilla bands—is the true method of warfare for all nations desirous of emancipating themselves from a foreign yoke," he explained. Just one year after the first revolt broke out in France, popular demonstrations brought down the papal government and forced Pius IX to flee Rome. Mazzini soon gained a foothold as head of the newly formed Republic of Rome.

THE RETURN TO ORDER

For the revolutionaries of 1848, a new, victorious age seemed to have dawned. Within a few months, the old governments almost everywhere had been swept from power or seriously weakened. The upheavals were so widespread that at one point Tsar Nicholas I

of Russia exclaimed to Britain's Queen Victoria, "What remains standing in Europe? Great Britain and Russia." Unfortunately for the revolutionaries, however, the forces of order showed resiliency and even new strength when events took more radical turns.

In France, divisions rose among those once unified against the monarchy. The more conservative peasantry and landowners in the countryside stepped back from the radical reforms demanded by Parisian artisans, shopowners, and intellectuals. The gap also widened be- *June Days in France* tween the middle class, which felt that reforms had gone far enough or even too far, and workers, who agitated for more social programs. These divisions reached a boiling point when the Constitutional Assembly, which had been elected in the late spring of 1848, abolished the national workshops. Officials told the workers to join the army or go look for work in the provinces. The desperate men and women of the Paris working class resorted to arms and barricades. For four days, war raged in the streets of Paris between the working class, armed with National Guard rifles, and the regular army. The French liberal writer and politician Alexis de Tocqueville (1805–1859), an observer of the events, described the June Days as "the revolt of one whole section of the population against another. Women took part in it as well as men . . . and when at last the time had come to surrender, the women were the last to yield."

Figure 18.12 depicts the fate of the revolutionary workers of Paris during the "June Days" of 1848. Here the paving stones used so successfully for the barricades in February, 1848, are scattered in the rout of the revolutionaries. The revolutionaries and the radical demands they represented—symbolized by the red, white, and blue of a fallen fighter's clothing—lie crushed by army troops, who this time have willingly fired on the people. When the last barricade had fallen during the bloody June Days, some 1500, mostly workingmen, had perished. Several hundred were sent overseas to French colonial prisons. Louis Blanc fled to Great Britain. The events widened the cleavage between radical urban Paris and conservative rural France—a cleavage that would long complicate France's public life. As a final insult to the revolutionaries, the December presidential elections swept Louis-Napoleon Bonaparte (1808–1873), nephew of Napoleon Bonaparte, to victory. Promising something for everyone and projecting an image of order and authority, Louis-Napoleon held office for

FIGURE 18.12
The June Days in France.

the Frankfurt Assembly, contemptuously calling it "a crown from the gutter." His rejection of the crown blasted the Frankfurt Assembly's hopes for a united, liberal Germany. He accused liberals in the Frankfurt Assembly of "fighting the battle of godlessness, perjury, and robbery, and kindling a war against monarchy," and his Prussian troops drove the point home by ousting the few remaining liberals determined to keep the assembly alive. Figure 18.13 depicts the street fighting in Frankfurt in September 1848. The king's well-ordered professional troops move up the street against a barricade thrown up by revolutionaries. The untrained revolutionaries and their supporters fire from windows and hurl stones, chairs, and bottles at the uniformed troops. This time, the revolutionaries proved no match for the king's forces.

WHAT HAPPENED?

By 1850 the conservative forces of order had regained control. What happened? How could so many victories by liberals, nationalists, workers, and students be turned into defeats so quickly?

There are several explanations. First, the alliances among middle-class liberals, radicals, socialists, artisans, and workers was one of convenience (their shared opposition to the status quo) *Internal divisions* rather than genuine fellowship. Once revolutionary forces gained power, the interests of the various groups proved too divergent for the alliances to endure. These divisions emerged most clearly in France, where the frightened middle class and conservative peasantry broke with the Parisian working classes. Lamartine, a poet and leading politician at the time, explained how the revolutionaries were divided into two groups: the republicans "were inspired by the hatred of royalty," while the socialists "were inspired . . . by the progress of humanity. The republic and equality was the aim of the one; social renovation and fraternity the aim of the other. They had nothing in common but impatience . . . and hope. . . ."

Second, liberal and nationalistic forces worked best together when out of power; once in power, they of- *Holding power: Liberalism vs. nationalism* ten stood at cross-purposes. This lack of harmony between liberals and nationalists was particularly pronounced in central Europe, where the nationalist aspirations of German, Polish, Magyar, Croatian, Serbian, and other groups conflicted with efforts to form new

three years and then destroyed the republic in 1851 by taking power for himself in a coup d'état.

In Austria, the revolutionaries' inexperience and the rivalries among various ethnic groups gave the Habsburgs the upper hand. Playing off one group *Austria and Hungary* against another and using their still formidable military force, the Austrian rulers beat down the liberal and national revolts one after the other. In Hungary, they had the help of the reactionary Nicholas I of Russia, whose army overwhelmed the Magyar rebels. In Italy, Austrian might (and, in Rome, French arms) eventually prevailed.

In Prussia, Frederick William IV fell under the influence of his militaristic and reactionary Junker advi- *Prussia* sors. Heartened by the news from Vienna that the Habsburgs had regained their position, he spurned the German crown offered him by

FIGURE 18.13
The forces of order in Frankfurt, September, 1848.

Third, the strength of conservatism should not be underestimated. With industrialization just beginning to emerge in central Europe, the middle and working classes—both discontented *Conservatism* with the conservative status quo— were still weak. Revolutionary leaders were inexperienced as well. In Germany, for example, the journalist Carl Schurz explained the failure of the Frankfurt parliament: "That parliament was laboring under an overabundance of learning and virtue and under a want of . . . political experience."

Finally, once the shock of initial defeat at the hands of revolutionaries had faded, the seasoned leaders of the forces of order marshaled their resources, drew on their own armies and those of allies, *Force* and overcame the divided revolutionary forces. Once they reestablished control, conservative leaders tore up most of the reforms and imprisoned, executed, or exiled revolutionaries. In December 1848, Pope Pius IX summarized the views of angry conservatives: "We . . . declare null and of no effect, and altogether illegal, every act" of reform during 1848. In fact, a few liberal reforms, such as the abolition of serfdom in Austria and Hungary and the limited constitutions in Piedmont and Prussia, would survive, but the great changes and power that for a few months seemed within the grasp of revolutionaries were gone.

governments with liberal institutions. For example, liberals in the Frankfurt Assembly who sought to unify Germany turned against other nationalities who rose up against German rule in Austria and Prussia.

Summary

In 1815, the conservative forces of order tried to secure their own survival by repressing all those heartened by the principles and reforms of the French Revolution and the Enlightenment. Change became the enemy of conservatives, but the industrial revolution and the growing strength of ideologies such as liberalism, nationalism, and socialism only strengthened demands for change.

In the early 1820s, a cycle of revolution and reform timidly emerged. In 1830, revolutionary forces posed a broader challenge, gaining some important victories in western Europe. The cycle returned in full force in 1848, as revolutions broke out through Europe and scored victory after victory. Those victories proved short-lived. By 1850, conservatives were back in power. This quick reversal of fortunes has led many historians to call the revolutions of 1848 "the turning point at which modern history failed to turn."

Yet the revolutions of 1848 left several important legacies. In a few cases, some liberal reforms were retained; in other cases, reforms in modified forms would be passed in succeeding years. Moreover, the overall failure of 1848 did not necessarily ensure a permanent victory for conservatism. As industrialization and urbanization spread year by year, traditional life and the old order it represented kept crumbling. Perhaps most significant, participants and observers had witnessed the power of ideologies, as well as economic and social realities, to galvanize people into political action.

Timeline: A Closer Look

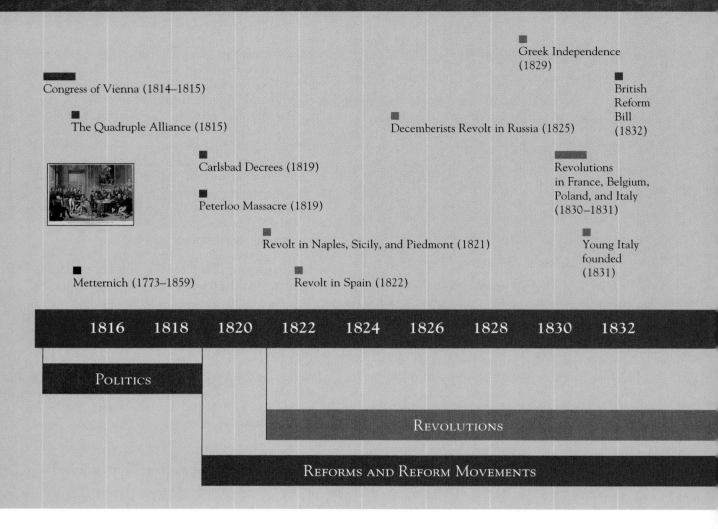

Greek Independence (1829)

Congress of Vienna (1814–1815)

British Reform Bill (1832)

The Quadruple Alliance (1815)

Decemberists Revolt in Russia (1825)

Carlsbad Decrees (1819)

Revolutions in France, Belgium, Poland, and Italy (1830–1831)

Peterloo Massacre (1819)

Revolt in Naples, Sicily, and Piedmont (1821)

Young Italy founded (1831)

Metternich (1773–1859)

Revolt in Spain (1822)

| 1816 | 1818 | 1820 | 1822 | 1824 | 1826 | 1828 | 1830 | 1832 |

POLITICS

REVOLUTIONS

REFORMS AND REFORM MOVEMENTS

However, the reestablished governments had learned important lessons from 1848, too, and would try to secure their positions with new vigor. They repaired the dam that broke in February, 1848. For the time being, at least, everything seemed under control.

REVIEW, ANALYZE, AND ANTICIPATE

REVIEW THE PREVIOUS CHAPTER

In Chapter 17—"Factories, Cities, and Families in the Industrial Age"—the industrial revolution and urbanization were analyzed. Chapter 16—"Overturning the Political and Social Order"—examined the

revolution whose consequences were felt throughout the West.

1. *In what ways might the developments described in Chapter 18 be considered a reaction to the French Revolution and industrial revolution discussed in the previous two chapters?*

2. *What forces stemming from the French Revolution and industrial revolution did conservatives try to*

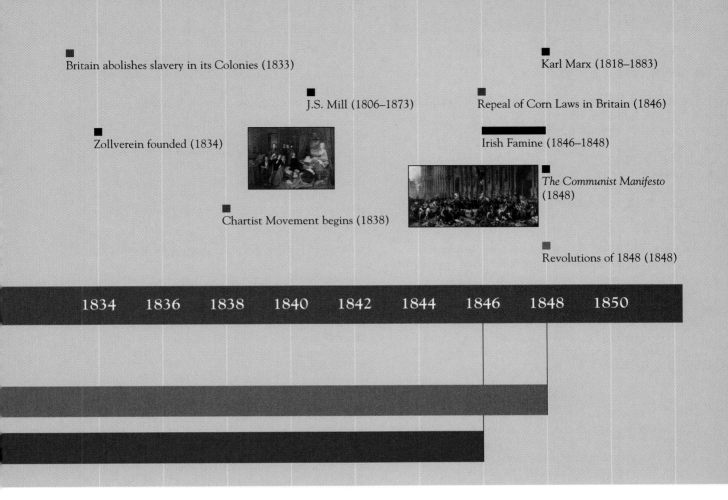

Britain abolishes slavery in its Colonies (1833)

Karl Marx (1818–1883)

J.S. Mill (1806–1873)

Repeal of Corn Laws in Britain (1846)

Zollverein founded (1834)

Irish Famine (1846–1848)

The Communist Manifesto (1848)

Chartist Movement begins (1838)

Revolutions of 1848 (1848)

| 1834 | 1836 | 1838 | 1840 | 1842 | 1844 | 1846 | 1848 | 1850 |

repress or contain? To what extent do you think conservatives succeeded?

ANALYZE THIS CHAPTER

Chapter 18—"Coping with Change"—analyzes the struggles between competing ideologies and political forces during the period between Napoleon's fall and the revolutions of 1848.

1. *Analyze the ideas of conservatism and policies of the forces of order in the years between 1815 and 1830.*

2. *In what ways did the ideas and actions of liberals, nationalists, and socialists challenge conservatives between 1815 and 1850?*

3. *In what ways did romanticism become a new cultural movement and an important ideology?*

4. *Analyze the commonalties in the several revolutions and movements for reform that developed between 1820 and 1848.*

ANTICIPATE THE NEXT CHAPTER

In Chapter 19—"Nationalism and Statebuilding"—the movements for national strength and unity will be examined.

1. *What "lessons" do you think governments and different social groups will have learned from the decades just preceding 1850 and, in particular, the revolutions of 1848?*

2. *Why might the ideologies of liberalism, nationalism, and socialism—which apparently suffered a stunning defeat between 1848 and 1850—persist and even grow in strength in the following decades?*

BEYOND THE CLASSROOM

THE CONGRESS OF VIENNA: A GATHERING OF VICTORS

Bridge, F. R. *The Great Powers and the European States System, 1815–1914*. London: Longman, 1980. A thorough diplomatic history of the period.

Nicolson, Harold. *The Congress of Vienna: A Study in Allied Unity, 1812–1822*. New York: Viking Press, 1961. A classic study of the Congress of Vienna and its accomplishments.

IDEOLOGIES: HOW THE WORLD SHOULD BE

Arblaster, Anthony. *The Rise and Decline of Western Liberalism*. Oxford, England: B. Blackwell, 1984. An analysis of the evolution and key components of liberalism.

Beecher, Jonathan. *Charles Fourier: The Visionary and His World*. Berkeley, CA: University of California Press, 1986. Traces the development of Fourier's ideas through his early years to his emergence as a political prophet and founder of one of the most significant early socialist movements.

Carlisle, Robert B. *The Proferred Crown: Saint-Simonianism and the Doctrine of Hope*. Baltimore: Johns Hopkins University Press, 1987. Studies the social philosophy of Saint-Simonianism.

Porter, Roy, and Mikulas Teich, eds. *Romanticism in National Context*. Cambridge: Cambridge University Press, 1988. A series of essays on romanticism by noted historians.

Smith, Denis Mack. *Mazzini*. New Haven, CT: Yale University Press, 1999. The most recent biography of this important figure by a well-known historian.

RESTORATION AND REPRESSION

Gildea, Robert. *Barricades and Borders: Europe 1800–1914*. New York: Oxford University Press, 1987. A broad survey stressing social and political developments during the period.

Jardin, André, and André-Jean Tudesq. *Restoration and Reaction, 1815–1848*. Cambridge: Cambridge University Press, 1988. A solid survey of France during this period.

Sheehan, James J. *German History, 1770–1866*. New York: Oxford University Press, 1989. A comprehensive, exhaustive examination of the changes in German social, political, and economic history.

Sked, Alan. *The Decline and Fall of the Habsburg Empire, 1815–1918*. London: Longman, 1989. Studies the growing problems facing the Habsburg Empire during the nineteenth century.

A WAVE OF REVOLUTION AND REFORM

Church, Clive. *Europe in 1830: Revolution and Political Change*. London: Allen & Unwin, 1983. Examines the revolutions that swept across Europe in a comparative context.

Thompson, Dorothy. *The Chartists: Popular Politics in the Industrial Revolution*. New York: Pantheon Books, 1984. An important and extensive treatment of the Chartist movement in Britain.

THE DAM BURSTS: 1848

Price, Roger. *The Revolutions of 1848*. Atlantic Highlands, NJ: Humanities Press International, 1989. A useful, wide-ranging survey.

Sperber, Jonathan. *The European Revolutions, 1848–1851*. Cambridge: Cambridge University Press, 1994. A brief yet thorough account that covers the tumultuous events throughout Europe.

GARIBALDI LANDING IN SICILY

In this painting, the lifelong nationalist Giuseppe Garibaldi (1807–1882) heroically lands at the island of Sicily to fight for Italian unification. In the background, his band of volunteer soldiers (the "Red Shirts") pour from three ships and march in rough formation. Carrying a sword and a flag representing Italian unity, Garibaldi is welcomed by admiring children, women, men, and a priest. The image, though stirring, still cannot convey the effort and anguish required to turn nationalistic sentiment into political reality.

CHAPTER 19

Nationalism and Statebuilding

Unifying Nations, 1850–1870

May 31, 1860: just three weeks after landing in Sicily, the Italian nationalist leader Giuseppe Garibaldi toured Palermo, Sicily's main city. He entered the city at the head of a band of 1,000 volunteer soldiers to begin the liberation of southern Italy from the old, Austrian-supported Bourbon king. He called for "Italians" to "put an end, once and for all, to the miseries of so many centuries," and "prove to the world that it is no lie that Roman generations inhabited this land." An eyewitness described how "the popular idol, Garibaldi, in his red flannel shirt, with a loose colored handkerchief round his neck … was walking on foot among those cheering, laughing, crying, mad thousands." As he moved through the streets, "the people threw themselves forward to kiss his hands, or, at least, to touch the hem of his garment, as if it contained the panacea for all their past and perhaps coming suffering."

In the decades between 1850 and 1870, millions of others in the Italian states—and in regions ranging from the Americas in the west to the Ottoman Empire in the east—would rally, fight, and die in the name of national unity. In Europe, maps had to be redrawn as new nation-states emerged. In the United States, a wrenching battle was entered in the name of preserving the Union. Political leaders would use nationalistic appeals to build stronger states as well as to tear apart multinational empires. Nationalism was evolving from the ideals of earlier decades to the realities of power politics.

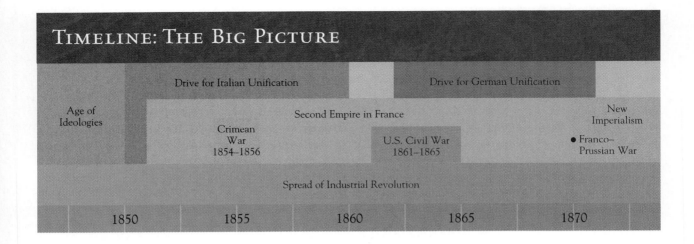

TIMELINE: THE BIG PICTURE

Drive for Italian Unification

Drive for German Unification

Age of Ideologies

Second Empire in France

New Imperialism

Crimean War 1854–1856

U.S. Civil War 1861–1865

● Franco– Prussian War

Spread of Industrial Revolution

1850   1855   1860   1865   1870

Building Unified Nation-States

"Every German heart hoped for it," wrote the baroness Spitzemberg in Berlin in 1871. "United into one Reich, the greatest, the most powerful, the most feared in Europe; great by reason of its physical power, greater still by reason of its education and the intelligence which permeates it!" So the baroness expressed her longing for national unification, a passion felt by many others in the West.

In the two decades after 1850, no political force was stronger than nationalism. It pushed people toward national unity in Italy and Germany, and

Nationalism threatened to tear the Habsburg and Ottoman Empires apart. In the United States, the principle of national unity helped spark a brutal civil war. In France and elsewhere, rulers enacted major reforms designed to bolster national unity and their authority as leaders of a nation of citizens. All these efforts were intended to build strong, unified nation-states led by central governments that could enjoy the support of their citizens.

Unlike in 1848, however, the nationalist political figures were neither revolutionaries nor idealists. As

Political realism one advocate of Italian unification observed, "To defeat cannons and soldiers, cannons and soldiers are needed." From positions of established power, this new generation of leaders molded nationalism to fit harsh political realities. They focused their eyes on practical policies, not ideals. They gambled, compromised, manipulated, and fought to achieve their goals. Few struggled more persistently and cleverly than Count Camillo di Cavour (1810–1861).

The Drive for Italian Unification

Cavour was born into a well-to-do, noble family living in Piedmont-Sardinia, a small, but relatively powerful independent state in northern Italy that also included the island of Sardinia. As a young **Cavour** man, he gambled, played the stock market, experimented with agricultural techniques, and succeeded in business—a pattern of taking calculated risks he would later try to follow in politics. By the 1840s, he had become committed to Italian unification. Shortly before the revolution of 1848, he founded the newspaper *Il Risorgimento* (*The Resurgence*), which passionately argued for a unified Italy. In 1850, Piedmont-Sardinia's king Victor Emmanuel II (r. 1849–1878) made Cavour his minister of commerce and agriculture and, two years later, prime minister.

Cavour's goals were clear. First, he wanted to modernize Piedmont economically and thereby win strength and respect for his homeland. Second, he sought to make Piedmont the **Piedmont's leadership** central engine of the drive for national unification. Third, he advocated forming a new Italian state as a constitutional monarchy under Piedmont's king rather than a democratic republic or a confederation under the pope. To achieve all these ends, Cavour lowered tariffs, built railroads, and balanced Piedmont's budget. He supported the nationalistic Italian National Society and its Feminine Committee, which worked toward national unification with Piedmont at the helm. Finally, he employed diplomacy and Piedmont's relatively small army to gain international support for the struggle against the primary obstacle to unification—Austria.

When the Crimean War broke out between Russia and the Ottoman Empire in 1854, Cavour saw an opportunity. He brought Piedmont in on the side of Great Britain and France, countries that had joined the Ottoman Turks against Russia. Cavour hoped to gain the friendship and support of France and Britain and thereby elevate Piedmont-Sardinia's status among the European powers. "I believe that the principal condition for the improvement of Italy's fate," he explained to the Parliament of Piedmont in 1855, "is to lift up her reputation once more . . . to prove that Italy's sons can fight valiantly on battlefields where glory is to be won." Victory in the east, he claimed, "will help the future state of Italy more than all that has been done by those people who hoped to regenerate her by rhetorical speeches and writings."

His risky plan may have paid off. At the Paris Peace Conference in 1856, which ended the war, he pleaded Piedmont's case against Austria so skillfully that he captured the attention of the international community. Two years later, Cavour and France's emperor Napoleon III met at a French resort to discuss ways to move against Austria, a competitor of France on the Continent and the chief barrier to Cavour's hopes for Italian unity. The two decided to provoke Austria into a war against Piedmont, and thereby bring France into the fray. "Together we began to . . . search of those grounds for war which were so difficult to find," explained Cavour in a note to his king. Then "we discovered what we had been trying so hard to find," a way to manipulate Austria into a war that "would not alarm the other continental powers." Once Austria declared war, France would help Piedmont drive the Austrians out of Lombardy and Venezia, and these two states would then be annexed to Piedmont-Sardinia. In return, Piedmont would cede the two small, French-speaking provinces of Savoy and Nice to France, and allow a kingdom of Central Italy to be created for Napoleon III's cousin.

In 1859, after Cavour mobilized the Piedmontese army and refused an Austrian demand to reverse the act, the unsuspecting Austrians declared war on Piedmont. French armies, using new railroad lines, poured across the Alps to fight alongside the Piedmontese. In the

War with Austria

bloody battles of Magenta and Solferino, the French and Piedmontese ousted the Austrians from Lombardy. But to the dismay of Cavour, Napoleon III suddenly made a separate peace at Villafranca with Austria that gave Piedmont Lombardy and left Venetia in Austrian hands. Cavour's side now had momentum, however. Nationalists in other Italian states, inspired by Piedmont's success, rose to the cause of national unity. By early 1860, most of northern and central Italy had joined Piedmont voluntarily.

At this pivotal point in the action, the rawboned nationalist Giuseppe Garibaldi made a daring exploit. Garibaldi had long struggled to create a unified and republican Italy—organizing people, conducting campaigns of guerilla

Garibaldi

warfare, and leading insurrections. Often in exile, he had become a well-known figure in Europe and the Americas. In May 1860, accompanied by a thousand civilian warriors dressed in red shirts, he sailed for Sicily in southern Italy, where many peasants had already launched a revolt. "It is the duty of every Italian to succor them [the Sicilians in revolt] with words, money, arms, and above all, in person," he announced. Garibaldi's goal was nothing less than the conquest of the Kingdom of Naples, the largest and most populous of the Italian states, and then Rome itself. Cavour officially condemned the seemingly foolhardy expedition but secretly assisted it. As we saw at the beginning of this chapter, Garibaldi's exploits read like an adventure novel. In rapid succession, he conquered Sicily, crossed the Strait of Messina, and triumphantly entered Naples (see Map 19.1). The opposing troops had little heart for their own cause. Many, along with civilian women and men by the thousands, joined Garibaldi after his first victories. Made ever bolder by his conquests, the confident Garibaldi advanced north toward Rome.

Not wanting to lose control of the rapidly changing situation and fearing that an attack on Rome by Garibaldi might lead France and Austria to come to the aid of the pope, Cavour sent troops southward in September 1860, gained control over the Papal States, and then skirted the area around Rome. King Victor Emmanuel, marching at the head of his army, met Garibaldi's forces south of Rome. Figure 19.1, an English engraving, portrays Victor Emmanuel—on the left in formal military attire—and the heroic adventurer Garibaldi—on the right informally dressed—shaking hands and thereby sealing the unification of

THINKING ABOUT GEOGRAPHY

MAP 19.1   *The Unification of Italy*

This map shows the unification of Italy in the years after 1859. ◧ **Locate** Lombardy and Nice. **Consider** how much Piedmont gave up and gained in its bargain for French support. ◧ **Find** the route of Garibaldi's campaign. **Why** might this have been so important—and threatening—to Piedmont's plans to unify Italy? ◧ **Consider** the importance of those territories still outside of the Italian state in 1860.

FIGURE 19.1
Victor Emmanuel and Garibaldi, 1860.

Germany "By Blood and Iron"

Like Italy, Germany as we understand it did not exist in 1850, except in the hearts of nationalists. Most of the many German states belonged to the loose Germanic Confederation, but this organization, under the dominance of Austria, did not function as a unified nation. Would someone like Piedmont's Count Cavour rise to overcome the obstacles to German unification? By 1860, no one of this caliber had yet stepped forward.

The best hope for German unity rested with Prussia, which had achieved a position of strength thanks to its economic expansion and leadership over the Zollverein, a German customs *Prussian leadership* union that fostered industrialization in Prussia and the Rhineland (see p. 579). By 1853, every German state except Austria had joined the Zollverein. However, Prussia was torn by the political struggle between liberals in the legislature and the conservative aristocracy. The two sides fought over plans to strengthen Prussia's military. When Prussia's new king, William I, and his military advisors proposed to double the size of the army, the liberals, who distrusted Prussian militarism and hoped to gain a stronger role for the legislature in the Prussian government, defeated the measure. Faced with a deadlock between these uncompromising forces and convinced that his royal authority was being threatened, William I called on Otto von Bismarck (1815–1898).

"I was born and raised as an aristocrat," Bismarck once explained. He would remain loyal to Prussia's landowning aristocracy for the rest of his life. As a young man, Bismarck showed little promise of future greatness. While attending uni- *Bismarck* versity, he spent more time gambling than studying. A religious conversion in 1846 and marriage seemed to give him more of a sense of purpose. He entered politics in 1847 and came to believe that only an alliance of conservatism and nationalism could preserve the aristocracy and strengthen Prussia. His enemies were the liberals, who had failed in 1848, and

Italy as their armies met in 1860. Uncertainty over whether Garibaldi and his forces would yield to Victor Emmanuel and his Piedmontese troops preceded this meeting. The artist emphasizes the significance of the moment by depicting Garibaldi as dignified, but with his hat in hand and his horse bowing in deference to the king. Two years later Garibaldi, hoping to annex Rome as the capital of Italy, fomented an unsuccessful uprising. The gallant patriot soon retired to his farm on the rocky island of Caprera.

The Kingdom of Italy was formally declared in March 1861, with Victor Emmanuel II as monarch *Kingdom of Italy* and the Piedmontese Constitution of 1848 as the national charter. The king, along with a parliamentary government elected by limited suffrage, would rule. The red, white, and green Piedmontese flag now flew over all of Italy, from the Alps to Sicily, except in Venezia and Rome (see Map 19.1). These two provinces joined the Italian state in 1866 and 1870, respectively.

Sadly, Cavour did not live to enjoy the fruits of his labors. Less than three months after the birth of his beloved Italian nation, he died. Paunchy, with ill-fitting glasses, he had never cut an impressive figure. Nor had he made a particularly powerful orator. "I cannot make a speech," he once said, "but I can make Italy."

Austria, Prussia's chief competitor and supposedly senior partner within the German states.

Bismarck assumed the office of chancellor (prime minister) of Prussia in 1862. With the backing of the king, the aristocracy, and the army, he promptly defied the liberals in the legislature, violated the constitution, and ordered taxes collected for military reform. "Necessity alone is authoritative," he argued. He would pursue a policy of realism—*Realpolitik*—to achieve his goals. "Not by speeches and majority resolutions," Bismarck rumbled, "are the great questions of the time decided—that was the mistake of 1848 and 1849—but by blood and iron." As the "Iron Chancellor" argued, Germans looked to Prussia for leadership not because of its liberalism, but because of its power.

Like Cavour in Italy, Bismarck sought out political opportunities, created them when they failed to materialize, and did not hesitate to take calculated risks, including war. In 1864, Den-

Wars for unification

mark provided his first opportunity when it tried to incorporate Schleswig and Holstein, two small provinces lying between Prussia and Denmark. The provinces' legal status had been disputed for decades. Posing as a defender of German nationalism, Prussia promptly declared war on Denmark, pulling Austria—anxious to retain leadership of the German Confederation—in as Prussia's reluctant ally. In the complicated settlement—Schleswig and Holstein were to be ruled jointly by Prussia and Austria—Bismarck shrewdly planted the seeds for a future conflict with Austria.

Bismarck soon used this unworkable arrangement to stir up trouble with Austria. He obtained the support of Italy by promising Austria's province of

Austro-Prussian War

Venezia as a prize. He gained Russia's sympathy by supporting its intervention against revolting subjects in Poland. Finally, he neutralized Napoleon III by personal persuasion and deception. In 1866 Bismarck took a risk by using threats and maneuvers to provoke Austria into declaring war on Prussia. Austria was twice the size and population of Prussia, and had long dominated central Europe. Nevertheless, Prussia's modern and mobile armies managed to overwhelm the surprised Austrian forces in just seven weeks. Austria suffered four times as many casualties as Prussia, in great part thanks to the fast firing needle-guns used by Prussian troops and the army's use of railroads to move

forces quickly to battlefields. Bismarck boldly expelled Austria from the German Confederation and even annexed several German states that had sided with Austria. Nevertheless, hoping for Austrian support in the future, Bismarck refused the desires of Prussia's king and army leaders to annex Austrian territories.

Prussia now controlled the newly created North German Confederation. Despite some democratic forms, such as a legislative body (the Reichstag) elected by universal male suf-

Franco-Prussian War

frage, the government was fundamentally autocratic. The legislature had no control over the chancellor—appointed by and responsible only to the king—or his cabinet, and little control over the budget or armed forces. However, some of the southern German states, with larger Catholic populations than Prussia, still lay outside Bismarck's grasp (see Map 19.2). He wisely recognized that these remaining, reluctant states might join the fold if German nationalism could be rallied against a common, foreign threat. France, Bismarck decided, might just fit the bill.

Bismarck's opportunity to confront France came in 1870, when the Spanish crown was offered to a Hohenzollern prince—a relative of Prussia's William I. When Bismarck persuaded the reluctant prince to accept the Spanish offer, the French immediately took alarm at the prospect of being surrounded by Hohenzollerns. The French exerted heavy pressure on Prussia, and both the prince and King William yielded. However, the unsatisfied French ministers demanded more. After a meeting at Ems between the French ambassador and the Prussian king, the chancellor saw an opportunity to provoke the French into war. Cleverly editing the Ems telegraph dispatch so as to make it appear that the French ambassador and the Prussian king had insulted each other, he published it to the world. The French government was offended and walked into Bismarck's trap. Buoyed by public demands for action, France declared war.

The chancellor had taken his greatest risk, for France seemed to possess enough military might and economic resources to humble Prussia. As France's confident prime minister stated, "We go to war with a light heart." Once again, however, the able Prussian troops quickly scored resounding successes. One French army was surrounded at the fortress city of Metz. The Prussians encircled another French army at Sedan, forcing it to surrender. Napoleon III himself

THINKING ABOUT GEOGRAPHY

MAP 19.2   *The Unification of Germany*

This map shows the steps taken to achieve German unification in 1871. **Notice** the positions of Prussia and Austria before 1866. **What** does this reveal about the rivalry between these two countries for control over the German states? **Notice** the changes in 1866, 1867, and 1871. **What** does this show about the importance of Prussia's triumph over Austria in 1866 and over France in 1871? **Who** might be most threatened by a powerful Germany after 1871?

was one of the captives. When this news reached Paris, the liberals overthrew the government of the Second Empire and declared the Third French Republic. Paris held out for a few more months, surrounded by the Germans, but finally surrendered in January, 1871.

On January 18, 1871, Bismarck called the heads of all the German states to Versailles in France. Gathering in the Hall of Mirrors, the dignitaries proclaimed Prussia's king William I, emperor of the new German Empire; he would rule until 1888. Figure 19.2 celebrates that moment. In this well-known painting,

FIGURE 19.2
Anton von Werner, *Proclamation of the German Empire*.

brant industrial economy, and a feared military. Bismarck, of course, remained chancellor and lived to rule over his creation for the next nineteen years. In Germany, as in Italy, a clever, realistic political leader had employed diplomacy and war to transform the unruly forces of nationalism into German unification.

The Fight for National Unity in North America

The struggle for unification flared up in other parts of the West besides Italy and Germany. Between 1800 and 1861, the United States' political institutions had evolved along democratic and nationalistic lines. Almost all white men had gained the right to *The United States* vote. A modern, broad-based political party system had formed and wrestled

Prussian officers hail William, who stands at the left. But the center of the painting belongs to Bismarck, dressed in white, the architect of this historical moment. He alone holds the document proclaiming the new empire that he, more than anyone else, had built. The dramatic scene is set in France's historic symbol of monarchical power, the Versailles palace. By choosing this location, Bismarck drove home the point that Prussia had achieved German unity by defeating France in war. He also wanted to make it crystal clear that Germany, now in possession of France's rich provinces of Alsace and Lorraine and owed a war indemnity of 5 billion francs in gold from the French, had replaced the humiliated France as Europe's leading continental power.

The constitution that Bismarck had drafted for the North German Confederation became the constitution for the new German Empire. Its twenty-five states retained control over many domestic matters, but Prussia dominated the union. Known as the Second Reich (Germans honored the old Holy Roman Empire as the First Reich), the powerful nation included a large and rapidly growing population, a vi-

political power from the elite circles of the old colonial well-to-do. The nation had expanded westward to the Pacific Ocean, conquering the Amerindians and displacing them to reservations. When Mexico stood in the way of expansion, it also lost its lands to the United States' armed forces. Finally, American culture began to free itself from strictly European influence. Citizens proudly thought of themselves and their institutions as having a distinct flavor within Western civilization.

However, as the nineteenth century progressed, the nation labored under growing regional differences. The North was an expanding, urban, industrial so- *North-South divisions* ciety based on free labor. Figure 19.3, a lithograph of the Stillman, Allen & Co. Novelty Iron Works of New York City, illustrates one of the many manufacturing facilities growing up in the North's cities in the middle decades of the nineteenth century. The South remained agricultural, dependent on plantation crops such as cotton, and based on slave labor. Figure 19.4, a painting by Charles Giroux, portrays this rural society with its large population of slaves. The North en-

FIGURE 19.3
A Northern factory.

decades before 1861, these two regions, with their increasingly different societies and interests, clashed politically on several occasions.

It was the issue of slavery, though, that gave these clashes a dangerous emotional intensity and tied together the other problems dividing the North and South. By the early 1800s, the northern states had eliminated slavery. However, the institution persisted in the South, where agriculture, and especially cotton plantations, reigned supreme. There slaveholders viewed slaves as the very basis of their wealth, power, and status. Meanwhile, in the free-labor North, antislavery sentiment grew. "[T]his government cannot endure permanently half slave and half free," declared Abraham Lincoln (1809–1865) in 1858, just two years before the nation elected him president.

Slavery

In 1861, all these regional differences, fueled by the question of whether to abolish slavery, ignited a bloody war between the North, led by Lincoln, and the South under Jefferson Davis (1808–1889). The conflict raged for four years until

The Civil War

joyed a growing population and generally favored federal over state power. The South, worried that its influence over national policies was slipping away, emphasized states' rights over federal power. In the

FIGURE 19.4
Charles Giroux, *Cotton Plantation*.

the North finally defeated the Southern armies. Ultimately the war took more than 600,000 lives, making it the bloodiest conflict in the Western world since the end of the Napoleonic Wars. Lincoln had achieved his primary goal: to reestablish national unity and affirm the power of the national government. In the aftermath, slavery was abolished in the United States.

Farther north, a different struggle for national independence and unity had been unfolding in Canada. William Lyon Mackenzie (1795–1861), a nationalist politician, called for Canadians to "put down the villains [the British] who oppress and enslave our country" and gain "freedom from British tribute." Britain responded to a rebellion in 1837 by granting Canada some control over its own domestic affairs.

Canada

Nevertheless, the Canadian territories were not yet joined into a single nation, and Canadians feared the growing power of the United States. Demands for union and complete nationhood increased. Finally, in 1867, the British North American Act united Canada into a single nation with its own constitution.

Divided Authority in the Austrian and Ottoman Empires

Nationalism pulled Austria's multiethnic empire apart rather than bringing it together (see Map 19.3). Czechs, Serbs, Romanians, Magyars (Hungar-

THINKING ABOUT GEOGRAPHY

MAP 19.3 *Language Groups of Austria-Hungary*

This map shows the concentrations of language groups in Austria-Hungary at the end of the nineteenth century. ✉ **What** does this map reveal about the difficulties facing the Austro-Hungarian Empire in an age of growing nationalism? In **what** areas is the empire most vulnerable? ✉ **Notice** the surrounding states. **What** language groups might find support from outside the empire's borders?

ians), and other ethnic groups wanted to form their own, independent nations rather than rally *Austria* behind Austria, which was predominantly German.

Austria's emperor, Francis Joseph (r. 1848–1916), was no reformer or politician in the mold of Bismarck, Cavour, or Lincoln. Under pressure from liberals and nationalists, he agreed in 1860 to a moder-*Austria-Hungary, 1867* ate decentralization of the empire and the creation of a parliament. After Austria's defeat by Prussia in 1866, the dominant German minority in Austria compromised with the assertive Magyars rather than fight them over issues of nationality. Their agreement, the Compromise of 1867, set up the Dual Monarchy of Austria-Hungary. Each country had its own separate parliament, but the two were united under a common ruler, the head of the House of Habsburg. This arrangement was essentially an alliance between the Germans of Austria and the Magyars of Hungary against other competing ethnic groups. The empire therefore divided authority in an effort to control even more threatening movements for national independence. This arrangement did not please other national groups, especially the Czechs who would persistently demand equality with the Hungarians.

Like the Austrians, the Ottoman rulers also had to struggle with the divisive forces of nationalism. In *The Ottoman Empire* 1850, the Ottoman Empire was still extensive. From its base in Turkey, it maintained control over much of southeastern Europe as well as over provinces stretching from North Africa to the Persian Gulf. However the empire, often referred to as "the sick man of Europe," was in decline. Powerful, ambitious neighbors—especially the Russians, who attacked the Turks in 1853 and again in 1877—maneuvered to take advantage of the *Balkan nationalism* Ottomans' weaknesses. But the greatest threats to the empire's integrity came from its restless Balkan provinces in southeastern Europe. In this area nationalism rose, producing the same sort of movements for independence that had weakened the Austrian Empire.

By 1830, the Ottoman Empire had already lost Serbia and Greece to independence movements (see Map 19.4). Nationalism had fueled an unsuccessful revolt by the Romanians in 1848 as well. In 1856, the Romanians gained international support as part of the settlement of the Crimean War. Over the next twenty years, they pressed the Ottomans for their freedom, finally winning full independence in 1878.

Nationalist movements also cropped up among the Bulgars. Encouraged by Serbia and Russia, the Bulgars revolted in 1876. Each side in the conflict committed atrocities, but those committed by the Turks especially shocked Europeans. That year, Bosnia and Herzegovina also rose against the Turks. Serbia and Russia then joined forces against the Ottoman Empire. By 1878 international agreements, most notably the Treaty of Berlin, had secured the independence of Bulgaria and placed Bosnia and Herzegovina under Austro-Hungarian rule. Movements for national independence, with the aid of powers eager to take advantage of the empire's declining strength, had ended Turkish control throughout most of the Balkans. However, these developments also left a jumble of dissatisfied groups and nationalities—a few who had their own states, some who longed for political independence, and others who did not like being annexed by Austria-Hungary.

Using Nationalism in France and Russia

The power of nationalism to motivate people to join revolutionary organizations, form new political allegiances, follow powerful politicians, and go to war in the name of national unity made itself clear in Italy and Germany. Under different conditions, nationalism weakened and dismembered long-established multinational states such as the Austrian and Ottoman Empires.

Nationalism also pushed governments in well-established states to reach out to citizens for support. These governments tried to justify and sustain their authority by performing public services, and they bolstered their power by promoting the idea of national greatness. They paid more attention to everyday life so as to maintain social peace and cultivate loyalty to the nation—and especially to its leaders. These efforts to channel nationalism into statebuilding are especially well illustrated by the paths that France and Russia took after 1850.

THINKING ABOUT GEOGRAPHY

MAP 19.4   *The Decline of the Ottoman Empire, 1683–1914*

This map shows the loss of territory by the Ottoman empire between 1683 and 1914. ◪ **Who** were the Ottomans' main European rivals in this region? ◪ **Notice** in particular those areas lost during the nineteenth and early twentieth centuries. **Consider** why the growth of nationalism became such a threat to the empire.

NAPOLEON III AND THE SECOND EMPIRE

In France, Louis-Napoleon Bonaparte, nephew of Napoleon Bonaparte, blended support from below, reform, and authoritarian nationalism in his Second Empire, which was established in 1852. Louis-Napoleon was originally elected president of France's Second Republic in 1848 (see pp. 629–630). He benefited from his *Napoleon III* illustrious name, his appeal to property owners longing for order, and his well-publicized promises to link democracy from below with reforming leadership from above. When the National Assembly refused to change the constitution so that he could run for a second term, he organized a coup d'état and seized power on December 2, 1851. Resistance was limited, though hundreds were killed and thousands were arrested and deported. He quickly granted universal male suffrage, and during the following year he held two plebiscites in which over 90 percent of the voters supported him and made him hereditary emperor—Napoleon III. "I believe," he confidently wrote, "that there are certain men who are born to serve as the means for the march of the human race. . . . I consider myself to be one of these."

Building upon his uncle's legend, Napoleon III tried to convince citizens that he would lead the nation to new heights in domestic as well as foreign affairs. His military uniform and opulent court served as images of authority. Figure 19.5 is typical of many paintings that portray the emperor in military dress. The order that Napoleon III stood for is represented by the balance of this scene. The emperor is astride a white horse just ahead of France's other military leaders. In the immediate background is an arch of triumph, and in the distant background the museum and palace of the Louvre, all symbolizing the glories of Napoleon Bonaparte's rule a half century earlier.

Napoleon III kept the elected legislature firmly under his thumb by minimizing its authority over his ministers and manipulating the electoral machinery. When it served his purposes, he encouraged industrialization and economic growth by promoting railroad construction, public works, and financial institutions—policies that appealed to the middle and working classes. His prefect of Paris, Georges Haussmann (1809–1891), rebuilt Paris into an envied model of a modern, wealthy, powerful capital (see Chapter 20). To project a progressive image, Napoleon also directed the building of hospitals, nurseries, and homes for the aged. To gain support from workers, he kept bread prices low, instituted a system of voluntary social insurance, encouraged cooperatives, and partially legalized labor unions.

The French emperor's foreign adventures gained him prestige at first, but lost him everything in the end. He brought France into the Crimean War and played the glorious host to the peace conference that ended that conflict. In addition, he tried to increase French influence in the Italian peninsula by joining Piedmont in a war against Austria, but he underestimated the strength of Italian nationalism; that nation unified without becoming beholden to France. In 1862 his armies marched into Mexico City and set up a Habsburg prince, Maximillian, as puppet emperor for France. A few years later, problems at home and a threatening army from the United States

FIGURE 19.5
Porion, *Napoleon III*.

Biography

FLORENCE NIGHTINGALE (1820–1910)

In October 1854, a British journalist in Constantinople reported the successes enjoyed by the British army in the Crimean War. He also described in dramatic detail the horrendous condition of the army's medical facilities where the wounded and sick languished and died.

One of the many readers outraged by the report was Florence Nightingale. Just three years earlier, in a private note, she had written, "What am I that their [other women's] life is not good enough for me? . . . why, oh my God, cannot I be satisfied with the life that satisfied so many people?" The war, which was causing so much suffering on and off the battlefield, suddenly created an opportunity for Nightingale to take control of her own life, gain fame as "the Lady with the Lamp," and be hailed as a national heroine.

Born in 1820 into an upper-class family, she received an unusual classical education—including several languages, philosophy, history, and science—from her father. Her mother tried to train her to conform to the domestic responsibilities of her class—the domestic rituals, long meals, and formal sociability Florence resisted. She complained that "daughters are now their mothers' slaves . . . they are considered their parents' property, they are to have no other pursuit, nor power, nor independent life, unless they marry." She rejected suitors, explaining, "I have a moral and active nature which requires satisfaction, and that would not find it in his [a husband's] life."

Instead, she pleaded with her family to allow her to train as a nurse. They responded with rage, for at the time nursing was considered a menial occupation reserved for the lowest classes. Her society offered few opportunities for "respectable" women to gain independence, and Florence described the suffering caused by these restrictions: "I see the numbers of my kind who have gone mad for want of something to do."

Her frustration and torment with family life became entwined with her anguished spiritual life. She first reported hearing God speak to her when she was sixteen. The depth of her despair is revealed by her petitions to God: "Forgive me, God & let me die—this day let me die." But she also looked to God for purpose: "God has something for me to do for him—or he would have let me die some time ago."

"Angel of the Crimea" and Medical Reformer

Her chance for a purposeful life came in 1854 when reports of the lack of proper medical care for sick and wounded British soldiers in the Crimean War appeared in the newspaper. Despite her family's opposition, Nightingale had managed to gain some training as a nurse in Germany, France, and Ireland. Now she was serving as superintendent of the Hospital for Invalid Gentlewomen in London. Using her family's wealth

---

forced Napoleon to withdraw his troops, leaving the doomed Maximillian to the mercy of Mexican forces, who executed him. The Mexican fiasco added to the growing unpopularity of Napoleon III with the French people.

Meanwhile, declining prosperity further weakened Napoleon's position within France. Trying to allay the mounting discontent of liberals and workers, he made one concession after another. By 1870 the liberal parliament had begun gaining the upper hand. That year, the ailing and discouraged Napoleon III blundered into a war with Prussia. Defeated and captured, he and his government fell.

Fall of Napoleon III

ALEXANDER II AND RUSSIA

Napoleon III had stood for order, reform from above, and national grandeur. Until he faltered, the French gave up their liberal sentiments for those ends. In and political connections, she obtained from the British government a commission to lead a team of thirty-eight nurses to Turkey.

On November 4, 1854, they arrived at the barrack hospital at Scutari—a suburb outside Constantinople on the Black Sea (see Map 19.4). In a November 14 letter, she described conditions at Scutari: "We have no room for corpses in the wards. . . . Not a sponge, nor a rag of linen, not anything have I left. . . . These poor fellows have not had a clean shirt nor been washed for two months before they came here. . . . I hope in a few days we shall establish a little cleanliness." She advocated fresh air, sunshine, hygiene, and diet. Figure 19.6, a lithograph of a ward at Scutari, shows Nightingale holding up her lamp and organizing care for the patients. Images such as this gave her the label "Lady with the Lamp."

Within six months and despite opposition, incompetence, and corruption within the British army, she transformed the medical facility, and the death rate fell from 40 percent to 2 percent. Her fame quickly spread. The *London Times* declared, "There is not one of England's proudest and purest daughters who at the moment stands on as high a pinnacle as Florence Nightingale."

The end of the war in 1856 did not end her efforts. Her best-selling *Notes on Nursing* (1859) became a primary text for nurses, and the nursing school she established in London (1860) became a model for similar institutions in Europe, Australia, and North America. Suffering from what she called "nervous fever," she spent much of the rest of her life in her own sickbed battling the sense of despair that had risen during her youth. Nevertheless, she used her prestige, political connections, and writings to campaign for reform of military healthcare, public sanitation, and social policy. In 1907, three years before her death, she was honored as the first woman to be awarded the British National Order of Merit. The "Angel of the Crimea" had revolutionized nursing and transformed military and public healthcare in the West.

▧ **Consider** how Nightingale's experience reveals the different ways war can alter people's lives. ▧ **How** does her life illustrate the problems caused by the social limitations on women during this period (see Chapter 17)?

FLORENCE NIGHTINGALE IN THE MILITARY HOSPITAL AT SCUTARI.

FIGURE 19.6
J.A. Benwell, Florence Nightingale in the military hospital, 1856.

Russia, Tsar Alexander II made similar appeals in an effort to overcome that country's troubles.

By 1850, Russia had earned a reputation as the most conservative of the European powers. Its government remained autocratic under the tsar, its feudalistic society still bound serfs to the land and their lords, and its large army enjoyed an aura of near invincibility. After the Crimean War, it became clear that things would have to change.

Russia's autocracy

In 1853, Russia's army and navy attacked the Ottoman Turks, hoping to snatch territory from the weakening Ottoman Empire. In addition, Russia sought to gain shipping access to the world from the Black Sea through the Turkish Straits, as well as influence in the Near East. Early the next year, France, Britain, and Piedmont-Sardinia, driven by their own ambitions rather than principles, joined the Ottoman Turks and poured their military forces into the Black Sea. They laid

Crimean War

siege to Russia's naval base, Sebastopol, on the Crimean Peninsula.

The war dragged on until 1856, and both sides fought with gross incompetence. Thanks to new telegraph lines and expanded press coverage, the public in the West could follow the conflict closely. People learned almost immediately, in graphic detail, about the horrific loss of life both on the Crimean battlefield and in the pitifully inadequate medical facilities (see Biography). More than 250,000 soldiers died, most of them from disease caused by poor sanitation, starvation, and lack of medical assistance. In the end, no one could claim much of a victory, but Russia, whose massive military no longer looked so formidable, was humbled.

Even before the Crimean disaster, peasant revolts and workers' protests had plagued Russia. In all of Europe, only Russia still allowed serfdom, which left millions tied to the land. Russia's serfs deeply resented the labor and dues they owed for the right to farm lands, and protests and insurrections broke out with alarming frequency. Between 1825 and 1855, more than 500 serf rebellions occurred in Russia. Food shortages struck all too often, yet most aristocrats took little responsibility for the suffering of their serfs. Many within the privileged class feared rebellion.

The peasants' low standard of living is revealed in Figure 19.7, a photograph of peasants in a Russian village during the second half of the nineteenth century. The man on the left wears tattered clothes. He and all the others stand barefoot in the mud street and aside the simple houses. This image contrasts sharply with Figure 19.8, an 1861 photograph that shows a noble landowner standing on the front steps of his mansion and reading a decree to some of his assembled serfs. Well-dressed members of his family watch from the stairs and the second-floor balcony, while household servants stand by attentively.

Not surprisingly, serfs conscripted into Russia's armies showed a distinct lack of enthusiasm. Their sullenness finally helped make Russia's leaders see that their country was being left behind by the other powers. The country simply lacked the social support, armaments, and railroads (it took Russia months in-

FIGURE 19.7
Peasants in a Russian village.

FIGURE 19.8
A noble's estate in Russia, 1861.

stead of weeks to move troops and supplies to the Crimean front) to win a modern war. Moreover, since serfs were bound to the land, Russia lacked a large mobile labor force to support industrialization and thereby keep up with nations to the west.

The new tsar, Alexander II (r. 1855–1881), was a complex, well-educated individual who recognized Russia's problems from the moment he took office. He

Alexander II's "Great Reforms"

was determined to introduce reforms to strengthen and modernize Russia and prop up his own rule. Like Napoleon III's policies, Alexander's "Great Reforms" came from above but proved much more far-reaching and dramatic. In 1861, Alexander freed Russia's 22 million serfs and, a few years later, 25 million state-owned peasants. "It is better to abolish serfdom from above than to wait until the serfs begin to liberate themselves from below," he told a group of his nobles. This bold move, occurring at almost the same time that millions of slaves were emancipated in the United States, put an end to a notorious form of human bondage and transferred land to the freed peasantry. In Figure 19.8, the noble landowner is reading the decree that abolished serfdom. However, emancipation did not make the peasants fully independent and self-sufficient. In general, they received the poorest land, owed payments for their land and freedom, and were tied by collective ownership to their village commune, the *mir*.

Other reforms made the judicial system more independent, created local political assemblies (*zemstva*) with elected officials, encouraged primary and secondary education by opening thousands of new schools, and reduced military service. However, expectations for further reform rose too fast for Alexander and came to haunt him. His efforts to relax control over Poland and grant amnesty to thousands of Poland's political prisoners seemed only to provoke a major Polish revolution in 1863, leading Alexander to repress the divisive nationalistic uprisings there and elsewhere within Russia's empire. To counter budding nationalism among minorities, he tried to force them to adopt the Russian language and culture. The universities he reopened became centers of intellectual discontent. Nor did his emancipation of the serfs end peasant rebellions.

Alexander intended to transform Russia into a modern authoritarian state that could command the allegiance of its citizens and wield power through a reformed, supported military. At best, he succeeded only partially. Certainly some of his reforms created important, long-lasting changes, but he did not turn his nation into a modern, national monarchy. Alexander himself, though called the "tsar liberator," was never popular. After an assassination attempt in 1866, he became more close-minded and increasingly turned Russia into a police state. Unrest still simmered among Russia's different nationalities. In addition, dissatisfaction among the peasantry and growing dissent among Russia's intellectuals, middle classes, and workers spelled trouble for the years ahead.

Summary

By the 1870s, the most successful political leaders had learned new lessons about the power of nationalistic sentiment. Nationalism was a mighty force more easily used than opposed. It could fuel successful movements for national unification, disintegrate multinational empires, enhance existing unity in already established nations, and strengthen central governments.

Shrewd political realists, rather than the idealists of earlier times, led successful nationalist struggles. These leaders relied on power politics, war, and diplomacy to achieve their aims. But such politicians, sometimes viewed as heroes who gamely shouldered the burden of unification, stood on ground that idealists and revolutionaries had broken in the years before 1850. Moreover, the hardest work was often carried out by nationalist groups, students, soldiers, intellectuals, journalists, and others who rose to the call of national unity. The costs for everyone were high. Many Italians, for example, lost their lives in the struggle for independence. Also tragic, those Italians who survived these turbulent years were left with a new nation that was far from rich and that still suffered from regional and political differences. Germany bought its unification with arms. From that point on, German nationalism remained

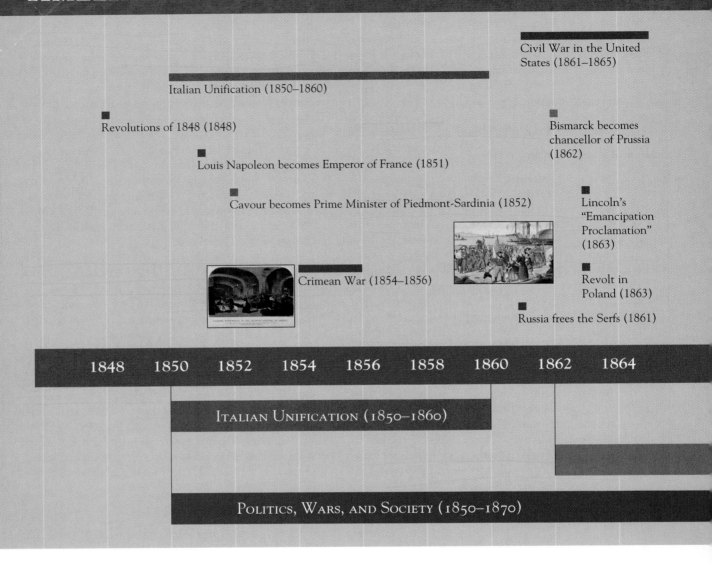

Civil War in the United States (1861–1865)

Italian Unification (1850–1860)

Revolutions of 1848 (1848)

Bismarck becomes chancellor of Prussia (1862)

Louis Napoleon becomes Emperor of France (1851)

Cavour becomes Prime Minister of Piedmont-Sardinia (1852)

Lincoln's "Emancipation Proclamation" (1863)

Crimean War (1854–1856)

Revolt in Poland (1863)

Russia frees the Serfs (1861)

| 1848 | 1850 | 1852 | 1854 | 1856 | 1858 | 1860 | 1862 | 1864 |

ITALIAN UNIFICATION (1850–1860)

POLITICS, WARS, AND SOCIETY (1850–1870)

linked with military prowess rather than liberal ideals. In the United States, Lincoln had preserved the Union—but only after a four-year nightmare that would mar American society for generations and cost Lincoln his life.

Other leaders, such as Napoleon III and Tsar Alexander II, recognized that reforms initiated from above could foster needed national unity and win them greater power. Moreover, Napoleon saw that real power flowed upward from a nation of citizens who deeply identified with their state and government. Increasingly, however, the cry "for the good of the nation" served as the only rationale for such leaders' policies and whims. As the era unfolded, even war could be presented to an unwary public as an act of national will and politics.

Austro-Prussian War (1866)

Canadian Independence and Unification (1867)

Creation of Austro-Hungarian Dual Monarchy (1867)

Franco-Prussian War (1870)

 German Unification (1871)

| 1866 | 1868 | 1870 | 1872 | 1874 | 1876 | 1878 | 1880 | 1882 |

GERMAN UNIFICATION
(1862–1871)

REVIEW THE PREVIOUS CHAPTER

In Chapter 18—"Coping with Change"—the struggles between competing ideologies and political forces during the period between Napoleon's fall and the revolutions of 1848 were analyzed.

1. *In what ways do you think the politics of this era reflect the efforts of governments to adjust to the changes initiated by the French Revolution and the industrial revolution?*

2. *How did the ideological struggles initiated during the first half of the century continue during the following decades?*

ANALYZE THIS CHAPTER

Chapter 19—"Nationalism and Statebuilding"—examines the efforts to build national unity and strength between 1850 and 1870.

1. *Analyze the methods used by leaders such as Cavour and Bismarck to achieve national unity. How do they compare with efforts during the revolutions of 1848?*

2. *How did leaders such as Napoleon III in France and Alexander II in Russia try to link nationalism and statebuilding?*

3. *In what ways was nationalism divisive in the Austrian and Ottoman Empires?*

ANTICIPATE THE NEXT CHAPTER

Chapter 19—"Mass Politics and Imperial Domination"—the spreading demands for democracy and the West's imperial expansion during the second half of the nineteenth century will be traced.

1. *What sorts of economic and social changes might be related to the rising nationalism and the increasing importance of politics during this period?*

2. *How might nationalism be related to both national and imperial expansion?*

BEYOND THE CLASSROOM

THE DRIVE FOR ITALIAN UNIFICATION

Beales, Derek. *The Risorgimento and the Unification of Italy.* London: Allen & Unwin, 1982. Offers a comprehensive account along with important documents from the period.

Coppa, Frank J. *The Wars of Italian Independence.* New York: Longman, 1992. A thorough discussion of the subject.

Mack Smith, Denis. *Cavour.* London: Weidenfeld and Nicolson, 1985. An excellent biography of this important figure in Italian unification.

GERMANY "BY BLOOD AND IRON"

Carr, William. *The Wars of German Unification.* London: Longman, 1991. Analyzes the three wars that led to the unification of Germany.

Craig, Gordon A. *Germany, 1866–1945.* New York: Oxford University Press, 1978. A respected survey of the course of German history from the establishment of Prussian hegemony and the creation of Bismarck's Second Reich to the fall of Hitler's Third Reich.

Pflanze, Otto. *Bismarck and the Development of Germany. I: The Period of Unification, 1815–1871.* Princeton, NJ: Princeton University Press, 1990. An exhaustive biography and history of Germany during the period.

THE FIGHT FOR NATIONAL UNITY IN NORTH AMERICA

Bensel, Richard Franklin. *Yankee Leviathan: The Origins of Central State Authority in America, 1859–1877.* Cambridge: Cambridge University Press, 1990. Discusses state formation and the extension of central state authority during the Civil War and Reconstruction.

Paris, P.J. *The American Civil War.* New York: 1975. While there are many more recent studies, this book remains a good one-volume survey of the war.

DIVIDED AUTHORITY IN THE AUSTRIAN AND OTTOMAN EMPIRES

Shaw, Stanford J. *History of the Ottoman Empire and Modern Turkey. II: Reform, Revolution and Republic: The Rise of Modern Turkey, 1808–1875.* 1977. Effectively analyzes the causes for the Ottoman decline during the nineteenth century.

Sked, Alan. *The Decline and Fall of the Habsburg Empire, 1815–1918.* London: Longman, 1989. A particularly strong analysis of the Habsburg Empire during this period.

USING NATIONALISM IN FRANCE AND RUSSIA

Goldfrank, David M. *The Origins of the Crimean War.* London: Longman, 1994. Analyzes the causes for the war, placing most of the blame on Russian Tsar Nicholas I.

Kolchin, Peter. *Unfree Labor: American Slavery and Russian Serfdom.* Cambridge, MA: Harvard University Press, 1987. A comparative study of the two experiences.

Lincoln, W. Bruce. *The Great Reforms: Autocracy, Bureaucracy, and the Politics of Change in Imperial Russia.* DeKalb, IL: Northern Illinois University Press, 1990. Puts the social reforms during the reign of Alexander II in a broad political, social, and intellectual context.

Plessis, Alain. *The Rise and Fall of the Second Empire, 1852–1871.* Trans. Johnathan Mandelbaum. Cambridge: Cambridge University Press, 1985. A broad analysis of France's Second Empire, stressing that it was a period of political and social transformation.

Opening of the Suez Canal, 1869

In 1869, after ten years of construction, the Suez Canal—linking the Mediterranean and Red Seas—opened. This drawing of the opening ceremony shows a crowd of traditionally dressed local inhabitants on the banks watching the line of new European boats, powered by steam as well as sails. European dignitaries, separated from this crowd, also attended the ceremonies. The canal, built by the French and later acquired by the British, shortened the sea route from Europe to India and the Far East by thousands of miles, and the new, large, smoke-belching steamboats carried cargo more rapidly and reliably than ever, facilitating the West's imperial expansion.

CHAPTER 20

Mass Politics And Imperial Domination

Democracy and the New Imperialism 1870—1914

"We have conquered for ourselves a place in the sun," announced Germany's Kaiser Wilhelm II (r. 1888–1919) in 1901. Addressing an audience from Hamburg's business community, he boasted that "it will now be my task to see to it that this place in the sun shall remain our undisputed possession, in order that the sun's rays may fall fruitfully upon our activity and trade in foreign parts, that our industry and agriculture may develop within the state." Wilhelm was referring to Germany's territories, gained in the scramble for overseas conquests that had been going on over the previous two decades. His audience and many others in the industrialized Western world expected to gain wealth from this recent imperial expansion.

He also may have been reminding his listeners that the German nation had been unified in the 1860s through war and conquest (see Chapter 19). Indeed, underlying his words was an appeal to pride in the growing power of this new nation. Like other political leaders in the West, Wilhelm had learned to use nationalism to gain support from listeners and readers.

Politicians such as Wilhelm could no longer ignore public opinion, for democracy was on the rise. Between 1870 and 1914, demands for democracy, or political participation by common people, spread as more and more people struggled to gain access to politics. Now the new politics of nationalism combined with industrialism to multiply the power of the West and push it outward into Africa and Asia in a great imperial expansion. The West was rising to a new level of world dominance.

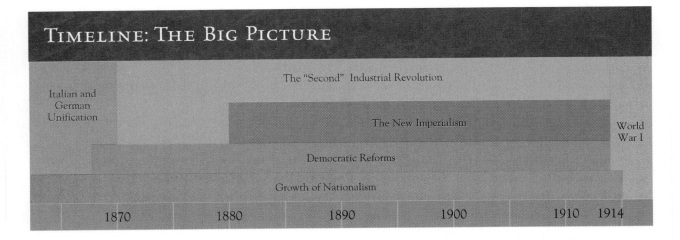

Italian and German Unification

The "Second" Industrial Revolution

The New Imperialism

World War I

Democratic Reforms

Growth of Nationalism

1870   1880   1890   1900   1910   1914

Demands for Democracy

In 1896, the Russian statesman Konstantin Pobedonostsev (1827–1907) published what would become a widely read attack on democracy. "What is this freedom by which so many minds are agitated, which inspires so many insensate actions, so many wild speeches . . . ?" His answer was democracy, "the right to participate in the government of the State." He complained that "the new Democracy now aspires to universal suffrage—a fatal error, and one of the more remarkable in the history of mankind."

However, between 1870 and 1914, it became increasingly clear to those who had long enjoyed political power in the West that, sooner or later, the beliefs of the masses counted in politics. Since the French Revolution in 1789, a widening pool of Europeans tasted political power, a trend that ruling elites had feared ever since. Some politicians, such as Pobedonostsev, tried to turn their backs on democracy. Others tried to tame it, and still others flourished with it.

During the 1870s and 1880s, three developments became entwined with demands for democracy. First, many governments established national systems of free *Public education* and compulsory public education at the primary-school level. With this policy, they hoped to create more patriotic citizens. They also wanted to provide citizens with the skills and discipline needed by modernizing economies and military establishments. Moreover, they wanted their voting electorate to be educated. To liberals especially, access to the schoolhouse and democracy went hand in hand.

Second, educated, voting citizens could read newspapers, and popular journalism responded to the call.

Before 1850, newspapers were few, small, expensive, and written for a limited readership. By the end of the century, a new kind of newspaper had popped up everywhere—one that was cheap, sensational, and wildly popular. In the United States, publishers such as Joseph Pulitzer (1847–1911) and William Randolph Hearst (1863–1951) built influential newspapers featuring screaming headlines, flag-waving patriotism, an easy style, sensational news, and attention-getting columns. Other *Popular journalism* newspapers throughout Europe, especially in the capital cities, followed the same pattern. They catered to the newly educated public's hunger for news and in turn powerfully molded public opinion.

Third, politicians realized they had to appeal to the new voters. They devised innovative campaign strategies, such as crisscrossing the country by railroads and delivering stirring campaign speeches to cheering crowds in large halls *Political campaigns* and outdoor forums. They listened to newly formed interest groups—whether business organizations, reformers, or labor unions. These interest groups held rallies on their own, to gather support and gain influence through newspaper coverage of their meetings. Finally, politicians began creating all sorts of state institutions, from census bureaus to social security administrations, to satisfy the demands of their politically aroused societies and persuade new voters to support them. All of these changes vastly reshaped parliamentary politics.

Such developments put pressure on politicians to adjust the way they conducted themselves, for democratic reform meant more than widening the right to vote and bringing new faces into government. To succeed in the new world of mass politics, politicians had to learn to monitor—and navigate—the shifting tides of public opinion. More and more, rising to and staying in political office meant pleasing interest groups, journalists, educated readers, and newly enfranchised voters.

§ LIBERAL DEMOCRACY IN WESTERN EUROPE

Would European societies ease toward a liberal democratic consensus? Many hoped so, particularly in western Europe, where Great Britain and France had experimented with democratic reforms, but in different ways.

Great Britain started the second half of the nineteenth century in a strong, stable position. It had avoided the revolutionary turmoil that swept over the European continent between 1848 and 1850, largely because the British adapted just enough to contain the pressures for radical change (see Chapter 18). Liberalism—stressing little governmental involvement in economic and social affairs, low taxes, and free trade—seemed to work well in Britain, and the island nation boasted the most modern economy in the world.

For most of the 1850s and 1860s, liberals controlled the British government. But they were more willing to call on national pride, sympathize with movements for national liberation abroad, and parade British naval might than to accommodate those who demanded entry into the political system. It was the Conservative Party, under Benjamin Disraeli (1804–1881), that finally decided to bend and take the credit for demo-

Reform Bills of 1867 and 1884

cratic reform before the Liberals themselves could grab it. The Conservatives passed a new measure—the Reform Bill of 1867—which doubled the electorate and gave the vote to the lower middle class for the first time. In addition, they gathered support from the working class by passing laws that limited working hours, established sanitary codes, created housing standards, and aided labor unions. In 1884, the Liberal Party under William Gladstone

(1809–1898) countered by pushing through another reform bill that gave two-thirds of adult males the vote. To sweeten the deal even further, the Liberals opened the army and civil service to talent and made primary education available to all.

Having both jumped on the reform bandwagon, British Conservatives and Liberals now had to compete for power in new ways. For the first time, politicians such as Gladstone used the railways to campaign throughout the nation, speaking before crowds of thousands. A growing corps of journalists followed the campaigns, shaping public opinion by reporting speeches and scandals daily in cheap newspapers with mass circulation. New interest groups, mostly from the middle class, bent the ears of politicians who wanted their support in return.

Figure 20.1, a painting by Alfred Morgan, reveals some of these trends in British politics. The artist depicts the political leader William Gladstone (wearing a tall hat, sitting stiffly, and staring straight ahead) riding in an omnibus. This form of transportation, which carried more than two dozen passengers at a time, was relatively inexpensive and available to all classes of people. The man (holding a newspaper), women, and children who share the bus with Gladstone are dressed

FIGURE 20.1
Alfred Morgan, *One of the People*.

well, but are not members of Britain's wealthy elite (who still ride in small carriages such as the one seen through the rear window). As this image indicates, Gladstone tried to appeal to the growing electorate by portraying himself as an upright, hardworking individual who allied himself with the people. Britain was moving toward democracy, but in ways that worried traditional politicians used to deciding things among their "own kind."

France's path toward democracy took more violent turns than Britain's. A birthplace of democracy, France nevertheless started the 1870s on a turbulent note. The Franco-Prussian War of 1870 spelled the end of Napoleon III's Second Empire and the emergence of the Third French Republic (see Chapter 19). The first elections, held in February 1871 after Napoleon III's fall and the surrender of Paris, resulted in a victory for the monarchists, who hoped to limit democracy and open the door for the restoration of a monarchy. Still the city of Paris refused to submit to the domination of conservative, rural France. It demanded home rule and set up its own city government, or commune.

France's Third Republic

The Paris Commune would gain a reputation as a democracy out of control or as an experiment in Marxist socialism. In reality, the Commune stood for decentralizing power in France, self-governance, support of working-class organizations, and greater equality for women. Its roots lay in the city's resistance to the Germans between September 1870 and January 1871. During those horrific months, Parisians had braved starvation and isolation in the face of the German siege. Most of the rich fled the city. The lower classes not only resented this exodus, they also took over positions of power that the wealthy had abandoned. The February 1871 elections ended the German siege, but not the division between Paris and the rest of the nation. Parisians felt betrayed by France's new conservative government when it concluded the peace with Germany. When government troops tried to disarm them, they rebelled and fighting erupted. The government troops withdrew, and again Paris was put under siege, this time by French troops. Two months later, the government troops attacked, killing some 25,000 Parisians, arresting thousands more, and deporting more than 5,000 to distant penal colonies.

The Paris Commune

Both sides in the Paris conflict committed bitter reprisals. In the photograph shown in Figure 20.2,

Communards execute hostages in response to an earlier execution of Communard leaders. The picture reveals how directly "civilians" involved themselves in the drama: women as well as nonuniformed men count among both the firing squad and the sixty-two hostages.

The fall of the Paris Commune ended the immediate threat to the integrity of France, but not the political and social uncertainties that still lurked below the surface. A period of restless political struggle followed. At first, monarchists almost regained power, but they failed to agree on which of three possible royal houses (the Bourbon, the Orleanist, or the Bonaparte) they should rally around. By the end of the 1870s, liberals, elected by universal male suffrage, controlled the French Republic. Conservatives, however, refused to give up. In the late 1880s, they joined nationalists, supporters of the military, and opponents of parliament to rally around a handsome man on horseback, General Boulanger, who became so popular that he might have overthrown the Republic had he been bolder and more skillful or had the republican leaders been less courageous. As it turned out, when he was summoned to answer charges of treason against the Republic, he fled to Belgium and eventually committed suicide on the grave of his late mistress.

Meanwhile, several forces reoriented politics toward the wider voting public. First, public schooling spread throughout France. Republican teachers replaced Catholic teachers, bringing in a common secular curriculum and promoting patriotism and republican virtues. Second, military service became compulsory and helped turn young, rural men into French citizens with new political awareness. Third, a popular national press took root in Paris and attracted readers throughout the nation. These papers reported all the political scandals, above all the sensational and far-reaching Dreyfus affair (see p. 669), and soon readers in the provinces began avidly following national politics. In France, as in Britain, democratic institutions were spreading throughout the nation and redefining the nature of politics.

Spread of democratic institutions

FOR AND AGAINST DEMOCRACY IN CENTRAL AND EASTERN EUROPE

In contrast to the western European governments, national leaders in central and eastern Europe were more autocratic. Monarchs and their ministers in these regions had the last word in political decision making. Like nations in western Europe, central and eastern Europe struggled with pressure to institute democratic reforms. In some cases, these nations took reluctant steps toward democracy; in others, they declined to change. In addition, the tensions between autocratic and democratic forces in central and eastern Europe became particularly entwined with aggressive nationalism. The cases of Germany, Austria, and Russia provide apt examples of the various ways in which this struggle manifested itself.

In Germany, the constitution stipulated universal suffrage, but real power rested with the king and his ministers. Bismarck, who dominated as Germany's *Germany under Bismarck* chancellor between 1870 and 1890, supported universal male suffrage from the beginning only because "in a country with monarchical traditions and loyal sentiments" such as Germany, "universal suffrage would lead to . . . eliminating the influence of the liberal bourgeois classes." Bismarck believed that most workers and peasants would vote for his conservative policies.

Bismarck solidified the German states and people under Prussia. He also brought the law codes, currencies, and military forces of the lesser states into conformity with those of Prussia. He then turned to issues of ethnic divisions and cultural unity. Laws and schools pressured non-German language groups to give up their languages and traditions. In 1872, Bismarck struck out against Roman Catholics for being insufficiently nationalistic. Known as the *Kulturkampf* (the struggle for civilization), the roots of Bismarck's attack lay in Germany's Protestant-Catholic religious divisions and the newly vigorous papacy of Pius IX, who declared papal infallibility in 1870, *Conflict with Catholic Church* opposed cooperation with Protestantism, and attacked the growth of state power. With support from liberals, Bismarck passed laws asserting the state's right to restrict religious orders, require civil marriage, and bring all education (including schools run by the Catholic Church) under state control. When the Roman Catholic clergy resisted, authorities arrested hundreds of priests and six bishops. Many of these measures backfired, however: they made the Roman Catholic Center Party stronger. In 1878 Bismarck repealed the most severe of the anti-Catholic *Conflict with Socialists* laws, but only because he wanted support for a more important struggle—the fight against the democratically minded and socially radical Socialists.

In a twelve-year crusade against the Socialists, who attacked the autocratic nature of Germany's government and were gaining popularity in elections, Bismarck outlawed the Social Democratic Party's publications, organizations, and meetings, and set the German police force on them. Figure 20.3, a satirical illustration from an 1878 edition of the British magazine *Punch*, shows German Chancellor Bismarck in military dress vainly struggling to keep down the frightening Socialist "Jack in the Box." When his repressive tactics did little to diminish Socialist votes, he tried to undercut the party's appeal to the working class by removing "the causes for socialism." Borrowing some of the Socialists' programs, between 1883 and 1889 he established a comprehensive system of social insurance that provided accident, sickness, and old-age benefits.

Ironically, in fighting against the Social Democrats, the conservative Bismarck made Germany a leader in enacting progressive social policies. Nevertheless, as the image in Figure 20.3, suggests, Bismarck's campaign against the Social Democratic Party

FIGURE 20.2
Executions during the Paris Commune.

would fail. The Socialists had built a solid following and continued to gain public support. In 1890, two years after the death of Kaiser William I, the new monarch, Kaiser William II dismissed the aging chancellor. William II, eager to rule himself, "dropped the pilot" of the German ship of state and ended an era in German history.

In Austria, liberalism spread during the 1870s along with the rise of the bourgeoisie in that country. Liberals supported the constitutional monarchy, parliamentary government, and restricted suffrage. They also believed

Nationalistic discontent in Austria

that it was possible to hold a multinational empire together. In the 1880s, nationalistic demands from different language groups began to overwhelm liberals and play into the hands of conservatives. Parliamentary sessions in Austria frequently degenerated into shouting matches, in which representatives from different language groups hurled inkstands at one

FIGURE 20.3
Bismarck and the Socialists.

another. This nationalistic discontent proved even more intense in Hungary than in Austria. Moreover, the partnership between Austria and Hungary threatened to disintegrate altogether (see p. 647). The introduction of universal male suffrage in 1907 only made the empire more difficult to govern. More often than not, the emperor and his advisors bypassed parliament and ruled by decree.

In Russia, Alexander II's "Great Reforms" did little to open the doors to democracy beyond the local level (see p. 653). Indeed, they may have sparked more dissatisfaction than celebration. For serfs, liberals, and intellectuals, the reforms did not go far enough. A group

Radical action in Russia

of sons and daughters of the aristocracy and middle classes decided to take action. In a well-intentioned but ill-fated movement, they traveled to rural areas in an effort to uplift the lives of country-dwellers. They received a rude welcome in several ways: rural people resented what they saw as condescending attention from inexperienced urban intellectuals, and the tsar's police promptly repressed them.

Some of the young idealists fled; others remained and turned to terrorism. One group, The People's Will, defined terrorism as "the destruction of the most harmful persons in the Government, the protection of the party from spies, and the punishment of official lawlessness and violence." Vera Zasulich became an early heroine in this movement when she attempted to assassinate the St. Petersburg chief of police in 1878. Her action initiated a series of violent eruptions and assassinations, in which terrorists killed numerous bureaucrats and police officials, and the government brutally suppressed the rebels. The cycle of terrorism and repression turned Alexander II to a more conservative course, and he halted all further reforms. In 1881, members of The People's Will retaliated by murdering Alexander II with a bomb.

The new tsar, Alexander III (r. 1881–1894), blamed his father's death on softness and set out to erase every trace of liberalism and democracy in Russia. His secret police arrested thousands of

Reaction under Alexander III

suspects, and the tsar himself initiated a sweeping program of Russianization. Authorities forced minority groups to use the Russian language and persecuted followers of non-Orthodox religions, especially Jews. Russia, much more so than Austria, would not yet bend to the democratic winds blowing from the west.

Insiders and Outsiders: Politics of the Extremes

During the late nineteenth century, those democratic winds in the West spread beyond what had been the mainstream of politics. New groups and causes emerged to challenge the established center of liberal and conservative politics. These new groups gained strength and complicated the trend toward democracy. To the political left of liberals stood the unions, socialists, and anarchists. To the political right of conservatives were anti-Semites and ultra nationalists. Still outside, without the vote, were women, who increasingly demanded a voice in national politics.

FIGURE 20.4
Paul Louis Delance, *Strike!*, 1908.

These groups and causes appealed to large numbers of people, particularly those who had previously been left out of politics. They became so prominent that established political leaders could not ignore them. With the political spectrum widening, it seemed less and less likely that Europe's nations would find some consensus or social peace.

THE SPREAD OF UNIONS

Until the 1880s, labor unions were limited chiefly to skilled workers, organized by crafts, who proved moderate in their aims and methods. In the 1880s, unionization spread rapidly to unskilled workers. These new union members adopted more radical methods, and turned toward socialist programs. Seeking more than mutual aid, they demanded a say in working conditions and wages. They went on strike and flexed their political muscle through the vote. One worker described an 1890 strike of textile workers in Bradford, England, that dragged on for six months. "Twice and sometimes three times a week we had pro-

cessions of the workpeople marching from near the millgates by several routes to the center of Bradford. The women strikers established a well-conducted soup kitchen, and the sympathy of the shopkeepers was very broad and the butchers gave their bones and greengrocers and grocers and bakers gave peas, lentils and loaves, and thus children were fed." As a man who employed thousands of dockers in Marseilles, France, explained, "The days of the employer's arbitrary power are past, unfortunately. . . . For long we could hope to subdue these trade unions that rose against our authority. . . . That too is finished, over."

Figure 20.4 captures some of the ideals of the new unions. This strike at Saint-Ouen, near Paris, France, is sympathetically portrayed by the artist, Paul Louis Delance. Workers, young and old, stream from smoke-belching factories carrying red flags, the symbol of their cause and of socialism. Their faces convey suffering and grim determination. The welfare of a woman and child—the core of the typical working-class family—represents the strikers' goal. The strikers are supported by humble people, heads bowed, upon whom a few rays of sunshine fall as if in blessing for the nobility of their cause.

Biography

JEAN JAURÈS (1859–1914)

One observer described the French politician Jean Jaurès as such a spellbinding orator that "he could raise the masses and enchant the elite at the same time." Figure 20.5 shows Jaurès standing beneath the red flag of socialism, addressing a crowd in 1913. Jaurès' speeches in France's Chamber of Deputies sometimes lasted for hours. He also wrote so prolifically that it would take ninety volumes, 400 pages each, to amass all his writing. Some called him an obvious genius. He called himself "a cultured peasant." Certainly an intellectual, he wore the typical middle-class long, black overcoat. However, the coat was usually dirty, his pants always too short, and his pockets forever stuffed with books and papers. Between the 1880s and 1914, he became one of France's most respected politicians.

Born in 1859 to a rural, middle-class family of little wealth, Jean excelled at school, winning a series of prizes and scholarships. He became a teacher in 1881, then a professor of philosophy at the University of Toulouse in southern France in 1883. In 1885 he was elected to the Chamber of Deputies as an unaffiliated republican. Just twenty-five, he was France's youngest deputy. That year he met Louise Bois, the daughter of a merchant, and a year later the couple married. Attracted to Paris by the political activity there, the couple settled in an apartment and eventually had two children.

Defeated in his 1889 bid for reelection to parliament, Jean became interested in socialism and made it the subject of his doctoral dissertation. He won fame for his support of striking miners at Carmaux in

Orator and Socialist Politician

1892. After this event, he was reelected to the Chamber of Deputies, this time as a socialist. He accepted the possibility of socialism by evolution rather than revolution: class struggle might properly be replaced by democratic political

---

As the end of the century approached, organized labor became a formidable force. Labor unions in Great Britain formed the National Trades Union Congress and became identified with the new Labour Party. In Germany, unions, especially among the unskilled workers, grew dramatically and coalesced into a national Marxist organization. In France, various unions banded together into the giant General Confederation of Labor, with a radical political program. In the United States, the abundance of cheap immigrant labor and the determined resistance by industrial capitalists hindered the emergence of unions. In 1886, however, Samuel Gompers founded the American Federation of Labor—the first successful national labor organization in America. By 1914, unions had become sufficiently large and organized to make them a major power, both in the workplace and at the polls.

SOCIALISM GAINS STRENGTH

Like the labor unions, socialism also became a major force within the working class and in politics during the late nineteenth century. Most socialists looked to the ideas of Karl Marx for inspiration (see Chapter 18).

The First International

Marx had argued that modern industrial society was splitting into two opposing classes: the capitalists, or owners of the means of production, and the workers. Capitalism, he explained, was bound to be replaced

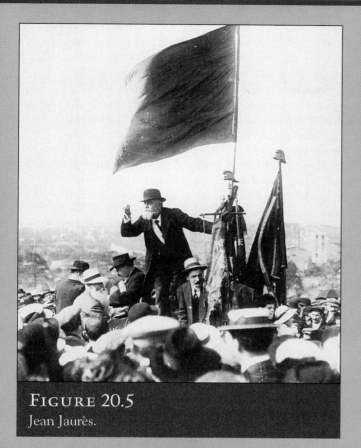

FIGURE 20.5
Jean Jaurès.

struggle. To Jaurès and a growing number of other socialists, the forces of history suggested that socialism was inevitable. He rose in the Socialist Party, becoming a leader by 1900. In 1904, he helped found a newspaper, *L'Humanité*, which became France's chief socialist periodical. By 1908 he had solidified the party.

Jaurès became increasingly concerned with the problem of war. He argued that France wasted its resources on military preparations. "What will the future be like when the billions now thrown away in war preparations are spent on useful production to increase the well-being of the people?" he asked. He saw the West's recent imperial expansion into the non-Western world as a primary cause for wars. "The fever of imperialism has become a sickness. It is the affliction of a badly organized society which cannot utilize its energies and productive forces at home." More and more, Jaurès championed pacifism and Franco-German reconciliation, but his stand won him and his followers ridicule and accusations of treason, particularly by right-wing nationalists.

During the evening of July 31, 1914, Jaurès began composing an antiwar appeal. At 9 P.M. he and a group of other socialist journalists met and decided to dine at a crowded cafe on the rue Montmartre. At 9:40 a young man, who was affiliated with a nationalist group, burst in and fired two shots, killing Jaurès. The French socialist leader was murdered on the very eve of the war he warned against.

◼ **Consider** how Jaurès' life reflects both the promises of democracy and the political problems faced by people in this era.

by a socialist system through revolution by the working class. Marx helped union organizers to form the International Working Men's Association (the First International) in 1864. The organization fell apart in the 1870s, but in 1889 socialists formed the Second International. These organizations helped socialists unify and spread their cause. A sense of shared struggle and beliefs inspired them to form unions, create political parties, and fight powerful employers and strong politicians.

Yet, the strength of socialism varied in each country. In Britain, established politicians excluded the working classes or socialist thinkers from politics until the 1880s. Then a group of well-known intellectuals formed the Fabian Society, which advocated the adoption of socialist policies through politics rather than revolution. Beatrice Webb (1858–1943), one of the founders of the Fabians, explained **The Fabians** that she became a socialist because of "the physical misery and moral debasement following in the tracks of the rack-renting landlord and capitalist profit maker in the swarming populations of the great centres of nineteenth century commerce and industry." Webb could see no way out of "the recurrent periods of inflation and depression—meaning for the vast majority of the nation, alternate spells of overwork and unemployment."

During the 1890s, both unions and socialists in Britain developed enough political muscle to form the Labour Party and elect members to Parliament.

By 1906, Labour had pressured the Liberals, led by David Lloyd George (1863–1945), to adopt new policies providing accident, sickness, old-age, and unemployment insurance for workers. As Labour members of Parliament argued, these old men and women were "the veterans of industry, people of almost endless toil, who have fought for and won the industrial and commercial supremacy of Great Britain. Is their lot and end to be the everlasting slur of pauperism?" To pay for the new policies, the Liberals shifted the "heaviest burden to the broadest backs." A steeply graduated income tax and high taxes on inheritances landed on the rich. When Conservatives in the House of Lords resisted, the Liberal and Labour Parties passed a bill that stripped the House of Lords of most of its former power.

Britain's Labour Party

In France, socialism gained strength during the 1890s. During the following decade, socialist parties helped push France's republican government to enact a limited program of unemployment, old-age, accident, and sickness insurance for workers. By this time, the different wings of the French socialists had joined to form the United Socialist Party under the leadership of scholar-orator Jean Jaurès (see Biography). By 1914, the United Socialist Party numbered 1.5 million voters and had 110 seats in the Chamber of Deputies.

France and Jaurès

Socialism enjoyed its greatest success in Germany. In 1890, Germany's main socialist party, the Social Democrats won the vote of 20 percent of the electorate. Officially the party adhered to the idea that revolution was historically inevitable. A party leader, August Bebel, expressed the optimism of this view: "Every night I go to sleep with the thought that the last hour of bourgeois society strikes soon." In practice, however, the party usually followed the ideas of the "revisionist" socialist Eduard Bernstein (1850–1932). This German writer and politician urged socialists to cooperate with the capitalist classes to obtain immediate benefits for labor and advocated a gradual approach to socialism. By 1914, the Social Democrats polled some 4.5 million votes, making it the largest political party in Germany.

German Social Democrats

Even in conservative Austria, socialists gained strength in industrial areas for the same reasons they did elsewhere in the West. The plight of workers was their top priority. Anna Maier, who started a life of work in a tobacco factory when she was thirteen, captured this concern when she explained that "young girls were often abused or even beaten" on the job. One day Maier read a copy of the *Women Workers'* newspaper smuggled into the factory by one of the older women. Eventually, she managed to join the Social Democratic Party. After taking part in demonstrations, her factory manager took her "off a good job" and put her "in a poorer one," but as she later reported, "nothing stopped me." When the tobacco workers union formed in 1899, she joined them and became "a class-conscious fighter." Maier's story was repeated by many other workers throughout the West in the decades before 1914.

ANARCHISM: FREEDOM FROM ALL AUTHORITY

While sometimes associated with socialists, anarchists made more radical demands. Drawing on the ideas of leaders such as the Russian activist Mikhail Bakunin (1814–1876) and Russian theoretician Pyotr Kropotkin (1842–1921), they stressed the elimination of any form of authority that impinged on human freedom. "So long as there exist States, there will be no humanity," Bakunin argued. "The masses of the people will be de facto slaves even in the most democratic republics." Anarchists believed that human beings, once freed from the corrupting institutions that oppressed them, would naturally cooperate with one another. "Life will be open to all," an anarchist leader explained. "Everyone will take what he needs—this is the anarchist ideal."

Bakunin

Anarchism became particularly influential in Spain, Italy, and France, where it appealed to trade unionists, artisans, agricultural laborers, and shopkeepers suffering from unemployment and declining wages. Its supporters favored direct action through unions and cooperatives rather than parliamentary politics. After the turn of the century, many anarchists hoped the grand solution to their problems would come with a "general strike," as described by the popular French writer Georges Sorel (1847–1922). Such a strike, they believed, would force the capitalist system to grind to a sudden halt. A small wing of the anarchist movement went beyond hoping for a general strike, and turned to violence. Among its victims were President Sadi Carot of France in 1894, King Umberto

I of Italy in 1900, and President William McKinley of the United States in 1901.

ANTI-SEMITISM AND ULTRANATIONALISM

Usually at the opposite end of the political spectrum from socialism and anarchism, anti-Semitism often appealed to conservative nationalists. Followers of Judaism had long suffered from anti-Semitism—hostility toward or hatred of Jews. Since the Middle Ages, Jews had been accused of murdering Christ, segregated into special quarters known as ghettos, and persecuted. However, between 1789 and the 1870s, the spreading ideals of the Enlightenment and the French Revolution had enabled Jews to gain new rights and a degree of legal equality, though rarely full acceptance. At least in western and central Europe, this progress led many Jews to believe that finally they could join their nation-states as full citizens.

During the last decades of the nineteenth century, however, nationalism took on militant and authoritarian tones. All too easily, this spreading strain of nationalism strengthened racist and anti-Semitic thought. Comte de Gobineau (1816–1882), a Frenchman, and Houston Stewart Chamberlain (1855–1927), an Englishman who became a German citizen, wrote widely read tracts arguing that race determined much of history. The two men helped formulate the Aryan myth, which held that Germans belonged to a special race and therefore possessed superior qualities: "[T]he Germanic races belong to the most highly gifted group, the group usually termed Aryan. . . . Physically and mentally the Aryans are pre-eminent among all people; for that reason they are by right . . . the lords of the world." Chamberlain's ideas veered off into anti-Semitism, as did the thinking of other well-known racist writers. Their pseudoscientific thought—which labeled Jews as a separate, inferior race—became increasingly popular, as indicated by this excerpt from a speech delivered by an anti-Semitic member of the German parliament: "A Jew who was born in Germany does not thereby become a German; he is still a Jew. Therefore it is imperative that we realize that Jewish racial characteristics differ so greatly from ours that a common life of Jews and Germans under the same laws is quite impossible."

During the same period, anti-Semitic politics gained force, especially among artisans, small shopkeepers, rural workers, and others who felt threatened by liberalism and capitalism and saw Jews as being linked to both. These people scornfully called Jews outsiders and capitalists, and blamed them for their own economic ills and fears. Ultranationalist politicians used anti-Semitism to rally crowds, shift the blame for failed policies away from themselves, and win votes. Figure 20.6, a derogatory caricature of a Jew, appeared on the cover of the French anti-Semitic newspaper, *La Libre Parole (The Free Word)*, in 1893. Using crudely drawn pictures on the head of this figure, it purports to depict "Jewish qualities" such as worshiping money, dishonesty, and laziness.

Right-wing newspapers such as *La Libre Parole* popularized scandals as well as anti-Semitic stories that coalesced most dramatically in the Dreyfus affair. People throughout France followed every development of "the affair" day after day and year after year. In 1894, a group of bigoted army officers falsely accused and *The Dreyfus affair* convicted a Jewish captain, Alfred Dreyfus, of treason, and sent him to solitary imprisonment on Devil's Island in South America. Three years later, evidence of Dreyfus' innocence appeared. Nevertheless, high-ranking officers refused to reopen the case. Newspaper articles, sensational trials, accusations, and huge public demonstrations divided the nation between the political Left and Right. Republicans, socialists, and intellectuals, inspired by the famous French writer Émile Zola, who attacked the judgment of the military and judiciary in the case, rallied for Dreyfus. Nationalist, conservative, monarchist, and anti-Semitic forces supported the army. In 1899, a second court-martial again convicted Dreyfus, despite evidence of another officer's guilt in the affair. The president of the Republic pardoned Dreyfus, but it took seven more years to get Dreyfus fully acquitted.

The Dreyfus affair marked not only the battle over anti-Semitism, but the evolution of French politics. The victory for Dreyfus became a victory for republicanism and anti-clericalism. Electoral victories made republicans strong enough to separate church and state in 1905 and initiate a program of social legislation. Socialists, who had joined republicans in the Dreyfus case, gained greater legitimacy and popularity. The political power of monarchists and the Catholic Church had been dealt a debilitating blow.

For Jews, persecution was worse in central and

FIGURE 20.6
Emile Courtet, *The Qualities of the Jew after Gall's Method,* 1893.

many's parliament explained in an 1895 speech that "every Jew who at this moment had not done anything bad may nevertheless under the proper conditions do precisely that, because his racial qualities drive him to do it."

In Austria, the Christian Socialist Party and the German National Party took a decidedly anti-Semitic stand. By the 1890s, a new breed of politics based on symbols, charisma, nationalism, racism, anticapitalism, and anti-Semitism had arisen. The election of Karl Lueger in 1897 as mayor of Vienna symbolized this political trend; Lueger campaigned on an anti-Semitic platform and triumphed even in this bastion of Austrian liberalism.

Some of the most violent anti-Semitic acts occurred in Russia. Tsars Alexander III and Nicholas II (r. 1894–1917) sanctioned the persecution of Jews and required them to live in designated areas. Officials labeled Jews as outsiders and excluded them from mainstream society. Whenever anyone wanted to assign blame for their problems, they could point to the Jews. This hostility culminated in a series of pogroms, or organized mass attacks on Jews, led by anti-Semitic groups and government officials. Between 1870 and 1914, this persecution helped push over 2 million eastern European Jews out of their homes and to the west, particularly the United States (see Map 20.1).

Concerns about persecutions in eastern Europe as well as the weakening of Jewish identity through assimilation in western Europe gave rise to Zionism, a Jewish nationalist movement to create an independent state for Jews in Palestine— *Zionism and Herzl* the ancient homeland of the Jews. The Hungarian writer Theodor Herzl (1860–1904) became the leading figure in the Zionist movement. While in Paris covering the Dreyfus affair for an Austrian newspaper, he gained a greater sense of the strength of anti-Semitism and his own identity as a Jew. In 1896, he published an influential pamphlet, *The Jewish State: An Attempt at a Modern Solution of the Jewish Question,* urging formation of an international movement to make Palestine a Jewish homeland. He envisioned the homeland transformed into a socialist community of hard working cooperatives. The following year he led the new World Zionist Organization to prominence. He gained a large following in eastern Europe, found financial support from several sources, and won cautious political support from British gov-

eastern Europe. These regions had the highest Jewish population and the most aggressive strain of nationalism. Nationalistic anti-Semitic organizations, such as *Central and eastern Europe* the Pan-German Association and the Christian Social Workers' Party, emerged in Germany. Anti-Semitic journals warned of the dangers to "the native-born Christian population" as Jews gained access to the press, to state offices, and to professions such as teaching and law. One anti-Semitic deputy in Ger-

The Pale: area where Russian Jews allowed to live

Other areas of large Jewish population

• Cities with large Jewish population

→ Typical Migration Routes

THINKING ABOUT GEOGRAPHY

MAP 20.1 *Jewish Migration, 1870–1914*

This map shows areas and cities with large Jewish populations along with typical migration routes to the west and south.

▣ **Notice** the heavy concentration of Jews are in eastern Europe. **Consider** the significance of the particularly harsh anti-Semitic policies in these areas. **Why** might Jews have migrated primarily to the west and south?

ernmental officials. "It might be many years before the founding of the State is under way," Herzl warned. "In the meantime, Jews will be ridiculed, offended, abused, whipped, plundered, and slain in a thousand different localities." After Herzl's death in 1904, other leaders advanced his aims and secured more support—including the financial aid of donors such as the French banker Baron de Rothschild, and the co-operation of Arthur Balfour (1848–1930), Britain's prime minister. By 1914 some 85,000 Jews had immigrated to Palestine, primarily from eastern Europe.

STILL OUTSIDERS: WOMEN, FEMINISM, AND THE RIGHT TO VOTE

By 1914, most of the political groups that had been outside the mainstream of politics had gained a political voice. In the majority of Western countries, universal male suffrage had become the rule by 1914. However women still remained on the political sidelines, hampered by an ideology that left them unequal economically, trapped in their own "separate sphere" by laws that declared them legally inferior, and excluded by political institutions that deprived them of the vote. Few men in any of the political parties, movements, or unions offered their support for women's suffrage.

During the last decades of the nineteenth century, many women finally turned to political activism. Numerous women—whether as individuals or as activist group members—were already calling themselves "feminist." Groups of feminists organized several movements to promote women's issues, demand legal equality of the sexes, and advocate social and political change. In 1878 representatives of these groups from twelve nations came together in Paris at the International Congress of the Rights of Women and initiated a period of increased activism and international cooperation. Although feminists were still a minority among women, their strength grew dramatically. In Britain and the United States, women with middle-class and aristocratic backgrounds fought especially hard for the right to vote. They argued that, without the vote, women would continue to suffer from a range of inequalities. "The idea that the possession of political rights will destroy 'womanliness,' absurd as it may seem to us, is very deeply rooted in the minds of men," British writer Frances Power Cobbe (1822–1904) pointed out in 1884. Men, Cobbe explained, "really prize what women now are in the home

Political activism

and in society so highly that they cannot bear to risk losing it by any serious change in their condition." A few years later Elizabeth Cady Stanton (1815–1902) expressed the views of many Americans in the woman suffrage movement: "If we are to consider [a woman] as a citizen, as a member of a great nation, she must have the same rights as all other members."

Another group of feminists tried to gain equality through social reform—focusing on the needs of the working class and often voicing socialist sympathies. Led by women such as Louise Michel (1830–1905) in France and Clara Zetkin (1857–1933) in Germany, they argued that only when workers as a whole gained freedom from economic and social oppression would women achieve justice. In 1885, Michel looked forward to a transforming revolution that would introduce a new era "when men and women will move through life together as good companions, and they will no more argue about which sex is superior than races will argue about which race is foremost in the world." Ten years later, Zetkin explained that proletarian women could attain "salvation only through the fight for the emancipation of labor."

The strongest women's suffrage movements arose in Great Britain. The movement was exemplified by organizations such as the National Union of Women's Suffrage Societies, led by Millicent Fawcett

Suffrage movements (1847–1929), and the more radical Women's Social and Political Union, led by Emmeline Pankhurst (1858–1928) and her two daughters. The leaders of these movements had reached a crucial conclusion: Being polite was not going to win them the right to vote. They worked as other political groups did, forming organizations, presenting petitions, pressuring politicians, forging alliances, holding demonstrations, publishing newspapers, and marching for the franchise. They continued despite scorn from men, ridicule by newspapers, rejection by politicians, cold shoulders from labor unions and socialists, and force by the police. Figure 20.7 shows a policeman arresting Emmeline Pankhurst. "We have tried every way," explained Pankhurst. "We have presented larger petitions than were ever presented for any other reform, we have succeeded in holding greater public meetings than men have ever had for any reform . . . we have faced hostile mobs at street corners . . . we have been ridiculed, we have had contempt poured upon us . . . we know that we need the protection of the vote even more than men have needed it."

In 1908 a rally for female suffrage drew some 250,000 women to Hyde Park in London. After 1910, feminism in Britain took a more public and violent turn as women resorted to window smashing, arson, assaults, bombing of railway stations, and chaining themselves to the gates of Parliament. Police arrested them, judges imprisoned them, and, when they went on hunger strikes, authorities force-fed them.

Still the British government as well as most other Western authorities refused to give in to the feminists' demands. Finland granted women the right to vote in 1906—the first victory for the women's suffrage movement—but other victories would take years. Women would not gain the vote until after 1918 in Britain, Germany, and the United States; until the 1940s in France; and until the 1970s in Switzerland.

FIGURE 20.7
Emmeline Pankhurst.

Emigration: Overseas and Across Continents

By 1914, most Western societies had taken great, often reluctant steps toward democracy. A swirl of forces—the growing pressures of nationalism, the spread of industry and commerce, and the competition for military might—fueled those steps and molded the politics that resulted. Some of those same forces also pushed a new wave of Europeans and their governments across the globe.

After the mid-nineteenth century, a great migration of people from Europe gained momentum. Europeans streamed overseas and across continents, hoping to start new and better lives. As they fanned across the globe, they brought money and great quantities of manufactured goods to nonindustrialized areas. Their governments did the same: Imperial powers raced to carve up Africa and establish control in Asia. With their new presence, wealth, and power, Europeans dominated the world as never before.

LEAVING EUROPE

Ever since the first sixteenth-century settlements, Europe had sent a sizable trickle of emigrants to the Americas. The trickle became a flowing stream in the mid-nineteenth century. Great numbers of British, Irish, and then German immigrants landed in the United States during the 1840s, 1850s, and 1860s. After 1870, the stream swelled into a rushing torrent, as peoples from southern and eastern Europe joined the flow. Between 1870 and 1914, some 30 million Europeans left their homelands and emigrated, mostly to the Americas and Australia.

In Figure 20.8, C. J. Staniland sentimentally portrays

FIGURE 20.8
C. J. Staniland, *The Emigrant Ship.*

the hopes and difficulties of these emigrants. Both men and women have boarded the ship, but in fact men outnumbered women emigrants 2 to 1. Despite the speed of the steam-powered ships of the day, most emigrants made their journeys under crowded conditions. On the English dock in this picture, the travelers leave behind their families, who sadly bid farewell. Emigration strained family ties. Sometimes those left behind later emigrated as well, and joined their families in the new land. In other cases, emigrants would return to Europe. Often, the separated couples and families never saw each other again.

Causes

What explains this immense migration? Some people wanted to leave Europe because it was simply becoming too crowded. In many parts of Europe, such as Scandinavia, the British Isles, and southern Italy, the land could no longer support the growing population. In addition, the shift to commercial agriculture throughout Europe left masses of small farmers landless and desperate to start new lives somewhere else. Natural catastrophes also played a part. A deadly potato famine in Ireland in the late 1840s forced many Irish to flee their homeland to escape starvation. Finally, human catastrophes drove people away. Millions of Jews, for example, left Europe to seek a haven from relentless persecution.

DREAMS VERSUS REALITIES

Many opportunities, both real and imagined, also beckoned from across the oceans. Visions of free or cheap land, already taken away from native peoples, attracted Europeans to the Americas, Australia, and New Zealand. People heard news of plentiful jobs in America's growing cities. Steamships and railroads made the trip faster and cheaper than ever, though not pleasant for the crowds who traveled in ships' bottom compartments with baggage and supplies.

Unfortunately for these hopeful travelers, reality often proved far less appealing than their dreams. New arrivals usually got only the most remote or poorest lands and the lowest-paying jobs. Lonely or adrift in their new world, they sent letters and money back home, maintaining ties to old communities for a while or asking others to join them. Millions gave up the search for a better life or found reason to turn back; about one-third of those emigrating overseas from Europe eventually returned home.

The New Imperialism: The Race for Africa and Asia

In the 1880s, this mass migration of individuals was paralleled by an expansion of Western power into non-Western parts of the world. European nations raced to gain control over Africa and Asia especially. They subdued local opposition and reshaped the existing societies to fit their own purposes. They brought Western culture and institutions to Africa and Asia whether those peoples wanted them or not. By 1914, imperial powers had seized most of Africa and much of Asia, taking direct or indirect control over almost half a billion people.

Imperialism was not new. Since the fifteenth century Europeans had been extending their influence over the globe. But the burst of expansion between about 1880 and 1914 was so rapid and extensive that historians call it the new imperialism.

MONEY AND GLORY

There were many forces driving this wave of imperialism. For one thing, people thought they could make money from it. "It is in order to foster the growth of the trade of this country, and to find an outlet for our manufacturers and our surplus energy, that our far-seeing statesmen and our commercial men advocate colonial expansion," concluded a British colonial administrator. Industrial nations hungered for new markets, cheap raw materials, and juicy investment opportunities. Western manufacturers, merchants, financiers, shippers, investors, adventurers, and settlers thought they would find all of these things in Africa and Asia, while European workers believed that the guaranteed markets would keep them employed. Political leaders, egged on by other pressures as well, usually agreed.

Economic causes

Yet the race for riches often proved more difficult than people expected. Many colonies cost European governments far more to acquire and maintain than riches received. The colonizing process got complicated politically as well. Imperial powers took some colonies not because they saw them as money-makers but because they wanted to protect the borders of other, more lucrative colonies. In many such "buffer" colonies, loans

Politics of imperialism

were never paid off, mines never yielded enough minerals to cover their expenses, and markets proved not worth the cost of building railroads to reach them. But in the beginning, people hoped for great profits or at least security for money-making ventures in distant lands. Competition and the optimistic taking on of risks were at the heart of capitalism, and this led many westerners and their nations into Africa and Asia.

A different, probably more powerful competition—the drive for international prestige—also drove governments, cheered on by millions of their citizens, to snap up colonies. The renewed burst of imperialism came at precisely the time when nationalism was on the rise in Europe. Nationalistic sentiment easily translated into a new struggle for imperial conquest—for remote islands, barren deserts, and impenetrable jungles as

Nationalism and imperialism

well as for more lucrative prizes. Governments used such conquests to display their muscle, especially when such a display was lacking at home. France's expansion, for example, helped French citizens feel compensated for losses suffered in the Franco-Prussian War. Italian conquests overseas promised to make up for Italy's failure to acquire first-rate power status on the Continent. Gaining colonies became a measure of status, proof of a nation's political and economic prowess. To be left behind in the imperial race marked a nation as second class. "[A]ll great nations in the fullness of their strength have desired to set their mark upon barbarian lands, and those who fail to participate in this great rivalry will play a pitiable role in the time to come," the nationalist German historian Heinrich von Treitschke announced. People in the West avidly followed the race for colonies. Newspapers reporting on incidents and conquests in Asia and Africa framed these developments as adventures and patriotic causes. Thrilling stories about action overseas sold countless papers. In books and classrooms, people could see their national colors spreading across oceans and continents.

This competition for economic gain and international prestige gained a life of its own, a momentum that became hard to curb. When one nation moved into a new area, others followed, for fear of being left with nothing. To protect established colonies, imperial powers seized adjoining territories. To ensure supply lines to distant colonies, nations grabbed up islands, ports, and bases. To form alliances and collect bargaining chips for when disputes arose, imperial powers made colonial claims.

Finally, people found ways to justify imperialism. Westerners saw themselves as bringing "blessings" of their civilization to "backward" peoples. The British writer Rudyard Kipling (1865–1936) expressed the belief of many westerners when he wrote of the "white man's burden" to civilize

Justification

the "lesser breeds" of the earth. Missionaries took to heart the injunction to "Go ye into all the world and preach the gospel to every creature."

Figure 20.9, a cover illustration from a French Catholic magazine, *The Pilgrim*, reveals westerners' idealized views of imperialism. Here a member of the White Sisters, a Catholic order, teaches already converted Ugandan girls how to use a sewing machine. The image plainly contrasts the devoted, beautiful European women and the humble, well-behaved children. The implied promise is that the West will bring the benefits of its technology, faith, and civilization to a new generation of thankful Africans.

Some people put imperialism in a less rosy context. These observers described colonial competition and conquest as part of an unavoidable, Darwinian strug-

FIGURE 20.9
A European vision of imperialism.

gle for survival of the fittest. In such a struggle, the white "race" would surely prevail, they believed. France's prime minister even claimed that "the superior races have rights over the inferior races," a view supported by many.

There were people who opposed imperialism. Intellectuals, reform clubs, and politicians such as Jean Jaurès called it an unjusti-

Opposition to imperialism fiably cruel and costly exploitation. However, such voices did not carry enough weight. Powerful economic interests and politicians had found imperial expansion irresistible, and most citizens were all too willing to support the adventure. Moreover, imperial conquest became so easy it seemed foolish not to take advantage of it.

THE TOOLS OF CONQUEST

Before 1850, it was either too difficult or not worth the effort for westerners to penetrate into Africa's interior or extensively expand colonial holdings in Asia. After 1850, science and technology gave the industrialized nations the tools they needed to conquer and control nonindustrialized lands.

Steam-powered iron ships conveyed messages, materials, and people across oceans quickly and cheaply. Smaller steamboats took travelers up rivers. Railroads

Transportation facilities carried them across vast stretches of lands. The Suez Canal cut thousands of miles off journeys to Asia, and the Panama Canal promised much the same (see the drawing on page 658). In 1800, mail took as long as one year to get from London to India. In 1880, a telegram took just hours.

Innovations in weaponry also gave the West new clout. Europeans had long possessed more firepower than non-Western peoples. The new breech-loading

Force rifles and machine guns multiplied that advantage. Local societies resisted, but with the destructive power of these new weapons, European soldiers numbering only a few hundred annihilated local forces in the thousands. Winston Churchill, Britain's future prime minister and an observer of the 1898 Battle of Omdurman in the Sudan, described the effects of the machine gun on natives: "It was not a battle but an execution. . . . The bodies were . . . spread evenly over acres and acres." In that particular battle, eleven thousand Muslim tribesmen died, while only 28 British soldiers lost their lives.

Disease, more than distance or resistance, had also kept Europeans out of most of Africa. But by 1830, the French had discovered the power of quinine to protect their soldiers from *Medicine* deadly malaria long enough to take Algeria in North Africa. After 1850, explorers, missionaries, traders, soldiers, and officials came into sub-Saharan Africa armed with the new medicine.

Various Europeans used these tools of conquest at different times. Sometimes missionaries and explorers entered new lands first; other times traders or even military officers made decisions on their own to move in. Once *Patterns of conquest* there, they called on home governments to provide support, enforce contracts, and protect private interests. Newspapers reported "atrocities" committed against the unwelcome intruders, and stirred up European cries for revenge and protection of national honor. Western governments that had requested the cooperation of local political leaders and been refused turned to force. Indirect control could quickly turn into direct control as problems arose. Control expanded even more as neighboring areas attracted the interest of the intruders.

THE SCRAMBLE FOR AFRICA

Imperial control spread most dramatically in Africa. In the early nineteenth century, Africa was the seat of several vital civilizations. In the north were the long-established Islamic societies. In sub-Saharan Africa—particularly in the western and central Sudan, where the Sahara Desert gave way to grasslands and trade flourished—a rich array of societies and states had developed over the centuries. In most kingdoms of the Sudan and western Africa, Islam had become a major cultural influence. Trade and contact with Europeans affected Africa, but except for coastal and certain other limited areas, such as South Africa, most of Africa remained free from European control.

By the middle decades of the nineteenth century, however, the French had conquered and annexed Algeria in North Africa, and had pushed up the Senegal River in the west. The British had taken the Cape Colony in South Africa from *North Africa* the Dutch during the Napoleonic Wars, and the Dutch settlers had moved northward into the interior (see Map 20.2). In the late 1870s, two developments initiated an international scramble to carve up Africa.

The first occurred in Egypt. This North African

state had long interested France and Britain as a market for European goods and investments, and as a bridge to Asia. European bankers financed the construction of port facilities, railroads, and telegraph lines in Egypt, granting high-interest loans to Egypt's government. In 1869 the Suez Canal, built by a French company, opened and became the vital link from the Mediterranean Sea through Egypt to the Red Sea and the Indian Ocean (see the drawing on p. 658). The British desired control over the canal so as to secure their lucrative position in India. In 1875, Great Britain took advantage of the Egyptian government's financial distress and purchased the Egyptian ruler's, or khedive's, controlling portion of the canal stock. Four years later, France and Britain seized Egypt's treasury to secure their investments. When nationalist groups in Egypt revolted, British troops occupied Egypt. Formally, the khedive remained in office, but after 1882, Britain held most of the real power. By then, 3,000 ships a year passed through the Suez Canal.

The British reshaped Egypt's economy so that it produced cotton, silk, and wheat for export in return for manufactured goods. They also disrupted local work life by hiring Egyptian laborers for their own projects—whether as railroad builders or servants. Worse, they insulted unfavored groups—such as Muslims and Arabs—by paying them less than favored groups.

The French reluctantly acquiesced to British control in Egypt in return for Britain's support of French ambitions in northwestern Africa. In the following years, Britain expanded south to secure Egypt and east to maintain its position in India and China. For similar reasons, France expanded from its stake in Algeria to Tunisia, Morocco, and most of northwestern Africa.

At the same time, King Leopold II of Belgium (r. 1865–1909), hungry for ivory, rubber, hardwoods, palm oil, and glory, initiated a new competition for acquisitions in sub-Saharan Africa by devouring the Congo. He had claimed that his purpose was "to open to civilization" central Africa, "to pierce the darkness which envelopes whole populations." In fact, his troops killed and mutilated thousands of local peoples in the process of conquest. Worried about missing out on the land grab, the other European powers voiced their own claims. The French centered their efforts in western Africa, the Germans in eastern Africa, and the British up and down the center "from Cairo to Capetown." The Berlin Conference of 1885 formal-

Sub-Saharan Africa

ized this scramble for Africa, setting ground rules for territorial acquisition on that continent. According to the conference, colonizers were supposed to have enough physical presence to control and develop an area before they could claim it. They also agreed to treat Africans according to humane standards, though they often used that declaration to disguise the exploitation and abuse they continued to commit.

By 1914, most of the huge continent had been carved up by the various European powers (see Map 20.3). The main exception was Ethiopia. There, Emperor Menelik II (r. 1889–1913) cleverly played one European power off against the other. In the process, he manipulated the Europeans into supplying his country with modern arms, which he then used to defeat the invading Italians in 1896.

For the Europeans, the costliest struggles occurred among themselves. The imperial powers averted most conflicts by diplomacy. In South Africa, however, even the most skilled diplomacy failed to keep the peace. British settlers began to move into the South African Cape Colony early in the nineteenth century. The Dutch Boers (Afrikaners), who had settled there in the seventeenth century and resented Britain's abolition of slavery, trekked northward far into the interior, slaughtering the resisting Zulus in their way. Eventually, the British recognized the independence of the two Boer states, Transvaal and the Orange Free State.

However, when rich gold mines were discovered in Transvaal in the 1880s, British immigrants flooded in. The British entrepreneur and empire builder Cecil Rhodes (1853–1902), backed by powerful interest groups concerned about growing German presence in southwestern Africa, decided to brush aside the two little Boer republics. But what the British thought would be an easy victory took three years (1899–1902) of military effort and involved severe casualties and enormous costs. Britain finally won the brutal contest, and in the end treated the defeated Boers leniently. The British took them into partnership in the Union of South Africa, and the Boer hero, General Louis Botha (1862–1919), was elected the Union's first prime minister. Botha's government announced that it would "permit no equality between colored people and the white inhabitants," a policy that South Africa would hold on to for the next eighty years.

Boer War

Europeans usually ruled directly over African societies so they could create the economic conditions they wanted. Colonial administrators trained cooperative

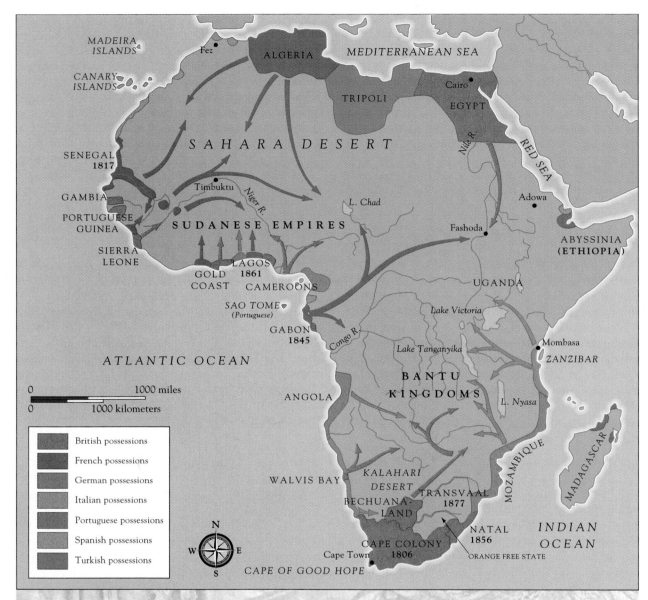

THINKING ABOUT GEOGRAPHY

MAP 20.2 *Imperialism in Africa, ca. 1885*

Comparing Map 20.2, which shows European holdings in Africa in 1885, and Map 20.3, which shows European holdings in 1914, reveals the results of the Europeans' grab for African lands. ▧ **Consider** which European nations became the main imperial powers in Africa. ▧ **Notice** the dates of acquisition by the European powers. **What** do these dates reveal about the timing of the "scramble" for African lands? ▧ **Locate** Britain's possessions. **How** do these reflect Britain's concern to protect its routes to India?

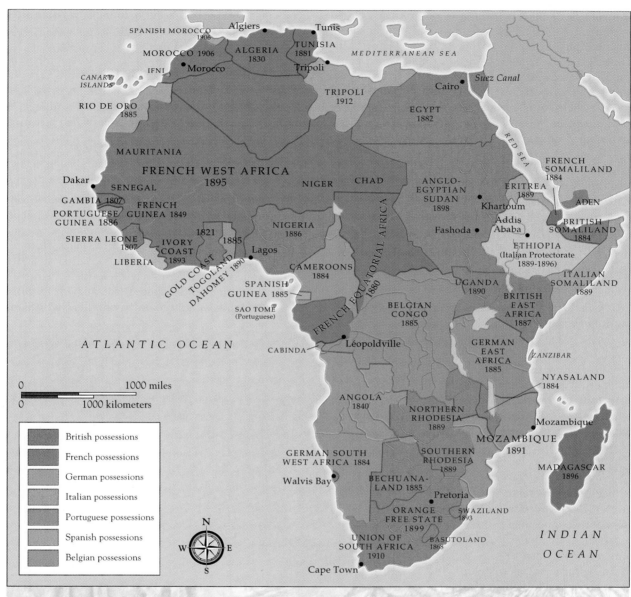

MAP 20.3 *Imperialism in Africa, 1914*

tribes as their clerks, soldiers, and favored workers. These preferences often sparked bitter tribal jealousies and rivalries. Throughout Africa, Europeans made it clear by their words and actions that they considered themselves, their civilization, and their "race" superior to the Africans. Their dominance established, Europeans prided themselves

Dominance, conflict, and consequences

on bringing Christianity and civilization to the "dark" continent. They had scant appreciation for the qualities of African societies and dismissed the Africans as inferior peoples useful only for manual labor. Often they treated them little better than slaves. They also established new political boundaries that ignored the long-standing social, cultural, and political realities of local peoples. Some officials even worked to "submerge"

Africans from different societies "into a single colored working class," a policy that prevented Africans from maintaining kinship and community ties. Those Africans who resisted might be decimated in armed battle or dispossessed and forced onto reservations. Yet resentment and desperation led many Africans to rebel against their conquerors, despite the hopelessness of their situation. A warrior in South Africa explained the reasons for one of these rebellions: "Our King gone, we had submitted to the white people and they ill-treated us until we became desperate and tried to make an end of it all. We knew that we had very little chance because their weapons were so much superior to ours. But we meant to fight to the last, feeling that even if we could not beat them we might at least kill a few of them and so have some sort of revenge."

ESTABLISHING CONTROL IN ASIA

In Asia, Western powers usually got what they wanted by ruling through local elites. In these large, well-organized societies, where the potential for effective resistance remained great, westerners' tampering with the established power structure was risky.

India was as linguistically and regionally diverse as Europe. Nevertheless, by the nineteenth century, the British had brought together a variety of states, territories, and tribal groups to create an Indian state under British control. The Indian subcontinent became Britain's richest imperial prize. Nearly twenty times larger than Great Britain and more than seven times as populous, India bought and sold more goods than any other British colony. Britain directed much of its imperial policy toward preserving this lucrative colony.

Until 1858, the British East India Company, a private-stock company, governed India. However, the great Sepoy Mutiny of 1857, the first large-scale uprising of Indians against British rule, prompted the British government to take direct control. Instead of meddling with the structure of Indian society, the British used India's elites to support their rule.

They employed a half million Indians to administer the huge country, and built railroads, canals, ports, schools, and medical facilities. In one sense, India benefitted in that population increased rapidly. On the other hand, living standards for most fell as population increases outstripped economic growth. The British paid low wages and labeled Indians as inferior—at best, in the words of the British historian and politician Thomas Macaulay, "a great people sunk in the lowest depth of slavery and superstition." Through use of tariffs, they forced India to collapse its own cotton industry and accept British imports of cotton cloth instead. They restructured India's economy to specialize in products the British wanted, such as jute, raw cotton, opium, tea, and wheat. As one Indian nationalist explained, "*Pax Britannica* [Britain's peace] has been established in this country in order that a foreign government may exploit the country."

Britain permanently altered this ancient civilization by creating a national unity whether the Indians

FIGURE 20.10
The British in India.

desired it or not. Moreover British men and women in India imported their own cultural standards, lived separately from the "inferior" native societies, and expected the Indians they dealt with—from elites to servants—to adjust to British ways. Figure 20.10, a photo of Indian servants catering to a British gentleman, indicates the gulf between the British ruling class and the Indians they governed. It also reveals the appeal of foreign service to the British, who at home may have enjoyed only modest social positions.

The British showed no inclination to grant India self-government. As a result, nationalism—already a potent force in Europe—rose in Asia. Indian dissatisfaction with British rule mounted steadily. In 1885, the nationalist Indian elite formed the Indian National Congress, which would launch a long struggle for Indian independence.

France followed the same pattern as Britain in its southeast Asia colonies. By the 1860s, open resistance to the intruding French became hopeless. As one of

Southeast Asia Vietnam's leading statesmen explained in 1867, "The French have come, with their powerful weapons of war . . . no one can resist them. They go where they want, the strongest ramparts fall before them." During the 1880s and early 1890s, France took what would become Vietnam, Cambodia, and Laos and grouped them into the Union of Indochina under French control. As in India, medicine, sanitation, canals, roads, and other projects financed by the French led to population growth in Indochina. French rule also spawned economic dependence and resentment against the European assumption of superiority. A southeast Asian elite arose that, as in India, would struggle to expel Western rule.

China, with its highly structured society, strong central government, and large armed forces, had long kept westerners at arm's length. Although the Chinese admitted some European traders and Christian

China missionaries in the sixteenth and seventeenth centuries, they closed their doors rather tightly thereafter. At the beginning of the eighteenth century, China ranked among the world's most prosperous and powerful societies. The Chinese still considered their huge, populous country the center of civilization surrounded by lesser civilizations. As late as 1793, China's emperor could easily dismiss a proposed trade agreement with Britain: "Our Celestial Empire possesses all things in abundance. We have no need of barbarian products."

However, during the nineteenth century, population explosion, famine, rebellions, and poor leadership under the declining Qing (Ching) dynasty weakened the ancient civilization. The country became a power vacuum that proved all too tempting to the Western powers. Armed with their guns and goods, westerners streamed into China.

First the British forced themselves on the Chinese. During the 1830s, Britain began trading Indian opium in China for tea, silver, silk, and other products. Soon opium became one of Britain's most important commodities. **Opium Wars** Chinese officials tried to stop the economic drain, addiction, and criminal activities stemming from the opium trade by making the drug illegal. As the Chinese official in charge exclaimed to the British, "You do not wish opium to harm your own country, but you choose to bring that harm to other countries such as China. Why?" In response, Britain sent gunboats and troops armed with modern weapons. They easily defeated the Chinese in a series of clashes known as the Opium Wars. By the terms of the Treaty of Nanking (1842), which ended the conflict, the Chinese ceded Hong Kong to the British, opened several tariff-free ports to foreign trade, exempted foreigners from Chinese law, and paid Britain a large indemnity.

At midcentury, disaster struck. China suffered a devastating civil war—the Taiping Rebellion (1850–1864). Other subsequent rebellions extended the internal conflict another ten years. In the end, these wars took perhaps **Taiping Rebellion** 40 million lives, and the famines that followed cost the lives of millions more. All this strife weakened the Qing dynasty and revealed the government's inability to control a nation threatened by external enemies and internal upheaval.

In the years that followed, China fought a series of wars against foreigners. It lost them all, and each defeat chipped away at its sovereignty and racked up yet more indemnities. The Western powers grabbed up spheres of influence and semi-independent treaty ports where all foreigners were exempt from Chinese jurisdiction. In addition, they built railroads to penetrate farther into China's heartland. As shown on Map 20.4, they also took lands on the huge country's periphery. By all these means, the French and British added to their possessions in south Asia, Russia gained territory in the north, and Japan snapped up Korea and Taiwan in the east.

Even the United States joined in the frenzy, grabbing the Philippine Islands after a war with Spain in 1898 and a long struggle against Filipino nationalist forces that cost the lives of perhaps 200,000 Filipinos.

THINKING ABOUT GEOGRAPHY

MAP 20.4   *Imperialism in Asia, 1840–1914*

This map shows the expansion of imperialism in Asia by the Western powers and Japan. ◘ **Which** powers gained the largest territorial interests in Asia by 1914? ◘ **Notice** in particular the lands controlled by Russia, Britain, and Japan. **Where** might conflicts break out between these powers?

President William McKinley explained that the United States had the duty "to educate the Filipinos and uplift and Christianize them." To protect its commercial interests in Asia, the United States called for an "Open Door" policy that would avoid further territorial annexations by the imperial powers. Rivalry among the great powers themselves, as much as Chinese resistance, saved China from complete loss of its independence.

The Philippines

Meanwhile, Chinese nationalism rose in response to foreign aggression. In 1899–1900 the Boxer Rebellion, a serious uprising against Western influences, erupted. Furious at those who had betrayed Chinese religion and customs, the Boxers, a secret organization that believed in the spiritual power of the martial arts, killed thousands of Chinese Christians and a number of foreigners—all with the encouragement of China's Dowager

Boxer Rebellion

FIGURE 20.11
John Clymer, *The Boxer Rebellion*, 1900.

Japan also had a sharply defined sense of identity: "[O]ur country is the source and fountainhead of all other countries, and in all matters it excels all the others," explained one Japanese writer.

In 1853, however, an American fleet under Admiral Perry (1794–1858) steamed into Tokyo Bay, uninvited and unwanted, and forced the Japanese to open their ports to westerners. Impressed by the Americans' technological superiority, the Japanese reacted differently than the Chinese to the foreigners. In 1868 a group of young Japanese overthrew the existing government and launched a social and political revolution from the top down. They ended the feudal structure of the country and began reorganizing Japanese society along modern Western lines (the Meiji Restoration). Taking what they considered the best features from the various Western nations, they patterned their business methods after those of the United States, their legal system after the French, and their navy after the British. They built an authoritarian government, an efficient military machine, and an educational system on the German model. They even required Western dress in court and imitated Western architecture in the rebuilding of Tokyo in 1872.

The Meiji Restoration

With stunning speed, Japan industrialized. Figure 20.12, a photograph of a Japanese silk-working factory, reveals how intensively—in form and substance—Japan adopted Western industrial methods. Men, dressed in formal Western attire, supervise women, who work on row after row of tightly spaced machines.

The industrialized nation soon began flexing its new muscle in Asia. Japan no longer viewed China as a source of culture to be respected, but a weakened land open to conquest and exploitation. In 1894, the Japanese invaded China, forcing it to pay a large indemnity and give up Korea and Taiwan. In 1904, after Russia angered Japan by increasing its presence in China's northern province of Manchuria, the Japanese attacked the tsar's troops. To the world's surprise, Japan defeated the inept Russian forces both on land and at sea, and became the dominant power in Manchuria. Industrialized, militaristic, and imperialistic, Japan took its place alongside other world powers by 1914.

Russo-Japanese War

Empress. Figure 20.11, a painting by American Artist John Clymer, depicts a battle between the Boxers—in the center, with swords and spears—and U.S. marines—in the lower right, with modern machine guns, rifles with bayonets, and revolvers. The Boxers seem to burst out of the heavily populated Chinese society, while the U.S. marines fire from the outside into that society. Combined forces from the imperial powers brutally suppressed this nationalist movement and forced China to pay large indemnities.

Even propped up by imperial powers, the corrupt Chinese central government could not last. In 1911, reformers led by Sun Yat-sen (1866–1925), a Western-educated doctor, launched a revolution aimed at freeing China from foreign exploitation and modernizing its society. Rebellions swept most of China and pushed the corrupt, inept, disintegrating dynasty to its final collapse. Sun proclaimed a republic, but power soon dispersed among imperial generals who became warlords. China's struggles to cope with the encroaching world and its internal problems were far from over.

Japan, even more than China, had long refused direct contact with the West. At the beginning of the nineteenth century, the island nation remained in great part a feudal society ruled by the shogun—a strong military governor—and his military chieftains. The Japanese emperor had only limited powers. Though long influenced by Chinese culture,

Japan

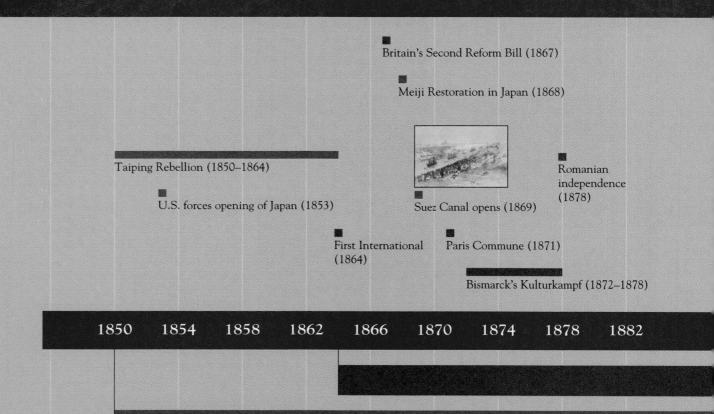

Britain's Second Reform Bill (1867)

Meiji Restoration in Japan (1868)

Taiping Rebellion (1850–1864)

U.S. forces opening of Japan (1853)

Suez Canal opens (1869)

Romanian independence (1878)

First International (1864)

Paris Commune (1871)

Bismarck's Kulturkampf (1872–1878)

| 1850 | 1854 | 1858 | 1862 | 1866 | 1870 | 1874 | 1878 | 1882 |

IMPERIALISM AND THE NON-WESTERN WORLD (1850–1904)

FIGURE 20.12
Japanese silk factory, 1905.

THE LEGACY OF IMPERIALISM

With its technology, its industrial capitalism, and above all its aggressive nationalism, the West had subjected most of Africa and Asia to its domination between 1870 and 1914. In Australia and New Zealand European powers had already established large settler colonies. However, in the Pacific the pattern of imperial conquest that the West had established in Africa and Asia held true. Western adventurers, missionaries, traders, gunboats, troops, and businesses came, took over, and destroyed the world that native peoples had long known. Worse, the westerners carried diseases that decimated Pacific populations.

Certainly, life in non-Western lands had not been idyllic before the intrusion of the West. As one Ndebele warrior in South Africa put it, "Even in our own time there were troubles, there was much fighting and many innocent people were killed." Many westerners

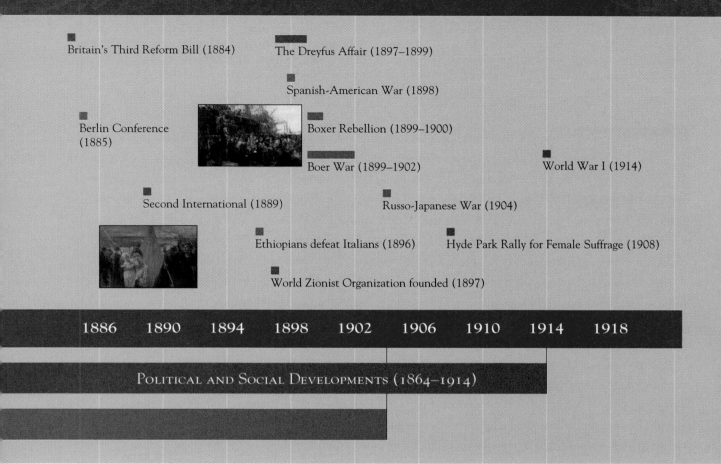

Britain's Third Reform Bill (1884)

The Dreyfus Affair (1897–1899)

Spanish-American War (1898)

Berlin Conference
(1885)

Boxer Rebellion (1899–1900)

Boer War (1899–1902)

World War I (1914)

Second International (1889)

Russo-Japanese War (1904)

Ethiopians defeat Italians (1896)

Hyde Park Rally for Female Suffrage (1908)

World Zionist Organization founded (1897)

| 1886 | 1890 | 1894 | 1898 | 1902 | 1906 | 1910 | 1914 | 1918 |

Political and Social Developments (1864–1914)

in these lands may have been well meaning, and they may have brought elements of Western civilization that were of some benefit to non-Westerners. In India, British rule probably prevented internal wars and promoted order. In Africa, westerners did abolish slavery. Yet rather than striving to understand and appreciate non-Western societies, most Westerners viewed them from a condescending, arrogant, or downright racist perspective. The colonized peoples had to endure being treated as menials and subordinates by men and women whose only necessary qualification was being Western. The insults to local peoples' self-respect and their relentless humiliation fueled resistance to Western control.

Western powers not only forcibly drew non-Western lands into a world economy, they also exploited the natural and human resources of the conquered lands and profoundly undermined the cultural, social, and religious traditions of the African and Asian peo-

ples. In addition, they distorted non-Western economies to serve the demands of their own commerce. They imposed what one observer called "the European system of monotonous, uninterrupted labour," in which industries such as mining and railroad building subjected native laborers to inhumane and dangerous working conditions. Forced to migrate to find jobs in the alien economy, local workers left behind shattered families and communities. Political structures that had long functioned effectively in these lands broke down in just a few years.

By 1914, tens of thousands of colonial administrators, soldiers, and settlers relied directly on imperialism for their careers, status, and livelihood. Indeed, most westerners had come to view imperialism as normal and harmless. Few recognized how destructive it could be—not only to colonial peoples but also to themselves. In Asia, for example, Russia's expansion south brought it to the borders of British India and nearly ignited a war with that nation. Farther east, Russia pushed to the Sea of Japan and Manchuria; the action sparked hostilities with Japan. More than once, Britain, France, and Germany narrowly avoided war in Africa. Imperialism extended the already intense economic and political competition among the European states, heightening the potential for major conflict among these powers.

In the years 1870–1914, more and more westerners gained access to the political process. Nationalism opened these doors for them, as did the movement toward democracy. But the combination of nationalism and democracy had its dangers. In Britain, J. S. Mill warned that "the sentiment of nationality so far outweighs the love of liberty that the people are willing to abet their rulers in crushing the liberty and independence of any people not of their race or language." Many political leaders recognized nationalism and democracy as forces that they could use to their advantage. Others simply adjusted to them. Those who resisted did so at their own peril.

Europeans were also moving, not only to their own cities but out of Europe by the millions. Industrialization and the promise of wealth in new places combined with nationalism and mass politics to push the imperial West throughout the world as never before. As a result, Western power—economic, political, military, and imperial—expanded in an environment of intense international competition.

In the years just before 1914, the strain of this competition on Western societies grew obvious. Labor unrest, the movement for women's suffrage, politics of the extremes, civil violence, diplomatic crises, military threats, and a growing sense of uncertainty all pointed to trouble in the making. Yet this was a complex era. During this same period, the civilization that produced such uncertainty also created new engines of wealth, transformed its cities, and supported an explosion of creative thought and culture.

REVIEW, ANALYZE, AND ANTICIPATE

REVIEW THE PREVIOUS CHAPTER

In Chapter 19—"Nationalism and Statebuilding"—the efforts to build national unity and strength between 1850 and 1870 were analyzed.

1. *In what ways did nationalism remain a powerful force in the decades after 1870?*

2. *Analyze how nationalism evolved during these later decades, comparing it with the nationalism of 1850–1870 as well as the ideology of nationalism of the early nineteenth century.*

ANALYZE THIS CHAPTER

Chapter 20—"Mass Politics and Imperial Domination"—examines the spreading demands for democracy, and the West's imperial expansion between 1870 and 1914.

1. *In what ways were large numbers of people incorporated into politics during this period?*

2. *Why were some areas and groups still left out of the political arena in 1914?*

3. *Analyze the various causes for the rise of imperialism during this period.*

4. *For both Western and non-Western peoples, what consequences flowed from imperialism?*

ANTICIPATE THE NEXT CHAPTER

In Chapter 21—"Modern Life and the Culture of Progress"—the changes stemming from new industrial transformations and urban growth, as well as the culture of the West, will be traced.

1. *What sorts of social changes might be related to the statebuilding and rise of democracy during this period?*

2. *How might the continuing rise of science and technology support the West's imperial expansion?*

BEYOND THE CLASSROOM

DEMANDS FOR DEMOCRACY

Harrison, J.F.C. *Late Victorian Britain, 1875–1901*. London: Routledge, 1991. Examines British society and the experiences of the different social classes during the period.

Mayeur, Jean-Marie, and Madeleine Réberioux. *The Third Republic—From Its Origins to the Great War, 1871–1914*. Cambridge: Cambridge University Press, 1987. A solid survey of France during this period, stressing the politics of the republican government.

Wehler, Hans-Ulrich. *The German Empire, 1871–1918*. Leamington Spa, England: Berg Publishers, 1985. An important and controversial work that argues for continuity between the Second and Third Reichs.

INSIDERS AND OUTSIDERS: POLITICS OF THE EXTREMES

Hause, Steven C., and Anne R. Kenney. *Women's Suffrage and Social Politics in the French Third Republic*. Princeton, NJ: Princeton University Press, 1984. Examines all aspects of the women's suffrage movement in France from its origins to the years after the end of World War I.

Levine, Philippa. *Victorian Feminism*. Tallahassee: Florida State University Press, 1987. Examines women's involvement in various campaigns for their rights.

Lindemann, Albert S. *A History of European Socialism*. New Haven, CT: Yale University Press, 1983. An overview of the European socialist tradition from the Enlightenment to the 1980s.

Pulzer, P. *The Rise of Political Anti-Semitism in Germany and Austria*. Cambridge, MA: Harvard University Press, 1988. Studies the role of anti-Semitism in the world of central European politics.

Schorske, Carl E. *Fin-de-Siècle Vienna: Politics and Culture*. New York: Alfred A. Knopf, 1980. A classic study of the creative intellectual climate of Vienna that emphasizes the connections between culture and politics.

EMIGRATION: OVERSEAS AND ACROSS CONTINENTS

Hoerder, Dirk, and Leslie Page Moch, eds. *European Migrants—Global and Local Perspectives*. Boston: Northeastern University Press, 1996. A collection of articles by several scholars on the migrations of Europeans across the land and overseas.

Wolf, Eric. *Europe and the People Without History*. Berkeley, CA: University of California Press, 1983. An important cross-cultural perspective on the process and consequences of imperialism.

THE NEW IMPERIALISM: THE RACE FOR AFRICA AND ASIA

Doyle, Michael W. *Empires*. Ithaca, NY: Cornell University Press, 1986. A comparative examination of imperialism.

Headrick, Danier R. *The Tentacles of Progress: Technology Transfer in the Age of Imperialism, 1850–1940*. New York: Oxford University Press, 1988. Argues that the poorer countries failed to develop under imperial rule despite the transfers of Western capital and technology.

Hobsbawm, Eric. *The Age of Empire, 1875–1914*. New York. Pantheon, 1987. A Marxist perspective on late-nineteenth-century Europe, excellent sections on imperialism.

Pakenham, Thomas. *The Scramble for Africa*. New York: Random House, 1991. A detailed and well-written narrative of this important area of imperial conquest.

William P. Frith, Many Happy Returns of the Day

In this painting, a family gathers for a birthday. The rich clothing, carpeting, paintings on the wall, heavy curtains, solid bricks showing through the window, and attentive servant on the left all mark this as an urban middle-class home. In the center, haloed by a wreath, is the innocent "angel" birthday girl. Here is the ideal of the happy home, the center of private life where men, women, and children celebrate together. Yet the scene also reflects the contrasting gender spheres. The women and children gather comfortably. But the father and grandfather—reading a newspaper—sit close to the window and to the outside, public world of the modern city.

CHAPTER 21

Modern Life and the Culture of Progress
Western Society, 1850–1914

In 1864, an observer described Milan in northern Italy as vibrant "without being feverish like Paris or London." Though Milan had become one of the great cultural centers in the newly unified Italian state, workers still lived along narrow, winding streets in the heart of this city. Everyone knew each other and spoke the local Milanese dialect. Citizens "huddled around the cathedral, like a family warming itself at the hearth."

This quaint image would not last long. Over the next thirty years, wide avenues and expensive "great white houses, all straight," replaced Milan's narrow streets and old dwellings. Each year thousands of immigrants—mostly peasants and artisans—streamed into the city looking for jobs and all kinds of other opportunities. In just one decade, the city's population grew by almost a third. By the 1890s, the center of Milan teemed with people from the city's outlying quarters and suburbs who traveled there to work, shop, or amuse themselves. They spoke the common Italian language and shoved "on and off the trams . . . day and night." More people purchased goods in the huge new department store near the cathedral than prayed in that Gothic church. Nearby, in the newly built Gallery, musicians, singers, businesspeople, shoppers, and diners congregated in the shops and cafes under a magnificent glass roof. Milan—like Paris, London, and other great cities in the West—had become a center of industry, growth, and culture—a thriving embodiment of modern life.

In the decades after 1850, industrialization pulled masses of westerners to new jobs in cities like Milan. Urban growth began to overwhelm the West's centuries-old land-based society. In cities, the continuing spread of liberal ideas and the optimism of wealthy urban leaders created a culture of progress. Dominated by science, which seemed to promise so much, and by competitive values that served the up-and-coming middle class so well, this urban culture altered the ways people thought about the world and their place in it. Those who recognized these engines of change saw their civilization being pushed to modernity. In 1850, however, few understood what modernity meant or even how difficult the ride there could be.

Romanticism	Italian and German Unification		"Second" Industrial Revolution				
Realism and Naturalism						World War I
			The New Imperialism		
Industrial Revolution		Spread of Democratic Reforms		
		Impressionism		Expressionism

| 1850 | 1860 | 1870 | 1880 | 1890 | 1900 | 1910 | 1914 |

The Second Industrial Revolution

"Steam and electricity have conquered time and space to a greater extent during the last sixty years than all the preceding six hundred years," gushed a special issue of *The Illustrated London News* in 1897. Yet in 1850, most people knew little about the industrial revolution. Outside Britain and a few limited areas in the West, more people still lived in the countryside than in the cities, and more worked at home or in home workshops than in factories. Most had never set foot in a railway car. Even in the cities, people probably made their living much as their parents had—as helpers in shops, domestics, artisans, merchants, and day laborers.

By 1914 this scenario had changed so drastically that even Britain had been left behind. Between 1850 and 1870, the coal mines, iron foundries, textile factories, steam engines, and railroads that had made Britain an industrial giant spread broadly into western and central Europe and North America. After 1870, new inventions, manufacturing processes, and methods for getting products to market and selling them rendered the earlier milestones of industrialization out of date. Science, technology, and industry marched hand in hand. Large-scale factories dwarfed the textile mills and iron foundries of the early industrial

era, and huge department stores displayed endless goods to entice consumers. For the first time in history, people began to expect continuing economic growth. According to some historians, these developments created a "second industrial revolution."

STEEL LEADS THE WAY

Steel led the way in this new wave of industrialization. The Bessemer processes for removing impurities from molten iron speeded up and cheapened steel production, transforming it from an expensive luxury product into a strong, affordable improvement over

FIGURE 21.1
The Krupp Steelworks, Germany, 1880.

iron. Figure 21.1, an 1880 photograph of the Krupp steelworks, reveals the new technology and massive factories that produced steel and enabled countries such as Germany to become industrial leaders. On the left are the huge converters that turned iron into steel. Dwarfed in comparison, workers (in the foreground and around the converters) toil to keep the process going. By 1914 the annual production of steel had risen more than fiftyfold since 1850. Figure 21.2 charts the growth of steel production between 1882 and 1912 and the countries that led in the creation of this crucial industrial material. Out of this steel, manufacturers made efficient tools and machines to fabricate metal, textile, leather, and wood products.

With advances in chemistry, textile manufacturers could now use inexpensive synthetic dyes to color their cloth, and paper manufacturers could process *Chemicals* wood pulp more efficiently than ever. By 1914, new chemical-based fabrics and processes had spawned a host of infant industries. Germany's chemical laboratories and their development of industrial uses for chemicals helped propel that nation ahead of Great Britain as an industrial leader.

Electricity and petroleum became practical sources of power, thanks to the invention of the electrical dynamo, the steam turbine, and the internal combus-*Electricity and petroleum* tion engine. By the end of the century, electric lamps glowed in city streets, large stores, and wealthy neighborhoods throughout Europe. Electricity powered factories and workshops and was the magic behind the refrigerators and vacuum cleaners starting to appear in middle-class homes.

New Transportation and Communication Networks

Getting around, moving things, and communicating became dramatically easier as well. Before 1850, few people had seen more of the world than they could *Railroad building* view on foot or by cart or horseback. By 1914, millions traveled enormous distances each year. Even in China, Turkey, and Brazil, trains chugged along hauling people for astonishing stretches. This was the greatest era of railroad building in history, and with the railroads came hundreds of bridges and long tunnels. At the same time, huge steamships with steel hulls, turbine engines, and screw propellers replaced sailing ships. The opening of the Suez Canal (between the Mediter-

ranean Sea and the Indian Ocean) in 1869 and the Panama Canal (between the Atlantic and Pacific Oceans) in 1914 cut thousands of miles off long sea voyages and brought the Western and non-Western worlds into closer contact.

However, the future lay with yet another revolutionary invention: the internal combustion engine. In 1887 the German inventor Gottlieb Daimler (1834–1900) attached his little combustion engine to a wagon—and the automobile was born. Two decades later in the United States, former bicycle mechanic Henry Ford (1863–1947) introduced the assembly line to the auto- *Internal combustion engine* mobile industry. By 1914 cars, taxis, and trucks jammed city streets in Europe and America, and created new demand for oil, rubber, and concrete.

Just as these new means of transportation linked millions of people physically, the telegraph and telephone connected them in a giant communication network. In 1844, Samuel *Telegraph and telephone* Morse sent a message by wire forty miles from Baltimore to Washington. In 1866, ships laid telegraph cable across the Atlantic, enabling news to travel from London to New York as quickly as it had moved from one side of London to the other. Ten years later, Alexander Graham Bell

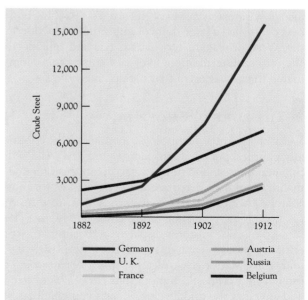

Figure 21.2
Steel production (thousands of metric tons).

(1847–1922), an American born in Scotland, invented the telephone.

THE BIRTH OF BIG BUSINESS

These telephone companies, railroads, shipping lines, steel mills, chemical plants, and new factories became too large for all but a very few individuals to finance. Capitalists now raised money by organizing corporations and selling shares of stock—partial ownership—to investors. Governments helped out by passing laws that limited stockholders' risk to only the money they invested. Luck helped, too, for the discovery of gold in California and Australia in the 1850s and 1860s and in Alaska and South Africa later in the century increased the supply of money. This was big business, and it was controlled by large banks and wealthy executives. These executives functioned much as heads of state, conferring with boards of directors and lesser executives. Under them were layers of managers who specialized in areas like sales, finance, and production, and who hired, fired, and supervised employees.

In this new world of business, the big and strong often destroyed the small and weak. Corporations combined into gigantic, monopolistic trusts (called "cartels" in Germany) that commanded markets, prices, and wages. Rockefeller's Standard Oil trust in the United States and the I. G. Farben chemical cartel in Germany are examples of the spectacular business successes of the age. By 1914, big business controlled a large share of industrial production in the West. In Japan, too, which adapted quickly to Western industrialization, five giant corporations dominated three-quarters of that nation's industry.

Monopolies

THE LURE OF SHOPPING

With all the new technology, manufacturers habitually churned out more products than they could sell. So, merchants found new ways to create customer demand. Grandiose department stores, such as the Bon Marché in Paris and Bocconi's in Milan, rose up in major cities across the West. The stores displayed a dazzling array of enticing goods—ready-made clothes, furniture, rugs, umbrellas, stationery, toilet paper—a cornucopia of foreign and domestic temptations. Prices were fixed and aimed at the middle classes, but even members of the working class might afford some items. Posters announced "sales" to draw more people to their stores'

Department stores

massive glass and iron emporiums. Glossy catalogues mailed to potential customers in other cities and the countryside encouraged people to order the practical goods and the luxuries of modern urban life for delivery by the new national postal services.

As Figure 21.3 suggests, the stores become tourist attractions, places to spend leisure time, and leading promoters of comsumption. This Parisian department store, with its dramatic central staircase, was designed like a theater for visitors as well as a building where a huge variety of goods could be purchased. Men, women, and children—themselves on display as much as the goods for sale—stroll through this monument to prosperity. By 1900 more than 15,000 people passed through the doors of the Bon Marché in Paris every day. Equally amazing, this shoppers' mecca was only one of twelve Parisian department stores that together employed almost 10,000 people. Department stores had come to represent the materialism of the cities.

FIGURE 21.3
A Paris department store.

WINNERS AND LOSERS IN THE RACE FOR WEALTH

In this intense economic struggle, some people flourished, others fell behind, and many worried about their future. Cycles of prosperity and recession made economic life precarious. New economic powers such as Germany and the United States rose to challenge and sometimes surpass mighty Great Britain, which failed to invest sufficiently in new processes and marketing techniques. Areas in southern and eastern Europe that held on to old ways of making a living fell further behind, though even in these poorer regions industrialization gained some footholds. By 1914, industrialization had penetrated outside of Europe and the United States into Japan, Canada, Argentina, and Australia.

Did this second industrial revolution make life better overall for westerners? As we saw with our discussion of the first industrial revolution in Chapter 17, *New wealth* this question is difficult to answer. Statistically, the answer is yes. It certainly paid to be living in the industrializing nations of the West. In these thriving regions, most people benefited from the new wealth—even those living outside the cities. Food prices came down, and larger farms, chemical fertilizers, and threshing machines boosted harvests and lowered costs. Agricultural producers in North America, Argentina, and Australia sent inexpensive grains and meat in new, refrigerated ships. Prices for manufactured products also dropped, as the new machines and processes made production more efficient. With declining prices came a rise in real wages for workers, which almost doubled in Britain between 1850 and 1914. Meat, dairy products, sugar, tea, and coffee were no longer luxuries. People snapped up previously out-of-reach manufactured goods. With care and luck, they even saved a bit of money for hard times.

Those hard times visited some more than others, and here the old pattern held true. The middle classes benefited more than the working classes, skilled workers more than unskilled, and owners of large farms more than agricultural laborers. Nor did the new wealth end misery for those at the bottom of the socioeconomic ladder. Many people remained mired in poverty. Among workers, few could expect to retire without sinking into dependence or impoverishment, let alone ease into the dream of a comfortable cottage with a small garden. The gaps between rich and poor were all too apparent. The upper 20 percent of the population generally received more of a nation's income than the remaining 80 per- *Hard times* cent. Every day the urban poor could see but not afford the fine apartments, carriages, and clothes of the wealthy.

The New Urban Landscape

City life became the new norm for masses of people in the West. Many rural villages declined or died, slowly in some areas, quickly in others. People from outside the local community moved in, bought the land, and hired migrant laborers to work it. Residents flocked to the cities, and those who had established themselves there stayed. An observer in 1899 reflected the experience of millions: "[T]he most remarkable social phenomenon of the present century is the concentration of population in cities." Europe's population ballooned from 270 million in 1850 to 450 million in 1914, and well over half of western Europeans lived in cities. In Britain, only 8 percent of the work force remained in the countryside. London, Europe's greatest urban center, grew from 2.5 million in 1850 to over 4.5 million in 1914.

REBUILDING CITIES

As these numbers multiplied everywhere, even the physical foundations of cities changed. Urban centers grew out, up, and below ground. Milan, the thriving Italian center described at the beginning of this chapter, was not the only city to rebuild. Governments, entrepreneurs, and speculators tore apart centuries-old housing and winding streets in Paris, Vienna, Brussels, Stockholm, Barcelona, Cologne, and Mexico City. In place of these older features, they constructed broad, tree-lined avenues, parks, fashionable apartment houses, department stores, fancy cafes, government buildings, museums, hospitals, opera houses, schools, and libraries. New neighborhoods, open spaces, transportation systems, and underground water and sewer systems transformed the face and substance of city life.

Paris led the way in this wave of reconstruction. In the French capital, Emperor Napoleon III and his technocratic administrator, Baron Haussmann, initiated the most ambitious plans for demolishing some of the oldest and poorest neighborhoods. Figure 21.4 shows just one of many large projects begun in Paris during the 1850s. Here workers tear down old tenements that lined the streets of Paris to make way for wide boulevards, new buildings, and parks.

According to Napoleon, Haussmann, and their advisors, these reconstruction efforts offered several important benefits. Doctors and reformers argued that filth from overcrowding caused the diseases that often swept though Paris. Wide streets and open spaces, they explained, would let in much-needed fresh air. But those wide streets also gave governments a political advantage: They deterred people from again throwing up revolutionary barricades to fight

Figure 21.4
Rebuilding cities.

the forces of order as they had in 1848 and afforded troops ready access to working-class areas. Finally, reconstruction projects generated untold wealth for investors, speculators, influence brokers, schemers, architects, engineers, and workers from all over France.

As in Milan, the new construction drove the poor out of the center of Paris to the east end or into working-class suburbs. Wealthier Parisians felt little sympathy. After all, they reasoned, the capital city represented the nation in the eyes of citizens and visitors alike. As Haussman explained, "The splendor of this city reflects on the whole country." The power, wealth, beauty, and modernity of Paris must not be marred by images of poverty and misfortune.

Sewers and Subways

Below Europe's city streets, less glamorous but no less important projects hummed along. In 1850, most houses in Europe's major cities did not have running water. Sewage in cities such as Berlin still ran in open gutters, creating an atmosphere of filth and tremendous stench. During the following decades, these standards began to change. First in London and then elsewhere, engineers and workers built water and sewer systems. Doctors, reformers, and planners led the drive to bring in freshwater in aqueducts or pipes

from sources upstream, and to create hundreds of miles of underground sewers to carry waste downstream. These measures made urban life healthier and more comfortable than before.

More than water and waste moved below the city, however. In 1863, London's underground railway opened. Over the next fifty years, Paris and New York built subways of their own. Along with carriages, trams, and railroads, the efficient, predictable subways enabled people to shop and work in places farther from home than ever. People moved their residences out of crowded urban centers to city fringes and suburbs—whether upscale neighborhoods for the middle class or less expensive areas for workers.

City People

Who were these people filling the cities of the West? How did they make their way in life, so far away from the land and surrounded by industrial advances and new wealth? Part of the answer is revealed in Figure 21.5, a midcentury engraving of a typical Parisian apartment house. At this time, the city's various social classes still lived in close proximity but in different conditions. The drawing portrays the wealthy

FIGURE 21.5
Bertall, The urban classes.

bourgeoisie living on the first (American second) floor in luxurious comfort; above them lives a bourgeois family of lesser means. The lower classes and aspiring artists—dancing and drinking instead of working, having too many children, and unable to pay their bills—live on the bottom and upper floors in increasing poverty, thanks to their imprudence.

ON TOP OF IT ALL: THE URBAN ELITE

At the top of the urban social order was a small, elite class of wealthy aristocrats and the richest of the bourgeoisie—the millionaire factory owners, mer-

chants, and bankers. Amounting to less than 1 percent of the population, these people socialized together, turned to each other for help, and intermarried. Through strategic matchmaking, new wealth from the daughter or son of an American captain of industry or banker might enable an aristocratic family to maintain its position. More often, however, aristocrats kept their positions by making shrewd investments, serving governments, holding on to top spots in the military and diplomatic corps, and wisely managing their lands and businesses. They, along with members entering their ranks, had prestige but not the formal privileges that their eighteenth-century predecessors had enjoyed.

Those who had been born into aristocratic families clung to what was left of the old lifestyle. Those aspiring to the aristocratic life used their money to copy that lifestyle. These newly rich bought estate houses in the country and opulent townhouses along the best avenues and parks, attended fancy balls, took hunting trips to Africa, and supported large staffs of servants. They also kept up with the latest fashions and made grand gestures toward cultural and philanthropic activities. However, a few rules of the aristocratic game had changed. Obvious arrogance was frowned upon, as this elite made an effort to comply with middle-class morality. At the very least, they strove to appear responsible, domestic, and religious. Of course, their children got the best of everything. In every way, these elites were truly the upper crust, on top and intent on staying there.

PRIDE AND SUCCESS: THE "SOLID" MIDDLE CLASS

Well below this upper crust, the "solid" bourgeoisie held the better jobs, lived in the finer apartments, dined at fashionable restaurants, and commanded at least one good servant. These were the families of small factory owners, merchants, managers, doctors, druggists, local bankers, lawyers, professors, and architects who earned and spent more money than most.

Worried about competitors from below, many middle-class men established "professional" associations designed to keep standards up and rivals down. Nor did they open their professions to women. Wives and daughters, they intoned, "best" not work for pay. Beliefs that women and men belonged in "separate spheres"—

Women and work

women at home, men in the public world of work—persisted. "Of all those acquirements, which more particularly belong to the feminine character," explained Isabella Mary Mayson Beeton in her best-selling advice book for women, "there are none which take a higher rank . . . than such as enter into a knowledge of household duties; for on these are perpetually dependent the happiness, comfort, and well-being of a family."

Some women managed to swim against the current, however. They engaged in philanthropic activities—in support of the poor and uneducated, or against alcohol and prostitution. British philanthropist Angela Burdette-Coutts (1814–1906), for example, gave away a fortune to schools and housing for the poor. In France, many wealthy women followed the example of Empress Eugénie (consort of Napoleon III), who supported societies that provided assistance to new mothers. In the United States, educated middle-class women staffed hundreds of settlement houses in urban centers that helped immigrants adjust to the customs and language of their new country as well as middle-class values. Only a few women managed to carve out careers in business, teaching, writing, or painting. Exclusion from universities kept most ambitious upper-middle-class women from pursuing lucrative professions, though schools such as Queens College in Britain and the Female Medical College of Pennsylvania promised some professional opportunities to women.

If not arrogant, this bourgeoisie was proud. Who else better represented their civilization? As they saw it, success flowed from character, ability, and effort; in a world open to talent, rewards came from achievement. These people praised discipline, control, and respectability, while attacking public drunkenness, emotional outbursts, and—especially in "Victorian" Britain—open displays of sexual affection. In addition, they respected Christian morality and marital fidelity. Cleanliness went hand in hand with purity and modernity, as did running water for regular baths and several changes of clothes. Certainly, they argued, all good people should live up to these standards, at least in appearance.

Values

HARDWORKING AND HOPEFUL: THE LOWER MIDDLE CLASS

Those just below the solid bourgeoisie probably tried as hard as any group to succeed in modern society. These lower-middle-class people performed skilled services as tellers in banks, sorters in mailrooms, and salespeople in department stores. Reading, writing, and mathematical skills (and for more and more, the new typewriter) enabled thousands to become schoolteachers, postal workers, and clerks in places from government agencies and insurance firms to accounting offices and train stations. Some of these lower-paying "white-collar jobs" came open to educated women, particularly if they were unmarried.

Lower-middle-class people made their living in settings that sometimes resembled factories. Figure 21.6 shows clerks working in the offices of Cadbury's, the chocolate firm described in Chapter 17. In this huge room, all the chairs, desks, and tasks seem the same. All the clerks are men, and even their clothes look almost identical. Figure 21.7 shows a French telephone exchange, also set in a large room in which the chairs, fixtures, and activities are similar. Here the employees are all middle-class women, with the exception of male supervisors and a boy who delivers messages. As this image shows, even when jobs

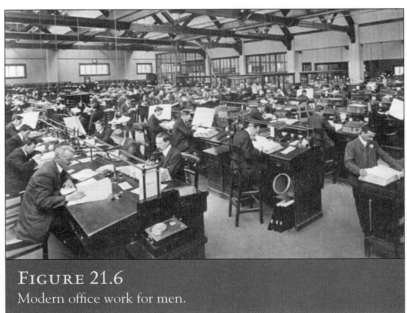

FIGURE 21.6
Modern office work for men.

opened for middle-class women, they were often separate from men's work and of lower status.

With the heightening tempo of industrialization, these lower-middle-class occupations multiplied. People might move up the economic ladder, and better-off workers could hope to see their *Social mobility* educated children rising into this class. In turn, a few children from lower-middle ranks might move into the also expanding solid middle class. Although moving up remained more the exception than the rule, the possibilities were far greater than before 1850. By 1914, the middle classes overall had grown from between 3 and 10 percent of the population to more than 20 percent in much of the West.

THE "OTHER HALF": THE WORKING CLASSES

Unlike the elites and the middle classes, the working classes lived on crowded side streets, the poorer east side of cities like London or Paris, or the edge of town where land and rents were cheaper. Though better off than before 1850, they still faced the threat of job loss, which could send them into poverty in an instant.

Even employed workers struggled to make ends meet. A new demand for certain skilled work helped some. Those who could read directions; build or re-

FIGURE 21.7
French telephone exchange.

pair machines; or who were printers, plumbers, or cabinetmakers earned respectable wages. They might also join unions and demand reforms. Other skilled workers lost out, for factory owners fit laborers to jobs that had become nothing more than mindless, repetitive tasks. Automaker Henry Ford expressed the views of many industrial managers toward this kind of labor: "I could not possibly do the same thing day in and day out, but . . . to the majority of minds, repetition holds no terrors. . . . The average worker, I am sorry to say, . . . wants a job in which he does not have to think." Whether former artisans with obsolete skills or migrants from the countryside, these workers earned paltry wages and worked at an exhausting pace. They and their children tended to remain low-paid industrial laborers for the rest of their lives.

Despite legislation restricting women from certain jobs, many labored outside and inside the home. Jeanne Bouvier, a French woman born in 1865, worked as millions of other working-class women. When she was eleven years old, she took her first job in a silk factory near Lyons. Three years later, she moved to Paris where she worked as a domestic and then in the hatmaking industry. Later, she worked a twelve-hour day as a seamstress while doing piece-work on her own.

In addition to their jobs in factories and small shops, many women took in work at home finishing clothes, polishing items for sale, wrapping chocolates, or decorating toys. Some of the new machines of industry even added to the demand for this older piecework. For example, Singer's sewing machine, invented in the 1850s, enabled entrepreneurs to hire women for low wages to work at home or in small "sweatshops." Such women proved especially appealing to these employers because they were easy to fire and posed little threat of forming a union or going on strike.

Still more women worked in traditional urban jobs. Domestic servants could count on meals and housing and perhaps even some savings from their salaries. On the other hand, they suffered from the whims of their employers and the threat of sexual abuse. Women in laundries, such as those in Figure 21.8, labored at drudgery for low wages, though some of them enjoyed the sense of comradeship that came with the job at times. The growth of cities may have increased the work available to these women, but the machinery of the industrial revolution did not yet ease job conditions for them.

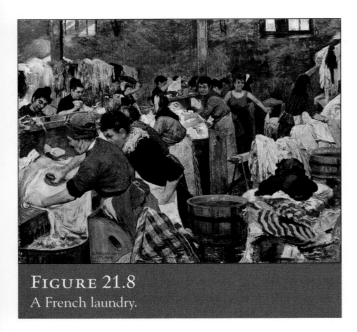

FIGURE 21.8
A French laundry.

WHAT TO DO ABOUT "THEM"

Members of the middle classes looked upon their working-class counterparts with a mixture of fear and sympathy: fear that these were "dangerous" people who might rise in revolt, commit crimes, or create disorder, and sympathy for the harshness of working-class life. Most middle-class people agreed with the popular writer Samuel Smiles that the working classes suffered from their own faults rather than injustices in the social system: "no laws . . . can make the idle industrious, the thriftless provident, or the drunken sober. Such reforms can only be effected by means of individual action, economy, and self-denial."

However, other members of the middle class—especially younger, college-educated people who were also connected to religious causes—joined organizations to ease the plight of the urban poor. With high optimism and idealism, they established clinics, settlement houses, and maternal-wellness societies. Thousands of middle- and upper-class women visited the poor; ran schools; and inspected asylums, workhouses, and prisons. One Spanish charity worker wrote a guide for visitors to the poor: "In viewing their faults, vices, and crimes, we must ask ourselves this question: Would the poor be what they are, if we were what we ought to be?" Some of these workers spread birth-control information; others touted the benefits of religion. Women's groups in particular distributed prayer books to the poor or sold Bibles to raise money to aid the needy—a reflection of the still close link between the churches and charitable work. Still others tried to help the poor through political activism, joining socialist organizations such as the Fabian Society in London, which decried the capitalist system as unjust and inefficient.

Sports and Leisure in the Cities

BUILDING CHARACTER THROUGH ATHLETICS

For turn-of-the-century Europeans who had the time and money, city life could be fun. New forms of recreation and sports not only offered entertaining diversions but also built character values important for industry and war. Soccer, rugby, and cricket, once games for only schoolchildren, became extremely popular, competitive team sports for adults. In 1901 over 100,000 attended a championship game of soccer in Britain. The emphasis on teamwork, competition, and discipline in the sports world reflected the qualities of industrial work and military service so prized during the era. Other new sports, such as bicycle and auto racing, stressed the speed and power of machines; by no coincidence, industrial firms sponsored some of these contests. Even the growth of scouting and, in Germany, the "wandering youth" clubs revealed the belief that good character required physical vigor and outdoor living. Accordingly, the modern Olympic games—stressing competition and nationalism—were established during this period, with the first games held in Athens in 1896.

Women's sports were less professional and less competitive than men's. Even scouting for girls was designed to instill homemaking values. But women did take to bicycles, despite warnings from the old guard that the loose clothing necessary for bicycling was unfeminine, that the activity would damage enthusiasts' ability to have children, and that women might inappropriately experience sexual pleasure from riding.

THE NEW TOURIST

Increasingly, people vacationed away from the cities. More and more, people left town. Those who had the means might imitate the eighteenth-century aristocratic habit of visiting the great cities, museums, and monuments of Europe. Others traveled to resorts on the Mediterranean coast, the Alps, or the shores of the Baltic Sea. By 1890, some 100,000 people visited the resort town of Vichy in central France to "take the waters" (cure their ills), relax, and socialize. Tourism became so popular that special books appeared and professionally organized tours formed to guide people on their travels.

Workers usually lacked the time or money for such luxuries. Some managed short trips on trains that left cities every day for the coast, perhaps to Dieppe in France or Brighton in England, where piers and amusement parks beckoned. Most, however, stayed in the cities. There, some went to café concerts to see singers, comedians, jugglers, and acrobats. Others attended theaters featuring fast dancing, or enjoyed boxing matches, vaudeville shows, and (after the turn of the century) movies.

Private Life: Together and Alone at Home

As the tempo of life in factories, stores, government offices, and streets increased, private life grew more precious. The individualism trumpeted by the liberal bourgeoisie accentuated the longing to withdraw from the public arena into the family, the home, and the self. The personal—one's body, sexuality, and internal life—became a subject of intense fascination. The home—the realm of the family protected by walls and locked doors—was the center of private life.

FAMILY: THE PROMISE OF HAPPINESS

People believed in the family. Like a religion, the family promised happiness in a difficult world, a meaning that would extend beyond death, and a sacred place free from intrusion by the outside world. As much as their means permitted, people celebrated the family through daily gatherings at meals and special occasions such as weddings, vacations, and birthdays (see the painting on p. 688). For individuals, these occasions marked points in their own life cycles. At more private moments, the family home served as a place where individuals shared emotions, or perhaps confessed silently or in a diary to themselves in the solitude of a bedroom.

More than ever, people recorded moments of private life in letters, diaries, and photographs. Families exchanged thousands of letters over a lifetime that told of children, deaths, visits, and health. Such correspondence held the family together when travel and migration to different cities threatened to pull it apart. Diaries of the day reveal much self-concern and introspection. One French woman explained, "When I am alone, I have plenty to do in following the movement of my ideas and impressions, in exploring myself, in examining my dispositions and my various ways of being, in drawing the best out of myself, in registering the ideas that come to me by chance or that are suggested to me by my reading." People took photographs to capture family occasions—from baptisms to Sunday meals and partings—especially after the invention of the small Kodak camera in the 1880s. They carefully enshrined these photographs in frames and collected them in well-organized albums.

Recording private life

A HOME OF ONE'S OWN

The dream of family life and privacy required having a home of one's own—a private kingdom apart from city and society. But home had another purpose as well: it announced the material success of the bourgeoisie and the pleasures of private life.

As revealed in the 1877 painting of a Paris interior shown in Figure 21.9, the typical bourgeois apartment resembled an antique shop, overdecorated in no par-

FIGURE 21.9
Mihaly Munkacsy, *Paris Interior*, 1877.

ticular style and bulging with possessions. Heavy drapes hang over the walls and windows, multiple carpets cover the floors, fabrics ornament the mantelpieces and furniture, and tassels dangle everywhere. In such a home, family members could gaze at the many prints and paintings, enjoy music played by an elder daughter on the piano, read a novel in the library, and stay informed by subscribing to journals. Small, private gardens or potted plants and painted landscapes completed the picture by offering a way to appreciate nature.

Servants shared middle-class homes, but remained on the fringes of the family's private life. Relegated to their own small quarters in the attic or basement, ser- *Servants* vants had little freedom to move about the house at their leisure or take part in their employers' lives. Indeed, with the era's emphasis on both individualism and privacy, employers increasingly saw servants as potential intruders into private life. The bedroom and bathroom became off limits, and people complained about how hard it was to find "good," affordable servants. By the turn of the century, many middle-class families managed with just a single female domestic, or none at all.

For the typical middle-class man, home was a retreat from public life, to be savored at the end of the workday or on weekends. For the middle-class woman, *Women's roles* it was much more. Society glorified her domestic role more than ever. No longer would she be praised for doing "productive" work such as managing a husband's shop. Instead, she orchestrated every aspect of the family's home life, managing the meals, chores, visits, and guests. Her highest duty, however, was to bear and raise children. No longer was reproduction regarded as simply a natural function: it had become a complex, demanding activity. Most likely, a middle-class woman had fewer children than her mother, but she was expected to lavish greater attention on them. Her children would probably remain at home through adolescence, though many families sent their offspring to boarding schools. To help women meet all these expectations, books, magazines, pamphlets, and advice columns offered tips on how to attract a man and marry well; manage a household; sharpen "home economics" skills; and cultivate an appropriate social life that included teas, afternoon visits, and dinner parties.

At the same time, disturbing cross-currents started to undermine this picture of the home and women's role in it. Many women demanded more independent lives, even choosing to live outside the confines of

the middle-class home. The British reformer Florence Nightingale (1820–1910) complained of "the petty grinding tyranny of a good English family," refused to marry, and helped found the modern profession of nursing (see the Biography in Chapter 19). A few occupations outside the home were gradually opened to middle-class women, and some women entered universities and professions. Growing numbers of "new women" lived in women's clubs or apartments, dressed more practically, and did more "daring" things such as traveling alone and entering the public space as activists.

POOR HOUSING

Workers could not afford to draw such sharp lines between public and private life. Their homes rarely fulfilled all their needs. Often they relocated from one residence to another, carrying what they could. In some cases, they moved so as to search for something slightly better; in others, they sought to avoid a landlord demanding back rent.

The loss of a job might well doom a family to homelessness. With little hope of saving enough to pay for decent housing, workers tended to spend their extra money on clothes to "cut a good figure" and thereby present a well-groomed image in their public lives. For them, the city streets held far more promise than the buildings in which they lived. While the bourgeoisie retreated into homes or private clubs, workers used the public buildings, streets, and spaces of the city for their social and even private lives.

Working-class women enjoyed neither the space, furnishings, nor servants that graced the typical middle-class home. They usually worked at a factory or did poorly paid piecework at home, where they could care for their children. If their chil- *Working-class women* dren seemed more unruly and independent than those of the middle classes, moralists condemned these mothers for failing to create a "proper" home life. Such critics ignored the fact that working-class women lacked the money needed to cultivate the "ideal" family life. Worse, this disapproval helped employers justify paying these women less than men and treating them poorly.

INTIMACY AND MORALITY

Private life for working-class families was burdened by tensions involving basic survival. Middle-class families experienced tensions, too, but of a different sort. Founded on love, companionship, and intimacy, the middle-class family could become a pressure cooker of conflicting feelings and desires, of guilt and shame, of misunderstood communication and resentment. Family members often fought over money, but the confining expectations of intimacy could be worse. "Do not admit anyone else into our private life, into our thoughts," counseled a French man to his prospective wife in 1873. People understood such warnings. The home was a center of secrecy. More often than not, at the heart of that secrecy was sex.

For Britain's middle classes in particular, this era witnessed the height of Victorian sexual morality. Sex was supposed to be little discussed and limited to the Victorian morality marriage bed, enclosed in a separate "master" bedroom with locked doors. Sexual problems "shouldn't arise," but if they did, "enlightened" sufferers might turn to their doctor—the expert on sex, hygiene, and morality all rolled into one. Mixing moralisms with an image of scientific authority, most doctors confirmed the standard views of other commentators: healthy and prudent sexuality could take place only within the marriage. Affairs risked scandal (especially for the woman) and illegitimacy. Sex with prostitutes was unhygienic and somehow dangerous to the race. Doctors vaguely connected prostitution, syphilis, tuberculosis, and alcoholism as physical and social "scourges," all resulting from "venereal excesses." Most often, they blamed women for being prostitutes, for forcing their husbands to visit prostitutes, or for having inappropriate sexual appetites.

Masturbation also caught the attention of doctors, priests, and parents. Physicians warned men that masturbation would drain their strength. They condemned masturbation by females even more strongly. To prevent youths from "abusing themselves," they prescribed orthopedic devices, special bandages, and belts.

As for homosexuality, people viewed it in an even worse light. Doctors labeled it a sickness or psychological disorder. Newspapers added to the public condemnation of homosexuality by reporting "scandalous" affairs among public figures and "uncovering" homosexual subcultures. The trial and imprisonment for gross indecency of the famed British author Oscar Wilde (1854–1900) in 1895 promoted a new awareness of homosexuality while revealing how far officials and the public would go to denounce it.

SEXUAL REALITIES

Despite these idealized, restrictive notions about proper sexual conduct, reality was quite different. Somehow people, especially the middle classes, discussed sex enough to limit births. While many used the old methods—abstinence and withdrawal—new information and methods also became available. Men began using condoms, and women douched or used diaphragms and sponges soaked in disinfectants. Many resorted to abortion as a method of birth control, particularly in cases of illegitimacy.

Birth control

These methods seem to have worked. The birthrate declined in these years. In France, for example, it dropped from thirty-three per thousand in 1800 to nineteen per thousand in 1910. Many people chose to limit births for economic reasons. As people moved from farms to the cities, they no longer needed so many children to help with the work. In the cities, the increasing costs of raising children deterred couples from having large families. Yet successful birth control among the middle classes caused concern, for many worried that the "best" of society were not reproducing themselves as quickly as the "poor" and "uncompetitive." Commentators argued that "good" families needed more children. Nationalists complained that competing states or "alien peoples" would overwhelm their nation or "race" if "the fittest" did not increase their fertility.

Certainly actual sexual behavior failed to live up to the standards of Victorian moralists. The "best" people had "affairs," and illegitimacy remained high. Deadly sexually transmitted diseases rose and spread widely among all classes. In addition, prostitution thrived in many urban areas. Tens of thousands of prostitutes in the largest cities displayed themselves on streets and in city parks, and in windows and doorways. Some worked in bars or elegant brothels for a more select clientele. Working-class women who lost jobs, domestic servants dismissed because of pregnancy, or young women on their own might turn to prostitution to survive. Men of all classes patronized prostitutes. Governments tried to control prostitution, requiring medical exams of prostitutes and limiting its practice to certain districts. Worse than these inconveniences were the risks of this life. Prostitutes were often subjected to violence, the most famous example of which was the serial killings committed by "Jack the Ripper" in London in the late 1880s.

By the end of the century, new attitudes or perhaps the weight of reality broke down some of the more restrictive notions of Victorian sexual propriety. More

New attitudes people accepted and expected mutual sexual enjoyment within marriage, and people became educated about the physical facts of sexual contact. Books, pamphlets, and talks about sex enabled women and men to read about the subject and sometimes even discuss it openly. Doctors, psychologists, and intellectuals began to study sex and see that it played a major role in individuals' sense of identity.

PSYCHIC STRESS AND ALCOHOLISM

Growing concern with sex and private life in this period reflected a broader preoccupation with psychological well-being. Anxieties and emotional disorders seemed all too common. Women especially suffered from fits, paralysis, convulsions, numbing, headaches, oversensitivity to light, digestive disorders, and fatigue. Doctors listened, prescribed pills, and suggested expensive cures such as surgery and health-spa retreats. They sometimes blamed the complexities of city life or the noise and speed of modern life for these disturbing health problems. Other commentators suggested different causes. Within the confines of middle-class life, perhaps people worried too much about being judged by others. Or maybe the rapid changes of the era led to insecurity. Whatever the causes, the evidence for psychic stress was growing in diaries, the rise of psychoanalysis, the new descriptions of proliferating "mental illnesses," the spread of psychiatric clinics, and the mounting number of chronic patients in insane asylums.

Was widespread alcoholism a sign of psychic stress? Figure 21.10, an 1876 painting by Edgar Degas (1834–1917) of a woman drinking absinthe (a strong alcoholic beverage) in a Parisian cafe, seems to indicate a link between drinking and stress. Although a man sits nearby, the woman's face suggests that she is alone and gloomy. In this evocative image, lines separating social drinking, addiction, and psychic stress blur. Drinkers now seemed more depressed than jovial, and drunkenness appeared to be everywhere—in the streets, at work, in bars, and, increasingly, behind closed doors. New temperance movements attacked the "scourge" of alcohol, and with legitimate reason. In France, the average person consumed more than 60 gallons of wine a year, not including the

FIGURE 21.10
Edgar Degas, *Absinthe*, 1876–1877.

brandy, beer, and the more addictive absinthe shown in this painting. Even drugs such as opium, morphine, heroine, cocaine, and hashish gained footholds, especially among artists. Fear of drug-induced suicides led France to ban such drugs in 1908.

By no coincidence, the practice of psychoanalysis emerged during this period (see pp. 712–713). Various other movements also focused on psychic stress. One of the most well-known and popular of these was Christian Science, founded in America by Mary Baker Eddy (1821–1910). Having suffered interminable ailments and nervous disorders as a youth, Eddy turned to a spiritual approach to healing in her adult years. As she explained in her best-selling book *Science and Health* (1875), "mind healing" could dispel sickness and pain. Whatever the causes and supposed cures, stress and emotional pain seemed too widespread to ignore, and many observers connected them to the pressures of modern life.

Science in an Age of Optimism

Despite these concerns about the pressures of modern life, most observers embraced the new age enthusiastically. "I see no limit to the extent to which intelligence and will, guided by sound principles of investigation, and organized in common effort, may modify the conditions of existence, for a period longer than that now covered by history," announced British biologist T. H. Huxley (1825–1895) in 1893. "And much may be done to change the nature of man himself," he added.

The eighteenth-century optimism about science spread during the second half of the nineteenth century. Many people—especially members of the rising middle classes—felt certain that their generation would find solutions to the problems that had plagued human beings from the beginning. Scientists confirmed this optimism by making discoveries that answered fundamental questions and that could be translated into practical products such as industrial goods and medicines. Intellectuals proffered new ways to explain the world and human beings' place in it. Writers and artists found answers to similar questions by looking hard at the lives of people in their changing world. These scientists, intellectuals, and artists thrived in big cities such as London, Paris, Berlin, Milan, and Vienna. In these cultural hubs, some taught in universities or conducted experiments in laboratories. Others might debate in learned societies, do research in libraries, or paint in studios. Still others chatted in cafés or simply wrote in back rooms. Their work generated provocative ideas and added to the sense that life could be understood more fully than ever before.

SCIENCE, EVOLUTION, AND RELIGION

The best news came from science. After 1850, word of scientific advances spread from elite circles to the broader public. Stunning discoveries emerged and directly affected people's lives. However, certain conclusions that appealed to some provoked outrage in others.

No one became a greater hero, or villain, than Charles Darwin (1809–1882). Born into a distinguished British family, Darwin studied medicine and theology. Yet these disciplines failed to challenge him. Instead, the world of plants and animals became his consuming passion. His answer to a single question—how have all living species come to be as they are today?—caused an intense controversy that still continues in some circles.

Darwin

In 1831, Darwin, despite frail health, began a voyage around the world as ship's naturalist on the *Beagle*. He observed and collected fossils and specimens in different environments. He made his most impor-

tant finds in South America and the Galápagos Islands off the coast of that continent. Gradually he developed his theory of evolution, which, for him, answered his question. In *On the Origin of Species by Natural Selection* (1859), he described the slow evolution of present plant and animal species from earlier, simpler forms through a process of natural selection. Survival, he explained, came from struggle. In the competition for survival, those that possessed the most useful characteristics in a given environment—for example, the horse with the longer legs—survived to produce the most offspring. Through this process, they transmitted their successful qualities to future generations.

These ideas were not completely new. By the mid-nineteenth century, many intellectuals had accepted the concept of a slow and gradual development of the earth's crust and its inhabitants. Liberalism included ideas about the competitive struggle among human beings for food and survival, something that Thomas Malthus had written about at the beginning of the century (see Chapter 17). In addition, Enlightenment thinkers had already popularized the notion of "progress." Many in the mid-nineteenth century already embraced the sense that the present had evolved in progressive stages from a lower past. But no one had ever before supplied an all-encompassing explanation, supported by convincing evidence, for the origin of plants and animals.

What about human beings? Most people believed that humans remained species apart from all others. At first Darwin avoided the delicate question. In his 1871 work *The Descent of Man*, he finally took the bold step, arguing that humans evolved from more primitive species by the same process as plants and animals. "Man still bears in his bodily frame the indelible stamp of his lowly origin," he proclaimed. No longer could people "believe that man is the work of a separate act of creation." Figure 21.11 , one of many satirical cartoons on this topic, ridicules Darwin's idea that humans descended from other species by showing Darwin holding up a mirror to his close relative—a monkey—and depicting Darwin with the body of a monkey.

Though many people already believed in evolution, Darwin's claims became front-page news. Few ideas have provoked such widespread controversy. To some people, his ideas made sense. Much of the scientific world, for example, quickly accepted Darwin's theory of evolution.

Controversy

found confirmation for their views that women were inferior to men and destined to play a dependent domestic role in the male-dominated family.

Philosophers also expanded Darwin's thesis and applied it to all human behavior. British philosopher Herbert Spencer (1820–1903) built a whole system of influential *Social Darwinists* ideas around the concept of evolution; he and other "Social Darwinists" extended Darwin's theory far beyond its scientific foundations by making it the key to truth and progress. Spencer even saw the notion of survival of the fittest as justification for the harsh competitiveness of human society: "Under the natural order of things society is constantly excreting its unhealthy, imbecile, slow, vacillating, faithless members," he explained. Helping such people "encourages the multiplication of the reckless and incompetent . . . and discourages the multiplication of the competent and provident. . . ." Other Social Darwinists, such as British criminologist Francis Galton (1822–1911), suggested that the human race could be improved through selective breeding, or eugenics.

Darwin's ideas threatened many people wedded to traditional Christian beliefs. He tried to reassure his alarmed readers: "I see no good reason why the views given in this volume should *Darwinism and religion* shock the religious feelings of anyone." Though many Christians accepted some of Darwin's ideas, his views offended numerous others. Specifically, the notion of a long and mechanistic evolution of all present species, including human beings, from simpler forms seemed to contradict the account of divine creation given in the Bible: "If the Darwinian theory is true," complained one theologian, "Genesis is a lie, the whole framework of the book of life falls to pieces, and the revelation of God to man, as we Christians know it, is a delusion and a snare." Evolution, Darwin's critics cried, left God out of the world and diminished the uniqueness of human beings in it.

Some of Darwin's opponents suppressed his books and the teaching of evolution in schools. The Catholic Church angrily rejected Darwin's theory along with many other ideas of the time. In 1864, Pope Pius IX (1846–1878) issued a *Syllabus of Errors* attacking the idea of evolution and secular education. He also railed against religious toleration, free speech, and much else: it is "an error to believe that the Roman Pontiff can and ought to reconcile himself to, and agree with, progress, liberalism, and modern civi-

FIGURE 21.11
The controversy over Darwin's theories.

Dominant social groups everywhere also derived comfort from it. The rising bourgeoisie, for instance, seized upon evolution as a way to explain and justify its own success. Scientists, including Darwin, also lization." In 1870 the First Vatican Council bolstered the pope's authority by declaring that, under certain circumstances, the pope's statements on issues of morality and faith should be considered divinely sanctioned truths.

Darwin's allies rushed to his defense. Thomas Huxley, a biologist, surgeon in the British navy, and president of a leading scientific society, popularized Darwin's work in dozens of vigorous and lucid books and pamphlets. Heaping withering scorn on opponents, Huxley called himself "Darwin's bull-dog." Alfred Russel Wallace (1823–1913), a Scottish naturalist, claimed that Darwin "is the Newton of natural history" who "established a firm foundation for all future study of nature."

Over time, many of Darwin's critics moderated their hostility to Darwin's findings. Toward the end of the century the Catholic Church, under Pope Leo XIII (1878–1903), even began taking the position that natural science was not the province of the church, that evolution could be taught as a hypothesis, and that parts of the Bible should be taken figuratively.

MYSTERIES OF THE MATERIAL AND HUMAN WORLD

Research multiplied in many fields besides natural science. Scientists focused especially on the nature of matter. Discovery after discovery in chemistry and physics led them to conclude that all matter was composed of atoms, that each atom **Physics and chemistry** was in turn made up of smaller particles that moved in circles like a miniature solar system, and that each chemical element of matter had a specific atomic weight. In 1870, the Russian chemist Dmitri Mendeleev (1834–1907) compiled a new chart showing the atomic weight of all the known elements and indicating by gaps the other elements that remained to be discovered. Chemists and physicists proved him right. Year after year, researchers discovered new elements that fit into the "Periodic Table." In the 1870s, James Clerk Maxwell (1831–1879) analyzed the relationship between gravity, light, magnetism, and electricity. His ideas led to a greater sense of physical unity in the universe and practical developments such as the development of the electronics industry.

The successes of Darwin and of chemists, physicists, and others in the natural sciences encouraged scholars to apply the same scientific techniques and principles to psychology, or the study of human behavior. One of the first to bring this discipline into the laboratory was Wilhelm **Psychology** Wundt (1832–1920). In his laboratory at Leipzig, Wundt and his enthusiastic students tested human reactions and carried out carefully controlled and measured experiments on cats and dogs, assuming that the findings would also apply to human beings.

The Russian scientist Ivan Pavlov (1849–1936), pursuing Wundt's line of inquiry, discovered the conditioned reflex. Pavlov showed meat to a hungry dog until the dog's mouth watered. Then Pavlov rang a bell while showing the meat. Eventually, the dog's mouth would water when only the bell was rung. The implication was that many of our human responses are purely mechanical reflexes prompted by stimuli of which we are often unaware.

The field of sociology also acquired status as a social science. Auguste Comte (1798–1857) named the new discipline. He argued that humankind was entering a stage of history in which truths would be discovered by the scientific gathering of factual data. Humans and society, he said, are **Sociology** as susceptible to scientific investigation as minerals, plants, and the lower animals are. He believed that his philosophy, which he called positivism, would reveal the laws of human relations and allow social scientists to engineer harmonious societies. Comte's followers, eager and numerous during the second half of the nineteenth century, placed great faith in statistics and amassed copious statistical data on numerous social problems. Like Comte, most of them believed that sure social knowledge would enable people to remake society for the better.

Historians such as the German Leopold von Ranke (1795–1886) strove to turn history into a social science. Ranke rejected history based on tradition or legend. He also attacked the notion that history could come in the form of a purposeful story **History** about the progress of humanity, the working out of God's will, or other such themes. He argued that historical accounts should be based on an exhaustive accumulation and analysis of documentary evidence. Conclusions could be drawn only from facts, he insisted. In this way, Ranke believed, history would become coldly scientific and morally neutral. His attitude and methodology spread widely, particularly in Germany and the United States.

These scholars believed that individual and social behavior could best be studied by careful, objective observation, experimentation, and analysis. Like scientists, they considered themselves professionals with specialties rather than amateurs. They also formed societies and published their findings in their own journals. Part of what drove them was their faith that these findings would point the way to improving the quality of human life, and they conveyed that faith to a wider public. In this sense, these scholars and scientists shared and promoted the optimism of the period.

GERMS, CURES, AND HEALTHCARE

No field of science promised more new understanding and dramatic applications than medicine. At mid-century, medicine entered a golden age. The most important discovery came not *Pasteur and germ theory* from a doctor, but from a chemist. Louis Pasteur (1822–1895), the son of a French tanner, became interested in what happened to wine and beer during the fermentation process. In the 1860s, he discovered the airborne microorganisms responsible for fermentation and showed that bacteria caused milk to sour. He demonstrated that heating milk—"pasteurizing" it—destroyed the bacteria that caused diseases. His long years of work eventually enabled him to identify disease-producing organisms in humans and create vaccines to prevent diseases such as rabies. Here, finally, was the explanation for how people caught infectious diseases: germ theory.

Many doctors and scientists, still wedded to old ideas and practices, dismissed Pasteur's findings. The German scientist, Robert Koch (1843–1910) confirmed the French chemist's conclusions, convincing doctors that bacteria indeed caused diseases. In the early 1880s, Koch discovered the bacteria responsible for two of the most deadly diseases of the time: tuberculosis and cholera. His students used the same research methods to find microbes that caused a list of other diseases from pneumonia and meningitis to syphilis.

Modern doctors of the late nineteenth century now understood that specific microorganisms ("germs") caused specific infectious diseases. In addition to this realization, new tools increased physicians' stature as scientists and improved their ability to diagnose ailments. The thermometer, for example, allowed them to measure body temperature, and the stethoscope let them hear what was going on inside the body. The microscope permitted examination of tissue samples, the X-ray (1896) revealed the body's internal structures, and the electrocardiograph (1901) recorded the workings of the heart.

The most advanced doctors realized that, while they may know more about illnesses and the inner workings of the body, they still could do little to cure diseases. Aspirin (1899) reduced *Remedies* fever, inflammation, and minor pain; morphine controlled more serious pain; and barbiturates might induce sleep—but none of these constituted a medical cure. The first great exception was an antitoxin against diphtheria developed in Robert Koch's Berlin laboratory in 1891. For most diseases, however, cures lay in the future. The best that doctors could do was to stop prescribing poisonous pills and dangerous procedures such as bloodletting and purges.

Within medicine, the field of surgery saw especially remarkable progress. During the 1860s and 1870s, the British surgeon Joseph Lister (1827–1912) developed procedures that included the use of antiseptics during operations. These procedures dramatically lowered the risk of infection *Surgery* from the operation itself. Over the following decades, surgeons applied Lister's methods with great success. No longer did they operate in dirty, blood-splattered back rooms, wearing black coats or street clothes. Increasingly, they washed their hands and worked in relatively sterile environments, and wore white surgical gowns, face masks, and rubber gloves to lessen the risks of infection.

In Figure 21.12, an 1890 painting of an operating room in a Vienna hospital, a patient is being prepared for surgery. The doctors wear white coats rather than street clothes, and the patient is being anesthetized. However, old practices died slowly. Even though Joseph Lister had developed antiseptic procedures more than twenty years earlier, the surgeon and his assistants do not yet wear masks or gloves, and the surgical instruments have not been sterilized. Everyone in the scene is male; most medical schools still denied access to women. The picture also lacks religious symbols. All in all, it conveys a sense of solid confidence in modern science.

Medical advances also made a huge difference in the field of nursing. In hospitals, emergencies, and war, nurses often had the most direct contact with sufferers and the wounded. During the Crimean War

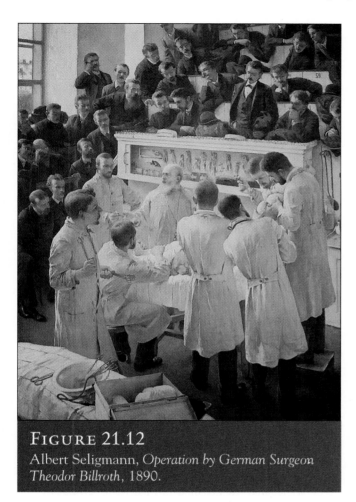

FIGURE 21.12
Albert Seligmann, *Operation by German Surgeon Theodor Billroth*, 1890.

(1853–1856), Florence Nightingale transformed nursing into a modern profession (see Chapter 19). Her reforms stressed cleanliness, fresh air, and disci-

Nursing pline, and helped make nursing an attractive path to independence and service. A few years later, the philanthropist Dorothea Dix (1802–1887) led similar reform efforts in the United States during the Civil War, and in Switzerland a banker established the International Red Cross, creating new demand for professional nurses.

By the turn of the century, much in medicine had gained the authority of science and was "professionalized." Better nursing gave the wounded a fighting chance at survival. Doctors who understood diseases and surgeons who performed operations safely now helped more than hurt their patients. Even so, many doctors insisted on practicing traditional medicine, and most remained too expensive for working-class families to afford except when they were in dire need. Many working-class women were forced to prescribe their own curative regime or find some inexpensive "cure."

Culture: Accepting the Modern World

Faith in science and technology reflected a growing sense that people could observe the facts of everyday life carefully, understand them, and use that understanding to control the world more successfully than ever before. Writers and artists also closely observed contemporary life in their books and paintings. During the second half of the nineteenth century, their focus included the methods of science and the realities of urban life. The romanticism of early-nineteenth-century culture—which had idealized love, religion, and the exotic—gave way to a gritty sense of realism (see Chapter 18). Realists felt free to look modern life full in the face and both praise its successes and criticize its failings.

REALISM AND NATURALISM: THE DETAILS OF SOCIAL LIFE

The age witnessed the rise of realistic and naturalistic literature, which explored the social dislocation brought about by the industrial revolution, commercial values, and city life. Eugène de **Literature** Vogüé (1848–1910), a nineteenth-century French writer, explained that a realist "observes life as it is in its wholeness and complexity with the least possible prejudice on the part of the artist. It takes men under ordinary conditions, shows characters in the course of their everyday existence." Authors, often focusing on the unpleasant, sordid side of human nature and society, examined how environment and heredity together shaped people's lives. With scientific thoroughness, these writers examined people's public and private lives, their individual and social failings, and the hypocrisy of their religious and moral values.

The French novelist Gustav Flaubert (1821–1880), for example, deftly captured the full flavor of realism. His *Madame Bovary* (1857) related the illicit sex life of the wife of a small-town French physician in such full and unblushing detail that it scandalized a public not yet accustomed to such unrestrained revelations. *Madame Bovary* became a model for other novelists. Few writers, however, were as popular as Charles Dickens (1812–1870). As we saw in Chapter 17, Dickens' novels presented realistic descriptions of the middle and lower classes in Britain's urban, industrial society. For example, in *The Old Curiosity Shop*, he refused to shy away from the realities of nighttime in impoverished sections of cities, "when bands of unemployed labourers paraded in the roads . . . when carts came rumbling by, filled with rude coffins . . . or when orphans cried, and distracted women shrieked and followed in their wake, . . . when some called for bread, and some for drink to drown their cares. . . ."

Mary Ann Evans (1819–1880), writing under the pen name George Eliot, also wrote popular novels examining the realities of British social life. In *Middlemarch*, for instance, she linked psychological conflict to the determining social realities surrounding her characters. The Norwegian playwright Henrik Ibsen (1828–1906) presented another perspective on such realities. Ibsen ridiculed bourgeois society in his popular dramas. In *A Doll's House*, probably his best-known play, the heroine Nora rebels against her expected role in the "doll's house" that her stodgy, hypocritical, middle-class husband Helmer has created for her:

Nora: What do you consider my holiest duties?
Helmer: Need I tell you that? Your duties to your husband and children.
Nora: I have other duties equally sacred.
Helmer: Impossible! What do you mean!
Nora: My duties toward myself.
Helmer: Before all else you are a wife and a mother.
Nora: That I no longer believe. Before all else I believe I am a human being just as much as you are.

The French writer Émile Zola (1840–1902) explained that the naturalist novel, having evolved from the realistic novel, "substitutes for the study of the abstract man . . . the study of the natural man, governed by physical and chemical laws, and modified by the influences of his surroundings; it is in one word the literature of our scientific age. . . ." He wrote in almost clinical detail about the social problems spawned by industrialism. In one series of novels, he portrayed several generations of a working-class family battered by the forces of heredity and the environment. They struggle to survive, fighting poverty, strikes, alcoholism, and conflict among themselves.

Russia produced some especially talented writers who created stunning realistic literature. An example is Leo Tolstoy (1828–1910) and his masterpiece *War and Peace* (1865–1869). This sweeping novel about Russia during the Napoleonic Wars features scores of characters who battle impersonal social forces and the overwhelming details of everyday life. Even the strongest individuals in the story become ensnared in forces beyond their control. In other writings that reflected the social realities of his own times, Tolstoy attacked capitalism and materialism: "Money is a new form of slavery, and distinguishable from the old simply by the fact that it is impersonal. . . ."

Fyodor Dostoyevski (1821–1881), another legendary Russian author, focused more on psychological and moral realities in his novels. His characters—such as the anguished student Raskolnikov in *Crime and Punishment* (1866) who murders an old woman—struggle with moral conflicts in an age marked by spiritual bankruptcy. Like other realistic writers, Dostoyevski shone a spotlight on the harshness of modern life, particularly its power to overwhelm individuals.

Innovative painters also turned to realistic depictions of life on their canvases. The French artist Gustave Courbet (1819–1877), who believed that an artist should "never permit sentiment to overthrow logic," led the attack on romantic art by painting sober scenes of urban life and rural labor. In *The Stone Breakers* (Figure 21.13), he portrays rural laborers as a passerby might see them. Courbet claimed he "saw these people every day on my walk." Here an old worker—with patches on his pants and holes in his socks—breaks up stones, probably for use in building a road. His young assistant, who is "suffering from scurvy" according to Courbet, carries the stones away in a basket. The two men's tattered clothing and averted faces make them seem anonymous and therefore representative of many other workers. While there is dignity in their work, Courbet does not glorify either the stonebreakers or nature. The scene, like the men's lives, is harsh. The image suggests that the young assistant is likely to end up the same as his old companion. Courbet and other realistic artists depicted everyday life on large canvases, and thereby earned the wrath of those artists and

Art

FIGURE 21.13
Gustave Courbet, *The Stone Breakers*, 1849.

critics who believed that only paintings of historical, mythological, religious, or exotic scenes should be considered "great art."

IMPRESSIONISM: CELEBRATING MODERN LIFE

Like the realists and naturalists, impressionist painters embraced modern life—but in a different way. Specifically, they applied a new understanding of color, light, and optics to their work. Their paintings—with their informal quality and emphasis on angles—suggested randomness of reality. Such artists ventured outside their studios to paint scenes. They especially sought to convey the impression of a view that the eye actually sees at first glance—the "impression" created by light reflected off a surface at a single moment—rather than what the knowing brain interprets from visual cues. The French artist Claude Monet (1840–1926) (see Biography) described the way he painted: "Try to forget what objects you have before you—a tree, a house, a field, or whatever. Merely think, here is a little square of blue, here an oblong of pink, here a streak of yellow, and paint it just as it looks to you . . . until it gives your own naive impression of the scene before you."

Monet's *The Pool at Argenteuil* (Figure 21.14) is an example of many paintings of the suburban countryside—the places to which the urban bourgeoisie might travel on Sundays or vacations. In this scene near his home just outside of Paris, middle-class women carrying parasols stroll down a wide, tree-lined path bordering the Seine or wander over to a dock on the right where boats might be rented. Sailboats on the river suggest pleasure, a bridge in the distance implies that the city is not far away. The bourgeoisie purchasers of Monet's paintings would recognize this sort of place, where civilization and countryside meet under a broad sky.

Impressionists also painted psychologically subtle portraits, bedroom and dance-hall interiors, urban parks, and city streets. *Boulevard des Capucines* (Figure 21.15), also by Monet, shows one of the straight, wide, tree-lined, fashionable boulevards constructed in Paris during the Second Empire under Napoleon III. Monet painted this winter scene while looking out the window of the studios where the first impressionist exhibition would be held in 1874 and where this painting would be shown. Only a few brush strokes suggest people, carriages, and building details—the impression that one might get glancing out an upper-floor window at an anonymous but vibrant urban scene below.

From Optimism to Uncertainty

The impressionists' delight in the beauty and charm of modern life fit well with the continuing belief in reason, individual rights, and progress that marked the decades after 1850. Economic growth, improving conditions in the cities, and new conquests by science buoyed a broad sense of moderate optimism about the world. However, from the 1880s on, signs of a disturbing new undercurrent rose to the surface of Western culture. Some of the West's best intellectuals, writers, and artists injected themes of pessimism and painful introspection into their work. They emphasized how strongly irrational forces guided human behavior. Though still a minority, these thinkers and critics undermined rather than overwhelmed the prevailing certainty and optimism of the period. They added to the growing social and political tensions of the turn-of-the-century decades described in Chapter 20.

FIGURE 21.14
Claude Monet, *The Pool at Argenteuil*, 1872.

EVERYTHING IS RELATIVE

In part, this disillusionment stemmed from the growing feeling of uncertainty creeping into elite scientific circles—the sense that the more people learned, the less solid and reliable the material world became. The work of Albert Einstein (1879–1955) exposed this uncertainty in physics. A German who later fled to America, Einstein assailed time-honored concepts about the stability of matter and the nature of the physical universe. In 1905, while still earning a living as a patent clerk in Switzerland, he proposed what would become the seminal theory of relativity. According to this theory, time, space, and motion were relative to one another as well as to the observer—they were not the absolutes scientists had believed in for so long.

Building on the work of the German physicist Max Planck (1858–1947), who had shown that heated bodies emit energy in irregular packets ("quanta") rather than a steady stream, Einstein also derived a groundbreaking formula, $E = mc^2$ (E = energy; m = mass; c = speed of light). This formula blurred the distinction between mass and energy and described the immense energy contained within each atom. The atomic energy in a lump of coal, for example, was revealed to be some three billion times as great as the energy obtained by burning the coal. This unsettling notion later contributed to the development of the atomic bomb. By showing that matter could be transformed into energy,

Einstein

CLAUDE MONET (1840–1926)

As a boy growing up in Le Havre on France's north coast, Oscar Claude Monet was rebellious and daring. "My youth was essentially that of a vagabond," he wrote. "Never would I bend to a rule."

That pattern of assertive rebellion would stay with him. In 1857, the sixteen-year-old Claude announced to his father, a prosperous merchant, that he was going to Paris to become a painter. His father refused to help him financially, but Claude left home anyway. In Paris he rejected academic art training, instead working with other young artists such as Pissarro and Renoir, with whom he would remain connected for many years.

In 1864, he met the eighteen-year-old Camille Doncieux, and the two moved in together. That year, Claude had his first paintings accepted at the official Salon, where prominent artists entered their paintings to be judged and—if accepted—offered for sale. Success at the Salon meant the possibility of earning a living as an artist. Despite this triumph, financial problems plagued the young Monet. He often had to hide in Paris or flee to the suburbs to escape from creditors. He perpetually wrote letters begging his family, friends, and other artists for money.

In the following years, Monet enjoyed some successes, but was disappointed whenever his paintings were turned down by the Salon. Depression often haunted him: "I am like a man going down the third time. . . . I see everything black. . . . Money is always lacking. Disappointments, insults, hopes, new disappointments." But in good times, he lived the bourgeois life and experienced private joys. In 1868 he wrote: "I am surrounded here by all that I love. I pass my time outdoors on the flint beach when the seas are heavy or when the boats go off to fish, or I even go into the country, which is so beautiful here. . . . I find in my tiny house a good fire and a good little family." Though he had a one-year-old son, Jean, with Camille, it took the prospect of money from an inheritance by Camille, guaranteed by a contract, before he finally married her in 1870.

In 1872 the Monets moved to Argenteuil, twenty minutes from Paris by train. Camille played the role of a middle-class housewife, rising early to serve breakfast to her husband and son, shopping, buying bread just before lunch, cleaning the house, preparing dinner, and reading the newspapers daily. Their son Jean, dressed in long skirts as was the style of the time and riding his tricycle with a stuffed horse mounted on its front end, appeared on several of Monet's canvases, as did Camille. Every day, Monet painted by the shore of the river, sometimes accompanied by other visiting impressionists.

By 1874 Monet had turned his back on the official Salon. That year he and other artists formed a group and mounted their own exposition. Monet was at the head of the group, which included Renoir and Pissarro. Critics attacked the paintings at the exposition, particularly one by Monet entitled *Impression: Rising Sun*, for rejecting accepted standards of good art. Yet the group continued to paint and show together, earning a reputation for being rebellious artists and "bohemians" with inappropriate lifestyles.

Impressionist Painter

In 1878, the ailing Camille gave birth to a second son. A year later she died. Soon Monet became involved with another woman, Alice Hoschede, already married to a successful merchant and the mother of several children. The couple soon moved in together.

Monet was happy living with Alice, and his paintings began to sell well. He stopped showing his paintings with the other impressionist painters and moved to Giverny, northwest of Paris. There he created a large garden and pond, which he would paint for the rest of his life.

Monet gained a public reputation for being both brilliant and unyielding. When the government tried to award him the Legion of Honor, he refused. By 1890 he was recognized as France's premier painter, far more popular than any of his colleagues. His paintings commanded high prices. Now sporting a long, white beard, he became a revered figure. Despite his failing eyesight, he painted almost up until his death in 1926.

Monet made the bourgeoisie both the subject and the assumed audience of his paintings. Many of his landscapes featured the suburban fields, gardens, walks, and riverbanks that the bourgeoisie loved to visit (see Figure 21.14). Even his landscapes of southern France or the north coast were presented from the point of view of a tourist. Monet always emphasized the "modern" in his work. There was no horror in his depictions of the city, only a celebration of its boulevards, railway stations, and parks.

❧ **Consider** how Monet's life, his paintings, and his popularity reflected European society during the second half of the nineteenth century.

FIGURE 21.15
Claude Monet, *Boulevard des Capucines*, 1873.

Einstein again challenged Newtonian physics. More conservative scientists, wedded to time-honored Newtonian physics, dismissed his theories. Eventually, however, Einstein's views gained support, further undermining scientists' assumptions about the physical nature of the universe.

SEX, CONFLICT, AND THE UNCONSCIOUS

Ideas about the human mind—the internal, mental universe—also took a disturbing turn in these years. Sigmund Freud (1856–1939), the Viennese neurologist, concluded that nervous disorders stemmed from psychological causes, not physiological sources as most doctors had believed. Basing his ideas on the words, experiences, and dreams of troubled patients, he founded psychoanalysis, which he described as "the *Freud and psychoanalysis* scientific method by which the unconscious can be studied."

Freud argued that much of human behavior was irrational, unconscious, and instinctual. Conflict, he claimed, was a basic condition of life, particularly when it occurred between people's innate biological drives (such as sex or aggression) and their social selves. According to Freud, these conflicts developed on a mostly unconscious level, and in stages during childhood. At war within all people are what Freud called the *id,* the *superego,* and the *ego.* The id is the source of our basic desires, the most important and disturbing of these being sexual. The superego imposes socially acceptable standards of behavior on the individual. The ego tries to find ways to satisfy both the demands of the id and the restraints of the superego. Typically, the mind responds to this conflict by repressing the id's desires from consciousness. However, the unconscious psychic struggle continues, creating a mental life of great tension.

Freud added fuel to his already controversial ideas by emphasizing the importance of sexual conflicts originating in childhood. He argued that children inevitably come into conflict with their parents, competing with the same-sex parent for the love of the opposite-sex parent. At an unconscious level, he claimed, this competition for the parent of the opposite sex strongly shapes the development of an individual's personality.

Freud believed that much psychic pain and many emotional disorders stemmed from the suppressed and frustrated drives of early life—frustrations that then festered outside of people's awareness. He concluded that the correct therapy for such disorders was to make the sufferer conscious of the facts and circumstances of his or her original frustration. Hence, he encouraged patients to talk about their dreams, for by interpreting dreams the unconscious could be revealed.

Freud's controversial explanation of human behavior had several disturbing implications: neither adults nor children were innocent beings after all; too few people led happy lives; sex and aggression played powerful roles in children and adults alike; people cannot escape from internal conflict and frustration. Although he hoped that reason and understanding would ease humanity's psychological plight, Freud was far from an optimist. He eventually concluded that "the price of progress in civilization is paid in forfeiting happiness."

FEAR OF SOCIAL DISINTEGRATION

The French scholar Émile Durkheim (1858–1917), a founder of modern sociology, offered a different sort of warning about trends in modern society. Though a strong believer in science, Durkheim argued that industrial society—especially with its competitive individualism and lack of collective values—was weakening the ties that connected people with one another. As people became more concerned with their own freedom and advancement, he believed, the restraints and the spiritual beliefs that held traditional societies together would break down. This trend toward social disintegration, Durkheim warned, disoriented individuals, made them feel cut off from others, and left them without a sense of purpose. As a result, more and more people were experiencing despair, which in turn led to rising suicide rates. Like Freud, Durkheim believed that advancing civilization left psychic pain in its wake.

Durkheim

DISENCHANTMENT SETS IN

Perhaps the deepest sense of disenchantment with the optimistic, bourgeois, urban society of the nineteenth century emerged in philosophy. Friedrich Nietzsche (1844–1890), a brilliant German philosopher, is one example. Reason could not solve human problems, Nietzsche concluded. Instead, he believed in "will," which in his view enabled people to survive and the strongest among them to achieve power. Great leaders, he argued, rose through strength, intelligence, and above all, "the will to power." Nietzsche further claimed that if a superior society were to emerge, it would have to come about through the efforts of gifted individuals who would rise to positions of leadership because of their superior strength, will, and intelligence. Anything that contributes to power is good, he explained—be it strength of will, boldness, cunning, or intelligence. Likewise, whatever leads to weakness is bad—be it gentleness, modesty, generosity, or compassion.

Nietzsche

In Nietzsche's view, Christianity stood in the way of a better human society. "Christianity has taken the side of everything weak, base, ill-constituted; it has made an ideal out of opposition to the preservative instincts of strong life," he announced. "God is dead; we have killed him." For Nietzsche, the idea of the death of God was liberating: Now humans could cast off all conventions. Nietzsche also decried democracy for amounting to rule by the supposedly mediocre "masses . . . or the populace, or the herd, or whatever name you care to give them." He went on to attack many other accepted tenets of nineteenth-century civilization, such as liberalism, rationalism, and science. Although Nietzsche was not a nationalist or racist himself, others would later use his ideas to support militant nationalism and racism.

In France, the philosopher Henri Bergson (1859–1941) also questioned the limits of rational and scientific thinking. Gaining a large following by lecturing at the University of Paris, he argued that truth is best grasped through intuition and unconscious feelings rather than reason: "Science can teach us nothing of the truth; it can only serve as a rule of action." Society, Bergson said, needed the energy that only a spontaneous following of the "life force" could provide. His views, like those of Nietzsche and others, reflected a growing criticism of the dominant ideas of middle-class society in the West.

Bergson

ART TURNS INWARD

Many talented artists also turned away from the mainstream of nineteenth-century civilization. Their work grew more pessimistic and critical of middle-class life. The slogan "Art for art's sake" reflected the trend of various artistic movements such as expressionism and symbolism. They self-consciously attacked social and artistic taboos in ways that mystified much of the public. Their often introspective works proved understandable mainly to themselves and a small artistic elite. The Russian abstract expressionist painter Wassily Kandinsky (1866–1944) spoke for many of his fellow artists when he explained that his work was not intended to represent how things looked. "Look at the picture as a graphic representation of a mood and not as a representation of objects," he suggested.

Expressionism

Many artists focused on peripheral members of a society that seemed to be disintegrating, painting prostitutes, solitary drinkers, blind beggars, and circus performers. Moreover, threatening symbols of science, ma-

chinery, and speed began to crop up on canvases. Photography had already displaced traditional representation art. Now avant-garde painters created distorted, subjective, and abstract images.

We can see evidence of these trends in expressionist paintings such as those by the Belgian artist James Ensor (1860–1949). In *Intrigue* (Figure 21.16), Ensor shows people as indistinct from the obnoxious masks they wear. In their everyday world of pretense, they gather together and exchange false smiles. Behind their masks lurk isolation and anxiety.

Like Ensor, the Norwegian artist Edvard Munch (1863–1944) expressed a deep current of horror in middle-class life, but in a deeper, more personal way. In *The Scream* (Figure 21.17), a wide-eyed figure standing on a bridge lets out a terrified shriek. The land, water, and sky—all distorted and painted in alarming colors—echo the cry of the figure. Munch described the feelings that inspired the scene: "I was tired and ill—I stood looking out across the fjord—the sun was setting—the clouds were colored red—like blood—I felt as though a scream went through nature. . . ." In this painting, themes of death, anxiety, loneliness, and fear coalesce. Munch once exclaimed, "How much of my art I owe to suffering!" Many other artists painted

FIGURE 21.16
James Ensor, *Intrigue*, 1890.

FIGURE 21.17
Edvard Munch, *The Scream*, 1893.

similarly anguished scenes, emphasizing social anxieties, urban loneliness, violence, horror, and a turning inward toward the unconscious. Their paintings penetrated through surface-level appearances into a deeper, disturbing psychic reality.

In music, expressionism also challenged artistic conventions and public tastes. The Russian composer Igor Stravinsky (1882–1971) led this movement in his music for the ballet *The Rite of Spring*. The premiere **Music** of the ballet on May 29, 1913, in Paris has been called the most notorious event of the twentieth century. Upon hearing the music—with its offbeat rhythm and unrestrained, dissonant sounds—the audience rose in outrage. Fights broke out, and many listeners stormed from the theater after complaining loudly. Yet among certain elites, Stravinsky became the leading composer of the day.

Like science and philosophy, art and music was slipping away from the grasp of ordinary people. The new understandings of modern life that seemed so promising a few decades earlier now appeared shadowed by doubt and even foreboding.

Summary

By 1914, industrialization, urban growth, and the culture of progress had pulled much of the West into new territory. Life in large parts of Europe and North America had undergone a huge transformation. Someone who had lived during the late eighteenth century would have found virtually everything about the turn-of-the-century West strange or even shocking. Most of us, however, would readily recognize early-twentieth-century Paris, Berlin, or New York as modern. Those cities—like our cities today—were part of a widespread urban society and culture dominated by the middle classes and marching to the quickening pace of economic transformation. The variety of public and private life within those cities has persisted to the present day.

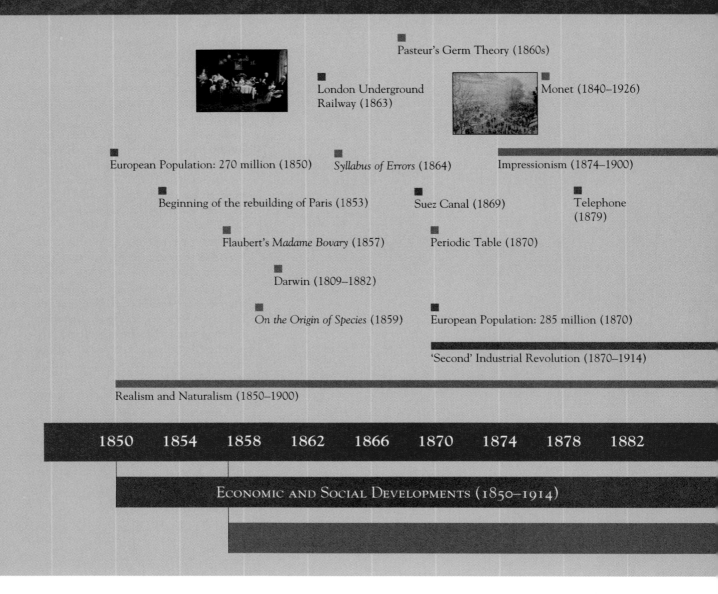

Pasteur's Germ Theory (1860s)

London Underground Railway (1863)

Monet (1840–1926)

European Population: 270 million (1850)

Syllabus of Errors (1864)

Impressionism (1874–1900)

Beginning of the rebuilding of Paris (1853)

Suez Canal (1869)

Telephone (1879)

Flaubert's *Madame Bovary* (1857)

Periodic Table (1870)

Darwin (1809–1882)

On the Origin of Species (1859)

European Population: 285 million (1870)

'Second' Industrial Revolution (1870–1914)

Realism and Naturalism (1850–1900)

| 1850 | 1854 | 1858 | 1862 | 1866 | 1870 | 1874 | 1878 | 1882 |

Economic and Social Developments (1850–1914)

People have called the years 1850–1914 the Age of Progress. The reasons are clear. Income for most people rose at least a little, and for some quite considerably, while the machines of industry pumped out endless new products that promised to ease the burdens of everyday life. Science promised even more and delivered findings that seemed to unlock the mysteries of both the physical and social world. Many of the cultural forms of the period gazed directly at the modern world and embraced it. In the 1920s, the French would look back to the two decades surrounding the turn of the century as "La Belle Époque"—the beautiful era.

Yet as we have seen, darker forces of change simmered below the optimistic surface during these same years. Just how much progress was achieved in politics is not so clear. Events in the summer of 1914 would expose that

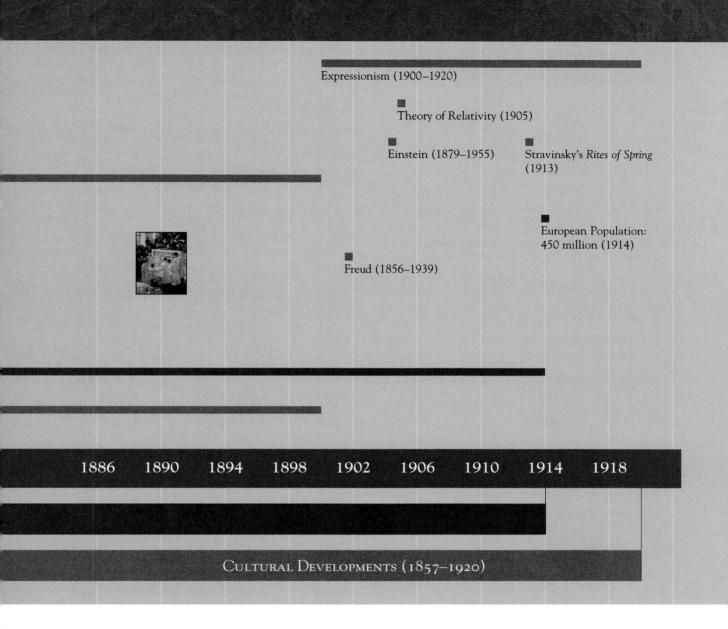

Expressionism (1900–1920)

Theory of Relativity (1905)

Einstein (1879–1955)

Stravinsky's *Rites of Spring* (1913)

European Population: 450 million (1914)

Freud (1856–1939)

| 1886 | 1890 | 1894 | 1898 | 1902 | 1906 | 1910 | 1914 | 1918 |

CULTURAL DEVELOPMENTS (1857–1920)

sense of dangerous uncertainty as all too well founded. Whether progress was made in the West's relations with the rest of the world is also in doubt. From outside the West, some questioned the very value of Western civilization. "In order to estimate the value of a civilization," explained a high Chinese official educated in European universities, "the question we must finally ask is not what great cities . . . it has built . . . what clever and useful implements . . . it has made . . . what institutions, what arts and sciences it has invested: the question . . . is what type of humanity, what kind of men and women it has been able to produce." These complex questions, too, would be immediately recognizable to us today. Modern times had arrived.

REVIEW, ANALYZE, AND ANTICIPATE

REVIEW THE PREVIOUS CHAPTER

In Chapter 20—"Mass Politics and Imperial Domination"—the spreading demands for democracy and the West's imperial expansion during the second half of the nineteenth century were traced.

1. *How did politics adjust to the new industrial and urban realities of this period?*
2. *In what ways did imperialism support and reflect both the nationalism and industrialism of this period?*

ANALYZE THIS CHAPTER

Chapter 21—"Modern Life and the Culture of Progress"—traces the changes stemming from new industrial transformations and urban growth, as well as the culture of the West.

1. *Considering the material in this chapter and Chapter 17 (which focused on the industrial revolution), why do you think industrialization so quickly doomed traditional society in the West?*
2. *Analyze the impact of spreading industrialization on the various social classes during this period.*
3. *How did people adjust to the opportunities and pressures of life in the West's modernizing cities?*
4. *Do you think the title "The Culture of Progress" is an apt description of Western culture during this period? Why or why not?*

ANTICIPATE THE NEXT CHAPTER

In Chapter 22—"Descending into the Twentieth Century"—the story of World War I and the Russian Revolution will be told.

1. *What political and social tensions developing during the years before 1914 might have made Europe ripe for war?*

BEYOND THE CLASSROOM

THE SECOND INDUSTRIAL REVOLUTION

Hobsbawm, Eric J. *The Age of Capital, 1848–1875.* New York: New American Library, 1979. Includes detailed sections on industrialism as well as its social consequences.

Ville, Simon P. *Transport and the Development of the European Economy, 1750–1918.* Houndmills, UK: Macmillan, 1990. A comparative study of the major forms of transportation from 1750 to 1918 and their relationship to economic development.

Williams, Rosalind H. *Dream Worlds: Mass Consumption in Late Nineteenth-Century France.* Berkeley, CA: University of California Press, 1982. An exploration of the mental evolution of consumer society in late-nineteenth- and early-twentieth-century France.

THE NEW URBAN LANDSCAPE

Olsen, Donald J. *The City as a Work of Art—London, Paris, Vienna.* New Haven, CT: Yale University Press, 1986. A well-illustrated examination of nineteenth-century urban growth and design.

Pinkney, David. *Napoleon III and the Rebuilding of Paris.* Princeton, NJ: Princeton University Press, 1972. A classic study of one of the most important urban renovations of the nineteenth century.

CITY PEOPLE

Cocks, Geoffrey, and Konrad H. Jarausch, eds. *German Professions, 1800–1950.* New York: Oxford University Press, 1990. Essays on the rise of professions in Germany such as law, medicine, social work, and architecture.

Joyce, P. *Visions of the People: Industrial England and the Question of Class, 1848–1914.* Cambridge: Cambridge University Press, 1991. An examination of working-class culture and language.

Pilbeam, Pamela. *The Middle Classes in Europe, 1789–1914.* Chicago: Lyceum Books, 1990. A thorough treatment of middle-class life in the major European nations.

PRIVATE LIFE: TOGETHER AND ALONE AT HOME

Gay, Peter. *The Bourgeois Experience: Victoria to Freud,* 2 volumes. New York: Oxford University Press, 1984–1986. An exhaustively researched series of volumes dealing with the varied experiences of middle-class life in America and Europe.

Perrot, Michelle, ed. *A History of Private Life, IV: From the Fires of Revolution to the Great War.* Cambridge, MA: Harvard University Press, 1990. Richly detailed and well-illustrated essays on the nineteenth century and its division between public and private life.

Peterson, M. Jeanne. *Family, Love, and Work in the Lives of Victorian Gentlewomen.* Bloomington, IN: Indiana University Press, 1989. A portrayal that defies the stereotype that Victorian gentlewomen led productive lives, were well-educated and sexually knowledgeable.

SCIENCE IN AN AGE OF OPTIMISM

Bowler, Peter J. *Evolution—The History of an Idea*, rev. ed. Berkeley, CA: University of California Press, 1989. An outstanding survey of the subject that argues that the Darwinian revolution never really occurred.

Bynum, W.F. *Science and the Practice of Medicine in the Nineteenth Century*. Cambridge: Cambridge University Press, 1994. Examines the impact of the sciences on medicine.

Kern, Stephen. *The Culture of Time and Space, 1880–1918*. Cambridge, MA: Harvard University Press, 1983. A lively discussion of the impact of the new technology.

CULTURE: ACCEPTING THE MODERN WORLD

Dale, Peter A. *In Pursuit of a Scientific Culture: Science, Art, and Society in the Victorian Age*. Madison, WI: University of Wisconsin Press, 1989. Examines the connections between science, culture, and society during the second half of the nineteenth century.

Pool, Phoebe. *Impressionism*. New York: Thames and Hudson, 1985. A thorough analysis of impressionism, stressing its origins and legacy.

FROM OPTIMISM TO UNCERTAINTY

Gay, Peter. *Freud—A Life for Our Time*. New York: Norton, 1988. Has become a standard biography of Freud.

Hughes, H. Stuart. *Consciousness and Society: The Reorientation of European Social Thought, 1890–1930*. New York: Vintage Books, 1979. A classic examination of the intellectual revolt against scientific certainty.

Teich, Mikulas, and Roy Porter, eds. *Fin de Siècle and Its Legacy*. Cambridge: Cambridge University Press, 1990. A collection of essays on the subject by noted historians.

Otto Dix, War, 1929–1932

The German expressionist painter Otto Dix (1891–1969) fought in the trenches of World War I and was wounded several times. In this triptych he depicts the destructiveness of war. In the panel on the left, soldiers march toward the bleak battlefront. Their fate is depicted in the following panels: the gore and destruction of the front lines, trenches that serve as coffins for the numberless dead, and the endless haunting nightmares of those who somehow survive. This painting all too accurately captured the reality of the period as experienced by millions of people.

CHAPTER 22

Descending into the Twentieth Century

World War and Revolution, 1914–1920

"Millions of men are going to be massacred in a War of the Worlds." As late as the first days of August 1914, only a few westerners voiced such ominous warnings as these words by the French writer Marcel Proust. In 1917, the third year of the war that Proust had foretold, the young British poet and soldier Wilfred Owen became trapped in a hole on the still-raging battle lines with the shattered body of a fellow officer. As Owen put it, the officer "lay not only near by, but in various places around and about." Owen returned to England suffering from "shell shock," as nervous breakdowns were known. Yet, a year later, he chose to return to the front. In a letter to his mother, he explained why: "I came out in order to help these boys . . ." He hoped "by watching their sufferings that I may speak of them as well as a pleader can."

Suffer the young soldiers did, and much of Western civilization agonized along with them. The "Great War" ended the era that had begun 125 years earlier with the French and industrial revolutions. It spawned a new round of revolution, destroyed several empires, and altered politics and society for the rest of the twentieth century. The consequences of this war even spread into the non-Western world, drawing in troops from Asia and Africa and changing how people around the globe viewed the West.

Why did entire nations send their people into this conflict? After all, the war was not inevitable, nor was it an accident. At the same time, some of the combatants reasoned that they had no choice in the matter. Indeed, the outbreak of the war seemed to pivot on something that happened one June day in 1914. By itself, that event would not have led nations to commit to such a costly endeavor. But people turned the event into a spark that ignited a deadly fire they could not put out.

The Alliance System						The Versailles Settlement		Rise of Fascism
Rising Nationalism and Militarism			World War I					
The "New" Imperialism						Russian Revolution and Civil War		Communism in the Soviet Union
The "Second" Industrial Revolution								

1914	1915	1916	1917	1918	1919	1920

On the Path to Total War

On June 28, 1914, nineteen-year-old Gavrilo Princip, gun in hand, waited along a parade route in Sarajevo, the capital of the Austro-Hungarian province of Bosnia. Princip was a member of a Bosnian nationalist organization that had been trained by the Black Hand, a Serbian terrorist group. He was not alone. That day, Archduke Ferdinand, the heir to the Austro-Hungarian throne, was visiting Sarajevo. Princip, waiting with several conspirators, planned to kill the archduke to promote Slavic liberation from Austro-Hungarian control. As Ferdinand's open car passed by, Princip's co-conspirators lost their nerve and did not shoot. Then Ferdinand's driver took a wrong turn. Realizing his mistake, he stopped the car and, by chance, backed up to where Princip stood. Figure 22.1, dramatically depicts the event. On an otherwise sunny, peaceful day, Princip holds his gun up at point blank range to fire at the occupants of the stopped car. The artist shows Ferdinand seeing the danger and heroically moving to protect his wife, Sophie. Princip fired, killing both of them.

In those years, several political leaders had been assassinated without great risk of war. Yet in just four weeks, this incident would lead Austria-Hungary, a second-rate power, to declare war on Serbia, a third-rate power in the southeast corner of Europe—the Balkans. Within one more week, most of Europe was engulfed by war. How could this incident in Sarajevo, far from the heart of Europe and not directly involving any of Europe's major powers, result in an all-out war that would end an era and transform Western society?

RIVALRIES AND ALLIANCES

Part of the answer lies in the national, economic, and imperial rivalry percolating in Europe at the time. Militant nationalism, intensifying since the mid-nineteenth century, encouraged countries to view one another as dangerous rivals in the struggle for power and prestige. Politicians used this nationalism to glaze over domestic problems and win public support. The growth of industrial capitalism created an environment of competitive economic struggle as nations tried to promote their industries and gain markets. The outburst of imperialism in the decades before 1914 pitted these rivals against one another in a race to acquire colonies and expand their arenas of influence around the world.

These rivalries fueled international affairs and pressured European states to form a system of alliances among themselves. The German statesman Otto von Bismarck initiated the alliances in the 1870s. Concerned about being encircled by enemies, he allied Germany with Austria-Hungary and Russia to avoid any possibility of a two-front war—to the east against Russia and to the west against France. With Bismarck's departure from office (see p. 664), the new German kaiser—hoping to extend German influence over areas of concern to Russia—allowed the reinsurance treaty with Russia to lapse. This opened the door to major shifts in international relations. New alliances formed as European states tried to protect themselves and pursue their ambitions. Italy, looking for support against France in the competition for colonies, joined Germany and Austria-Hungary in 1882 to form the Triple Alliance. Russia, hoping to

The alliance system

expand into southeastern Europe and gain access to the Mediterranean at the expense of the declining Ottoman Empire, came into conflict with Austro-Hungarian and German ambitions in the Balkans. By 1894, Russia had joined in a new alliance with France, which eagerly sought an ally in case of a clash with Germany. In 1904, Britain, threatened by the rise of Germany as a new naval, industrial, and imperial power, joined its old rival France in an alliance called the Entente Cordiale. In 1905 and again in 1911, German challenges to French sovereignty over Morocco in North Africa created international crises that drew France and Britain closer together.

By 1914, Europe had divided itself into two powerful alliance systems: the Triple Entente, comprising France, Russia, and Great Britain; and the Triple Alliance, made up of Germany, Austria-Hungary, and Italy. On one hand, these alliances may have encouraged Europeans to believe that they could avert major wars. Between 1870 and 1914, a balance of power did generally prevail. Statesmen solved most conflicts diplomatically, and military scuffles remained brief and local. On the other hand, the alliance system gave smaller powers an opportunity to influence the decisions of larger powers; everyone feared that losing an ally—even a relatively weak supporter making decisions in its own interests—would upset the balance of power and make strong nations vulnerable.

Meanwhile, military might played a large part in politics in this world driven by competition and a struggle for international stature. Germany built a new navy; Britain kept ahead and in 1906 launched the Dreadnought, *Military buildup* the first of a new class of battleships armed entirely with big guns; and most powers reinforced their armies. Between 1870 and 1914, France and Germany more than doubled the size of their standing armies by requiring citizens to serve for set periods of time. Politicians justified huge expenditures for the military buildup with nationalistic slogans and claims that military spending promoted industry, jobs, and trade. Military staffs made plans emphasizing quick offensive thrusts and drew up timetables for mobilizing their forces in case of war. Most people assumed that any war that broke out would be short, like the Franco-Prussian War of 1870 (see p. 642), and that their own nation would win it. This armaments race and military planning only heightened the suspicion and fear brewing between nations. It also made national leaders feel ever more dependent on their allies for support in case of war.

CRISES IN THE BALKANS

These rivalries and hardening alliances became enmeshed in a series of crises that exploded in the Balkans (see Maps 22.1 and 22.2). Why the Balkans? This was Europe's most unstable area—a land of strong nationalistic aspirations felt by several peoples who had been long dominated by the declining Austro-Hungarian and Ottoman Empires. As the Ottoman Empire disintegrated during the late nineteenth and early twentieth centuries, various Balkan peoples, such as the Romanians, Bulgarians, and Serbs, had established independent nations. Peoples still under Ottoman or Austro-Hungarian rule agitated for

FIGURE 22.1
The assassination of Archduke Ferdinand and his wife.

THINKING ABOUT GEOGRAPHY

MAP 22.1   *The Balkans, 1878.*   ## MAP 22.2   *The Balkans, 1914.*

Map 22.1 shows the Balkans in 1878, and fighting and territorial changes to 1913. Map 22.2 shows the same region in 1914 after new fighting resulted in further territorial changes. ◗ **Notice** the shifting alliances and battle fronts indicated by the red arrows. **Consider** who gained the most and who lost the most. **Why** might this region be such a complex political and military cauldron?

their own independence or sought support from their linguistic kin—especially the Serbs—in these new Balkan states. The Ottoman Turks, newly united after a 1908 revolution led by the nationalistic Young Turks, struggled to maintain what power they still had in the area. The Austro-Hungarians feared dismemberment of their multinational empire by these nationalistic sentiments. They hoped to expand into the Balkans and thereby weaken any movements for independence among their own ethnic minorities. These hopes

brought Austria-Hungary into conflict with Russia, which had long hungered for influence and expansion in the Balkans. Russia had fought two limited wars in pursuit of these aims during the second half of the nineteenth century. It also envisioned itself as the protector of Slavic peoples in the Balkans.

The first Balkan crisis erupted in 1908, when Austria-Hungary suddenly annexed two provinces, Bosnia and Herzegovina, which were home to Serbs, Croats, and others. Serbia had wanted to annex these territories, peopled by its own linguistic kin. Serbia appealed to Russia, and Russia threatened Austria-Hungary, whereupon Germany joined its ally and forced Russia to back down. The second Balkan crisis occurred in 1912–1913. The various Balkan states defeated Turkey in a war and then fought among themselves over the spoils. Victorious Serbia longed for more territory. Austria-Hungary thwarted the small country's expansion to the Adriatic Sea and threatened to annihilate Serbia. Again Serbia appealed to Russia, and again German pressure forced Russia to back down.

The assassination of Archduke Ferdinand on June 28, 1914, precipitated the third Balkan crisis. The government of Austria-Hungary, certain of Serbian involvement in the assassination, decided to crush *Germany's blank check* Serbia and establish its own dominance in the Balkans once and for all. But this plan would require the backing of Germany, for Russia might come to the support of its Serbian allies and defend its own interests in the Balkans. At a fateful conference in Berlin eight days after the Sarajevo shooting, the German government encouraged Austria-Hungary's scheme with a "blank check" of full support. Emboldened by Germany's backing and advice to act quickly, Austria-Hungary presented Serbia with an ultimatum that Serbia could not hope to meet. Upon hearing of Austria's demands on Serbia, Russia's foreign minister told Austria's ambassador, "You are setting fire to Europe." On July 28, even after Serbia had yielded on all but one of the ultimatum's terms (which would have allowed Austria to investigate Serbian involvement in the assassination plot), Austria-Hungary declared war.

To back Serbia against Austria-Hungary, Russia ordered its clumsy military establishment to mobilize. However, Russian military planning, which assumed a *Mobilization* war against both Austria and Germany, did not allow for only partial mobilization against Austria. Russia's order of full mobilization on July 29 was almost the same as a declaration of war—especially to German military leaders.

Germany's only war plans assumed a two-front war against Russia and France, requiring the German army to knock France out of the fighting before Russia could bring the weight of its slow-moving forces against Germany. Therefore, Germany mobilized and sent ultimatums to Russia, demanding demobilization, and France, requiring a declaration of neutrality. When Russia failed to reply and France gave an unsatisfactory response, Germany declared war on Russia on August 1 and on France two days later. On August 4, when German troops violated Belgian neutrality on their way to attack France, Great Britain declared war on Germany.

Thus the great powers of Europe were sucked into a general war they did not want by the very alliances they had formed to protect themselves and feared to violate. Nationalism, imperialism, and economic competition had fostered the military buildup, alliances, and the suspicious state of mind that created this explosion. The growing tensions in European societies—violent domestic politics, strikes, threats from the political Left and Right, and themes of uncertainty and disintegration expressed in the arts—all worsened matters. These tensions made many Europeans welcome war as a quick, all-encompassing relief. At the time, they could not know how long the brutality would last.

The Front Lines

OFF TO BATTLE

Almost everywhere in Europe, people greeted the declarations of war with outbursts of nationalistic joy. As the Austrian writer Stefan Zweig (1881–1942), a volunteer himself, recalled, "There were parades in the street, flags, ribbons, and music burst forth everywhere, young recruits were marching triumphantly, their faces lighting up at the cheer- *Celebrating war* ing." Young men volunteered in droves, "honestly afraid that they might miss this most wonderful and exciting experience of their lives; that is why they hurried and thronged to the colors, and that is why they shouted and sang in the trains that carried them to the slaughter." Figure 22.2, a photograph of German volunteers marching down a Berlin street during the first weeks of the war, reveals the enthusiasm, optimism, and naivete of the young men. Well-dressed and raising their hats, they announce their bravery and celebrate their good fortune at being able to fight for their nation.

Here, suddenly, was a way to end domestic divisions and renew one's sense of purpose in the world. Political opponents set their differences aside and came together to support the war effort. Even socialists, long opposed to war and nationalistic calls, joined in the effort to promote national defense. In Germany the socialists voted

FIGURE 22.2
German volunteers, August 1914.

for war credits and agreed to suspend strikes until the end of the war. In France, socialists joined their old opponents to support a government of national defense, called the "Sacred Union." Russia's leading socialist party proclaimed, "Our first duty is to preserve our nation's unity and integrity, and to defend her position as a world power." Most feminists also suspended their political demands and offered ardent support for the military cause. The troops, people assumed, would surely be home by Christmas. Indeed, the British government promised that life would go on as usual with no shortages and no new regulations. Each combatant expected to win.

Nations initially on the sidelines soon enlisted with one side or the other (see Map 22.3). Hoping to gain territory in a victorious fight, Turkey and Bul-

The Central Powers versus the Allies garia joined Germany and Austria-Hungary to become the Central Powers. Italy, long a member of the Triple Alliance with Germany and Austria-Hungary, had declared its neutrality at the beginning of the war, claiming that Austria had violated the alliance by launching a war of aggression on Serbia. Italy shifted its loyalty to France and Britain after receiving better promises of victory spoils. This side, eventually joined by many other nations from the Americas and the non-Western world, became known as the Allies. The Allies had the advantage of sheer numbers, but the Central Powers were led by Germany's better equipped, well-trained army and could more easily move troops and coordinate military strategies.

THE SCHLIEFFEN PLAN

Anticipating a confrontation with both Russia and France, the German high command had committed itself to a military strategy known as the Schlieffen Plan. This plan called for a holding action against the slow-moving Russians while the main German forces thrust through neutral Belgium to knock out France. Then the Germans could concentrate on destroying Russia. Great Britain, her allies hobbled, would sue for peace, the Germans expected.

Day after day, the Schlieffen Plan worked. Four weeks after the outbreak of hostilities, German forces arrived just outside Paris ahead of schedule. Some surprises, however, lay in store for them. Stubborn Belgian resistance had held up the Germans long enough for the French to redeploy their forces to the north and for the British to send their small army across the Channel. Germans suffered unanticipated casualties and transportation problems. At a critical moment, the German command detached 100,000 of their best troops under generals Hindenburg (1847–1934) and Ludendorff (1865–1937) and sent them east to fight the Russians, who had invaded Germany with unexpected speed. Nearing Paris, the German First Army detoured from its planned route in order to concentrate its force on the French capital. This move opened a gap in the Germans' eastern flank and exposed its western flank. At this juncture, the desperate French armies seized the opportunity and turned on the Germans. Parisian taxicabs rushed army reserves to the front in the effort to save Paris. Units of Britain's army arrived to enter the fray at a crucial moment. In the bloody seven-day Battle of the Marne, the Allies at last halted the Germans, drove them back several miles, and shattered German hopes that the Schlieffen Plan would succeed. As Map 22.4 indicates, both sides extended their lines more than 300 miles from the Swiss border to the North Sea and dug in for the winter. Germany was now stuck with what it had tried so hard to avoid—a war on two fronts.

SLAUGHTER AND STALEMATE ON THE WESTERN FRONT

The defensive lines proved superior to offensive thrusts. To the surprise of almost everyone, the armies on the western front fought a war of attrition from their networks of trenches protected by barbed wire,

THINKING ABOUT GEOGRAPHY

MAP 22.3   *World War I*

This map shows the two alliances and the major fronts in World War I. ⬛ **Consider** what this map reveals about the surrounded position of the Central Powers and the importance of Turkey during the war. ⬛ **Locate** the major areas of fighting on the western and eastern fronts. **What** do these reveal about the different nature of the war on these two fronts? **Which** areas in Europe were most directly affected by the fighting?

THINKING ABOUT GEOGRAPHY

MAP 22.4 *The Western Front*

This map shows the western front at various stages of World War I. ◼ **Notice** how far the Germans penetrated in their 1914 offensive and how close they came to capturing the French capital. ◼ **Locate** the western front at the beginning of 1915—that line would change little over the next three years. ◼ **What** countries were most directly affected by the fighting on the western front?

1916 but did not manage to use them effectively to cross trenches until the end of the war.

Despite the defensive advantages of trench warfare, military commanders remained wedded to notions of an offensive breakthrough. Again and again, they sent troops scrambling out of their trenches, "over the top" and into "no man's land," where enemy machine-gun fire mowed them down by the thousands. Fritze Franke, a German soldier, described his experience of trench warfare in a November 1914 letter: "Every foot of ground contested, every hundred yards another trench; and everywhere bodies—rows of them! All the trees shot to pieces; the whole ground churned up a yard deep by the heaviest shells; dead animals; houses and churches . . . utterly destroyed . . . And every troop that advances in support

mines, and machine guns. The trenches, up to thirty feet deep, became filled with mud, rats, human bodies, lice, waste, poison gas, and the stench of death.

Trench warfare But they also served as homes and protection for troops under fire, as shown in Figure 22.3. Along with their rifles and grenades, soldiers carried wire cutters and gas masks. Between the trenches, mortar and massive artillery bombardments created a barren, pockmarked landscape of mud and death that few soldiers could cross and still hope to live. The British introduced tanks in

FIGURE 22.3
Trench warfare.

must pass through a mile of this chaos, through this gigantic burial ground and the reek of corpses." Wilfred Owen, the British poet whom we met at the beginning of the chapter, related how the brutal reality of the war wiped out old images of its glory. Owen warned that anyone who saw the suffering

"... [W]ould not tell with such high zest
To children ardent for some desperate glory,
The old Lie: Dulce et decorum est
Pro patria mori." ("It is sweet and proper
to die for one's country.")

Military leaders failed to realize that machine guns, modern artillery, mass mobilization, and trenches had utterly changed the nature of warfare. Acting on old assumptions and oblivious to these new military realities, generals ordered offensives again and again. Each time the charges moved lines only yards if at all, and each time the human costs were staggering. "We lie under the network of arching shells and live in a suspense of uncertainty," wrote German war veteran Erich Maria Remarque (1898–1970) in his novel *All Quiet on the Western Front*. "Over us Chance hovers." The wartime life expectancy of a front-line officer such as Wilfred Owen was only two months. After a year and a half of this mutual slaughter, nothing had changed.

In 1916 the Germans tried for a draining victory by attacking the French fortress at Verdun (see Map 22.3). Their plan was, in the words of the German commander, to "bleed to death" the French by forcing them to sustain massive casualties defending this historic *Great battles of 1916* strongpoint. During the ensuing nine-month battle, the Germans sometimes fired as many as a million shells in one day. The French managed to hold off the Germans, but 700,000 men on both sides lost their lives in the effort. "You found the dead embedded in the walls of the trenches, heads, legs, and half-bodies, just as they had been shovelled out of the way by the picks and shovels of the working party," recalled one French soldier.

That same year the British attempted a breakthrough in the Battle of the Somme in northeastern France (see Map 22.3). They suffered 60,000 casualties, with more than 20,000 killed, in just one day. "As far as you could see there were all these bodies lying there—literally thousands of them ... It didn't seem possible," wrote a British soldier. By fall, Britain had endured 400,000 casualties; France, 200,000; and Germany, 500,000 in this one battle. It ended in a stalemate. "Here chivalry disappeared for always," wrote

the German Ernst Jüger. In the Passchendaele offensive (see Map 22.3), the British again tried to break through the German "crust," losing some 400,000 soldiers in the effort. Like other great battles in the west, Passchendaele scarcely moved the front lines at all.

Neither the politicians nor the generals found the will to call a halt to the slaughter. Anything short of complete victory, they feared, would mean that all the deaths and casualties were in vain. The troops were not so stubborn. Sometimes they agreed to avoid battles. They even occasionally fraternized across the trenches, sang together, and allowed each other to eat meals in peace or collect the bodies of fellow soldiers in no-man's-land. They also were capable of making their outrage known to their superiors. After a new, disastrous offensive ordered by France's commander General Nivelle in April 1917, mutinies broke out in half the French divisions on the front. Thousands of soldiers were court-martialed and more than 500 sentenced to death, though most executions were never carried out. New commanders and troops tacitly agreed to stop these hopeless offensive onslaughts.

Figure 22.4 illustrates how all means, old and new, were used to fight this war. Here soldiers with plumed helmets sit astride horses while an *Weapons of war* airplane, used for bombing and intelligence, flies overhead. Armies would use poison gas, flame throwers, and tanks for the first time. Even dogs—75,000 of them—were employed to search for wounded men on the battlefronts.

On the seas, both sides in the war hoped for decisive victories. The British navy set up a blockade of Germany, and the Germans responded with the submarine. Germany and Britain never met in a conclusive naval showdown, however. In the Battle of Jutland, the only major naval battle of the war, the British fleet prevented the German fleet from breaking the blockade—but suffered serious losses as a result. Most of the massive struggle took place on the ground. After three years of fighting, neither side could break through on the western front. By then, the French alone had sustained more than 3.5 million casualties. Yet, the war dragged on.

VICTORY AND DEFEAT ON THE EASTERN AND SOUTHERN FRONTS

On the eastern front, as Map 22.3 indicates, the war proved far more mobile and offensive than in the west. In eastern Europe, the terrain did not favor trench warfare, and in any case the Russians lacked

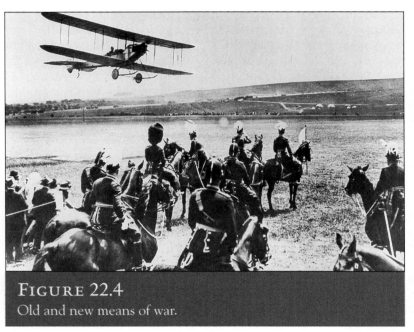

FIGURE 22.4
Old and new means of war.

the resources to sustain such a defensive effort. Initially, Russia, with its huge but inadequately supplied army, pushed into German and Austro-Hungarian lands. By the end of August 1914, however, the reinforced German armies, bolstered by their superior technology and leadership, trapped the Russians at Tannenberg and administered a crushing defeat. The Russian commander, General Samsonov, committed suicide on the spot. Farther south, the Russians defeated an Austro-Hungarian army at Lemberg only to bring in a German army that delivered a series of hammer blows to the Russians. The Germans drove deep into Russia and inflicted immense casualties, making Generals Hindenburg and Ludendorff heroes. In the Balkans, German, Austrian, and Bulgarian forces eliminated Serbia from the war by the end of 1915. That same year, a disastrous Anglo-French effort to help the hard-pressed Russians by landing at Gallipoli and breaking through Turkish defenses at the nearby Dardanelles was beaten back by the Turks with heavy losses to the Allies (see Map 22.3).

In 1916 Russia made one more great effort against the Austro-Hungarian forces in the south. Under General Aleksei Brusilov, Russian armies almost forced the Austro-Hungari-

Russia's military collapse

ans to withdraw from the war. The Austro-Hungarians resorted to recruiting men over the age of fifty into the army, and in the end kept going only with German support. But the Rus-

sians could not sustain the effort. Lack of effective leadership, insufficient supplies, and desertions plagued Russia's armies. "Half of them have no rifles," tsar Nicholas admitted, "the troops are losing masses and there is nobody to collect them on the battlefields." Germany's renewed push against the Russians in 1917 finally prompted Russia's military collapse. These losses, along with internal strife that toppled the tsar and his government, knocked Russia out of the war in December 1917. Nevertheless, for more than two years, the Russian effort had drawn German troops east, weakening the German forces in the west.

Meanwhile, in northeastern Italy, Austrian and German troops won some costly battles, but the Italian forces limited the Central Powers' advances (see Map 22.3). Farther south

Southern fronts

and east, Allied forces suffered serious defeats at the hands of the Ottoman Turks. Even more crippling, malaria, cholera, dysentery, and other diseases spread among the troops fighting in the Middle East. Eventually, the British, most notably the charismatic officer and writer T. E. Lawrence (1888–1935), stirred up Arab resentment into a desert revolt against Turkish rulers. Together, British and Arab forces gradually gained the upper hand against the Ottoman Turks.

THE WAR SPREADS ACROSS THE GLOBE

The war itself soon spread outside of Europe and the Mediterranean basin, in great part thanks to the West's colonies and imperial interests throughout the world. In Africa, minor battles erupted around Germany's colonies. In East Asia, Japan joined the war on the Allied side and promptly seized German holdings in the Pacific and China. When Russia seemed on the verge of falling apart, Japan also sent soldiers into the tsar's far eastern provinces. Britain and France drew troops from Canada, Africa, Asia, and Australia to fight on several fronts. The Western nations also called on laborers from these lands to work in France and elsewhere in the war effort.

However, non-Western peoples often resisted the European powers' efforts to gain their support. Nomadic tribes fled Russia's central Asian provinces rather than serve in the tsar's army. In French West Africa, local tribes revolted when the French tried to mobilize labor brigades. Moreover, non-westerners did not automatically favor the Allied cause. Most of those who followed the conflict in Asia viewed World War I as a European civil war. In addition, they were likely to favor Germany over France and Britain, two nations who had a tradition of Asian conquest. Indeed, for the most part, the first world war remained a European affair. Raging on year after year, the conflict shattered the lives of soldiers and civilians alike.

War on the Home Front

No Western society could come through such a protracted war unscathed. As the toll on lives and supplies climbed, whole societies had to mobilize to support the military effort. In this sense, World War I became the first total war, blurring the traditional distinctions between combatants and civilians, and between battle lines and the home front. The first world war transformed whole economies, societies, and governments, as well as the lives of soldiers.

Total war

MOBILIZING RESOURCES

After the first few months of hostilities, armies began to run out of ammunition, supplies, and troops. The French alone were firing more than 100,000 artillery shells a day—far more than their armaments factories could supply. Entire economies were reorganized to churn out huge quantities of bullets, guns, and machines in just days and weeks rather than the usual months and years. The war effort required untold quantities of other materials as well—everything from food and uniforms to trucks and coffins. Over all, the war demanded unprecedented industrial capability and organizational agility to produce and move supplies for the armed forces.

To varying degrees, the governments of the major powers took control of their economies. Government agencies, rather than the free marketplace, determined production, consumption, wages, and prices. In Germany, the War Raw Materials Board located, rationed, and distributed raw materials. To meet the

Governments take control

need for products that Germany could no longer import, such as rubber, the Board helped develop synthetic substitutes. In Britain, the Ministry of Munitions, led by David Lloyd George, supervised the armaments industry. The ministry's bureaucracy of 65,000 clerks controlled prices, supplies, and production of war material.

This tightly controlled mobilization of resources also included people. Not only were men drafted into the armed services, but women and men on the home fronts were often required to work in accord with priorities determined by the government. Labor unions were brought into partnership with business and government. In addition, governments suspended laws limiting the length of the workday and controlling workplace conditions. People were thus forced to work longer hours under dangerous circumstances.

Demand for troops on the front lines and labor on the home front altered traditional social and national boundaries. Although the war did not eliminate class conflict, social distinctions blurred as people from all walks of society joined the war effort and worked or fought side by side. Conventional national distinctions were sometimes violated: For a while, the hard-pressed Germans forced thousands of Belgians to move and work in German factories. The war effort could even include children: Some German teachers organized their students to go through garbage and collect anything that might be useful. Perhaps most striking, officials challenged traditional gender roles by calling women into the labor force.

NEW GENDER ROLES

Gender roles changed radically under the pressures of all-out war. At first, many women were left on their own financially as their husbands marched off to battle. Later, when economies began straining with the war effort, women got new jobs previously reserved for men. Figure 22.5 shows women working in a large British armaments plant, producing the huge quantity of shells needed on the battle lines. Such women participated in all aspects of the munitions industries. They became army clerks and streetcar conductors and drove taxies and ran farms. Some served as firefighters at home and as nurses at the front. Others gained entry into white-collar jobs in banks, commercial businesses, and urban offices. In Great Britain, the number of women working outside the home increased twenty

FIGURE 22.5
Women war workers.

fold to some 5 million by 1918. In Russia women made up over 40 percent of the labor force. Similar patterns held in other European countries.

These shifting labor patterns created new tensions over women's roles as men began fearing they would lose their jobs to women permanently. "Workmen have to be handled with the utmost tenderness and caution lest they should actually imagine . . . that women could do their work equally well," wrote a female British munitions factory worker in 1916. Women themselves often had conflicted feelings about their new role. Many gained a new sense of independence from earning a paycheck. Some displayed their newfound freedom by living alone, going out socially on their own, wearing shorter dresses, cutting ("bobbing") their hair, and smoking ciga-

rettes. Others felt torn by the dual demands of service and family. "What exhausts women in wartime is not the strenuous and unfamiliar tasks that fall upon them, nor even the hourly dread of death for husbands or lovers or brothers or sons," recalled British writer Vera Brittain (1896–1970), who served as a nurse on the front lines. "It is the incessant conflict between personal and national claims which wears out their energy and breaks their spirit." By no coincidence, several nations would grant women the right to vote at the war's end.

MAINTAINING THE EFFORT

As the war persisted, governments became more involved in manufacturing consent and less tolerant of dissent. Propaganda specialists tried to inspire support for the war and hatred for the enemy. The more the propaganda succeeded in its aims, the harder it became for governments to compromise or withdraw *Propaganda* from the conflict. Officials deliberately manipulated information and censored private letters in order to shape public opinion about the war. In particular, they tried to create the impression that their own country was completely virtuous and that it was the other nations that were committing crimes against humanity. To combat war weariness, governments painted the enemy as evil incarnate, and whipped up people's sense of outrage. There was no way, political leaders declared, that "good" people could ever make peace with such diabolical opponents.

Figure 22.6, a cover from a French magazine, is an example of such propaganda. The image depicts Germans as having committed atrocities during their march through Belgium and northern France. Here an innocent, horror-stricken, assaulted woman kneels on a blood-soaked crib and cradles the body of her murdered child. The empty wine bottles and helmet scattered on the ground around her leave no doubt that immoral German soldiers have committed these acts. The illustrator also blames the Germans for setting the homes and church of this village on fire while passing through. The glaring headline exhorts people to "Never Forget."

Governments also tried to promote dissent among their opponents and turn neutral countries into allies. Germany supported the Irish in their 1916 Easter Rebellion in Dublin for Irish independence, which British forces brutally crushed. Germany also aided the Bolsheviks against Russia's government. The British promoted rebellion among the Arabs against the Turks and used propaganda to help bring the Americans in on their side.

Victories or defeats on the front lines reflected the abilities of civilian societies to mobilize effectively for the war effort—materially, politically, and psychologically. Those nations less able to develop and sustain this vast home-front effort—such as the Austro-Hungarian and Russian empires—faltered first. They lacked the solid industrial base and organizational strength of Germany, France, and Great Britain. Over time, however, even the strongest nations weakened under the strains of total war. Food shortages spawned malnutrition, disease, and high infant mortality, especially in Germany, which acutely felt the impact of

Britain's naval blockade. Governments tried to pay for the war by printing more money, thereby creating an inflation of prices.

By 1917, hunger and war weariness ignited strikes and domestic disorders throughout Europe. Beleaguered governments suspended civil liberties, ignored democratic *Rising dissent* procedures, and ruled by emergency police powers. In France, Georges Clemenceau (1841–1929) became a virtual dictator after November 1917. He sent troops against strikers and arrested those agitating for peace. "I wage war," he declared. "I wage nothing but war!" In Austria, political unity unraveled as different nationalities clamored for independence. In Germany, some socialist and Catholic

FIGURE 22.6
French propaganda picture.

Biography

KÄTHE KOLLWITZ (1867–1945)

By the eve of World War I, Käthe Kollwitz's prints, drawings, and posters had made her one of Germany's leading artists. "[M]y art has purpose," she said. "I want to be effective in this time when people are so helpless and in need of aid."

Käthe Schmidt was born in East Prussia in 1867. As a child, she often suffered from periods of depression, and these episodes continued well into her adulthood. Early on she learned to express her feelings in art. In 1891, Käthe married Dr. Karl Kollwitz, whom she would praise years later as her "life's comrade." Karl shared Käthe's socialist sympathies. That year, the couple moved to Berlin, where Karl took a job as a physician for a workers' health insurance fund, and where Käthe gave birth to Hans in 1892 and Peter in 1896. Reflecting on the role of love in her life, she would later describe silently falling in love with women as well as men and the influence of bisexuality on the themes in her art.

Käthe earned her first public success as an artist between 1895 and 1898 with the publication of a series of prints, "The Weavers." These images recorded a doomed revolt of handloom weavers in the 1840s. Indeed, most of her works explored the plight of victims of social injustice, the cause of peace, and the sufferings of war and death. Not surprisingly, her art often offended the authorities, including the kaiser.

In early August 1914, just after World War I broke out, the Kollwitz family heard German soldiers singing as they marched in the streets (see p. 725). Käthe wept in horror. During those same days, her youngest son Peter, only eighteen years old, volunteered for the army. On August 27, 1914, she wrote, "Where do all the women who have watched so carefully over the lives of their beloved ones get the heroism to send them to face the cannon? I am afraid that this soaring of the spirit will be followed by the blackest despair and dejection." A month later, she wrote, "It seems so stupid that the boys must go to war . . . how can they possibly take part in such madness?" Three weeks later, on October 22, 1914, Peter was killed in the war.

This loss of her son haunted Käthe for the rest of her life. In letters and diaries, she expressed endless grief for her fallen boy. She expanded her sorrow to embrace grieving mothers in all countries. Reflecting on the causes of the war, she described how Peter and others she knew had "subordinated their lives to the idea of patriotism. The English, Russian and French young men have done the same. The consequence has been this terrible killing and the impoverishment of Europe."

After her son's death, Käthe began a long struggle to create monumental sculptures in memory of Peter and other sons killed in the war. It would take her ten years to start work on the final forms for these sculptures, and another eight years before the figures were completed in stone. Figures 22.7 and 22.8 are photographs of the two sculptures. At the opening ceremony, held in the Belgian cemetery where Peter was buried, Käthe stood before her stone figure of the mother: "I looked at her, my own face, and wept and stroked her cheeks."

Artist and Witness to War

When the war ended, she worried that "the peace will probably be very bad." For her the war, fought by Europe's youth, had destroyed "all that is most beautiful in Europe." In 1919, she became the first woman elected to the Prussian Academy of Arts. In 1928, she was further honored by being appointed head of a master class for graphic arts. In 1930, as the Nazis rose in strength, she wrote that "evil reaction is creeping into all areas." Käthe was forced to resign her prestigious position when Hitler came to power in 1933, and

---

legislators came out for peace, and generals Hindenburg and Ludendorff assumed control over the German war effort. By the end of 1917, Russia's whole war effort had collapsed. Clearly, World War I would be won or lost on the home front as well as on the battle lines.

To the Bitter End

Early in 1917, the German high command grew desperate to bring the draining war to a victorious conclusion. The generals decided to launch an unre-

FIGURE 22.7
Käthe Kollwitz, *The Mourning Father*.

FIGURE 22.8
Käthe Kollwitz, *The Mourning Mother*.

the Führer banned her work. In 1940 her grandson, Peter, the namesake of her son Peter killed in World War I, joined Germany's army as World War II erupted. He was killed on the Russian front in 1942. She continued her work almost until her death on April 22, 1945.

Like so many other people, Käthe Kollwitz had witnessed the great enthusiasm as soldiers first marched off to the Great War in August, 1914. Also like countless millions of people,

she had lost a loved one in that conflict. She too would live long enough to witness a terrible renewal of war. In her last letter, she wrote, "the war accompanies me to the end." She, along with far too many in the West, would never fully recover from the scars of World War I.

Consider how Kollwitz's life reflected the impact of World War I on European society.

stricted submarine campaign against enemy and neutral shipping alike. Germany's leaders knew this policy could bring the United States into the war. Up to that point, the United States had remained neutral but had become increasingly invested in the Allied cause through trade and loans. The sense that Germany and

its partners were the aggressors, along with the 1915 sinking of the passenger liner *Lusitania* during a German submarine blockade of Britain, had also nudged American public opinion toward support of the Allies. Now Germany's high command gambled that they could defeat Britain and France before the Americans could send enough supplies and troops to Europe to make a difference. Indeed, Ludendorff and Hindenburg promised victory within only six months.

At about the same time, British intelligence turned over to the United States an alarming note that it claimed to have intercepted. In that document, called the Zimmermann note, Germany offered to grant U.S. territory to Mexico if Mexico agreed to attack the United States. When German submarines began sinking American cargo ships, U.S. entry into the conflict was assured. On April 6, 1917, the United States declared war on Germany. President Woodrow Wilson promised to "make the world safe for democracy."

The U.S. enters the war

The Germans had good reason to think that they might prevail. By the beginning of 1918, the United States' contribution to the war was still relatively small. In addition, the Italians had suffered a disastrous blow at the Battle of Caporetto, almost putting them out of the war. Romania and Serbia had been defeated and Russia had withdrawn from the war. Now Germany could at last focus its efforts on a one-front war. In the Atlantic, its U-boats (submarines) were sinking one-fourth of all ships taking supplies to Britain—350 ships went down in one month alone.

On the other hand, Germany's allies—the Austro-Hungarian and Ottoman Empires—were teetering, and Germany was suffering from lack of materials and food, thanks to Britain's naval blockade. The British had also discovered a way to foil the U-boats by using heavily escorted convoys armed with depth charges. Now the race was between Germany and the United States. Germany transferred troops from the Russian front in an effort to overwhelm Great Britain and France before waves of American troops could arrive, while the United States struggled to raise, train, and transport sufficient forces to France to stem the German tide.

Final battles

In March 1918, Field Marshall Ludendorff launched the first of a series of massive German blows on the western front designed to end the war. The British and French were driven back with heavy losses. Desperate, they finally agreed to a unified command under France's General Ferdinand Foch (1851–1929). By mid-June, after the fourth of the great drives, the Allied lines were so badly battered that when the climactic fifth drive began along the Marne River in mid-July, Ludendorff wired the kaiser: "If the attack succeeds, the war will be over and we will have won it." When Foch heard the opening German barrage, he wired his government: "If the present German attack succeeds, the war is over and we have lost it." The Allies stopped the Germans by a narrow margin. Foch, now receiving a swelling stream of fresh American troops—more than 250,000 troops a month—immediately ordered a counterattack. British tanks helped break through German lines. The balance shifted. Suddenly, the Germans were in retreat. German strength and morale waned rapidly. That spring and summer, Germans suffered more than 2 million casualties.

At the end of October, Germany's Bulgarian and Turkish allies surrendered. On November 3, Austria-Hungary, its ethnic minorities in revolt, also surrendered; a week later, the last Austro-Hungarian emperor abdicated. The next day, mutiny broke out in the German navy and spread to workers in German cities. Popular uprisings brought down the kaiser's government, and on November 9 he fled the country. On November 11, the new German Republic government accepted an armistice.

For many, however, even the last days of the war were too long. In Britain, Wilfred Owen's mother, like so many others, received news of her son's death (he was machine-gunned in a final attack) just as church bells began ringing for victory. Those last days would also leave a haunting legacy in Germany. German commanders manipulated reports from the front so that most of Germany's population remained unaware of the extent of their country's military collapse. The new civilian government of republicans and socialists in Germany would later be blamed by many Germans for the surrender. This development would in turn set the stage for future charges that Germany had not really lost the war but had been "stabbed in the back" by the very political forces that would rule Germany during the 1920s.

Assessing the Costs of the War

The war had shattered much of Europe. Some 10 million soldiers and another 10 million civilians perished from the war and its hardships. More than 50 percent of the Allied soldiers and 60 percent of the Central Powers soldiers mobilized became casualties. In France, half the men between the ages of eighteen and thirty-two were killed. Russia lost almost 2 million soldiers, as did Germany. All across northern France and Belgium, war cemeteries spread, many with unmarked graves, others with elaborate monuments to the fallen such as those in Figures 22.7 and 22.8. Europe lost the cream of a generation of its future leaders. Colonial troops from Asia and Africa also suffered. Figure 22.9, showing a Senegalese soldier learning to use artificial limbs with the help of a Red Cross nurse, indicates the price many such veterans paid for their service. Almost 30,000 Senegalese soldiers died in the trenches fighting for France.

For those left behind, the hardships persisted. Many survivors would have to spend the rest of their lives in veterans' hospitals. In many places, mutilated people, widows, and spinsters seemed the rule rather than the exception. In addition to all the death and misery, the fighting brought incalculable financial and material losses. The war laid to waste a tenth of the richest region of France and devastated the most developed part of Russia. It also saddled European nations with heavy debts, especially to a new international creditor—the United States.

The Peace Settlement

No peace settlement could make up for the losses of World War I. Nevertheless, delegates who gathered at Versailles near Paris in January 1919 and the people they represented expected a resolution that could somehow justify those losses. Other burdens weighed on the delegates as well. The end of fighting did not stop wartime hatred and suffering. Starvation threatened central and eastern Europe. In addition, a growing fear of revolutionary communism haunted the delegates, who primarily represented the forces of order and wealth in their nations. Already in power in Russia, communists had a real chance of triumphing in Germany and the newly independent states of eastern Europe.

GATHERING AT VERSAILLES

Although all thirty-two of the victorious Allies participated in the peace conference, the leaders of France, Great Britain, the United States, and Italy made the major decisions. Representatives of colonized peoples, ethnic and religious groups, women's organizations, and various national groups went to Versailles hoping for a hearing but received none. The vanquished Germany and Austria-Hungary were excluded from the talks, as was Russia, which had dropped out of the war a year earlier.

Figure 22.10 is one of many paintings, photographs, and newsreels made of the peace conference. The political leaders of the major powers sit at the table in the center of this painting. Around them stand representatives of smaller powers, who had less say in the negotiations. The conferees are gathered in the Hall of Mirrors at Versailles, quite consciously the same place where the Germans celebrated their victory in the Franco-Prussian War almost fifty years earlier.

Premier Georges Clemenceau, the aged "Tiger of France," headed the French delegation. As host of the conference and leader of the nation that

FIGURE 22.9
Casualities from the colonies.

FIGURE 22.10
Signing of the Treaty of Versailles, 1919.

had done the most to defeat Germany, Clemenceau expected to dominate the decision making. The eloquent and fiery Prime Minister David Lloyd George led the British delegation. He also intended to dominate the conference. Premier Vittorio Orlando (1860–1952), head of the Italian delegation, wanted all the territory that the Allies had promised to draw Italy into the war in the first place. The idealistic President Woodrow Wilson (1856–1924), expecting approval of his "Fourteen Points" as the basis for peace, led the American delegation. The United States had attained much prestige during the war and was the first non-European country in centuries to influence the fate of European nations.

A VICTORS' PEACE

A fundamental and bitter clash immediately developed between Clemenceau, who wanted a "hard peace" that would render Germany harmless, and Wilson, who wanted a "just" peace free of vindictiveness. Wilson and his advisors feared that a harsh settlement would leave Germany resentful, eager for re-

venge, or ripe for takeover by extreme political forces. He also believed that secret diplomacy and the alliance system had caused the war in the first place, and urged "open covenants of peace, openly arrived at." *Wilson's Fourteen Points* In his Fourteen Points, Wilson also called for the self-determination of peoples, armaments reduction, and a "general association of nations" to guarantee the safety of "great and small states alike." Lloyd George often sided with Wilson, but like Clemenceau wanted a victory worthy of the sacrifices made during the war.

It took six months of hard work and wrangling to draw up the peace terms. Although the Treaty of Versailles reflected many of Wilson's ideals, it was more of a victors' peace reflecting France's desire for security and an eagerness to punish Germany. In what came to be known as the "war guilt" clause, the agreement forced Germany "and her allies" to accept full responsibility for the war. Germany lost all its overseas colonies and concessions; several victorious nations gained control over these territories in Africa and the Pacific. France regained Alsace and Lorraine, lost in the Franco-Prussian War of 1870. In addition, the victors would occupy German territory on the west bank of the Rhine for the next fifteen years. The Polish-speaking areas of eastern Germany were ceded to the resurrected Polish state, and a "Polish corridor" was cut through German territory to give Poland an outlet at Danzig to the Baltic Sea. Germany's armed forces were limited to 100,000 soldiers and saddled with severe armament limitations. Finally, Germany was held liable for an indemnity that in 1921 was set at $33 billion.

REDRAWING THE MAP OF EUROPE

As Map 22.5 reveals, the treaties dealt the harshest blow to Germany's allies because the territorial rearrangements were usually based on the principle of unifying national language groups. Austria-Hungary was cut down from a polyglot empire of 50 million— second in area only to Russia among the nations of Europe—to an Austria of 6.5 million German-speaking Austrians and a Hungary of 8 million Magyars. Many in Austria wanted their new country to merge with Germany, but the settlement specifically forbade this arrangement. The Czechs and Slovaks were joined into the new state of Czechoslovakia, which included sizable German and other minorities. Serbs,

THINKING ABOUT GEOGRAPHY

MAP 22.5 *Europe, 1923*

This map shows Europe after the settlement that ended World War I. **⬛ Notice** the territorial losses suffered by the German, Russian, Ottoman, and Austro-Hungarian empires. **Do** these losses support the argument that the Versailles settlement was a harsh one? **What** areas might suffer from instability stemming from these new territorial arrangements? **Consider** the strategic problems facing the new eastern European states that hoped for support from France and Great Britain.

Croats, Slovenes, Bosnians, and others populated the new state of Yugoslavia. Turkey lost its far-flung non-Turkish territories. Great Britain took administrative control over Mesopotamia and Palestine, while France took Lebanon and Syria. Perhaps unavoidably, all these new national boundaries created many internal ethnic divisions and pockets of discontent that would breed future conflicts.

Woodrow Wilson had placed his chief hopes for peace in an association of countries—the League of

Nations—that he expected would guarantee borders and peaceably settle the tensions and conflicts that were certain to arise in the future. The League was incorporated into the treaty with Germany but had no military forces at its command. Its only weapons were economic sanctions and moral condemnations. Though perhaps well intentioned, the League was doomed almost from the beginning. The exclusion of Germany and the Soviet Union from the association weakened its potential effectiveness. In addition, the self-righteous President Wilson—reluctant to compromise with political opponents back in the United States and physically weakening—failed to persuade the isolationist American Senate to ratify the peace accords and join the League. What little faith Great Britain and France had in Wilson's ideas quickly disappeared.

The League of Nations

LEGACY OF THE PEACE TREATY

The peace settlement negotiated in Paris satisfied no one and left a legacy of deep resentments. France's Clemenceau considered the terms too lenient. Moreover, both Great Britain and the United States refused French pleas to join France in a defensive alliance. Not surprisingly, the French felt betrayed and abandoned. The Germans, for their part, considered the terms outrageous. Many Germans refused to believe that their armies had lost the war. The Germans also resented not being allowed to participate in the talks. Their representatives were presented with a humiliating settlement that they signed only after the Allies threatened to invade. Italy's leader, Orlando, walked out of the conference to protest broken Allied promises of more territorial gains. China refused to sign because the treaty gave the Japanese rights in the Chinese mainland, while Japan left offended because the conference refused to declare formally the equality of all races. Russia, which had suffered huge losses, had not even been invited to the conference, and the U.S. government refused to sign the treaty.

John Maynard Keynes (1883–1946), an influential British economist who attended the talks, perhaps best summed up the flaws in the Paris agreement in his book *The Economic Consequences of the Peace* (1919). "[T]he treaty," Keynes warned, "includes no provisions for the economic rehabilitation of Europe—nothing to make the defeated Central Empires into good neighbors, nothing to stabilize the new States of Europe, nothing to reclaim Russia . . ."

World War I had unleashed passions and destruction of such magnitudes that possibly no settlement could have sufficed. Nowhere in the West did those passions rage stronger than in Russia, defeated by Germany in 1917 and still reeling from internal upheavals. There, revolution and civil war were forging a new union that would alter world affairs for the rest of the twentieth century.

Revolutions in Russia

In 1914, the Russian tsar Nicholas II and his advisors hoped that a short, painless war in the Balkans would overcome domestic divisions within Russia, strengthen the tsar's regime, and improve Russia's international stature. Instead, the "short, painless" fight turned into a massive conflagration that only compounded Russia's internal discord and revealed how far Russia had fallen behind other powers to the west. In addition, the greatest fears of the tsar, his government, and the aristocracy whose interests he represented came true: World War I devastated Russia militarily and brought the centuries-old Romanov dynasty crashing down.

THE FIRST WARNINGS: 1905

Long-simmering discontent made Russia ripe for violent upheaval. This discontent had its roots in the Russian government's historical resistance to change. Throughout the nineteenth century, Russia's government had usually tried to ignore rather than adapt to the liberalizing movements that swept most of Europe. Industrialization, initiated in the 1880s and surging in the 1890s—encouraged by the aggressive policies of Sergei Witte (1849–1915), the finance minister, and an infusion of foreign capital into Russia—stimulated the growth of the middle and working classes in cities such as Moscow and St. Petersburg. These people chafed against Russia's traditional society and archaic government. Frustrated Russian intellectuals turned to revolutionary doctrines and even terrorism in an effort to promote rapid change. Others hoped for more moderate liberal reforms. Still the tsarist government, particularly under Nicholas II (1894–1917), refused to bend.

A turning point came with the embarrassing defeat of the tsar's army and navy by Japan in the 1904–1905 Russo-Japanese War. The various liberal and radical groups took advantage of the government's weakness and clamored for reform. The mounting pressures for change finally exploded early in 1905. On Sunday,

January 22, thousands of workers gathered in front of the tsar's palace in St. Petersburg to protest economic hardships. Marchers sang "God save the tsar," but the tsar's troops fired on them, killing and wounding hundreds of women, men, and children. The violent event, known as "Bloody Sunday," was dramatically depicted by the Russian artist N. Vladimirov (Figure 22.11). On the right, a line of Tsar Nicholas II's troops fire on the procession of workers, killing hundreds of women, men, and children. On the left, the unarmed workers, who sought to present peacefully a petition to the tsar at the Winter Palace in St. Petersburg, fall. Their blood darkens the snow as well as faith in the tsar as a protector of the people.

Demands for reform increased, and in October a general strike paralyzed the country for ten days. In the cities, workers organized themselves into councils, or "soviets." Sailors mutinied on the battleship *Potemkin* as did soldiers in the army. At the same time, peasants in the countryside revolted and attacked wealthy landowners. Several officials were even assassinated. With much of its army pinned down thousands of miles away in the Russo-Japanese War, the tsar's government wavered. Surrounded by dissension and revolt, Nicholas II yielded at last and issued a manifesto that promised civil liberties, a popularly elected Duma (parliament), and legalization of unions. These concessions had little lasting meaning, however. The return of the Russian troops from the Far East and a fresh round of governmental repression restored order by 1907. The tsar and his advisors reduced the Duma to a nondemocratically elected body.

THE FALL OF THE TSAR

The few, half-hearted reforms were not enough, and discontent persisted in the years after 1905. In the months before the outbreak of World War I, strikes proliferated in Russia's cities. This turmoil probably encouraged the tsar to bring Russia into the war, for he immediately banned strikes and suspended the Duma, whose members still agitated for liberal reforms. As we saw earlier, Russia soon suffered staggering losses at the hands of the German armies. Its leadership, transportation facilities, supplies, and armaments simply could not withstand the demands of total war. Moreover, many non-Russian subjects living within the empire became more interested in establishing their own independent states than supporting the war effort.

In August 1915, a desperate Nicholas made a fatal mistake: He left the capital to take personal command of the army. The severity and depth of this error is revealed by the reaction of Russia's war minister. Reporting on the dire military situation to the council, the minister concluded, "Considering the present situation at the front and in the rear of the armies, one can expect an irreparable catastrophe momentarily." However, he added, "a far more horrible event threatens Russia." His stunned colleagues on the Council of Ministers waited for the grim news. "This morning, His Majesty told me of his decision to personally assume the supreme command of the army." As a result of Nicholas' actions, the Russian people blamed the tsar for their country's military losses. Equally problematic, the inept, unpopular government in the capital now fell under the sway of Nicholas' wife Alexandra. When the tsarina came under the influence of Grigori Efimovich Rasputin (1871?–1916), a corrupt Siberian mystic who claimed to have the power to heal the tsar's hemophiliac son, things took a more bizarre turn. Even the tsar's aristocratic supporters, a group of whom finally murdered Rasputin late in 1916, demanded fundamental change.

In early March 1917, the dam broke. The strains of war drove hungry working women to initiate strikes and

FIGURE 22.11
Bloody Sunday, January 22, 1905.

demonstrations. With industrialization, Petrograd (St. Petersburg), Moscow, and other Russian cities had grown rapidly. Women, who made up more than half of the labor force in Petrograd, had to work long hours for low wages and then stand in long bread lines to buy food for their families. Rising prices and shrinking supplies, especially during the winters, translated into hunger and starvation. Figure 22.12, is a photograph of one of these demonstrations. Here women march down a Petrograd street demanding an increase of rations to soldiers' families.

The March Revolution

Women rightly blamed the government for Russia's continuing involvement in the war and for the food shortages. On March 8, in recognition of International Women's Day, they made their voices heard. That day, 10,000 women marched into Petrograd, shouting, "Down with war and high prices! Down with starvation! Bread for workers!" The protesters also demanded an end to the rule of Nicholas II. Thousands of sympathizers, both women and men, joined the demonstrations in the wintry days of March 1917. Yet police and troops were reluctant to fire on the crowds, especially because so many of them were women. Many troops actually joined the demonstrators. The French ambassador to Russia reported watching "a disorderly mob carrying a red flag" marching toward an oncoming regiment of troops. But instead of restoring order, "the army was fraternizing with the revolt." Too many people had lost their respect for the rigid, poorly led autocracy. As Russia's Minister of Foreign Affairs put it, "The Emperor is blind!" Many of his colleagues agreed. On March 12, the Duma organized a provisional government, and three days later Nicholas II abdicated. Railroad workers took him and his family into custody.

THE PROVISIONAL GOVERNMENT

Most members of the provisional government hoped that Russia would move toward constitutional parliamentary democracy. Led by moderate liberals Pavel Milyukov (1859–1943) and Prince Georgi Lvov (1861–1925), these politicians represented the upper classes. The provisional government enacted into law civil liberties, religious freedom, equality before the law, union rights, and other liberal reforms. They also promised more fundamental social reforms and a constitution.

However, in addition to its inexperience, its rival factions, and the intensifying pressures for change, the provisional government labored under three key burdens. First, it had to share power with the soviets—the political organizations of workers, soldiers, and radical intellectuals—particularly the strong Petrograd soviet. The soviets favored socialist self-rule and stood against the upper classes represented by the provisional government. Second, the government chose to continue Russia's draining involvement in World War I. The links between these first two burdens came to light with the Petrograd so-

The soviets

FIGURE 22.12
Demonstrations in Petrograd, March 1917.

viet's issuance of Order Number 1 on March 14. This significant mandate declared that military officers would be democratically elected by soldiers and that military decisions would be democratically made. Order Number 1 further unraveled authority and discipline within Russia's armed forces. Third, neither the provisional government nor the soviets could control the peasantry, which made up some 80 percent of the population. Peasants refused to wait for the land-redistribution legislation that the government had promised. They seized land and hoarded food for themselves, worsening hunger in the cities as prices rose and supplies became more scarce. The peasantry's defiance also attracted soldiers, who deserted the front to make land claims of their own.

The provisional government failed to satisfy many. The peasants wanted still more land, and workers demanded more bread. Russia could no longer support the unpopular war effort, yet the government could not find a way to withdraw gracefully from it. Again and again the provisional government tried to rally the Russian troops to victory. In desperation, it even created the Women's Battalion of Death in an effort to shame male soldiers into greater effort. More than 80 percent of these women became casualties. The desertions continued.

In May, the liberal heads of the provisional government resigned and the moderate socialist Alexander Kerensky (1881–1970) became the leading figure in the government. Kerensky, however, faced new political divisions, for by this time many radical in-

Kerensky leads

tellectuals had returned to Russia from the west, where they had fled from the tsar's repression, or rose from Russia's social ranks. They tried to push ideas and events in one direction or the other. Those who proved most influential came from a group of Marxist revolutionaries, the Social Democrats—in particular their minority faction, the Bolsheviks. This faction was led by Vladimir Ilich Ulyanov (1870–1924), known by his revolutionary name, Lenin.

THE RISE OF THE BOLSHEVIKS

Marxism had become influential among some Russian intellectuals toward the end of the nineteenth century. In 1898 Russian Marxists had formed the Social Democratic party, whose principal leaders were Georgi Plekhanov (1857–1918) and his disciple Lenin. Repression by the tsar's government forced the Social Democrats into exile. At a London conference in 1903, the radical Bolshevik wing under Lenin split from the more moderate Mensheviks.

Until 1917, Lenin's Bolsheviks remained only a minor party within Russia. Its leaders were hunted down by the state police and shot, imprisoned, or exiled. For seventeen years, Lenin remained in exile in Switzerland, keeping his party alive from a distance and plotting the eventual overthrow of the tsar's government. During that time, he developed theoretical and tactical principles that the Bolsheviks would later use. Three

Lenin's principles

of these principles set forth the most crucial guidelines and, for the most part, set Lenin's Bolsheviks apart from other Marxist organizations. First, the party should be an elite, highly trained, and constantly purged (cleaned of disloyal ideas and people) group of dedicated Marxist revolutionaries capable of instructing and leading the masses. This elite would not be seduced by short-term gains. Second, contrary to what Marx had argued, the socialist revolution need not include only the industrial working class. In Russia, it could be a dual revolution of workers and poor, land-hungry peasants—all part of an even broader socialist revolution that would sweep through other European countries. Third, the party should firmly oppose participation in World War I, which Lenin considered a product of imperialist rivalries and a continuing civil war among capitalists.

In April 1917, the German government secretly transported Lenin from his place of exile in Switzerland to the Russian border in an effort to worsen the chaos in Russia and remove Russia from the war. The Germans had good reason to consider Lenin a threat to stability in Russia. John Reed, a sympathetic American journalist and observer, described Lenin as "a strange popular leader—a leader purely by virtue of intellect; colorless, humorless, uncompromising and detached; without picturesque idiosyncrasies—but with the power of explaining profound ideas in simple terms, of analyzing a concrete situation." Once back in Russia, Lenin refused to cooperate with the provisional government. Instead, he unleashed a barrage of compelling slogans such as "Peace to the Army," "Land to the Peasants," "Ownership of the Factories to the Workers," and "All Power to the Soviets." He argued that the time was ripe for a socialist revolution against capitalism. To achieve this revolution, he urged his followers to gain control over the soviets, particularly the powerful Petrograd soviet.

When Kerensky failed to extract Russia from the war, Bolshevik influence grew, especially among the Petrograd workers and soldiers. In July 1917, a massive

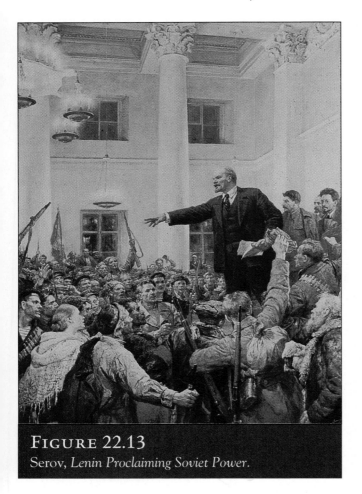

FIGURE 22.13
Serov, *Lenin Proclaiming Soviet Power.*

turn of events helped the Bolsheviks, under the leadership of Lenin and the brilliant Leon Trotsky (1877–1940), finally gain control over the Petrograd and Moscow soviets. Bolshevik women created a network to call for demonstrations, organize women in factories, and do paramilitary work. Lenin judged the time right for his next move.

On November 6, he and Trotsky launched a well-organized seizure of power. His Red Guards (workers' militia units) took over crucial control centers and arranged for the transfer of power to the soviets and Lenin. Within just hours, the deed was complete. Kerensky, unable to reorganize his forces, fled. Although some of the fighting was violent, the success of the Bolshevik revolution stemmed mostly from the revolutionaries' organizational talents, a lack of effective resistance by the provisional government, and Trotsky's success in portraying the uprising as *defense* of the soviets rather than a Bolshevik *offensive*.

The November Revolution

On November 7 the Bolshevik majority enthusiastically elected Lenin the head of the new government. The revolution won the endorsement of soviets throughout Russia. Figure 22.13, a painting by the Russian artist Serov, shows Lenin, with Stalin and Trotsky, proclaiming to the revolutionary forces the Bolsheviks' assumption of power in 1917. In this idealized re-creation of events, the artist has elevated Stalin to a prominent position just behind Lenin. The artist also portrays Lenin as a powerful orator towering above all others. The serious, impassioned crowd below, made up of women, sailors, soldiers, and workers, listens intently. The red flag of communism is held aloft in victory.

COMMUNISM AND CIVIL WAR

The Bolsheviks, who now called themselves Communists, immediately moved to fulfill their promises and consolidate their power. In place of the old tsarist hierarchy, they set up a pyramid of people's soviets, or councils. These councils were elected by universal suffrage but were actually dominated by relatively few Communist Party members. When national elections failed to return a Communist majority to the Constituent Assembly, Lenin had the Red Army disperse that elected body. Capitalism was abolished outright. A barter system of exchange replaced money, the value of the ruble having been destroyed by inflation and devaluation. Committees of workers responsible to party commissars took over management of industry and commerce. The government nationalized the land and turned over its

popular demonstration against the provisional government erupted in that city. Most members of the Bolshevik Party supported the demonstration, though in the end the leadership did not. In these bloody "July Days," the provisional government put down the demonstrators with force. The Kerensky government arrested many Bolsheviks and impelled others, including Lenin, to flee to Finland.

Russia's July Days

Yet Kerensky soon suffered a fresh round of failures in the war as well as the threat of an impending coup d'état by General Lavr Kornilov (1870–1918). To avert disaster, in September the desperate Kerensky released the Bolsheviks and relied on the soviets to defend the capital against Kornilov. Kornilov's plans failed when most of his soldiers refused to follow his orders to attack Petrograd.

By October, many leading figures from larger socialist parties had become discredited through their association with the provisional government. This

management to local peasant committees, who then distributed it to individual peasants to be worked by their own
labor. All crop surpluses were to be
given to the state. Finally, the state ex-
propriated church lands and enacted
laws to establish the legal equality of
the sexes—the first Western government to do so.

To buy time and free the new
regime for the enormous task of re-
fashioning Russian society, Lenin immediately opened peace negotiations
with Germany. The Germans, realizing Russia's helplessness, demanded
the harshest of terms. Lenin attempted to stall them, but in March
1918, when the Germans threatened
to attack Petrograd and Moscow, he
signed the Treaty of Brest-Litovsk.
Russia lost Finland, Estonia, Latvia,
Lithuania, the Ukraine, Bessarabia,
the Polish provinces, and some of the
Trans-Caucasian territory. Lenin had
paid a high price for peace. These
lands contained one-third of Russia's
European population, three-fourths
of its iron, and nine-tenths of its coal.
In addition, Germany compelled
Russia to pay a heavy indemnity.
Lenin gambled that a socialist revolution in Germany would reverse
some of these losses and provide the
support that the fledgling socialist
system desperately needed to survive
in Russia.

Nevertheless, these hard peace
terms were not the worst of Lenin's
woes. A bitter civil war broke out in
Russia following the peace with Germany (see Map 22.6). The Russian
aristocracy, including most of the
higher army officers, launched a series
of uncoordinated attacks against the
Bolshevik regime. These "White" forces were aided
by various other groups disaffected by the revolution.
They also had the support of French, British, Greek,
Polish, Japanese, Czech, and U.S. troops that were in
Russia for various reasons, but in great part to oppose
the anticapitalist Bolshevik government. For decades
afterward, the communists would remember how the

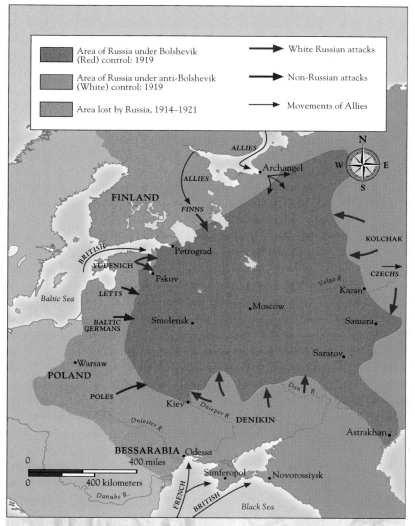

THINKING ABOUT GEOGRAPHY

MAP 22.6 *Civil War in Russia, 1919*

This map shows Russia during the civil war. ◙ **Notice** the
different forces threatening the area controlled by the Bolsheviks.
Consider why the Bolsheviks might emerge from the period with
a sense of isolation from the West. ◙ **What** strategy might have
helped the forces opposing the Bolsheviks?

outside world had turned against them during this
vulnerable time.

Creating an emergency policy of "war communism," the Bolshevik government mobilized Russia's
economy and society for the civil-war effort. Urban
workers and troops swept through the countryside
and confiscated grain from the peasantry to feed the

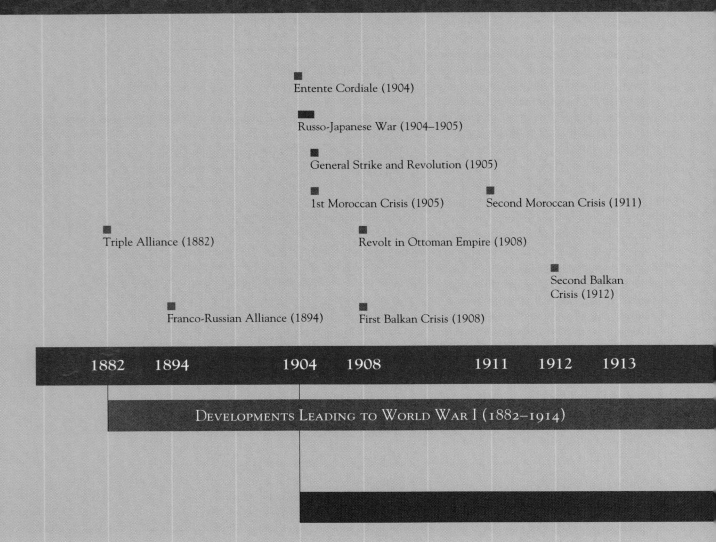

Entente Cordiale (1904)

Russo-Japanese War (1904–1905)

General Strike and Revolution (1905)

1st Moroccan Crisis (1905)   Second Moroccan Crisis (1911)

Triple Alliance (1882)   Revolt in Ottoman Empire (1908)

Second Balkan Crisis (1912)

Franco-Russian Alliance (1894)   First Balkan Crisis (1908)

| 1882 | 1894 | 1904 | 1908 | 1911 | 1912 | 1913 |

Developments Leading to World War I (1882–1914)

cities and the army. The Bolsheviks sharply suppressed any internal opposition. A secret police force—the Cheka—unleashed the "Red Terror" to hunt down "class enemies" and ensure internal conformity to the Bolshevik regime. To avoid the possibility of White forces freeing the imprisoned Nicholas II and his family, the Bolshevik government ordered them executed. However, the "Red" armies faced numerous obstacles in their all-out effort to defeat the "Whites." When peasants realized that the government intended to seize their surpluses, for example, they resisted or refused to raise more crops than they needed for themselves. Moreover, the government had to contend with violent ethnic hatreds that further divided the country. Only with the greatest difficulty did the "Red" armies, well organized by Trotsky, finally defeat the "Whites." In doing so, the Bolsheviks regained the Ukraine.

By 1920, World War I and the Russian civil war had ended. In addition to the deaths of two million Russian soldiers in the world war, some four to six million had lost their lives in the civil conflict. The once powerful nation lay defeated, impoverished, and exhausted. Starvation hung like a specter over millions. The fighting was over, but Russia and other Western nations now faced the challenge of rebuilding social stability in an environment of continuing political and economic turmoil.

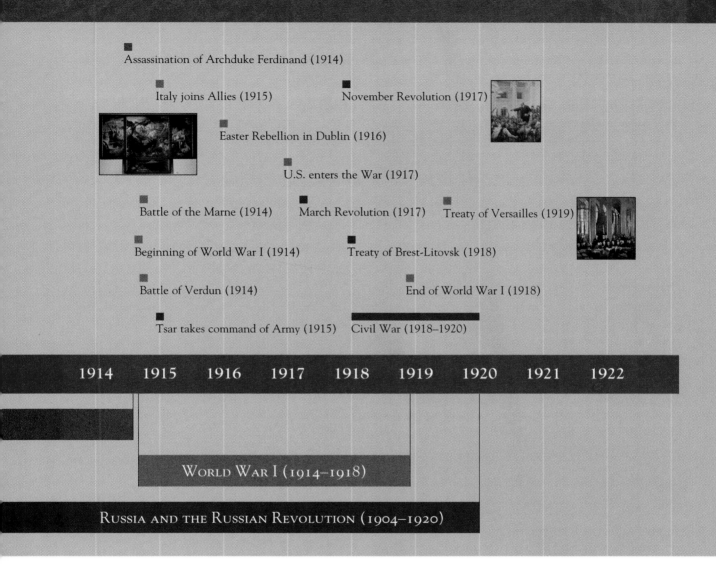

Assassination of Archduke Ferdinand (1914)

Italy joins Allies (1915)   November Revolution (1917)

Easter Rebellion in Dublin (1916)

U.S. enters the War (1917)

Battle of the Marne (1914)   March Revolution (1917)   Treaty of Versailles (1919)

Beginning of World War I (1914)   Treaty of Brest-Litovsk (1918)

Battle of Verdun (1914)   End of World War I (1918)

Tsar takes command of Army (1915)   Civil War (1918–1920)

1914	1915	1916	1917	1918	1919	1920	1921	1922

WORLD WAR I (1914–1918)

RUSSIA AND THE RUSSIAN REVOLUTION (1904–1920)

Summary

British historian Arnold Toynbee said that in the years before 1914, his generation expected that "life throughout the World would become more rational, more humane, and more democratic . . . that the progress of science and technology would make mankind richer . . . that all this would happen peacefully." World War I shattered that vision. The very technology and industrial prowess that had fueled the West's growth and sense of progress was turned to unimagined destruction. The war ended dreams of heroic battles and courageous military deeds: "Words such as glory, honor, courage, or hallow [became] obscene" in the face of how the war was fought and the carnage that resulted, wrote the American author and veteran Ernest Hemingway. Indeed, many survivors of World War I were haunted for the rest of their lives with a sense of belonging to a "lost generation."

Along with millions of human lives, the war destroyed or weakened European empires. The German, Austro-

Hungarian, Ottoman empires collapsed. Military losses and revolution ended the Russian empire, replacing it with the Soviet Union and Communist rulers who were transforming that society and would alter the political landscape throughout the world in the next decades. In the Far East, the Japanese gained lands and stature by expanding their empire at the expense of German colonies and China. In the Middle East, Africa, and Asia, the war and vague Allied declarations in support of national liberation stimulated struggles for national rights and independence. Even in the West, faith in imperialist ideals waned during and after the war. As one Indian diplomat explained, "there was no conviction left of the Europeans' superiority or sense of vision." From the outside looking in, Europe now seemed shrunken, vulnerable, and subject to unreasonable passions.

The calamities of those years were not limited to the war itself. In Turkey, the nationalistic government responded to Armenian demands for independence by deporting some 2 million Armenians from eastern Turkey. Probably one-third of these were massacred in what amounted to modern mass genocide; another third may have died during the forced march to Syria. In 1918 an influenza epidemic hit, killing some 27 million people worldwide. In central and eastern Europe, postwar starvation threatened millions despite relief efforts by the United States and the International Red Cross. The peace treaties "to make the world safe" and "to end all wars" left a legacy of disappointment and resentment. In the next two decades, these sentiments would draw Europe and the world once again into a maelstrom of violence.

REVIEW, ANALYZE, AND ANTICIPATE

REVIEW THE PREVIOUS CHAPTERS

In Chapter 20—"Mass Politics and Imperial Domination"—nationalism, the spreading demands for political inclusion, and imperialism during the second half of the nineteenth century were analyzed. In Chapter 21—"Modern Life and the Culture of Progress"—new industrial transformations and urban life during this same period were examined.

1. *In what ways did nationalism, industrialism, and imperialism create the forces underlying World War I?*
2. *After the experience of World War I, why might people look back on the decades preceding the war so longingly?*

ANALYZE THIS CHAPTER

Chapter 22—"Descending into the Twentieth Century"—tells the story of World War I and the Russian revolution.

1. *How might it be argued that several nations should bear responsibility for plunging the West into World*

War I? Which countries, if any, do you think were most responsible?
2. *Why was this war so devastating, physically and psychologically?*
3. *Analyze the role of the home fronts. How did problems at the home fronts relate to problems on the battlefronts?*
4. *It is perhaps easier to understand why there was a revolution in Russia that toppled the tsar than why the Bolsheviks came to power several months later in a second revolution. How do you explain this?*

ANTICIPATE THE NEXT CHAPTER

In Chapter 23—"Darkening Decades"—the rise of fascism, the development of the Soviet Union, and the trials of nations struck by the Great Depression will be analyzed. World War II, which came at the end of these difficult decades, will also be examined.

1. *What potential problems did the peace settlement at the end of World War I create for the future? What might have been done differently?*
2. *What threats did the Russian revolution pose to other Western nations, and what might be the consequences of those threats?*

BEYOND THE CLASSROOM

ON THE PATH TO TOTAL WAR

Joll, James. *The Origins of the First World War*. New York: Longman, 1984. A succinct survey of a complex subject.

Robbins, Keith. *The First World War*. Oxford: Oxford University Press, 1984. A wide-ranging examination of the effects of the war on the belligerent nations.

THE FRONT LINES

Ellis, John. *Eye-Deep in Hell: Trench Warfare in World War I*. New York: Pantheon Books, 1989. An examination of the daily experiences of the trench soldier.

Keegan, John. *The First World War*. New York: Alfred A. Knopf, 1999. A highly respected military historian examines the realities of warfare, stressing experiences on the western front.

Leed, Eric J. *No Man's Land: Combat and Identity in World War I*. Cambridge: Cambridge University Press, 1979. A fascinating treatment of the psychological effects of warfare on its combatants.

WAR ON THE HOME FRONT

Brayborn, Gail, and Penny Summerfield. *Out of the Cage: Women's Experiences in Two World Wars*. London: Pandora Press, 1987. Analyzes women's experiences in the two world wars and finds that the wars were economically and socially liberating for women.

Coetzee, Frans, and Marilyn Shevin-Coetzee, eds. *Authority, Identity and the Social History of the Great War*. Providence, RI: Berghahn Books, 1995. A comparative study of the experience and significance of the war in people's lives, especially for those on the home fronts.

Williams, John. *The Homefronts: Britain, France and Germany, 1914–1918*. London: Constable, 1972. Studies the effect of the on-going struggle on the British, French, and German populations.

TO THE BITTER END

Becker, Jean-Jacques. *The Great War and the French People*. New York: St. Martin's Press, 1986. An examination of the impact of the war on the French.

Schmitt, Bernadotte E., and Harold C. Vedeler. *The World in a Crucible, 1914–1918*. New York: Harper & Row, 1984. Analyzes World War I as a total war and traces its economic, social, cultural, and diplomatic consequences.

ASSESSING THE COSTS OF THE WAR

Fussell, Paul. *The Great War and Modern Memory*. Oxford: Oxford University Press, 1975. A fascinating study of the British experience on the western front from 1914 to 1918 and the literary means by which it has been remembered.

Winter, J.M. *The Experience of World War I*. New York: Oxford University Press, 1988. A well-written examination of how the war was experienced by the peoples of the belligerent nations.

THE PEACE SETTLEMENT

Nicolson, H. *Peacemaking 1919*. New York: Grosset & Dunlap, 1965. A standard treatment of the peace process by a participant.

Sharp, Alan. *The Versailles Settlement: Peacemaking in Paris, 1919*. New York: St. Martin's Press, 1991. A balanced overview that stresses the difficulties facing participants at the conference.

REVOLUTIONS IN RUSSIA

Fitzpatrick, Shelia. *The Russian Revolution, 1917–1932*, 2nd. ed. Oxford: Oxford University Press, 1994. A brief and insightful treatment of this complex subject.

Lincoln, W. Bruce. *Red Victory: A History of the Russian Civil War*. New York: Simon and Schuster, 1989. Examines the Bolshevik triumph over internal conflicts.

Pipes, Richard. *The Russian Revolution*. New York: Vintage Books, 1991. Argues that the Bolshevik Revolution was an authoritarian coup d'état.

Service, Robert. *Lenin: A Political Life*, 3 volumes. Bloomington, IN: Indiana University Press, 1985, 1991, 1995. An exhaustive biography.

Two Fascist Leaders

Benito Mussolini of Italy and Adolf Hitler of Germany stand together in the late 1930s. Virginia Woolf (1882–1941), a famed British author, described authoritarian men such as these: "His eyes are glazed; his eyes glare. His body, which is braced in an unnatural position, is tightly cased in a uniform. Upon the breast of that uniform are sewn several medals and other mystic symbols. His hand is upon a sword. He is called in German and Italian Führer and Duce; in our language Tyrant or Dictator."

CHAPTER 23

Darkening Decades

Dictators, Depression, and World War II, 1920–1945

"The Storm has died away," wrote French poet Paul Valéry in the years just after World War I, "and still we are restless, uneasy, as if the storm were about to break ... we do not know what will be born, and we fear the future ...." Many in Europe shared Valéry's sense of "terrible uncertainty." The Great War was finally over, and people longed for the return of "normal" life. In 1919, almost any memory of the days before the war seemed rosy. Too much had changed, though; the pre-World War I era was gone forever.

In fact, the immediate postwar years would bring frustration and turmoil. In the victorious democracies, growing disillusionment and political bickering rather than dynamic action seemed the rule. Moreover, some of these nations faced dramatically rising resistance to foreign rule in their overseas holdings. Millions of people living in communist Russia still struggled just to survive, let alone transform that troubled nation. Elsewhere in the West, union, socialist, and communist movements alarmed those who feared change. Many Europeans, especially in Italy, Germany, and east-central Europe, turned to right-wing leaders who attacked parliamentary government and raised the compelling banner of militant nationalism. The photo on p. 750 shows the two most predominant of these right-wing leaders and reveals some of the values they represented. Ahead, still unseen by most, lay the very dangers that people thought were over when the Great War ended.

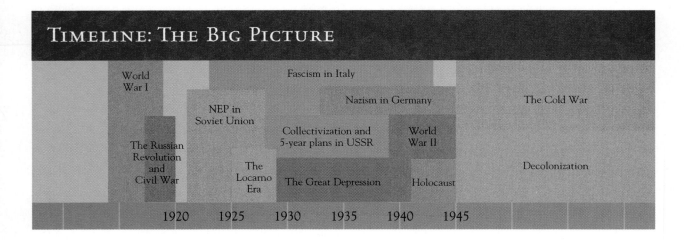

TIMELINE: THE BIG PICTURE

World War I

Fascism in Italy

Nazism in Germany

The Cold War

NEP in Soviet Union

Collectivization and 5-year plans in USSR

World War II

The Russian Revolution and Civil War

The Locarno Era

The Great Depression

Holocaust

Decolonization

1920   1925   1930   1935   1940   1945

Trying to Recover from the Great War, 1919–1929

In a haunting preview of troubles lurking over the era, Erich Maria Remarque, a German author and war veteran, described his life in Berlin during the early 1920s. "Prices have been soaring everywhere" and "poverty is greater than it was during the war." One afternoon he heard that demonstrations had been called for. In the streets, ominous rumors circulated that "troops have been concentrated at the barracks." Groups of strikers began marching through the streets. A disturbance broke out, people were yelling, and on corners speakers harangued small crowds. "Then suddenly everywhere is silence." A procession of maimed and wounded war veterans in the "faded uniforms of the front-line trenches" moved slowly toward him. Men with one arm carried white placards: "Where is the Fatherland's gratitude? The War Cripples are starving."

For Remarque and millions of others living in the post-World War I West, reality soon undermined the sense of liberation that the end of the war had brought. Families tried to care for their wounded sons, fathers, and brothers, and to endure the loss of those who had perished in battle. Many veterans came home angry. They had been promised moral "purification" during the war and compensation for their service after. Now they sensed that, in some ways, civilians did not fully appreciate their sacrifices. Too often, their old jobs had disappeared. For some, their wives or lovers had deserted them or developed a new, disturbing sense of independence. Many veterans, returning to homelands whose economies lay in ruins, struggled just to get enough food.

Indeed, economic uncertainty had settled like a pall over most of Europe. In the decades after the war, nations struggled to retool their economies from wartime needs back to ordinary requirements, and to reestablish international trade. Enormous sums in veterans' pay, war-widow benefits, and unemployment insurance burdened government treasuries. In vain, the victors had hoped that high reparation payments from Germany would be enough to help them rebuild their economies or at least cover debts from the war. So, governments borrowed when they could and printed money that had no basis in actual wealth. The resulting inflation hurt the middle classes in particular. They watched in panic as rising prices drained away their life savings. Between 1914 and 1928, France's currency alone lost four-fifths of its value. Still more unlucky were the thousands of western European investors, especially in France, who had invested in Russian bonds and saw them turn worthless when the Bolsheviks came to power.

Economic uncertainty

Across Europe, recessions followed short periods of relative prosperity all too quickly. Unemployment persisted—in Britain, it remained above 10 percent in both good times and bad. Governments and employers pressured women to give up their wartime jobs or accept lower-paying positions so as to make way for men. Inflation and unemployment spun Germany's economy out of control. Among the Western powers, only the United States emerged from the war richer than ever. Europeans now looked to their governments for relief and leadership.

THE VICTORS JUST HOLD ON

Solutions to Europe's economic problems depended greatly on the politics of the postwar era. However, within the democracies, no one seemed to step forward with innovative ideas for change. Some people hoped that the addition of women to the voting roles in these countries (with the notable exception of France, Italy, and Sweden) would improve politics. In fact, however, women's suffrage seemed to change politics little if at all. Most women voted as men did, and relatively few women gained political office.

International relations showed the same lack of innovation as domestic politics. Although the dominant military power on the Continent, France still feared a resentful Germany and defensively **Defensive France** held on to what it salvaged in the Versailles treaty following the war. A bloc of conservative parties generally held power and domestic policies changed little from the prewar period. The conservatives concentrated on rebuilding France and trumpeting anti-German nationalism.

Great Britain might have worked with its ally France to find solutions to postwar problems, but each nation usually acted alone or in opposition to one another. Various political parties—Conservatives, Laborites, and Liberals—alter- **Britain and its empire** nated in power in Britain. Sometimes they formed coalitions with each other, but none came forth with fresh solutions to the economic and diplomatic problems plaguing the British. Instead, Britain pulled away from extensive involvement in European affairs and tried to solve the Irish problem and to hold on to its restless colonies in Asia and Africa.

In the decades before World War I, British governments had attempted in vain to enact home rule for Ireland to quell growing demands for Irish independence. In 1914, Parliament had finally passed the Irish Home Rule Bill, but postponed its implementation until after the war. In 1916, impatient Irish nationalists in Dublin rose up against the British, but were crushed (see p. 733). Executed leaders quickly became national martyrs, and the extremist organization Sinn Fein ("Ourselves Alone") gained leadership in the nationalist cause. Its military wing became the Irish Republican Army. When the Sinn Fein Party declared Irish independence in 1919, fighting broke out between the IRA and the British army. With the British cast in the role of oppressors, the bloodshed persisted for two years. In December 1921, a treaty created the Irish Free State, though the six predominantly Protestant counties of Ulster (Northern Ireland) remained tied to Great Britain. Even then, a civil war broke out between protreaty and antitreaty forces. This legacy of violence would haunt the British and Irish again and again.

The British also faced nationalist problems elsewhere in the world. In North Africa, opposition to foreign rule forced the British to grant independence to Egypt in 1923. In Asia, nationalist parties developed into powerful political forces. Perhaps the strongest movement for national liberation emerged in India. Many Indians, hoping they would be rewarded with self-government, had fought for Britain in World War I, and the Indian economy had grown with India's support of Britain's war effort. Indian leaders, such as Mohandas Gandhi (1869–1948) and Jawaharlal Nehru (1889–1964), who had been westernized by education and experience while employed by British rulers, led the drive for independence. Even Britain's leaders, reacting to these pressures, began talking about granting self-rule to India.

The United States, for its part, could have taken a leadership role in international affairs. However, it refused to sign the Versailles treaty, join the League of Nations, or involve itself extensively in tensions overseas. **The U.S. turns inward** Europe's troubles came to center more and more on events in Germany, an unstable nation that would soon become enmeshed in a round of political and international turmoil.

CONTINUING CRISES IN GERMANY

Germany emerged from World War I defeated and angry. However, it had the potential to regain its strength quickly. More populous than France, Germany still had an intact industrial infrastructure. It also occupied an advantageous position in the postwar rearrangement of the European map. On its eastern borders lay weak nations newly created at the end of World War I. Farther east, Russia was isolated and preoccupied with shoring up its struggling new communist society.

Soon after the war, the Germans set up the Weimar Republic (named after the city where its constitution was drawn up) as a model liberal democracy. Moderate Social Democrats **The Weimar Republic** led the republic, but they had inherited the taint of defeat from the outcome of the war. Moreover, many officials in the bureaucracy, judiciary, and army were the same people who had occupied these positions before 1918. They were not particularly dedicated to the new republic. Nationalists and right-wing parties looked on the new parliamentary system with contempt.

Challengers within Germany arose almost as soon as the Social Democrats came to power. From the Left, Rosa Luxemburg (1870–1919) and Karl Liebknecht (1871–1919) led an uprising of radical Marxists (Spartacists). The government responded with repression, using the Free Corps—right-wing paramilitary groups made up mostly of veterans—to murder the two leaders and put down the communist threat. Nevertheless, communists continued to stir discord for several more years. In 1920, the German government faced a new threat, this time from right-wing nationalists under Wolfgang Kapp (1858–1922). A general strike by workers in support of the government paralyzed the economy and ended Kapp's effort to take over Berlin.

Then economic and international crises added to Weimar's political woes. In January 1923, after the German government defaulted on the huge war reparations bill, French and Belgian troops responded by occupying the Ruhr Valley, Germany's richest industrial area. The Germans struck back with passive resistance—opposing the occupiers in every way but violence. Enraged, the French tried to create a secession movement from Germany in the Rhineland. Although the occupying forces failed to collect any reparations, the occupation paralyzed Germany's economy, and wild inflation swept the country. At the crest of the inflation wave, 4 trillion German marks were worth only one dollar. People literally took wheelbarrows full of money to go shopping. Figure 23.1 reveals the extent of the inflation. Here children, apparently unaware of the economic turmoil throughout Germany, play with stacks of their nation's nearly worthless paper money. Within days, the inflation wiped out countless Germans' life savings.

Wild inflation

CONCILIATION AND A GLIMPSE OF PROSPERITY

Germany's international and economic picture looked bleak in 1923. But near the end of that year, a series of events unfolded that held out hope for international cooperation and a return to prosperity, not only for Germany but also for other nations in the West. In August, Gustav Stresemann (1878–1929) rose to leadership in the German government and offered to reconcile its differences with France. Having lost more money and international standing than it had gained from its occupation of the Ruhr, France reversed its policy and agreed to cooperate with Stresemann. An international commission headed by Charles Dawes (1865–1951) of the United States drew up a plan for the occupying forces' withdrawal from Germany. The commission also arranged for international loans to Germany, and set up a system by which Germany would pay lower reparations in installments. In 1925 Germany signed the Treaty of Locarno with France, Great Britain, Italy, and Belgium—an agreement that guaranteed Germany's existing frontiers with France and Belgium. Optimistic headlines in the *New*

The Dawes Plan

FIGURE 23.1
German inflation, November 1923.

York Times declared, "France and Germany <u>Ban War Forever.</u>" In 1926 the League of Nations admitted Germany and elected Stresemann its president. With international relations apparently normalized, France retreated, hoping that alliances with smaller eastern European states and the Maginot Line—a string of defensive fortresses on the French/German border it began building in the late 1920s—would contain the economically revived Germany.

Most of the remaining Western economies also perked up after 1924. In several countries, automobile manufacturing, aviation, synthetics, and electronics took off. Vacuum cleaners, washing machines, refrigerators, and electric irons—now often purchased on installment plans—became the norm in middle-class homes. New production techniques spread, especially among big-business employers who began using the principles and methods of "scientific management," promoted by the American efficiency engineer Frederick W. Taylor (1856–1915). After conducting time and motion studies, Taylor and other industrial psychologists recommended a sharper division of labor and detailed control over every aspect of work in order to boost worker productivity. Taylor especially emphasized the division between thinking by managers and physical labor by workers: "We do not want any initiative [from workers]," he wrote. "All we want of them is to obey the orders we give them, do what we say and do it quick." These techniques may have made production more efficient, but for laborers work became more mindless, dull, and repetitive than ever.

| Uneasy prosperity |

Outside of manufacturing, many people found jobs in the fast-growing service and housing sectors. Women in particular took positions as salesclerks, social workers, nurses, telephone operators, manicurists, hairdressers, and processors of convenience foods such as pudding mixes and dried cereals. Housing projects with indoor plumbing, electricity, and central heating sprang up throughout Europe—many of them boasted common-use day-care centers, laundries, and gardens. With all these developments, the West seemed to be back on the path of material progress that characterized the decades before World War I.

At the same time, several industries declined, unable to keep up with the new products, enhanced technology, and stiffer competition. Britain especially clung to its old expertise in metals and textiles, and failed to invest in the rising new technologies. Its coal industry sank dramatically, sparking massive strikes

that in 1926 turned into a general strike by miners and other industrial workers. The economies of nations outside of Europe—particularly in the United States, Canada, Australia, and Japan—benefited at Britain's and Europe's expense.

THE ROARING TWENTIES?

The popular culture of the 1920s reflected these complex political and economic changes of the postwar era. This uneasy, worrisome time has been called the "Jazz Age" and the "Roaring Twenties." Both terms convey the exuberance of the period's popular culture. They also hint at the superficial nature of the gaiety. This glittering culture had an edgy, frenetic quality that suggested a people haunted by a profound insecurity.

In Figure 23.2, a depiction of a cabaret scene, the German expressionist painter Otto Dix captures these contradictions of life during the 1920s. Berlin in particular became famous for cabarets such as this. In the painting, a couple dances to the music of a jazz band made up of black and white musicians, probably from America. European interest in American jazz and culture reflected the new international stature of the United States. To the right poses a "flapper," a fashionably thin woman whose dress and hair are cut short. She and the woman behind her smoking a cigarette stand alone, apparently independent. The scene suggests sexual abandon, yet the expressions on most people's faces are stiff, even apathetic. The picture conveys more of a sense of frenzy, decadence, and artificial celebration than relaxed happiness. The artist's deeper message is especially clear in the first panel (left) of this painting. In this smaller section, a crippled veteran leans on a crutch outside the cabaret and begs for assistance as the revelers pass him by with scarcely a glance in his direction.

While millions of people read the proliferating practical books, popular fiction, and newspapers, no new forces of popular culture shaped and reflected national attitudes more than the radio and movies. In France, | *The radio and movies* | the first radio broadcast station opened in 1920. It transmitted poor-quality sound to a limited audience, but by 1939 the number of radios in France had reached almost 5 million. The movie industry also flourished, particularly in Germany, Russia, France, and the United States. More than 100 million people saw a film each week.

FIGURE 23.2

Otto Dix, *Metropolis*, 1927.

Filmmaking itself became an art form, a visual record of social attitudes, and an account of people's ambitions and dreams. Increasingly, creating movies involved specialized roles, such as producer, director, and editor. Marketed actors became envied celebrities, and millions followed the lives and careers of these "movie stars." Many filmmakers projected their nations' self-images in stunning, creative ways—perhaps none more so than the legendary Russian Sergei Eisenstein (1898–1948). His epic films about the 1905 and 1917 revolutions in Russia represented the Soviet view of events in those "heroic" years.

Other films revealed deep-seated concerns about modern society. Figure 23.3, for example, shows an eerie, futuristic scene from the German director Fritz Lang's (1890–1976) film *Metropolis* (1925). This image emphasizes the overwhelming power of urban architecture and technology, and demonstrates cinema's potential to serve as an artistic medium. Here a solitary airplane flies through the stark canyons of buildings in a futuristic city. Humans are dwarfed out of sight in the impersonal world they have created. The image seems to complement visually lines from "The Waste Land" (1922), a work by one of the period's leading poets, T. S. Eliot (1888–1965):

> *"Unreal City,*
> *Under the brown god of a winter dawn,*
> *A crowd flowed over London Bridge, so many . . .*
> *And each man fixed his eyes before his feet."*

On another level, this scene also hints at other harbingers of modernity: the advent of skyscrapers, already rising in New York City, and the daring flights being made in small planes. Just two years after this film was made, the solo flight across the Atlantic of the American pilot Charles Lindbergh (1902–1974) won acclaim on both sides of the ocean. Americans and Europeans alike saw embodied in Lindbergh and New York the promise of something young, exciting, and dynamic that just might push the West forward into a bright future.

Indeed, throughout the West, cities such as Berlin,

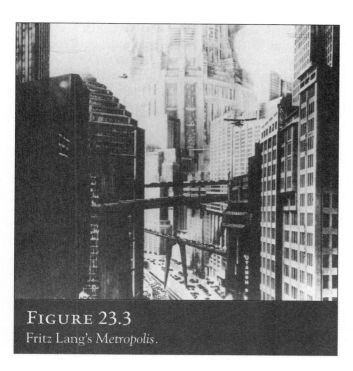

FIGURE 23.3
Fritz Lang's *Metropolis*.

styling, became more revealing. Along with the briefer fashions, women's hairstyles grew progressively shorter as well. Women discarded confining corsets that had long been in fashion and even donned trousers for sporting activities. Bathing suits, too, became increasingly skimpy. The "flapper," whom we saw in Figure 23.2, was now the new symbol of the ideal, free, sexually liberated working woman.

The new focus on body image and sexual appeal intensified concerns about hygiene. People began regularly using toothbrushes, deodorants, and cosmetics. In addition, they bathed more often than before and shaved more closely. Tanned, thin women and muscular men became the new standards of health and sexual attractiveness.

As sex became more openly discussed and encouraged, people also searched for ways to revive declining birthrates and thereby replace the lives lost during the war. In France, for example, the government made distributing birth-control information illegal and abortion punishable by death. The French proclaimed a new holiday, "Mother's Day," an innovation that other Western countries soon copied. Many governments provided maternity benefits, and increasingly, births took place in hospitals under the control of specialized nurses and doctors. Separate rooms for testing, labor, delivery, and recovery made the process of giving birth almost factory-like. Doctors, nurses, and social workers told women the "best" way to care for their children, and

Paris, and New York became even more dazzling cultural centers than before. Office buildings and skyscrapers shot up, some of them displaying striking *The Bauhaus school* new trends in architecture. Most influential was the German architect Walter Gropius (1883–1969), who in 1919 founded the Bauhaus school of art in Germany. This school created new standards for modern architecture and for the design of ordinary objects from chairs and lamps to dishes. In 1925, Gropius designed the building shown in Figure 23.4. Emphasizing clean, functional lines, this international style of architecture symbolized acceptance of the modern, industrial world. These buildings unabashedly displayed their efficient structure, prefabricated materials, and steel and glass features. Many architects would follow this new style over the next half-century in creating office buildings, workers' housing, and private homes in the new style.

In addition to trends in entertainment and the arts, the "Roaring Twenties" implied new attitudes toward sex. Especially in leading cities, clothing fashions, often popularized in movies, exhibited these changing attitudes. Women's clothing, featuring thinner fabrics, shorter skirts, and tight-fitting

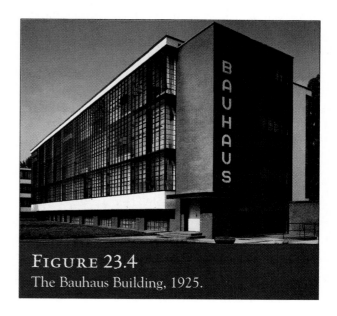

FIGURE 23.4
The Bauhaus Building, 1925.

child-rearing courses for girls became compulsory in some countries.

THE ANXIOUS TWENTIES

Of all the forms of culture that gained currency during these years, high culture most powerfully reflected the stressful undercurrents of the postwar period. Many writers, intellectuals, and artists emphasized the uncertainty of the era, and explored the widespread feelings of insecurity that people harbored.

Several philosophers, reacting to the horrors of the Great War, attacked nineteenth-century optimism and rationalism. These thinkers expanded on the ideas set forth earlier by Friedrich Nietzsche in Germany and Henri Bergson in France (see pp. 713–714). The most widely read of the post-World War I philosophers was German Oswald Spengler (1880–1936). In his book *The Decline of the West* (1918), Spengler argued that all civilizations were like biological organisms, each with its own life cycle. Western civilization, he claimed, had passed its high point, and World War I signaled the beginning of its end. This sense of decay and crisis emerged in many other works, most notably in the Spanish writer José Ortega y Gasset's (1883–1955) *Revolt of the Masses* (1930). Gasset lamented the decline of liberal elites and the "accession of the masses to complete social power." The masses, he warned, were not equipped to lead, yet they now took control from qualified elites and demanded a dangerous conformity: "Anybody who is not like everybody, who does not think like everybody, runs the risk of being eliminated."

Sense of decay and crisis

Sigmund Freud's ideas (see Chapter 21) about the irrational, unconscious, and instinctual aspects of human thought and behavior—which had first emerged just before World War I—gained more acceptance during the 1920s. The unconscious and irrational played particularly prominent roles in the most acclaimed literature of the postwar era. The Irish writer James Joyce (1882–1941), German author Franz Kafka (1883–1924), and French writer Marcel Proust (1871–1922) created disquieting, introspective works of literature that elevated personal psychological experience over reason. In *Ulysses* (1922), Joyce in particular mastered the "stream of consciousness" technique, which displayed to the reader the rambling thoughts, free associations, and erotic fantasies going on in the mind of a character. At first critics and the public dismissed the novel as "morbid," "nonsense," and "foul." Eventually, however, this book about a single day in the lives of a group of Dubliners, which also served as a commentary on the human condition, was hailed as one of the century's greatest works of literature. In her novel *Mrs. Dalloway* (1925), British author Virginia Woolf used similar techniques to describe one day in the inner life of a woman, including fragmented conversations, partial remembrances, and fantasies.

Novels and memoirs of the Great War also proliferated during these years. As in *All Quiet on the Western Front* by the German author Erich Maria Remarque, these works emphasized themes of brutality and suffering, disillusionment with civilian life, and a sense that the war had spawned a generation of "lost souls." At the same time, Remarque's and other's books revealed a longing for the sense of purpose and comradeship that so often arises during a war effort but subsides in times of peace.

Similar themes marked artistic styles of the day. The *dada movement* stressed the absence of purpose in life. Surrealist painters explored dreams and the world of the subconscious. Other painters such as Käthe Kollwitz (see the Chapter 22 Biography), and Otto Dix (Figure 23.2) created moving images of suffering, destruction, and social despair.

In the 1920s, then, Western democratic societies struggled mightily both to come to terms with the consequences of the war and to move on to better days. In the early postwar years, the difficulties seemed overwhelming. Even with the revival of healthier economies and easing of international tensions after 1923, underlying doubt and insecurity persisted and made themselves plain in the period's cultural expression.

Turning Away from Democracy: Dictatorships and Fascism, 1919–1929

The sense of unease and the difficult realities clearly burdened politics in the Western democracies, but things were far worse on the political front elsewhere in Europe. Among the states of east-central and southern Europe, the strain of the postwar years became too much for the fragile democratic systems budding there.

AUTHORITARIANISM IN EAST-CENTRAL EUROPE

In 1919, Admiral Miklos Horthy (1868–1957), the reactionary former commander of the Austro-Hungarian navy, led forces, aided by anticommunist Allies and ambitious Romanians, that overthrew the newly formed regime led by the communist Béla Kun (1885–1937) in Hungary. Horthy's rule, like other right-wing authoritarian regimes that followed in Poland (1926) and Yugoslavia (1929), amounted to a dictatorship backed by the nation's military and conservative forces—the bureaucracy, high church, and wealthy elites. Why did these east-central European nations, most of which emerged from the dissolution of the Austro-Hungarian Empire during World War I with new democratic regimes, turn away from parliamentary democracy?

Part of the answer may be that the newly created nations in this area faced enormous economic problems. Although the old Austro-Hungarian Empire had suffered from ethnic and political divisions, it had functioned as an economic whole—its industrial areas trading with its agricultural regions. Now split up, the individual nations were mostly agricultural and too unproductive to create prosperity. Only Czechoslovakia, whose parliamentary system would survive the longest, boasted an advanced industrial economy.

Struggling with these problems, the new democratic regimes seemed divided and ineffective. Many conservative groups feared the kind of change represented by liberal democracy, socialism, and communism. Such changes promised to dilute conservatives' power, diminish their economic base, and undermine their beliefs in the traditional social order. This lack of experience with democracy and the strength of these conservative groups made these nations vulnerable to authoritarian men like Horthy, who promised order and advocated nationalism backed by armed force. One by one, the democratic governments fell to authoritarian takeovers. As in Horthy's regime, the new rulers sometimes used "White Terror" to silence opponents and often repressed Jews and other minority groups.

This rise of authoritarian governments during the 1920s spread beyond east-central Europe. The most dramatic and ominous move came in Italy. There, the charismatic Benito Mussolini (1883–1945) took power, bringing with him a new governance system and ideology: fascism.

THE RISE OF FASCISM IN ITALY

At its core, fascism in practice meant dictatorship by a charismatic leader. However it was more than that. It included a set of antidemocratic, anti-individualistic, and anticommunist ideas or attitudes. Fascist doctrine hailed "the people" while denouncing the principles of the French *Fascist doctrine* Revolution. Fascist leaders such as Alfredo Rocco (1875–1935) viewed the state as "a living organism" and rejected liberal democratic forms of government, complaining that the liberal state "is dissolving into a mass of small particles, parties, associations, groups and syndicates that are binding it in chains." The fascist call was to nationalism and military prowess. In Italy, people angry and dismayed with events following World War I heard this call and followed it.

Italy had emerged from World War I a battered, disappointed victor. Its armies, on the verge of collapse, had nevertheless managed to hold on and ultimately contributed to the final Allied victory. However, the Treaty of *Turmoil in Italy* Versailles denied Italy some of the territories on the Adriatic coast that the Allies had promised in return for Italy's contribution to the war effort. Many Italians felt that at Versailles, their nation lost its rightful status as a great power. All this left Italian nationalists bitter and convinced many more Italians that the war had not been worth the price Italy had paid.

Near-chaos within this troubled nation multiplied these disappointments. Italy's already weak economy staggered under a huge national debt. Its inflated currency, together with a shortage of consumer goods, made prices skyrocket. Hundreds of thousands of veterans could find no jobs. In the summer of 1919, disorder spread. Farmworkers threatened property owners by joining unions called "red leagues." Veterans and poor families began seizing idle lands. Banditry in the south grew out of control, and strikes plagued the cities. During the winter of 1920–1921, workers seized control of several hundred factories. Socialists and communists gained strength within industrial and rural unions.

Italy's newly elected government, plagued by political divisions, seemed powerless in the face of these pressures. Frightened landlords and factory owners, along with thousands of veterans and a middle class ravaged by inflation and insecurity, longed for vigorous leadership and a strong, dependable government. The vigorous leader who stepped forward was Benito Mussolini. The strong government was his fascist dictatorship.

Mussolini was born into a family of socialist artisans, and received enough education to become a teacher and then a radical journalist. At the outbreak of World War I, he used the socialist paper he edited to advocate antimilitarism and *Mussolini takes power* to demand that Italy remain neutral during the war. A year later, he changed his mind, now convinced that "only blood makes the wheels of history turn." He broke from his socialist allies, started a new newspaper, and joined the army. After the war, he organized mostly unemployed veterans into the National Fascist Party—the term "fascist" alluding to Roman prowess, unity, and justice. His Fascist Party soon attracted enough support to bring down Italy's parliamentary government.

Why did Mussolini's political movement hold such appeal? The answer to this question is complex. Fascism attracted veterans hoping for a sense of renewal *The appeal of Fascism* after the disappointments of the war and the immediate postwar years and appealed to young men who felt they had "missed out" on the war experience and therefore responded to the call of wounded national pride. "When I returned from the war—just like so many others—I hated politics and politicians, who . . . had betrayed the hopes of soldiers, reducing Italy to a shameful peace," explained Italo Balbo, a future associate of Mussolini. These men became the members and muscle of the new party. Factory owners, merchants, and landowners also embraced fascism when Mussolini vowed to save Italy from communism. These groups provided Mussolini with money when he organized squads of black-shirted "Fascisti" to terrorize radical workers and their liberal supporters. Finally, those who blamed the parliamentary government for Italy's postwar woes warmed to fascist promises to act decisively and create unity through nationalistic policies. Fascism seemed to offer a "third way"—a path above socialism and conventional parliamentary democracy—to security and success for Italy.

Figure 23.5 reveals some of the qualities that made Mussolini's Fascist movement attractive. Mussolini stands on a platform dressed in a white paramilitary uniform, his arm raised in the Fascist salute of exaggerated bravery. Below him stands his bodyguard of black-shirted party members in their paramilitary uniforms, holding knives up in the disciplined salute. All are posing for the crowd of onlookers to the left and photographers. The whole scene has been self-consciously set up to present an image of strong leadership and military prowess, and it suggests the appeal of ritual and participation in a mighty movement. Similar scenes would become common as fascist movements and authoritarian governments spread across Europe.

In 1922, building on this support, squads of black-shirted Fascists marched on Rome under Mussolini's vow that "either we are allowed to govern or we will seize power." The indecisive Italian king Victor Emmanuel III (r. 1900–1946) buckled under the pressure and appointed Mussolini prime minister. With great speed, the Fascist leader acquired extraordinary powers.

Between 1924 and 1926, Mussolini turned his office into a dictatorship. Under his rule, only the Fascist Party could engage in organized political activity. Il Duce (the leader) sent his secret police everywhere. "Everything within the State," he *The Fascist system* demanded, and "Nothing outside the State." Mussolini next struck a deal with the powerful Catholic Church and signed the Lateran Treaty of 1929. In return for money and the right to teach religion in the public schools, the papacy finally recognized the existence of the Italian state. The agreement ended the sixty years of division between the church and the state since unification.

FIGURE 23.5
Mussolini and his Black Shirts.

To guide Italy's economy toward self-sufficiency and industrialization, while carefully protecting private property and profits, the Fascists worked closely with business leaders. They organized the different industries and trades into confederations, or "corporations." Each corporation included a syndicate of workers and one of employers, each in turn headed by a Fascist official. The Fascists also abolished all independent labor unions, strikes, and lockouts. Instead, compulsory arbitration under the party's direction now settled issues of wages and working conditions and disputes between labor and management. The complicated economic and political machinery that Mussolini put in motion for these purposes became known as the corporate state, or corporatism.

Although the state would gain a controlling hand in several major industries, Mussolini's corporate state mainly enlarged the bureaucracy and hamstrung workers' unions. A few well-publicized achievements, such as new railroads, highways, building projects, and educational reforms, hid more fundamental deficiencies. His ambitious agricultural policies generally failed to improve per capita output. People of property fared well, but workers, especially women, suffered declining income. Even though women flocked to hear him, Mussolini cut their wages by decree and banned them from several professions. Those who did not heed his call to take up their "maternal duties" were pushed toward low-paying jobs. Nevertheless, growing numbers of Italian women still managed to enter universities and find positions in the world of paid work.

By 1929, Mussolini stood unchallenged. Using films, radio addresses, biographies, newspapers, and schools, he amassed a huge following of supporters who repeated his reassuring phrase, "Mussolini is always right." Some artists and intellectuals supported at least his image of dynamic leadership. Mussolini also won a reputation among groups throughout Europe, South America, and the United States as someone who could "make the trains run on time," gain peace with the Catholic Church, and stand up to communist threats.

In reality, Mussolini—like many twentieth-century politicians—was more of an actor able to manipulate appearances than an effective ruler who could solve domestic or international problems. Many people immune to his charm saw him as merely a strutting, boasting carnival performer. Mussolini's vision of "historical destiny"—to create a Second Roman Empire and turn the Mediterranean into an Italian "lake"—perhaps most revealed a disturbing lack of touch with reality. Even with "Il Duce" in control, Italy was no major power.

To the east, the situation was entirely different. Russia had been a major power and might well rise again. Now transformed into a communist state and reformed into the Soviet Union by the Bolsheviks, its radical left-wing policies represented an even more frightening threat to capitalist democracies than the extreme right-wing politics of Italian Fascism.

Transforming the Soviet Union: 1920–1939

In 1920 Russia's bloody civil war had finally ended. The suffering, however, dragged on. Industrial production sank to only 13 percent of pre-World War I levels. A famine struck, taking 4 to 7 million lives. Countless thousands of veterans and city-dwellers roamed the countryside in search of food, shelter, and employment. "Green Armies" of peasants revolted against forced requisitions of their crops and restrictions against selling products at market prices. Workers struck against declining wages and lack of control over the factories. Sailors at the Kronstadt naval base mutinied, demanding political liberty. Many Communist Party and union members called for more democracy. How could Lenin's still vulnerable Communist government survive?

LENIN'S COMPROMISE: THE NEP

Lenin retreated. In 1921 he launched the New Economic Policy (NEP), a "temporary" compromise with capitalism. This policy allowed peasants to manage their own land and sell their own crops. In addition, small-scale industries could operate under private ownership, and money and credit were restored. Although the state still supervised the economy, the NEP provided enough capitalist incentive to pull the Russian economy out of chaos.

Lenin's retreat did not extend to politics, however. Russia remained a "dictatorship of the Proletariat," symbolized on Russia's flag by the red of socialism, the hammer of industrial workers, and the sickle of peasants. Lenin and the Communist Party elite maintained a tight grip on power and brutally suppressed any opposition. Local soviets submitted to the central government in Moscow, dominated by its sixteen-person Politburo and, above all, the secretariat of the Communist Party. The formal creation of the "Union of Soviet Socialist Republics" (USSR, or Soviet Union) in 1922 paid only lip service to desires for autonomy in "republics" such as the Ukraine, Armenia, and Georgia. Russia, home to four-fifths of the USSR's total population, dominated the Union.

Soviet society in the 1920s reflected its revolutionary origins as well as the temporary compromise with capitalism. The Communists had eliminated the old aristocracy, church, and traditional class distinctions. But party, military, and cultural elites enjoyed higher standards of living, better housing, and more educational opportunities than anyone else. Some peasants who took advantage of NEP opportunities also became relatively wealthy, as did their urban counterparts running small businesses.

Moreover, women enjoyed unprecedented legal equality. In addition to the right to vote, they received the right to equal pay, education, and professional opportunities. The government set up programs and agencies such as the Women's Bureau to promote equality, day care, housing, medical care, and information on birth control and divorce. Alexandra Kollontai (1872–1952), head of the Women's Bureau, urged collectivization of child-rearing and a new family form: "The narrow and exclusive affection of the mother for her own children must expand until it embraces all the children of the great proletarian family. In place of the indissoluble marriage based on the servitude of woman, we shall see rise in the free union [of two people] . . . equal in their rights and in their obligations. . . ."

These new policies all showed promise, but in fact the burdens on Soviet women probably increased. Programs to help them lacked the resources to make a real difference. Greater access to jobs rarely translated into higher-level positions. Women were still expected to retain their traditional burdens at home, their "second shift."

Although the NEP was a retreat from strict Communist policies, Lenin's regime still envisioned itself as leading the world into modernity. The government turned churches and great mansions into museums and meeting halls. Cultural activities promoted proletarian pride, the benefits of technology, and the glories of the future. Avant-garde artists created utopian visions by connecting images of mass production and social justice.

The NEP may have encouraged the outside world to end its isolation of Russia. Between 1922 and 1924, all Western nations recognized the Soviet Union except the United States, which remained aloof until 1933. Indeed, to many socialists throughout the West, the Soviet Union stood as a source of hope and inspiration.

THE STRUGGLE TO SUCCEED LENIN

Lenin would not live to witness the results of the NEP. After a series of paralytic strokes, he died in 1924. Three of his chief associates—Leon Trotsky (1877–1940), Nikolai Bukharin (1888–1938), and Joseph Stalin (1879–1953)—jockeyed to succeed him. Most observers assumed that the brilliant but arrogant Trotsky, who had led the Red Army during the civil war, would win. He argued that the Soviet Union must promote revolutions elsewhere in the West to survive, and that the Soviet economy should be tightly controlled and massively industrialized from above. By contrast, the popular Bukharin, who had been appointed by Lenin to lead the NEP, argued for socialism by slow, careful steps. The shrewd political manipulator Stalin claimed a middle-of-the-road position between these two, but believed that Russia must survive alone—"socialism in one country." His opponents vastly underestimated him.

Stalin (a pseudonym meaning "man of steel") was born in Georgia the son of poverty-stricken ex-serfs. His mother managed to get him into an Orthodox seminary school, where he received a formal education. Expelled from the *Joseph Stalin* seminary because of his Marxist views, he joined revolutionary groups. Repeatedly arrested, he kept managing to escape. In 1917, he took advantage of the revolutionary turmoil and hastened to Petrograd from his exile in Siberia. A poor speaker and writer, he used daring and organizational talents to rise in the party. He played a prominent role in Russia's civil war and became executive secretary of the Communist Party. In this key position, he made himself master of the all-important party machinery and pursued his drive for power.

Toward the end of his life, Lenin had warned that "Stalin is too rude" to lead. Nevertheless, after Lenin's death, Stalin cleverly played on the Soviet people's love of Lenin by posing as his heir and leading a movement to deify him. He also brought into the party new people, who thereby owed him a debt. Playing off his rivals against each other, he used his control over the Central Committee of the Communist Party to edge the overconfident Trotsky and his supporters on the Left out of powerful positions and, in 1927, expel them from the party. The next year, he turned against Bukharin and the Right. Party members who had doubts about Stalin accepted the need for party loyalty. By the end of 1928, Stalin had maneuvered himself into a position of dominance over the Communist Party, and of dictatorship over the Soviet Union. Now he set out to transform the nation.

STALIN'S FIVE-YEAR PLANS

By 1928 Soviet industry had attained no more than 1913 levels of production. Stalin and his party leadership wanted much more. That year, he ended the NEP and launched the First Five-Year Plan. The fundamental goal of the plan could not have been more ambitious: "We do not want to be beaten. . . . Old Russia . . . was ceaselessly beaten for her backwardness. . . . We are fifty or a hundred years behind the advanced countries. We must make good this lag in ten years . . . or they crush us." The plan called for the rapid, massive industrialization of the nation. Goals included more than doubling industrial production, increasing the generation of electric power almost fivefold, and building 1,500 new factories within five years. To achieve the goals, the State Planning Commission, or Gosplan, would strictly regulate all aspects of production, including targeting crucial industries such as steel, regimenting the industrial labor force, and hiring foreign engineers to help build the new factories. The 1930s Soviet propaganda poster shown in Figure 23.6, "The Five-Year Plan in Four Years," portrays the idea that Stalin will lead Soviet industrial development against the threatening reactionary forces of capitalism and religion. As if preparing for another war, Stalin ordered the USSR's entire society to mobilize for industrialization.

To help accomplish the Five-Year Plan's goals (which included doubling agricultural production), the state took agriculture out of the control of individual peasants by consolidating their lands into huge collective farms that used modern machines. Elected managers and party officials ran the farms. Individuals could own tools, keep small gardens for fruits and vegetables, and raise pigs and chickens for private use or sale. By determining prices and distribution of crops, the state expected to use agricultural "surpluses" to pay for industrialization—to buy the equipment to build factories, transportation facilities, and power plants. Collectivization, it was believed, would also push peasants to become industrial workers in the cities.

Collectivization

The process of collectivization proved ruinous. Hundreds of thousands of peasants, especially wealthier landowners derisively called *kulaks*, powerfully resisted the new policies. In protest, they even destroyed their own crops and livestock—some 50 percent of horses and cattle between 1929 and 1933. Officials terrorized such resisters into submission. "The expropriation of the kulaks is an integral part of the formation . . . of the collective farms," announced Stalin. The kulaks should be "eliminated as a class." Hundreds of thousands of peasants were killed and far more were exiled to Siberia, never to return. This violent battle of wills was accompanied by plummeting agricultural production and government pressure to

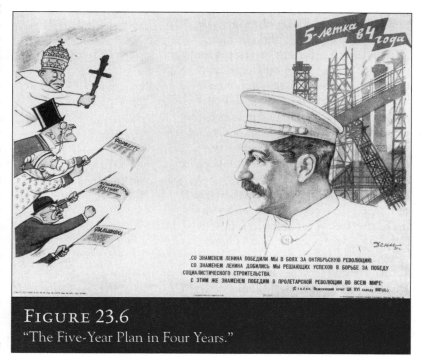

FIGURE 23.6
"The Five-Year Plan in Four Years."

increase agricultural exports at all costs to finance industrialization. The results were disastrous: Between 1930 and 1933, famine struck, taking the lives of 4 to 6 million people. An observer reported that in Ukrainian villages, peasants resorted to eating "dogs, horses, rotten potatoes, the bark of trees, grass—anything they could find . . . and no matter what they did, they went on dying, dying, dying." The effort to collectivize agriculture and the deadly hunger tore apart rural families, communities, and established ways of life. Nevertheless, Stalin finally got his way: more than half the land was collectivized within the first year, and over 90 percent after ten years.

To industrialize the Soviet Union, planners had to start almost from ground level and build up. They concentrated on producer goods such as engines and tractors rather than consumer goods such as shoes and clothes. Gradually, steel mills, dams, power plants, foundries, mines, refineries, chemical factories, and railroads sprang up all over the Soviet Union. Technocrats and officials faced pressure to produce targeted results. The government fostered a sense of emergency to inspire people, especially the young, to work hard. Presenting the effort as a great adventure, officials pointed out that those who most contributed to the industrialization drive could achieve a status similar to that of the heroes of the 1917 revolution. The government moved "shock brigades" of enthusiastic, efficient workers from factory to factory to stimulate production, while the press celebrated new "Heroes of Labor" who exceeded production targets. Officials encouraged women to work on both the collective farms and in factories; by 1940, women made up almost half the labor force.

Mobilizing for industrialization

All elements of Soviet society were mobilized to support the effort to make the USSR an industrial power. Schools, adult education classes, newspapers, union meetings, and youth associations became saturated with official doctrines of Soviet communism, efficiency, and class pride. "We must make every school child aware of . . . how the great people of our epoch—Lenin, Stalin, and their companions in arms—organized the workers in the struggle for a new and happy life," explained a Soviet text on teaching methods. Officials, minor bureaucrats, and members of the secret police ranged everywhere and monitored progress. Within families—the "school for socialism"—mothers were urged to raise their children to fit into communist society. Earlier policies supporting women's' choices were reversed. The state made abortion illegal and promoted traditional marriage and relationships. In this more repressive era, homosexuality became a crime.

The state also tightened controls over cultural productions, ending the experimentation of the 1920s. The Central Committee of the Communist Party told publishing houses that "books must be an instrument for the mobilization of the workers for the tasks of industrialization and collectivization." Socialist realism became the required orthodoxy in art. In this style, approved murals, art, and literature portrayed realistic images of people carrying out the dreams of a communist society. Figure 23.7 is an example of this effort to make art relevant and compelling to the working masses. In this idealized image, the sun of a new day streams in as women workers and architects confer over plans for a new factory. The men listen attentively, but as was usually the case in real life, they (in authoritative suits), not the women (wearing work-

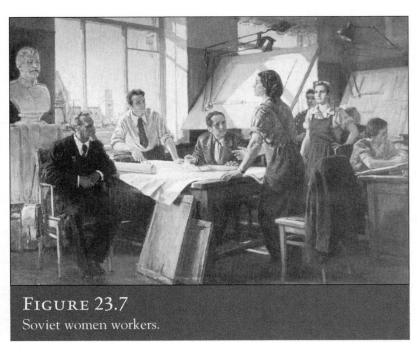

FIGURE 23.7
Soviet women workers.

ers' kerchiefs), are in charge. On the left, above everyone, a bust of Stalin looks on.

At the end of 1932, Stalin announced that all goals of the First Five-Year Plan had been accomplished several months ahead of time. He recited a list of accomplishments in iron, steel, tractors, automobiles, machine-tools, chemicals, and aircraft production. "Our country has been converted from an agrarian into an industrial country," he proclaimed. These gains, however, came at a high price. For the hard-pressed workers, consumer goods beyond the necessities remained scarce. Clearly, some Soviet citizens—namely party members—benefited more than others. One refugee cynically compared life before and after the Bolshevik Revolution: "In Tsarist times there were the rich and the poor; under Soviet power there were the party members and the non-party members." Similar Second and Third Five-Year Plans would follow, this time with more emphasis on consumer goods and armaments. The terrifying Great Purges would also follow.

BLOOD AND TERROR: THE GREAT PURGES

In 1934, someone assassinated Sergei Kirov (1888–1934), a high Soviet official. Stalin used the murder as an excuse to eliminate potential rivals. The incident introduced a long period of party purges, marked by terror, house arrests, bizarre show-trials, torture, imprisonments, and executions—all approved by Stalin.

Historians still debate Stalin's motives for the Great Purges. Stalin and party officials blamed difficulties during the five-year plans on many—engineers, technocrats, army officers, older party members, regional nationalists, foreign conspirators, saboteurs—and purged the accused. Lower-level officials probably contributed to the waves of purges by trying to rise at the expense of higher-level officials. Certainly Stalin worried about threats from within the party. He eradicated all potential opposition—real or imagined, and even on foreign soil. In 1940, Soviet agents assassinated Trotsky in Mexico.

By the time the Great Purges ended in 1939, authorities had killed some 1 million people. Another 7 million died or languished in forced-labor camps; still more had been sent into exile. The terror spread throughout Soviet society, for everyone knew of someone accused and arrested. Almost all the original

Bolshevik leaders and the Red Army's top officer corps were gone. New, younger figures beholden to Stalin now staffed the government, Communist Party, and military.

In the end, Stalin got most of what he wanted. By 1939, the Soviet Union had a fully planned economy, with the state determining production, prices, and distribution. Although officials announced successes whether they occurred or not, the USSR had in fact become the third greatest industrial power in the world. More than 90 percent of peasants lived on collective, mechanized farms. Millions more had moved to the cities, where new housing, schools, libraries, and hospitals had sprung up. For the first time, most of the population could now read. Within the Soviet Union, no one dared oppose Stalin, and now he had the armaments to face a new challenge already rising in the west. But the cost had been tremendous. Up to 20 million people had died and far more had suffered as a result of Stalin's policies.

The Great Depression, 1929–1939

The forces to the west creating that challenge to the USSR had begun to coalesce and gather momentum, and the Soviets were not the only ones threatened by them. As we saw earlier, authoritarianism and fascism—fierce opponents of communism—had already started to rise in the 1920s. In 1929, a new crisis struck the Western democracies: the Great Depression. Reeling from years of hard times and pulling much of the world with them, Western societies began edging toward a new darkness that would more than rival the horrors of World War I.

CRASH!

In October 1929, the New York stock market crashed. In one month, stocks lost almost two-thirds of their value. The financial crisis quickly spread from the United States, the world's leading industrial nation and creditor, to Europe, where nations depended heavily on American loans and trade. The crash ended the relative prosperity since 1924, and provoked an unprecedented global depression. Within two years, thousands of banks and businesses throughout the West failed. Spending, production, employment, and income all dropped sharply. Plant closings, farm foreclosures, and joblessness haunted the Western nations. People's confidence in the economy died, and too often with it went their faith in themselves.

A complex series of events had led to the disaster. The postwar economic order was built on a fragile foundation of international credit, reparations payments, and foreign trade. Much of Europe remained dependent on the United States for credit. Germany in particular relied on American loans to support its reparation payments.

Causes of the economic collapse

In 1928, American investors began pulling their money out of Germany and demanding repayment of loans to invest in the unregulated, soaring U.S. stock market. Credit dried up in Germany and in east-central European nations tied to the German economy. The 1929 crash sent people running to banks to withdraw funds, further undermining credit. Soon the West's entire economic house of cards collapsed.

The collapse took much of the globe with it. Over the years, non-Western lands had become important suppliers of raw materials—such as rice, cotton, cocoa, rubber, oil, copper, and tin—for Western industry and urban populations. With their economies more and more dependent on international trade, these regions were now tied to the economic fate of the West. Ties to the West particularly marked industrialized Japan's economy. The lure of increasing trade with the United States during the 1920s had persuaded Japan to halt its imperial expansion in Asia. The Great Depression—which quickly slashed exports to the United States in half and left 3 million people unemployed—brought an end to Japan's prosperity and revived its imperial ambitions. Japan's leaders looked to make East Asian markets their own, by conquest if necessary.

IN THE TEETH OF THE DEPRESSION

By 1932, Europe's economies had shrunk to one-half their 1929 size. Unemployment in the West rose to a shocking 22 percent, leaving 30 million people out of work. Along with their jobs, people lost their savings, their farms, and their homes. In Germany, Heinrich Hauser described how "an almost unbroken chain of homeless men extends the whole length of the great Hamburg-Berlin highway." One British woman echoed the feelings of many: "These last few years since I've been out of the mills . . . I've got no spirit for anything." Masses of people sank into poverty, and

malnutrition and diseases spread. Families suffered from new tensions as men lost their traditional role as breadwinners. "When he was out of work," lamented a woman from Liverpool, "we were always having rows over the children."

Scenes of despair could be found everywhere. Figure 23.8, a painting by Isaac Soyer, shows people in a New York employment agency. Their faces reveal little hope as they wait—reading a newspaper, looking away in distraction, or staring ahead in resignation. The dreary room offers no consolation, and the scene through the window suggests there is little to look forward to on the city streets.

In eastern and central Europe, hard-pressed farmers and unemployed workers looked for scapegoats. They blamed Jews, whom they saw as controlling the banks, bureaucracy, jobs, and policies responsible for the depression. People also pointed their fingers at socialists, communists, big business, and even modernity. Ethnic groups and major powers turned on one another, and throughout the West, popular protests by desperate, angry people spread.

SEARCHING FOR SOLUTIONS

At first, governments met the depression the old way: balance the budget and increase tariffs on imported goods. However these policies just made matters worse by dampening spending and hindering trade. A moratorium on reparations and war debts in August 1931 came too late to do much good. Imperial powers such as Britain and France turned to their colonial holdings for secure trade and profits, only to meet rising demands for independence in India, Iraq, Vietnam, Algeria, and elsewhere. The British economist John Maynard Keynes (1883–1946) argued for new policies—more government expenditures financed by budget deficits to stimulate consumer spending and raise employment—but few listened to his still little-known ideas.

After 1932, new regimes in the United States, Britain, and Germany adopted policies to increase government spending and provide some relief. Similar policies had already enabled Scandinavian democracies to weather the depression with relative ease. However, even with these measures, most Western democracies recovered slowly and not fully until the late 1930s, thanks to spending for rearmament. Figure 23.9 indicates that France and the United States in particular had difficulty raising industrial production

FIGURE 23.8
Isaac Soyer, *Employment Agency*, 1937.

to figures approaching pre-1929 levels. By then, these democracies faced new threats that made even the anxious 1920s look like "roaring" good times. The most ominous menace came from Germany.

Nazism in Germany

In 1928, Germany's fascist party, the Nazis (National Socialists), won less than 3 percent of the vote in national elections. Five years later, the party and its leader, Adolf Hitler, gained power and ended German democracy—all through legal means. How did this happen?

THE YOUNG ADOLF HITLER

The story of Nazism's rise begins with the life of Adolf Hitler (1889–1945). Hitler was born to a middle-aged Austrian customs official and his much younger wife. When his father died in 1905, Hitler quit school and traveled to Vienna, where he hoped to become an artist or architect. Denied admission to the art academy, he lived on his orphan's pension, selling postcards and hanging wallpaper. He compulsively followed daily routines, and would so for the rest of his life. He also picked up nationalistic, anti-Semitic,

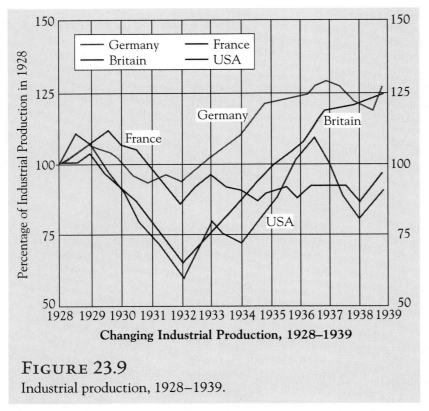

FIGURE 23.9
Industrial production, 1928–1939.

and racist ideas circulating in Vienna that he would embrace with deadly seriousness.

When World War I broke out, Hitler "thanked heaven out of an overflowing heart." For this ardent German nationalist, here was a righteous crusade to end a life of drifting. He served as a courier in the German army and was decorated three times. War's end found him in a hospital recovering from a poison gas attack. He revered World War I as "the greatest of all experiences." As for Germany's defeat at the end of the conflict, he blamed Jews and Marxists, who he felt sure had "stabbed Germany in the back."

THE BIRTH OF NAZISM IN GERMANY'S POSTWAR YEARS

Hitler spotted opportunities in Germany's turbulent postwar years. Several right-wing groups had formed that offered extreme solutions to Germany's problems and that threatened the newly formed parliamentary government of the Weimar Republic. In 1919, while working in Munich as an informer for the army, Hitler joined one of those groups—the German Workers' Party. A year

later, he rose to leadership in the party and renamed it the National Socialist German Workers' Party, or the Nazi Party (despite the party's name, it was neither socialist in the traditional sense nor well-supported by urban workers). Hitler also organized a paramilitary wing—the SA "stormtroopers"—to back the party. Copying Mussolini's techniques, the SA troopers wore brown shirts and carried pagan symbols (the swastika). They marched through the streets, sang patriotic songs, and beat up communists, socialists, and anyone else they considered their opponents.

Nothing yet marked this small group as destined for success. Nevertheless, in 1923 Hitler and the popular war hero Field Marshal Ludendorff made an ambitious grab for power. From a beer hall in Munich, the Nazis marched on the local government. Republican troops easily put down this "Beer Hall Putsch," and Hitler, after a highly publicized trial, spent nearly a year in jail. While in prison, he wrote *Mein Kampf* (*My Struggle*), a work that set forth the core of his Nazi doctrine.

Nazism, like other brands of fascism, assaulted the liberal, democratic tradition in the West. According to Nazi doctrine, the political order should be dominated by a single party headed by a dictatorial leader (Hitler) who appealed to *Nazi doctrine* the masses. In addition, Germany should rearm, redress the "injustices" of the Versailles treaty, and conquer the Slavic people to the east to gain "living space" (*Lebensraum*). At the center of Hitler's beliefs lurked biological racism and anti-Semitism. He glorified the mythical German "Aryan race" as superior and destined to conquer all other peoples in the struggle for racial supremacy. He also condemned the Jews as corrupt, landless parasites who created Marxist communism, caused Germany's humiliating defeat in World War I, and propagated liberalism.

THE GROWTH OF THE NAZI PARTY

Hitler exited jail in 1924 determined to acquire power from within, "legally." Between 1925 and 1929, the Nazi Party grew in numbers somewhat, but still remained a small splinter group. Then in October 1929, Germany's foreign minister, Gustav Stresemann, whose effective leadership for five years held center parties of the Weimar Republic together, died. That same month, the New York stock market crashed. Soon the Great Depression had Germany in its grip. It spelled the end of American loans and ignited unemployment and panic. Internal divisions immobilized parliamentary government, and the political extremes on both the Left and Right rapidly gained strength.

In 1930, the aged president Paul Hindenburg, Germany's military commander during World War I and no friend to democracy, authorized rule by decree over Germany's unstable parliament. In elections held that year, the Nazis won a startling 18.3 percent of the vote—up from 2.6 percent in 1928. Hindenburg turned to conservative politicians to lead the republic, but they failed to govern effectively. The moderates, socialists, and communists, for their part, could not unify into a strong political force. In 1932, the Nazi Party became the largest political organization in Germany, wining an astonishing 37.3 percent of the vote. In elections for the office of president, Hitler gained 13.5 million votes against Hindenburg's 19 million.

THE APPEAL OF NAZISM

Hitler and the doctrine of Nazism captured the imaginations of many Germans, especially young people and displaced veterans eager to achieve some measure of social stature in the new elite. Indeed, Hitler presented Nazism as "the organized will of the youth." He also appealed to the millions of Germans—the lower middle class in particular—who had been traumatized by the Great Depression.

Much of Hitler's appeal stemmed from the alluring promises he made—promises that offered comfort and reassurance to a people in desperate need. He claimed that he would get rid of the despised war reparations, economic hardship, incompetent leadership, threats from the Left, and parliamentary government. In addition, he vowed to restore national unity and order in Germany and revive both the German people's shattered pride and their military might.

To wealthy industrial leaders and landowners who feared the growing strength of unions, socialists, and communists, Hitler and his party held less of a personal attraction. Instead, Nazism represented the lesser of two distasteful options in the minds of these groups. Many such people who voted for the Nazis did so as a way to vote *against* the Weimar Republic, the terms of the Versailles treaty, and the communist path, rather than *for* the Nazi ideology. Indeed, most of these Germans probably would have preferred to elect more traditional conservatives, but none of the existing candidates passed muster.

Whatever the appeal, those drawn to Hitler and the Nazis either ignored the party's strident nationalism, racism, and anti-Semitic fervor or embraced those sentiments. After all, such calls had been heard throughout central and eastern Europe for decades. However, many Germans failed to detect the especially virulent quality of the Nazis' version of these feelings. Even experienced politicians never saw the danger in the situation. In fact, some conservative leaders such as Franz von Papen supported Hitler under the assumption that they could control him. As they would discover, they were greatly mistaken.

HITLER TAKES POWER

In January 1933, President Hindenburg offered Hitler chancellorship, and the Nazi leader accepted. Jubilant stormtroopers marched through Berlin's streets, holding their blazing torches high. In his new position, Hitler immediately called for another round of parliamentary elections. Now in official control of the state police and the agencies of information, the Nazis used propaganda and terror to confuse and frighten voters. As Hitler explained it, "Terror at the place of employment, in the factory, in the meeting hall, and on the occasion of mass demonstrations will always be successful."

Five days before the elections, Hitler discredited the communists by accusing them of burning the Reichstag building (a fire that the Nazis may have set themselves). He used the fire to justify the suspension of civil liberties and the arrest of many communists. On election day, the Nazis gained 44 percent of the vote; with their nationalist allies, they now had enough for a majority. The Reichstag quickly passed an enabling act granting Hitler the power to make laws on his own for four years. He soon outlawed all other political parties, and when Hindenburg died in 1934, Hitler became the sole leader of the German government. That same year, Hitler ordered Heinrich Himmler (1900–1945) and a handpicked private armed force, the elite SS, to "blood purge" his own paramilitary organization, the SA. Hitler saw the leader of the SA, Ernst Röhm (1887–1934) as a rival with plans to establish control over the army. That "Night of the Long Knives" eliminated potential opponents to Hitler within the party and the powerful SA as a rival to the reviving German army. Now the army swore allegiance to Hitler. The Nazi leader's dictatorship was complete.

LIFE IN NAZI GERMANY

His power consolidated, Hitler proceeded to turn Germany into a police state. The government abolished freedom of speech, press, and assembly. An elaborate and all-powerful secret police, the Gestapo, uncovered and destroyed opposition. Nazi officials took over top positions in the government and pressured churches to conform to the new order. Professional organizations of doctors, teachers, lawyers, and engineers were transformed into Nazi associations. Officials even pushed people into joining Nazi leisure-time organizations.

The Nazis set out to bring family and private life under their control. As one step, the German Women's Bureau established guidelines for "proper" womanhood. Women, the bureau

Family and private life

proclaimed, belonged at home where they could fulfill their primary duties as homemakers, as subordinates to their husbands, and as producers of children. According to Guida Diehl, the leader of a pro-Nazi women's organization, "A woman's honor rests on the province specifically entrusted to her . . . love, marriage, family, motherhood . . . . The German man wants to know . . . that it is worthwhile to live and die for such German womanhood." Officials launched campaigns to honor and reward pregnant women, prevent birth control, and "improve racial stock." The government provided subsidies for large, "racially German" families. Women who gave birth to more than four children received the bronze Honor Cross of the German Mother; more than six warranted a silver medal, and more than eight, the coveted gold. In 1937 the Nazi Art Council of the Reich demanded that

painters cease depicting families with only two children. A new program in 1938 went so far as to encourage SS soldiers to breed children with "racially fit" women outside of marriage.

Nazi youth organizations such as the Hitler Youth and the League of German Girls expanded rapidly, absorbing the majority of teenage boys and girls by the late 1930s. Boys were molded into Nazi support-

Nazi youth organizations

ers with military values and sometimes encouraged to spy on their teachers and parents. "I don't want an intellectual education" for boys, Hitler said. "They must learn in the face of the most difficult trials to conquer the fear of death for my sake." Girls were trained to become housewives and mothers, which the Nazis saw as the perfect complement to the loyal, fearless German soldier.

Hitler inspired and manipulated people with his stirring, inflammatory speeches, rallies, parades, and symbols. His organizers choreographed mass meetings such as the one at Buckeberg in 1934,

Promoting Nazism and Hitler

shown in Figure 23.10, to whip up excitement and a sense of belonging among the populace. In this photograph, Hitler leads a procession of Nazi elites between two lines of honor guards and swastika banners. At

FIGURE 23.10
Adolf Hitler at Buckeberg.

such rallies, Hitler made a carefully staged, dramatic entrance and delivered a long, emotionally charged speech. "It is the belief in our people that has made us small men great, that has made us poor men rich, that has made brave and courageous men out of us wavering, spiritless, timid fold," he proclaimed at the Nuremberg rally in 1936. Listeners described feeling "eternally bound to this man." The ministry of propaganda, under Joseph Goebbels (1897–1945), reinforced the psychological power of the rallies by controlling information and spreading Nazi ideology through the press, radio, films, textbooks, pamphlets, and posters. Goebbels also painted an image of Hitler as the people's heroic leader, the one who could even be trusted to limit any excesses by overzealous extremists within the Nazi Party itself.

In addition to promoting enthusiasm for their leader and ideology, the Nazis attacked "decadent" modern art and the popular culture of the Jazz Age. Only those whose works conformed to Nazi tastes—usually sentimental, pro-Nazi subject matter—could exhibit, publish, or perform. Officials promoted the burning of liberal books, sometimes even those of Germany's greatest literary figures of the eighteenth and nineteenth centuries such as Goethe and Schiller. The Nazi minister of culture told university professors, "From now on it will *not* be your job to determine whether something is true but whether it is in the spirit of the [Nazi] revolution." While some intellectuals and artists supported these policies, many opposed them and left Germany.

Both to solidify their power and to carry out their racist ideas, the Nazis targeted many groups for repression. For example, they sent communists, socialists, resisting Catholics, Jehovah's Witnesses, and Gypsies to concentration camps. Mixed-race children, criminals, prostitutes, alcoholics—

Nazi repression and persecution

all considered genetically inferior or "community aliens"—became candidates for sterilization. Homosexuality warranted at least incarceration or castration. A frightening glimpse of the future for all these groups came in 1939 when the Nazis created euthanasia programs designed to eliminate the mentally ill, handicapped, aged, and incurably ill.

No group, however, was more systematically repressed than the Jews. According to Joseph Goebbels, Jews had "corrupted our race, fouled our morals, undermined our customs, and broken our power." He blamed them as "the cause and the beneficiary of our misery." In 1933 the government excluded Jews from higher education and public employment. By 1935, most Jewish professionals in Germany had lost their jobs. That year the Nuremberg Laws took citizenship away from Jews, forced them to wear a yellow Star of David on their clothes, and forbade marriage or sexual relations between Jews and non-Jews. In 1938, an episode of unrestrained violence revealed the mounting intensity of the Nazis' anti-Semitism. Incited by Goebbels, who blamed Jews for the assassination of a German diplomat in Paris, Nazi stormtroopers vandalized Jewish residences, synagogues, and places of business, smashing windows and plundering shops during the night of November 9–10. The troops then attacked Jews themselves, killing dozens and imprisoning tens of thousands in concentration camps. After this attack—known as *Kristallnacht*, or Crystal Night, for its images of shattered glass—the Nazi government increasingly restricted Jews' movements, eliminated their jobs, and confiscated their assets. By 1939 over half of Germany's Jews had emigrated, even though they had to leave their possessions behind, pay hefty emigration fees, and face rejection in other countries. Soon, though, it became too late to escape Germany.

Figure 23.11 depicts the repression closing in on the Jews. The man in this painting—a self-portrait of

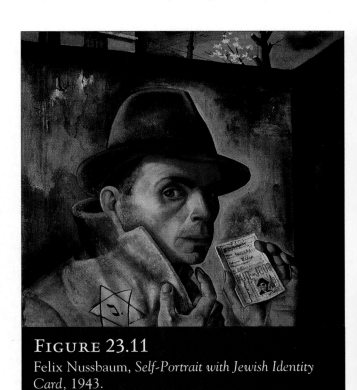

FIGURE 23.11
Felix Nussbaum, *Self-Portrait with Jewish Identity Card*, 1943.

the German artist Felix Nussbaum (1904–1944), grimly regards the viewer. In one hand, he holds up his identity card, which in red letters states that he is Jewish. The yellow Star of David on his coat also identifies him as Jewish to the public. The walls of a prison yard tower above him. Beyond the walls, barbed wire, a truncated tree, and a blackening sky all hint at the dark future facing this man and others like him. Nussbaum completed this painting in 1943 while in hiding from the Nazis; less than a year later the Nazis arrested, imprisoned, and then killed him, along with his parents and brother.

What did ordinary Germans think of this repression and persecution? Historians still debate this question. While many people seemed to share Hitler's attitudes, at least to a degree, most people outside the persecuted groups may not have understood Hitler's extreme, ultimate purpose. Certainly some knew and many should have known. A few Germans objected. However open resistance was dangerous. For those who disagreed with Hitler, it was much easier and safer to retreat into private life and apathy. Moreover they, and many other Germans, found reason to overlook Hitler's repressive measures and support him in his efforts to revive their prostrate nation.

REBUILDING AND REARMING THE NEW GERMANY

Governmental expenditures fueled economic recovery, but Hitler's main goal was rearmament. Superhighways, hospitals, sports stadiums, and apartment houses sprang up all over Germany; so did rearmament plants that created jobs for millions. To make Germany self-sufficient in case of another war, the Nazis supported the development of synthetics for the manufacture of such items as rubber and petroleum that Germany would otherwise have to import. The planned conquest to the east, Hitler hoped, would provide needed raw materials and eventually pay for Germany's government expenditures.

For the most part, the Nazis left business organizations and the capitalist economy alone. However, big business, forced to bow to the will of governmental policy, did lose some freedom. The real assault was on independent labor unions, which the government abolished and replaced with the Nazi Labor Front.

All these efforts worked. Germany regained the economic and military strength to make it a great power. By 1935, Hitler had taken Germany out of the League of Nations and the Geneva Disarmament Conference. Unwilling to back the letter of the Versailles treaty with force, the Allies offered only muted opposition to Hitler's renunciation of Versailles disarmament provisions. The next year, he initiated a secret Four-Year Plan to prepare Germany for war. By 1939, the Nazis had increased armaments expenditures thirtyfold. Hitler felt ready to flex his newly developed muscles. His aggressive ambitions, combined with disturbing events outside Germany, were pushing the world toward war.

The Road to War, 1931–1939

As we saw earlier, in these tense years a new wave of authoritarian governments had washed across eastern and southern Europe; by 1938, only Czechoslovakia remained a parliamentary democracy. Many of these regimes included elements of fascism, but most were simple dictatorships by royal or military figures. Fascist movements, such as the Cross of Fire organization in France and the "Rex" Party in Belgium, also sprouted up in western Europe.

The democratic nations turned inward as they grappled with the depression and political divisions within their own borders. After 1934, communists in those nations sought to form alliances with socialists and moderates against the growing strength of fascism. The Popular Front in France is an example of such a partnership. The Front governed from 1936 to 1938. It was unable to pull the nation out of the depression, however, and ultimately fell from power. Its defeat left France more politically divided and discouraged than ever.

INTERNATIONAL AFFAIRS BREAK DOWN

For France and the other democracies, international affairs soon slipped out of control. Rearmament spread, aggression became the order of the day, and neither the democratic powers nor the League of Nations responded forcefully to stop it.

In 1931, Japan initiated the new pattern. On the orders of young officers, the Japanese army invaded Manchuria in northern China and began a drive for conquest. *Japan on the march* Crowds in Japan cheered the news of the Manchurian campaign, and a heightened sense of nationalistic militarism gradually pervaded Japanese political life. The League of Nations condemned Japan but took no action. In 1937, full-scale war broke out between Japan and China. By this time, China had managed to shake off the most onerous Western controls over the country but still bore the scars of decades of sporadic, bloody civil war. China's dominant Nationalist Party under Jiang Jieshi (Chiang Kai-shek) (1887–1975) had expended much of its strength opposing the growing Chinese Communist Party, led by Mao Zedong (1893–1976). In the early 1930s, Jiang almost vanquished the Communists, but Mao and the core of his movement held on. Although the two sides finally forged an alliance against the Japanese in 1937, and the Soviet Union provided military assistance to China against its powerful rival in the east, city after city in China fell to Japanese bombs and invading armies. With its expanding industrial economy hungry for new markets, Japan was determined to create "a new order in East Asia" under its domination. To secure its position, it moved to form an alliance with two other aggressive, authoritarian states: Italy and Germany.

In 1935 Mussolini ordered his troops to invade Ethiopia in East Africa, hoping to win popularity at home despite the unemployment and failing social policies there. Ethiopia appealed to the League of Nations for protection. The League condemned Il Duce's actions, but the democratic powers did not follow up with enough action to stop him. Indeed these responses to his aggression only pushed Mussolini toward *Italy invades Ethiopia* Hitler, and in 1936 the two leaders agreed to a friendship alliance—the "Rome-Berlin Axis." In 1939 that alliance solidified into the military "Pact of Steel." To show unity with Hitler, Mussolini promptly adopted anti-Semitic racial laws for Italy. To further his own military ambitions, he invaded Albania.

CIVIL WAR IN SPAIN

In 1936, civil war broke out in Spain. Five years earlier, Spain had become a democratic republic for the first time. But when the Popular Front, made up of radicals, socialists, and communists, won election in 1936, a group of generals led by the conservative Francisco Franco (1892–1975) launched an armed rebellion against the new government. Franco's nationalist rebels enjoyed the support of the fascist Falange Party, the army, the church, and most of the wealthy elites; nevertheless, they could not easily overturn the popular Loyalists—the supporters of the Popular Front government.

The Spanish civil war soon became an international battlefield. Hitler and Mussolini, spotting an opportu-

FIGURE 23.12
Pablo Picasso, *Guernica*, 1937.

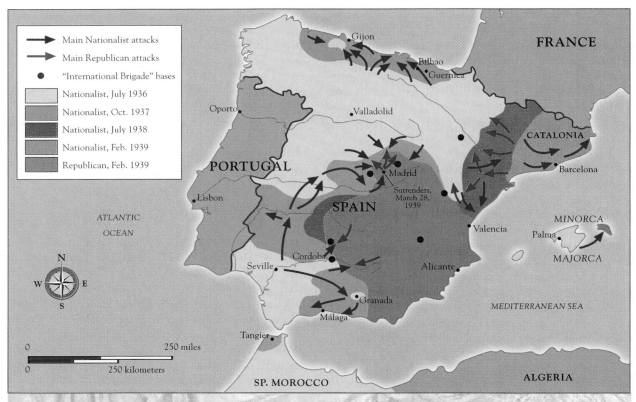

THINKING ABOUT GEOGRAPHY

MAP 23.1 *The Spanish Civil War, 1936–1939*

This map shows the evolution of the Spanish civil war between 1936 and 1939. ■ **Notice** that Franco's Nationalist forces first moved north from Spanish Morocco and southern Spain, then east to Republican strongholds. **Consider** the importance of France's unwillingness to help the Republican forces.

nity to advance the cause of fascism, gain an ally, and test their new weapons, sent arms and troops to aid Franco. At one point in 1937, Germans manning new airplanes on behalf of Franco's nationalists attacked the small Spanish town of Guernica, raining death on the civilian population there. The slaughter became the subject matter of one of the most haunting paintings of the twentieth century, *Guernica* (1937), by the Spanish artist Pablo Picasso (1881–1973). This twenty-five-foot-long mural in black and white (Figure 23.12) captures the worst features of this war—terror, brutality, disjointedness, lack of direction, and despair. On the left, a woman shrieks while holding a dead child. In the center, a warrior and horse lie shattered into fragments as the wounded sorrowfully look on. On the right, a

woman plummets from a burning building. The image expresses both a wailing lament and a warning: modern war not only kills indiscriminately, but targets civilians in order to terrorize all into submission.

The Loyalists appealed to the other Western democracies for aid, but no help came. These nations hoped to maintain good relations with Italy and Germany, and thus committed to a policy of neutrality even though the fascist powers only pretended to agree. Unofficial Loyalist support came from some 40,000 idealistic volunteers, such as the Garibaldi Brigade and the Lincoln Brigade, who traveled to Spain from abroad and fought as individuals in the Loyalist cause. Otherwise, only the Soviet Union (until 1938) and Mexico provided assistance. The Loyal-

Legend:
- International boundaries, 1936
- Germany in 1933
- Remilitarized in 1936
- Annexed in 1938
- Satellite states, March 1939
- Conquered by Germany in September 1939
- Annexed by Soviet Union in September 1939

THINKING ABOUT GEOGRAPHY

MAP 23.2 *German Expansion, 1936–1939*

This map shows German expansion between 1936 and September 1939, as well as territory annexed by the Soviet Union thanks to the Nazi-Soviet nonaggression pact of August 1939. ❧ **Consider** how vulnerable these developments left Poland. ❧ **How** might the steps in Germany's expansion be distinguished? ❧ **What** nations might feel most threatened by further German aggression?

ists also suffered from internal divisions between competing communists, anarchists, and liberals. In 1939, after three years of slaughter and atrocities on both sides, Franco's rebels finally beat down the last of the Loyalist resistance (see Map 23.1). The authoritarian Franco would rule Spain until his death in 1975.

TRYING TO COPE WITH GERMANY

In March, 1936, Hitler gambled by ordering his armed forces into the Rhineland, that part of Germany on the west bank of the Rhine River that the Treaty of Versailles had deemed a demilitarized zone (see Map 23.2). France fretted and fumed but, lacking Britain's support, did nothing. Hitler's bold gamble had paid off. With a new confidence, he turned to the three countries that bordered Germany to the east: Austria, Czechoslovakia, and Poland.

In 1938, the Nazis incorporated Austria without opposition, annexing the 6.5 million Austrians to the German Reich (empire) (see Map 23.2). Hitler then claimed a portion of Czechoslovakia—the Sudetenland—that included 3.5 million German-speaking people. The Czechs, however, surprised him by rushing to their defenses. For months, Hitler churned out a barrage of propaganda that painted the German-speaking Czechs as a persecuted minority. He threatened and roused his people to readiness for war, finally vowing to march if the Sudetenland was not surrendered to him.

A difficult question now arose for the rest of Europe as it watched Hitler's actions: what should be done? For complex reasons, no one had the nerve to oppose Hitler with force. For one thing, World War I had made many Europeans reluctant to risk general war again. In addition, disagreement swirled over the justice of Hitler's demands. Some people agreed with Germany that the Versailles treaty was too harsh, and sympathized with those who wanted to appease Germany's injured feelings. Many other people saw Hitler as sometimes reasonable, and as at least a force that might be used to stop the spread of communism. British prime minister Neville Chamberlain (1869–1940), aware of Britain's lack of armed forces and public support to halt Hitler, tried for a compromise with the German ruler.

The leaders of Germany, Italy, France, and Britain met at Munich to come to some resolution of the Sudetenland question. They did not consult the Soviet Union, and they left Czechoslovakia with little alternative but to go along with any agreement that might arise from the meeting. In the end, Britain and France chose appeasement—giving in to Hitler's demands in hopes of satisfying him—and Hitler got the piece of Czechoslovakia that he wanted. Back in Britain, Prime Minister Chamberlain announced that the Munich agreement "has saved Czechoslovakia from destruction and Europe from Armageddon." Across Europe, crowds cheered, celebrating what they saw as the preservation of peace. A few months later, Hitler's forces overran the remainder of the Czechoslovakian Republic without warning (see Map 23.2).

Appeasement at Munich

When Hitler next threatened Poland, Great Britain got tough and promised to come to Poland's aid. They turned to the Soviets for help, but it was too late. Isolated or excluded for too long from international affairs and disillusioned by France's and Britain's weak response to German aggression, Stalin stunned the world by signing a nonaggression pact with Hitler on August 23, 1939. In return for the Soviet Union's neutrality while Germany carved up Poland, Hitler gave Stalin a free hand to reannex territories in eastern Europe—including eastern Poland—that Russia had lost during World War I (see Map 23.2). By making this cynical pact with his greatest ideological enemy, Nazi Germany, Stalin may have gambled that the Soviet Union could stay on the sidelines, growing in strength, while the fascist and democratic capitalists destroyed one another.

Nazi-Soviet Nonaggression Pact

At dawn on September 1, the Germans launched an all-out attack on Poland by land, sea, and air. Hitler remained convinced that France and Britain would not go to war over Poland. He was wrong. Two days later, Great Britain and France declared war on Germany. In a poem entitled "SEPTEMBER 1, 1939," American poet W. H. Auden (1907–1973) moaned that

> *"The unmentionable odor of death*
> *Offends the September night"*

World War II had begun.

World War II, 1939–1945

Perhaps the war initiated in 1914 never quite ended, and the 1920s were just a pause in three decades of fighting and crises after 1914. Maybe if the depression had not struck, Hitler and the Nazis would not have come to power, the democracies would have continued to grow, and war could have been averted. Tragically, the war that did break out in September 1939 would blaze six long years and encompass the globe as never before.

TRIUMPH OF THE GERMAN BLITZKRIEG

The German "blitzkrieg"—a "lightning war" of highly coordinated air strikes and rapid deployment of tanks and motorized columns—overwhelmed Polish forces. The French and British mobilized their armies along the German border, and the British fleet blockaded Germany by sea—all to no avail.

For the next six months, in what became known as the "phony war," almost no military action took place. France and Great Britain seemed paralyzed. Meanwhile, the Soviet Union took advantage of its agreement with Hitler and reannexed territories in Poland and eastern Europe—including Estonia, Latvia, and Lithuania—that Russia had lost in World War I. When Finland refused to yield strategic territories, the Soviets attacked. The Finns put up a determined resistance, and it took several months for the Soviet army finally to defeat these stubborn soldiers.

In April 1940, the Germans suddenly overran both Denmark and Norway. German planes fended off Britain's fleet, inflicting heavy losses. The next month, German armies assaulted Luxembourg, the Netherlands, Belgium, and France. The tiny Luxembourg offered no resistance, while the Dutch fought heroically but fell after six days. To support the beleaguered Belgians, the British army and a large part of the French army moved into Belgium. The French trusted that their Maginot Line of fortresses would hold along the German border. However, the line proved useless against the highly mobile German tanks. The Germans skirted the fortresses to the north through the Ardennes Forest. The German blitzkrieg drove quickly to the English Channel, cutting off Allied armies in Belgium and then trapping them at Dunkirk, a seaport in Northern France. A flotilla of military and civilian ships, including fishing boats and pleasure craft, rescued 330,000 British and French troops off the beach at Dunkirk.

The Battle of France

The Battle of France ended after only five weeks. Although almost equal in numbers to the Germans, the French seemed demoralized from the beginning of the war. According to one French journalist, they felt abandoned by the British, "who were ready to fight to the last French soldier." On June 16, 1940, the aged, right-wing Marshal Philippe Pétain became premier of France and quickly surrendered to Hitler. Germany took the northern half of France and the entire Atlantic coast. The new authoritarian French regime would govern the remaining unoccupied portion of France from the city of Vichy. French general Charles de Gaulle escaped to Great Britain and declared himself leader of the Free French government in exile.

The collapse of France left Great Britain to face Germany alone. To gain control of the English Channel and prepare for an invasion of Britain, the Germans unleashed massive air attacks against Britain in July 1940. For almost two months that fall, the Germans bombed London every night. The audacious and eloquent Winston Churchill (1874–1965), who had replaced Neville Chamberlain as prime minister, rallied his country, offering his "blood, toil, tears, and sweat," and vowing "we shall never surrender." Figure 23.13 reveals some of the effort involved in the Battle of Britain. A group of three women and one man pull in a barrage balloon. Weighted cables dangling beneath the balloon hinder low-level flights by German bombers. In the background are buildings destroyed by bombings, but numerous smokestacks in the distance indicate that Britain's ability to fight survives. In cellars and subway stations, the British people holed up while their planes and antiaircraft guns, now aided by radar, fought off the Germans. Boosted by the high morale of the people, the increased output of aircraft factories, and Churchill's leadership, the island nation miraculously held. By November, the British had won the Battle of Britain.

The Battle of Britain

WAR IN NORTH AFRICA AND THE BALKANS

Even though Italy was not yet ready to take on another major war, Mussolini did not want to miss out on the spoils of an easy victory. He too invaded France as

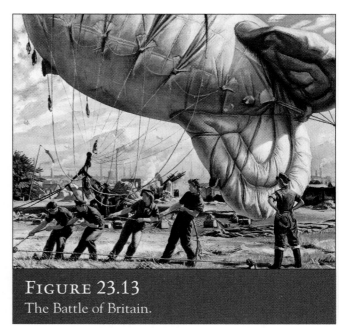

FIGURE 23.13
The Battle of Britain.

it fell to the Germans. Then in September 1940, his armies in Africa moved east from Libya into Egypt. A few weeks later, they attacked Greece from Albania.

However, Mussolini's forces met disaster at every turn. Mobile British forces routed Italian armies in North Africa, and British planes crippled the Italian fleet in southern Italy. The Greeks also contributed to the rout, driving the Italians back into Albania.

In response, Germany's forces streamed into the Balkans and North Africa. Hitler had several goals in mind for this move. He coveted the Balkans for their rich supplies of raw materials, especially the Romanian oil fields. He also hoped to save the Italian forces in North Africa and take the Suez Canal, Britain's lifeline to its empire. Hungary and Romania yielded to Hitler's threats and joined the Axis alliance in November 1940; Bulgaria did the same in March 1941. Yugoslavia and Greece refused, and were overrun by German forces within a few weeks. Germany's Afrika Korps drove the British back into Egypt. Pro-German movements broke out in Iraq, Iran, and French Syria. At this point, however, Hitler hurled his main forces against the Soviet Union, giving the British a breathing spell to recoup their strength in North Africa and the eastern Mediterranean.

OPERATION BARBAROSSA: GERMANY INVADES THE SOVIET UNION

The eventual conquest of the Soviet Union had always been uppermost in Hitler's thoughts, despite his deceptive pact with the USSR. Still, he had hoped to subdue the British before turning on the Soviets. Failing that, he decided to invade the Soviet Union anyway. In June 1941, the Germans launched Operation Barbarossa, sending 3 million troops against the USSR. Hitler expected to crush Soviet resistance in six weeks, well before the notorious Russian winter set in.

For a few days, the stunned Stalin disappeared from the public eye. Finally he called the Soviet people to rally to "the Great Patriotic War." Not everyone rose to the challenge. Indeed, the Ukrainians and some other Soviet groups initially greeted the Germans as liberators. However, most Soviet peoples rallied and put up a determined resistance. Nevertheless, the German war machine crunched forward. By December 1, it was within sight of Moscow and almost surrounded Leningrad. The Soviets had suffered staggering casualties. A confident Hitler announced the permanent destruction of the Soviet Union.

Then the Russian winter set in. Hitler's troops lacked adequate clothing and supplies to conduct a winter war. The weather and Russian counterattack forced the Germans to halt and in some places retreat—temporarily.

JAPAN ATTACKS

Farther east, events were brewing that would add yet another dimension to the war. Specifically, Western imperial presence in Asia and the Pacific had frustrated Japan's dreams of expansion. The resource-poor island nation depended on foreign raw materials and markets to fuel its industrial economy. During the 1930s, the Great Depression had weakened Japan's democratic regime and made the army a more potent political as well as military force. As military men gained control of the government, Japan's foreign policy shifted to expansionism. By 1939, Japan had conquered the populous coastal areas of China and pushed Chinese forces well into the interior. When the war in Europe weakened European colonial powers—which controlled much of southeast Asia, with its wealth of essential resources such as oil, tin, and rubber—Japan joined the Rome-Berlin Axis. It quickly occupied French Indochina and threatened the Dutch East Indies. The United States responded with a total economic embargo on all exports to Japan, threatening Japan's oil supplies in particular.

Hoping that the war in Europe would induce the United States to cede dominance to the Japanese in southeast Asia, Japan struck. On December 7, 1941, Japanese air forces surprised the American fleet anchored in Pearl Harbor, Hawaii, crippling the U.S. naval and air forces. President Franklin D. Roosevelt (1882–1945) called it "a day that will live in infamy." *The U.S. enters the war* The United States immediately declared war on Japan and within days was at war with the other Axis powers as well. Several Latin American nations joined the United States in the Grand Alliance against the Axis.

The long-isolationist United States had an army with limited capabilities. In addition, it had sent huge quantities of arms, equipment, and food across the Atlantic in its role as "the arsenal of democracy." Roosevelt agreed with Churchill to make the war in Europe the United States' first priority, and Americans started mobilizing their country's vast resources for the fight.

Meanwhile, the Japanese conquered a vast area in

southeast Asia and the Pacific (Map 23.4), creating "The Greater East Asia Co-Prosperity Sphere." Japan claimed to be liberating Asia from the imperial West, but it dominated the new territories through nationalist leaders ready to collaborate with Japan's occupation forces, and treated the conquered peoples as inferior subjects. Scoring victory after victory, the Japanese and Germans seemed to be winning the war.

BEHIND THE LINES: THE STRUGGLE AND THE HORROR

By 1942, Hitler ruled most of continental Europe from the English Channel to the outskirts of Moscow (see Map 23.3). In administrating his lands, he pursued two primary goals. First, he hunted for ways to *Hitler's "New Order"* keep Germany supplied with war materials and maintain the standard of living for Germans without having to call on them to make unpopular sacrifices. Second, he sought to fulfill his racist agenda. To these ends, he implemented his "New Order," a program of economic exploitation and racial imperialism in the lands that he now controlled. He used conquered peoples according to their ranking in his racial hierarchy. Those most directly related to the Nazi conception of the "Aryan race," such as Scandinavians, Anglo-Saxons, and Dutch, were treated well and might be absorbed into the Nazi Empire as partners with the Germans. He considered the "Latin races," such as the French, inferior but tolerable as supportive cogs in the New Order. Slavs ranked toward the bottom of Hitler's hierarchy; they were to be isolated, shoved aside, treated like slaves, or killed.

Lowest on this racial scale were the Jews, and they fared the worst in Hitler's scheme. Nazis herded Jews into ghettos in German, Polish, and Russian cities. For a while, the Nazis envisioned forced emigration of *The Holocaust* Jews, perhaps to the island of Madagascar off the east coast of Africa, to solve the "Jewish problem." In 1941, such ideas ended and Hitler initiated a policy of extermination. SS squads under Reinhard Heydrich (1904–1942) and Heinrich Himmler began the wholesale killing of Jews, along with Slavic prisoners of war, in Poland and Russia. Firing squads shot victims en masse. Dissatisfied with the pace of the killings, the Germans began using mobile vans that exterminated people by gas. Finally, when that method still did not seem effi-

cient enough, the Nazis used large gas chambers that murdered thousands at a time.

The Nazis built six great death camps in what had been Poland. From gathering points all over Europe, unknowing victims were crowded into cattle cars where they soon became dehydrated, disoriented, and terrorized; many died in transit. Upon their arrival, officials divided families, segregated people by sex, and made the first "selection." "Inside the camp, one's first view was fixed on a mountain of children's shoes," recalled a woman survivor. "To tell the truth I did not understand what that meant." Those who could not work as the Nazis wanted—therefore more women, children, and elderly—were sent to the "showers"— the Nazis' euphemism for the gas chambers. Officials especially targeted pregnant women to prevent the birth of more Jews. They sent the rest, now physically and mentally terrorized, to the work camps.

The scale and depravity of this programmed inhumanity, torture, and death were so unprecedented that the victims simply could not grasp it until it was too late. Some Jews rebelled—in the Warsaw ghetto and the Treblinka camp, for example—but in vain. The Nazis trapped their victims in a powerful, thoroughly organized system.

Struggling to survive in the camps, many people tried to help one another, though the desperate conditions at times also brought out the worst in people. In this surreal world, the Germans applied assembly-line methods to the destruction of millions of *Life and death in the camps* human beings. A French doctor described the process of extermination at the Auschwitz-Birkenau camp: Once prisoners were herded and forced into the gas chambers, "the massive oak double doors are shut. For two endless minutes one can hear banging on the walls and screams which are no longer human. . . . Five minutes later the doors are opened. The corpses, squashed together and distorted, fall out like a waterfall." In a particularly brutal twist, the Nazis forced Jewish prisoners to carry out much of the dirty work of extermination. Nazi guards subjected their captives to torture and abuse, and German doctors conducted gruesome experiments on camp prisoners.

In the end, almost all prisoners slaved in the camps on starvation rations until they died or were sent to the gas chambers when no longer useful to their captors. In Auschwitz alone, the largest of these camps, the Nazis murdered more than 12,000 people a day

Map legend:
- Hitler's Greater Germany
- Allied with Germany
- Occupied by Germany and its allies
- Grand Alliance
- Neutral Nations
- Major battles

THINKING ABOUT GEOGRAPHY

MAP 23.3 *World War II in Europe*

This map shows Hitler's empire at its height in 1942, the front lines in the following years as the Allies closed in on Germany in 1945, and major battles of the war. ❧ **What** does this indicate about the military problems facing Hitler after 1942? ❧ **Compare** the eastern, southern, and western fronts. **How** might the fighting have differed in these three areas? ❧ **Locate** the western, Italian, and Russian fronts in February 1945, just a few months before the end of the war. **What** might these troop locations suggest about spheres of influence during the postwar decades?

and more than 1 million Jews by the end of the war. Although Jews were the Nazis' main target for extermination, many people from non-Jewish groups—communists, gypsies, Jehovah's Witnesses, Soviet prisoners of war, Slavs, homosexuals—suffered the same fate. Ultimately these genocidal efforts took priority over even the war effort and continued right up until the last days of the war.

THINKING ABOUT GEOGRAPHY

MAP 23.4 *World War II in the Pacific*

This map shows Japan's empire at its height in 1942 and the course of the Allied counteroffensive that led to Japan's defeat in 1945. ◙ **What** problems did the Japanese face trying to control their far-flung territories? ◙ **Consider** what strategy the Allies used in their counteroffensive against the Japanese. **Why** did this strategy differ from that used in Europe?

Figure 23.14 is a photograph taken after World War II ended. Here American officials force German civilians living near the Landsberg camp to stand witness to the Nazis' shocking atrocities. Who knew about the brutal realities of the camps during the war? The Nazis had gone to great lengths to cover up the extermination process, swearing everyone involved to secrecy, and presenting more benign concentration camps outside Poland for international inspection. As reports of what really was happening filtered out, many people expressed disbelief. Atrocities on such a mass scale seemed impossible. But it had taken thousands of officials, bureaucrats, soldiers, police, and SS guards to carry out the murders. At least these thousands knew. Indeed, many concentration- and death-camp officials followed orders with enthusiasm, competing for approval from their superiors. Several large German companies, including the industrial giant I.G. Farben, benefited from contracts with the camps. Authorities on the outside who might have tried to help did nothing. At some point British and American commanders probably knew and could have

FIGURE 23.14
Landsberg concentration camp, 1945.

forces that might have been used on the war fronts. Communists, such as those in Yugoslavia under the command of Josip Broz (Tito—the Biography), often formed the core of the most determined resistance movements. Figure 23.15 shows Tito, standing on the far right, with his staff of fellow fighters. His organization became one of the most effective resistance forces in Europe. But the price of fighting back was high. In one case, the Nazis massacred 7,000 people in one town in retaliation for the killing of ten Germans by Yugoslav partisans.

Even more than in World War I, whole societies mobilized for the war effort in the 1940s. Governments controlled production and rationed goods. As labor shortages arose, women again assumed jobs normally reserved for men. Political leaders acquired unusual powers and discouraged dissent. Even outside the Nazi Empire, some groups of citizens fell victim to the suspicion that the war engendered. In the United States, for example, government agents *Mobilizing the home fronts* removed Japanese Americans living on the West Coast from their homes and businesses and placed them in camps. Propaganda on all sides painted distorted, racist pictures of the enemy and whipped up civilian support of the troops.

Britain, taking the brunt of German aggression early on, mobilized thoroughly. The government drafted men between the ages of eighteen and fifty and women between twenty and thirty into military or civilian war service. Women accounted for most of the increase in Britain's labor force. The government also enlisted scientists to help break the German code and work on an atomic bomb.

The Soviet Union tried everything to brace itself against the Germans. Hundreds of thousands of Russian women served in the Soviet armed forces; millions took jobs, replacing men sent to the front. In October 1941, the Soviets managed an astounding feat: they dismantled more than 500 factories in Moscow and elsewhere and reassembled them in the east, away from the encroaching German troops. By 1943, Soviet factories were turning out 2,000 tanks a month.

agreed with pleas from Jewish leaders to bomb gas chambers or railway lines to the death camps, but the Allied governments claimed that other military targets were more important.

Collaborating governments often copied or cooperated with the Nazis. In some countries, such as *Collaboration and resistance* Croatia, officials willingly rounded up Jews and carried out the killing themselves. The anti-Semitic government of Vichy France under Pétain transported thousands of Jews to Nazi death camps. In almost all conquered lands, the Nazis managed to find individuals who would collaborate with them.

However, many others resisted. The Danes saved most of the Jews living in their lands. In Italy, officials often ignored Nazi directives, despite Mussolini's alliance with Hitler. Numerous stories, such as the experience of the young Anne Frank hiding in the Netherlands, record individual heroism and tragedy. Resistance organizations rose in almost every occupied territory, particularly in France, Yugoslavia, and the Soviet Union. At great risk, men and women alike established underground networks, provided intelligence to the Allied forces, conducted guerrilla actions, aided escaping prisoners, sabotaged German military installations, and engaged Nazi this time in the southern sector of the USSR. In August they reached the outskirts of Stalingrad on the Volga River. There the battle, the greatest of the war, raged for *The eastern front and the Battle of Stalingrad* six months. Stalin spared no resource, including the many women who served on the front lines as combat soldiers, tankers, and snipers. Indeed, some airforce regiments were made up entirely of women. The most revered pilot, Lily Litvak, shot down twelve German planes.

Though the Russian winter again approached, Hitler ordered his army not to retreat. That decision took a huge toll on the German army. In a diary, a German soldier complained that "everybody is racked with hunger. Frozen potatoes are the best meal." Just before his death, this same German wrote, "The soldiers look like corpses or lunatics, looking for something to put in their mouths. They no longer take cover from Russian shells; they haven't the strength to walk, run away and hide." They fought on street corners and even over houses already turned into rubble. In February 1943, the Russians finally surrounded the remainder of the 300,000-man German army, now reduced by casualties to 80,000, and gained victory. The Soviets lost 1 million in the bitter struggle over Stalingrad. Over the next two and a half years, they slowly beat the Germans back (see Map 23.3).

In North Africa, the German general Rommel's (1891–1944) tough Afrika Korps fought to within sixty-five miles of the Egyptian coastal city of Alexandria. But in August 1942, at the Battle of El Alamein, the British forces, bolstered by supplies from the United States, *The Mediterranean* held. Over the following months, British and newly arriving American forces managed to push the Germans back, and in May 1943, the cornered Afrika Korps surrendered.

The war-weary Stalin now urged Britain and America to open up a major western front in France to take the pressure off his forces. Instead the Allies attacked Italy, moving from the island of Sicily up into the southern Italian mainland. In July 1943, the Italian

FIGURE 23.15
Tito and the Yugoslav resistance.

The United States, less threatened geographically by the war, mobilized unevenly; still, it boosted its wartime production by 400 percent in two years and sent large quantities of supplies to its British and Soviet allies. Germany was also slower to mobilize its citizens. In the early years, Hitler instead relied on quick victories and spoils from conquered lands to fulfill his nation's needs. Millions of conscripted foreigners and prisoners of war served as Germany's laborers. Only after 1942 did Hitler turn to full mobilization, multiplying Germany's production over the following two years despite concentrated Allied bombing.

TURNING THE TIDE OF WAR

The now global war was fought in three major theaters: the Soviet Union, the Mediterranean and western Europe, and the Pacific. The turning points in all theaters came between June and August 1942. The largest, bloodiest battles occurred in the Soviet Union and involved some 9 million soldiers.

The Germans, refreshed and reequipped, resumed their offensive against the Soviet Union in June, 1942,

Biography

JOSIP BROZ (TITO) (1892–1980)

Josip Broz was as a hunted resistance leader for years. Born in Croatia in 1892 to a peasant family, the young Josip became an apprentice to a locksmith and then worked as a mechanic. In World War I, he served as a platoon leader in the Austro-Hungarian army, was severely wounded, and was taken prisoner by the Russians. Already a socialist, he joined Russia's Red Army during the revolution and civil war. He also married a Russian woman, with whom he would have a son. In 1920, he returned to Croatia, became a trade-unionist, joined the Communist Party of Yugoslavia, and soon rose to a position of leadership. Eight years later, he was arrested and imprisoned for six years for his communist activity—the police had discovered bombs in his apartment. He again traveled to the Soviet Union, where he rose through the ranks as a loyal Stalinist during the purges. In 1937, he became the head of Yugoslavia's Communist Party. During his underground party work, Josip assumed the pseudonym Tito.

When Hitler invaded Yugoslavia and the Soviet Union, Tito announced, "We do not recognize the various Fascist puppet governments." He called on the Communist Party of Yugoslavia to organize the "partisans," a guerrilla resistance movement against Axis forces. At the same time, he entered into a virtual civil war with a competing, more conservative resistance movement. Although Tito won this struggle between resistance movements, it may have cost more lives than the battle against the Nazis. While fighting occupying forces, he organized a provisional communist government that would stand ready to take over at the end of the war. With the help of Soviet troops, Tito's forces drove the retreating Germans from Yugoslavia.

In 1945, Yugoslavia became a federal republic, with Tito as its leader and virtual dictator. He turned the new republic into a one-party, communist state on the model of the Soviet Union. Eventually balking at Stalin's plans to purge Yugoslav leadership and undermine his authority, Tito led Yugoslavia on a separate course after 1948. Unlike Stalin, he emphasized more relaxed, decentralized control over his nation and its economy, yet he tolerated no opposition to his rule. In the 1950s and 1960s, he became a spokesperson for nations such as Egypt, Indonesia, and India who

Communist Leader and Yugoslav Dictator

refused to align themselves with either the United States or the Soviet Union in the Cold War. He served as president of Yugoslavia until his death in 1980.

Yugoslavia would not long survive his passing. Conflict between ethnic groups had long plagued this region of Europe. Such tensions had helped ignite World War I, had contributed to the rise of authoritarian leaders of both the Right and Left during the 1930s and 1940s, and had taken thousands of lives during the resistance struggles of World War II. Now that conflict led to the undoing of the federation. Yugoslavia broke up in 1991 in a series of bloody civil wars that would drag on for years.

Consider how Tito's life reveals the ties between war, ideology, and politics during this period.

---

government arrested Mussolini, and two months later Italy surrendered. However, strong German forces still held most of the country. German commandos rescued Mussolini and set him up as the head of a puppet government in the north. The Allies' progress slowed through the Italian mountains, and the rest of the Italian campaign became a long and costly effort.

On June 6, 1944 (D day), the primarily Anglo-American forces under General Dwight Eisenhower (1890–1969) finally assaulted the German forces holding France. Hitler, overextended in Russia and the Mediterranean, had to defend a 3,000-mile coastline in the west. Forced to gamble on where the Allies would invade, he bet on Calais, where the English Channel was narrowest. Instead, the invasion came on the Normandy beaches. Nevertheless, Hitler's "Atlantic Wall" of defenders took a huge toll on the invaders. In many cases, lead companies suffered 90 percent casualties; boats and tanks were often destroyed before their troops could even fire a shot. Despite these losses, the Allies established a

The western front and the D-day invasion

northwestern European front. Two months later, the Allies opened a new front in southern France. Aided by French forces and resistance fighters, the Allies pushed the Germans out of most of France before year's end. Meanwhile, Allied bombs pulverized German cities and crippled Germany's transportation network.

Under the steady onslaught, Germany began running out of oil and soldiers. Early in 1945, American and British forces at last succeeded

Germany defeated

in crossing the Rhine into Germany. By that time, the Russians had swept through most of eastern and southeastern Europe. Along the 1,500 miles between Stalingrad and Berlin lay the wreckage of Hitler's once mighty war machine.

Germany surrendered on May 8, and the war in Europe ended. Hitler, his wife Eva Braun, and several other top Nazis committed suicide. In Italy, Italian partisans had already shot Mussolini and his mistress.

In the Pacific, the turning point of the war came in the late spring of 1942 (see Map 23.4). American and Australian troops stopped the Japanese army in New Guinea, and the Americans turned back Japanese naval forces in the Battle of the Coral Sea, northeast of Australia. Shortly thereafter, in the Battle of Midway, a U.S. fleet inflicted heavy losses on the Japanese, forcing them to retreat. In August 1942, the Americans assumed the offensive by attacking Guadalcanal in the Solomon Islands northeast of Australia. Capitalizing on their growing naval superiority, and having broken the Japanese code, the Americans conducted an island-hopping campaign toward Japan. In October 1944, the Japanese fleet made a final, desperate effort near the Philippines, but American forces annihilated it in the Battle of Leyte Gulf. However, as the United States and its allies closed in on the Japanese home islands, the most savage land battles of the war lay ahead: Iwo Jima and Okinawa. During these bat-

The war in the Pacific

tles, Japanese soldiers often fought to the death or took their own lives rather than surrender. During the battle of Okinawa, Japanese pilots volunteered to fly almost 2,000 *kamikaze* missions in which they dive-bombed their planes into Allied ships. The Allies lost dozens of ships and thousands of soldiers to these desperate tactics.

Isolated, exposed, and subjected to ceaseless air and sea attacks, Japan was doomed. In February, 1945, the United States began massive bombing raids on Japan's home islands, igniting huge firestorms that destroyed vast sections of Japan's cities and killed hundreds of thousands of people. After Germany surrendered in May 1945, American and British troops rushed to the Far East. In mid-July, American and British scientists finished developing and testing the atom bomb, a

The atomic bomb

new, powerful weapon the two countries had been working on for several years. To avoid the heavy casualties that a direct assault on the Japanese home islands would cause, the United States decided to use the bomb to shock Japan into surrender—a decision that has sparked controversy ever since. On August 6, 1945, a U.S. plane dropped an atomic bomb that destroyed the Japanese city of Hiroshima and some 80,000 of its inhabitants; tens of thousands more died later from the effects of radiation. One survivor, Yamaoka Michiko, described the horror: "There were people, barely breathing, trying to push their intestines back in. People with their legs wrenched off. Without heads. Or with faces burned and swollen out of shape. The scene I saw was a living hell." Three days later, a second atomic bomb demolished the industrial city of Nagasaki, killing an additional 50,000. On August 8, the Soviet Union declared war on Japan and sent troops into Manchuria. The Japanese finally surrendered on August 15, 1945.

Summary

During the post-World War I years of the 1920s and the Great Depression of the 1930s, the West had divided into three camps: the capitalist democracies, the fascist and authoritarian nations of central and eastern Europe, and the communist Soviet Union. By 1941, all three camps—along with much of the rest of the world—had once again been pulled into a violent vortex that wrought unprecedented destruction.

Fifty million people were killed during World War II, more of them civilians than soldiers. The Soviet people and

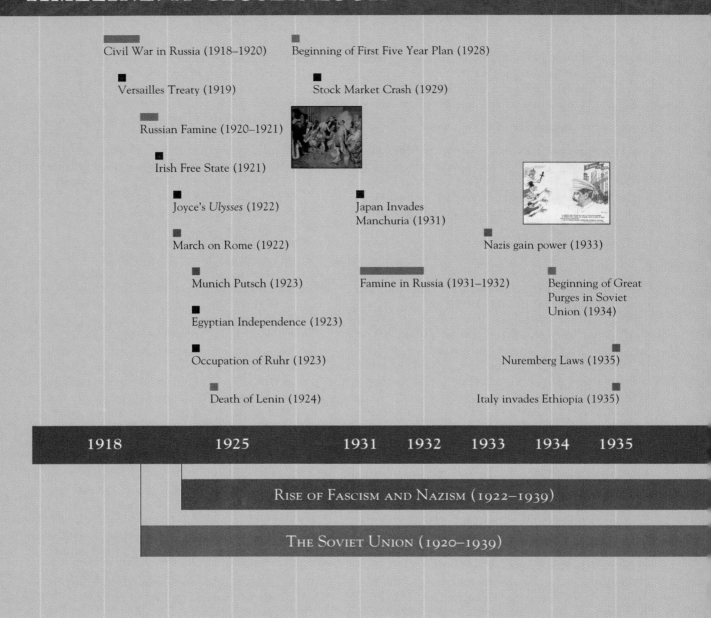

Civil War in Russia (1918–1920)

Beginning of First Five Year Plan (1928)

Versailles Treaty (1919)

Stock Market Crash (1929)

Russian Famine (1920–1921)

Irish Free State (1921)

Joyce's *Ulysses* (1922)

Japan Invades Manchuria (1931)

March on Rome (1922)

Nazis gain power (1933)

Munich Putsch (1923)

Famine in Russia (1931–1932)

Beginning of Great Purges in Soviet Union (1934)

Egyptian Independence (1923)

Occupation of Ruhr (1923)

Nuremberg Laws (1935)

Death of Lenin (1924)

Italy invades Ethiopia (1935)

| 1918 | 1925 | 1931 | 1932 | 1933 | 1934 | 1935 |

RISE OF FASCISM AND NAZISM (1922–1939)

THE SOVIET UNION (1920–1939)

government understandably felt that they had sacrificed more than any other nation to defeat Germany. Twenty million Soviets—an appalling 10 percent of the population—perished in the struggle. Despite crucial aid from the United States and Great Britain, the Soviets produced 90 percent of their supplies themselves. They had turned the tide against the Germans in Europe well before the Americans and British opened a western front in France. Other countries also sustained terrible losses. Germany gave up 6 million lives; Japan, almost 2 million. Poland suffered horribly—in addition to the deaths of hundreds of thousands of ordinary citizens, its elites were systematically rounded up and executed by both the Soviets and the Germans. At war's end, tens of millions of Europeans were uprooted and homeless.

World War II witnessed the introduction of devastating new weaponry—jet planes, rockets, and, most omi-

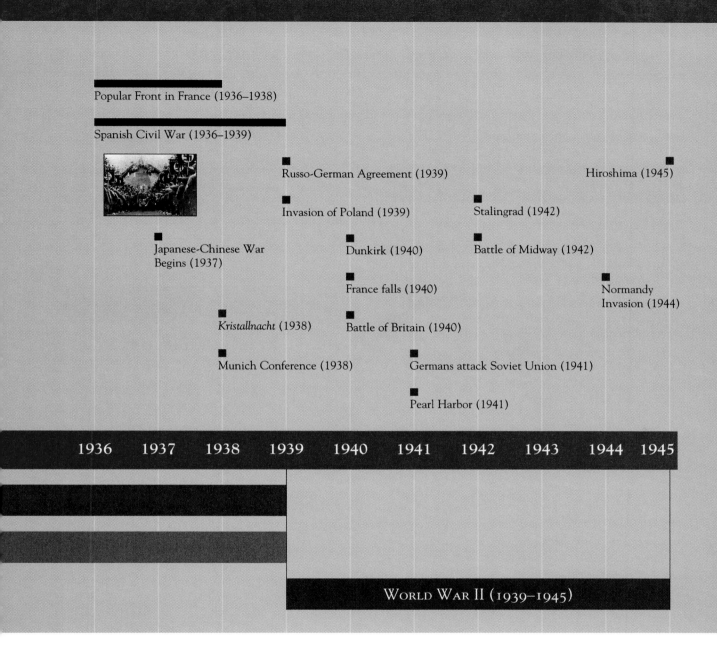

Popular Front in France (1936–1938)

Spanish Civil War (1936–1939)

Russo-German Agreement (1939)

Hiroshima (1945)

Invasion of Poland (1939)

Stalingrad (1942)

Japanese-Chinese War Begins (1937)

Dunkirk (1940)

Battle of Midway (1942)

France falls (1940)

Normandy Invasion (1944)

Kristallnacht (1938)

Battle of Britain (1940)

Munich Conference (1938)

Germans attack Soviet Union (1941)

Pearl Harbor (1941)

| 1936 | 1937 | 1938 | 1939 | 1940 | 1941 | 1942 | 1943 | 1944 | 1945 |

WORLD WAR II (1939–1945)

nously, the atomic bomb. Terror—of combatants and civilians alike—had become a standard tactic. Allied fire-bombings of German and Japanese cities caused hundreds of thousands of civilian deaths, and soldiers sometimes deliberately targeted women and children. Officially sanctioned mass rape—in particular by advancing Russian forces in retaliation against the Germans, and by Japanese soldiers against the Chinese—made the experience of war all the more vicious. And in the end, the Nazi death camps became the settings of unimaginable brutality and inhumanity. The camps left 6 million Jews dead along with an estimated 6 million victims from various other groups; only a few people survived to "tell the story, to bear witness."

Western and non-Western societies, weary and bloodied, now faced an overwhelming task: to recover from the devastation of the war and to regain some sense of order. The road ahead looked hard. In Asia, rumblings of national revolutions had already begun to appear. There, the Japanese invaders had inadvertently emboldened nationalists by showing that Western overlords could be defeated by a non-Western people. All these developments were unfolding under the shadow of a sobering new realization: that modern warfare truly had the potential to engulf and obliterate the entire world.

REVIEW, ANALYZE, AND ANTICIPATE

REVIEW THE PREVIOUS CHAPTER

In Chapter 22—"Descending into the Twentieth Century"—the story of World War I and the Russian revolution was told.

1. *In what ways were the forces unleashed by World War I responsible for the rise of authoritarian governments in Europe?*
2. *How might one argue that World War II stemmed directly from World War I and the Great Depression?*

ANALYZE THIS CHAPTER

Chapter 23—"Darkening Decades"—traces the rise of fascism, the development of the Soviet Union, and the trials of nations struck by the Great Depression. This story culminates with World War II.

1. *Do you think the 1920s was a period of real recovery and cultural flowering, or more of a haunted, anxious decade? Why?*
2. *Analyze the main qualities of German Nazism. How do you explain its rise and the acquisition of power by Hitler?*
3. *Why do you think Stalin initiated the Five-Year Plans? What were the purposes of those plans?*
4. *How and why do you think the Allies were able to turn the tide and achieve victory against the Axis powers in World War II?*

ANTICIPATE THE NEXT CHAPTER

In Chapter 24—"Superpower Struggles and Global Transformations"—the Cold War competition between the United States and the Soviet Union and the recovery of the West from the war will be examined. Changes stemming from the end of colonialism will also be analyzed.

1. *What problems faced negotiators trying to design a settlement at the end of World War II?*
2. *Do you think the course of World War II and its consequences would make conflict and competition between the United States and the Soviet Union inevitable? Why?*

BEYOND THE CLASSROOM

TRYING TO RECOVER FROM THE GREAT WAR, 1919–1929

Kitchen, Martin. *Europe Between the Wars: A Political History.* London: Longman, 1988. An economic and political history of the interwar period.

Mommsen, Hans. *The Rise and Fall of Weimar Democracy.* Chapel Hill, NC: University of North Carolina Press, 1996. Argues that Weimar collapsed because of a skewed political culture inherited from imperial Germany.

TURNING AWAY FROM DEMOCRACY: DICTATORSHIPS AND FASCISM, 1919–1929

Lyttelton, Adrian. *The Seizure of Power: Fascism in Italy, 1919–1929,* 2nd ed. New York: Scribners, 1988. A narrative history of how Mussolini came to power and consolidated it, with in-depth chapters on ideology.

Nolte, Ernst. *Three Faces of Fascism.* New York: Holt, Rinehart & Winston, 1965. A study and comparison of French, Italian, and German fascism.

Payne, Stanley G. *A History of Fascism, 1914–1945.* Madison, WI: University of Wisconsin Press, 1995. Excellent in its European and global perspective on fascist movements.

TRANSFORMING THE SOVIET UNION: 1920–1939

Lewin, Moshe. *The Making of the Soviet System: Essays in the Social History of Interwar Russia.* London: Methuen, 1985. A thoughtful analysis by a noted scholar.

Thurston, Robert W. *Life and Terror in Stalin's Russia, 1934–1941*. New Haven, CT: Yale University Press, 1996. An attempt to revise accepted interpretations of Stalin and the Great Terror as the product of an evil mastermind.

Tucker, Robert C. *Stalin in Power: The Revolution from Above, 1928–1941*. New York: Norton, 1990. The second volume of an exhaustive and acclaimed analysis of Stalin, stressing the policies of collectivization and industrialization.

THE GREAT DEPRESSION, 1929–1939

Eichengreen, Barry. *Golden Fetters: The Gold Standard and the Great Depression, 1919–1939*. New York: Oxford University Press, 1992. Argues that the gold standard was the obstacle to financial stability and economic prosperity in the interwar period.

Kindleberger, Charles. *The World in Depression, 1929–1939*. 2nd ed. Berkeley, CA: University of California Press, 1986. A wide-ranging account that argues that problems in the system of international exchange played the most important role in causing the Great Depression.

NAZISM IN GERMANY

Bullock, Alan. *Hitler: A Study in Tyranny*. New York: Harper & Row, 1971. The standard biography.

Fischer, Klaus P. *Nazi Germany: A New History*. New York: Continuum, 1995. A highly regarded examination of Nazi Germany.

Kershaw, Ian. *The Nazi Dictatorship, 3rd ed*. London: Edward Arnold, 1993. A thoughtful examination of the historiography of Nazism.

Koonz, Claudia. *Mothers in the Fatherland: Women, the Family, and Nazi Politics*. New York: St. Martin's Press, 1987. Studies Nazi ideology regarding women as well as women's responses to it.

THE ROAD TO WAR, 1931–1939

Alexander, M.S., and H. Graham. *The French and Spanish Popular Fronts: Comparative Perspectives*. Cambridge: Cambridge University Press, 1989. A comparison of the antifascist movements in France and Spain.

Jackson, Michael. *Fallen Sparrows: The International Brigades in the Spanish Civil War*. Philadelphia: American Philosophical Society, 1994. A study of the foreign volunteers on the antifascist side of the Spanish civil war.

WORLD WAR II, 1939–1945

Keegan, John. *The Second World War*. New York: Viking, 1990. Particularly good on battles and strategy.

Weinberg, Gerhard L. *A World at Arms: A Global History of World War II*. New York: Cambridge University Press, 1994. Excellent in its global perspective and its examination of the Nazi plan for world order.

Yahil, Leni. *The Holocaust: The Fate of European Jewry*. New York: Oxford University Press, 1990. A comprehensive look at the persecution of the Jews before and during World War II.

Don Eddy, *New Shoes for H*, 1974

In this 1974 painting, Don Eddy uses the artistic style known as photo-realism to depict a shoe-store display in New York City. Reflected in the store window are cars, buses, a department store sign (S. Klein), office and apartment buildings, and a pedestrian in blue jeans—all in all, a typically vibrant street scene in a leading Western city of the era.

CHAPTER 24

Superpower Struggles and Global Transformations

The Cold War, 1945–1980s

In 1974 a retired French woman, Françoise Giroud, contrasted her early life as a stenographer in the 1930s with the lives of young women of the 1970s. "[T]here is simply no comparison. . . . A month of paid vacation, . . . organized travel, . . . paperback books, . . . blue jeans and the T-shirts, instant mashed potatoes, the transistor, . . . the boyfriend who has a [used car], . . . and the Pill! It's not a better world; it's another world altogether." This new world that Giroud described boasted unheard-of material well-being, international peace throughout most of the West, innovative day-to-day conveniences, and striking new medical knowledge. The painting on page 790 is an apt illustration of this new age. The image reveals a wealthy, commercial society awash in consumer goods. In effect, the painting offers a view of reality from different perspectives, paralleling the efforts that many westerners made to understand their rapidly changing world.

Yet these decades also had their dark side. Nations around the world labored to recover from the devastation of World War II. As they did so, a new menace emerged—growing tensions between the United States and the Soviet Union that for decades would overshadow international relations and everyday life. At the same time, colonial peoples took advantage of Europe's weakness and changing attitudes toward imperialism and demanded their independence in ways the West could not ignore. New nations and international organizations soon emerged throughout the world, and global interactions grew so complex that the traditional lines between Western and non-Western societies blurred more than ever.

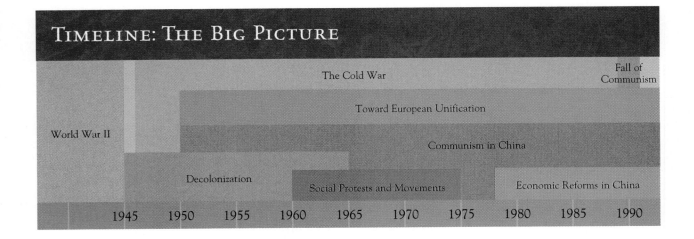

The Cold War

Fall of Communism

Toward European Unification

World War II

Communism in China

Decolonization

Social Protests and Movements

Economic Reforms in China

1945　1950　1955　1960　1965　1970　1975　1980　1985　1990

From Peace to Cold War

On a poignant night in August 1945, 300 frail, tired boys liberated from Nazi concentration camps arrived by plane in England. Each was greeted with a cup of hot chocolate. One of these survivors later described that moment: "The return to humanity began. Clean clothes, a normal bed and bedding, and kind people to talk to." The worst was over for these boys and millions of other surviving victims of the war, but peace did not end the suffering. Europe lay prostrate as some 50 million refugees drifted across the land and countless people faced starvation and homelessness. Memories of lost loved ones and homes, the horrors of the concentration camps, the hardships of occupation, and the echoes of mass bombings would haunt people for the rest of their lives.

Europe in shambles

Outrage, fear, and violence continued to stalk Europe. Many resistance fighters and Soviet troops executed surrendering Nazi soldiers on the spot. Angry officials and ordinary people hunted down and punished collaborators after only summary trials. To shame women they suspected of sleeping with German soldiers, irate citizens shaved off women's hair and marched them through the streets. The Soviets, Poles, and Czechoslovakians pushed 13 million ethnic Germans out of homes in Eastern Europe toward the west. One eyewitnesses described how "families with children, packages, hand wheelbarrows, horse-drawn wagons, and bicycles were making their way, and were being assaulted" as they fled along the roads to Germany. Stalin's officials sent thousands of returning Soviet prisoners to forced-labor camps or to the executioner for being "contaminated" by dangerous, anti-Soviet ideas. Jews who had managed to survive often found their homes destroyed and still suffered from flagrant anti-Semitism.

With agricultural and nonmilitary industrial production at a fraction of their prewar levels, Western Europe looked to the United States for loans, relief, defense, and leadership. Eastern Europe, in even worse shambles, was falling under the dominance of the Soviet Union. Political leaders and diplomats involved in the peace settlement hoped this time to avoid the "mistakes" made at the close of World War I. The main challenge facing them was to find a way to deal with defeated nations without spawning new conflicts.

THE SETTLEMENT

The leaders of Great Britain, the United States, and the Soviet Union shaped postwar Europe in two wartime conferences at Teheran in December 1943 and Yalta in February 1945, and one postwar conference at Potsdam in July 1945. They agreed to accept only unconditional surrender by Germany and Japan, and to require complete restructuring of the aggressors' governments. Germany, which had proved so powerful in two world wars, would be disarmed and divided. The Soviet Union, having suffered so much from Germany's massive invasion, demanded and received pledges of territories on its western border as well as reparations from Germany (see Map 24.1). To further weaken Germany and recognize the impact of the war, Poland's border with Germany was pushed westward. Finally, a United Nations organization was founded in 1945 by fifty-one nations to promote international peace and cooperation. Figure 24.1, a 1947 poster marking the second anniversary of the organization's birth, reveals the high hopes of its founders. Caring hands plant a tree of peace and union, each leaf representing the flag of a member nation. People hoped that as the "sapling" grew, new "leaves" and maturity would strengthen the young organization.

On other matters, however, discord among the wartime allies created a more ominous view of the future. The most crucial disagreements came over the fate of the Eastern European countries. Stalin argued that because the Soviet Union had endured invasions ***Discord over Eastern Europe*** through these countries in both world wars, he needed them to serve as a "buffer zone" of states loyal to the USSR. The United States and Great Britain demanded complete independence and democracy for these countries. Concessions on both sides at the Yalta Conference in February 1945 left Eastern Europe vaguely "democratic" but "friendly" to the Soviet Union. This arrangement quickly proved unworkable. Two nations—Poland and Bulgaria—were already under communist control, and pro-Soviet "coalition governments" quickly formed in other Eastern European states.

At the final conference at Potsdam in July 1945 (the war ended without a formal peace treaty), Stalin had the upper hand. President Roosevelt had died. Although the American president, Harry Truman, firmly demanded free elections in all of Eastern Europe, he had been in office only three months. Churchill might have been able to exert more pressure on Stalin, but the newly elected Clement Attlee replaced him during the conference. Stalin, insisting that the Soviet Union must obtain complete security against Germany and any potential Eastern European allies, refused to budge on the issue: "A freely elected government in any of these East European countries would be anti-Soviet," he admitted, "and that we cannot allow."

ORIGINS OF THE COLD WAR

U.S. leaders had trouble swallowing the reality behind Stalin's words. In fact, Eastern Europe was already behind Soviet lines and occupied by Soviet troops by war's end, just as Western Europe remained behind Anglo-American lines and within the United States' and Britain's sphere of influence. "Everyone imposes his own system as far as his armies can reach," observed Stalin privately. "It cannot be otherwise."

The conflict over the fate of Eastern Europe drove a sharp wedge between the World War II allies. Long-standing antagonisms and new differences soon combined to break down further any cooperation between the Western democracies and the Soviet Union. Ever since the communists had come to power in 1917, they and the capitalist democracies had viewed each other as opponents (see Chapter 23). As ideologies, communism and capitalism had always been in direct opposition. As practiced in the Soviet Union under Lenin and Stalin, the political system of communism took a dictatorial form, in sharp contrast to the democracies of Great Britain and the United States. Hitler's invasion of the Soviet Union in World War II and the United States' entry into the war only temporarily united Great Britain, the United States, and the Soviet Union. The three powers joined as allies more in opposition to Nazi Germany than in agreement over principles or goals. Not surprisingly, when negotiations over war aims and settlement terms took place, the history of hostility, distrust, and fear between the capitalist and communist powers caused problems. After the war, when the threat of Nazi Germany no longer held the Allies together, tensions worsened.

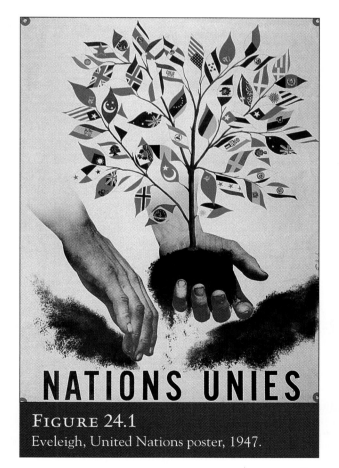

NATIONS UNIES

FIGURE 24.1
Eveleigh, United Nations poster, 1947.

THINKING ABOUT GEOGRAPHY

MAP 24.1 *Europe After World War II*

This map shows Europe after World War II and the dates communists gained control of governments in Eastern Europe. ▣ **Notice** the territories acquired by the Soviet Union as well as those lost by Germany. ▣ **Notice** that Austria, Germany, and Berlin were divided into American, British, French, and Soviet zones. ▣ **Locate** Berlin. **Why** might this city be of such strategic, political, and symbolic importance? **What** predicament faced the western zones of Berlin when the Soviets cut off land traffic from the west? ▣ **Evaluate** the size and potential importance of a unified Western Germany and Eastern Germany.

In 1945, the U.S. cut off all aid to the USSR. The rhetoric of discord between the powers increased. The next year, Winston Churchill, speaking at a small college in Missouri, warned the world of "an iron curtain" descending from the Baltic to the Adriatic Seas, dividing Europe between communist East and capitalist West.

Churchill's warning proved apt. Within the next few years, Soviet-backed communist parties in Eastern Europe pushed their opponents aside and rose to power; only communist Yugoslavia and Albania would manage to follow independent courses. In Western Europe, despite the presence of popular communist parties, American-backed anticommunist politicians controlled the governments. In Greece, the two sides clashed as the British and the Americans supported the repressive anticommunist monarchy in an armed conflict against the Greek communists. The Cold War had begun.

THE HEART OF THE COLD WAR

At the heart of the Cold War lay a troubled Germany. As Map 24.1 indicates, the peace settlement had divided the aggressor nation into four occupation zones: American, Soviet, British, and French. The city of Berlin, in the Russian zone, was also divided into the same four sectors. Sharp disagreements soon surfaced among the occupiers. The Soviets alarmed their allies by grabbing valuable resources from Germany, including entire factories, and transporting them to the Soviet Union as reparations for war losses rather than waiting for cash payments. The Soviets also hoped to keep their old enemy Germany economically weak and fully divided. The United States and Britain, on the other hand, set out to restore and integrate economically the western sectors of Germany, seeing those regions as essential allies in the growing split with the USSR.

Matters came to a head in 1948 when the U.S. and Britain tried to spur economic recovery by introducing a new currency in the western zones of Germany

The Berlin blockade and the division of Germany

despite Soviet opposition. Stalin countered by blockading the three western zones of Berlin. From June 1948 to May 1949, the Soviets stopped all land traffic across their zone from the West to Berlin. In response, the Western powers mounted a daring and continuous airlift that carried supplies to the city. If "Berlin falls," warned the American military commander General Lucius Clay, "western Germany will be next . . . if we withdraw, our position in Europe is threatened. . . . Communism will run rampant."

Figure 24.2 shows one of the 277,000 flights that carried supplies to the city. Children stand on a pile of rubble left over from the devastation of World War II and look up at the American cargo plane. The children gather here to pick up candy dropped in small handkerchiefs before the plane lands. This well-publicized photograph presented to the world an image of a mission of mercy saving the grateful children of Berlin. The airlift eventually prompted the Soviet Union to back down.

In September 1949, the Western allies followed through on their plan to merge the three western zones of Germany and to create an independent West German state—the German Federal Republic. One month later, the Soviet Union established the German Democratic Republic in its eastern zone, completing the division of Germany into the capitalist West and communist East.

Meanwhile, the Cold War chill was already spreading across the rest of Europe. In 1947, U.S. president Harry Truman (1884–1972) initiated the Truman Doctrine, *The Cold War spreads* a policy that offered military and economic aid to countries threatened by a communist takeover. "The peoples of a number of countries of the world have recently had totalitarian regimes forced upon them against their will," he warned. "[I]t must be the policy of the United States to support free peoples who are

FIGURE 24.2
The Berlin airlift, 1948–1949.

resisting attempted subjugation by armed minorities or by outside pressures." His immediate concern was the civil war in Greece, where local communists aided by neighboring Yugoslavia were making gains against the royalist government. His larger goal was to create a military ring of "containment" around the Soviet Union and its satellite states.

That same year, Truman's secretary of state, George Marshall (1880–1959), launched the Marshall Plan, a package of massive economic aid to European nations designed both to strengthen them and tie them to American influence. The Soviet Union forbade Eastern European governments to accept the aid and soon established the Council for Mutual Economic Assistance (COMECON), a Soviet version of the Marshall Plan for Eastern Europe.

In 1949 the United States organized the North Atlantic Treaty Organization (NATO), a military alliance among the United States, Canada, and most of the nations of Western Europe against the Soviet Union. Within a few years, Greece and Turkey had joined the alliance. After West Germany signed on in 1955, the Soviet Union countered NATO by creating its own military alliance in Eastern Europe, the Warsaw Pact. Now thousands of troops in each alliance— backed by the presence and might of the two superpowers—faced each other along a line dividing Eastern and Western Europe. It had taken only a few years for each side in the Cold War to forge economic, political, and military ties among its allies and form two hostile camps (see Map 24.2).

The Cold War would color international relations and everyday life for more than four decades. Andrei Zhdanov (1896–1948), a powerful Soviet official, described the official Soviet view of the Cold War in 1947: U.S. goals were "domination in all countries marked out for American expansion" and "the creation in peace-

THINKING ABOUT GEOGRAPHY

MAP 24.2 *Europe During the Cold War*

This map shows how the Cold War had divided Europe by the 1950s. ◨ **What** connections between military and economic cooperation are revealed by this map? **Consider** why the Soviet Union was so anxious to maintain control over its Eastern European allies. **Why** was Turkey such an important member of NATO? ◨ **Notice** what nations are not part of the alliance organizations. **Consider** the possible reasons for this.

time of numerous [military] bases . . . for aggressive purposes against the USSR." John Foster Dulles (1888–1959), President Dwight Eisenhower's secretary of state, presented the U.S. view in 1953: "Soviet communism . . . is the gravest threat that has ever faced. . . . Western civilization, or indeed, any civilization . . . dominated by a spiritual faith." Compromise between such extreme, hostile views seemed impossible.

Terror lurked just below the surface of the Cold War. By 1949, both superpowers had the atomic bomb; by 1953, the hydrogen bomb. Each country *Cold War weapons* supported growing military budgets and stockpiled huge caches of weapons, including intercontinental ballistic missiles (ICBMs) that could carry nuclear warheads. The danger rippled outward as other nations—Britain, France, India, China, Israel, and Pakistan—also developed nuclear weapons. As U.S. President John F. Kennedy (1917–1963) admitted in 1962, "The decision to use any kind of a nuclear weapon . . . presents such a risk of it getting out of control so quickly. . . ."

In fact, the Cold War was fought in all ways except open military conflict between the United States and the Soviet Union. Networks of spies fanned out over the globe. Political struggles anywhere, even purely internal matters, became arenas for defining a victory or defeat in the Cold War. The competition expanded to include nonpolitical activities as well, such as space exploration and the Olympic Games.

Cold War posturing and imagery also saturated the media. In Figure 24.3, a 1948 poster created for the French Communist Party, atomic bombs hover over the prostrate victim, spreading death (the crosses in the background) and destruction (the crumbling buildings). The poster warns France against any form of alliance with Germany, which the communists claimed would amount to preparation for war against the Soviet Union. From the United States, the Voice of America radio station spread anticommunist messages throughout Europe, while the station's Soviet counterpart presented its own views. Most European governments controlled the news on their radio and television programs.

All this led to a pervasive sense of suspicion and fear. Novels, movies, and television shows featuring spies and international intrigue proliferated. In the United States, for example, Senator Joseph McCarthy (1908–1957) led a massive name-calling campaign between 1950 and 1954 "to uncover" communists and communist sympathizers; these "fellow travelers," McCarthy claimed, had infiltrated every aspect of American life, from the armed services to Hollywood movie studios. Atomic bomb drills in American schools and bomb shelters in city basements and suburban backyards completed the picture of a Western democratic nation menaced by communism and the Soviet Union.

THE GLOBAL IMPACT OF THE COLD WAR

The Cold War quickly spread around the globe as each side searched for allies and victories wherever they could find them (see Map 24.3). No area escaped from the worldwide competition, but events in Asia and Latin America especially reveal the far-reaching impact of the Cold War. In both areas, the United States forged anticommunist alliances, while the Soviet Union supported communist governments and revolutionary movements. More than once, the contest fueled crises and armed conflict in these areas.

Japan had emerged from World War II defeated on sea and land, the shocked victim of history's first two atomic bombs used for military purposes. Because the United States by far had played the major role in the

FIGURE 24.3
André Fougeron, *Peace Must Be Saved*, 1948.

THINKING ABOUT GEOGRAPHY

MAP 24.3 *Cold War Alliances and Conflicts*

This map shows the Cold War alliances that spread across the globe during the 1940s and 1950s and areas where conflicts related to the Cold War broke out. ◼ **Notice** which countries are part of anticommunist organizations, and that several of these nations are members of more than one organization. **Consider** the geopolitical advantages and disadvantages held by each side.

defeat of Japan, it refused to share the occupation and governing of the Japanese islands with its former allies. The U.S. quickly promoted political democratization and used financial aid to help Japan rebuild and conform to U.S. policies. In this way, Japan, like West Germany, would become a link in the Cold War containment "chain" that the U.S. was forging around the Soviet Union. The strategy paid off handsomely. During the 1950s and 1960s, Japan became a firm ally and used its modern industries and skilled labor to make an astounding economic recovery that surpassed that of even West Germany.

The Cold War in Asia

China, just across the Sea of Japan, moved in a different direction. The civil war between Mao Zedong's zealous Communist forces and Jiang Jieshi's conservative Nationalist forces was suspended during World War II. Mao's forces waged a more incessant guerrilla warfare against the Japanese than the Nationalists did and thereby gained a growing following among the Chinese people. After the surrender of Japan in 1945, the bitter, internal struggle for the control of China began anew. The United States supported the Nationalists, while ever increasing numbers of Chinese supported the Communists. In 1949, the victorious Communists swept over the entire Chinese mainland. Jiang's Nationalists fled to the nearby island of Taiwan, where they came under the protection of the U.S. navy. Mao promptly proclaimed the People's Republic of China and joined in an alliance with the Soviet Union. With Soviet aid, he began the daunting task of industrializing and communizing China.

Less than a year later, the Cold War merged with simmering internal forces in nearby Korea to produce a major conflict that embroiled both the new Chinese communist regime and the United States. At the end of World War II, in accordance with the Yalta agreements, Soviet troops occupied Korea north of the thirty-eighth parallel while American forces controlled the south. The Soviets and Americans withdrew by 1949, leaving North and South Korea as armed client states rather than a united Korean nation. The new governments of the North and South, each ruled by dictators, talked loudly of conquering each other.

The Korean War

In 1950, the Soviet-backed North Korean communists—with the approval of both Stalin and Mao—suddenly invaded U.S.-backed South Korea. The determined, well-armed North Korean communists easily defeated the South Koreans. Supported by the UN, the U.S. quickly intervened. The American and UN forces soon overcame the North Koreans, but as their troops approached the Korean-Chinese border and threatened to bomb North Korean sanctuaries in China, the Chinese entered the fray. They pushed the U.S. and UN forces back to the thirty-eighth parallel, where a stalemate developed. By the time of the armistice in 1953, the war had cost some 1.5 million casualties on each side and had left much of Korea in ruins.

These experiences with Korea and China prompted the U.S. to involve itself in nearby Vietnam, Laos, and Cambodia. The U.S. feared that the fall of one nation in that region to communism would, like a row of dominoes, lead to the fall of other adjacent nations. "Vietnam represents the cornerstone of the Free World in Southeast Asia, the keystone to the arch, the finger in the dike," warned then Senator Kennedy in 1956. "Burma, Thailand, India, Japan, the Philippines, and obviously Laos and Cambodia are among those whose security would be threatened if the red tide of Communism overflowed into Vietnam. . . ."

Accordingly, the U.S. helped the French prop up the unpopular anticommunist regime in southern Vietnam as it fended off insurgents and the North Vietnamese communists. Vietnam had been a French colony before *The Vietnam War* World War II and, under the leadership of Ho Chi Minh (1890–1969) and his Vietnamese Communist Party, had fought for its independence from France in the years after World War II. After suffering a series of defeats, France finally agreed to withdraw in 1954. The nation was divided between the North, ruled by the victorious Ho Chi Minh, and the South, under an authoritarian, anticommunist government that tried to maintain the aristocratic society of a vanishing era (see Map 24.4).

The unpopular regime in the South relied for its survival on the economic and political support of the United States and its allies. Military aid and armed forces soon followed, as the United States sought to increase its influence not only in South Vietnam but also in Laos and Cambodia, which had gained freedom from the French. During the mid-1960s, the U.S. sent more than 500,000 troops to Vietnam. American planes dropped more explosives there than had been used by all combatants during World War II, pummeling the tiny nation. Still, the opposing North Vietnamese—helped by material aid from the Soviet Union and China—proved skilled and tenacious fighters, and the war dragged on.

Throughout the West, the United States drew harsh criticism from antiwar demonstrators for its

THINKING ABOUT GEOGRAPHY

MAP 24.4 *Vietnam and Southeast Asia*

This map shows Vietnam and its neighbors during the 1950s, 1960s, and 1970s, when war wracked the area. ❽ **Consider** why Cambodia and Laos became involved in the conflicts. ❽ **Notice** China to the north. **Why** might the U.S. bombings of Hanoi and Haiphong have been strategically risky?

relentless—and apparently futile—assaults on Vietnam. Figure 24.4, a 1968 collage titled *Miss America*, is one example of the reproach aimed at the United States. In this disturbing image, the well-known German artist Wolf Vostell uses photojournalism to convey his message. In the center, a Viet Cong suspect in South Vietnam is being executed. At the bottom, U.S. troops loom over crumpled corpses. Above is a mutilated image of a woman. The title of the work implies a mangling of American innocence, beauty, and honor by the daily, brutal realities of Vietnam published in newspapers and beamed into televisions around the world.

The cost, futility, and unpopularity of the Vietnam War put increasing pressure on U.S. leaders to end American involvement in the conflict. In 1973, after long negotiations, the U.S. and Vietnamese forces finally signed peace agreements, and the United States withdrew its forces. The civil war in Vietnam, however, persisted for another two years before the communists swept to victory—not only in Vietnam but also in neighboring Laos and Cambodia.

The Cold War tide shifted in Asia several times. China, which had backed the Vietnam communists, had continued in its own direction. During the 1950s, China was engaged in trying to meet overly *China's "Great Leap Forward"* ambitious goals in industry and agriculture. To that end, it communized its society even more completely than had ever been attempted in the Soviet Union. In a plan called the "Great Leap Forward," China's huge and burgeoning population was set to building irrigation dams and ditches, steel mills, factories, railroads, schools, and hospitals at a frenetic pace. In 1959, an alternating cycle of droughts and flooding struck, producing one of the deadliest famines in history; some twenty million Chinese may have died of starvation and malnutrition over the next three years. Overzealous local party officials provoked resentment and resistance among the already harried populace, and for years the Communist Party hierarchy was wracked by a power struggle between moderates and radicals. In 1966 Mao tried *Mao's cultural revolution* to reignite the revolutionary spirit by launching the Great Proletarian Cultural Revolution. He empowered youthful zealots to cleanse China of those who did not enthusiastically support him. Over several years, millions of people suffered humiliation or death.

At the same time, relations between China and the Soviet Union began to cool. As early as 1956, China

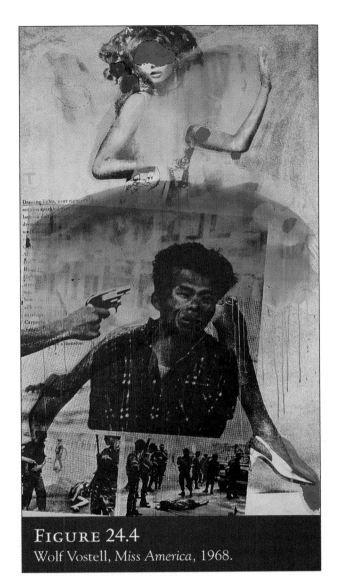

FIGURE 24.4
Wolf Vostell, *Miss America*, 1968.

tions with the U.S., replaced Taiwan in the UN, and, after the death of Mao in 1976, initiated policies emphasizing economic decentralization and free-market activities. Figure 24.5 symbolizes the new, assertive strength of communist China. In this striking photograph, a ninety-foot statue of Chairman Mao Zedong towers over marchers celebrating the twenty-first anniversary of the communists' victory in China.

The Cold War soon took another turn in central Asia, where the Soviet Union became entangled in its own version of the Vietnam War. In 1979, Soviet troops intervened to support a communist coup in Afghanistan, a nation on the USSR's southern border that *Soviets in Afghanistan* the Soviets considered within their own sphere of influence. They promptly became locked into a ten-year war against tenacious guerrilla forces backed by the U.S. Central Intelligence Agency. In 1989 the Soviets finally withdrew, leaving Afghanistan in shambles and wracked by internal violence.

Even the Latin American countries, far from the conflicts in Asia and long considered "friends" by the United States, got pulled into the Cold War. At the end of World War II, *The Cold War in Latin America* the governments of independent Latin American states were republics in name. In reality, however, most of them were right-wing dictatorships, representing the interests of the well-to-do bourgeoisie, the landowning classes, and the professional military. The Roman Catholic church, which had been a powerful conservative force in this region during the nineteenth century, had grown more liberal during the twentieth century. Sometimes it even exerted its influence in social and economic

started criticizing the USSR, which that year under Nikita Khrushchev (1894–1971) began backing away from Stalin's harshest policies. Mao denounced Moscow for softening toward the capitalistic, imperialist West and for abandoning *The Chinese-Soviet split* strict Marxist-Leninist principles. In 1960, the Soviet Union began to withhold promised economic and technological aid to China. When China exploded its first nuclear device in 1964, the two communist nations moved further apart, and by 1968, they were embroiled in border disputes.

With the Soviet Union a common enemy, China and the U.S. tentatively looked to one another for support. During the 1970s, China normalized rela-

FIGURE 24.5
Victory parade in China, 1970.

reform movements. In the years following World War II, the poor in Latin America became increasingly restless. Many of them turned to communism, encouraged by the Soviet Union. The United States, on the other hand, supported the conservative governments.

Over the next four decades, the U.S. intervened in or invaded several Latin American nations to shore up conservative forces in its global struggle against communism. The Soviets, for their part, supported sympathetic revolutionary movements and regimes. Of all the Latin American countries, Cuba became the most volatile staging ground for the intensifying feud between the superpowers. In 1959, Marxist rebel leader Fidel Castro ousted the American-supported dictatorship in Cuba and launched a sweeping program of social and economic reforms. The new program included the seizure of property owned by citizens and corporations of the United States. The U.S. government promptly terminated aid to the island nation, and Castro turned to the Soviets for help. These developments threatened the Americans in two crucial ways. First, a revolutionary, left-wing regime backed heavily by the Soviet Union had suddenly gained a beachhead in Latin America— a mere ninety miles away from the U.S. mainland. Second, the Americans worried that Castro's success would embolden other opposition and revolutionary movements—also typically led by Marxists—throughout Latin America. Such uprisings would lead to more Cold War victories for the communists. Three years after the Cuban revolution, the U.S. government sponsored the Bay of Pigs invasion, an ill-fated attempt by Cuban refugees to topple the Castro regime.

Crisis in Cuba

Tensions soon reached a new high in the Caribbean. On October 12, 1962, a U.S. spy plane discovered Soviet missiles being installed in Cuba. Privately, President Kennedy admitted: "What difference does it make? They've got enough to blow us up now anyway. . . . This is a political struggle as much as military." Although the U.S. had missiles on Russia's border in Turkey, the Americans decided that Soviet missiles in Cuba were intolerable. With the USSR's ships steaming toward the Caribbean, the U.S. navy under orders to intercept them to prevent the arrival of more missiles in Cuba, and American forces mobilizing, people around the world braced themselves for a possible nuclear war. On October 27, the U.S. Joint Chiefs of Staff urged an all-out attack on Cuba if the Soviets did not immediately remove the missile bases. Two days later, USSR leader Nikita Khrushchev backed down, and an agreement ended the crisis.

 DÉTENTE

The two superpowers would not again come so close to war with each other. Indeed, at times Cold War tensions relaxed as each side backed away from the sort of conflict that promised to devastate each nation and much of the world. Nuclear test-ban treaties in the 1960s and strategic arms limitation talks in the 1970s eased fears of confrontation. The Helsinki agreement in 1975 confirming Europe's political frontiers and recognizing certain human rights seemed to solidify a period of *détente*—growing cooperation between Cold War adversaries. But détente went only so far. The 1980s witnessed a return to combative rhetoric and policies with the Soviet invasion of Afghanistan and the tougher anticommunist policies of the Reagan administration in the United States. By the middle of that decade, few saw any end to the Cold War.

East and West: Two Paths to Recovery in Europe

Under the long shadow of the Cold War, Europeans once again tried to return to normal life after World War II. Beyond the astounding number of deaths and widespread destruction, whole cities—such as Berlin, in the heart of Europe—had been devastated. "Nothing is left in Berlin," wrote a reporter for the *New York Herald Tribune* in 1945. "There are no homes, no shops, no transportation, no government buildings. . . . Berlin can now be regarded only as a geographical location heaped with mountainous mounds of debris." Realists declared that economic recovery alone might take twenty-five years. Others wondered whether European society would ever recover.

European nations followed two main paths toward recovery that reflected Cold War differences and the politics underlying those differences. In the Soviet Union and Eastern Europe, communist governments promised clear planning and an unquestionable sense of direction under firm party direction. In Western Europe, the capitalist democracies relied on an alliance of the free market and governmental controls to transform their societies from the wartime devastation. Each path would have its successes and problems.

Tight Control in the Soviet Union and Eastern Europe

Nowhere was the damage and upheaval from World War II worse than in the Soviet Union and Eastern Europe. Soviet citizens longed for an end to wartime deprivations and Stalin's strict controls. Eastern Europeans living along the USSR's border wondered uneasily what to expect as their governments and economies came under the rule of communist parties controlled by Moscow.

Stalin refused to relax his grip over the Soviet Union. He asserted dictatorial control, crushing the merest hint of political dissent and purging those whom he perceived as potential threats. Prisons and forced-labor camps overflowed with his victims. Nor did his economic policies—tight planning and extreme sacrifice for heavy industrialization—change. To help rebuild what the war had destroyed in the Soviet Union, Stalin drained off economic resources from the Eastern European states.

Those countries under Soviet dominance—the "satellite" states—were required to cooperate with the Soviet Union. Single-party "people's democracies" in Poland, East Germany, Czechoslovakia, Hungary, Romania, Yugoslavia, and Albania initiated Soviet-style economic planning, nationalization, collectivization of agriculture, and industrialization. Officials allowed little contact with Western Europe.

Nevertheless, Eastern Europe refused to become a mere appendage to the Soviet Union. These nations harbored strong desires for national autonomy and they often resented Soviet restrictions. Within these states, discontent also rose over the persistent shortage of consumer goods, low wages, and poor working conditions. The Soviets and their followers often had difficulty maintaining control as resistance flared into open rebellions.

Yugoslavia snapped first. The Soviet Union had a weak foothold there because the Yugoslav Resistance had liberated the nation from Nazi control almost on its own. In 1948, Yugoslavia's strong and popular dictator, Tito (see Biography in Chapter 23), stood up to Stalin's threats and headed his nation on an independent course. Tito's decentralized form of communism stressed more local control and worker participation in management than the Soviet model.

In 1953, Joseph Stalin, the man who had led the Soviet Union for a quarter-century, died. In the Soviet Union, millions mourned Stalin as the leader who had saved them from Nazism. However, some Eastern Europeans saw his death as an opportunity to step up their demands for greater independence. Workers in East Berlin initiated protests against governmental efforts to *The death of Stalin and new opportunities* increase workloads without raising wages. Crowds soon gathered in the streets, demanding political reform and a loosening of ties to the USSR. Police and Soviet tanks promptly crushed these uprisings.

In Moscow, potential successors to Stalin jockeyed for power. They quickly agreed to eliminate the dreaded head of the secret police, Lavrenti Beria (1899–1953), and restricted that organization's terrorist activities. After two years of collective leadership, Nikita Khrushchev, the son of a miner, moved up from the party bureaucracy to emerge as Stalin's successor. In a 1956 unpublished speech to startled communist leaders, Khrushchev denounced the "cult of personality" fostered by Stalin. He also accused Stalin of using "the most cruel repression, violating all norms of revolutionary legality . . . mass arrests and deportations of many thousands of people, executions without trial." Khrushchev slightly loosened government control of Soviet cultural life; authors such as Boris Pasternak (1890–1960) even managed to publish works that implied some criticism of the Soviet regime. New policies also stressed the production of consumer goods, increased housing, and better healthcare. Workers throughout the USSR gained more freedom to move from one job to another.

Eastern Europeans hoped that this de-Stalinization would spell a relaxation of Soviet control over their nations. In Poland, worker strikes against wage cuts expanded into demands for *Protests and uprisings in Eastern Europe* political change in 1956, and the Soviets threatened to intervene. Nevertheless, Poland's Communist Party elected the moderate Wladyslaw Gomulka (1905–1982) instead of the Soviet candidate. Gomulka refused to cave in to Soviet demands but promised military loyalty. A compromise left Poland within the Soviet sphere of control while enjoying some new levels of economic and cultural independence—including increased toleration of the Roman Catholic Church.

Next, Hungarians issued a challenging demand for independence. When Hungary's communist leaders called on troops to put down protesters in the streets, the troops refused to fire and switched sides. A new government under the reforming communist Imre Nagy (1896–1958) initiated major economic and political reforms that included the introduction of a multiparty system. Nagy even proposed to withdraw Hungary from the Warsaw Pact—Moscow's military alliance with its Eastern European satellites. The Hungarians had crossed the line. The Soviets sent in tanks and troops, slaughtering thousands and forcing hundreds of thousands to flee to the west. Nagy was hanged, and the lesson was made crystal clear: cooperate with Moscow, or pay the highest penalty.

In 1961, relations between East and West hit a new low. Under orders from Khrushchev, the East German government erected a 100-mile, heavily armed wall in Berlin to keep its citizens from fleeing to the West. **The Berlin Wall** Berlin had served as an escape route for 2.6 million people, especially professionals and the well educated who sought a higher standard of living in Western Europe. Figure 24.6 shows the Berlin Wall, topped by barbed wire, as it curves around the historic Brandenburg Gate. To the left is East Berlin. Between the wall and a wire fence is the lane where guards were ordered to shoot anyone trying to flee west. The wall graphically marked the division of Germany and symbolized the hostility between Western and Eastern Europe.

In 1964 competitors within the Communist Party's Central Committee suddenly ousted Khrushchev, who had been weakened by foreign policy embarrassments such as the Cuban Missile Crisis, and installed the more conservative Leonid Brezhnev (1906–1982). The new Soviet leader took a firm line in dealing with Soviet satellites in Eastern Europe. Most of these states posed no problem for him. East Germany, for example, closely followed the Soviet line while developing its industrial capacity, and became the richest nation in Eastern Europe. Hungary remained tranquil, orienting its economy toward consumer goods, loosening state control, and introducing limited capitalistic practices at the local level.

Other satellite states caused conflict—none more than Czechoslovakia. In 1968 reformers gained control of the Czechoslovak Communist Party and replaced the country's Stalinist leader with Alexander **The Prague Spring** Dubcek, who believed that communism could be made compatible with internal party democracy and personal freedom. In this "Prague Spring" uprising, the Dubcek government initiated economic decentralization, greater national independence, democratic reforms, and elimination of censorship—"socialism with a human face." The reforms gained enthusiastic support within Czechoslovakia, especially among optimistic students and intellectuals thirsting for free speech.

Like Hungary in 1956, Dubcek's reforms went too far for the USSR's comfort. Especially fearful that the Prague Spring could inspire similar movements throughout Eastern Europe, the Soviets sent in Warsaw Pact troops to reverse Dubcek's policies and halt Czechoslovakia's steps toward independence. Figure 24.7 shows Soviet tanks rumbling through Prague in August 1968. Czechoslovakian citizens stand on the sidewalks watching as the tanks overwhelm any potential resistance in the streets. Fire burns in the background, adding to this image of the Soviets using brute force to compel Czechoslovakia back into line. The Czechs reacted with passive resistance; they could do little more. The Soviets removed Dubcek and his liberal supporters from power, and Brezhnev established his "Doctrine": Soviet intervention is justified in order to ensure the survival of socialism in another state. The conservative Brezhnev would make sure that Eastern Europe, like the Soviet Union itself, would not stray too far from the tightly controlled communist path followed since the early post–World War II years.

PARLIAMENTARY POLITICS AND PROSPERITY IN THE WESTERN DEMOCRACIES

Western European nations proceeded on a strikingly different course to recovery, dictated both by Cold War considerations and the internal histories of those soci-

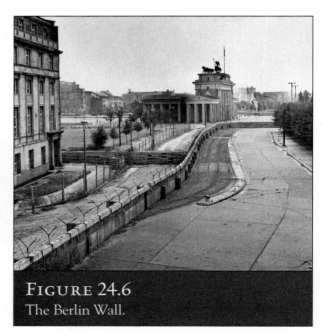

FIGURE 24.6
The Berlin Wall.

eties. In 1945, most Western European nations quickly returned to prewar democratic forms of government, and political parties leaning toward the center of the political spectrum soon gained control. In some countries, one political party dominated for long stretches of time—the Christian Democrats reigned in West Germany for two decades, for example, and in Italy for four decades following World War II. In other countries, major parties alternated in power, as the Labor and Conservative parties did in Britain. Some governments lasted only months, as happened in France, though the same group of well-known politicians usually rotated into the high offices of new governments and worked with a stable bureaucracy that carried out policy.

Initially, communist parties also gained strength after the war, especially in France and Italy. In France, elections in 1945 resulted in a sweeping victory for parties of the Left, including the communists, as well as the retirement of the conservative general Charles de Gaulle, who had set up a government in Paris in 1944. In Italy, the communists also emerged from World War II strong. For decades, the Italian Communists would command 25 to 35 percent of the vote and win local elections. But after 1947, when the Cold War heated up, these communist parties in France, Italy, and elsewhere were systematically excluded from participation in national governments.

In the struggle to repair their broken economies, European nations benefitted greatly from U.S. aid. Having emerged from the war the world's preeminent economic power, the U.S. pumped almost $13 billion of Marshall Plan aid into Western Europe between 1947 and 1952. More than a sense of humanity motivated the Americans. The economic aid also served U.S. Cold War interests by supporting anticommunist forces. *U.S. aid and economic recovery* The aid came with strings attached: international cooperation and freer trade by the recipients. By demanding these conditions, the U.S.—now producing more than half the world's industrial goods—gained unprecedented access to large European markets.

Europeans helped themselves as well. Drawing on lessons from the Great Depression, World War II, and the British economist John Maynard Keynes, governments adopted policies to dampen recessions by deficit spending ("priming the pump") and to counter inflation by tightening expenditures and interest rates. Several European states, from France to Norway, went even further by engaging in economic planning. This typically included nationalizing certain industries. In France, for example, major banking and insurance companies, coal mines, and gas and electrical utilities came under government control. In such countries, technocrats—bureaucrats with technological or scientific expertise—made economic decisions that were once the province of business owners or parliaments. Other nations avoided such extensive planning. West Germany, for example, broke up prewar corporate cartels instead and pressured labor and management to cooperate for industrial peace.

At the same time, most European nations created social programs to protect citizens from severe hardship and to promote social peace. These "welfare state" programs had roots in *The welfare state* the late nineteenth century, when governments had begun taking responsibility for the inequities of capitalism. Concerned about declining population growth, Europeans also wanted to encourage women to have more children. In the years after World War II, many governments followed Sweden's early lead and initiated programs providing healthcare benefits and family allowances as well as prenatal care, maternity benefits, childcare, and nursery schooling.

Nowhere was the welfare state more dramatically introduced than in

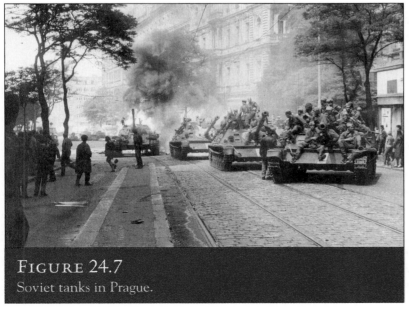

FIGURE 24.7
Soviet tanks in Prague.

Britain. Having shared the toil and suffering of World War II under the effective governmental direction of the economy, British citizens believed that everyone should get a piece of the prosperity that they expected would follow the war. In 1945, they elected a Labor government under Clement Attlee (1883–1967). The new government soon nationalized some 20 percent of Britain's economy and initiated what some called "cradle-to-grave" social-welfare policies. All British citizens could now look to governmental support during times of need—whether those times involved raising children, suffering job loss or accidents, paying for adequate housing, or insuring adequate resources for retirement. Above all, Britain's National Health Service guaranteed free medical care to all.

Scandinavian countries continued to lead, going the furthest in ensuring a decent standard of living for everyone in both good times and bad. By contrast, the Americans bucked against the tide. Prosperous, with its high-spending military in close alliance with big business, the United States strenuously resisted programs smacking of socialism. Not until the 1960s did it pursue moderate social reform, such as new educational programs, low-income housing projects, and limited governmental support of medical services.

Of course, all social programs came at a price. Taxes rose, particularly for the middle and upper classes, and government bureaucracies ballooned. Moreover, critics questioned the quality of the services provided, particularly medical care. Yet once established, most social programs served enough people and gained sufficient political backing to become permanent fixtures.

The nations of Western Europe recognized that cooperation offered the best hope for competing economically in a world of superpowers. Encouraged by the Marshall Plan, these countries moved toward economic integration. In 1950, France and West Germany created the French-German Coal and Steel Authority to re-

Beginning European economic integration move tariff barriers and manage coal and steel resources regionally. Jean Monnet (1888–1979), the architect of this organization, held some of the same hopes reflected in the United Nations poster shown in Figure 24.1: "If only the French could lose their fear of German industrial domination, then the greatest obstacle to a united Europe would be removed. . . . It could, in fact, become the germ of European unity." In 1952, the organization expanded into the European Coal and Steel Community with the addition of Italy, Belgium, Luxembourg, and the Netherlands. Five years later, these same six nations

signed the Treaty of Rome establishing the European Economic Community (the EEC, also referred to as the Common Market). The treaty proposed to eliminate tariff barriers, cut restrictions on the flow of labor and capital, and integrate the economies of the member nations.

The Common Market ended tariff and immigration barriers ahead of schedule, and its member nations enjoyed increased trade, productivity, and industrial production. In 1967 the organization combined with other cooperative bodies to form the European Community (EC) to work toward even greater economic and political integration. Optimistic supporters hoped that the European Community would make Western Europe an independent regional power that might economically and even politically challenge its superpower ally, the United States, as well as the opposing Soviet bloc in Eastern Europe.

ASSESSING THE PATHS TAKEN

Throughout Europe, early fears about how long reconstruction would take proved unfounded (see Figure 24.8). The Soviet and East European economies expanded after the war, though not as rapidly as Eastern Europeans expected or hoped. The Soviets applied advanced science, technology, and engineering to establish a strong industrial base, support a huge military, and build large urban projects. Some Eastern European nations, such as East Germany and Czechoslovakia, also developed extensive industrial bases and even outperformed the Soviets.

The Eastern-bloc nations

Country	1938	1953	1963	1980
Britain	181	258	330	441
France	74	98	194	362
Germany	214	224	416	747
West Germany		180	330	590
East Germany		44	86	157
Italy	46	71	150	319
Poland	19	31	66	169
Sweden	21	28	48	83
Soviet Union	152	328	760	1630

FIGURE 24.8
European industrial production, 1938–1980.
Figures are a percentage of British industrial output in 1900.

Although communism stood for the end to class differences, some citizens within each nation were, in the words of British author George Orwell, "more equal" than others. Certainly the Communist Party elite and professionals enjoyed better services and a higher standard of living than everyone else. But all citizens gained access to education, free medical care, and job security under communism. Subsidies made their usually overcrowded housing inexpensive, and unemployment and abject poverty virtually disappeared.

Women participated fully in economic life in these nations, often outnumbering men in the labor force. Moreover, a majority of doctors and teachers were women. Far more women engaged in manual labor such as logging and heavy construction work than their counterparts did in the West. They also received family allowances, maternity benefits, and childcare support. Outside the higher levels of government, Soviet women gained widespread political representation in parliamentary bodies, especially in local government. Nevertheless, women's pay lagged behind men's and women usually remained responsible for traditional domestic duties.

But even with all these improvements, Eastern-bloc nations could not keep up with their citizens' growing desires for a higher standard of living and more independence. Eastern Europeans had relatively few choices in consumer goods, food, and housing. In satellite nations, longing for autonomy from the Soviet Union persisted. Within each nation, Soviet-backed regimes—for the most part dictatorships—labored under questions about their political legitimacy. For many people, a sense of isolation from the West and a stifling of free expression within their own societies dampened cultural life in those nations.

In the capitalist democracies of Western Europe, government spending and welfare-state programs, as well as U.S. aid, fueled a strong revival (see Figure 24.8). Europeans used this money, **Western Europe** their growing store of new technology, and their skilled work force to rebuild factories and transportation networks into models of efficiency. Falling tariff barriers and a population enlarged by increased birthrates created new demand for consumer goods. Food and clothing prices declined, jobs abounded, and wages rose. By 1955, the standard of living for even those in the bottom half of society rose. In just a decade, Western Europe had recovered fully from the economic devastation of the war.

During the 1960s, some Western European nations achieved unimagined levels of prosperity. West Germany, Switzerland, and Sweden became the wealthiest nations in Europe. People in northern Italy spoke of their own "economic miracle." On the other hand, areas farther south still wedded to more traditional agricultural economies lagged behind, and once-mighty Britain—reeling from the loss of overseas trade and investments, and hampered by the antiquated state of most of its mines and factories—suffered a relative decline.

Overall, however, Western Europe took on the look and substance of wealth. Industries such as electronics, automobiles, plastics, petroleum, prefabricated housing, and airlines flourished. Newly restored city centers attracted hordes of shoppers, suburban commuters, tourists, and pedestrians. The number of cars on Europe's streets jumped tenfold from fewer than 5 million in 1945 to over 50 million by 1970. Stores overflowed with a cornucopia of foods and clothing. Electronic gadgets—from electric can openers to hand-held audiotape players—cropped up everywhere. The proliferation of restaurants, theaters, travel, and hotels reflected the affluence and the widespread standard of a forty-hour workweek and four weeks of paid vacation each year.

The good economic news outweighed almost everything else in Western Europe, and nothing helped its politicians more, for economic growth became the key measure of political success. Moreover as observers and visitors looked at the paths to recovery taken in Eastern and Western Europe, the West's stunning prosperity clearly contrasted with the slower growth in the East. However Western Europe also had problems that reflected its decline from the heights of power and certainty. Not only had these nations forfeited leadership to the United States, they lost their colonial empires as well.

The Twilight of Colonialism

Even before World War II, national liberation movements around the globe had gathered momentum. When Germany defeated imperial nations such as France and the Netherlands, and Japan conquered Western holdings in Asia and the Pacific, Europe's control over its colonial territories weakened. The United Status further undermined the imperial powers by pushing them to dismantle their empires at war's end. At the same time, the Soviet Union continued to spread its decades-old denunciation of Western imperialism throughout the world. In the

United Nations, sentiment grew toward the view that colonial "subjugation, domination and exploitation constitutes a denial of fundamental human rights." In the colonies, people seethed with anger against the Europeans. "Leave this Europe where they are never done talking of Man, yet murder men everywhere they find them," wrote the French West Indian philosopher Frantz Fanon (1925–1961) in his widely read book *The Wretched of the Earth*. "For centuries they have stifled almost the whole of humanity . . . . Look at them today swaying between atomic and spiritual disintegration." The last emperor of Vietnam, Bao Dai, warned his French overlords about "this desire for independence which is in everyone's heart and which no human force can any longer restrain."

Despite the intensity of these sentiments, many European settlers felt they had lived in the colonies too long to cede control to the local populations. Several political leaders in Europe agreed with Winston Churchill's sentiments: "I did not become the king's first minister in order to preside over the liquidation of the British Empire." The French announced that "the attainment of 'self-government' in the colonies, even in the distant future, must be excluded." The struggle to end colonialism was on.

REVOLTS IN SOUTHERN ASIA

At the end of World War II, national liberation revolts threatened the huge British, Dutch, and French empires in southern Asia. Of the Western imperial powers, only the United States escaped direct embroilment in this revolt by granting independence to the Philippines in 1946.

In India, the world's second most populous country, Mohandas K. Gandhi (1869–1948) led the independence movement. Educated in Great Britain, this *India* astute middle-class Hindu used passive resistance and civil disobedience rather than direct violence to pressure British officials to grant Indian independence. In 1947, Britain's Labor government finally freed India, partitioned into the separate states of India and Pakistan because of growing political divisions between Hindus and Muslims. Great Britain also relinquished Ceylon (Sri Lanka), Burma (Myanmar), and Malaya.

Independence, however, did not end problems in this troubled region. Religious and national strife soon broke out between Hindu India and Muslim Pakistan. Gandhi tried to quell the hostilities, but a fanatical Hindu nationalist assassinated him in 1948.

Open war between the two states erupted in 1949 over possession of the disputed state of Kashmir. The United Nations managed to stop the shooting but failed to resolve the dispute, which would simmer for decades. This conflict, as well as border clashes with China, persuaded India to accept military aid from both the United States and the Soviet Union. India and Pakistan also faced the huge tasks of unifying their populations—divided by languages, caste, and class—and helping their millions of poverty-stricken and illiterate citizens.

In the rich and populous Dutch East Indies, nationalist leaders had established underground organizations during the wartime Japanese occupation. These leaders now stepped in and declared *Indonesia* independence when the invaders left. The Dutch resisted fiercely for four years before yielding control. In 1949, they finally recognized the Republic of Indonesia as an independent nation.

A similar but more painful pattern emerged in France's Asian empire after the Japanese left Indochina in 1945. As we have seen (pp. 799–800), the popular Indochinese nationalists, led by So- *Vietnam* viet-educated communist Ho Chi Minh (1890–1969), proclaimed the independent Democratic Republic of Vietnam. Heavy fighting between the French imperialists and communist nationalists ensued. In 1954, France finally admitted defeat, pulling out of Vietnam and freeing the neighboring countries of Laos and Cambodia.

CONFLICT IN THE MIDDLE EAST

In the Middle East, Britain had been the dominant imperial power since World War I. However, under pressure from nationalists who had agitated for full independence since the first decades of the twentieth century, the British relaxed their control in the years before World War II. At the end of the war, British influence remained strong in several states, but only Cyprus, Palestine, and the Suez Canal were still official British possessions. Moreover, Britain was making a pronounced bid for Arab friendship, and to that end helped to form the League of Arab States in 1945. Yet, the admission of tens of thousands of Jews into Palestine under the Balfour Declaration of 1917—a British promise to create a "national home" for Jews in Palestine—made Palestine a new trouble spot.

Palestine was the ancient home of the Jews—a people with a long history of being displaced by others. In the seventh century, the Islamic Arabs conquered

Palestine and lived there until the twentieth century. In the late nineteenth century, a new movement— Zionism—emerged to restore Palestine as the national

Palestine

home for the Jews (see pp. 670–671). During the anti-Semitic persecutions of the Hitler era, Jewish refugees poured into Palestine and bought land, enraging the dispossessed Arabs. The British were caught between their obligations to both the Arab nationalists in Palestine and Jewish settlers eager to reclaim Palestine as their homeland.

In 1948, the beleaguered British finally turned Palestine over to the United Nations. The Jews im-

Israel founded

mediately proclaimed the State of Israel and accepted the boundary lines that the United Nations drew up dividing Palestine between the Jews and the Arabs. However, the League of Arab States protested this arrangement, and fighting broke out between the two sides. Although outnumbered, the well-organized Jewish forces held on. After a year, the United Nations brokered a truce. During the conflict, Israel had gained some territory and had expelled more than a half-million Palestinian Arabs. Most of these refugees, not welcomed by neighboring Arab states, settled in rough camps just outside Israel's new borders. The vigorous new nation, with financial help from abroad and a social-democratic government at home, began building modern cities and a strong economy. The Arab nations, however, refused to recognize Israel, and Palestine nationalists, without a country of their own, continued to conduct border raids on the fledgling nation. Conflicts stemming from the birth of the Israeli state would drag on for decades (see Map 24.5).

These conflicts only compounded the broader anti-Western sentiment percolating in the region, especially in nearby Egypt, where Britain still

Egypt

controlled the Suez Canal. In 1952, a military coup in Egypt brought the dynamic nationalist leader Gamel Abdul Nasser (1918–1970) to power. Although Nasser kept much political power for himself,

he promised parliamentary institutions, drew up a constitution guaranteeing individual rights, and distributed land to the poorer peasantry. In 1956, when the United States refused to support his plans to develop the Egyptian economy, he seized the Suez Canal. As he saw it, control of the canal would not only enrich Egypt but would also symbolize Egypt's independence and Arab nationalism.

Nasser's bold action provoked a military attack by Israel, Britain, and France. Cold War rivalries quickly came into play when the Soviet Union threatened to intervene on the side of Egypt. At this point, the United States pressured the three invading powers to retreat. Though defeated militarily, Nasser ended up a

THINKING ABOUT GEOGRAPHY

MAP 24.5 *The Arab-Israeli Conflict, 1947–1982*

This map shows some of the results of the various Arab-Israeli conflicts between 1947 and 1982. ▪ **Consider** which states in the area might be most involved in these conflicts. **Who** gained the most and suffered the greatest losses of territory? **Why** might Jerusalem, the West Bank, and the Golan Heights be of such importance to the parties involved?

national hero and the leader of the Arab world for standing up to Israel and the Western powers. Moreover, Britain lost the canal and soon its last holdings in the Middle East, while the Soviets gained influence in the region.

When war broke out again in 1967 and 1973—between Egypt (with its Arab allies) and Israel—the Soviet Union and the United States rushed billions more dollars of arms and advisors to their respective allies. The area had become another crucible of superpower competition that would continue to generate anti-Western resentment.

LIBERATING AFRICA

As in Asia and the Middle East, movements for national liberation stirred in Africa, where France and Britain held the most territory. France faced its greatest challenge in North Africa, where the largely Islamic population seethed with nationalistic unrest.

The French in North Africa

In the face of this growing force, France granted independence to Morocco and Tunisia in 1956 but drew the line at Algeria. The imperial power had held Algeria for over a century and considered it part of France rather than just a colony. In addition, more than a million French settlers lived there. They feared loss of property and reprisals from the 8 million Islamic Algerians in the case of France's withdrawal. Complicating matters, the French military was determined to hold Algeria so as to repair the damage that France's reputation had sustained in Vietnam. At the same time, Arab nationalists living in Algeria believed that, with enough resolve, they just might oust the colonialist regime.

A long, bloody stalemate resulted. As one French soldier noted, "There's this staggering fact: The entire Arab population is joining the resistance against us." When the French government eventually showed a willingness to compromise, disgruntled colonial army officers threatened to overthrow the government in Paris. In 1958, as France's government teetered on the verge of collapse, retired general Charles de Gaulle was recalled to power. The World War II hero alone had the stature and legitimacy to negotiate with the forces of Arab nationalism. He granted Algeria independence in 1962, and freed almost all the other remaining French colonies. Figure 24.9 shows Algerians celebrating the independence they gained on July 3, 1962. Algerian flags are held high, and children dressed in the colors of the new state march in the parade. Reflecting their background as a French colony and an Islamic people with a long history, women and men wear both traditional and Western dress.

Britain experienced similar challenges to its authority in its African colonies. The Labor government tried to prepare for the gradual freeing of British territories by sharing power with Africans in the civil service and bolstering funds for educational and economic development. The experience with Nasser in Egypt and a rebellion in Kenya from 1951 to 1956 finally persuaded the British to hasten their departure from Africa. By 1965, Britain had formally dismantled its African empire.

Britain dismantles its empire

Yet even with most imperialists gone, trouble still brewed on the African continent. Sizable white minorities living in Rhodesia and South Africa clung desperately to their power over black majorities. In Rhodesia, despite persistent guerrilla attacks by angry

Rhodesia and South Africa

FIGURE 24.9
Algerian independence, 1962.

members of the black majority, the exclusively white regime held on until 1980. In long-independent South Africa, the prosperous white minority held fast to its power over the nonwhite majority. Starting in 1948, the white minority harshly suppressed the increasingly restless black majority and enforced *apartheid* (racial segregation). This policy earned the all-white South African government decades of heated protests from nonwhites and condemnation throughout the world. Only in the 1990s would the white government under F. W. de Klerk at last allow the popular African National Congress, headed by the venerated Nelson Mandela, to assume leadership. By then, all European powers had pulled out of Africa. As Map 24.6 shows, their departure ended Europe's domination of Africa and Asia.

Decolonization did not end Western influence in the non-Western world or bring peace and prosperity to the previously subject peoples. Newly independent nations were often left with illogical borders

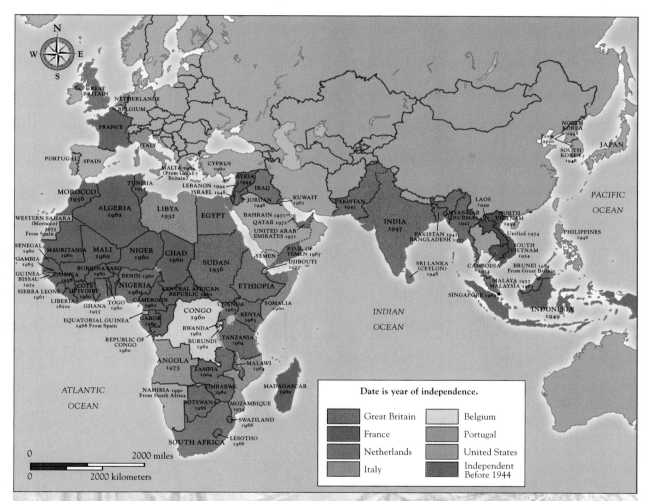

THINKING ABOUT GEOGRAPHY

MAP 24.6 *Decolonization*

This map shows the colonial empires held by Western powers before World War II and the dates when the former colonies gained their independence. ❧ **Consider** how decolonization diminished the political reach of Europe. ❧ **Which** former colonies became particularly volatile zones of conflict? **How** might that be related to decolonization?

drawn arbitrarily by nineteenth-century European imperialists, depleted economies, and internal polit-ical divisions that drew in Cold War agents from both sides to exploit the chaos. Especially in Africa, eth-nic conflict sometimes flared up into bloody civil wars, such as in Nigeria where the Ibos in the eastern region attempted to secede and set up the indepen-dent Republic of Biafra. Because the newly freed countries—especially in Africa—were generally left without internally generated political institutions, instability, bloodshed, and rule by military strong-men often resulted. In southern and southeastern Asia, religious and political differences broke out into wars in the years after liberation. Growing but impoverished populations lived under the threat of hunger, and in bad weather, starvation. Droughts, for example, in the huge sub-Saharan region of north-ern Africa during the 1970s, 1980s, and 1990s, brought famine and death to tens of thousands. Most former colonies remained "Third World" nations—relatively poor, supplying raw materials to industrial-ized nations, and dependent on the wealthier coun-tries' goods and aid. Interaction between Western and non-Western peoples had transformed life on both sides, and resentments nurtured by years of colonial suppression still lingered in many non-Western nations.

The legacy of colonialism

A Sense of Relativity in Thought and Culture

Decolonization forced Western Europeans to reevalu-ate themselves and their civilization. So did the rise of the United States and the Soviet Union as superpowers and the ensuing Cold War that quickly cast its shadow over the West and the world. In these decades of such accelerating change, thoughtful people struggled to un-derstand and define their lives and the culture in which they lived. The idea of universal truths that had pre-vailed in earlier times gave way to a growing sense that truth was relative—to the individual, to time, and to place. Increasingly, intellectuals, scholars, and writers argued that values were defined by the cultures in which they arose, judgments stemmed from individual percep-tions, and conclusions hinged on the evidence selected. In these subtle senses, the postwar decades stressed shifting meanings rather than certainties.

EXISTENTIALISM: RESPONSIBILITY AND DESPAIR

During the 1940s and 1950s, the philosophy of exis-tentialism captured much attention in the West. Originating in an era marked by war, depression, mass death, and the decline of traditional standards of morality and religious beliefs, ex-istentialism offered a stark inter-pretation of reality. France's Jean-Paul Sartre (1905–1980) (see Figure 24.12) became the most in-fluential proponent of this body of thought. In novels, plays, and philosophical works, Sartre argued that there is no meaning to existence, no universal right or wrong. As he saw it, individuals are born and sim-ply exist. They must make their own decisions, define their own purpose and values, and take responsibility for their actions. "Man cannot escape from the sense of complete and profound responsibility . . . one ought always to ask oneself what would happen if everyone did as one is doing." In the end, according to Sartre, one simply dies without there being any philosophical meaning to death. The French writer Albert Camus (1913–1960) also popularized existen-tialism in novels and plays such as *The Stranger* (1942) and *The Plague* (1947). He stressed the plight of the responsible individual seeking understanding and identity in an amoral, purposeless world.

Sartre and Camus

The sense of despair that existentialist assumptions often engendered came forth graphically in the Theater of the Absurd, which dispensed with linear plots, definable ac-tion, and conventional sets and costumes. Samuel Beckett's (1906–1989) plays are good examples of this genre. In "Waiting for Godot" (1952), two tramps wait for someone who never arrives. There is no purpose in what they do, for people in this culture no longer shared a sense of meaning. In Beckett's "Endgame" (1958), one character adrift in a world out of control describes his situation: "All life long the same questions, the same answers." In this absurd life, all responsibility rested with individuals, who had to make their own choices and decide how best to use their time on Earth.

Theater of the Absurd

A CULTURE OF CONTRASTS AND CRITICISM

The uncertainty and relativity implied by existential-ism emerged not only in theater but in other cultural forms as well. Writers, artists, and critics often dis-

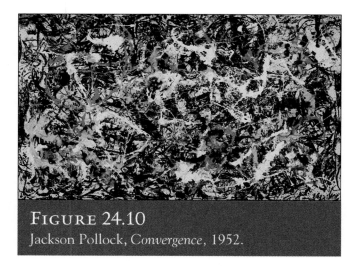

FIGURE 24.10
Jackson Pollock, *Convergence*, 1952.

In the more traditional cultural fields, a similar pattern of conflict over new works emerged. Some of the most critically acclaimed works seemed inaccessible to ordinary people. In art, abstract expressionistic paintings, such as those created by the American artist Jackson Pollock (1912–1956), who dripped paint onto canvases, drew attention but not crowds. Figure 24.10 is an example of Pollock's best-known works. Pollock explained why he avoided realistic representations of recognizable objects: "The modern artist is living in a mechanical age and we have a mechanical means of representing objects in nature such as the camera and photograph. The modern artist . . . is working and expressing an inner world . . . expressing his feelings rather than illustrating."

Art

Pop art, with its images of everyday objects such as hamburgers in advertisements, also gained attention but bewildered audiences. Figure 24.11, by the American artist Andy Warhol (1928–1987), looks like nothing more than rows of soup cans. From another perspective,

agreed with each other and with popular taste. In cinema, a stream of what critics dismissed as undistinguished movies nevertheless poured forth year after year. Yet cinema was perhaps the most original art form produced during the twentieth century. In the late 1940s and 1950s, several thoughtful movies, such as *The Bicycle Thief* by Italian filmmaker Vittorio de Sica, stressed the realistic struggles of ordinary people. During the 1960s and 1970s, the works of filmmakers such as Ingmar Bergman in Sweden, Federico Fellini and Liliana Cavani in Italy, Jean-Luc Godard in France, and Stanley Kramer in the United States exemplified the potential of cinema as a sophisticated, creative, artistic medium. These films contrasted sharply with the flashy artificiality of innumerable Hollywood movies—although many Hollywood motion pictures did feature stunning re-creations of the past, finely honed acting, and a creative mix of lighting, sound, and special effects.

Cinema

Many educators and commentators hoped that television would become a worthy cultural and educational medium as well. By the 1960s, people spent on average fifteen to thirty hours per week watching television. To be sure, numerous situation comedies, adventure shows, dramas, and game shows celebrated the joys, anguish, and pains of everyday life—as well as violence, romance, and fantasy. Yet most television critics were disappointed. Like radio and newspapers, television crossed lines between serious news, politics, and entertainment alike. TV had an especially powerful impact on politics. Politicians sought or purchased TV exposure, shortened and simplified their messages, and cultivated an image created with the help of media and advertising professionals.

FIGURE 24.11
Andy Warhol, *100 Campbell Soup Cans*, 1962.

however, viewers might interpret it as an image of striking, colorful unity that reproaches our commercial, prepackaged society with its standardized tastes.

Such paintings sometimes drew popular ridicule. One American news magazine, *Time*, called Jackson Pollock "Jack the Dripper." On one level, this popular rejection of bold new artistic forms was nothing new. Indeed, artistic styles that were once unpopular and considered avant-garde or elite—such as nineteenth-century postimpressionism and the twentieth-century paintings of Pablo Picasso—now attracted admiring crowds.

A related, but more puzzling pattern emerged in literature and music. For example, the "new novel," which consciously avoided clear plots and well-defined characters, gained critical acclaim but attracted little popular attention. Yet other, hard-to-categorize Literature and music novels that critics praised just as heartily—for example, works by German author Günter Grass, French author Marguerite Duras, and British author Doris Lessing—won wide popularity. In music, the dissonant, atonal music of Arnold Schoenberg (1874–1951) garnered few fans compared with the hugely popular rock and roll, whereas jazz—a creation of African-American culture that emphasized sophisticated improvisation and rhythm—enjoyed a large following.

Perhaps cultural products and tastes, like the civilization they reflected, were changing too fast for most people. To be sure, many westerners worried about the speed of and the forces behind cultural Americanization changes. In Europe especially, people talked about maintaining their own cultural tastes and identities in the face of "Americanization." They complained about the Hollywood movies, blue jeans, Coca-Cola, hamburgers, and fast food that poured from the United States into Europe. They also bemoaned the drain of intellectuals and artists moving to the United States. However, they could do little about the rapid spread of ideas, tastes, talent, and culture across political boundaries. Western Europeans found themselves losing the control they once had, and even the relative stability and prosperity gained in the 1950s and 1960s came under attack.

Protests, Problems, and New Politics: The 1960s to the 1980s

As the two postwar decades came to a close, the course of history in the West shifted. Events in the 1970s and 1980s unfolded in a context similar to that of the earlier decades: Cold War competition led by the United States and the USSR. Each side represented different political and economic systems that divided Europe and much of the world. Each side also marched to the beat of economic growth—more rapid in the capitalist West than the communist East. However, within this same context, economic and political trouble was afoot. During the late 1960s and early 1970s, the road to social peace grew bumpy.

A FLURRY OF SOCIAL PROTESTS AND MOVEMENTS

During these years, the gap between the ideals and realities of democracy, equality, and prosperity became more obvious and irritating than before. In some cases, unprecedented access to education fueled a growing awareness of this gap, while in others prosperity itself gave people the confidence to demand change. Often the well-publicized efforts of one group to force change inspired similar efforts by others. Protest movements frequently began in the United States and attracted close attention throughout the West. These dissatisfied groups voiced their demands with an assertiveness that shook several Western societies and even threatened governments.

The first of the great social movements began in the United States during the 1950s. There, African Americans initiated the civil rights movement, The civil rights movement which inspired several other protest and liberation efforts in the West. The civil rights movement stemmed from America's long failure to integrate its large black population. African-American veterans returning from World War II felt particularly frustrated with the discrimination they once again faced at home.

In 1954 the Supreme Court took a major step in the fight against discrimination by outlawing racial segregation in public schools. "Separate educational facilities are inherently unequal," the court concluded. A year later, a quiet act by a courageous individual set a series of additional changes in motion. A black civil rights activist, Rosa Parks, took a seat in the white-only section of a bus in Montgomery, Alabama. A year-long boycott of segregated public transportation by African Americans in Montgomery followed, the first of many mass actions throughout the U.S. in the 1950s and 1960s.

White resistance to the black struggle for equality flared up in the American South, and more than once the federal government had to send troops and marshals there to overcome white resistance. White opposition also mounted in the large industrial cities of the North. Many whites fled to the suburbs to avoid integration. In 1964 and 1965 Congress passed a series of civil rights acts that guaranteed voting rights for all and broadly outlawed racial discrimination. Still, the turmoil continued. Racially charged riots broke out in major cities. The violence reached a climax in 1968 following the murder of Martin Luther King, Jr. (1929–1968), the prominent African-American leader.

In the face of growing opposition and divisions within its own ranks, the civil rights movement lost steam in the 1970s, but not before inspiring other groups such as Spanish-speaking Americans, Native Americans, young people, and women. The protests by youths became especially threatening. Like the civil rights movement, these protests began in the United States. Soon, however, they spread throughout the West.

College students, whose numbers in the West more than tripled during the 1950s and 1960s, created movements of their own. The sheer mass of this *Student movements* first postwar generation of students and the emergence of a separate youth culture helped give these young people an acute sense of their own power. The civil rights movement and growing opposition to the Vietnam War provided causes and experiences for many. In 1964, students at the University of California at Berkeley attacked the restrictive values, social inequities, and competitive impersonality of the university and the traditional society it represented. Many found support in the writings of well-known social theorists such as Herbert Marcuse (1898–1979), who criticized modern Western society as too restrictive and overly commercialized. They also decried racism, poverty, and the growing American participation in the Vietnam War. Sometimes the protests turned into riots when authorities used force. Similar demonstrations soon boiled up across the United States.

In 1968, the unrest spread to the campuses and streets of capitals from Tokyo and Mexico City to London, Amsterdam, Milan, and Berlin. Even in Eastern Europe—especially in Czechoslovakia—youthful protesters added to dissident movements demanding social change and political democratization. "We are intensely aware, in a way perhaps not possible for the older generation, that humanity stands on the edge of a new era," declared students at the University of British Columbia in Canada. The most dramatic confrontations took place in Paris—the "Days of May" uprisings. Fed up with the rigid, overcrowded university system and fearing that many would miss out on France's new prosperity after graduation, Parisian students rampaged through the streets of the French capital. Charles de Gaulle, president of France since 1958, met the demonstrators with police repression. The students then gained the support of sympathetic workers, who in turn demanded higher wages and an end to police brutality. This alliance between students and workers paralyzed France and even threatened to overturn the government. But the danger was short-lived. Agreements to raise wages appeased workers and siphoned them off from the movement, and the government once more regained control. However, the protests provoked major reforms in higher education and probably played a role in de Gaulle's resignation a year later.

Like the civil rights movement, student activism waned in the 1970s. As universities adopted reforms that met many of the protesters' demands and the war in Vietnam came to an end, the sparks of protest faded. Among women, however, an international feminist movement was still gaining momentum.

Although feminism had a lengthy history in the West, the traditionally defined domestic role of women still had not changed much, even as late as the 1950s. In *The women's liberation movement* 1956, a London journalist wrote, "Today, the spirit of the old pioneers [of feminism] is so dead it seems a miracle it ever existed." In most Western nations, the dominant message from pulpits, welfare offices, doctors, and governmental officials was the same: Women should stay at home and serve as the anchor of the family, defining their social identity through their husband and focusing on raising children. But that age-old message increasingly came under attack as women gained access to higher education, experience in various protest and liberation movements, and greater awareness of the social restrictions on their lives.

One key to this increasing awareness came from new books. In 1949, the French writer Simone de Beauvoir (1908–1986) (see Biography) published *The Second Sex*, the century's most pivotal analysis of the condition of women (Figure 24.12). In this powerful book, de Beauvoir uncovered the myths that had relegated women to second-class status relative to men. "There is an absolute human type, the masculine . . . He is the Subject, . . . she is the Other." de Beauvoir argued that women remained in cultural and economic dependence to men and therefore did not live as free human beings. The passive role assigned to women, she explained, forced them to live according to standards set up by men. de Beauvoir recommended a difficult, but rewarding role for women: a life of work, self-definition, and independence.

The Second Sex became the fundamental text for feminist movements in the 1960s. Other writers, such as the American Betty Friedan, popularized de Beauvoir's ideas and added to them. In her widely read book *The Feminine Mystique* (1963), Friedan urged women to escape the confines of home, go back to school, get new careers, and become more independent.

These ideas struck a chord, especially among many middle-class women. Increasing life expectancy and fewer children meant that more of these women than ever were living longer and devoting less of their lives to raising a family. They now had the time and resources to seek fulfillment outside the home—if they could find a way to break down traditional barriers. As more women enrolled in universities and pursued careers, discrimination against them on the job because of their gender only heightened their sense of injustice and outrage.

Starting in the late 1960s, women in several Western nations founded organizations, conducted marches, held rallies, started journals, opened feminist bookstores, and pressured officials to recognize their needs. Figure 24.12 shows one of many demonstrations. Women—many in slacks and jeans rather than traditional dresses—along with a few supporting men march through the streets of Paris. Carrying banners, signs, and balloons, they announce their purposes—equal pay with men for equal work—and unity. In 1969, an English women's group described the essence of the women's liberation movement: "We are economically oppressed: In jobs we do full work for half pay, in the home we do unpaid work full time. We are commercially exploited by advertisements, television and the press; legally we often have only the status of children. We are brought up to feel inadequate, educated to narrower horizons than men.

This is our specific oppression as women. It is as women that we are, therefore, organizing."

Such efforts inspired a barrage of specific demands, including full citizenship in the political arena, equitable wages, and access to new careers. Despite opposition from conservative and religious groups, women pushed controversial issues such as day care, maternal leave, abortion, and liberalized divorce into the spotlight of public discourse. They also protested stereotypical portrayals of femininity and widespread assumptions—among women and men alike—that raised the barriers facing them. Finally, they persuaded universities to introduce women's studies programs and prompted scholars in numerous academic disciplines to include feminist perspectives in their books.

By the early 1980s, the sharp edge of women's movements had dulled, but many long-term victories were already theirs. Women had gained greater control over fertility and sexuality from governments, churches, and male-dominated medical establishments. Moreover lesbians demanded and received some recognition of their rights. As French author Monique Wittig noted in 1979, without feminism, lesbian culture and society "would still be as secret as they have always been." More women than ever flocked to universities, began careers in law, medicine, education, government, and business, and won political office. "Every girl now thinks in terms of a job. This is progress," said one Swedish vocational counselor. "They don't intend to be housewives for some future husband."

FIGURE 24.12
The women's movement in France.

Biography

SIMONE DE BEAUVOIR (1908–1986)

Simone de Beauvoir was born in 1908 to a devoutly Catholic mother and an intellectual father who practiced law. Later, after rebelling against her family's middle-class values, Simone wrote that her mother "held dear all those bourgeois, Catholic, pious, well-thinking ideas which I was learning to detest," while her father gave her "a taste for the intellectual life." World War I ruined the family financially. Realizing that she needed to support herself, de Beauvoir went to college. Reforms in 1924 gave women new access to higher education, and de Beauvoir, a brilliant student, seized the opportunity.

In 1929, while completing her degree in philosophy at the Sorbonne, Simone met and fell in love with Jean-Paul Sartre—a dazzling speaker and leader of a circle of rebellious intellectuals. "What is unique between Simone de Beauvoir and me," Sartre would later say, "is the equality of our relationship." The two vowed that "neither of us would conceal anything from the other." de Beauvoir had already concluded that "bourgeois marriage is an unnatural institution . . . that doubles one's domestic responsibilities, and, indeed all one's social chores." Neither did she want children: "I was too self-sufficient."

Through the 1930s, the couple's teaching careers in various parts of France kept them apart. de Beauvoir admitted that she and Sartre avoided getting involved in politics until 1939 when "history took hold of me and never let go thereafter." When the Germans invaded France the following year, de Beauvoir fled Paris along with thousands of others. Shortly thereafter, the Germans captured and imprisoned Sartre. Freed in 1942, he joined de Beauvoir, who had returned to Paris.

In 1944, de Beauvoir became a full-time writer. By then she had already published the successful novel, *She Came to Stay* (1943), in which she discussed connections between personal life and existentialism—the philosophy she, Sartre, and their intellectual circle often discussed. Sartre had also published numerous well-received works. In 1946, the couple founded and edited the influential review, *Les Temps Moderne*. Between 1946 and 1949, de Beauvoir

Writer and Feminist

researched and wrote her thousand-page study of women, *The Second Sex* (1949). By this time, de Beauvoir and Sartre had become France's—and perhaps the West's—leading intellectual couple (see Figure 24.13).

During the 1960s, de Beauvoir rejected formal participation in feminist groups, believing instead that socialism would lead women and men alike to full liberation. In the 1970s, disillusioned with socialism and impressed with the strength of the feminist movement, she changed her mind. She served as president of the French League of Women's Rights and editor of feminist journals and remained active in the feminist cause for the rest of her life.

In 1980, Sartre died. Their fifty-year relationship was not idyllic. Both had lovers, and their relationship was not equal. Much of the time, the companionship of Sartre and de Beauvoir had more of a verbal than physical intimacy. "That was why it lasted so long," said de Beauvoir just weeks before her own death in 1986.

📎 **Consider** what de Beauvoir's life reveals about the position and role of intellectuals during the twentieth century.

FIGURE 24.13
Simone de Beauvoir and Jean-Paul Sartre.

STAGNANT GROWTH AND RISING INFLATION

While the protest movements inspired optimism among their proponents and anger among conservative opponents, disturbing economic developments spawned worry and doubt. A new phenomenon that became known as "stagflation"—stagnant economic growth paired with rising inflation—spread in the West. The main culprit was oil and its central role in providing cheap energy for the Western economy. During the 1950s and 1960s, Western interests had kept oil prices low by expanding production and discouraging oil-producing countries in the Middle East, Africa, and South America from presenting a united front to raise prices. The low prices encouraged many users of coal to switch to oil and helped control inflation.

In 1973, a war broke out in the Middle East between Israel and its Arab opponents. Middle Eastern oil-producing states, now organized into the Arab-dominated Organization of Petroleum Exporting Countries (OPEC), began to *The oil crisis* punish the West for supporting Israel in this conflict. As they limited production and increased prices, the cost of oil rose sixfold between 1973 and 1975. Prices again surged in 1979, spurring global inflation that particularly distressed the poorer nations of Asia and Africa and sent Western nations into a downward spiral of debt. Western economies, also facing disruptions in the international monetary system and growing competition from Japan, fell into recession.

In Europe and the U.S., expectations of perpetual economic growth and limitless natural resources gave way to doubt. Indeed, the very forces that had brought prosperity for some threw others out of work. For example, the increased automation of industrial plants, substitution of oil for coal, and growing use of computers often eliminated more jobs than they created. The "green revolution" in agriculture boosted productivity but also forced people off the land and into the urban labor market. Equally alarming, large transnational corporations cut jobs as they moved their plants to regions offering cheap labor.

All these forces worsened unemployment, which by the early 1980s hit a whopping 10 percent and *Growing unemployment* higher in many Western nations. In Britain—once an economic giant—unemployment stayed at more than 12 percent year after year through the 1980s.

Unions weakened, unable to protect workers in this perilous economic climate. The gap between rich and poor widened, and for many people—especially lower wage earners—the economic good times seemed over. Least able to protect themselves were immigrant workers.

As is common during periods of economic uncertainty, wealthier nations turned against "outsiders." During the prosperity of the 1950s and 1960s, Western Europeans had opened their doors to desperate immigrants from southern Europe, Turkey, *Turning against immigrants* North Africa, and former colonies lured north by the promise of work. Immigrants filled the jobs that British, French, German, and Swiss workers passed over—the hardest, lowest-paid work in factories and fields, undesirable night shifts, street cleaning, and garbage collecting. Immigrant women were particularly vulnerable to exploitation in these jobs and in positions as domestics. Immigrant workers also labored under obligations to send money back home. Many, having heard myths about "lands of plenty," assumed that some day they would return home rich.

In fact, officials often denied them social services and discouraged them from settling permanently. West Germany refused to grant citizenship to even those "immigrants" born in Germany. In the 1970s and 1980s, many governments, fearing worsening unemployment in their own countries, slammed the door shut against immigrants. The millions of foreign-born residents or "outsiders" who managed to arrive in the West increasingly suffered racial and anti-immigrant attacks.

THE NEW POLITICAL LANDSCAPE

Reacting to social movements and uneasy about their economic fate during the 1970s and 1980s, voters throughout the West turned to political parties that they had once ignored or even disdained. Socialists, who accommodated these voters *Turning to the Left* by toning down their radical message, gained the most from this new development. In 1969, the Social Democrats in West Germany won control for the first time in almost fifty years. During the 1970s, under Willy Brandt (1913–1992) and Helmut Schmidt, they eased Cold War tensions by pursuing a policy of increased diplomatic and economic relations with Eastern Europe and the Soviet Union. By the late 1970s and early 1980s, Spain, Portugal, and Greece had also elected new Socialist governments that endured and led these nations into the European Common Market. In 1981, socialists under the leadership of François Mitterrand (1916–1996) came into power in France for the first time since the 1930s. They nationalized industries, shortened working hours, and enacted progressive social programs. However, persisting inflation and high unemployment soon led them to reverse some of these policies.

Communist parties in Western Europe also tried to adapt to voters' demands so as to garner popularity. In Italy, Spain, and France, the communists turned to "Eurocommunism," supporting more moderate policies and vowing to cooperate with other leftist parties. They even gave up the Soviet model and its call to worldwide revolution, and promised to work within Western democratic institutions and economic systems that blended free enterprise and state planning. For a while during the late 1970s and early 1980s, communists gained strength in Italy and played roles in governments in Spain and France.

Britain turned the other way. In 1979, voters handed a sweeping victory to the Conservatives and their right-wing leader, Mar-

Turning to the Right garet Thatcher, Britain's first female prime minister. Thatcher initiated policies to diminish state control over the economy, crush union power, and cut spending for Britain's welfare state. Some state-owned and subsidized industries were "privatized"—sold to private enterprise. Thatcher also cut taxes on the wealthy, hoping to encourage investment and a "trickling down" of wealth to the rest of British society. Bitter strikes and urban riots by workers and the unemployed decrying her hard policies did not dissuade her.

Across the Atlantic, Thatcher found an ideological ally in Ronald Reagan, elected president of the United States in 1980. Reagan pursued similarly conservative policies, reversing some of the liberal social policies of the 1960s, moving against unions, privatizing governmental services, cutting taxes, increasing military spending, and reviving Cold War posturing against the Soviet Union. Thatcher's and Reagan's partially successful efforts in the 1980s to limit governmental spending on social programs marked the beginning of a gentle but broad turn toward conservative politics in the West.

Despite the changes, some groups still felt left out of politics. They demanded attention, even at the

Terrorism price of violence. In the 1970s and 1980s, political terrorism spread across the West, conducted by groups such as the Red Brigades in Italy,

the Red Army Faction in West Germany, and the Palestine Liberation Organization (PLO). Many of these groups had radical political goals. Others, such as the militant Basque separatists in Spain and Kurdish rebels in Turkey, demanded national liberation. All desperately wanted recognition and had concluded that only assassinations, abductions, and bombings would achieve their aims. Terrorists killed several prominent Western businessmen and politicians. The most stunning of these incidents occurred in Italy, where in 1978 the Red Brigades murdered Aldo Moro (1916–1978), Italy's leading politician.

No area in Europe suffered more from terrorism than Northern Ireland. There the Roman Catholic minority struggled fiercely to gain equality with the Protestant majority. Many Roman Catholics demanded total separation from Britain and union with Ireland. The Provisional Wing of the Irish Republican Army (IRA) conducted a long campaign of terror to this end. As the Protestants fought fiercely to maintain their supremacy, violence begot even more violence. Hundreds on both sides died, and hopes for a harmonious solution sank.

Governments responded to terrorists, sometimes with violence and occasionally by making deals. Security measures increased, as did the presence of armed police, and occasionally governments were able to penetrate the urban anonymity of modern society to capture terrorists. For the most part, however, terrorism remained an exceptional means of protest that never gained enough support to threaten governments.

Postindustrial Society

The political fluctuations of the 1970s and 1980s reflected more than just economic ups and downs or politicians' efforts to garner popular support. Underlying many changes during this period was a fundamental development: the industrial societies of the West had begun transforming themselves into "postindustrial" societies. This term refers to a culmination of economic and social changes occurring in the West over several decades. Traditional manufacturing industries declined in importance as more competitive plants employing cheap labor opened outside of Europe and North America. In place of manufacturing, demand for financial, health, educational, informational, and consumer services mushroomed—all services at which the West excelled.

Well-educated and handsomely paid professionals, managers, and financiers rose to prominent positions in corporations and government, joining or replacing property owners and entrepreneurs as key economic figures. The bulk of the middle class—most of them well educated and with white-collar jobs—also grew in number and wealth. Industrial workers saw their jobs disappearing while demand for service employees expanded. Yet many of these service employees, who seemed "white collar" or "middle class" in their appearance or lifestyle, made the same income or even less than blue-collar workers. Traditional class lines were blurring.

Changing Fortunes in the Postindustrial Society

Some people gained more than others in this mobile society. The gap between rich and poor may have narrowed between the 1940s and 1960s, but that gap remained formidable and even increased in the 1970s and 1980s. Only the growing numbers of married women entering the paid work force maintained or improved most families' standard of living after the early 1970s. Nor did overall prosperity solve problems of economic discrimination. Women generally received only two-thirds to three-fourths of men's salaries for the same work. Minority and immigrant groups still occupied the most poorly paid jobs. In many Western cities, a core of impoverished slum-dwellers remained. Often without regular jobs and marked by their race or ethnic origin, they suffered the worst problems of urban life.

For most people in postindustrial societies, however, material life improved. Housing mushroomed, in France alone increasing to a half-million new units per year during the 1970s. New apartments had distinct rooms—bedroom, kitchen, living room, bathroom—and were not just for the middle class. Most homes boasted running water, indoor toilets, a bath or shower, and heating as well as an array of appliances. In the 1980s, one Italian woman reflected in amazement how her children "have grown up in a world in which washing machine, refrigerator, vacuum cleaner, and television set are taken for granted."

Daily patterns of life also changed as more and more people lived and worked in different parts of the cities and their expanding suburbs. People commuted on crowded trains or by car through traffic jams. "I'm running, running . . . from home to bus, from bus to metro, bus again. Metro again. To work and back," complained a Soviet woman in 1969. The neighborhood cafés or pubs where people used to gather after work steadily lost customers, as did local, small stores where shoppers knew the merchants and each other. In their place, restaurants, supermarkets, and shopping malls sprang up, adding to the sense of urban anonymity.

The Baby Boom and the Booming Cities

Underlying the development of this postindustrial society were shifting populations that fueled economic growth and transformed patterns of life. Skyrocketing birthrates that had started during the war years led to the so-called baby boom soon after. An increase in life expectancy and the influx of immigrants added to the population growth. Europe, for example, increased from a population of 264 million during the war to 320 million in the early 1970s. But the baby boom and the rapid jump in population did not last long. By the 1960s, birthrates began to decline as people returned to the long-term pattern of choosing to have fewer children. In the 1970s, these rates fell to less than half the pre-World War II figures in some areas.

Fewer of those populations lived on farms anymore. By 1955, less than a quarter of the population worked in agriculture. Over the next thirty years, that figure would fall to below 10 percent almost everywhere. Thanks to mechanization, fertilizers, pesticides, new seeds, and larger farms, these dwindling numbers of farmers produced more than enough for everyone else, as well as surpluses for export. Rural economies could no longer offer employment to more than a small minority of the population. Once the heart of Western civilization, rural areas became places that city people traveled through and nostalgically imagined. Small country towns dominated by church steeples tried to stay viable by attracting tourists, people wanting second homes, or small industries looking to relocate. With the spread of highways, telephones, televisions, and computers, rural life retained only a hint of the isolation that once so distinguished it from city life.

As they had for decades, people left rural areas and small towns in droves and headed for the cities. These migrations spread well beyond national borders.

Wealthy northern European cities absorbed waves of newcomers from southern Italy, Greece, Turkey, and Africa, just as cities in North America took in Latin Americans and Asians. These immigration trends added to the traditional urban problems of congestion, overburdened transportation systems, pollution, and crime. Large parts of great cities deteriorated while the surrounding suburbs, with their own industrial plants, corporate offices, apartment complexes, and housing projects, expanded. Despite these problems, cities and suburbs generally boasted more comfortable housing and working conditions than ever before.

THE SHIFTING FOUNDATIONS OF FAMILY AND PRIVATE LIFE

Along with this movement of people and transformation of cities, the very foundations of family and private life within postindustrial society began to shift. After the baby boom years of the 1940s and 1950s, families became smaller as people, aided by more widely available birth-control devices, chose to limit births. Families also became less stable, as married people used changing attitudes and laws concerning divorce to break apart more often. Many people decided to put off or avoid marriage altogether. Increasing numbers of single parents and same-sex partners now headed households.

The old family structure, in which the man wielded authority, weakened and began to be replaced by a sense of the family as a democratic partnership of equals. Married women streamed out of their roles as housekeepers, child rearers, and supporters of their "breadwinning" husbands. They now took paying jobs outside the home not only for the income, but also for the equality and independence that paid employment offered. Especially within the middle classes, work outside the home became a sign of emancipation for women. With these changes, some homes became zones of domestic cooperation; others witnessed new battles between couples over household chores and child rearing. Overall, however, the burdens of housework and childcare still rested primarily with women.

The process of raising children also changed. Children spent more years than ever in school to acquire the skills to excel in the competitive postindustrial society, a shift that made them financially dependent on their parents into their late teens and even early twenties. With nursery schools becoming standard, children now started school at age three rather than age six. More than ever, the socialization, training, and career choices of youths were taking place outside the home.

Within the home, an individual's private life became no longer secondary to family life. Figure 24.14 presents the image of the small family together watching television. The television as much as the kitchen became a center of nightly family gatherings. But this image may also depict a *Growing concern for private satisfactions* decline of family interaction. Larger apartments and houses let family members spend more time than ever in separate rooms, coming together only for meals or TV watching. Much of home life became private, with individuals spending most time apart and alone rather than joining other family members.

This growing concern for private satisfactions, which fit so well with the competitive economic individualism of postindustrial society, also played a role in the frequent separation of families. More often than ever, the ties holding marriages together began breaking apart. With love as the primary motive for marriage, the declining intensity of love that often occurs with time seemed enough to warrant divorce. As the sexual satisfaction of both partners became a core purpose of marriage, trouble in this domain also became a volatile source of discord and divorce.

FIGURE 24.14
Family watching television.

Legal changes and statistics reflected these new realities. The grounds for divorce eased in most places to the point where mutual consent was enough. By the 1980s, between 25 and 50 percent of those who married would eventually get divorced. The old image of the breadwinning father, the homemaking wife, and the dependent children bonded together in a life-long relationship remained true for only a minority of the population.

THE "SEXUAL REVOLUTION" AND THE YOUTH CULTURE

Within or outside marriage, people gained new degrees of sexual freedom. Innovative methods of contraception, particularly the birth-control pill and the intrauterine device (and abortion, especially in Eastern Europe), achieved widespread acceptance in the 1960s and further separated sexual pleasure from reproduction. Manuals, sex education in schools, and the portrayal of sex in movies, books, magazines, and marketing materials became far more explicit than ever, reflecting the changing attitudes toward sex. Many conservative and religious groups strongly opposed these developments and the increase in premarital sex, though they were losing this battle by the 1970s. They also lost ground to gays, lesbians, and others who demanded respect and freedom.

Young men and women coming of age in the late 1950s and the 1960s, sometimes called the era of "the sexual revolution," led these widespread changes in sexual values. Their new clothing—flowered shirts and beads for men, blue jeans and mini skirts for women—and long hairstyles symbolized their new sexual freedom as well as the wider challenge of their youth culture to "the older generation."

Young people's taste in music and movies also announced a break between generations. In the United States, Elvis Presley led the explosion in rock and roll's popularity in the late 1950s. With his suggestive dancing, slicked back hair, and devoted following of young, screaming fans, Presley embodied eroticism and sexual abandon. The Beatles and other popular rock groups had a similar impact. Social dancing evolved from a carefully choreographed, chaste ritual to a no-holds-barred celebration of the body and sexuality. In popular movies, brooding, sullen young actors such as James Dean and Marlon Brando portrayed rebellious youths and became icons of the expanding youth culture.

Breakthroughs in Science

The postindustrial society and the changing patterns of urban life that characterized it owed much to the many scientific breakthroughs of the period following World War II. More than ever, science became linked to economics and the needs of large institutions—from governments and industrial corporations to universities. These links were particularly strong in "big science." Before World War II, most scientific research was carried out by individuals or small groups of scientists in a university setting. The application of their discoveries by engineers and technicians came later. After the war, funds for scientific research poured in from government and big business, forming what some called the military-industrial-university complex. With the influx of money and interest, the number of scientists jumped fivefold between 1945 and 1985, and the fields they entered divided into more and more subspecialties. Organized teams of scientists, technicians, and managers worked in large research laboratories, using expensive equipment and aiming for specific goals. The results were stunning.

The rise of big science

FROM THE UNIVERSE ABOVE TO THE UNIVERSE WITHIN

Cold War competition especially fueled the massive effort to put satellites and humans into space. By the 1960s, satellites spun around the earth, providing a steady stream of military surveillance, weather observations, communications, and scientific information. The "space race" between the United States and the Soviet Union climaxed with a televised walk on the moon's surface in 1969. While taking his first step, the American astronaut Neil Armstrong spoke his now-famous words: "That's one small step for man, one giant leap for mankind." Figure 24.15 shows an American astronaut standing on the surface of the moon. One of the first things he did was to plant the United States flag and pose with it for a photograph. The image announced how daring and powerful the combination of government, science, and nationalism could be. Subsequent unmanned voyages carried spacecraft to planets throughout the solar system and beyond.

Government money funded other scientific and technological efforts as well. Teams of physicists used powerful particle accelerators to explore the subatomic world. From innovations in radar systems during World War II came microwave technology, which became central to the television and long-distance telephone industries. Work on the atomic bomb led to nuclear power plants.

Similar efforts by teams of scientists and individuals led to fundamental discoveries in fields such as genetics. In 1953 the structure of DNA, the material in chromosomes that contains hereditary information, was discovered. This implied that the characteristics of all living things, including humans, could be controlled, and opened the controversial possibility of tampering with this molecule to create new forms of life. Research into gene splitting and genetic engineering would turn this possibility into reality. During the 1980s and 1990s, scientists introduced cloning—reproducing an organism from cells of that organism in a laboratory.

The Information Revolution

Much of the new scientific work depended on computers, which became the core of the "information revolution." The computer first emerged in the 1940s as a tool for storing and manipulating information. Encouraged by business and government during the 1950s and 1960s, its scientific and economic impact widened. With miniaturization during the 1970s and 1980s, computers the size of a notebook could out-

Figure 24.15
Americans on the moon, 1969.

power their room-size predecessors. These new "personal computers" cropped up on desktops and in briefcases everywhere. Now most people involved in science, scholarship, and business relied on computers, and the new devices became the core of a booming, worldwide industry.

Transforming Medicine

In the decades after World War II, medicine also entered new territory—itself becoming a big business with strong links to science and economics. Long gone were the days of visits by horse-and-buggy doctors. Now most physicians saw patients in offices, clinics, and especially hospitals, which employed medical personnel working in coordinated teams with complex machines. The age of the family doctor also faded. Now patients consulted more prestigious specialists. Finally, doctors gained a new degree of power to battle medical problems. Whereas in earlier centuries physicians may have done more harm than good with their treatments, now medicine became a major lifesaver in the Western and non-Western world.

The keys to these changes were antibiotic drugs and vaccines. In the 1930s, researchers discovered that sulfa drugs could cure infectious diseases. Penicillin and other antibiotics soon followed. By the 1940s, once fatal illnesses such as meningitis and pneumonia could be cured by antibiotic drugs. Tuberculosis, a disease so deadly that it was called the "white plague," was almost eliminated by a vaccine and antibiotics. In 1977 smallpox was literally eradicated throughout the globe. The spotlight on medicine shifted from traditional infectious diseases to cancer, heart disease, arthritis, and AIDS.

New surgical techniques also offered more hope than in previous centuries. Antibiotics let surgeons perform lung and other operations that had been too risky before because of the danger of infection. By the 1960s, open heart surgery and heart bypass operations became almost routine. Then organ replacement—first kidneys and then even hearts—became possible. Dr. Jan H. Louw described the first successful human heart transplant in 1967 and the use of electric shock to start the transplanted heart: "It was like turning the ignition switch of a car." Surgery became more a process of continuous repair and replacement than cutting and removing.

Expensive new machines for diagnosis and treatment complemented all the new medical techniques.

TIMELINE: A CLOSER LOOK

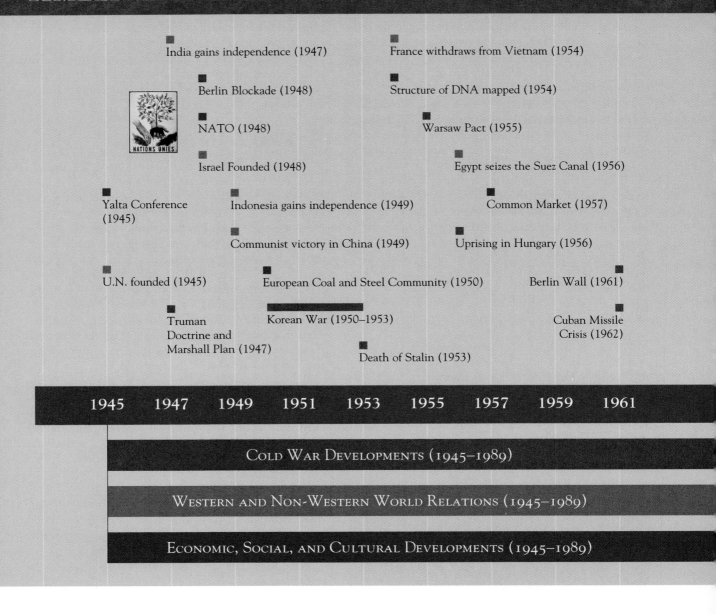

India gains independence (1947)

Berlin Blockade (1948)

NATO (1948)

Israel Founded (1948)

Yalta Conference (1945)

Indonesia gains independence (1949)

Communist victory in China (1949)

U.N. founded (1945)

European Coal and Steel Community (1950)

Truman Doctrine and Marshall Plan (1947)

Korean War (1950–1953)

Death of Stalin (1953)

France withdraws from Vietnam (1954)

Structure of DNA mapped (1954)

Warsaw Pact (1955)

Egypt seizes the Suez Canal (1956)

Common Market (1957)

Uprising in Hungary (1956)

Berlin Wall (1961)

Cuban Missile Crisis (1962)

| 1945 | 1947 | 1949 | 1951 | 1953 | 1955 | 1957 | 1959 | 1961 |

COLD WAR DEVELOPMENTS (1945–1989)

WESTERN AND NON-WESTERN WORLD RELATIONS (1945–1989)

ECONOMIC, SOCIAL, AND CULTURAL DEVELOPMENTS (1945–1989)

Ultrasound machines, CT scanners (which combined X rays with computer analysis), and MRI devices that used radio waves gave doctors a window into the body without having to open it up. Dialysis machines and pacemakers offered new hope to kidney and heart patients.

For those suffering from mental illnesses, effective medications emerged in the 1950s. Doctors prescribed a growing list of these psychotropic drugs for people with schizophrenic and manic-depressive conditions. Though the success of these drugs was far from complete, they contributed to the closing of many mental hospitals and asylums.

By the 1980s, medicine had become dominated by large hospitals, groups of doctors, insurance companies, and governmental agencies. Health "consumers" expected more and more from medicine—including "cures" for most ailments and what many saw as a right to live to retirement and a robust old age. Nations devoted more resources than ever to medicine—often more than 10 percent of the national income. Britain's minister of health once

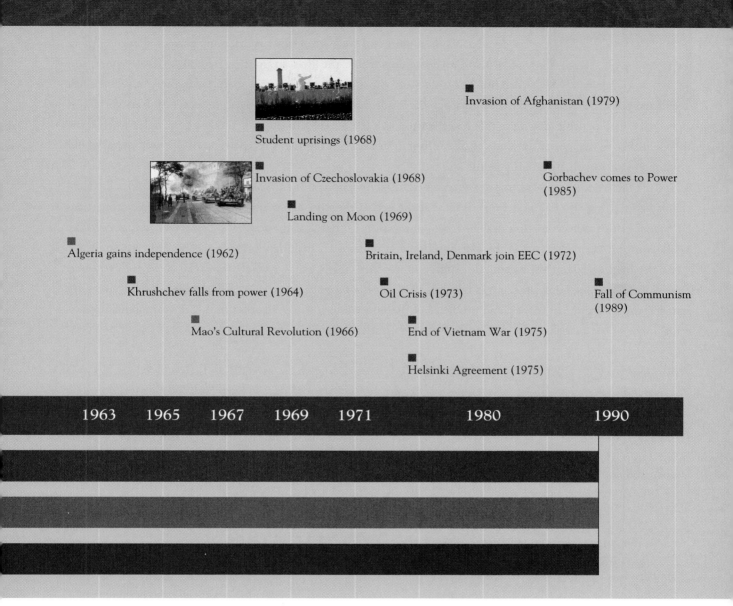

Student uprisings (1968)

Invasion of Afghanistan (1979)

Invasion of Czechoslovakia (1968)

Gorbachev comes to Power (1985)

Landing on Moon (1969)

Algeria gains independence (1962)

Britain, Ireland, Denmark join EEC (1972)

Khrushchev falls from power (1964)

Oil Crisis (1973)

Fall of Communism (1989)

Mao's Cultural Revolution (1966)

End of Vietnam War (1975)

Helsinki Agreement (1975)

| 1963 | 1965 | 1967 | 1969 | 1971 | 1980 | 1990 |

complained, "There is virtually no limit to the amount of health care an individual is capable of absorbing."

In several senses, then, the evolution of medicine since World War II reflected broader qualities of the era. Science, and especially "big science," enabled doctors to expand and even revolutionize the field. Medicine also relied on the overall prosperity and governmental support of those decades, which enabled people to demand and the healthcare industry to provide so many services. The very growth of this service industry as well as the high status and income enjoyed by its leading practitioners echoed the development of the postindustrial society, with its stress on services and technical expertise. Finally, like much else, Western medicine spilled across borders and into the non-Western world—though also in ways that highlighted the disparities of wealth between the Western and non-Western worlds and the conflicts that often arose when those different cultures met.

Summary

The decades between 1945 and 1989 witnessed a quickening pace of change as more people than ever were drawn into the swirl of politics, economic development, and urban life. The Cold War, whose contours came into sharp focus after 1945, cast a pall over the entire era. Each side represented different paths to recovery after World War II as well as competitive ideologies that had their roots in the nineteenth century. Yet despite people's worst fears, the Cold War never ignited into an actual conflagration between the two superpowers. As we will see, it would evaporate with surprising rapidity in the late 1980s.

During these decades, Western society became more technocratic, affluent, welfare-oriented, and culturally open, characteristics that also had first come to light at the end of the nineteenth century. Western Europe, in particular, managed this transformation despite ceding leadership to the United States and losing its colonial empires. While Western Europe's status in the world declined, it remained a strikingly prosperous, dynamic region.

As the final decade of the twentieth century approached, the West as a whole remained powerful and often envied abroad. At the same time, it had become clear that the Western powers could no longer act without taking into account the concerns, power, and problems of the non-Western world. Soon, stunning developments in Eastern Europe would mark 1989 as the dawn of a new historical era.

REVIEW, ANALYZE, AND ANTICIPATE

REVIEW THE PREVIOUS CHAPTER

In Chapter 23—"Darkening Decades"—the rise of fascism and communism and the impact of the Great Depression were analyzed. The period ended with a devastating war that encompassed the world.

1. *In what ways did World War II set the stage for the Cold War and the different paths followed by Western and Eastern Europe?*

2. *In what ways did World War II hasten decolonization in the following decades?*

ANALYZE THIS CHAPTER

Chapter 24—"Superpower Struggles and Global Transformations"—traces the Cold War competition between the United States and the Soviet Union. Within this context, the recovery of the West and the end of colonialism are examined.

1. *How did Cold War tensions influence international affairs in the Western and non-Western worlds?*

2. *In what ways did Western life during these decades represent a triumph of Western industrialization and political democracy? What sorts of problems persisted despite this triumph?*

3. *Compare and evaluate the two paths followed by Western and Eastern Europe during this period.*

4. *Evaluate the process of decolonization. What problems faced the newly independent nations of the non-Western world?*

ANTICIPATE THE NEXT CHAPTER

In Chapter 25—"Into the Twenty-First Century"—the collapse of communism and the intense interaction between the Western and non-Western worlds will be examined.

1. *What forces developing in these decades might lead to the collapse of communism in Europe?*

2. *Which of the major developments during the decades between 1945 and the 1980s seem most relevant to today's world? Which seem like part of the already distant past? Why?*

BEYOND THE CLASSROOM

FROM PEACE TO COLD WAR

Gaddis, John Lewis. *We Now Know: Rethinking Cold War History.* New York: Oxford University Press, 1997. An examination of the Cold War based upon newly released and declassified Soviet and U.S. documents.

Patterson, Thomas G. *On Every Front: The Making and Unmaking of the Cold War.* New York: W.W. Norton, 1992. Analyzes both the domestic and foreign policy aspects of the Cold War.

EAST AND WEST: TWO PATHS TO RECOVERY IN EUROPE

Dedman, Martin J. *The Origins and Development of the European Union, 1945–1995: A History of European Integration.* London: Routledge, 1996. A concise, useful survey of the topic.

Ellwood, David W. *Rebuilding Europe: Western Europe, America and Postwar Reconstruction.* London: Longman, 1992. Examines the Marshall Plan and weighs its overall effects on Europe.

Hosking, Geoffrey. *The First Socialist Society: A History of the Soviet Union from Within.* Cambridge, MA: Harvard University Press, 1990. A comprehensive history of the USSR from its origins to its demise.

Rothschild, Joseph. *Return to Diversity: A Political History of East Central Europe Since World War II,* 2nd ed. New York: Oxford University Press, 1993. A history of states in this region that stresses the growing conflicts between nationalist ambitions and communist rule.

THE TWILIGHT OF COLONIALISM

Ansprenger, Franz. *The Dissolution of the Colonial Empires.* London: Routledge, 1989. Stresses the legacy of inequality and cells of poverty created by imperialism, but also asserts that imperialism helped to create a global economy.

Holland, R.F. *European Decolonization, 1918–1981: An Introductory Survey.* New York: St. Martin's Press, 1985. A good overview of the topic.

A SENSE OF RELATIVITY IN THOUGHT AND CULTURE

Hughes, H. Stuart. *Between Commitment and Disillusion: The Obstructed Path and the Sea Change, 1930–1965.* Middletown, CT: Wesleyan University Press, 1987. A study of European dissent in the interwar and postwar period.

Maltby, R., ed. *Passing Parade: A History of Popular Culture in the Twentieth Century.* New York: New Oxford Press, 1989. Excellent in its breadth of coverage.

Stromberg, Roland N. *After Everything: Western Intellectual History Since 1945.* New York: St. Martin's Press, 1986. An excellent survey of ideas and ideology in the postwar period.

PROTESTS, PROBLEMS, AND NEW POLITICS: THE 1960s TO THE 1980s

Caute, David. *The Year of the Barricades: A Journey Through 1968.* New York: Harper & Row, 1988. Examines the revolutionary upheavals in a period called "year one" of the revolution.

de Beauvoir, Simone. *The Second Sex.* New York: Knopf, 1963. A classic and important examination of women's confinement to the periphery throughout history.

Lovenduski, Joni. *Women and European Politics: Contemporary Feminism and Public Policy.* Amherst, MA: University of Massachusetts Press, 1986. Compares the movement for women's liberation in the 1960s with previous women's movements.

Pulzer, Peter. *German Politics, 1945–1995.* Oxford: Oxford University Press, 1995. Examines both West and East Germany during the period and covers the process of reunification.

Rubinstein, Richard. *Alchemists of Revolution: Terrorism in the Modern World.* New York: Basic Books, 1987. Analyzes the causes for modern terrorism and stresses the role of disaffected intellectuals.

POSTINDUSTRIAL SOCIETY

Hoffman, Stanley, and Paschalis Kitromilides. *Culture and Society in Contemporary Europe.* London: Allen & Unwin, 1981. A wide-ranging, interpretative survey connecting cultural and social developments.

Ruggie, Mary. *The State and Working Women: A Comparative Study of Britain and Sweden.* Princeton, NJ: Princeton University Press, 1984. Compares the legislative and political events affecting women in Britain and Sweden.

BREAKTHROUGHS IN SCIENCE

Porter, Roy. *The Cambridge Illustrated History of Medicine.* Cambridge: Cambridge University Press, 1996. A well-written and well-illustrated survey by several noted scholars.

Ziman, John. *The Force of Knowledge: The Scientific Dimension of Society.* Cambridge: Cambridge University Press, 1976. A useful examination of connections between science and society during the postwar years.

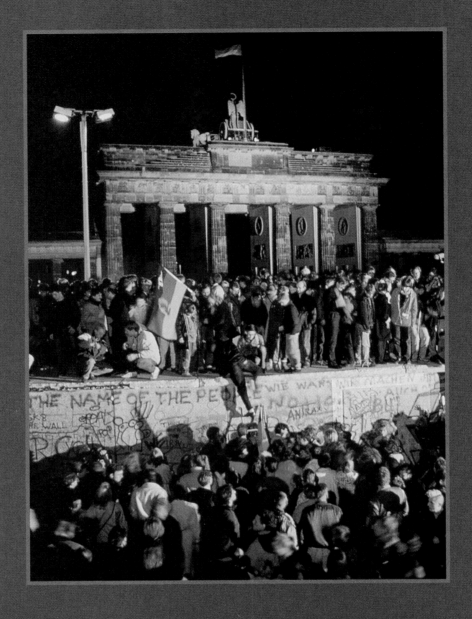

The Berlin Wall, November 1989

In November 1989, as revolutions swept Eastern Europe and ended the Cold War, Germans from East and West climbed over the Berlin Wall near the Brandenburg Gate. Demonstrators wrote "In the Name of the People" on the wall, crediting popular will for finally tearing down the decades-old barrier. By writing in English, they announced the importance of this historical event to the watching world.

CHAPTER 25

Into the Twenty-First Century

The Present in Perspective

"The 20th century is now over." The historian John Lukacs made this announcement in a 1991 issue of the *New York Times*. By "20th century," Lukacs meant the seventy-five-year era that began in 1914 and ended in 1989. The year 1914 marked the outbreak of World War I, which for most historians represented the beginning of the twentieth century. That conflict and World War II dominated the period. "The Russian Revolution, the atom bomb, the end of the colonial empires, the establishment of the Communist states, the emergence of the two superpowers, the division of Europe and of Germany—all of these were the consequences of the two world wars, in the shadow of which we were living, until now," wrote Lukacs. The year 1989 saw the nations of Eastern Europe break from their Soviet ties and from communism. In just two more years, the Soviet Union itself would fall apart.

Other developments, also with roots in the past, added to the sense that the world had just lived through the closing of one historical era and the opening of another. The movement toward economic integration in Western Europe, the growing strength of the newly unified Germany, and the changing position of the United States altered international relations. Beyond the West, the Pacific Rim—particularly East Asia—gained enormous economic clout. From a global perspective, three regional power centers had emerged—Europe, North America, and East Asia. Almost everywhere, people, problems, cultures, and histories spilled across national borders, challenging those living in the Western and non-Western worlds to broaden their understanding of the world and their place in it.

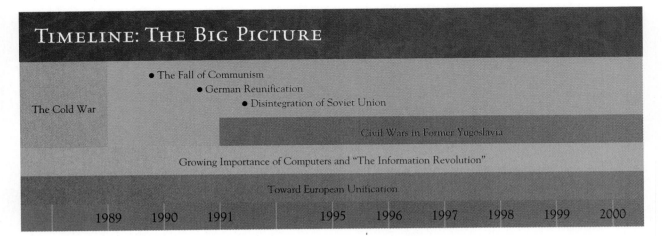

TIMELINE: THE BIG PICTURE

The Cold War

● The Fall of Communism
    ● German Reunification
      ● Disintegration of Soviet Union

Civil Wars in Former Yugoslavia

Growing Importance of Computers and "The Information Revolution"

Toward European Unification

| 1989 | 1990 | 1991 | 1995 | 1996 | 1997 | 1998 | 1999 | 2000 |

The Collapse of Communism

Of all these developments, the collapse of communism in the Soviet Union and Eastern Europe arguably had the most dramatic and far-reaching global impact. In a startling public announcement early in November 1989, East Germany's communist leader succumbed to months of growing pressure and ordered the Berlin Wall, the most powerful symbol of the Cold War, torn down. A reporter described the scene (see the photo on page 828): "Nearby, before the Brandenburg Gate . . . people climbed up onto the rim of the wall during the night of November 9 . . . taking pickaxes to it." Then the cranes and bulldozers came. "People stared unbelieving, as East German cranes lifted away the slabs of concrete . . ." As the wall crumbled, another observer described the Berlin border crossings: "The streets were packed with people streaming past the East German border guards. . . . Cars from East Berlin slowed to a crawl alongside the crowds of West Berliners waiting just over the white stripe painted on the asphalt, cheering every car . . . handing cans of beer to the drivers." In those first heady days, millions of East Germans crossed the border, some to stay, others to return again and again "loaded down with full plastic shopping bags." The mayor of West Berlin declared, "This [is] the greatest historical event since the French Revolution."

Everywhere in Eastern Europe, communist governments were collapsing. The Soviet bloc, which had seemed so impenetrable, quickly dissolved. Soon the Soviet Union itself would break apart.

UNDERMINING COMMUNISM IN THE SOVIET UNION

What explains this massive historical reversal? The story begins in the Soviet Union where communist power was most firmly entrenched. During the two or three decades following World War II, the Soviet Union, like other communist nations, enjoyed economic growth and relative prosperity (see Chapter 24). The USSR boasted impressive factories and elaborate technical projects such as dams, railway systems, military hardware, and manned rockets. Rapid industrialization, which pulled peasants and women into the urban work force by the millions, boosted productivity.

However, during the 1970s and 1980s, central planning and collectivization—the hallmarks of the Soviet economic system—failed to match new consumer demands. Keeping up with the rapidly changing, technologically sophisticated economy of the 1970s and 1980s required flexibility, a *Problems with central planning* willingness to experiment with new production methods, and local decision making—all of which the Soviet economic system lacked. Instead, economic decisions came from high officials more sensitive to political pressures than economic realities. Central planners, pursuing out-of-date strategies or unaware of changes in grassroots needs, often ordered factories to produce goods that did not meet consumers' demands. Local plant managers, struggling to get needed materials and labor, suffered long delays while distant officials made decisions. Workers, their jobs guaranteed, had little incentive to work hard or even show up consistently. Similar problems plagued agriculture, where collectivization discouraged effective decision making and hard work. As the rate of economic growth declined, embarrassed Soviet planners had to import grain again and again from the capitalist West. Government leaders worried that the Soviet economy would never catch up with formidable capitalist competitors such as the United States, Germany, and Japan.

Worse, everyday dissatisfactions spread. Soviet workers had money but not the selection or quality of goods that they wanted and that they knew were available to people in the West. Instead, they regularly stood in lines for as long as two hours a day just to buy basic supplies. Even urban professionals, managers, and technicians, although relatively wealthy and well educated, experienced similar frustrations. Far too obviously, only a small corps of Communist Party officials and privileged elites enjoyed access to the most desirable goods and services in this supposedly egalitarian society, fueling resentment. For everyone else, the only alternative was the thriving, but expensive and illegal, black market. Faith in the communist system, even among members of the Communist Party, began to evaporate. "I'm not a good Party member because I don't believe in Communism . . . nor do a lot of Party members," admitted one forty-year-old Communist in 1990. "Joining the Party was for me entirely a calculated way of furthering my career."

Spreading dissatisfaction

Three pivotal developments during the late 1970s and 1980s exacerbated the problems undermining the Soviet brand of communism. First, the spread of modern communications broke down the old Stalinist policy of enforced isolation from the rest of the world and fueled the growing dissident movement. By watching television, people saw for themselves the material wealth enjoyed by Western nations. They also perceived the swirling cultural and intellectual currents that officials tried to stifle within the Soviet Union. Yet photocopiers and computers spread information easily, making censorship difficult. Privately published manuscripts criticizing Soviet life circulated among the educated elite. The dissident movement grew, led by the Nobel Prize-winning physicist Andrey Sakharov (1921–1989) and others. Dissidents demanded more democracy, greater civil liberties, and some independence for nationalities within the Soviet Union. Although such demands earned Sakharov and others exile, the dissident movement persisted. Moreover, among many people not yet ready to join the dissident movement, the increasingly obvious contradictions between the official party line and the harsh realities of Soviet life engendered cynicism and apathy.

Growth of dissent

Second, military and wartime expenditures increasingly burdened the Soviet economy. In the 1980s, the United States under President Ronald Reagan vigorously pursued the Cold War arms race, forcing the Soviets—with their fundamentally weaker economy—to struggle to keep up. At the same time, the 1979 Soviet invasion of Afghanistan turned into a costly military quagmire. The widely condemned conflict wore on for years, straining the USSR's economy and diminishing the Soviet leadership's popularity.

Military burdens

Third, the quality of the Soviet leadership declined in the 1970s and 1980s. Leonid Brezhnev weakened noticeably and repeatedly fell ill in the seven years before his death in 1982. Most of his colleagues were long established in their offices. Brezhnev's immediate successors, Yuri Andropov (1982–1984) and Konstantin Chernenko (1984–1985), each died shortly after assuming office. These older men were reluctant to alter the USSR's course or to make way for a younger generation of reformers. But in 1985, a new leader—Mikhail Gorbachev—was appointed head of the Soviet Union. Just fifty-four years old, he had very different ideas about how the Soviet Union should operate.

Declining leadership

GORBACHEV LAUNCHES REFORMS

Born into a peasant family, Mikhail Gorbachev studied law as a youth at the University of Moscow. He moved rapidly up through the Communist Party ranks, eventually taking responsibility for agricultural policy. Charming and astute, he became a capable manipulator of people and events. Britain's prime minister Margaret Thatcher recognized him as a man "with whom we can do business." Gorbachev also had bold plans to lead the Soviet Union in new directions. Soon after assuming power in 1985, he replaced a third of the old party leadership with new supporters. By then, he shared the views of reformers who recognized the fundamental economic problems plaguing the Soviet Union. In his willingness to grapple with problems, Gorbachev echoed Khrushchev's attack on Stalinism some thirty years earlier. Nevertheless, he had no intention of loosening the party's hold on power.

Gorbachev embarked on a three-pronged policy: *perestroika* ("restructuring"), *glasnost* ("openness" to discussion), and disarmament. All three were intended to bring the Soviet economy up to the standard of Western capitalist societies. No one—not even Gorbachev—imagined the consequences that would flow from these daring reforms.

Perestroika

Perestroika involved a thorough restructuring of the Soviet economy. The program's goals included decentralizing planning, allowing market forces rather than officials to set prices, and putting control of land and agricultural practices into the hands of families and cooperatives rather than large state farms. In short, *perestroika* would create a mixed economy featuring a blend of socialist planning and a capitalist, free market. Gorbachev knew that the transformation would take time and cause short-term pain, including further shortages of consumer goods, inflation, and unemployment. To gather the political backing and the financial resources he needed to carry out the program, he initiated *glasnost* and an arms-reduction plan.

Glasnost curtailed censorship, encouraged freer discussion of everything from culture to politics, and opened the doors to the partial democratization of the Communist Party and the Soviet political system. Officials freed dissidents such as Andrey Sakharov. Some governmental proceedings were made visible to the public and even televised. In the spring of 1989, the government held the first open elections since 1917, which resulted in the defeat of numerous communist dignitaries. Gorbachev hoped that *glasnost* would elevate his prestige internationally, win him foreign political and financial support, and inspire intellectuals and workers at home to accept his bold restructuring of the Soviet economy.

Glasnost

His arms-reduction plan served the same ends. In meetings with U.S. presidents almost every year between 1985 and 1991, Gorbachev pushed for more and more reductions in both countries' military stockpiles. These meetings bore fruit: both the USSR and the U.S. agreed to limit nuclear weapons and conventional forces not only on their own soil but also in Europe. At the same time, Gorbachev tried to extract Soviet forces from the war in Afghanistan. The effort took four years, but in 1989 the last Soviet troops finally came home. These feats burnished Gorbachev's reputation at home and abroad, and promised to ease the USSR's heavy burden of military expenditures.

Arms reduction

Figure 25.1 shows Gorbachev, standing next to his wife, at the height of his popularity. On this visit to Prague, he reaches out to greet people in the crowd. Czechoslovakian officials, including the nation's president, Gustav Husak (just behind Gorbachev), smile and seem to back him up. Gorbachev made many visits such as this to make his policies known and to drum up support.

However, implementing *perestroika* proved more difficult than Gorbachev and his supporters expected. Entrenched officials resisted the changes, as did many Soviet individuals whose jobs and incomes were threatened by economic restructuring. Gorbachev's promises also raised the Soviet people's expectations to impossible heights. Some reformers even criticized him for moving too slowly.

To complicate matters, ethnic groups and republics within the Soviet Union began agitating for national autonomy and the freedom to express their own cultural beliefs. Peoples from central Asia and Armenia to the Baltic republics had long harbored resentments against the Soviet state. Most of these republics had been forced to join the Soviet Union during the devastating civil wars of 1917–1921. When Gorbachev weakened the monopoly power of the Communist Party, he undermined the principal institution holding the multinational Soviet Union together. Emboldened by Gorbachev's promised leniency in Eastern Europe, the republics took action. The greatest threat came from elites in Latvia, Lithuania, and Estonia on the Baltic coast who led demands for political autonomy. As tensions mounted, events in Eastern Europe took a dramatic turn, overshadowing developments in the Soviet Union.

Demands for autonomy

REVOLUTIONS IN EASTERN EUROPE

Ever since coming under the USSR's control, many people living in the communist nations of Eastern Europe had yearned to reclaim their national autonomy. Moreover, economic and cultural problems similar to those undermining communism in the Soviet Union plagued these societies and their governments. Though dissent did not always result in public protests, strikes, or demonstrations, it still sim-

FIGURE 25.1
Gorbachev in Czechoslovakia, 1987.

mered. In 1978, the Czechoslovakian playwright Václav Havel (see Biography) mocked the words of the *Communist Manifesto*: "A spectre is haunting eastern Europe: the spectre of what in the West is called 'dissent.'" Underground publications demanding honesty and civil rights circulated through intellectual and artistic circles in Poland, Hungary, and Czechoslovakia.

Two developments in the late 1980s strained the communist regimes trying to maintain control over these satellite states. First, economic difficulties **Economic problems** mounted as Eastern European governments labored to keep prices artificially low. To make matters worse, foreign loans from the West to Eastern European nations such as Poland became more expensive and began drying up. When those governments finally tried to increase prices without raising wages, public opposition mushroomed. Second, Gorbachev revoked the long-standing Brezhnev Doctrine. In 1989, he made his intentions clear: "Any interference in domestic affairs and **Revoking the Brezhnev Doctrine** any attempts to restrict the sovereignty of states, both friends and allies or any others, are inadmissible." Gorbachev had decided to let events in Eastern Europe unfold without Soviet intervention. For reformers and dissenters, this policy was a green light to action.

Poland led the way in the rush for liberation. This nation already had a history of protest movements that made it a weak link in the Soviet chain. In 1980, **Poland leads** shipyard workers in Gdansk struck against rising consumer-goods prices. The strikers organized a noncommunist union, Solidarity, under the leadership of Lech Walesa. Support for Solidarity spread throughout the nation, forcing the government to recognize the new organization and accede to some of its demands. When the union pushed for more, resistance from Moscow and conservative elements in the Polish government stiffened. In late 1981, General Wojciech Jaruzelski, the new leader of the Polish Communist Party, declared martial law, arrested Walesa, and outlawed Solidarity.

However, the union survived these reversals. Early in 1989, with the Polish economy in crisis, negotiations began between Jaruzelski and Solidarity, still led by Walesa. The Polish Catholic Church, which had maintained a position in the nation and indeed enhanced its own prestige with the visit of Pope John Paul II in 1979, helped mediate discussions. The talks resulted in the legalization of Solidarity and, in June,

new elections. Solidarity's stunning victory at the polls prompted Jaruzelski to ask the union to form a new government. A few months later, the communist leader stepped down, and the Communist Party gave up power in Poland without a fight.

Hungary soon followed suit. This satellite state already had a mixed economy, with almost one-third of its wealth coming from a private sector of small **Hungary** enterprises, crafts, and family agriculture. Reformers within the Hungarian Communist Party gained some power in 1988 and removed the old leader, János Kádár, from office. In the summer and fall of 1989, Hungary held elections, established a multiparty political system, and initiated economic reforms to open the country to private enterprise. Figure 25.2, a poster published by the Hungarian Democratic Forum, captures the sense of ushering out a bygone era. The poster announces the

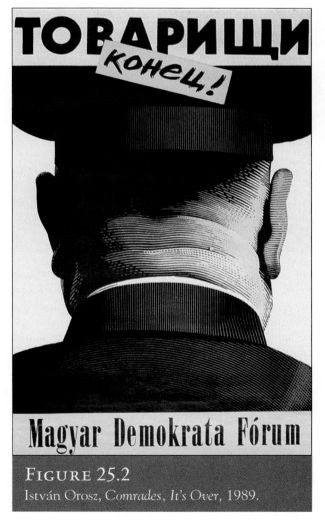

FIGURE 25.2
István Orosz, *Comrades, It's Over*, 1989.

Biography

VÁCLAV HAVEL (1936–)

In May 1989, Czechoslovakian authorities released the playwright and dissident leader Václav Havel from jail. Just seven months later, the nation elected him as its new president. The well-known American author Arthur Miller called Havel "the world's first surrealist president" in reference to his unusual literary and intellectual background. *Time* magazine described him as "the conscience of Prague." Havel referred to himself as a mere writer who lacked "any of the necessary qualities" of a politician. "I've always understood my mission to be to speak the truth about the world I live in, to bear witness to its terrors and its miseries—in other words, to warn rather than hand out prescriptions for change."

Václav was born in 1936 into a well-known, middle-class family of engineers. With the advent of the communist regime in 1948, the family lost much of their property and position. Havel thanked "the apparent disadvantage of coming from a bourgeois background and growing up in a Communist state" for enabling him to see "the world . . . as it really is."

At age thirteen, Havel began writing poetry and philosophy. Over the next several years, he developed an interest in the theater and started writing plays. In 1956, he met his future wife, Olga Splichalova, who would become the first person to read each of his manuscripts.

In the early 1960s, Havel wrote plays and articles while attending night classes at the Academy of Performing Arts. The boyish, blue-eyed writer often stayed up all night working or talking with friends in beer pubs. Soon he earned acclaim as one of Czechoslovakia's most successful playwrights. His best-known works included *The Garden Party*, *The Increased Difficulty of Concentration*, *The Memorandum*, and *Largo Desolato*.

Havel also acquired a reputation as a dissident in 1965 by publicly criticizing the Writers' Union for acting "as a broker between politics and literature" rather than "defending the right of literature to be literature." During the "Prague Spring"

Playwright, Dissident, and Politician

of 1968 (see Chapter 24), Havel published a bold article suggesting the end of single-party rule in Czechoslovakia. Warsaw Pact troops crushed that moment of liberation, and the new, repressive regime banned Havel's works.

---

fall of communism in Hungary with the words "Comrades, it's over," and with the depiction of the back of a departing man's head. The military hat symbolizes the confining authority of the old regime, and the wide neck perhaps represents the resentment against communist officials who had enjoyed special privileges.

Next came Czechoslovakia. In the fall of 1989, student demonstrators took to the streets demanding academic freedom and human rights. When police re-

The "velvet revolution" in Czechoslovakia sponded with clubs and tear gas, the demonstrators turned against them and other authorities. Workers and employers alike joined the students in the streets of Prague and in the great St. Wenceslas Square in the city center. In November, the call went out for a general strike. Within a

few days, the hard-line Communist government resigned. Václav Havel, the playwright and dissident leader who had been imprisoned for his views, and Alexander Dubcek, who had tried to liberalize Czechoslovakia in 1968, quickly rose to power. As in Poland and Hungary, the fall of the communist regime in Czechoslovakia was bloodless—a *"velvet revolution."*

In East Germany, the wealthiest and most powerful of the Eastern European states, even people who did well under communism wanted to head west by the thousands. An American woman residing in East Germany described the growing dis-

East Germany satisfaction. "Too many . . . things were wrong . . . Too much was missing from the shops . . . There were no spare parts to fix home appliances or cars. Assembly lines were halted for want of sup-

In the 1970s, Havel helped establish an underground press that published many disapproved and hard-to-find works. He wrote several influential essays on totalitarianism and dissent, including "The Power of the Powerless." Further, he argued that the communist regime in Czechoslovakia was based on fundamental lies, though he had faith that truth could penetrate these lies. In 1977 he became a founding spokesman for Charter 77, signed by hundreds of Czechs, Slovaks, and intellectuals from other countries. The charter called for people to do all they could for human rights in Eastern Europe. Officials labeled the publication as "reactionary," something "delivered to Western agents as instructed by anti-Communist and Zionist headquarters." Police quickly rounded up and interrogated signers.

FIGURE 25.3
Václav Havel addressing the crowd, 1989.

Havel spent most of the period from 1977 to 1983 in prison for his human rights activities. Nevertheless, his wife Olga continued the underground publishing. Václav would later publish a book of his letters to her. Not long after his release, he reflected on his prison experience: "[A]ll that heroic time in prison was in fact one long chain of worries, fears, and terrors . . . and despite all this, I know that, if it were necessary, I would go back to prison again. . . ."

His words were prophetic. In February 1989, Havel once more languished in a prison cell for his criticisms of the communist regime. Yet his fortunes were about to change. Not far from the walls of his prison, student demonstrators marched angrily through the city streets. A petition campaign somehow persuaded authorities to release Havel in May. He soon took up his role again as a leader of the dissidents, circulating petitions demanding democratic reforms.

In November 1989, he helped found the Civic Forum, which led the opposition movement in Czechoslovakia. Before the end of the year, the Czech parliament elected Havel president, completing his stunning transition from prison cell to the halls of government. Figure 25.3 shows Havel in December 1989. Newly elected president of Czechoslovakia, he reads the names of the nation's new, noncommunist government members to the crowd. In his 1990 New Year's address, he announced, "People, your government has returned to you!"

Through the 1990s, the people again and again reelected Havel president. Some critics saw him as too much of an intellectual. Still, he gained a worldwide reputation as a moral spokesperson for Europe who stressed "the tolerant coexistence of different cultural identities" and the "ties that link everything in this world together."

◙ **Consider** how Havel's life reveals the forces behind the fall of communism in Eastern Europe.

plies from auxiliary plants. It was the same on building sites, and the workers stood idle and furious. What good was this kind of socialism? Why did everything work so smoothly in the Germany next door?" When Hungary opened its borders with Austria in September 1989, tens of thousands of East Germans used that escape route to stream into the West. "They had been watching it longingly on West German television all their young lives. They knew from the commercials exactly how they would furnish their homes and make them shine."

In October 1989, antigovernment demonstrations spread throughout East Germany. People brandished signs proclaiming "We are the people." Long-suppressed criticism of the state's feared "security" forces surfaced. The hard-line communist leader was ousted from office. In November, 1989, his communist successor bowed to the inevitable and ordered the Berlin Wall torn down. Joyful demonstrators celebrated for days. Soon, communists lost power, and within a year East and West Germany had reunified.

The rest of Eastern Europe also quickly followed. In Bulgaria an internal coup deposed the Stalinist ruler. In Romania, the relatively independent but dictatorial communist leader Nicolae Ceausescu ordered troops to fire on demonstrators, setting off a bloody revolution. His overthrow cost many lives and ended with the execution of Ceausescu and his wife. The following year, Albania's independent but highly Stalinist regime also collapsed.

The freeing of Eastern Europe took less than a year. One after another, these nations cut the ties binding them to the USSR, enacted democratic reforms, and introduced capitalism into their economies (see Map 25.1). The repercussions of these events echoed throughout the Soviet Union, quickly pushing developments beyond the control of Gorbachev and his supporters.

THE SOVIET UNION DISINTEGRATES

The Soviet leader had managed only halting steps in his effort to restructure the Soviet economy—*perestroika*. High officials announced plans to move the economy away from central planning *Problems with reform* and then delayed the plans in the face of determined opposition by hard-liners. These officials also worried about the difficulties—including unemployment, inflation, and dislocation—that the transition would cause. Gorbachev watered down his reforms to the satisfaction of no one. The waffling and controversy only worsened the frustrations of hard-liners and reformers alike. Reformers who wanted Gorbachev to move faster grew disgusted with the moderate pace of change, while the old communist guard became increasingly alienated. As the economy began to spin out of control, the Soviet leader's popularity dwindled.

Gorbachev tried pushing through promising political reforms as part of his *glasnost* policy, but, as with *perestroika*, each step taken to enact reforms opened the door further for new expressions of dissatisfaction. In 1990 he persuaded the Communist Party's Central Committee to eliminate the party's constitutional monopoly on political power. He created a new, strong presidency—an office separate from the Communist Party hierarchy. Equally daring, he called for new elections.

All these changes democratized Soviet politics and undermined the power of the Communist Party—in the process exposing the corruption of the old Soviet

THINKING ABOUT GEOGRAPHY

MAP 25.1   *Eastern Europe, 1989*

This map shows the upheavals that toppled the communist regimes in Eastern Europe. ◙ **Notice** the extent of public protests and demonstrations. ◙ **Consider** which Western European states might gain more influence in Eastern Europe as Soviet control over the area disappeared. **Why** might several of these states be interested in joining Western European organizations such as NATO and the European Community?

regime. Party members resigned in droves. These policies also facilitated the rise of Gorbachev's chief rival, Boris Yeltsin, the newly elected president of the Russian Republic. A charismatic, liberal reformer, Yeltsin publicly resigned from the Communist Party in July 1990. In another bold move, he declared the Russian Republic an independent state.

At the same time, movements for independence gained momentum within several ethnic groups and nationalities throughout the USSR. The Soviet Union contained more than a hundred ethnic groups, as well as some 50 million Muslims in central Asia. Many of these groups considered themselves separate nations and the Soviet Union as a collection of nations rather than a single whole. The republics of Estonia, Lithuania, and Latvia led in pressing Moscow for independence. In 1991 the Ukraine joined the Russian Republic in declaring itself independent. Ethnic conflict and nationalistic demands spread in the Soviet republics of Armenia, Azerbaijan, Moldova, Georgia, and elsewhere. Though Gorbachev resisted these demands and tried to quell the ethnic conflicts, the situation had gone beyond anyone's control. In the spring of 1991, he proposed a compromise: the "Treaty of Union," in which all the Soviet republics would be independent but held together as a confederation.

Independence movements

In August 1991, with the treaty of union about to take effect, communist hard-liners from inside the government and the KGB tried to oust Gorbachev. Within three days, the hard-liners' ineptitude and the opposition marshaled by Russian president Yeltsin doomed the coup to failure. Figure 25.4 shows Yeltsin interrupting the restored Gorbachev as he addresses the Russian parliament just after the failed coup. Indeed, Gorbachev's authority was slipping away to Yeltsin even

Hard-liners coup

FIGURE 25.4
Mikhail Gorbachev and Boris Yeltsin, 1991.

at this moment. In late 1991, after the two leaders stripped the Communist Party of much of its power, Gorbachev resigned.

In the end, no one, including the once dominant Russians, wanted to save the old Soviet Union. Gorbachev had unleashed the forces of revolution, and he—along with the USSR itself—became revolution's victim. In 1999, Gorbachev would look back and explain, "Communism—as the inventors of the theory imagined it—never existed anywhere. . . . What did exist was Stalinist socialism. That system had exhausted itself and was doomed to disappear." Map 25.2 shows what became of the former Soviet Union. Most of the republics within the old structure joined the new Commonwealth of Independent States, a loose confederation. A few republics, such as the Baltic states, broke away altogether.

LIFE AFTER THE COLLAPSE OF COMMUNISM

Once the celebrations in the former communist bloc ended, people awoke to new, dismaying realities. In his 1990 inaugural address, Václav Havel had issued a warning that applied just as much to other nations in Eastern Europe as it did to Czechoslovakia: "Our country is not flourishing. . . . Entire branches of industry are producing goods which are of no interest to anyone, while we are lacking the things we need. A state which calls itself a workers' state humiliates and exploits workers. Our obsolete economy is wasting the little energy we have available. . . . We have polluted our soil, our rivers and forests. . . ." Leaders in Eastern Europe and the former USSR faced a crucial problem: how to institute capitalism and liberal democracy in nations with little experience of either.

The economic transition proceeded quickly in Poland and Hungary, but more moderately in Bulgaria, Romania, and Albania. Almost everywhere, however, it brought pain. When governments closed the doors of inefficient state industries or sold them, many workers lost their jobs. The removal of price controls also provoked instant inflation that especially hurt those living on fixed incomes. Some people took advantage of new opportunities that came with the transition; for example, former communist officials in particular benefitted from lucrative insider deals. Several cities—such as Prague in the Czech Republic, with its domes, spires, cobblestone alleys, pubs, cafes, and

Eastern Europe

THINKING ABOUT GEOGRAPHY

MAP 25.2 *The Dissolution of the Soviet Union, 1991*

This map shows the division of territory resulting from the disintegration of the former Soviet Union. ◼ **Notice** which states became the largest and potentially the most powerful in the former USSR. **Which** areas might be most influenced by European states to the west and Islamic states to the south? ◼ **Notice** the ethnic divisions in the former Soviet Union. **What** problems might ethnicity pose after the breakup of the USSR?

secondhand bookstores—also fared well with the heightened tourism to such areas. But too many people had let themselves expect more than the eradication of communism could deliver. In the face of widespread bitterness, governments struggled to gain stability and institute unpopular but apparently necessary economic policies such as closing state industries and allowing prices to rise.

In the former Soviet Union, people were unaccustomed to democratic politics, managers were unfamiliar with the market economy, and many officials resisted reform. The economy stumbled badly. Year after year, Russia's economic output decreased, as did its population. Removing price controls and privatiz-

The former Soviet Union

ing industry had eliminated lines in front of stores and created economic opportunities for some. However, prices skyrocketed beyond the reach of average consumers, the Russian currency lost its value, and some 30 percent of the population struggled to subsist on approximately $1 per day.

The collapse of communism proved particularly stressful for Russian men. From Communist Party officials and generals to physicists and professors, men who had once enjoyed status, security, and relative wealth lost these benefits in the turmoil of the postcommunist era. Life expectancy for Russian men plummeted to fifty-eight years, a decline that was "the steepest and most severe ever documented anywhere in the world" according to one researcher. Alcoholism more than tripled in the years after the collapse. For women, the story was different. Although many women suffered from unemployment when state industries folded, perhaps their losses were not so great and were eased by new opportunities. In any case, they seemed to manage the transition better than men, maintaining a life expectancy of seventy-three years. Indeed, a growing elite of women entered managerial positions and earned increasing salaries.

Boris Yeltsin retained a precarious hold on power as president of Russia, and despite illnesses was re-elected in 1996. But the Russian *Yeltsin's problems* people resisted his inconsistent efforts at reform. In the parliament, with its tangled array of different political parties, fragmentation ruled. Moreover, "reformed" communists retained positions of power, as they did in Eastern European states such as Serbia, Bulgaria, and Lithuania. With control disintegrating, lawlessness—from street crime to organized crime—rapidly spread. By 1998, the fumbling Yeltsin had lost his popularity and much of his power as the Russian economy verged on collapse. When he resigned on the last day of 1999, many Russians yearned for the power, order, and stability that communism had brought.

NATIONALISM UNLEASHED

Despite its drawbacks, communism had provided many people with a sense of unity and security. Its fall opened a void that nationalistic sentiments rose to fill. As had often been the case in nineteenth- and twentieth-century history, nationalism provoked heated conflict along with a feeling of belonging. Ethnic and cultural struggles raged in several republics of the former Soviet Union. In Azerbaijan, the Azerbaijanis and Armenians clashed. The most violent outburst came in secessionist Chechnya, where Russians fought an unpopular war with Chechnyans demanding their independence. The indecisive two-year conflict cost some 80,000 deaths and a quarter-million wounded, though the Chechnyans gained many of their goals. In 1999, another draining war broke out between Chechnyans and Russians.

In Eastern Europe also, nationalistic, ethnic, and religious rivalries opened old wounds and created new divisions. Maps 25.3 and 25.4 reveal some of these problems. In 1993, the Slovak minority in Czechoslovakia, pushed by ambitious Slovak politicians, voted for independence. Czechoslovakia reluctantly agreed to divide itself into the Czech Republic and Slovakia.

In Romania, ethnic friction between the Romanian majority and the Hungarian minority flared up.

The bloodiest conflicts broke out in Yugoslavia, where chaotic civil wars marked the disintegration of that country. Figure 25.5, a chart listing the many ethnic groups living in Yugoslavia, reveals the complexity of *Civil wars in Yugoslavia* ethnic divisions in the country. In some regions, one ethnic group made up the vast majority of the population, but in other areas several ethnic groups lived as large minorities. The six republics that constituted Yugoslavia had been held together under communist rule since World War II (see Map 25.4). With the death of Tito in 1980 and the fall of communism in the rest of Eastern Europe in 1989, Yugoslavia began to crack. In 1991, Slovenians, angered by the refusal of the dominant Serbian communists to liberalize economic and political policies, detached themselves from Yugoslavia. Peoples in Croatia, Bosnia-Herzegovina, and Macedonia followed suit. War soon erupted between the religiously Orthodox Serbs, attempting to expand the territory they controlled, and their long-time Catholic Croatian rivals to the northwest. Trapped between the two antagonists were the mostly Muslim Bosnians and other peoples who lived as minorities in these areas.

The war for a "Greater Serbia" raged with appalling brutality. The worst fighting took place in Bosnia-Herzegovina. On this bloody battlefield, the Serbs initiated a policy of "ethnic cleansing," driving Muslim Bosnians from their homes; placing them in concentration camps; and raping, murdering, and starving

Ethnic group	Percentage
Serbians	36
Croatians	20
Bosnians (Muslim)	9
Slovenes	8
Albanians	8
Macedonians	6
Montenegrins	3
Hungarians	2
Others	8

FIGURE 25.5
Ethnic groups in Yugoslavia, 1991.

Disintegration of Czechoslovakia and Yugoslavia in the 1990s
These maps show how Czechoslovakia divided into the Czech Republic and Slovakia, and the disintegration of Yugoslavia. ■ **Compare** the maps. **How do you explain the different paths to the breakup of these two nations?**
■ **Consider** why problems in this area of Europe led to war at the beginning as well as the end of the twentieth century.

Former border of Yugoslavia

Border of Bosnia-Herzegovina

Dayton Agreement inter-entity boundary (November, 1995)

Bosnian Serb territory, after Dayton

Croat-Muslim Federation portion of Bosnia, after Dayton

on top of another . . . The bodies eventually were gathered with a forklift . . . this happened almost every day." Figure 25.6 reveals the suffering from the war and the international effort to do something about it. In the foreground, a woman throws her arms and head back in anguish. Behind her is a white United Nations truck and blue-helmeted soldiers—one carrying a medical kit. Almost surrounded by barbed wire, the troops try to provide aid to civilians—all women and children—standing along the road.

The Bosnians, supported by aid from the Islamic world, fought back desperately for more than four years. Only a Western embargo and NATO intervention brought an uneasy end to the violence and peace accords in 1996. The conflict had killed 250,000 people, displaced 3 million, and left 800,000 antipersonnel mines embedded in the land. Moreover, peace still depended on the continued presence of international troops. In 1997 a NATO commander in Bosnia warned that "if we withdraw our forces, there will be slaughter in the streets," and predicted that complete recovery would take decades.

Just two years later, the brutality unleashed in Bosnia rose again in nearby Kosovo—another region within Yugoslavia. Serbians, led by President Slobodan Milosevic, met rising demands for independence from the Albanian majority in Kosovo with overwhelming military force. Renewing the practice of "ethnic cleansing," Serbian troops slaughtered thousands of Kosovar Albanians and forced hundreds of thousands to flee to neighboring states.

them. In 1992, a Serb guard at one concentration camp proudly explained, "We won't waste our bullets on them . . . They have no roof. There is sun and rain, cold nights, and beatings two times a day. We give them no food and no water. They will starve like animals." A survivor reported seeing "corpses piled one

After diplomacy failed, NATO unleashed its military resources for the first time in its fifty-year history. Member air forces, led by the United States, opened a three-month bombing campaign on Serbian forces and on Serbia itself. President Havel of the Czech Republic reflected the views of many in the West when he declared, "this is probably the first war that has not been waged in the name of 'national interest,' but rather in the name of principles and values." Milosevic finally agreed to terms and withdrew his forces. Protected by NATO troops, the Kosovar Albanians streamed back to their badly damaged land, bringing with them few hopes for ethnic cooperation in the region.

Repercussions and Realignments in the West

Repercussions from the collapse of communism spread around the world. As communism lost its credibility, nations still committed to the Soviet model, such as Cuba and North Korea, were left isolated. Capitalism gained renewed respect and even inspired awe in both the Western and non-Western worlds. For many, the collapse of communism in eastern Europe and the USSR signified the final triumph of capitalism. With the end of the Cold War, the contours of domestic and international politics began to shift.

THE UNITED STATES UNCHALLENGED AND GERMANY RISING

With the former Soviet forces in decline and the Warsaw Pact dissolved, the United States and Germany rose in stature. The United States emerged as the world's only military superpower. It flexed its military muscle in 1991 by leading a United Nations-authorized coalition that repelled Iraq's invasion of tiny, neighboring Kuwait. In the short war, the U.S.-dominated coalition easily defeated Saddam Hussein's forces. The U.S. also contributed to international peacekeeping efforts by sending forces to troubled areas such as Somalia, Haiti, Bosnia, and Kosovo. Despite years of large budget deficits and apparent decline, the U.S. economy rebounded in the mid-1990s to a position of leadership that inspired envy the world over.

Germany's influence and potential also rose. In 1990, German unification confirmed Germany as a European and world economic leader—in exports, in balance of trade, and in gross domestic product. Emerging

victorious from the first national elections, the former West German chancellor Helmut Kohl and his conservative Christian Democrats vowed to bring eastern Germany's economy up to the high standard enjoyed in the West. The costs of the transition mushroomed far beyond expectations; as state industries collapsed in the East, unemployment and the cost of welfare benefits shot up. Nevertheless, the reunified state still ranked as the top economic power in Europe. Clearly, Germany stood poised to exert new influence in Eastern Europe and the European Community.

POLITICS SHIFT TO THE RIGHT

In the United States, Germany, and elsewhere in the West, politics shifted to the Right. The reasons behind this change were complex, but economic forces played a major role. Despite the continued overall prosperity enjoyed in the West, many nations suffered from high unemployment and declining growth rates during the 1980s and 1990s. In part, the free flow of trade and capital had created a new international labor market that operated outside the control of national governments and labor unions, resulting in the loss of many business opportunities and manufacturing jobs in the West. As global economic competition stiffened and nations struggled to stay in the game, many people blamed costly social programs—often supported by the political Left—for their nation's economic problems. The changes wrought by the postindustrial society, especially the shift from manufacturing to services, also weakened labor unions—the Left's traditional source of support. The previous

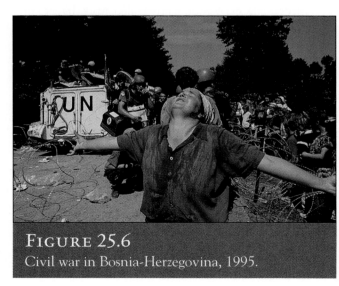

FIGURE 25.6
Civil war in Bosnia-Herzegovina, 1995.

sense that government was obligated to provide for rich and poor alike—a belief that had fueled the post–World War II welfare state—faded along with memories of those older times. Government regulation of economic affairs and the cost of social programs came under question everywhere.

Conservatives began scoring record successes at the polls. Citing the apparent triumph of capitalism, they attacked expensive programs and sometimes fanned the flames of anti-immigrant sentiments, playing on the popular perception that foreign-born newcomers took jobs. France's right-wing National Front, led by Jean-Marie LePen, attained particular prominence by blaming immigrants from North Africa and elsewhere for France's economic problems. The traditional communist parties in Western Europe declined, and socialist parties, whether in power or not, moderated their policies to shore up their popularity. In Austria, Italy, Germany, and Spain, conservative and right-wing politicians gained popularity. Even when traditional parties of the Left regained power, as they did in many countries during the late 1990s, their platforms were more muted and conservative than in the past. No nation ventured as far down the conservative path as Great Britain and the United States. In Great Britain, the Conservatives led by Margaret Thatcher and her successor dominated throughout most of the 1980s and 1990s, cutting taxes, attacking social programs, and selling state-owned industries to private investors. When the Labor Party finally came to power in Great Britain in 1997, it promised only mild changes. In the United States, Republicans rolled back liberal programs and Democrats scrambled to adopt more conservative platforms.

Questioning traditional politics

By the mid-1990s, this conservatism merged with a broader questioning of traditional politics in the West. As anxieties over economic problems intensified and as scandals rocked governments, people voted for unknowns or stopped voting altogether. Especially in France, Italy, and Austria, candidates who voiced disenchantment with the standard politics of the Left and Right attracted popular support. In 2000, for example, a populist right-wing party in Austria gained enough support to join with conservatives and form a government—much to the dismay of traditional parties throughout Europe. All these shifts in domestic politics gained much attention. However, events beyond state borders would soon overshadow these internal concerns throughout Europe.

TOWARD EUROPEAN INTEGRATION

The end of the Cold War may have left the United States the world's sole superpower, but it also strengthened the movement toward unity that had been unfolding in Europe since the 1950s. Many Europeans agreed with Michel Albert, a leading French official and industrialist, who in 1991 argued, "If the aim is to harness capitalism without impairing its efficiency, it is no longer to the nation-state that we must look, but to Europe."

In 1992, the twelve members of the European Community eliminated all major internal barriers to trade, the flow of capital, and the movement of people. That same year, the EC joined with the seven-member European Free Trade Association to form the European Economic Area, creating the world's largest trading bloc and paving the way for several new countries to seek full membership (see Map 25.5). A number of Eastern European nations, such as Poland, Czechoslovakia, and Hungary, lined up to join to the European Community as well as NATO. Also in 1992, France and Germany formed a joint army corps, the European Corps, open to other participants in the European Union. With the Maastricht Treaty of 1992 (which changed the name of the EC to the European Union), most members of the European Union agreed to establish a common currency (the Euro) controlled by a central European bank by 1999. The plan required great economic discipline, above all controlling the large yearly budget deficits most nations ran.

Figure 25.7 shows the new monetary unit of the European Union. In the center of the print are Euro bills

FIGURE 25.7
The Euro, 1999.

Member of the European Union
Accepted for Membership
Applied for Membership

N
W E
S

SWEDEN   FINLAND
NORWAY
ESTONIA   RUSSIA
BALTIC SEA   LATVIA
NORTH   DENMARK   LITHUANIA
SEA   RUSSIA
IRELAND   GREAT   BELARUS
BRITAIN   NETH.   POLAND
BEL.   GERMANY   UKRAINE
ATLANTIC   LUX.   CZECH REP.
OCEAN   SLOVAKIA
FRANCE   SWITZ. AUSTRIA HUNGARY   MOLDOVA
SLOVENIA   ROMANIA
CROATIA
BOSNIA   SERBIA
PORTUGAL   ITALY   MONT. KOS. BULGARIA
MACEDONIA
SPAIN   ALBANIA
GREECE   TURKEY

M E D I T E R R A N E A N   S E A

MOROCCO   ALGERIA
TUNISIA
600 miles
0
0   600 kilometers
LIBYA   EGYPT

THINKING ABOUT GEOGRAPHY

MAP 25.5   *The European Union, 1999*

This map shows the European Union in 1999 and nations that applied for membership. ❂ **Notice** how inclusive membership is. **Which** nations form the most important core of a potentially united Europe? **How** economically and politically powerful might a united Europe be? ❂ **Consider** the significance of several Eastern European nations' joining this association.

colorful nations with their own flavors into a bland, homogenized union controlled by faceless bureaucrats.

The potential of the European Union seemed tremendous. The member nations had more than 340 million inhabitants and a combined gross national product greater than that of the United States. Perhaps in response, the United States joined with Mexico and Canada in 1994 to create a new free-trade zone—the North American Free Trade Agreement. Not everyone embraced the idea of such alliances. Many Europeans opposed further integration, clinging to national preferences and warning against the dangers of giving up sovereignty to an international body of bureaucrats. To be sure, the European nations had great difficulty joining forces to put down the crisis in Bosnia, but their joint action as part of a NATO force to quell the violence in Kosovo in 1999 led to a vow by the leaders of fifteen European countries to make the European Union a military power for the first time. The Union adopted plans to build its own military of up to 60,000 troops. Moreover, by that same year, the European Union had opened its arms to possible membership for Turkey as well as virtually all of central and eastern Europe. Despite many reservations, most Europeans seemed willing to cooperate more than ever.

The World and the West from a Global Perspective

As they took further steps toward unity, Europeans had more in mind than competing with the United States. They also knew that they had to meet the changes sweeping through much of the Western and non-Western worlds. Since the end of colonialism, European nations could no longer rely on colonies as controllable markets. By the 1990s, all nations faced a global economy marked by the presence

of various denominations, designed simply and neutrally so as not to favor any country. Swirling around them are the currencies—represented by colorful bills with historical and national symbols—the Euro replaced. To some critics, this image represented a danger of European integration—the merging of unique, of multinational enterprises beyond the command of individual states. Waves of huge corporate buy-outs and mergers only increased this concentration of economic power. By 2000, small handfuls of these corporations controlled more than half the global market in oil, automobiles, electronics, multimedia, and personal computers. Westerners also confronted new competitors, from Latin America to East Asia, who wielded growing economic and political clout. Finally, the pace of global economic integration and change had quickened, complicating international business for everyone. Certain technological advances, above all the development of the computer, the internet, and genetic engineering, had the potential of creating the equivalent of a third industrial revolution. By 2000, the mushrooming use of computers and the internet in business and commerce had already transformed many economies. All these changes called into question the very issue of national identity. Even in the poorest nations, signs of this blending proliferated. As just one example, workers in new manufacturing plants owned by multinational corporations wore the same brand-name athletic shoes and drank the same beverages as their Western counterparts. Moreover, thanks to films, television, radio, computers, and travel, ideas flowed across international borders as easily as money, goods, and services, further blurring the distinctions between cultures.

EAST ASIA AND THE RISE OF THE PACIFIC RIM

The greatest challenge to the West's economic dominance came from East Asia. Since the 1960s, Japan had grown into a major economic power. Year after year, this island nation enjoyed the world's largest favorable balance of trade. By the 1980s, it boasted the world's second-largest gross domestic product. A giant in automobile production and electronics, Japan replaced the United States as the world's topmost creditor nation. Although reversals brought Japan's economic momentum to a virtual standstill during the 1990s, the nation still led the world in per capita gross domestic product.

By the 1990s, other regions on the periphery of the Pacific Ocean attracted wealthy investors with their political stability, cheap and disciplined labor force, and openness to capitalism. Multinational corporations opened offices and made investments throughout this so-called Pacific Rim. Hong Kong, Taiwan, South Korea, Malaysia, Indonesia, and Singapore all boomed, drawing manufacturing jobs away from Europe and the United States in industries such as elec-

tronics, textiles, plastics, metals, computers, automobiles, and leather goods. Visitors found thriving cities such as Kuala Lumpur in Malaysia—with the world's two tallest buildings marking its skyline and its high-rise apartment houses serviced by climate-controlled malls—"unrecognizable to anyone who knew it 30 years ago." On the outskirts of such glittering urban centers, satellite communities and industrial parks rose where jungles used to thrive. Similar developments transformed other great cities of East Asia, from Singapore and Bangkok to Jakarta and Hong Kong.

Yet no country experienced a more stunning economic transformation than China. In 1978, the successors to Mao, led by Deng Xiaoping (1904–1997), had initiated the "Four Modernizations" program to foster rapid economic development and greater productivity. The program de- *The economic transformation of China* parted dramatically from Mao's economic policies by decentralizing decision making and introducing a market-oriented economy into the countryside and, later, into some urban areas. By the mid-1980s, these policies had opened China to tourism and foreign investment, stimulated new economic growth, and created greater economic freedom within China. Agreements with Japan and the United States rapidly expanded trade as well. For the first time, Chinese farmers produced a surplus of food for export. In certain areas of the country, particularly the "New Economic Zones" in the southeast, capitalistic investments and manufacturing practices spurred high rates of growth.

Nevertheless, China made these economic reforms without corresponding political reforms. Whether that practice could continue was called into question in 1989, when students and intellectuals demanding political reform organized massive demonstrations in Beijing. After a brief standoff, the government, supported by China's rural population and most of the army, violently crushed the demonstrations and jailed the leaders. In the 1990s, as China's leadership aged and pressures for political reform persisted, analysts watched carefully for change within the great Asian country.

THE CHALLENGE OF ISLAM

Other areas of the world presented different challenges to the West. In particular, several Islamic nations in North Africa and the Middle East developed a new assertiveness and a willingness to make their dissatisfaction with Western ways known. They had long resented the former Western imperial powers' condescension toward them. The West's support of Israel only irritated an already raw nerve. The emergence of combative leaders in states such as Libya, Syria, Iran, and Iraq—some of whom advocated Islamic or Pan-Arab unity against Israel and Western influence—stepped up tensions further. Moreover, in nations from Algeria and Turkey to Afghanistan and Pakistan, Islamic fundamentalists had gained strength. Condemning westernization and the secularization of life in their countries, they demanded a return to traditional symbols of their conservative views, such as the veil that they required women to wear in public. Iran's fundamentalist leader Ayatollah Ruholla Khomeini (1900–1989), who had come to power as the leader of a revolution in 1979, epitomized rejection of the West. He especially castigated the United States, labeling it the "great Satan" because it had supported Israel and had intervened several times in the region. Finally, many Middle Eastern Islamic states possessed the crude-oil reserves on which the West and Asia depended, and used the precious resource to command international respect and attention. The potential of Middle Eastern states to pull Western nations into armed conflict was made all too clear in 1990 when Iraq invaded oil-rich Kuwait, prompting a UN-backed military response.

All these developments—in the Middle East, North Africa, and East Asia—revealed the West's inextricable ties with the non-Western world. They also *Resistance to globalization* posed new challenges to the dominance that the West had enjoyed for so long. Perhaps most important, they illustrated a problem that spread well beyond any one region: the chafing of local cultures against global and even national influences. On one level, globalization meant the invasion of Western culture into centuries-old but vulnerable non-Western cultural legacies. Figure 25.8 reveals this tenuous mixture and clash of cultures in Mexico. A descendant of the Olmecs, who once dominated parts of Mexico some three thousand years ago, prepares to dance as a jaguar to bring rain. The boy's clay-covered body is being stamped with ashes by an adult using a Coca Cola bottle—one of the most recognized symbols of Western commerce. This image was soon transmitted by a Western photographer to a magazine with circulation in the millions, perhaps encouraging Western tourists and companies to invade this traditional culture even further. On another level, nationalism and religious fundamentalism revealed a deep resistance to globalization. The struggles of minorities to retain their own sense of identity in the face of de-

mands for national and religious conformity within their own nations reflected a parallel resistance to outside meddling. In a terrifying variation of this pattern, in the central African state of Rwanda, ethnic Hutu extremists slaughtered some half a million ethnic Tutsi during the mid-1990's; fighting and civil war plagued the area for years. In the West and elsewhere, these multilayered resentments and struggles formed a complex backdrop for other emerging developments.

ACROSS BORDERS: CULTURAL CONFLICT AND CONVERGENCE

While ethnic conflict and nationalism intensified in several parts of the globe, cultural differences among Western nations and between Western and non-Western peoples also softened with an increase in international contacts. Peo- *Immigration* ple migrated in droves to the West and other wealthier areas of the world, such as the oil-rich Middle East, and crossed countless borders in the search for work. The new immigration opened doors for many people, but it also had its dark side. The opening of frontiers within Europe during the 1990s and the desperation of

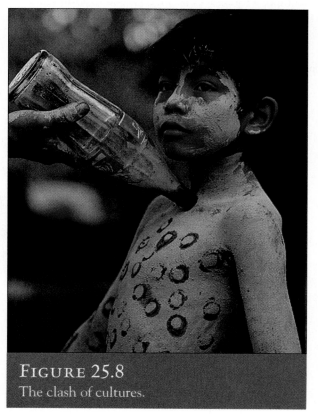

FIGURE 25.8
The clash of cultures.

millions throughout the world made the movement of people difficult to control. Illegal immigration skyrocketed to more than 10 million people a year globally. For example, immigrants from Iran, Turkey, Iraq, Pakistan, Bangladesh, Albania, and elsewhere risked dangerous boat passages and expulsion to reach places such as Italy's long, exposed southern coast. "We lived like animals. . . . If we had not brought some biscuits and water, we would have starved," said a Kurdish immigrant in 1997. Some of the thousands who crossed North American borders each year—legally and illegally—told similar stories.

Germany in particular drew people from Turkey, Yugoslavia, Italy, Eastern Europe, and Russia, and attracted asylum-seekers from many other parts of the world. In 1997, almost 9 percent of Germany's population were immigrants, many of whom remained unassimilated and yet alienated from their lands of origin. One Turkish woman who worked in her father's pizzeria in Berlin described the situation: "People like me are foreigners in Turkey . . . There you are not a real Turk, and here you are not a complete German. We are somewhere in between." Her father agreed: "Even if I had a German passport, I would still feel like a foreigner and be regarded as a foreigner."

At the same time, a common popular culture, especially among the youth in American, European, and non-Western cities, spread with increasing speed across all borders. The worldwide popularity *Popular culture* of Hollywood movies, Disney products, soccer, Nintendo computer games, hamburgers, pizza, shopping malls, noodle soup, Nike shoes, Benetton clothes, TV series, and rock and roll all reflected this standardization of cultural tastes. The spread of English as the world's second language and the beaming of television shows across borders by satellite facilitated the convergence of cultures. No medium offered more potential for this crossing of cultural lines in the future than the computer "information superhighway." Instantaneous electronic communication and access to burgeoning informational, commercial, and scientific resources on the World Wide Web seemed to have dissolved time and space as well as national borders, spawning what some observers called the "global village."

The easing of more traditional forms of travel also added to the meeting of cultures, particularly for middle-class tourists who journeyed throughout the world, visited museums, and absorbed at least visual images of different nations' cultural past and present. Figure 25.9, an illustration for the *Sophisticated Traveler* supplement to the *New York Times*, captures this sense of historical and cultural convergence. In this composite of six masterpieces of Western art, the artist makes a playful statement about the blending of Western cultures. Most of this image's components, which span 3,000 years of Western history, are probably familiar to the millions of museum-going, "sophisticated" middle-class travelers for whom this magazine is intended.

Other cultural changes also set off the 1990s as unique. In the arts, what was once seen as modern in 1914 or even as late as midcentury—the glass skyscrapers and the abstract paintings of Mondrian and Pollock, for example—now *Post modernism* seemed old and taken for granted. Artistic and intellectual movements adopted the "postmodern" label. In the arts, followers of postmodernism became less concerned with austere principles. Architects, for example, rejected the pure forms and plain glass walls of the modern style in favor of buildings with elaborate shapes and ornamentation. Intellectuals and critics sympathetic to postmodernism attacked all ideologies—from liberalism to Marxism—and even the intellectual foundations of most academic disciplines as outmoded, oppressive distortions of the truth. Skeptical that objective truth was possible, they claimed that science itself was infected by the dominant values and beliefs of the culture that produced it.

BEYOND BORDERS: UNCERTAINTY AND OPPORTUNITY IN A SHRINKING WORLD

The spreading webs of communications and the goods and services radiating out from the West promised satisfactions galore for anyone who wanted to—and could afford to—participate. However, the 1980s and 1990s reminded westerners and nonwesterners alike that economic growth could not be taken for granted. Despite the West's overall prosperity, inflation and declining personal incomes for the bottom half of society spawned social discontent in these decades. In most of Europe, unemployment continued to hover above 10 percent and reached as high as 20 percent during the 1990s. Unions everywhere lost membership and clout, leaving more workers than ever without protection in a shifting, competitive marketplace.

In addition, with international economic ties proliferating, problems in one area of the world quickly made themselves felt in other regions. For example, the financial crisis and economic turmoil that struck

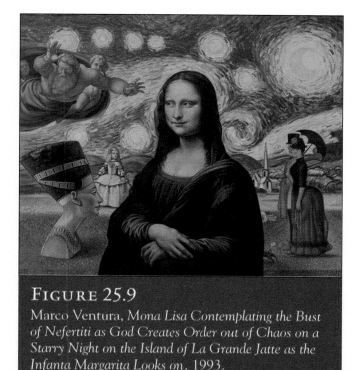

FIGURE 25.9

Marco Ventura, *Mona Lisa Contemplating the Bust of Nefertiti as God Creates Order out of Chaos on a Starry Night on the Island of La Grande Jatte as the Infanta Margarita Looks on*, 1993.

process of urbanization (see Map 25.6). While the wealthy areas of the West once experienced the most rapid urban growth, other parts of the world gained the lead during the last half of the twentieth century. Moreover, in 1950, six out of the ten largest cities were in Europe and the U.S.; by 2000 most of the world's largest cities were in the non-Western world, a trend likely to grow in the future.

Economic growth, population increases, and urbanization created alarming environmental problems in the late twentieth century (see Map 25.7). The earth's air, water, and seas became more and more polluted, while acid rain, caused by *Environmental costs* smoke and fumes, damaged more than one-third of Germany's remaining forests. Great rivers such as the Rhine and the Danube became like sewers, while waters such as the Mediterranean and Black Seas were fouled by runoff from industrial sites and cities. Even the monuments of ancient Greece and Rome were rapidly deteriorating and crumbling from the onslaught of fumes and vibrations of city life. In Eastern Europe and the Soviet Union, environmental problems had been virtually ignored for decades. The collapse of communism in those areas revealed staggering environmental degradation.

As Map 25.6 shows, environmental problems extended well beyond the West. Thirteen of the fifteen cities with the worst air pollution in the world were in Asia. Of the estimated 2.7 million people worldwide who died each year from illnesses caused by air pollution, the majority were Asians. Each year, Asia lost 1 percent of its forests. Depletion of the protective ozone

Asia in 1998 spread rapidly, creating huge losses for investors and trading partners throughout the world. The relatively affluent West, with its multinational corporations, could no *Growing international economic ties* longer ignore nations scourged by crushing debts, pressing economic needs, and unmet demands. The evolving global economic landscape added to the uncertainty. Despite the rise of East Asia, the gap between the affluent, industrialized nations of the northern latitudes and the poorer, developing nations of the south widened. Incomes in most nations in sub-Saharan Africa and Latin America actually declined from 1960s levels. In 1999, over 2 billion people in the world subsisted on the equivalent of less than $1 per day.

As world population in 1999 passed 6 billion—more than double that at the end of World War II—the poorer southern half of the globe carried the heaviest burden of population growth. Figure 25.10 shows population changes for major areas of the world since 1900 and estimates population figures for the mid-twenty-first century. Europe alone is expected to experience a decline of population, while Asia and Africa will gain the most.

The distinction between Europe and the rest of the world in population trends is also reflected in the

Major Area	1900	1950	1998	2050
	Population (in millions)			
Asia	947	1402	3585	5268
Africa	133	221	749	1766
Europe	408	547	729	628
Latin America	74	167	504	809
North America	82	172	305	392
Oceania	6	13	30	46
World (total)	1650	2522	5902	8909

FIGURE 25.10

Population changes across the twentieth and twenty-first centuries.

layer and a heating up of the atmosphere threatened coastal areas, agriculture, and wildlife everywhere. As humanity consumed more and more resources and disrupted the globe's natural balance, thousands of plant and animal species became extinct each year. Humanity's need for more and more energy also led many nations to rely increasingly on nuclear power. The 1986 accident at the Chernobyl plant in the Soviet Union shed new light on the potential dangers of nuclear power—the accident released 200 times the radiation of the two bombs dropped in World War II.

People turned to science and government to solve these environmental problems, but the results were mixed at best. On one hand, scientists and governmental officials finally recognized the severity of these problems and began to address them by committing more funds to research and coming to agreements on new regulations to minimize the damage. On the other hand, anxieties about the environment often conflicted with a stronger desire of many people for continued economic growth. Businesses and governments, reflecting this desire, proved reluctant to commit to expensive environmental-protection programs.

Like the environment, health issues also received an ambivalent response. Many officials and commentators recognized that an aging population, particularly in the West, presented a growing health problem that would strain medical facilities and budgets, but they were unsure what to do. With certain **AIDS** health problems—the worldwide AIDS epidemic is just one example—recognition of the dangers often came too late. Even then, many efforts to address such crises proved half-hearted. Again, AIDS is an apt example. Between 1980 and 1996, some 12 million peo-

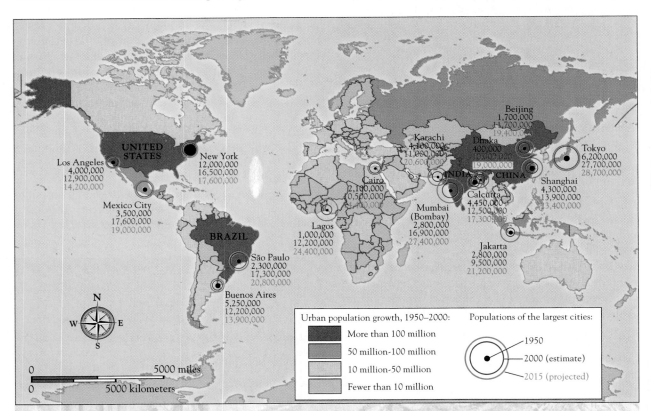

THINKING ABOUT GEOGRAPHY

MAP 25.6   *The Growth of Cities*

Map 25.6 shows those areas with the largest urban populations and the growth of population in the world's largest cities. ◙ **Notice** where the greatest growth of large cities has been and is expected to occur. ◙ **Consider** what problems this growth of urban population poses for the West and the world.

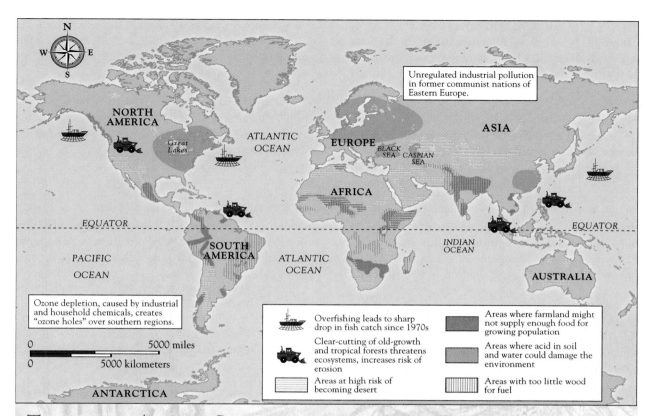

THINKING ABOUT GEOGRAPHY

MAP 25.7 *Global Environmental Problems*

Map 25.7 indicates widespread environmental problems, most stemming from industrialization, exploitation of natural resources, urbanization, and population increases. ◙ **Which** areas of the world are affected more than others by environmental problems? **How** interconnected are these difficulties? ◙ **What** environmental problems are not adequately revealed by this map? ◙ **Consider** what might be done to diminish these problems.

ple died from this disease—610,000 in North America and Western Europe, though far more in Africa and other areas of the world. AIDS became the most deadly epidemic in recent global history, yet many people initially denied its existence or criticized those who had contracted it. The AIDS poster in Figure 25.11, *Love Aids People,* uses Renaissance painter Tanzio da Varallo's painting of the Christian martyr Saint Sebastian, to protest these attitudes. In this poignant image, a modern-day AIDS victim has been wounded by the "arrows" of officials and social attitudes that condemn both the third-century martyr and the twentieth-century AIDS victim as "morally dirty" and "sinful." The poster makes an urgent plea for assistance for AIDS sufferers. After several years, some help began to arrive, but not nearly enough. In 1997 the United Nations estimated that 30.6 million people in the world were living with AIDS or HIV, the virus that causes AIDS. Sixteen thousand people were being infected each day—a shocking 5.8 million new victims per year. By the turn of the century, in some sub-Saharan countries of Africa 1 in 4 adults were infected.

In the face of frightening diseases, environmental degradation, economic uncertainty, and devastating weaponry, many people looked to the new century with cynicism or dread. Some found it all too easy to imagine even the violent destruction of the entire Earth, as Figure 25.12 suggests. This painting, by American artist Jennifer Bartlett, shows a firestorm sweeping away everything in its path. Sculptural objects are dashed to the floor between the viewer and the canvas. In a world that still had unimaginably destructive weapons of war at its fingertips, this scene may well have offered a visual warning of the potential for holocaust that hung over the West and the rest of the world as the twentieth century closed.

Perhaps in response to these anxieties, the end of the century saw a renewal of religious commitment among *Movements of religious revival* many people. In the United States and Europe, evangelical Christianity—with its emphasis on personal salvation and spiritual experience—became the fastest growing religious movement. In Russia, an outpouring of religious sentiment within the Orthodox Church followed the collapse of communism. Islamic fundamentalism, calling for a return to traditional ways and a rejection of alien ideologies, intensified in lands from West Africa to East Asia. All of these movements reflected a hunger for a sense of meaning and a clarity of values by which to live in an uncertain time.

Yet, despite these anxieties, there were also reasons to look to the coming century with hope and optimism. After all, the West had surmounted major obstacles. It had enjoyed fifty years of relative peace and had managed to avert the *Accomplishments and optimism* dreaded clash of superpowers during the Cold War. In Eastern Europe most nations had gained their long-sought independence with a minimum of violence. In some areas, seemingly hopeless problems showed signs of being solved. For example, in Northern Ireland Protestants and Catholics created a power-sharing government, promising an end to a decades-long bitter conflict.

For many people around the world, the standard of living had risen to unprecedented levels. Although social equality still remained only an ideal, the Western promise of continually improving well-being for everyone seemed to hold firm. The increasing human life span and rising numbers of elderly—in part thanks to the global increase in food production and better access to healthcare—attested to that well-being. Moreover, many women gained access to opportunities once available only to men: by the late 1990s, roughly equal numbers of women and men in the West received higher education and pursued paying careers. Women's presence in professional life and in politics continued to grow. True, traditionalists worried about the destruction of the family as an institu-

FIGURE 25.11
AIDS poster by Charles Michael Helmken, 1989.

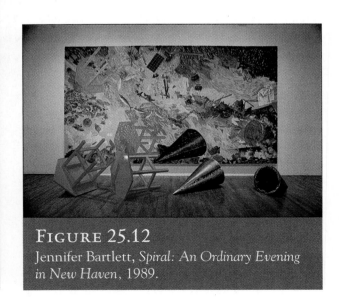

FIGURE 25.12
Jennifer Bartlett, *Spiral: An Ordinary Evening in New Haven*, 1989.

tion, citing the growing prevalence of two-career parents, a rise in cohabitation and single motherhood, and accelerating divorce rates. Nevertheless, family structures persisted, though many of them took new forms such as "an emotionally bound partnership."

Continuing scientific discoveries suggested that the West and the rest of the world could look forward to dramatic developments in the future. Perhaps most stunning was the prospect of changes stemming from the decoding of the human genome—determining the chemical sequence of the DNA in every cell of the human body. By the spring of 2000, this costly, long-term project carried out by hundreds of scientists in 6 countries neared completion. With this "blueprint" of human life, scientists hoped to revolutionize medicine and gain new insights into human nature.

Overall, the West has gained a much needed appreciation of its place in the world, and human beings around the globe have new tools to understand themselves within a widening universe. Technology, trade, and instant communications provide growing opportunities for cooperation across national boundaries. As the twenty-first century opens, life offers more options to more people than ever.

In 1989, history in the West abruptly shifted course. The communist regimes in Eastern Europe fell, severing these nations' ties to the Soviet Union and sparking unprecedented political and economic reforms. Two years later, the Soviet Union itself disintegrated. The Cold War ended, and along with it a sharply defined historical era stretching back to 1914. The end of the Cold War renewed the commitment to democracy and capitalism in the West, accelerated the existing movement toward unification in Europe, and left the United States standing as the sole military superpower in the world.

But the collapse of communism did not end all the anxieties present during the Cold War era. The transition in Eastern Europe and the Soviet Union proved rocky, and westerners realized that despite their lofty global position, they could no longer keep the rest of the world at arms' length. Indeed, the West's global status began to change, as statistics reveal. In 1950, some 30 percent of the world's population lived in Europe and North America. In 1997, that figure dropped below 20 percent and continued to decline. As peoples around the world interacted more and more, cultures mingled, producing both conflict and convergence: our time may mark the beginning of a new global society. The relentless human desire for limitless economic growth and material security also left its mark on the environment in ways that spread concern across national boundaries. Western civilization, so long centered on the western tip of the Eurasian continent, now seemed to be just one of many lights shining on this shrinking globe. As one era closed and another opened, great challenges faced all of humanity. Whether and how the West—and the world—would embrace these challenges remained to be seen.

REVIEW, ANALYZE, AND ANTICIPATE

REVIEW THE PREVIOUS CHAPTER

In Chapter 24—"Superpower Struggles and Global Transformations"—the Cold War competition between the United States and the Soviet Union was examined. Within the Cold War context, the recovery of the West and end of colonialism were analyzed.

1. *How might you argue that developments since 1989 are not the beginning of a new historical era, and that instead they are a continuation of trends that first emerged in the post-World War II decades?*

2. *Do you think that the collapse of communism and the end of the Cold War should have been predictable by the early 1980s? Why?*

ANALYZE THIS CHAPTER

Chapter 25—"Into the Twenty-First Century"—traces the collapse of communism and the intense interaction between the Western and non-Western worlds.

1. *Analyze the consequences of the collapse of communism outside Eastern Europe and the Soviet Union.*

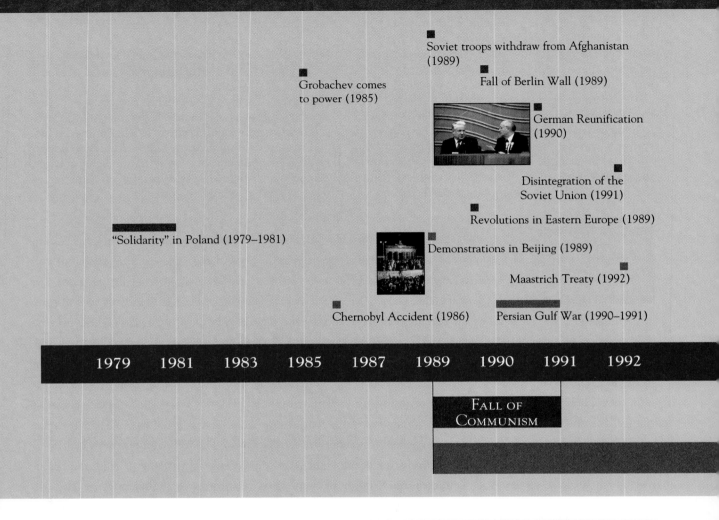

Soviet troops withdraw from Afghanistan (1989)

Fall of Berlin Wall (1989)

Grobachev comes to power (1985)

German Reunification (1990)

Disintegration of the Soviet Union (1991)

Revolutions in Eastern Europe (1989)

"Solidarity" in Poland (1979–1981)

Demonstrations in Beijing (1989)

Maastrich Treaty (1992)

Chernobyl Accident (1986)

Persian Gulf War (1990–1991)

| 1979 | 1981 | 1983 | 1985 | 1987 | 1989 | 1990 | 1991 | 1992 |

FALL OF COMMUNISM

2. In what ways has much of Europe become integrated, and what steps remain to achieve full integration?

3. What forces are pulling the world together? How do these forces compare with those dividing the world?

ANTICIPATE THE FUTURE

It is always difficult to predict the future, but perhaps history can sometimes provide grounds for reasonable guesses.

1. In the near future, what might be the consequences of continuing steps toward the unification of Europe?

2. Judging from developments since 1989, which problems do you think will prove the most serious in the years to come? Why? Do you think there is good reason for optimism? Why?

BEYOND THE CLASSROOM

THE COLLAPSE OF COMMUNISM

Brown, Archie. *The Gorbachev Factor.* New York: Oxford University Press, 1996. An examination of Gorbachev's role in the collapse of communism.

Donia, Robert J., and John V. A. Fine, Jr. *Bosnia and Herzegovina: A Tradition Betrayed.* New York: Columbia University Press, 1994. A chronological survey of the region from the medieval Bosnian state to the wars of Yugoslavian secession.

Elster, Jon, ed. *The Roundtable Talks and the Breakdown of Communism.* Chicago: University of Chicago Press, 1996. An examination of the historic summits of 1987.

World population 6 billion (1999)

Division of Czechoslovakia (1993)

NAFTA created (1994)

Euro introduced (1999)

| 1993 | 1994 | 1995 | 1996 | 1997 | 1998 | 1999 | 2000 |

OTHER DEVELOPMENTS (1989–2000)

Garton Ash, Timothy. *In Europe's Name: Germany and the Divided Continent*. London: Jonathan Cape, 1993. Stresses the history of tensions between the two Germanys as background to their reunification.

Malia, Martin. *The Soviet Tragedy: A History of Socialism in Russia, 1917–1991*. New York: Maxwell Macmillan International, 1994. A compact history of the Soviet period from 1917 to the collapse of communism in 1991.

Remnick, David. *Lenin's Tomb: The Last Days of the Soviet Empire*. New York: Random House, 1994. Journalistic coverage of the final period before the collapse of the Soviet empire, stressing the role played by Yeltsin.

Silber, Laura, and Little, Allan. *Yugoslavia: Death of a Nation*. New York: TV Books/Penguin USA, 1996. An account of the nation's ethnic troubles.

Stokes, Gale. *The Walls Came Tumbling Down: The Collapse of Communism in Eastern Europe*. Oxford: Oxford University Press, 1993. Analyzes the decline and fall of communism in Eastern Europe since 1968.

REPERCUSSIONS AND REALIGNMENTS IN THE WEST

Caplan, Richard, and John Feffer, eds. *Europe's New Nationalism: States and Minorities in Conflict*. New York: Oxford University Press, 1996. A collection of essays by scholars on the growth of nationalism in Europe after the collapse of communism.

Cheles, Juciano, et al., eds. *The Far Right in Western and Eastern Europe, 2nd ed.* London: Longman, 1995. A comparative study of fringe movements in these areas.

THE WORLD AND THE WEST FROM A GLOBAL PERSPECTIVE

Campos, Jose Edgardo, and Hilton L. Root. *The Key to the Asian Miracle: Making Shared Growth Credible.* Washington, D.C.: Brookings Institution, 1996. An interesting analysis of economic development in Asia and its connections to the West.

Cleveland, William L. *A History of the Modern Middle East.* Boulder, CO: Westview Press, 1994. A broad, useful survey that provides good background to the current period.

Kroes, Rob. *If You've Seen One, You've Seen the Mall: Europeans and American Mass Culture.* Urbana, IL: University of Illinois Press, 1996. A study of the international effects of American consumer culture.

Glossary

Note to users: Terms that are foreign or difficult to pronounce are transcribed in parentheses directly after the term itself. The transcriptions are based on the rules of English spelling; that is to say, they are similar to the transcriptions employed in the *Webster* dictionaries. Each word's most heavily stressed syllable is marked by an acute accent:

A

Absolute monarch (máh-nark) A seventeenth- or eighteenth-century European monarch claiming complete political authority.

Absolutism (áb-suh-loo-tism)(Royal) A government in which all power is vested in the ruler.

Abstract expressionism (ex-présh-un-ism) A twentieth-century painting style infusing nonrepresentational art with strong personal feelings.

Acropolis (uh-króp-uh-liss) The hill at the center of Athens on which the magnificent temples—including the Parthenon— that made the architecture of ancient Athens famous are built.

Act of Union Formal unification of England and Scotland in 1707.

Age of Reason The eighteenth-century Enlightenment; sometimes includes seventeenth-century science and philosophy.

Agora In ancient Greece, the marketplace or place of public assembly.

Agricultural revolution Neolithic discovery of agriculture; agricultural transformations that began in eighteenth-century western Europe.

Ahura Mazda In Zoroastrianism, the beneficial god of light.

Ahriman In Zoroastrianism, the evil god of darkness.

Akkadian (uh-káy-dee-un) A Semitic language of a region of ancient Mesopotamia.

Albigensians (al-buh-jén-see-unz) A medieval French heretical sect that believed in two gods—an evil and a good principle—that was destroyed in a crusade in the thirteenth century; also called Cathars.

Allies (ál-eyes) The two alliances against Germany and its partners in World War I and World War II.

Anarchism (ánn-ar-kizz-um) Late-nineteenth- and early-twentieth-century ideology and movement standing against all governmental authority and private property.

Ancien Régime (áwn-syáwn ráy-zhéem) The traditional political and social order in Europe before the French Revolution.

Antigonids (ann-tíg-un-idz) Hellenistic dynasty that ruled in Macedonia from about 300 B.C. to about 150 B.C.

Anti-Semitism (ann-tye-sém-i-tism) Prejudice against Jews.

Appeasement Trying to satisfy potential aggressors in order to avoid war.

Aramaic (air-uh-máy-ik) A northwest Semitic language that spread throughout the region. It was the language that Jesus spoke.

Archon (áhr-kahn) A chief magistrate in ancient Athens.

Areopagus (air-ee-áh-pa-gus) A prestigious governing council of ancient Athens.

Arete (ah-ray-táy) Greek term for the valued virtues of manliness, courage, and excellence.

Arian (áir-ee-un) **Christianity** A fourth-century heresy that taught that Jesus was not of the same substance as God the father, and thus had been created.

Assignats (ah-seen-yáh) Paper money issued in the National Assembly during the French Revolution.

Astrolabe (áss-tro-leyb) Medieval instrument used to determine the altitudes of celestial bodies.

Autocrat (áuto-crat) An authoritarian ruler.

Axis World War II alliance whose main members were Germany, Italy, and Japan.

B

Baby boom The increase in births following World War II.

Bailiffs Medieval French salaried officials hired by the king to collect taxes and represent his interests.

Balance of power Distribution of power among states, or the policy of creating alliances to control powerful states.

Balkans States in the Balkan Peninsula, including Albania, Bulgaria, Greece, Romania, and Yugoslavia.

Baroque (ba-róak) An artistic style of the sixteenth and seventeenth centuries stressing rich ornamentation and dynamic movement; in music, a style marked by strict forms and elaborate ornamentation.

Bastard feudalism (feúd-a-lism) Late medieval corruption of the feudal system replacing feudal loyalty with cash payments.

Bastille (bas-téel) The royal prison symbolizing the old regime that was destroyed in the French Revolution.

Bauhaus (bóugh-house) An influential school of art emphasizing clean, functional lines founded in Germany by the architect Walter Gropius just after World War I.

Bedouin (béd-oh-in) An Arab of any of the nomadic tribes of the deserts of North Africa, Arabia, and Syria.

Berlin airlift The airborne military operation organized to supply Berlin's Western-occupied sectors during the Soviet Union's 1948 Berlin blockage.

Berlin Wall The wall erected in 1961 to divide East and West Berlin.

Bessemer (béss-uh-mer) **process** A method for removing impurities from molten iron.

Blackshirts Mussolini's black-uniformed Fascist paramilitary forces in the 1920s and 1930s.

Blitzkrieg (blíts-kreeg) "Lighting war," a rapid air and land military assault used by the Germans in World War II.

Boers (boars) Dutch settlers in south Africa.

Bolshevik (ból-shuh-vick) "Majority faction," the Leninist wing of the Russian Marxist Party; after 1917, the Communist Party.

Bourgeoisie (boor-zhwa-zée) The middle class.

Boxers A nineteenth-century Chinese secret that believed in the spiritual power of the martial arts and fought against Chinese Christians and foreigners in China.

Boyar A Russian noble.

Brezhnev (bréhzh-nyeff) **Doctrine** Policy that justified Soviet intervention in order to ensure the survival of socialism in another state, initiated by USSR leader Brezhnev in 1968.

Brownshirts Hitler's brown-uniformed paramilitary force in the 1920s and 1930s.

Burschenschaften (bóor-shen-shàhf-ten) Liberal nationalist German Student Unions during the early nineteenth century.

C

Cabinet system Government by a prime minister and heads of governmental bureaus developed by Britain during the eighteenth century.

Cahiers (kye-yéah) Lists of public grievances sent to the French Estates General in 1789.

Caliph (káy-liff) A title meaning "successor to the Prophet" given to Muslim rulers who combined political authority with religious power.

Capitalism An economic system characterized by freedom of the market with private and corporate ownership of the means of production and distribution that are operated for profit.

Capitularies (ka-pít-chew-làir-eez) Royal laws issued by Charlemagne and the Carolingians.

Caravel (care-uh-véll) A small, light sailing ship of the kind used by the Spanish and Portuguese in the fifteenth and sixteenth centuries.

Carbonari (car-bun-áh-ree) A secret society of revolutionaries in nineteenth-century Italy.

Cartel (car-téll) An alliance of corporations designed to control the market place.

Cathars (cáth-arz) A medieval French dualist heretical sect; also called Albigensians.

Central Powers World War I alliance, primarily of Germany, Austria, and the Ottoman Empire.

Centuriate (sen-chúr-ee-ate) **Assembly** An aristocratic ruling body in ancient Rome that made the laws.

Chancellor A high-ranking official—in Germany, the prime minister.

Chartists English reformers of the 1830s and 1840s who demanded political and social rights for the lower classes.

Checks and balances A balanced division of governmental power among different institutions.

Civil Constitution of the Clergy New rules nationalizing and governing the clergy enacted during the French Revolution.

Classical style A seventeenth- and eighteenth-century cultural style emphasizing restraint and balance, and following models from ancient Greece and Rome.

Cold War The global struggle between alliances headed by the United States and the Soviet Union during the second half of the twentieth century.

Comecon (cómm-ee-con) The economic organization of communist eastern European states during the Cold War.

Committee of Public Safety Ruling committee of twelve leaders during the French Revolutionary period of the Terror.

Common market The European Economic Community, a union of western European nations initiated in 1957 to promote common economic policies.

Commonwealth of Independent States A loose confederation of several former republics of the disintegrated Soviet Union founded in 1991.

Commune (cómm-yune) A medieval or early modern town; a semi-independent city government or socialistic community in the nineteenth and twentieth centuries.

Complutensian Polyglot (comm-plue-tén-see-an pólly-glàht) **Bible** An edition of the Bible written in 1520 that had three columns that compared the Hebrew, Greek, and Latin versions.

Compurgation (comm-pur-gáy-shun) A Germanic legal oath taken by twelve men testifying to the character of the accused.

Concert of Europe The alliance of powers after 1815 created to maintain the status quo and coordinate international relations.

Conciliar (conn-síll-ee-ar) **movement** The belief that the Catholic Church should be led by councils of cardinals rather than popes.

Concordat (conn-córe-dat) A formal agreement, especially between the pope and a government, for the regulation of church affairs.

Congress of Vienna The peace conference held between 1814 and 1815 in Vienna after the defeat of Napoleon.

Conservatism An ideology stressing order and traditional values.

Constitutional monarchy Government in which the monarch's powers are limited by a set of fundamental laws.

Consuls (cónn-sul) The appointed chief executive officers of the Roman Republic.

Continental System Napoleon's policy of preventing trade between continental Europe and Great Britain.

Copernican (co-pér-nick-an) **revolution** The change from an Earth-centered to a sun-centered universe initiated by Copernicus in the sixteenth century.

Corn Laws British laws that imposed tariffs on grain imports.

Corporate state Mussolini's economic and political machinery to manage the Italian economy and settle issues between labor and management.

Corsair A swift pirate ship.

Cossacks The "free warriors" of southern Russia, noted as cavalrymen.

Cottage industry Handicraft manufacturing usually organized by merchants and performed by rural people in their cottages.

Coup d'état (coo-day-táh) A sudden taking of power that violates constitutional forms by a group of persons in authority.

Creoles (crée-ohlz) People of European descent born in the West Indies or Spanish America, often of mixed ancestry.

Cult of sensibility The eighteenth-century emphasis on emotion and nature forwarded by several European artists and authors.

Cuneiform (cue-née-uh-form) A writing system using wedge-shaped characters developed in ancient Mesopotamia.

Curia Regis (kóo-ree-uh régg-ees) A medieval king's advisory body made up of his major vassals.

Cynicism (sín-uh-sism) A hellenistic philosophy that locates the search for virtue in an utter indifference to worldly needs.

Cyrillic alphabet An old Slavic alphabet presently used in modified form for Russian and other languages.

D

Dada (dáh-dah) An early-twentieth-century artistic movement that attacked traditional cultural styles and stressed the absence of purpose in life.

Dauphin (dough-fán) Heir to the French throne.

D-Day The day of the Allied invasion of Normandy in World War II– June 6, 1944.

Decembrists (dee-sém-brists) Russian army officers who briefly rebelled against Tsar Nicholas I in December, 1925.

Declaration of the Rights of Man and Citizen France's revolutionary 1789 declaration of rights stressing liberty, equality, and fraternity.

Deductive reasoning Deriving conclusions that logically flow from a premise.

Deism (dée-iz-um) Belief in a God who created the universe and its natural laws but does not intervene further; gained popularity during the Enlightenment.

Demotic A form of ancient Egyptian writing used for ordinary life. A simplified form of hieratic script.

Détente (day-táhnt) The period of relative cooperation between Cold War adversaries during the 1960s and 1970s.

Devotio moderno (day-vóh-tee-oh moh-dáir-noh) A medieval religious movement that emphasized internal spirituality over ritual practices.

Diet The general legislative assembly of certain countries, such as Poland.

Directory The relatively conservative government during the last years of the French Revolution before Napoleon gained power.

Division of labor The division of work in the modern process of industrial production into separate tasks.

Domesday (dóomz-day) **Book** A record of all the property and holdings in England commissioned by William the Conqueror in 1066 so he could determine the extent of his lands and wealth.

Drachma (dróck-mah) Hellenistic coin containing either 4.3 grams (Alexander's) or 3.5 grams (Egypt's) of silver.

Dreyfus (dry'-fuss) **case** The political upheaval in France accompanying the unjust 1894 conviction of Jewish army officer Alfred Dreyfus as a German spy that marked the importance of anti-Semitism in France.

Dual monarchy The Austro-Hungarian Empire; the Habsburg monarchy after the 1867 reform that granted Hungary equality with Austria.

Il Duce (ill dóoch-ay) "The Leader," Mussolini's title as head of the Italian Fascist Party.

Duma Russia's legislative assembly in the years prior to 1917.

E

Ecclesia (ek-cláy-zee-uh) The popular assembly in ancient Athens made up of all male citizens over eighteen.

Edict of Nantes (náwnt) Edict grated by French king Henry IV in 1598 granting rights to Protestants, later revoked by Louis XIV.

Émigrés (em-ee-gráy) People, mostly aristocrats, who fled France during the French Revolution.

Emir (em-éar) A Muslim ruler, prince, or military commander.

Ems (Em's) **Dispatch** Telegram from Prussia's head of state to the French government, edited by Bismarck to look like an insult, that helped cause the Franco-Prussian War.

Enclosure Combining separate parcels of farmland and enclosing them with fences and walls to create large farms or pastures that produced for commerce.

Enlightened absolutism (áb-suh-loo-tism) Rule by a strong, "enlightened" ruler applying Enlightenment ideas to government.

Entente Cordiale (on-táhnt core-dee-áhl) The series of understandings, or agreements, between France and Britain that led to their alliance in World War I.

Entrepreneur (on-truh-pren-óor) A person who organizes and operates business ventures, especially in commerce and industry.

Epic (épp-ik) A long narrative poem celebrating episodes of a people's heroic tradition.

Epicureanism (epp-uh-cúre-ee-an-ism) A Hellenistic philosophy which held that the goal of life should be to live a life of pleasure regulated by moderation.

Equestrians (ee-quést-ree-ans) A social class in ancient Rome who had enough money to begin to challenge the power of the patricians.

Ethnic cleansing The policy of brutally driving an ethnic group from their homes and from a certain territory, particularly prominent during the civil wars in the Balkans during the 1990s.

Eugenics (you-génn-iks) The study of hereditary improvement.

Euro (yóu-roe) The common currency of many European states, established in 1999.

Eurocommunism The policy of western European Communist parties of supporting moderate policies and cooperating with other Leftist parties during the 1970s and 1980s.

European Economic Community The E.E.C., or Common Market, founded in 1957 to eliminate tariff barriers and begin to integrate the economies of western European nations.

European Union The community of European nations that continued to take steps toward the full economic union of much of Europe during the late twentieth century.

Evolution Darwin's theory of biological development through adaptation.

Existentialism (ekk-siss-ténn-sha-lism) A twentieth-century philosophy asserting that individuals are responsible for their own values and meanings in an indifferent universe.

Expressionism A late-nineteenth- and early-twentieth-century artistic style that emphasized the objective expression of inner experience through the use of conventional characters and symbols.

F

Fabian (fáy-bee-an) **Society** A late-nineteenth-century group of British intellectuals that advocated the adoption of socialist policies through politics rather than revolution.

Factory system Many workers producing goods in a repetitive series of steps and specialized tasks using powerful machines.

Falange (fa-láhn-hey) A Spanish fascist party that supported Francisco Franco during the Spanish civil war.

Fascism (fáh-shism) A philosophy or system of government that advocates a dictatorship of the extreme right together with an ideology of belligerent nationalism.

Fealty (fée-al-tee) In the feudal system, a promise made by vassals and lords to do no harm to each other.

Fibula (pl. fibulae) An ornamented clasp or brooch, favored by the ancient Germanic tribes to hold their great cloaks closed.

Fief (feef) In the feudal system, the portion—usually land—given by lords to vassals to provide for their maintenance in return for their service.

Five Year Plan The rapid, massive industrialization of the nation under the direction of the state initiated in the Soviet Union in the late 1920s.

Fourteen Points U.S. president Wilson's plan to settle World War I and guarantee the peace.

Frankfurt Assembly Convention of liberals and nationalists from several German states that met in 1848 to try to form a unified government for Germany.

Free Corps (core) Post—World War I German right-wing paramilitary groups made up mostly of veterans.

Free trade International trade of goods without tariffs, or customs duties.

Fronde (frawnd) Mid-seventeenth century upheavals in France that threatened the royal government.

G

Galley A large medieval ship propelled by sails and oars.

General will Rousseau's notion that rules governing society should be based on the best conscience of the people.

Gentry People of "good birth" and superior social position.

Geocentric Earth-centered.

Gerousia (gay-róo-see-uh) Ruling body in ancient Sparta made up of male citizens over age sixty.

Gestapo (guh-stóp-po) Nazi secret police in Hitler's Germany.

Girondins (zhee-roan-dán) Moderate political faction among leaders of the French Revolution.

Glasnost (gláz-nost) Soviet leader Gorbachev's policy of political and cultural openness in the 1980s.

Globalization Twentieth-century tendency for cultural and historical development to become increasingly worldwide in scope.

Gosplan The Soviet State Planning Commission charged with achieving ambitious economic goals.

Grand tour An educational travel taken by the wealthy to certain cities and sites, particularly during the seventeenth and eighteenth centuries.

Great Chain of Being A traditional Western-Christian vision of the hierarchical order of the universe.

Great Depression The global economic depression of the 1930s.

Great fear Panic caused by rumors that bands of brigands were on the loose in the French countryside during the summer of 1789.

Great Purges The long period of Communist Party purges in the Soviet Union during the 1930s, marked by terror, house arrests, show-trials, torture, imprisonments, and executions.

Greek Fire A Byzantine naval weapon made of combustible oil that was launched with a catapult or pumped through tubes to set fire to enemy ships.

Guild An association of persons of the same trade united for the furtherance of some purpose.

Guillotine (ghée-oh-teen) A device for executing the condemned used during the French Revolution.

H

Haj (hodge) The Muslim annual pilgrimage to Mecca, Medina, and other holy sites.

Hasidim (hah-see-déem) Sect of Jewish mystics founded in Poland in the eighteenth century in opposition to the formalistic Judaism and ritual laxity of the period.

Heliocentric (hee-lee-oh-sén-trick) **theory** Theory that the sun is the center of the universe.

Hellenes (Héll-eenz) The name ancient Greeks assigned to themselves, based on their belief that they were descended from a mythical King Hellen.

Hellenistic Of or related to the period between the fourth century B.C. and the first century B.C.

Helot (héll-ots) A serf in ancient Sparta.

Hermetic doctrine Notion popular in the sixteenth and seventeenth centuries that all matter contains the divine spirit.

Hieratic A form of ancient Egyptian writing consisting of abridged forms of hieroglyphics, used by the priests in keeping records.

Hieroglyph (hígh-roe-gliff) A picture or symbol used in the ancient Egyptian writing system – means "sacred writing."

Hijra (hídge-rah)(also Hegira) Muhammad's flight from Mecca to Medina in A.D. 622.

Holocaust (hóll-o-cost) The extermination of some 6 million Jews by the Nazis during World War II.

Holy Alliance Alliance of Russia, Austria, and Prussia to safeguard the principles of Christianity and maintain the international status quo after the Napoleonic Wars.

Homeopathy (home-ee-áh-pa-thee) Medical treatment emphasizing the use of herbal drugs and natural remedies.

Hoplites (hóp-light) Ancient Greek infantrymen equipped with large round shields and long thrusting spears.

Hubris Excessive pride, which for the ancient Greeks brought punishment from the gods.

Huguenots (húgh-guh-nots) French Protestants of the sixteenth, seventeenth, and eighteenth centuries.

Humanism Renaissance intellectual movement based on a deep study of classical culture and emphasizing the study of the humanities as a means for self-improvement.

I

Icon (éye-con) A sacred image of Jesus, Mary, or the saints that early Christians believed contained religious power.

Iconoclasm (eye-cónn-o-claz-um) A term literally meaning "icon breaking" that refers to an eighth-century religious controversy in Byzantium that argued that people should not venerate icons.

Ideogram (eye-dée-o-gram) A hieroglyph symbol expressing an abstract idea associated with the object it portrays.

Ideograph A written symbol that represents an idea instead of expressing the sound of a word.

Ideology (eye-dee-áh-lo-gee) A set of beliefs about the world and how it should be, often formalized into a political, social, or cultural theory.

Imperialism The policy of extending a nation's authority by territorial acquisitions or by the establishment of economic and political control over other nations or peoples.

Impressionism A nineteenth-century school of painting originating is France that emphasized capturing on canvas light as the eye sees it.

Indo-European Belonging to or constituting a family of languages that includes the Germanic, Celtic, Italic, Baltic, Slavic, Greek, Armenian, Iranian, and Indic groups.

Inductive reasoning Drawing general conclusions from particular concrete observations.

Industrial revolution The rapid emergence of modern industrial production during the late eighteenth and nineteenth centuries.

Information revolution A rapid increase in the ability to store and manipulate information accompanying the development of computers during the second half of the twentieth century.

Intendant (ann-tawn-dáunt) A French official sent by the royal government to assert the will of the monarch.

Ionia (eye-ówn-ee-uh) Ancient district in what is now Turkey that comprised the central portion of the west coast of Asia Minor, together with the adjacent islands.

Iron curtain The dividing line between Eastern and Western Europe during the Cold War.

Islamic fundamentalism A movement within Islam calling for a return to traditional ways and a rejection of alien ideologies that gained strength during the second half of the twentieth century.

J

Jacobins (ják-o-bins) A radical political organization or club during the French Revolution.

Jansenism A religious movement among French Catholics stressing the emotional experience of religious belief.

Jihad (jée-hod) Islamic holy war in which believers feel they have the authority to fight to defend the faith.

Journeyman A worker in a craft who has served his or her apprenticeship.

Joust A medieval contest in which two mounted knights combat with lances.

Junkers (yóong-kers) Prussian aristocracy.

Justification by faith The belief that faith alone—not good works—is needed for salvation. This belief lies at the heart of Protestantism.

K

Kristallnacht (kriss-táhl-nahkt) The "night of the broken glass"—a Nazi attack on German Jewish homes and businesses in 1938.

Kulak (kóo-lock) A relatively wealthy Russian peasant labeled by Stalin during the period of collectivization as a "class enemy."

Kulturkampf (kool-tóur-kahmpf) Bismarck's fight against the Catholic Church in Germany during the 1870s.

L

Laissez-faire (léss-say-fair) "Hands-off." An economic doctrine opposing governmental regulation of most economic affairs.

Laudanum (láud-a-numb)—Opium dissolved in alcohol, used as a medicine in the eighteenth and nineteenth centuries.

League of Nations A post–World War I association of countries to deal with international tensions and conflicts.

Lebensraum (láy-benz-rowm) "Living space." Hitler's policy of expanding his empire to the east to gain more land for Germans.

Legume (lég-yoom) A pod, such as that of a pea or bean, used as food.

Levée en masse (le-váy awn máhss) General call-up of all men, women, and children to serve the nation during the French Revolution.

Levellers Democrats who tried to "level" the social hierarchy during the English civil war.

Liberalism A nineteenth- and twentieth-century ideology supporting individualism, political freedom, constitutional government, and (in the nineteenth century) laissez-faire economic policies.

Liege (léezh) **lord** In the feudal system, a lord who has many vassals, but owes allegiance to no one.

Linear perspective An artistic technique used to represent three-dimensional space convincingly on a flat surface.

Lollards Followers of the English church reformer John Wycliffe who were found heretical.

Long March An arduous Chinese communist retreat from south China to north China in 1934 and 1935.

Luddism The smashing of machines that took jobs away from workers in the first half of the nineteenth century.

M

Ma'at (máh-aht) An Egyptian spiritual precept that conveyed the idea of truth and justice, or, as the Egyptians put it, right order and harmony.

Magi (máyj-eye) Ancient Persian astrologers or "wise men."

Maginot (máh-zhin-oh) **Line** A string of defensive fortresses on the French/German border that France began building in the late 1920s.

Marshall Plan A package of massive economic aid to European nations offered in 1947 to strengthen them and tie them to American influence.

Marxism A variety of socialism propounded by Karl Marx stressing economic determinism and class struggle—"scientific socialism."

Megalith An archaeological term for a stone of great size used in ancient monuments.

Meiji (máy-jee) **Restoration** The reorganizing of Japanese society along modern Western lines; initiated in 1868.

Mercantilism (mírr-kan-till-ism) Early modern governmental economic policies seeking to control and develop the national economy and bring wealth into the national treasury.

Mesolithic Of or belongng to the period of human culture from about 15,000 years ago to about 7,000 B.C. characterized by complex stone tools and greater social organization. "Middle Stone Age."

Methodism A protestant sect founded in the eighteenth century that emphasized piety and emotional worship.

Metics (métt-iks) Foreign residents of Athens.

Miasma (my-ázz-ma) Fumes from waste and marshes blamed for carrying diseases during the eighteenth and the first half of the nineteenth centuries.

Minoan (mínn-oh-an) A civilization that lived on the island of Crete from 2800 to 1450 B.C.

Mir (mere) Russian village commune.

Missi dominici (mée-see do-min-ée-kee) Royal officials under Charlemagne who traveled around the country to enforce the king's laws.

Mithraism (míth-ra-ism) A Hellenistic mystery religion that appealed to soldiers and involved the worship of the god Mithra.

Moguls (móe-gulls) Islamic rulers of much of India in the sixteenth, seventeenth, and eighteenth centuries.

Munich conference The 1938 conference where Britain and France attempted to appease Hitler by allowing him to dismantle Czechoslovakia.

Mycenean (my-sen-ée-an) A civilization on the Greek peninsula that reached its high point between 1400 and 1200 B.C.

N

Napoleonic (na-po-lee-ón-ik) **Code** The legal code introduced in France by Napoleon Bonaparte.

Nationalism A nineteenth- and twentieth-century ideology stressing the importance of national identity and the nation-state.

NATO North Atlantic Treaty Organization. A military alliance against the Soviet Union initiated in 1949.

Natural law Understandable, rational laws of nature that apply to the physical and human world.

Nazi Party Hitler's German National Socialist Party.

Neolithic (nee-oh-líth-ik) Of or denoting a period of human culture beginning around 7,000 B.C. in the Middle East and later elsewhere, characterized by the invention of farming and the making of technically advanced stone implements. "New Stone Age."

Neoplatonism (nee-oh-pláy-ton-ism) Views based on the ideas of Plato that one should search beyond appearances for true knowledge; stressed abstract reasoning and was popular during the fifteenth, sixteenth, and seventeenth centuries.

New Economic Policy Lenin's compromise economic and social policy for the USSR during the 1920s—the NEP.

New imperialism The second wave of Western imperialism, particularly between 1880 and 1914.

New Nominalism (nóm-in-al-ism) A popular late medieval philosophy based on the doctrine that the universal, or general, has no objective existence or validity, being merely a name expressing the qualities of various objects resembling one another in certain respects.

Night of August 4 Surrender of most privileges by the French aristocracy at a meeting held on August 1, 1789.

North American Free Trade Agreement The 1994 agreement between the United States, Mexico, and Canada to create a free trade zone.

Nuremberg Laws Hitler's anti-Jewish laws of 1935.

O

Ockham's razor A principle that says between alternative explanations for the same phenomenon, the simplest is always to be preferred.

October Revolution The 1917 Bolshevik revolt and seizure of power in Russia.

Old regime (re-zhéem) European society before the French Revolution.

Oligarchy (áh-luh-gar-kee) Rule by a small group or by a particular social class—often wealthy middle classes, as in ancient Greek or medieval European cities.

OPEC The Arab-dominated Organization of Petroleum Exporting Countries that became effective during and after the 1970s.

Operation Barbarossa (bar-bar-óh-ssa) The German invasion of the USSR during World War II.

Ostracism (áhs-tra-sism) A political technique of ancient Greece by which people believed to be threats to the city-state were chosen for exile by popular vote.

P

Paleolithic (pay-lee-oh-líth-ik) Of or belonging to the period of human culture beginning with the earliest chipped stone tools, about 750,000 years ago, until the beginning of the Mesolithic, about 15,000 years ago. "Old Stone Age."

Paris Commune The revolutionary government of the city of Paris, first in the 1790s and then in 1871.

Parlement (parl-máwn) A French court of law during the Old Regime.

Parliament Britain's legislature, including the House of Commons and House of Lords.

Parthenon (párth-uh-non) A famous Doric temple of Athena on the Acropolis in ancient Athens.

Patricians The ancient Roman aristocracy who populated the Senate and were particularly powerful during the Republic.

Peace of Paris The 1919 peace settlement after World War I.

Peers Members of the House of Lords in England.

Perestroika (pair-ess-trói-ka) Gorbachev's policy of "restructuring" the Soviet economy during the 1980s.

Phalanstery (fa-láns-ter-ee) The model commune envisioned by the French utopian socialist Fourier.

Phalanx (fáy-langks) An ancient Greek formation of foot soldiers carrying overlapping shields and long spears.

Philosophes (fee-low-zóff) Leading French intellectuals of the Enlightenment.

Phonogram A character or symbol used to represent a speech sound used in ancient writing.

Physiocrats (fízz-ee-oh-crats) Eighteenth-century French economic thinkers who stressed the importance of agriculture and favored free trade.

Pictogram A picture representing an idea used in ancient writing.

Pietism (píe-uh-tism) An eighteenth-century Protestant movement stressing an emotional commitment to religion.

Plebeians (pleb-ée-an) The members of the urban lower classes in ancient Rome.

Plebiscite (pléb-uh-sight) A direct vote that allows the people to either accept or reject a proposed measure.

Pogrom ('puh-grúhm'; also 'póe-grom') An organized persecution or massacre of Jews, especially in eastern Europe.

Polis (póe-liss) (*pl.* Póleis [póe-lease]) An ancient Greek city-state.

Poor Laws Eighteenth- and nineteenth-century British laws enacted to deal with the poor.

Popular Front The political partnership of parties of the left, particularly in France and Spain, during the 1930s.

Post-industrial societies Late twentieth-century societies that moved from manufacturing to services led by professionals, managers, and financiers.

Postmodernism A later twentieth-century approach to the arts stressing relativism and multiple interpretations.

Pragmatic Sanction The international agreement secured by the Habsburg emperor in the 1730s to insure that his daughter would succeed him without question.

Prague Spring The brief period of democratic reforms and cultural freedom in Czechoslovakia during 1968.

Prefect Powerful agents of the central government stationed in France's departments.

Principate (prínce-a-pate) The governmental system of the Roman Empire founded by Octavian (also known as Caesar Augustus).

Privateer An armed private vessel commissioned by a government to attack enemy ships.

Protestants Members belonging to any branch of the Christian church excluding Roman Catholicism and Eastern Orthodox.

Ptolemaic (ptah-luh-máy-ik) **system** The traditional medieval earth-centered universe and system of planetary movements.

Ptolemies (ptáh-luh-meez) Hellenistic dynasty that ruled in Egypt from about 300 B.C. to about 30 B.C.

Purge Expelling or executing political party members suspected of inefficiency or opposition to party policy.

Q

Quadrant An instrument for taking altitude of heavenly bodies.

Quadrivium (quad-rív-ee-um) The medieval school curriculum that studied arithmetic, music, geometry, and astronomy after completion of the trivium.

Quadruple (quad-róo-pull) **Alliance** Alliance of Austria, Prussia, Russia, and France in the years after the Napoleonic Wars to maintain the status quo.

Qur'an (also Koran) The Muslim holy book recorded in the early seventh century by the prophet Muhammad.

Quietism (quíet-ism) A movement among 17th century Spanish Catholics that emphasized the emotional experience of religious belief.

R

Racisim Belief that racial differences are important and that some races are superior to others.

Raison d'état (ráy-zawn day-táh) "Reason of state." An eighteenth- and nineteenth-century principle justifying arbitrary or aggressive international behavior.

Rationalism The belief that, through reason, humans can understand the world and solve problems.

Realism A medieval Platonist philosophy that believed that the individual objects we percieve are not real, but merely reflections of universal ideas existing in the mind of God. In the nineteenth century this referred to a cultural style rejecting romanticism and attempting to examine society as it is.

Realpolitik (ray-áhl-po-lee-teek) The pragmatic politics of power; often a self-interested foreign policy associated with Bismarck.

Redshirts Garibaldi's troops used in the unification of Italy.

Reform Bill of 1832 English electoral reform extending the vote to the middle classes of the new industrial cities.

Reichstag (ríkes-tahg) German legislative assembly.

Reign of Terror The violent period of the French Revolution between 1792 and 1794.

Relativity Einstein's theory that all aspects of the physical universe must be defined in relative terms.

Resistance movements Underground opposition to occupation forces, especially to German troops in conquered European countries during World War II.

Restoration The conservative regimes in power after the defeat of Napoleon in 1815 that hoped to hold back the forces of change or even turn back the clock to pre-revolutionary days.

Risorgimento (ree-sor-jee-mén-toe) A nineteenth-century Italian unification movement.

Rococo (roe-coe-cóe) A style of art developed from the baroque that originated in France during the eighteenth century that emphasized elaborate designs to produce a delicate effect.

Romanticism A cultural ideology during the first half of the nineteenth century stressing feeling over reason.

Rostra The speaker's platform in the Forum of ancient Rome.

Royal absolutism The seventeenth- and eighteenth-century system of elevated royal authority.

S

Salon (suh-láhn) Seventeenth- and eighteenth-century social and cultural gatherings of members of the upper and middle classes.

Sans-culottes (sawn-key-lóht) Working-class people of Paris during the French Revolution.

Sarcophagus (sar-kóff-a-gus) A stone coffin.

Satellite states Eastern European states under the control of the Soviet Union during the Cold War.

Satrap (sát-trap) An ancient Persian governor in charge of provinces called "satrapies."

Schlieffen (shléaf-en) **Plan** German military strategy in World War I that called for a holding action against Russia while German forces moved through Belgium to knock out France.

Scutage (skyóot-ij) Medieval payment in lieu of military service.

Seleucids (se-lóo-sids) Hellenistic dynasty that ruled in Asia from about 300 B.C. to about 64 B.C.

Semitic (sem-ít-ik) Of or pertaining to any of a group of Caucasoid peoples, chiefly Jews and Arabs, of the eastern Mediterranean area.

Serfs Medieval peasants who were personally free, but bound to the land. They owed labor obligations as well as fees.

Shi'ite (shée-ite) **Muslims** Those who accepted only the descendants of 'Ali, Muhammad's son-in-law, as the true rulers. It was not the majority party in Islam but did prevail in some of the Muslim countries.

Shire An English county.

Sinn Fein (shín féign) "Ourselves Alone." A twentieth-century Irish nationalist organization.

Skepticism (skép-ti-cism) The systematic doubting of accepted authorities—especially religious authorities.

Second Reich (rike) German regime founded in 1871 and lasting until the end of World War I.

Sepoy (sée-poy) **Mutiny** The 1857 uprising of Indians against British rule.

Social Darwinism The effort to apply Darwin's biological ideas to social ideas stressing competition and "survival of the fittest."

Socialism A nineteenth- and twentieth-century ideology stressing cooperation, community, and public ownership of the means of production.

Socratic method The method of arriving at truth by questioning and disputation.

Solidarity A Polish noncommunist union that became the core of resistance to the communist regime during the 1980s.

Sophists (sóff-ists) Fifth-century B.C. Greek philosophers who were condemned for using tricky logic to prove that all things are relative and success alone is important.

Sovereignty (sóv-rin-tee) The source of authority exercised by a state; complete independence and self-government.

Soviet A workers' council during the 1905 and 1917 Russian revolutions and part of the structure of government in the Soviet Union.

SS The Schutzstaffel, Hitler's elite party troops of the 1930s and 1940s.

Stadholder (stáhd-holder) A governor of provinces in the Dutch United Provinces.

Stoicism (stów-i-cism) A hellenistic philosophy that advocated detachment to the material world and an indifference to pain.

Strategoi (stra-táy-goy) Generals in ancient Athens who eventually took a great deal of political power.

Sturm und drang (shtúrm unt dráhng) "Storm and stress." A literary movement in late-eighteenth-century Germany.

Sunna (sóon-a) A collection of sayings and traditions of the prophet Muhammad that delineates the customs adhered to by Muslims.

Supply and demand Adam Smith's liberal economic doctrine that demand for goods and services will stimulate production (supply) in a free-market system.

Surrealism (sur-rée-a-lism) A twentieth-century literary and artistic style stressing images from the unconscious mind.

Symphony A long sonata for orchestra.

Syncretism (sín-cre-tism) The attempt or tendency to combine or reconcile differing beliefs, as in philosophy or religion.

Syndicalism (sín-di-cal-ism) A late-nineteenth-century anarchist ideology envisioning labor unions as the center of a free and just society.

T

Tennis Court Oath Oath taken by members of the French Estates General not to dissolve until they had created a constitution for France.

Tetradrachma (tet-ra-drák-ma) Hellenistic coin worth four drachmas.

Tetrarchy (tét-rar-key) The governmental system of the Roman Empire founded by Diocletian that divided the empire into four administrative units.

Theme A division for the purpose of provincial administration in the Byzantine Empire

Thermidorian (ther-mi-dór-ee-an) **Reaction** The overthrow of Robespierre and the radicals in July, 1794, during the French Revolution.

Third Estate Commoners, or all people except the nobility and clergy, in early modern European society.

Third French Republic The republican government established in 1871 and lasting until Germany's defeat of France in 1940.

Tories A conservative British political party during the eighteenth and nineteenth centuries.

Totalitarianism A twentieth-century form of authoritarian government using force, technology, and bureaucracy to effect rule by a single party and controlling most aspects of the lives of the population.

Triangular trade Trade routes carrying manufactured goods from Europe to Africa, slaves to the Americas, and agricultural products to Europe.

Tribune An official of ancient Rome chosen by the common people to protect their rights.

Triple Alliance Alliance of Germany, Austria-Hungary, and Italy in the years before World War I.

Triumvirate (try-úm-vir-ate) A group of three men sharing civil authority, as in ancient Rome.

Trivium (trív-ee-um) The basic medieval curriculum that studied grammar, rhetoric, and logic; after completion, students could proceed to the quadrivium.

Truman Doctrine U.S. policy initiated in 1947 that offered military and economic aid to countries threatened by a communist takeover with the intention of creating a military ring of containment around the Soviet Union and its satellite states.

Tsar The emperor of Russia.

U

Ultra-royalism The nineteenth-century belief in rule by a monarch and that everything about the French Revolution and Enlightenment was contrary to religion, order, and civilization.

Unconscious According to Freud, that part of the mind of which we are not aware; home of basic drives.

Universal A metaphysical entity that does not change, but that describes particular things on earth—for example, "justice" or "beauty." Explained by the ancient Greeks and examined by subsequent philosophers. (Also called "forms" or "ideas.")

Utilitarianism (you-till-a-táre-ee-an-ism) A nineteenth-century liberal philosophy that evaluated institutions on the basis of social usefulness to achieve "the greatest happiness of the greatest number."

Utopian (you-tópe-ee-an) **socialism** A form of early-nineteenth-century socialism urging cooperation and communes rather than competition and individualism.

V

Vassal In the feudal system, a noble who binds himself to his lord in return for maintenance.

Versailles (ver-sígh) **treaty** Peace treaty between the Allies and Germany following World War I.

Victorian Referring to the period of Queen Victoria's reign in Britain, 1837–1901.

Vulgate (vúll-gate) A version of the Latin Bible, primarily translated from Hebrew and Greek by Jerome.

W

Warsaw Pact A military alliance in Eastern Europe controlled by the Soviet Union and initiated in 1955.

Waterloo Site in Belgium of a decisive defeat of Napoleon in 1815.

Weimar (wy'e-mar) **Republic** The liberal German government established at the end of World War I and destroyed by Hitler in the 1930s.

Wergeld (véhr-gelt) In Germanic law, the relative price of individuals that established the fee for compensation in case of injury.

Whigs A British political party during the eighteenth and nineteenth centuries.

Witan The ancient Anglo-Saxon men who participated in the Witenagemot.

Witenagemot Ancient Anglo-Saxon assembly of nobles.

Z

Zemstva (zémst-fah) Municipal councils established in Russia in the second half of the nineteenth century.

Ziggurat (zíg-gur-raht) A pyramid-shaped Mesopotamian temple.

Zionism A late-nineteenth-and twentieth-century Jewish nationalist movement to create an independent state for Jews in Palestine.

Zollverein (tsóll-ver-rhine) Nineteenth-century German customs union headed by Prussia.

Zoroastrianism (zorro-áss-tree-an-ism) An ancient Persian religion that had a belief in two gods: a god of light named Ahura Mazda, and an evil god named Ahriman.

PHOTO CREDITS

Cover Photos (left to right)
(1) Queen Elizabeth of England. Super-Stock; (2) Washington Appointed Commander in Chief by Currier & Ives. SuperStock; (3) French Revolution: The Assault of the Bastille by Lallemand. Musee Carnavalet, Paris, France/A.K.G., Berlin/SuperStock; (4) Family of Peasants by LeNain. Musee Du Louvre, Paris/SuperStock; (5) Huge City by Dix. Gallery of the City, Stuttgart/A.K.G., Berlin/SuperStock; (6) Mao Zedong at the 9th National Congress, Beijing China. Jack Novak/SuperStock.

Chapter 13
Opener: © Scala/Art Resource; 13.1: © Scala/Art Resource; 13.2: © Bibliotheque Nationale; 13.3: © Giraudon/Art Resource; 13.4: © Herve Lewandowski/Reunion des Musees Nationaux; 13.5: © The National Gallery, London; 13.6: © Historical Museum; Moscow/The Art Archive; 13.7: © Metropolitan Museum of Art, Marquand Collection, Gift of Henry G. Marquand, 1889; 13.8: © Granger Collection; 13.9: © Bridgeman Art Library; 13.10: © New York Public Library; 13.12: © Giraudon/Art Resource; 13.13: © Rijksmuseum, Amsterdam; p.460: © Granger Collection; p.461(top): © Herve Lewandowski/Reunion des Musees Nationaux; p.461(bottom): © Historical Museum; Moscow/The Art Archive.

Chapter 14
Opener: © Houghton Library, Harvard University; 14.1: © British Museum; 14.2: © Houghton Library, Harvard University; 14.3: © British Museum; 14.4: © New York Public Library; 14.5: © Dibner Library/Smithsonian Institution; 14.6: © Houghton Library, Harvard University; 14.7: © Giraudon/Art Resource; 14.8: © Biblioteque Nationale, Paris; 14.9: © Houghton Library/Harvard University; 14.10: © Fitzwilliam Museum, University of Cambridge; 14.11: © Bettmann/Corbis; 14.12: © Houghton Library, Harvard University; 14.13: © Giraudon/Art Resource; 14.14: © Giraudon/Art Resource; 14.15: © Musee des Beaux Arts, Dijon. p.492(top): © Dibner Library/Smithsonian Institution; p.492(middle): © New York Public Library; p.492(bottom):

© Biblioteque Nationale, Paris; p.493: © Houghton Library, Harvard University.

Chapter 15
Opener: © Scala/Art Resource; 15.1: © Novosti/Sovfoto; 15.2: © Bildarchiv Preussischer Kulturbesitz; 15.3: © Mary Evans Picture Library; 15.4: © Sir John Soane Museum; 15.5: © National Maritime Museum, London/Bridgeman Art Library; 15.6: © British Library/Bridgeman Art Library; 15.7: © The Granger Collection; 15.9: © Germanisches Nationalmuseum, Nuremberg; 15.10: © Corbis-Bettmann; 15.11: © Erich Lessing/Art Resource; 15.12: © Giraudon/Art Resource; 15.13: © Giraudon/Art Resource; 15.14: © The Metropolitan Museum of Art, Harris Brisbane Dick Foundation, 1932; 15.15: Gift of Joseph W. Revere, William Revere, and Edward H. Revere, Museum of Fine Arts, Boston; p.530(left): © Scala/Art Resource; p.530(right): © Giraudon/Art Resource; p.531: © Novosti/Sovfoto.

Chapter 16
Opener: © Musee Carnavalet/Photo Bulloz; 16.1: © Corbis-Bettmann; 16.2: © Giraudon/Art Resource; 16.3: © Giraudon/Art Resource; 16.4: © Giraudon/Art Resource; 16.5: © Musee des Beaux-Arts de Quimper, France; 16.6: © Bibliotheque Nationale; 16.7: © The Granger Collection; 16.8: © Erich Lessing/Art Library; 16.9: © Art Resource; 16.10: © The Granger Collection; 16.11: © Erich Lessing/Art Resource; p.564(left): © Musee Carnavalet/Photo Bulloz; p.564(right): © Giraudon/Art Resource; p.565: © Art Resource.

Chapter 17
Opener: © The Royal Collection, Royal Collection Enterprise; 17.1: © National Railway Museum, York/Bridgeman Art Library; 17.2: © The Bridgeman Art Library; 17.3: © Musee des Arts Metiers, Paris/Photo P. Faligot, Seventh Square; 17.4: © Science and Society Picture Library, Science Museum, London; 17.5: © Guidhall Library, London/Bridgeman Art Library; 17.6: © Guidhall Library, London/Bridgeman Art Library; 17.8: © New York Public Library; 17.9: © Trades Union Congress,

London/Bridgeman Art Library; 17.10: © Print Collection, Miriam & Ira D. Wallach Division of Art, Prints, & Photographs, New York Public Library, Astor, Lenox, and Tilden Foundation; 17.11: © The Wellcome Institute Library, London; 17.12: © William H. Helfand Collection, Philadelphia Museum of Art; 17.13: © The Detroit Institute of Arts; 17.14: © Cadbury, Ltd; p.596(left): © The Bridgeman Art Library; p.596(right): © Science and Society Picture Library, Science Museum, London; p.597: © Guidhall Library, London/Bridgeman Art Library.

Chapter 18
Opener: © Historisches Museum, Vienna; 18.1: © AKG, London; 18.2: © British Library; 18.3: © Neue Pinakothek, Munich/Artothek; 18.4: © Yale Center for British Art/Bridgeman Art Library; 18.5: © Bildarchiv Preussischer Kulturbesitz; 18.6: © Archiv fur Kunst und Geschichte; 18.7: © Granger Collection; 18.8: © Giraudon/Art Resource; 18.9: © Lauros-Giraudon/Art Resource; 18.10: © Mary Evans Picture Library; 18.11: Musee du Petit Palais, Paris/Giraudon/Bridgeman Art Library; 18.12: © Giraudon/Art Resource; 18.13: © Granger Collection; p.632: © AKG, London; p.633(left): © Bildarchiv Preussischer Kulturbesitz; p.633(right): Musee du Petit Palais, Paris/Giraudon/Bridgeman Art Library.

Chapter 19
Opener: © Scala/Art Resource; 19.1: © Culver Pictures; 19.2: © Bismark Museum/Bildarchiv Preussischer Kulturbesitz; 19.3: © Museum of the City of New York; 19.4: © Museum of Fine Arts, Boston; 19.5: © Photo Bulloz; 19.6: © Wellcome Institute Library, London; 19.7: © Granger Collection; 19.8: © Novosti/Sovfoto; p.654(top): © Scala/Art Resource; p.654(middle): © Bismark Museum/Bildarchiv Preussischer Kulturbesitz; p.654(bottom): © Wellcome Institute Library, London.

Chapter 20
Opener: © Mary Evans Picture Library; 20.1: © Bridgeman Art Library; 20.2: © BBC Hulton/Gamma Liaison; 20.3: © Corbis/Bettmann; 20.4: © Erich

Lessing/Art Resource; 20.5: © Roger-Viollet/Gamma Liaison; 20.6: © Jewish Museum, New York/Art Resource; 20.7: © Culver Pictures; 20.8: © Bradford Art Galleries & Museum/Bridgeman Art Library; 20.9: © Mary Evans Picture Library; 20.10: © BBC Hulton/Bettmann Archive; 20.11: © Defense Department/Marine Corps/National Archives; 20.12 © California Museum of Photography/University of California at Riverside.

Chapter 21
Opener: © Harrogate Museum and Art Gallery/Bridgeman Art Library; 21.1: © Ullstien Bilderdienst; 21.3: © Tallandier; 21.4: © Mary Evans Picture Library; 21.5: © Bibliotheque Nationale, Paris; 21.6: © Cadbury, Ltd.; 21.7: © Musee de la Poste, Paris; 21.8: © Goteborg Konstmuseum/Edimedia; 21.9: © Magyar Nemzeti Galeria, Hungarian National Gallery, Budapest. Photo, Mester Tibor; 21.10: © Erich Lessing/Art Resource; 21.11: © AKG/London; 21.12: © Erich Lessing/Art Resource; 21.13: © Sachsische Landesbibliothek–Staats–und Universitatsbibliothek Dresden/Duetsche Fotothek; 21.14: © Erich Lessing/Art Resource; 21.15: © Scala/Art Resouce; 21.16: © Erich Lessing/Art Resource; 21.17: © Erich Lessing/Art Resource; p.714(left): © Harrogate Museum and Art Gallery/Bridgeman Art Library; p.714(right): © Scala/Art Resouce; p.715: © Erich Lessing/Art Resource.

Chapter 22
Opener: © Erich Lessing/Art Resource; 22.1: © Corbis-Bettmann; 22.2: © Ullstein; 22.3: © Roger-Viollet/Gamma Liaison; 22.4: © Imperial War Museum,

London; 22.5: © Imperial War Museum, London; 22.6: © Mary Evans Picture Library; 22.7: © Sachsische Landesbibliothek–Staats–und Univesitatsbibliothek Dresden/Deutsche Fotothek; 22.8: © Sachsische Landesbibliothek–Staats–und Universitatsbibliothek Dresden/Duetsche Fotothek; 22.9: © Corbis-Bettmann; 22.10: © National Portrait Gallery, Smithsonian Institution/Art Resource; 22.11: © Sovfoto/Eastfoto; 22.12: © Sovfoto/Eastfoto; 22.13: © Sovfoto/Eastfoto; p.747(left): © Erich Lessing/Art Resource; p.747(middle): © Sovfoto/Eastfoto; p.747(right): © National Portrait Gallery, Smithsonian Institution/Art Resource.

Chapter 23
Opener: © Corbis-Bettmann; 23.1: © Archiv fur Kunst und Geschichte; 23.2a: © Erich Lessing/Art Resource; 23.2b: © Erich Lessing/Art Resource; 23.3: © British Film Institute; 23.4: Erik Bohr/Archiv fur Kunst und Geschichte; 23.5: © AP/Wide World Photos; 23.6: © Fotomas Index, London; 23.7: © Sovfoto/Eastfoto; 23.8: © 2000: Whitney Museum of Art; 23.10: © Heinrich Hoffman/Life Magazine © Time, Inc.; 23.11: © Felix Nussbaum Haus, Kulturgeschichtliches Museum, Osnabruck, Germany; 23.12: © Museo Nacional del Prado/ARS, NY/Spadem, Paris; 23.13: © Imperial War Museum; 23.14: © AP/Wide World Photos; 23.15: © The Imperial War Museum; p.786(left): © Erich Lessing/Art Resource; p.786(right): © Fotomas Index, London; p.787: © Heinrich Hoffman/Life Magazine © Time, Inc.

Chapter 24
Opener: © Cleveland Museum of Art, 2000, Purchase with a grant from the National Endowment for the Arts and matched by gifts from members of The Cleveland Society for Contemporary Art, 1974.53; 24.1: © Musee d'Histoire Contemporaine, BCIC, Universite de Paris; 24.2: © Consulate General of Germany; 24.3: © Musee d'Histoire Contemporaine, BCIC, Universite de Paris; 24.4: © Museum Ludwig, Cologne; 24.5: © Gocksin/Sipa; 24.6: © Corbis-Bettmann; 24.7: © Josef Koudelka/Magnum; 24.9: © AP/Wide World Photos; 24.10: Albright-Knox Art Gallery, Buffalo, NY; 24.11: © Albright-Knox Art Gallery, Buffalo, NY; 24.12: © G. Pierre/Sygma; 24.13: © Martine Franck/Magnum; 24.14: © Lambert/Archive Photos; 24.15: © NASA; p.824: © Musee d'Histoire Contemporaine, BCIC, Universite de Paris; p.825(top): © Gocksin/Sipa; 24.6: © Corbis-Bettmann; p.825(bottom): © Josef Koudelka/Magnum.

Chapter 25
Opener: © Regis Bossu/Sygma; 25.1: © Aventurier/Gamma Liaison; 25.2: Musee d'Histoire Contemporine BDIC, Universite de Paris; 25.3: © AP/Wide World Photos; 25.4: © Agence France-Presse; 25.6: © J. Jones/Sygma; 25.7: © Antony Edwards/The Image Bank; 25.8: © Kenneth Garrett/National Geographic; 25.9: © Marco Ventura/The Artworks; 25.11: © National Library of Medicine; 25.12: © Jennifer Bartlett; p.852(top): © Agence France-Presse; p.852(bottom): © Regis Bossu/Sygma; p.853: © Antony Edwards/The Image Bank.

Index

Note: Entries printed in *italic* type and followed by a lower-case letter refer to figures (f), maps (m).